FIFTH EDITION

The Social Services:
An Introduction

FIFTH EDITION

The Social Services:
An Introduction

H. WAYNE JOHNSON   *University of Iowa*
and contributors

F. E. PEACOCK PUBLISHERS, INC.
Itasca, Illinois

Cover image:
PhotoDisc, Kaz Chiba

Copyright © 1998
F. E. Peacock Publishers, Inc.
All rights reserved
Library of Congress Catalog Card No. 97-76283
ISBN 0-87581-413-1
Printed in the U.S.A.
Printing: 10 9 8 7 6 5 4 3 2 1
Year: 03 02 01 00 99 98

Contents

Part 1
BACKGROUND

Part 2

SOCIAL PROBLEMS AND SOCIAL SERVICES

Part 3

METHODS OF SOCIAL WORK PRACTICE

Part 4

SPECIAL GROUPS, ISSUES, AND TRENDS

Contributors

H. WAYNE JOHNSON (Chapters 1, 2, 3, 4, 12, 15, 16, 26, Epilogue) is Coordinator of the undergraduate program of the School of Social Work at the University of Iowa. Teaching, research, and interest areas include the introductory course, juvenile/criminal justice, field experience, and rural social work. He has served on the boards of two national social work education organizations, as an accreditation site visitor for the Council on Social Work Education (CSWE), and as Vice President of CSWE. He serves on local agency boards.

CRAIG ABRAHAMSON (Chapter 27) is Assistant Professor of Social Work at James Madison University. His research interests are in future developments in direct services. He teaches in both direct service and policy areas.

B. ELEANOR ANSTEY (Chapter 23) is University of Iowa Professor Emeritus in the School of Social Work. She continues to teach courses about women in national and international social welfare, social development, and human behavior. Her publications focus on women in rural areas and international settings.

GARY ASKEROOTH (Chapter 24) is Special Projects Manager, Neighborhood Reinvestment Corporation, Washington, D.C. He designs and manages the training of staff working to revitalize communities and develop affordable housing. He has also managed housing programs and taught community development.

JUDITH LEE BURKE (Chapter 25) is Professor in the School of Social Work at the University of Missouri-Columbia. She has written about women's participation in development programs, in community development, and in family therapy. Her international research experience is in Mexico and South Vietnam.

N. YOLANDA BURWELL (Chapter 22) is Associate Professor in the School of Social Work at East Carolina University in Greenville, North Carolina. She has extensive experience in cross-cultural and empowerment practice issues. In addition, she is a social welfare historian with a focus on community building activities in early African-American communities.

JAY J. CAYNER (Chapter 8) is an Assistant Hospital Director at the University of Iowa Hospitals and Clinics (UIHC). He served as President of the National Association of Social Workers (NASW) from 1995 to 1997 and formerly directed the Social Service Department at UIHC.

JUDITH I. GRAY (Chapter 10) is Associate Professor of Social Work at Ball State University, Muncie, Indiana, where she teaches social work practice and human behavior courses and supervises practicum students. She directed a National Institute of Mental Health–funded project, which focused on preparing undergraduates for entry-level careers in community mental health.

GILBERT J. GREENE (Chapters 5, 6) is Associate Professor at Ohio State University College of Social Work, where he teaches courses in the clinical social work concentration. He has extensive professional experience working with families and has published a number of articles on this topic in social work and family therapy journals.

JAMES A. HALL (Chapters 8, 21) is Associate Professor of Social Work at the University of Iowa and Director of Practice Research at the University of Iowa Hospitals and Clinics (UIHC). He has worked in health care settings for over 21 years and is assisting the social service staff at UIHC to integrate research with their practice.

THOMASINE HEITKAMP (Chapter 19) is Associate Professor of Social Work at the University of North Dakota. She teaches community organization classes at the undergraduate and graduate levels. She currently coordinates the department's Distance Education Program, which utilizes interactive television for instruction.

MICHAEL JACOBSEN (Chapter 19) is Chairperson of the Department of Social Work at the University of North Dakota. He served on the board of the Association on Community Organization and Social Administration and has worked in community organization.

GREGORY V. JENSEN (Chapter 8) is Director of the Department of Social Service at the University of Iowa Hospitals and Clinics. He is also on the Board of Directors of the National Association of Social Workers (NASW) and in the Society of Social Work Administrators in Health Care where he served as past President.

PATRICIA KELLEY (Chapter 18) is Professor in the School of Social Work at the University of Iowa, where she chairs the curriculum clinical concentration. She has published in the areas of therapy with individuals, families, and groups, and she maintains a private therapy practice.

VERNE R. KELLEY (Chapter 9) is retired Executive Director of the Mid-Eastern Iowa Community Mental Health Center. He serves on accreditation teams for the CSWE and is former president in Iowa of the NASW. His publication topics include civil liberties, rural mental health delivery, natural helpers, and treatment outcome of adolescents.

STEVEN KRAFT (Chapter 19) is Assistant Professor of Social Work at the University of North Dakota. He has taught community organization at four schools of social work and worked in agency administration and as a community organizer. He teaches in both direct service and policy areas.

TERESA K. FULLER KULPER (Chapters 5, 6) is a psychotherapist at Marchman Psychology Associates in Iowa City. She is an approved supervisor of the American Association for Marriage and Family Therapy and an adjunct faculty member of the School of Social Work at the University of Iowa.

JANET JOHNSON LAUBE (Chapter 17) of Madison, Wisconsin, has been the Director of outpatient services at a community mental health center and is currently in private practice. She represents social work practitioners on the Commission on Accreditation of the Council on Social Work Education.

JEANNE HOWELL MANN (Chapter 13) has been the Executive Director of Elderly Services Agency in Johnson County, Iowa, for 13 years. She has taught courses in anthropology and gerontology at the University of Iowa and Cornell College and has published in anthropology and social work.

WILLIAM P. McCARTY (Chapter 20) is Vice President for Behavioral Health Services for Four Oaks, Inc., of Iowa, a nonprofit child and family service agency. He has been involved in human services administration and management for 25 years.

GLENDA DEWBERRY ROONEY (Chapter 14) is Associate Professor/Chair in the Department of Social Work, Augsburg College, Minneapolis. She has taught occupational social work and conducted research on employee assistance programs.

MARLYS STAUDT (Chapter 7) is Assistant Professor at the University of Tennessee-Knoxville School of Social Work. She has extensive school social work practice experience and has authored several articles on the subject of school social work.

ROBERT VANDER BEEK (Chapter 10) is a Clinical Professor in Social Work at the University of Iowa, where he is Director of Field Education. His practice experience includes directing a neighborhood center in a low-income housing project, providing support services to students with special needs, and working on an interdisciplinary team serving people with disabilities.

THOMAS WALZ (Chapter 27) is Professor and former Director of the University of Iowa School of Social Work. He teaches in the areas of aging and public policy and has written over 75 articles and six books on a variety of social welfare topics. His interests include the future of social services.

FRANK H. WARE (Chapter 11) is Executive Director of the Janet Wattles Community Mental Health Center in Rockford, Illinois. Formerly he directed a therapeutic community for substance abusers. He has published, lectured, and taught on substance abuse and dual diagnosis of mental illness and substance abuse.

Preface

When the first edition of this book was written in the early 1980s it never occurred to me, nor probably to the various chapter contributors, that we would still be involved with this project so many years later. Nor was it realized how often it would be necessary to have new editions of the text. But this should not be surprising, given the times in which we live. More than anything else, perhaps, it is a time of great change.

The theme of this text as we move into a fifth edition continues to be *change*. As a pervasive fact of modern life, change is clearly seen both in our social problems and in the services/programs designed as responses to such problems. Many have expanded or emerged just in the last few years since we prepared the last edition. When change occurs at such a rapid pace, academic tools such as textbooks for describing and analyzing the phenomena cannot stand still. They too must evolve. Hence this new edition.

Like the four previous editions, this revised text is intended for the first course in an undergraduate social work program, whether in a four-year program or a two-year community or junior college. In some institutions, this will be the only social work course available to students, and it will most likely be offered within a sociology department or other social or behavioral science area. In other schools, this will be the first in a series of courses constituting a program, and it will probably come at the freshman/sophomore level. Some of these courses enroll students of various levels, most of whom are taking the course as an elective, whereas in others a majority are taking the first course required for a major in social work, the human services, or some similar designation.

Some schools have a two-semester or three-quarter introductory course. Patterns vary, but in such cases, one term is often devoted essentially to social welfare as a social institution and another to social work as a profession. This text could be used for either or both, but it is designed more for the institutions approach. Instructors and students will need to decide how to make best use of the book, given particular needs, objectives, and patterns.

Why produce a text revision when books already exist? The field of social work and social work education are in infinitely better shape today than 25 years ago relative to available texts for the introductory course. Although several options exist now for instructors of this course, and some are of good quality, there remain deficiencies that many perceive to be important and that I attempted to remedy in the first editions and do so now again. Considerable new content has been added on managed care and case management, technological change and its ramifications, privatization of services, physician-assisted suicide, AIDS, homelessness, and other social problems. A major development since the last edition has been welfare reform, and this is presented in some detail, along with updating in income maintenance generally. There is new content in every chapter and extensive updating throughout the entire volume.

The new code of ethics of the profession is included, along with changes reflecting the newest accreditation requirements. The generalist thrust is preserved and extended. Emerging contexts of social work practice are retained as a chapter with expanded and updated content on such topics as the human-animal bond and displaced people, that is, immigrants, refugees, migrants. Both rural and urban areas are explored relative to problems and services and human diversity is stressed. Three new coauthors have joined this edition.

At the same time that we are careful to include contemporary concerns, in an introductory text, we have the responsibility to cover thoroughly the large, traditional, commonplace social services, and we have done so. In fact, the only field allowed more than one chapter is services to families and children, the core of social work for decades. Similarly, social services are examined in the context of public welfare, schools, health, mental health, disabilities, substance abuse, criminal justice, and the elderly. The major thrust in this new edition is updating to make the information as current as possible.

Virtually every chapter could be a book in itself in view of the scope of the topics. Obviously there is much that must be omitted in each chapter in order to prevent the book as a totality from being a tome of thousands of pages. This necessitates making judgments, setting priorities, emphasizing the important (recognizing that notions of what is important vary from person to person), and at the same time including material for breadth and balance. An ever-present challenge in the introductory course is the vast territory to be covered. Hence, a text for the course is faced with the same challenge.

The chapters individually can be read as independent entities if the reader wishes, because each can stand alone at the same time that each is an integral part of the whole. Although the order and sequence of chapters and parts is always arbitrary, there is a logical flow. Content does not have to be read in the order presented, and instructors may desire to assign reading in a different pattern. This is particularly true with regard to Parts 2 and 3, which are often reversed in other books and can easily be shifted here. Clearly this book should be adapted to one's own uses, preferences, and style.

A suggestion about supplementing the text may be useful. Each instructor and many students will have ideas from their own reading and experience on appropriate supplementation. Examples I find useful are a book(s) on history of social welfare/social work and such writings as *A Welfare Mother* and *Blaming the Victim*. Over the years I have also used Michael Harrington's books, most recently *The New American Poverty*. In the 1990s I have used such books as *Rachel and Her Children, The Color Purple, The Broken Cord, There Are No Children Here, Living on the Edge,* and *Amazing Grace*.

A word about the title is in order. The title is different from that of some more-or-less comparable texts in its uses of *social services* rather than *welfare* or *social work*, all terms defined in Chapter 2. Some such books end up dealing with both social welfare and social work but do not reflect this fact in their titles. Hence, there is a degree of inaccuracy in some titles. This is one reason to use a different phraseology. I see social services as relating to both welfare and social work, and therefore it is an acceptable term. Second, *welfare* is an emotion-laden term in the United States, and there may be value in promoting a more neutral concept. In addition, *social work* is an awkward term; physicians are not medical workers nor are attorneys legal workers. The terms *work* and *worker* are not generally used in occupational labels except for social work/er, and therefore it may be preferable to cultivate another way of thinking, at least in the title. The traditional terms are used frequently throughout the book, but the title carries a different one.

Case vignettes are again included for purposes of illustration. A major effort has been made to use realistic portrayals. Therefore, not all persons or situations described in the vignettes change in desired directions; not all consumers of social services are transformed and "live happily after." Such is life in the human services and in the real world.

We continue to place at the end of each chapter the "Notes," which include citations, comments, and various pieces of hopefully pertinent information that we did not want to include in the body of the chapter. These and the following "Additional Suggested Readings" have all been updated. The latter are for the reader who would like to pursue a particular subject further. The two listings do not duplicate each other, so readers should consult both lists in determining what one might wish to read.

A genuine effort has again been made throughout to avoid sexist language. In spite of such endeavors, the reader may find that occasionally we still say "he" or "she" when there is no intention to refer to one sex more than the other. It is sometimes awkward to use language that is not sexist, but a serious attempt has been made to do so.

Acknowledgments

It is humbling to consider how much is owed to so many. As was true of the first four editions, this book would, in all probability, not exist were it not for the generous and thoughtful contributions of the chapter authors. Most chapter authors' interest continues, and their revised work appears again in this new version. A few new authors have appeared to replace those who have retired. Each author is an expert on the respective topic(s), and each continues to be willing to subject her or his work to my editing so that the final product is my responsibility.

Faculty from around the country were especially helpful with their constructive criticisms and suggestions expressed at meetings and conferences and elsewhere. Some of these had used previous editions of the text extensively and others had not, but they took time to review the book and provide feedback. The publisher also arranged through Jack Pritchard for ten reviewers to examine the fourth edition and make suggestions. From all of this, the scholarly, penetrating observations and ideas are greatly appreciated. Some of these people will recognize their thoughts and comments incorporated in the new edition. Of course, it is not possible to be totally responsive to all suggestions, partly because there is not unanimity among them. But every idea was considered, and many were used.

A special word of thanks to the ultimate consumers, the students, who read and work with the book. It is gratifying to have feedback and reactions, both from our own students here at the University of Iowa and from others all around the country. These students are in colleges and universities, large and small, public and private, in a wide range of situations. It is especially for them that I first became interested in undertaking this endeavor and it is still for them that I continue with another edition.

Typing is a large part of this task and not very exciting for those who do all of the tedious work. Always with efficiency and good humor, the job has been done so well by Jo Conroy, Madelyn Bowersox, and Beverly Sweet. University of Iowa librarians have been most helpful. Publishers play a special role in producing a textbook. I have found all of those associated with F. E. Peacock Publishers, Inc., with whom I have dealt, to be consistently competent, cordial, and supportive. This is true from Ted Peacock and Dick Welna through the entire staff. John Beasley did an outstanding job of editing the manuscript and moving the project through to completion.

Finally, as always, the person who is my greatest source of assistance, inspiration, and support is my wife, Donna. It is to her, and to the memory of two friends, colleagues and outstanding social work educators, Ralph E. Anderson and Frank Z. Glick, that the book is dedicated.

H. Wayne Johnson

Part 1

Background

1

Introduction

H. WAYNE JOHNSON

Welcome to the study of the social services or, more accurately, contemporary American social services. While in this book we do concern ourselves with both the historical development and future trends relative to social work and welfare, the emphasis is on current social problems, services, and methods of practice. Further, despite some consideration of international social welfare, we are most concerned with the United States.

It is important to understand that the social services constitute an extremely broad and diverse collection of endeavors. In comparison with most professions, social work is a more expansive umbrella covering a tremendous array of activities and dealing with a wide variety of problems. While all of this will be examined at greater length later, here we can note that most, though not all, of social work has in the past been divisible into one of three categories that traditionally were termed *methods* and now are often described as *practice approaches*. These are social casework, social group work, and community organization. Later we will suggest modification and refinement of this threefold construct reflecting the trend toward generalist practice, but it will suffice for now. Much social work is direct or personal service, one-to-one or with families or other small groups, with persons variously labeled clients, patients, residents, members, and so on. This *micro* activity is casework and/or to a considerable degree group work, some of which is clinical. On the other side is indirect, *macro* level, community-oriented activity involving social planning, organizing, social action, and other related efforts.

Both of these major aspects are aimed at helping people, either individually or collectively, and both are directed at bringing about change. When change in a positive direction is not possible, as is sometimes the situation, the goal in the human services is to preserve or maintain the status quo. More about purposes and objectives will come later. For now it is well to keep in mind the idea of the social worker as an enabler generally, a person who empowers and who helps others to make desired things happen. Any way they are conceptualized, social workers are helpers—helping people in myriad ways to help themselves.

To be a helper requires understanding people's psychosocial situations and humans as bio-psycho-social creatures. It necessitates developing the ability to intervene in people's lives and situations in constructive ways and to build strategies for such intervention. To become this kind of a professional requires a combination of certain knowledge, skill, and attitudes/values. Much of the remainder of the book deals with these.

To illustrate the kind of knowledge required to work competently with people in a helping capacity, two aspects of human motivation and human development will be noted. The psychologist Abraham Maslow and others have postulated the idea that humans are motivated by certain basic needs. According to Maslow, there is a hierarchy beginning with physiological needs and progressing to the need for safety, belongingness and love, esteem, and self-actualization or self-fulfillment (and potential). As the more basic ones are satisfied, subsequent needs replace them in importance. If the needs go unsatisfied, they remain a major force in the personality and behavior of the person in typically negative ways, just as their gratification tends to have positive consequences for the person.[1]

Erik Erikson, a neo-Freudian, has contributed to our understanding of human development in important ways. He conceptualizes "eight ages of man" ranging from infancy through old age. Each developmental stage builds on and moves forward from all previous life stages. Erikson also suggests that there are major issues of living to be resolved at each developmental level. For example, in infancy the issue is "basic trust versus mistrust," in adolescence "identity versus role confusion," and in old age "ego integrity versus despair."[2] This notion of human development acknowledges the biological realities of humankind and places these within a cultural and historical context.

Important understandings of human behavior are derived from integrating the contributions of social and behavioral scientists. In the case of Maslow and Erikson, for example, relating the idea of a hierarchy of basic needs to the notion of stages of development produces an image of the human as dynamic and changing and as possessing potential for further accomplishments. The work of Maslow, Erikson, and many others furthers the comprehension of human service workers and others dealing with people in the context of social problems.

SOCIAL CHANGE

A central theme in this book is *social change,* which is ever present in society and, as we move toward and into the twenty-first century, comes at a breathtaking pace. The change is multifaceted and exists on several levels. Perhaps the most conspicuous change is technological, as illustrated by the information/computer revolution, to cite just one of many developments. But change is not restricted to tangibles in this age of technology that has been termed the *postindustrial* and/or *information era.* Just as striking are some of the modifications taking place in social institutions such as the family where, to mention only a few aspects of this phenomenon, we are experiencing much higher rates of cohabitation, divorce, single parenthood, employment of women outside the home, and early retirement than were traditionally the case. In addition, such movements as children's rights and women's rights, while not new historically, have new impetus and implications.

Long ago the sociologist William Ogburn spoke of a tendency toward what he called "culture lag" in societies in which the various cultural elements do not change at the same rate; the intangible components often tend to lag behind the material.[3] A classic illustration is our sophisticated instruments of warfare, which are so far in advance (or at least seem to be) of our methods of peacekeeping and international relations. The concept of culture lag is a useful one in considering social change as it relates to social work. One reason is that social work itself is changing just as are the problems and conditions with which it attempts to cope. Some facets of the helping disciplines are advanced while others are relatively primitive. For example, technologically, medicine is a highly advanced and sophisticated field; yet, much is unknown about mental illness or about how to pay the physician's and/or hospital's bill for treatment.

That there would be value conflicts at such a time should not be surprising. Perhaps no field of endeavor is more enmeshed in these than are the social services. One need merely mention abortion, national health insurance, crime and delinquency penalties, and guaranteed annual income to suggest how extremely complex and value-conflict–laden problems and services involving social work are.

A specific example warrants mention. World population is viewed by some as an out-of-control "explosion" and potential disaster whereas others apparently see little reason for concern. The population of the Earth more than doubled from 2.5 billion in 1950 to 5.8 billion in 1997. I t is growing at the rate of 87 million each year and is projected to double again in the twenty-first century despite reductions in growth in such countries as India, Indonesia, Brazil, and China.[4] This growth has implications for food supply, water, natural resources, ecology, and the environment, along with sheer space. While the growth in the United States is smaller than many developing nations (almost 1 percent annually, nearly half from immigration) the "annual increase in the U.S. population of 2.6 million people puts more pressure on the world's resources than do the 17 million people added in India each year."[5] This is because we Americans are such disproportiuonately heavy consumers of resources. Regardless of one's stance on these complex issues, value conflicts abound, and the implications for social work, both here and abroad, are profound.

In 1992, Barbara White, then president of the National Association of Social Workers (NASW), drawing from the *World Development Forum,* noted a way to see what our world is like—assume that it were a village of 1,000 people. Of this group, 564 are Asians, 210 Europeans, 86 Africans, 80 South Americans, and 60 North Americans. Of the 1,000, half of the total income would be controlled by 60 people, hunger would affect 500, shantytowns would be home for 600, and 700 would be illiterate. At least five of our neighbors in the village would be infected with HIV and AIDS.[6] This is our world today. Chapter 25 deals further with the international realm.

Social work can be conceptualized as helping people to cope with change.[7] One advantage of this view is that it assumes that everyone is influenced by, and is an integral part of, change. Furthermore, since many social problems result from change and because it is human to have such problems, the idea that any of us may be potential users of social services becomes more acceptable. Any of us, then, might have occasion to need a social worker, not just the "poor," the people from the "wrong side of the tracks," or of some particular age, ethnic, or other group. This concept of social work may tend to bring about more humility and realism in our thinking, for troubles can, indeed, "happen to any of us."[8]

At the same time that there is pervasive change, there is also, on the other hand, a simultaneous force toward stability. While tomorrow is never exactly like yesterday, neither is it entirely different. Such continuities make a good deal of prediction possible, but the likelihood of change requires that various qualifications and caveats frequently must accompany the predictions. We will be noting in a number of ways that social work is a relatively young field (as professions go) and that it is very much in ferment, which is part and parcel of this social change.

TECHNOLOGY

Technological change is particularly striking currently, and some of these changes have profound significance for a profession such as social work. Scientific developments in such fields as biochemistry, physiology, and genetics have far ranging ramifications. For example, embryo adoption programs in which infertile couples receive embryos from couples who have completed their families have been instituted. Such programs offer new hope to infertile couples but simultaneously present complex questions and issues—legal, moral, and ethical. One university hospital has a committee developing guidelines for this activity. On the committee are a social worker, chaplain, pediatrician, psychologist, a nonuniversity physician, a lawyer, and two lay people.[9]

DNA researchers are working rapidly, and gene therapy is growing phenomenally. But the related ethical systems evolve more slowly than scientific knowledge.[10] But with or without the ethical developments, genetaceuticals (new pharmaceutical treatments resulting from genetic research) emerge. In a very different area of concern there is the possibility of the chemical castration of sex offenders as both punishment and prevention of further offenses.

In February 1997, the world was stunned with the news that Scottish scientists had cloned a lamb from a single cell of a sheep, the first clone of an adult mammal. This development could have great significance for animal agriculture, but most of the discussion on implications focused on the moral and cultural aspects of cloning humans. This could legally be done in the United States but not in some European countries.[11] President Clinton quickly prohibited the use of federal funds for human cloning research. Implications of these developments for social work appear profound in this "information era" of electronic technology.

BUREAUCRACY

Today, in this country and in much of the world, we experience industrial, urban, mass society. These qualities tend to make for bureaucracy. We use the term *bureaucracy* not in a negative judgmental sense, as is the case when it is so often used in conjunction with government. Rather we use it in the dictionary, neutral sense to mean "a body of officials and administrators," each of whom is responsible to his or her superiors.[12] Characteristics attributed to bureaucracy typically have a negative hue: devotion to routine, inflexibility of rules, red tape, procrastination, and reluctance to assume responsibility and to experiment.[13]

Instead of emphasizing these and other undesirable attributes of bureaucracy, it is useful to understand this phenomenon as a function of bigness. It is not just government that is bureaucratic; so also are large business, industry, labor, education, religion, and social welfare institutions. Such is the almost inevitable nature of mass organizations and social institutions.

In the 1980s and 1990s there was a strong antigovernment, especially anti–federal government, attitude and movement in the United States. This permeated up and down the public sector and included calls for *privatizing* previously governmentally provided services. Implementation of these calls has been far from an unqualified success, and the evidence mounts that, while privatization is sometimes useful, it may be ineffective, even destructive.[14] Furthermore, private organizations can be and often are as bureaucratic, if not more so, than governmental ones. Nonetheless there is a place for privatization if done rationally and with consideration for and sensitivity to the human dimension.

From a human services point of view, one of the most bothersome and problematic aspects of bureaucracy is the insensitivity it may bring on the part of some personnel who are supposed to be serving others and facilitating the meeting of human needs. This should, however, be related to a larger, more generalized societal insensitivity toward people in need generally. Large cross sections of the United States population are ready and waiting to engage in what has been termed *victim blaming*.[15]

BLAMING THE VICTIM

Blaming the victim takes place in connection with the poor, minorities, the elderly, children, and people with assorted problems. To delineate a group of people as problematic and then to place responsibility and criticism on them for the condition(s) that lead to their labeling is all too commonplace. As Ira Glasser notes, "private troubles become a reason for public punishment."[16] William Ryan popularized the concept of victim blaming with his 1971 book. He demonstrated the usefulness of the concept in such diverse areas as racial and ethnic minority groups, schools/education, medical care/health, illegitimacy, housing, and crime/justice.[17] Actually it goes far beyond these broad considerations in that in a deep and profound sense, we tend to condemn those who are the products of forces and practices over which they have little or no control, such as racism, discrimination, sexism, unemployment, poverty, poor health and inadequate medical care, and so on.

In view of these developments, it is not particularly surprising that we come to issues of social control, of "regulating the poor," to cite one consequence of victim blaming.[18] Such activity is not limited to the poor but includes other recipient groups as well. But we do much more than openly, conspicuously, and all too often destructively regulate some of the people we "serve." In less visible ways, many social welfare programs serve social-control functions. This is often subtle but nonetheless real. That this is a fact is not necessarily bad; social control is inherent in much of what social work is and does. The corrections and mental health fields are significant examples; both are dealt with in later chapters. What is important is that this fact be recognized and that those of us working in such fields acknowledge the power and potential we have for destructiveness as well as for constructiveness. This is one of the reasons that self-awareness is stressed so much in social work education.

SOCIAL JUSTICE

Since the responsibility of a profession such as social work is to further social justice, it becomes necessary to consider this concept. Beverly and McSweeney define justice as "fairness in the relationships between people as these relate to the possession and/or acquisition of resources based on some kind of valid claim to a share of those resources."[19] They adopt from Perelman the "formal principle of justice," which holds that "all human beings, because they belong to the category of being human, must be treated in the same way."[20] In order for this rather abstract and nebulous concept of social justice to become more meaningful, it may be useful to continue on a bit further with the three Beverly/McSweeney "concrete principles" of justice[21]:

1. The allocation of resources by government must give priority to meeting basic human needs in the areas of food, clothing, and shelter for all people within the jurisdiction of that government.
2. All demands or claims on resources are valid and just if and only if they satisfy either of the following conditions:
   a. Those demands serve to enhance the conditions of humanness required in terms of providing for food, clothing, and shelter.
   b. The quantity of resources available is such that additional resources are available to meet demands beyond those postulated to maintain humanness.
3. It is the responsibility of our national government to ensure that fairness prevails in the allocation of resources, and that resources are allocated in accord with Principles 1 and 2.

These basic ideas are central to what social work is all about, and we will have opportunity to examine them in numerous contexts as we move along in the course of this book. How important the concept of social justice is to social work is seen in the NASW Code of Ethics. Revised in 1996 and effective in 1997, the Code contains a "Preamble" that is reprinted here.

The preamble of the Code of Ethics reflects values that are integral to social justice. But social justice does not come easily. There is a social class system in America. Perhaps it is useful to reflect on the annual earnings of some individuals as compared to the poverty of large numbers of children, elderly, and others. In 1997, a baseball player was paid $10 million a year in spite of a difficult disciplinary record and heavy gambling on sports.[22] This is more than the entire payroll of some major league teams, but the average baseball salary was $1.3 million.[23] A major television newsman was offered $7 million by another

---

CODE OF ETHICS
Preamble

The primary mission of the social work profession is to enhance human well-being and help meet the basic human needs of all people, with particular attention to the needs and empowerment of people who are vulnerable, oppressed, and living in poverty. A historic and defining feature of social work is the profession's focus on individual well-being in a social context and the well-being of society. Fundamental to social work is attention to the environmental forces that create, contribute to, and address problems in living.

Social workers promote social justice and social change with and on behalf of clients. "Clients" is used inclusively to refer to individuals, families, groups, organizations, and communities. Social workers are sensitive to cultural and ethnic diversity and strive to end discrimination, oppression, poverty, and other forms of social injustice. These activities may be in the form of direct practice, community organizing, supervision, consultation, administration, advocacy, social and political action, policy development and implementation, education, and research and evaluation. Social workers seek to enhance the capacity of people to address their own needs. Social workers also seek to promote the responsiveness of organizations, communities, and other social institutions to individuals' needs and social problems.

The mission of the social work profession is rooted in a set of core values. These core values, embraced by social workers throughout the profession's history, are the foundation of social work's unique purpose and perspective:

*   service
*   social justice
*   dignity and worth of the person
*   importance of human relationships
*   integrity
*   competence

This constellation of core values reflects what is unique to the social work profession. Core values, and the principles that flow from them, must be balanced within the context and complexity of the human experience.

Source: National Association of Social Workers.

---

network.[24] Some actors and actresses received $20 million for appearing in a single movie. A basketball player received $30 million, only a minor portion of his income when product endorsements are included, and a university coach in this sport earned almost $900,000 a year.[25] IBM's "downsizing" of 13,000 jobs was seen as a good business practice, whereas efforts to close unneeded and costly military bases and to eliminate 8,000 jobs in California were greatly criticized.[26]

Business Week, in reporting the pay of top executives in large U.S. companies and corporations in 1996, termed the situation "out of control." One chief executive officer (CEO) received $102.4 million. Between salaries, bonuses, and stock-option deals many CEOs have remuneration in the multimillions. Stock options are supposed to provide CEOs incentive for outstanding performance, but they often also reward "so-so" records, and they dilute return to stockholders. The average total compensation of CEOs in 1996 rose 54 percent, while factory employees received 3-percent raises. Some executives do not exercise their stock options but let them accumulate. The value of these in one case exceeded half a billion dollars.[27] According to *Forbes* magazine, in 1982 there were only 13 billionaires in the United States, whereas in 1997 there were 170, up from 135 the previous year.

A frequent response to all of this is that, "It's the market." This, of course, is obvious, but what does it say about societal values, priorities, justice, and equity? Can a society that affords these sums afford to neglect its needy elderly, children, and other people—as so often occurs?

A LOOK AHEAD

What can be accomplished in a single volume is limited in a number of ways. Much information is provided here, but it can go only so far. No book can be all things to all its readers. For example, we do not attempt to include an in-depth treatment of the how-to-do-its of working with people who have problems. Rather, this content is covered largely in a descriptive way. With other content more oriented to social policy matters, for example, we often do more than describe, analyze, and explain. Sometimes we take a position, making it clear, hopefully, that we are doing so. We do have views on many matters of public concern as far as human social well-being is concerned, and to deny this fact or to act as though this were not the case would be counterproductive when there are areas of genuine controversy and divided opinion.

Because of these limitations in almost any single title, students reading this text who believe they may want to move toward social work as a career are invited to test their interest by going beyond the book. One way to do so is to engage in volunteer work in the community, in its agencies and organizations. Spend some time volunteering (paid employment is fine, of course) with children or the elderly, for example. Work in a hospital or some other institution. Help out in a day-care center, crisis hotline, group home, or any one of the numerous possibilities in communities. In the introductory social work course with which the author is most familiar, students do 45 hours of volunteer work. There is nothing sacred about this figure. What is important is acquiring experience and, if possible, working at a variety of things over a period of time. By the time they graduate, some students have accumulated a rich background of experiences. The more, the better. Talking to social workers about their work, visiting agencies, and spending a day observing one or more professionals can all be worthwhile and valuable.

No assumption is made by the author or contributors that all readers will or should ultimately become social workers. But all can gain an understanding of social work and take it with them into other fields where the knowledge is useful and can be shared. It is essential that people be informed, so that we can all work together in our communities and society toward shared goals. Partly as a result of taking courses like the one for which this book was planned, students will someday have decision-making and leadership responsibilities greater than could have been imagined during student days. The fact of holding a degree (associate, baccalaureate, or graduate) almost inevitably makes for larger community roles. Certainly it is important to be informed taxpayers, voters, and citizens. This, at a minimum, we have a right to expect of ourselves and of each other. The author hopes the time together will be fruitful in these respects.

SUMMARY AND CONCLUSIONS

In this first chapter, we have briefly initiated some preliminary exploration of what the study of social work/social welfare is all about and what this may mean for the interests and goals of at least some readers. The presence of social and technological change has been noted, and it was suggested that social work attempts to help people to cope with change. The fact of bureaucracy and the phenomenon of blaming the victim were discussed briefly. Finally, the idea of social justice as a responsibility of social work has been introduced and the preamble to the NASW Code of Ethics has been considered. Some of what has been discussed in this chapter is rather abstract, but it will take on more meaning as we move along. May your journey through the remainder of the book be a pleasant and rewarding voyage.

Notes

1. A.H. Maslow, *Motivation and Personality* (New York: Harper & Row, 1954), pp. 80–106.
2. Erik H. Erikson, *Childhood and Society*, 2nd ed. (New York: W.W. Norton, 1963), p. 273.
3. William F. Ogburn, *Social Change* (New York: Viking Penguin, 1922), pp. 200–201.
4. Christopher Flavin, "The Legacy of Rio," chapter 2 in *State of the World 1997*, Lester R. Brown et al., World Watch Institute Report (New York: W.W. Norton, 1997), pp. 3–22.
5. Ibid., p. 19.
6. National Association of Social Workers, *NASW News* 37, no. 8 (September 1992): 2.
7. H. Wayne Johnson, *Rural Human Services* (Itasca, IL: F.E. Peacock Publishers, 1980), pp. 5–6.
8. For example, see P.B. Horton, G.R. Leslie, R.F. Larson, and Robert Horton, *The Sociology of Social Problems*, 12th ed. (Englewood Cliffs, NJ: Prentice-Hall, 1997).
9. "Embryo Adoption Program Offers Hope—and a Thicket of Questions," *Des Moines Register*, September 1, 1996, p. 1A.
10. Karrie Higgins, "The Ethics of New Medicine," *Daily Iowan,* October 8, 1996, p. 4A.
11. "Scientists Clone Lamb from 1 Cell," *Corpus Christi Caller-Times*, February 24, 1997, pp. A1, A10.
12. *The Random House Dictionary of the English Language*, 2nd ed. (New York: Random House, 1987), p. 279.
13. Henry Pratt Fairchild, *Dictionary of Sociology* (Savage, MD: Littlefield, Adams, 1964), p. 29.
14. For example, see "Study Says Privatizing Schools Hasn't Worked," *USA Today*, October 29, 1996, p. 1A; and "Escape Spurs Call for Halt to Privatization," *Des Moines Register*, September 5, 1996, p. 3A.
15. William Ryan, *Blaming the Victim*, 2nd ed. (New York: Vintage Books, 1976).
16. Ira Glasser, "Prisoners of Benevolence," in Willard Gaylin, Ira Glasser, Steven Marcus, and David Rothman, eds., *Doing Good* (New York: Pantheon Books, 1978), p. 114.
17. Ryan, *Blaming the Victim*.
18. Frances Fox Piven and Richard A. Cloward, *Regulating the Poor* (New York: Vintage Books, 1971).
19. David P. Beverly and Edward A. McSweeney, *Social Welfare and Social Justice* (Englewood Cliffs, NJ: Prentice-Hall, 1987), p. 5.

20. Ibid., p. 7.
21. Ibid., pp. 8–10.
22. "Belle Likely to Face Year of Probation If Didn't Gamble on Baseball Games," *Corpus Christi Caller-Times*, February 14, 1997, p. D1.
23. "Belle's Salary Tops Entire Team's," *Des Moines Register*, April 3, 1997, p. 1S.
24. "CNN Offers Brokaw $7 Million a Year Deal," *Corpus Christi Caller-Times*, February 19, 1997, p. A6.
25. "Olson Deal Extended," *Des Moines Register*, September 21, 1997, p. 1D.
26. "Americans Must Accept Need to Close Facilities," *Corpus Christi Caller-Times*, February 19, 1997, p. A6, Letter to the Editor.
27. *Business Week*, April 21, 1997, pp. 58–66.

Additional Suggested Readings

Anderson, Ralph E., and Irl Carter. *Human Behavior in the Social Environment*. 4th ed. Hawthorne, NY: Aldine, 1990.

Berger, R.L., J.T. McBreen, and Marilyn J. Riflain. *Human Behavior*. 4th ed. White Plains, NY: Longman, 1996.

Chess, Wayne A., and Julia Norlin. *Human Behavior and the Social Environment*. 3rd ed. Needham Heights, MA: Allyn & Bacon, 1997.

Dolgoff, Ralph, Donald Feldstein, and Louise Skolnik. *Understanding Social Welfare*. 4th ed. White Plains, NY: Longman, 1996.

Furr, L. Allen. *Exploring Human Behavior and the Social Environment*. Needham Heights, MA: Allyn & Bacon, 1997.

Gambrill, Eileen, and Robert Pruger, eds. *Controversial Issues in Social Work: Ethics, Values, and Obligations*. Needham Heights, MA: Allyn & Bacon, 1996.

Lipsky, Michael. *Street-Level Bureaucracy*. New York: Russell Sage Foundation, 1980.

Longres, John. *Human Behavior in the Social Environment*. 2nd ed. Itasca, IL: F.E. Peacock Publishers, 1995.

Perrucie, Robert, and Marc Pilisuk. *The Triple Revolution Emerging*. Boston: Little, Brown, 1971.

Public Concern Foundation. *The Washington Spectator*, New York.

Schriver, Joe M. *Human Behavior and the Social Environment*. Needham Heights, MA: Allyn & Bacon, 1995.

Zastrow, Charles, and Karen Kirst-Ashman. *Understanding Human Behavior and the Social Environment*. 4th ed. Chicago: Nelson-Hall, 1997.

2

Basic Concepts: Social Welfare, Social Work, and Social Services

H. WAYNE JOHNSON

Three terms are basic for this discussion and for the entire book: social welfare, social work, and social services. Numerous definitions of *social welfare* are found in the literature, but they tend not to differ from each other substantively. For our purposes social welfare refers to societally organized activities aimed at maintaining or improving human well-being. This very broad concept involves a number of professions, including, but not restricted to, social work. Among other occupations involved are those having to do with health, education, recreation, and public safety, to mention only a few. Social welfare encompasses both governmental and voluntary sectors and cuts across all levels of each. Since these activities are organized, it should be noted that this means both those formally and those informally organized. For example, in the United States we find rural social welfare in general less formally organized than its urban counterpart.[1]

Explicit in this definition of social welfare is the goal of human well-being. That this is a highly relative purpose is seen in the statement about the activities aiming at *maintaining* or *improving* social functioning. While improvement is the ideal, in the real world it is not always possible. Often one must settle for maintenance. The dying patient, for example, is probably not going to improve; yet, increasingly there is the notion of death with dignity. In other words, much can often be done to be helpful to people in the sense of maintaining them and thus enhancing their well-being.

A second term, *social work*, requires definition, and as with social welfare, various definitive statements exist. Boehm's, developed in the late 1950s, follows:

> Social work seeks to enhance the social functioning of individuals, singly and in groups, by activities focused upon their social relationships which constitute the interaction between man and his environment.[2]

Twenty years later Baer and Federico defined social work this way[3]:

> Social work is concerned and involved with the interactions between people and the institutions of society that affect the ability of people to accomplish life tasks, realize aspirations and values, and alleviate distress.

In this book, social work is taken to mean a profession concerned with the relationships between people and their environments and the influencing of these relationships toward maximal social functioning. Boehm found social work's "distinguishing characteristic" to be its focus on social relationships.[4] Here we take a similar position. This means that social work is concerned with human interactions and the interchange between people and their surroundings, their psycho-social situations. That this is still central to social work is seen in current developments having to do with the revision of Council on Social Work Education (CSWE) accreditation standards for undergraduate and graduate programs to accompany the revised Curriculum Policy Statement of 1992. The analytic model for social work practice is seen to be the "person at the interface with the environment."[5] What this means is that the social worker focuses on the points at which the various levels of social systems come together and their effect on the person: individual, family, other groups, community, organizations, and society. These are the major social systems.[6] This is why, with the move to more of a social systems approach in this profession, social work is being seen as *boundary work*, that is, the boundaries between the systems and/or their component parts. Social work tends to deal with exchanges between the components of these systems, for example, between family members, between an individual and a person(s) in other systems such as education or employment, between two or more groups in a community, or between several organizations.[7]

The distinction between social welfare and social work is one between social institution or system (social welfare) and occupation or profession (social work). Social welfare, a far broader concept than social work, is what sociologists call a *social institution*.[8] It encompasses a number of occupational endeavors, including social work. On the other hand, social work refers to professional activities—what certain people do as their practice in their vocational roles.

Social services is the last concept for analysis. It is defined here as the programs or measures employing social workers or related professionals and directed toward social welfare goals. Social workers operate in many different fields: in the corrections services the worker may be a probation officer; in family social services a marriage counselor; in the field of the elderly the worker is perhaps a planner of programs, an advocate, or an organizer.

SOCIAL WORK AND SOCIOLOGY

Partly because social work courses in colleges and universities are often offered within sociology departments, but for other reasons as well, a question frequently arises as to the relationship between sociology and social work. Sociology is basically an academic discipline, a social science, with a body of scientific knowledge, while social work is professional practice.[9] Whereas sociology is a theoretically based and research-oriented study of human groups, social work

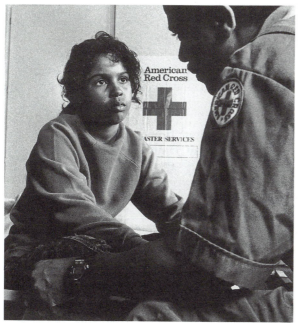

American Red Cross

Social workers try to meet the needs of people afflicted by floods, earthquakes, and other natural disasters. During a mock emergency in Virginia, a "victim" is comforted by a volunteer at a Red Cross shelter.

represents technology or social engineering and the application of knowledge, sociological as well as other. Berger puts it well: "Social work…is a certain *practice* in society. Sociology is not a practice, but an attempt to understand."[10]

A rough analogy may help to make the point. Sociology is to social work approximately what biology is to medicine. Biology and sociology are bodies of knowledge, while the other two are professional services or practices. Of course, the physician must study and know more than biology; so also the social worker's sources of knowledge include, but go beyond, sociology. Other important parts of the knowledge base are psychology, human development, political science, and economics.

One difference between sociology and social work has to do with values. The sociologist, like any scientist, is committed to the "search for truth" and thus attempts to be objective and practice "value neutrality" apart from devotion to knowledge (which, incidentally, is a value in itself). The social worker functions from a different value base, one that reflects the Judeo-Christian heritage and the American and Western world humanitarian and democratic influences.

VALUES

Like any profession, social work practice entails knowledge, skills, and attitudes or values. The core values are those having to do with human worth and dignity. Social workers generally deal with people experiencing problems of one kind or another and often see people who are not at their best. This makes commitment to humanitarian values especially important. Take the intoxicated person as an example; the inebriate in the gutter, untidy, irrational, uncooperative, is still a human being, and this quality gives him or her worth. The drunk is important not because of the drunkenness but because of the humanness. We are all fallible and capable of falling short of our potential. The social worker's professional values acknowledge both the strengths and weaknesses of humankind.

What are the other philosophical values upon which modern social work stands? Friedlander categorized these into a fourfold scheme, simplified as follows:[11]

1. The humanistic values having to do with the dignity, integrity, and worth of the individual human being just alluded to.
2. The right of self-determination—the idea that the individual has the right to determine his or her own needs and how to meet them.
3. Equality of opportunity, limited only by the innate capacities of the individual.
4. People's social responsibilities toward themselves, their families, their community, and society.

The value orientation of a profession can be understood in many ways. One is to examine some of the formalized statements, creeds, and documents that are developed by organizations. In the case of social work, the Code of Ethics of the NASW is perhaps the best example. Summarized here is a revision and expansion of the code adopted by NASW in 1996 that took effect in 1997. The democratic humanistic core of social work values appears rather conspicuously in this code and in the Preamble included in Chapter 1.[12]

CODE OF ETHICS
Summary of Ethical Principles
(Each principle is elaborated in the complete code.)

The following broad ethical principles are based on social work's core values of service, social justice, dignity and worth of the person, importance of human relationships, integrity, and competence. These principles set forth ideals to which all social workers should aspire.

Value: *Service*

Ethical Principle: Social workers' primary goal is to help people in need and to address social problems.

Value: *Social Justice*

Ethical Principle: Social workers challenge social injustice.

Value: *Dignity and Worth of the Person*

Ethical Principle: Social workers respect the inherent dignity and worth of the person.

Value: *Importance of Human Relationships*

Ethical Principle: Social workers recognize the central importance of human reltionships.

Value: *Integrity*

Ethical Principle: Social workers behave in a trustworthy manner.

Value: *Competence*

Ethical Principle: Social workers practice within their areas of competence and develop and enhance their professional expertise.

Summary of Ethical Standards
(Each standard is discussed in the complete code.)

1. SOCIAL WORKERS' ETHICAL RESPONSIBILITIES TO CLIENTS
   1.01   Commitment to Clients
   1.02   Self-Determination
   1.03   Informed Consent
   1.04   Competence
   1.05   Cultural Competence and Cultural Diversity
   1.06   Conflicts of Interest
   1.07   Privacy and Confidentiality
   1.08   Access to Records
   1.09   Sexual Relationships
   1.10   Physical Contact
   1.11   Sexual Harassment
   1.12   Derogatory Language
   1.13   Payment for Services
   1.14   Clients Who Lack Decision-Making Capacity
   1.15   Interruption of Services
   1.16   Termination of Services

2. SOCIAL WORKERS' ETHICAL RESPONSIBILITIES TO COLLEAGUES
   2.01   Respect
   2.02   Confidentiality
   2.03   Interdisciplinary Collaboration
   2.04   Disputes Involving Colleagues
   2.05   Consultation
   2.06   Referral for Services
   2.07   Sexual Relationships
   2.08   Sexual Harassment
   2.09   Impairment of Colleagues
   2.10   Incompetence of Colleagues
   2.11   Unethical Conduct of Colleagues

3. SOCIAL WORKERS' ETHICAL RESPONSIBILITIES IN PRACTICE SETTINGS
   3.01   Supervision and Consultation
   3.02   Education and Training
   3.03   Performance Evaluation
   3.04   Client Records
   3.05   Billing
   3.06   Client Transfer
   3.07   Administration

Source: National Association of Social Workers.

SOCIAL WORK: ART OR SCIENCE?

Another question that sometimes surfaces has to do with whether social work is an art or a science. Much of the rest of this book addresses this question, at least implicitly, but we will deal with it briefly now: The only possible answer is that it is both. To the extent that there is a transmittable body of verifiable relevant information and knowledge integrated within a subject, it is a "science."

The scientific aspect of social work is real and growing, especially as the social and behavioral sciences, on which it so heavily depends, mature. But just as the field of medicine has its individual, subjective, "bedside manner" nonscience components, so social work is partially an "art." It is an art in that some people appear to be "naturals" or possess a "knack" or talent for working with others in a helping capacity. Whatever qualities these terms are used to characterize—warmth of personality, dedication to a helping goal, empathy, and so forth—the fact remains that social work is not all science. Ideally a person possessing the personality qualities and motivation so important to this profession (art) is able to capitalize on formal education and profit from present knowledge (science).

RESIDUAL AND INSTITUTIONAL SOCIAL WELFARE

Wilensky and Lebeaux presented two useful conceptions of social welfare, which they termed the *residual* and the *institutional*.[13] The older, residual view sees a place for social welfare services only after the breakdown of the family or the market, the proper sources for meeting needs. The newer, institutional position, looking at contemporary industrial society, calls for these services as a regular societal function. These two views are philosophically at opposite ends of a scale, but in actual practice social work today is somewhere between them, mixing elements of each. Powerful social forces are at play impacting on individuals and families: population growth, industrialization, urbanization, the human rights "revolution," mobility, changes in the structure of the family, scarcity of natural resources and energy, among others. From all this, the long-term historical trend appears to be from the residual toward the institutional. Some components of each conception are as follows:

Residual	*Institutional*
The needs are seen as abnormal.	The needs are expected, given industrialization.
Problematic situations are an emergency, a crisis.	Problems are inherent in the complexity of modern life.
People are helped only after the exhaustion of their resources.	Help is provided before a breakdown
The problem and the service carry a stigma.	There is no stigma in either the problem or the service.
Help tends to take the form of temporary amelioration, a reluctant, last-resort dole or charity and is terminated as early as possible.	Service is institutionalized to emphasize prevention and rehabilitation and may be permanent.
Philosophy of rugged individualism.	Emphasis on security, humanitarianism.

Wilensky and Lebeaux conclude their discussion with this prediction: "The 'welfare state' will become the 'welfare society,' and both will be more reality than epithet."[14] With conservative presidents having been in power in the United States from 1981 to 1993 and the regressive aspects of "welfare reform" of 1996, it may be difficult to accept this historical assessment. Over the long haul, however, this does seem to be the direction in which we are moving. The thrust of modern societies is toward viewing social services as what Kahn and Kamerman called "*social utilities,*" an investment in people to meet their normal needs "arising from their situations and roles in modern social life" in industrial communities.[15]

Some people find this trend disconcerting and bemoan our movement toward "socialism" or some other "ism" seen as threatening to free enterprise, capitalism, and freedom. The critics of welfare argue that its beneficiaries "become its victims, after dependence on government has turned into bondage...." Welfare opponents contend that helping people in need should be a private matter or a concern of state and local government rather than federal, and they purport to be concerned about the "spiritual as well as material well-being of our citizens."[16]

The word *welfare,* as we use it, connotes the general well-being of people collectively. In our society, to attain general well-being, mass (federal governmental) action is often necessary. Why do we have federal highways and a postal system, among the many other measures, except for the common good? On other governmental levels we seldom deplore our use of public educational systems, either primary/secondary or college/university. Nor do we seem distressed over our "socialized" municipal fire and police protection or water supply, sewage disposal, and garbage removal. All represent accepted general needs and expected collective governmental actions. Why should it be different in such areas as income maintenance and health, for example? Many other industrial nations do not understand the American preoccupation and obsession with the evils of socialism. They seem to understand far better than we do that such programs, in part, make capitalism and free enterprise workable by, among other things, providing a framework of protection for vulnerable individuals in mass societies. The "victims" and "slaves" that welfare critics refer to are such only when ignored by the communities and societies for which, incidentally, they perform much of the dirty work through typically low-wage and high-risk, but essential, occupations. The concern for the "spiritual" well-being of people and their freedom seems strange; where is the spirituality and freedom in hunger, poverty, illness, and all the other threats to human decency? Where is the human dignity in this? Finally, those opposed to welfare naively suggest that all money not appropriated by government for welfare is available potentially for private charities. This assumes a pervasive altruism, evidence for which appears lacking. Even if such altruism existed, private charities are generally designed to meet narrower, specific needs, not mass problems.

SOCIAL AGENCIES

Most social work is carried out within the context of an agency or organization of some kind. Collectively these are usually thought of as social agencies. A growing amount of social work is done outside the framework of an agency, in the form of private practice.[17] Social workers in private practice are generally engaged in such activities as counseling, psychotherapy in some form, consultation, or educational/training endeavors. While social workers in industry and some other contexts are in nontraditional settings, these are organizations. They influence the activities of professionals and are influenced by them in the same manner as agencies in general.

Agency settings can be classified into various categories with regard to social work practice. In some settings social workers are the principal professionals present and social work is of the essence—no social work, no agency. These are termed *primary agencies*. Examples are a welfare department, family service agency, and children's program offering adoption and foster care services. In other agencies the social work role is subordinate to that of other professionals from such fields as medicine, education, or law, and these agencies are called *secondary* or *host settings*. They are hosts to social work and can operate without this profession although we, of course, would argue that the service is of better quality when social work is present. Examples of these are hospitals (medical and psychiatric social workers), courts (probation officers), and schools (school social workers).

One of the most basic distinctions made relative to social work programs is whether they are *public* (tax-supported) or *private* (voluntary). In an earlier era this separation was clear and distinct. Now, however, it is much less so in that governmental (public) funds permeate many, if not most, formerly private agencies. This is so extensive, in fact, that some so-called private services could not exist today without public funding.[18] A common form that this takes is for public organizations such as a state department of public welfare, social services, or human services to purchase needed defined services from private providers such as a day-care center, group home, or rehabilitation program. This enables the provision of services that the department is not equipped to provide or could offer only at great expense. Once in existence, the service is available not only to the government department but often to other community entities as well.

Public agencies may be funded by local governmental units such as municipalities, counties, school districts; by regional bodies or states; by the federal government; or by some combination. The sources of funds for private agencies are often many and complex. Some combination of the following may be found: United Way money, fees, purchase-of-service charges, church or other contributions, bequests and annuities, interest from endowments, and others.

Private or voluntary agencies are of two types, sectarian (that is, church- or religious-related) and nonsectarian. Examples of the former are Lutheran Social Services, Catholic Charities, Jewish Community Centers, and many others, sometimes bearing a denominational name, but often not. Some private agencies, particularly organizations serving groups and communities, but also family and children's services, are not church-related. In view of the ecumenical movement of recent decades, the distinction between church-related and non-church–related agencies is not necessarily terribly significant. Many denominational agencies serve numerous clients, sometimes actually a majority, from outside their own groups. The infusion of public funds into private agencies noted above includes church-connected organizations, so this tends to diminish the importance of the sectarian/nonsectarian line further.

Social agencies also differ in age and size. Some go back to the beginning of the century or earlier, and others may reflect in their programs the factors and forces from the 1960s, 1970s, or later that led to their creation. In size, some agencies are so small that the director may also be heavily involved in direct service. On the other end of the scale are large organizations with more than one

administrative person, several supervisors, and numerous direct service workers in addition to a sizable clerical staff and perhaps others.

A social agency is often more than a single local entity; many are part of a
network of organizations, stretching across a state, the nation, or even several
countries. Local welfare or public social service departments, for example, are
units of similar state agencies. Some states have two or more intermediate district
or regional offices encompassing several counties each. Outside of a single state
we next encounter the federal regional unit of this system. There are ten such
multistate regions with headquarters in Boston, New York City, Philadelphia,
Atlanta, Chicago, Dallas, Kansas City, Denver, San Francisco, and Seattle. Finally, at the top of the pyramid there is, in Washington, D.C., the U.S. Department
of Health and Human Services (HHS) or what until 1980 was the Department of
Health, Education and Welfare (HEW).

Another example, this one from the private sector, is Family Service America (FSA) in Milwaukee. Some 245 local, mostly private, family service agencies
across the nation are affiliated with FSA, which provides various supports to
the local units. The Child Welfare League of America (CWLA) is a further illustration. This Washington, D.C.-based organization accredits agencies serving
children. Organizations like these two set standards for agencies in their fields
and engage in publication, education, information assembly and distribution,
program development, research, and advocacy.

DIMENSIONS

A number of dimensions can be delineated in social work that facilitate our understanding. Included are fields, age groups, populations, and social problems.
It is true that there is considerable overlapping and interrelatedness among
these, but they are nonetheless useful constructs.

Bartlett points out that *field* may refer to either programs/settings/services
on one hand or different kinds of social work practice in these contexts on the
other.[19] In examining the so-called fields of practice, it is advantageous to differentiate further between settings and fields. *Settings* refer to the agencies or organizations themselves rather than the larger fields of which the settings are a
part. To illustrate, health and mental health are fields, whereas a hospital and a
mental health center are settings. In both cases the context (setting and field) is
important.

Another dimension in the social services results from categorizing people
served by *ages*. Some programs focus on a single age group and others on several
or even all ages. The usual groups when separating by age are infants, preschool-
ers, children, adolescents, young adults, middle-aged, and elderly or some variation of these. A day-care center for youngsters and a nursing home for the aged
point up the importance that social welfare attaches to age factors.

A related and somewhat overlapping approach is concerned with *populations*. Examples are single parents, college students, widows, and the handicapped. Programming often revolves around a particular population(s) and is
directed toward meeting needs and problem resolution within this context. Some
problems are unique to one population, whereas others are characteristic of several groups.

Finally, one way to look at social welfare measures that also relates to those just described is in terms of *social problems*. The list is long but includes crime, poverty, alcoholism, and mental illness, to cite a few. Social work may be thought of as a profession concerned with social problems and their remedy and control. The interrelatedness of these various dimensions or levels is seen if we take the case of crime (social problem): Consider for example victims of offenders (populations), the youth or young adults who commit much of our crime (ages), corrections (a field of service), and a prison (a specific setting). Similar relationships exist with many, but not all, social service areas.

Interrelationships exist between what may appear to be largely unrelated social problems. For example, survey results releaed in 1996 indicated that, of homeless men in a group of shelters, one third were military veterans.[20] This is a disproportionately high percentage perhaps reflecting such factors as the posttraumatic stress of, especially, Vietnam war service, the difficulty in making the transition from military life, and alcohol and drug abuse. Relationships between human services and social problems also exist. An example was reported by the Gannett News Service.[21] A downturn in the murder rate nationally is attributed in part to the expansion in the number of hospital trauma centers. There is now a 90-percent survival rate of hospitalized victims of gunshot wounds. There are other examples of these interrelationships.

OTHER CONCEPTS, PRINCIPLES, TRENDS

There are a number of developments in social welfare and the broad field of human services at this time, some of which have profound implications for a field like social work. Some of these are further along than others and are far beyond the idea stage; others are still emerging. Many are interrelated with others. The order in which these principles and concepts are presented here is of no particular importance. They all are important themes, thrusts, and issues in social work currently.

1. *Least drastic or restrictive alternative.*[22] Developments of the last couple of decades have given many Americans pause as we have become increasingly aware that too much of our past programming for people in the name of helping has had damaging consequences or side effects. Hence it is now being perceived that the general principle should be followed of always using the least drastic or restrictive alternative available. Historically we have passed through a series of eras in our notions of proper treatment. Clearly from the present view some of these were harmful.

Child care is a good example. Today's view is that children should be kept at home if at all possible and supports provided to keep the family intact. If part-time arrangements such as day care do not suffice and a youngster cannot remain at home for whatever reason and if relatives are not available, foster family care may be the next possibility, a less drastic alternative than institutional care of the kind associated with the orphanage era at the turn of the century.

Another example is corrections. Incarceration of offenders is a drastic and restrictive action. There is clear evidence that most offenders do not require such severe handling and that there can and should be a variety of ways of keeping the offender in the community with less cost to the taxpayers, adequate protection for the public, potential help for the victim, and a better prognosis for the perpetrator of the illegal act. This will be discussed in greater detail in Chapter 12.

2. *Community-based services and deinstitutionalization.* A closely related trend is that of developing programs in the community that often, but not always, bring services out of distant institutions and place them closer to home. Not only does this mean that newly created programs today are more likely to be in the open community than in the more closed environment of a physical institution, but it also implies a reduced need for institutions. There is, therefore, a move toward reduction in size and numbers. Deinstitutionalization has happened in mental health, retardation, corrections, and child welfare, among other fields, but is uneven around the country both geographically and in the social problem being addressed. In general, community-based programs are perceived as less drastic and less restrictive than institutional programs.

It should be noted that the picture is complex, that "everything is relative," and definitions are required. For example, what about day care; are not such centers in effect institutions? The answer must be no if we recognize that day-care centers are typically community-based, often actually serving local neighborhoods. Furthermore, day care can keep some children out of institutions. A sizable number of children in day care are from single-parent families, and historically it was youngsters such as a portion of these who could not be cared for at home and were living in orphanages (institutions) with their regimentation, anonymity, depersonalization, and other limitations.

That "trends" are complex and mixed is seen in a proposal of no less significant a national figure than Speaker of the U.S. House of Representatives, Newt Gingrich. In the mid-1990s he suggested placing poor children in orphanages, a practice largely abandoned decades earlier. Another complication is correctional institutions; many states are building more rather than deinstitutionalizing. At the same time, there has been significant deinstitutionalization of juvenile delinquents and although more institutions are being erected for adult offenders, and to a lesser extent for juveniles, these are often more widely dispersed. There also are some highly important community measures for both youth and adult deviants.

Sometimes the view is advanced that deinstitutionalization has gone too far, especially in such areas as mental health.[23] It is alleged that parts of our large cities have become "psychiatric ghettos," where often homeless, formerly hospitalized patients idle away their time, at best unproductively, if not destructively, in neighborhoods, flophouses, and nursing homes. This view seems an exaggeration of a genuine problem and concern. Rather than being taken as an argument for more institutionalization/hospitalization, it can be seen as the case for more adequate, efficient, and creative locally based services and facilities such as mental health centers, sheltered workshops, and structured housing.

Intertwined with community-based services is the emergence of home-based services, sometimes termed *family-based services* or *family preservation programs*.[24] There is striking evidence that heavy social service input into families in their own homes can substantially reduce the need for substitute care for family members, including the need for institutionalization.

3. *Permanence.* Since the 1970s there has been a thrust in child welfare toward greater permanence in the care of children. All too often children have gone from natural home to foster home, back to natural home, and through a whole series of foster homes and other substitute care arrangements such as group homes and institutions.[25] There is a variety of reasons for this, but the experience is generally and understandably not a positive one for the child or for other persons involved. As there has come to be more awareness of the problem, more professionals are devoting themselves to solutions. An example of the problem is children who, in adoption circles, have traditionally been labeled "hard to place." Now some agencies are having success placing youngsters for adoption who formerly would never have had the continuity of growing up in one family. Permanence is a relative concept that goes beyond children. The elderly are another example. It is now quite clear that the day of institutional care such as a nursing home or other out-of-home arrangements can be delayed or prevented altogether for large numbers of older persons if supportive services are offered in communities. The result may not be complete permanence but certainly continuity can be attained.

4. *Comprehensiveness of services and continuity of care.* Closely related to permanence are the further interrelated yet separate ideas of continuity of "care" and comprehensiveness of services. These are goals rather than accomplished facts in the social services, and there is anything but a steady progression toward these ends. Social welfare programs are in many respects a hodgepodge, a collection of pieces that do not always mesh together well. Examples of some movement toward comprehensiveness, even if not total attainment, are some of the types of public assistances that are now more integrated and less categorical, and some mental health centers that have broadened their services beyond those that are strictly clinical.

A field in which continuity of care is essential but does not currently exist for millions of Americans is health. A high price is paid for what has often been referred to as our health nonsystem. One of the products of this nonsystem is that significant numbers of people needing health care are falling between the cracks, receiving no medical services or only piecemeal ones, and lacking continuity. Still another concept is *prevention*, which in part may be an outgrowth of quality services that are comprehensive in nature and provide for continuity. While prevention, continuity, and comprehensiveness are not synonymous, they are highly interrelated. Collectively they go hand in hand with the *holistic* notion of viewing persons and situations in their entirety as totalities.

5. *Case management.* In recent years there has been a marked movement related to comprehensiveness and continuity of care for clients, residents, and patients that is termed case management. A *Journal of Case Management* commenced in 1992 as part of a growing literature on the subject. This term has multiple meanings and connotations. Five functions are typically involved: (1) identification of and/or outreach to persons needing service; (2) assessment of needs; (3) planning for service; (4) linking service consumers with resources; and (5) monitoring cases.[26]

Case management is a social work practice model that has expanded extensively since the 1980s. It is used with such diverse client populations as the mentally ill, developmentally disabled, elderly, immigrants, children, those needing long-term care, and people with human immunodeficiency virus (HIV) and acquired immune deficiency syndrome (AIDS). One reason for the increase of case management is the deinstitutionalization of client populations, along with the growth of poverty and unemployment.[27] People experiencing these complex problems present challenges to social welfare and the human service systems.

6. *Right to treatment and to refuse treatment.* Implicit in the act of becoming a "client," "patient," "resident," or whatever else a social welfare "consumer" may be termed is the idea of such person's right to treatment. All too often, for example, people have been hospitalized, incarcerated, or institutionalized in the name of care, rehabilitation, or some other facet of treatment only to find that actual treatment is nonexistent or of inferior quality. Certain mental hospitals and correctional institutions in the United States have, in recent years, been reprimanded by courts for failing to provide treatment and have been mandated to institute programs to provide it.

And as the right to receive treatment has received the attention of the courts, the individual's right to refuse treatment is also coming to be recognized. Such refusal can be an issue in a variety of settings and situations. With offenders, for example, a strong case can be made that, while the state can incarcerate as punishment, the prisoner should be free to decline "treatment" in prison and that participation in various institutional programs should be voluntary rather than mandatory. This in spite of the view that some of the treatment programs may reduce recidivism and hence benefit offender and society.

Related to this is the movement with respect to assisted suicide. An issue is whether terminally ill patients have or should have the right to medical assistance in ending their own lives. This highly controversial matter is as emotionally laden as abortion and has some similar implications for social work. The U.S. Supreme Court held in June 1997 that there is no constitutional right to doctor-assisted suicide, but the court suggested that the national debate on this issue continue. In 1990 the court had held that terminally ill people could refuse treatment that would prolong life.[28]

7. *Do no harm.* It may appear contradictory that social workers who are sometimes referred to as "do-gooders" by unsympathetic elements of the public should be cautioned to avoid doing harm. But this is an important idea, given the extent to which some of the social worker's actions and programs contain at least the potential for damage. The sociologist Robert Merton suggested that behavioral practices have both "manifest" (intended and recognized) and "latent" (unintended and unrecognized) functions.[29] For example, young people go to college to attain an education and gain entry into certain kinds of life pursuits (manifest functions). But there may also be latent functions such as keeping them out of the labor market for a time and finding spouses.

Some of the latent functions may actually be dysfunctional, that is, they may be harmful or destructive. In medicine there is the phenomenon of iatrogenic illness, that is, illness caused by the treatment.[30] Loeb and Slosar described "sociatrogenic dysfunctions" as negative consequences resulting from social intervention activities.[31] They discussed various instances of sociatrogenic dysfunctions, grouped under psychotherapy, corrections, mental hospitals, school dropouts, and urban renewal. In each of these contexts the destructive potential is real. Obvious examples are the stigmatizing labels used in corrections and mental hospitals. A principal point of the Loeb and Slosar article is that it is unwise to proceed as "though doing anything is better than doing nothing." In some situations, taking no action is actually preferable. And so we conclude that the idea and admonition to do no harm is important for social work.

8. *Managed care.* Related to case management and to other recent developments is managed care, which is appropriate to consider along with the idea of doing no harm since managed care is frequently alleged to be, in fact, sometimes harmful.[32] While the idea of managed care is generally associated with the organization of health care and of health insurance, it is broader than this, encompassing other fields as well and having ramifications even more broadly. Much of the focus of managed care is on the principle of prepayment for certain health services. This puts insurance companies and other entities in powerful positions relative to who is served, how, and the nature and the duration of service. For example, there are controversies over how long a woman can remain in a hospital after giving birth; legislators and governmental administrators in 1996 sided with consumers against some insurance companies, resisting the latter's attempts to force women out of hospitals after one-day stays following delivery of a baby. The short-term treatment model espoused by managed care simply does not fit all medical treatment, certainly not in the mental health field, which is another controversial arena. In this field it is sometimes argued that managed care means denial of care or inappropriate limitations on treatment. It appears clear that dealing with insurance companies often means, for the consumer, loss of choice and, for the social worker, less autonomy.[33] It is also clear that managed care in some form is here to stay. Further discussion of managed care and its related issues comes later in several chapters.

9. *Accountability.* There can be little doubt that we are now in an era of significant demands for accountability. Various segments of the public are questioning social welfare programs and services. Funding, of course, is a central issue and concern. People understandably want to know what they are receiving for their money, whether tax funds or private contributions. But it is far more complex than this. Often it is not enough for an agency to demonstrate that it provided a certain number of units of service in a specified time period. The agency must also document quality and effectiveness of services. There may be skepticism about efficiency in program administration and about effectiveness. While this trend may complicate the lives of social workers and present demands that are difficult to meet, it is generally healthy, if appropriate and reasonable.

The human services should be accountable, especially in such inflationary times. But the general public may also need to be educated to understand some of the problems and limitations of this field and what can realistically be expected. Accountability is not a one-way street but one of reciprocity and mutuality. Communities, too, have accountability responsibilities. Social welfare institutions cannot be fully productive and effective without support from the society and communities of which they are a part and to whose problems they are addressed. Sometimes the obvious must be restated and stressed. Social work does not make social problems—communities and societies do, and they must provide the solutions and pay the costs. For example, one price of industrialization is unemployment; hence, there is a societal responsibility to provide some sort of income maintenance protection. These dynamics must be spelled out as often as necessary to build public understanding and support.

SUMMARY AND CONCLUSIONS

In this chapter we have considered some of the key concepts and principles in the field under study. Basic terminology is important in coming to grips with the fundamentals of any field, and this one is no exception. We have also examined a few of the dimensions and issues of social welfare/work/services today. There will be ample opportunity throughout much of the remainder of the book to flesh these out, to illustrate and explore them in greater depth and detail. In the next chapter we will take a historical look at our subject and, hopefully, gain a better understanding of how all this came to be.

Notes

1. H. Wayne Johnson, ed., *Rural Human Services* (Itasca, IL: F.E. Peacock Publishers, 1980), pp. 50, 144–45. See also Leon Ginsberg, ed., *Social Work in Rural Communities* (Alexandria, VA: Council on Social Work Education, 1993).
2. Werner W. Boehm, "The Nature of Social Work," *Social Work* 3, no. 2 (April 1958): 18.
3. Betty L. Baer and Ronald Federico, *Educating the Baccalaureate Social Worker* (Cambridge, MA: Ballinger Publishing, 1978), p. 61.
4. Boehm, "The Nature of Social Work."
5. *NASW News* 25, no. 10 (November 1980): 10.
6. Ralph E. Anderson and Irl Carter, *Human Behavior in the Social Environment*, 4th ed. (Hawthorn, NY: Aldine Publishing, 1990).
7. Gordon Hearn, "General Systems Theory and Social Work," in Francis J. Turner, ed., *Social Work Treatment*, 2nd ed. (New York: Free Press, 1979), pp. 333–359. See also William E. Gordon, *The General Systems Approach: Contributions toward an Holistic Conception of Social Work* (New York: Council on Social Work Education, 1969), and Robert Jackson and John Else, "Social Work as Boundary Work: Implications for Clinical Practice," a presentation (Washington, DC: NASW Professional Symposium, 1983).
8. Social institutions are defined as "the major spheres of social life, or society's subsystems, organized to meet basic human needs" by John Macionis, *Sociology*, 6th ed. (Upper Saddle River, NJ: Prentice-Hall Inc., 1997), p. 105.
9. One definition of sociology is "the systematic study of human society." The primary subject matter is the group. John Macionis, *Sociology*, 6th ed., p. 2.
10. Peter L. Berger, *Invitation to Sociology: A Humanistic Perspective* (Garden City, NY: Anchor Books, 1963), p. 4.
11. Walter Friedlander, ed., *Concepts and Methods of Social Work*, 2nd ed. (Englewood Cliffs, NJ: Prentice-Hall, 1976), pp. 2–6.
12. The complete text is available from the National Association of Social Workers, 750 First Street, N.E., Washington, DC 20002-4241.
13. Harold L. Wilensky and Charles N. Lebeaux, *Industrial Society and Social Welfare* (New York: Free Press, 1965), pp. 138–140.

14. Ibid., p. 147.

15. Alfred J. Kahn and Sheila B. Kamerman, *Social Services in International Perspective* (Washington, DC: U.S. Department of Health, Education and Welfare, 1976), pp. 6–7.

16. Barry Goldwater, *The Conscience of a Conservative* (New York: Macfadden Books, 1961).

17. Robert L. Barker, *Social Work in Private Practice*, 2nd ed. (Silver Spring, MD: NASW, 1991); *NASW News*, October 1987, p. 5, indicates that about one-third of NASW members have a part-time or a full-time private practice.

18. Ralph M. Kramer, *Voluntary Agencies in the Welfare State* (Berkeley, CA: University of California Press, 1981).

19. Harriet M. Bartlett, "Social Work Fields of Practice," *Encyclopedia of Social Work*, 16th ed. (New York: NASW, 1971), p. 1477.

20. "A Third of Homeless Men in Shelters Are Military Vets," *Des Moines Register*, November 10, 1996, p. 6A.

21. "Trauma Centers Keep Murder Rate Down," *Iowa City Press Citizen*, October 14, 1996, p. 3A.

22. Joseph Goldstein, Anna Freud, and Albert J. Solnit, *Beyond the Best Interests of the Child* (New York: Free Press, 1973).

23. "Mentally Ill Homeless Moved into Hospitals in New York City," *Des Moines Register*, October 30, 1987, p. 3A.

24. *Children and Youth Services Review* 19, no. 1/2, 1997. Entire issue on family preservation.

25. National Association of Social Workers, "Foster Care Up Despite 'Permanency' Efforts," *NASW News*, July 1993, p. 9.

26. Stephen M. Rose and Vernon L. Moore, "Case Management," *Encyclopedia of Social Work*, 19th ed. (Washington, DC: NASW, 1995), p. 336.

27. Ibid., p. 335.

28. "Bans on Assisted Suicide Upheld," *Des Moines Register*, June 27, 1997, p. 1A.

29. Robert K. Merton, *Social Theory and Social Structure* (New York: Free Press, 1957).

30. Peter C. Loeb and John A. Slosar, Jr., "Sociatrogenic Dysfunctions: A Concern for Social Work Education," *Journal of Education for Social Work* 10, no. 2 (Spring 1974): 52.

31. Ibid., pp. 51–58.

32. As an example, the CBS television program, *Sixty Minutes*, January 5, 1997.

33. Golda M. Edinburg and Joan M. Cottler, "Managed Care," *Encyclopedia of Social Work*, 19th ed. (Washington, DC: NASW 1995), p. 1641.

Additional Suggested Readings

Bailey, Roy, and Mike Brake, eds. *Radical Social Work*. New York: Pantheon Books, 1975.

Billups, James O. "Unifying Social Work: Importance of Center-Moving Ideas." *Social Work* 29, no. 2 (March–April 1984): 173–80.

Federico, Ronald C. *Social Welfare in Today's World*. New York: McGraw-Hill, 1990.

Galper, Jeffrey H. *The Politics of Social Services*. Englewood Cliffs, NJ: Prentice-Hall, 1975.

Haynes, Karen S., and James S. Mickelson. *Affecting Change*. 3rd ed. New York: Longman, 1997.

Loewenberg, Frank, and Ralph Dolgoff. *Ethical Decisions for Social Work Practice*. 5th ed. Itasca, IL: F.E. Peacock Publishers, 1996.

Reamer, Frederic C. *Ethical Dilemmas in Social Service*. 2nd ed. New York: Columbia University Press, 1993.

Reid, Nelson P., and Philip R. Popple. *The Moral Purposes of Social Work*. Chicago: Nelson-Hall, 1992.

Rosenfeld, Jona M. "The Domain and Expertise of Social Work: A Conceptualization." *Social Work* 28, no. 3 (May–June 1983): 186–191.

Rothman, Jack. *Guidelines for Case Management: Putting Research to Professional Use*. Itasca, IL: F.E. Peacock Publishers, 1992.

Tomlinson, Ray J. "Something Works: Evidence from Practice Effectiveness Studies." *Social Work* 29, no. 1 (January–February 1984): 51–56.

Wells, Carolyn Cressy, and M. Kathleen Masch. *Social Work Ethics Day to Day*. Prospect Heights, IL: Waveland Press, 1991.

3

Historical Development

H. WAYNE JOHNSON

To understand the contemporary social welfare/social work scene in this country, it is necessary to examine the record of the historical evolution of these fields in the United States and elsewhere. Not surprisingly, the present situation has been influenced substantially by earlier events and forces here and in various parts of the world, particularly in Europe and especially in England. This chapter gives a brief summary of this historical development. The subject is vast, and for those who want to delve into it in greater depth or detail, additional sources are suggested at the end of the chapter.

ENGLISH BACKGROUNDS

The development of social welfare as a social institution and social work as a profession needs to be seen in the broad context of social change. There are always various social, economic, and political factors and processes relative to social welfare activities whether the time under consideration is now or several centuries ago. Hence, there is no actual "beginning point" except as an arbitrary selection.

Karl de Schweinitz initiates his discussion of the English situation with the year 1349, because he saw an interlinked set of events tying that time in English history to the present.[1] In 1348–1349 an extremely severe epidemic of bubonic plague (the so-called Black Death) swept England, killing one-fourth of the populace. Through the balance of the century, in a period of labor shortage resulting from the plague, attitudes toward the needy changed and hardened. The church had played a large part in caring for the poor, handicapped, and disadvantaged in earlier times. There was considerable benevolence growing out of religious motives and the desire for salvation.[2] Following the plague, however, a distinction came to be made between the able-bodied poor and those seen as unable to work, including pregnant women, young children, the handicapped, the elderly, and the ill. With the labor shortage, mobile needy persons, particularly those perceived as able to work, came to be viewed negatively. As Coll states, "for more than two hundred years the problem of poverty was intimately and formally linked to the problem of vagrancy."[3]

Social changes underlying and accompanying these developments were the decline of feudalism, the enclosure of land, and the Reformation.[4] While from a contemporary viewpoint feudalism may be thought of as a kind of servitude, it provided a great deal of security and met the needs of the workers. With the gradual disappearance of feudalism, new needs arose. Similarly, the Reformation brought a reduction in church organizations such as monasteries and hospitals that previously provided extensive aid for paupers.

The Statute of Laborers of 1349 was designed to curb mobility. It prohibited giving alms to able-bodied beggars; required that able-bodied persons accept any employment offered; and prohibited such persons from leaving their parishes. A restrictive negative stance was replacing the earlier more positive and benevolent views of the indigent.

The next significant development came in the reign of Henry VIII in 1531 in what paradoxically is a more positive development, even though it provided for licensing of begging. From a twentieth-century perspective, such a change would hardly seem constructive. But it was an effort to impose some control on a situation at that time of indiscriminate begging. Beggars unable to work were registered and assigned specific areas in which to seek alms. Since this function was a task of mayors and justices of the peace, Friedlander and Apte note this as the "beginning of a recognition of public responsibility for the poor."[5]

From this point on through the rest of the 1500s came a number of important developments that culminated in the famous Elizabethan Poor Law of 1601. From the 1530s through the rest of the century, various measures provided a plan of public relief, labor regulation, public taxation to provide funds for poor relief, and appointment of overseers of the poor to administer the law. The 1601 statute, following a major economic depression and widespread unemployment, was largely a codification and restatement of existing measures and contained little that was actually new. For the first time the poor law was entirely secular, and it was comprehensive.[6] It affected social welfare practices in the American colonies as well as in England, and our public welfare system today is still influenced by this legislation.

Elizabethan Poor Law

The principal provisions of the Elizabethan Poor Law, or the Great Poor Law as it is sometimes known, were (1) local public responsibility, (2) relative responsibility, (3) administration by the "overseer of the poor," and (4) classification of the poor into three categories. Although this measure was a far cry from a federal system, which did not emerge in most nations until near or in the twentieth century, it did provide for public (governmental) responsibility on the local level for the poor. Relief could come from tax sources. This was a clear departure from using largely voluntary sectarian funding and personnel as had been done earlier.

Relative responsibility was the doctrine that parents were responsible for the support of their children and grandchildren, and similarly children must care for their dependent parents and grandparents. The overseer of the poor was a local public official appointed by magistrates or justices of the peace. The term *overseer of the poor* is still used in some American communities and, like relative responsibility, is problematic as implemented. Coll makes the point that the Elizabethan Poor Law was actually intended to be "standby" legislation.[7] The preference still was for voluntary charity, and the Elizabethan plan afforded a backup if and when necessary.

Three groups of poor were delineated by the Elizabethan Poor Law:

1. The able-bodied poor or "sturdy beggars" were dealt with punitively and repressively, being forced to work in the workhouse or house of correction. Giving alms to such people was prohibited. Anyone refusing to work in the house of correction was to be jailed or put in stocks. The problem of vagrants was handled by providing that indigents who came into a community from other parishes were to be returned to the last place where they had lived for a year.
2. The impotent poor were those unable to work. Two forms of care were possible for them. They could be cared for in the poorhouse or almshouse where they were expected to work within their capacities. On the other hand, if the impotent poor had a place to live and it was felt to be less expensive to keep them there, they were given "outdoor relief" (that is, aid in their homes rather than in institutions). This was nonmonetary aid or relief-in-kind in such forms as fuel, food, or clothing.
3. Dependent children were children whose parents were absent or were too poor to support them. They were to be placed with an adult who would take them without a charge or to the lowest bidder, that is, the person charging the least for their care. Boys were to learn a trade through apprenticeship, and girls were brought up as domestic servants.

Separating the poor into "deserving" and "undeserving" becomes quite pointed with the Elizabethan Poor Law, making it clear that to be poor is no longer acceptable; it is a sign of immorality or criminality, at least for the able-bodied. This profound development still impacts upon us centuries later in the United States and other parts of the world.

Post-Elizabethan Era

Two-thirds of a century later, in 1662, the Law of Settlement and Removal was enacted, dealing with the matter of residency, which is still an issue today.[8] Under this statute, it was possible to eject from the parish persons who it was thought might become dependent upon the community in the future. This legislation was a reaction to the view of officials and lay people of the time, often mistaken, that indigent people entered certain geographical areas in order to receive more generous aid. Removal proved to be more of a problem than a solution, and it was often easier to grant assistance than to send individuals and families to their place of legal residence.

During the 1600s and 1700s, the workhouse became a major center of activity. Conditions in these facilities were often deplorable, and reformers called for improvements. The workhouse was essentially a punitive place. To receive even this punitive help, needy people were required to give up their homes and enter the workhouse for employment. This is often termed the *workhouse test*; one had to demonstrate willingness to work.

An interesting development occurred in 1795 with the passage of the Speenhamland Act, which provided for partial outdoor relief or wage supplementation. Without entering an almshouse or workhouse, a poor person's earnings could be supplemented using a formula. The *bread scale* was used to determine what a family needed for sustenance based on the local cost of bread. Since there was no minimum wage as we are accustomed to today, employers had no reason to pay a living wage, and the Speenhamland Act had the self-defeating effect of increasing taxes for poor relief and encouraging substandard wages. That parallels in social welfare exist over the centuries is seen in the title of an article published in 1969 at the time of the Nixon administration's proposal for a family assistance plan: "Mr. Nixon's Speenhamland."[9]

The seventeenth through the nineteenth centuries were dynamic times of social change impacting significantly on human well-being and social welfare arrangements. Protestantism, the Industrial Revolution, and capitalism all became intermeshed to emphasize the work ethic and laissez-faire economic ideas. Individuals and families were exploited by mass business/industrial enterprises in an era of urbanization. Child labor was one social problem illustrative of many others as wealth was amassed at the expense of common citizens who often experienced alienation in the process. Help given to persons in distress through this era was generally handled by volunteers.

The pendulum swung again in England with the reform known as the New Poor Law of 1834. Reform is a relative term; in this case most of the change was backward-looking and repressive rather than progressive and forward-moving. Based on a biased investigation of the Poor Law, it was concluded that the existent system was "a bounty on indolence and vice."[10] Hence, the core of the new poor law was the prohibition of partial home or outdoor relief to the able-bodied. Thus, it was an undoing of the Speenhamland provisions. All able-bodied needy were to be aided only in workhouses. Only the elderly, the ill, the invalid, and widows with young children could receive outdoor relief. Finally, a new principle was added to the poor law, known as *less eligibility*, which holds that no recipient of relief could be as well off as the lowest-paid worker in the community.[11] This was an effort to make relief unattractive and uncomfortable. The reader may profit from reflecting on whether such philosophy exists in any way in the United States today.

With all this negativism, there was one respect in which the new poor law was progressive, that is, more efficient. This had to do with organization and administration. Several parishes were to be combined for purposes of relief administration into a *poor law union*, and a central board of control was to be appointed by the king.[12] For the time this centralization represented progress, but today, in an era of mass organization, we often desire the opposite—decentralization.

England and other parts of Europe saw various reforms in the nineteenth century in such areas as public health, child labor, prisons, housing, charity organization, and settlement houses, among others. Not until the twentieth century, however, were income maintenance programs generally instituted. Germany became a pioneer in this field in the 1800s, preceding parallel developments of the Great Depression in the United States by a number of decades. Among the famous pioneers who contributed to the growing reforms early in the century in England were Beatrice and Sidney Webb. Later in the decade, the Beveridge Report of 1941 led to the elements of the welfare state found in England today.

AMERICAN DEVELOPMENTS

Early settlers brought to our eastern seaboard social welfare ideas and practices that had taken centuries to evolve in Europe. There was much hardship in the colonial period because many people were poor when they arrived and conditions were often harsh. The Elizabethan Poor Law and the Law of Settlement were adopted here, and from the beginning there was present the notion of public aid as a "right."[13]

Forms of aid included almshouses, relief in the home, contracting out the needy as a group, and auctioning off to the lowest bidder. There were arguments for and against use of the almshouse, and its role varied over time, but there were almshouses for those unable to work and workhouses for the able-bodied. Concern about indiscriminate grouping of people into almshouses with deplorable conditions eventually led to the removal from these facilities of certain groups, such as children, and to making more specialized provisions for them.[14] There was also public outdoor relief as well as assistance from voluntary sources. Residency requirements to be eligible for aid were an early practice. Persons who were thought likely to become dependent upon the community were "warned out," that is, given notice to leave or, failing to do so, did not gain eligibility for assistance by remaining.

Prior to the twentieth century in the United States, voluntary or private social welfare activities were more extensive and generally significant than those of the public sector. One major movement was the Charity Organization Society (COS), starting in London in 1869, and based on the earlier ideas of the Rev. Thomas Chalmers. Chalmers advocated dividing the community into districts and meeting the poor personally, on a friendly basis, but he held to the notion that individual failure was the reason for poverty. The COS moved quickly to numerous American communities by way of Buffalo, New York, in 1877, where S.H. Gurteen was the founder. But in spite of all its effort to constitute a new approach to charity, the COS continued judgmental attitudes toward the poor. Paupers were seen as being to blame for their condition (victim blaming), and the COS held relief (or aid) in low esteem. Such attitudes were expressed by Josephine Shaw Lowell, a leader in the New York City COS and a nationally known figure in their movement.

Initially the COS stayed out of the relief-giving business. Central in its approach was the idea of organizing and coordinating existing relief-giving units,

The Industrial Revolution, which began in the eighteenth century, caused great misery among poor working people. Child workers are shown in an American textile factory in the early 1900s.

developing a central register of the needy, and using *friendly visitors*, volunteers to visit applicants for help. In these activities, the COS represented early roots of two modern social work methods: friendly visiting was a forerunner of social casework with the idea of working with people one-to-one, and the coordinating function was an early form of what is now called *community organization.*

As the COS gained experience with human need and suffering in various communities, it felt a growing awareness that social problems were more complex than simply results of immorality and lack of initiative and thrift on the part of individuals, as had been the view. Hence, COS workers joined social action efforts to obtain legislation for improving conditions in such areas as housing, health, and prisons. They also played a part in bringing about the first formalized training program for social work in 1898.[15] In some communities the COS also began to dispense relief itself rather than restrict itself to the coordination of other relief-giving bodies.

Other significant social welfare/social work developments appeared in the mid-1800s with the founding of a number of group-serving agencies, often focused on youth work. All were voluntary and became national movements. Included were the Young Men's Christian Association (YMCA), Boys' Clubs, Jewish Centers, and Young Women's Christian Association (YWCA). After the turn of the century, the scouting movement emerged, for both boys and girls, as did Campfire Girls, Junior Red Cross, and the 4-H Clubs. Some of these organizations had European forerunners. The purpose and focus differed somewhat among these movements, but all came to be important voluntary resources and remain so today.

One of the most fascinating social innovations in urban centers on both sides of the Atlantic was the *settlement house*. This movement started with the work of Samuel Barnett and others at Toynbee Hall in London and spread quickly to the United States in the 1880s. One of the best known was Hull House in Chicago, established in 1889 by Jane Addams, one of the striking early personalities in American social work. Settlement houses were typically located in the inner city in areas populated by working people and immigrants. The staff of the settlements were often well-to-do people like Jane Addams who lived in the facility and set about becoming neighbors to those who lived in their neighborhoods. These dedicated leaders offered a variety of services as well as friendship and counsel, helping to acclimate foreigners as well as people who had moved into the cities from smaller communities for jobs in mushrooming industries.

The settlements provided educational and cultural programs. Naturalization activities for immigrants and training in English were important as were recreational opportunities for people of all ages. Day nurseries and kindergartens were developed. Because the social problems related to poverty were so massive and oppressive at that time, settlement house personnel became active in promoting social legislation for improved housing, factory regulation, labor laws, and health and sanitation control. Urban slums were almost indescribable in their misery; water and milk were impure, streets were unpaved and filthy, and deplorable conditions abounded. In this context, settlements worked—directly serving people and also attempting to improve social conditions affecting them. Settlements also impacted upon other social movements such as the juvenile court that started in Chicago in 1899. The term *settlement house* is no longer very common, and such facilities today are more often known as *neighborhood* or *community centers*. They are still private (voluntary) as they were originally, and many are affiliated with the National Federation of Settlements and Neighborhood Centers. Other community centers have developed under public, often municipal, auspices and often focus mainly on recreation.

The two decades preceding U.S. involvement in World War I make up the Progressive Era. As Robert Bremner observes, it was a hopeful time of confronting social problems, with social workers taking leading roles in the reform efforts.[16] Many of these workers were active in the COS, settlements, and other movements. Social justice became a clear goal in this dynamic period.

Governmental Social Welfare Activities

While government, especially on the federal level, did not play a significant role in social welfare in this country until the Great Depression of the 1930s, there were some beginnings prior to this century that served as important precedents for what was to come later. On the state level, specialized facilities, usually hospitals, "asylums," schools, and prisons appeared as early as the late 1700s but expanded particularly in the nineteenth century. These represented efforts to remove certain groups of needy people from the almshouses and to provide separate treatment for them. Included in these groups were the mentally ill and retarded; the blind, deaf, and deaf-mute; and offenders.[17] In parallel developments the federal government took responsibility for certain programs for Native Americans, immigrants, health, veterans, and federal offenders.[18] All these endeavors collectively were a far cry from the kind of governmental responsibility to be seen later, but they did constitute a beginning.

After the turn of the century, mothers' or widows' pensions appeared in some states. They were an early form of assistance that later was to be incorporated into the nation's Social Security framework as Aid to Dependent Children and in the form principally of survivor insurance benefits.

Although the colonists had brought to America some notion of local public responsibility toward the poor, not until the severe economic crisis of the Great Depression, following the stock market crash in 1929, did the federal government come to assume a large role in social welfare matters. Some of this change originated in the Herbert Hoover administration as it grappled with the horrendous problems of the depression from 1929 to 1933. Hoover's conservatism, however, left his proposals unsuited to cope with the seriousness of the problems confronting the nation. The major changes came with the administration of President Franklin D. Roosevelt and his New Deal beginning in 1933. Roosevelt was determined to meet the crises of massive unemployment, poverty, and an immobilized economy and immediately instituted a series of reforms. Collectively these often were experimental trial-and-error efforts, and some were abandoned after relatively short periods of time. An alphabet soup era of new programs: FERA (Federal Emergency Relief Administration), CWA (Civil Works Administration), WPA (Works Progress Administration), CCC (Civilian Conservation Corps), NYA (National Youth Administration), and others focused on work relief, employment, conservation, help for youth and rural dwellers, and related activities. Conspicuous in the administration of some of these federal efforts was Harry Hopkins, a professional social work administrator. His participation symbolized a move toward using educationally qualified persons to staff social welfare programs.

It should also be noted that the New Deal was sympathetic with and supportive of the organized labor movement. This movement is perhaps as significant historically as any single factor in an improved standard of living and better conditions for workers generally. For this reason the current situation relative to organized labor is of interest to social work.

Not only was the role of government in social welfare transformed by the depression of the 1930s, so also was that of the private agencies. Until that time, a major function of private agencies was the provision of relief to those in financial need. Because of the broad scope of the depression, funds were exhausted in the voluntary sector, and it was not possible to raise more money to assist those in distress. With the passage of the Social Security Act in 1935, private agencies generally reduced or ended their relief-giving role, which was taken over by the public sector. In the next chapter we will examine the income maintenance programs that have evolved, mostly since 1935.

War and the Postwar Era

In the twentieth century, two world wars and other conflicts, especially that in Vietnam, have affected human needs and social services. Military service placed individuals and families in stress.[19] Disequilibrium results from war-created

mobility as people move to work in defense industries, and numerous other social problems arise when nations are at war. In this country both public and private agencies have been involved in the response to such problems.

For social welfare purposes, the World War II era, the immediate postwar
years, and the Korean conflict of the early 1950s constituted a relatively quiet period. When the nation is embroiled in major warfare, priorities tend to emphasize
matters other than social welfare considerations. This is not to say that there are
no social problems or services at these times. Obviously war is disruptive to a nation even when bombs do not fall on its territory, and social programs reflect
these national tensions. But significant social welfare legislation is less likely to
be enacted in this context.

Dwight D. Eisenhower was a moderate Republican president (1953 to
1960). While this administration was not associated with major federal social
welfare developments, some striking social movements had their roots in this
decade. For example, the bus boycott in Birmingham, Alabama, in 1955 initiated
the civil rights movement that was to expand nationally in the 1960s.

The 1960s to the 1990s

The 1960s and early 1970s constituted a time of great ferment in this country
with a number of powerful social movements, including what collectively may
be termed the *human rights revolution*. Some aspects of this are still very much
present as we move into the twenty-first century. Few of these movements were
actually new but were reappearing with new emphases and impetus. The civil
rights movement sought equal rights for racial minorities. The *war on poverty*
attempted to bring millions of deprived Americans into the economic mainstream, and with it came the welfare rights movement. As the 1960s progressed,
the antiwar movement expanded, aimed at terminating the involvement of the
United States in the Vietnam conflict. New chapters were written in the decades-
old women's rights activities. At various times, attention has been and is being
focused on rights of children, prisoners, veterans, mental and other patients,
those favoring access to abortion, nursing home residents, homosexuals, the
handicapped, aged, and others.[20] The children's rights movement illustrates the
complexity of these controversies, since increased rights for children may also
have the effect of increasing their vulnerability. This kind of value conflict often
accompanies social change. Collectively, what all of these developments tend
to do is to increase the visibility of certain groups and their needs, often fairly invisible otherwise, and the injustices experienced by large numbers of persons
who are all too often discriminated against, exploited, or otherwise abused
through stereotyping and scapegoating prejudice. Generally, these groups are
made up of people at risk in varying degree. Social work has an important part
to play in helping people secure their rights and to safeguard these rights against
infringement. Social justice is a primary concern of social work.

By comparison with their immediate predecessors, the administrations of
Gerald Ford and Jimmy Carter in the 1970s were somewhat quiescent. In 1981, a
profoundly more conservative administration came into office in Washington.
Federal expenditures for military defense were greatly expanded and human

service funds were reduced substantially. There is general agreement that a major problem confronting most Americans is inflation (even though inflation has been relatively modest in the 1990s), but there is disagreement on what should be done about it and what the role of the federal government should be. Once again, it is being said or implied that the poor should work; that welfare programs are too generous; and that if the economy can just become more healthy (which some may say translates into the rich becoming richer), something is bound to trickle down to the less well-off. This development demonstrates convincingly that these centuries-old issues were not settled for all time with the humanitarianism of the New Deal in the 1930s, but the pendulum continues to swing.

The Clinton administration is attempting to institute reforms in health, welfare, and other areas but the outcome, in part, is unknown at this writing. "Welfare reform" was enacted by Congress and signed by the president (after two vetoes of earlier bills) in 1996, and is now being implemented. (This development is examined in the next chapter.) The most certain thing about the remainder of the century and beginning of the next appears to be uncertainty, as Alvin Toffler described in *Powershift*, with continuing rapid technological change and profound modifications in our social institutions, as he has noted subsequently.[21]

Chapter 27 considers the future of social services. But at this juncture a general observation can be made. In some respects it made little difference which political party prevailed in the 1996 elections and who occupies the White House as the nation ends the 1990s. The reason in part is the national debt and federal deficit, casting a shadow over the financing of many (but not all) social welfare measures. Even the ever-present debt and deficit are not written in stone, however (the deficit has been sharply reduced in the 1990s), and change may make the picture appear quite different in years to come.

SUMMARY AND CONCLUSIONS

To understand the present and to have some reasonable notions about the future, one must turn to the past for enlightenment. This is what we have attempted to do in this chapter. Social welfare history is a vast subject with an extensive literature of its own. Because of many priorities, it has been necessary to present a highly summarized portrayal.

Without subscribing to the "few great persons" theory of history, we have included the role and contributions of such figures as the Webbs, Thomas Chalmers, S.H. Gurteen, Josephine Lowell, Samuel Barnett, Jane Addams, and Harry Hopkins. These people, of course, were products of their times, but they also made a difference in those times and what followed.

More important than most of the specific events sprinkled throughout the centuries are the ongoing themes, developments, and evolution of social welfare and human services broadly. Always occurring within some context and never in a vacuum, these social problems and helping measures are usually very much bound up in and influenced by wider political, economic, and other processes, and institutions. For this reason, in order to be a student of the social services, one's study must cover a wide horizon of information and knowledge.

Notes

1. Karl de Schweinitz, *England's Road to Social Security* (New York: A.S. Barnes, 1961, Perpetua Edition), p. 2.
2. Walter A. Friedlander and Robert Z. Apte, *Introduction to Social Welfare*, 5th ed. (Englewood Cliffs, NJ: Prentice-Hall, 1980).
3. U.S. Department of Health, Education and Welfare, *Perspectives in Public Welfare* by Blanche D. Coll (Washington, DC: U.S. Government Printing Office, 1969), p. 4.
4. Lucy Komisar, *Down and Out in the U.S.A.*, 2nd ed. (New York: New Viewpoints, 1977), pp. 2–4.
5. Friedlander and Apte, *Introduction*, p. 13.
6. Coll, *Perspectives*, p. 5.
7. Ibid., pp. 6–7.
8. Ralph E. Pumphrey and Muriel W. Pumphrey, eds., *The Heritage of American Social Work* (New York: Columbia University Press, 1961), pp. 17–18.
9. Edith G. Levi, "Mr. Nixon's 'Speenhamland,'" *Social Work* 15, no. 1 (January 1970): 7–11.
10. Coll, *Perspectives*, pp. 10–11.
11. Friedlander and Apte, *Introduction*, p. 21.
12. Ibid.
13. Coll, *Perspectives*, p. 19.
14. Friedlander and Apte, *Introduction*, pp. 61–62.
15. Ibid., p. 75.
16. Robert H. Bremner, *From the Depths: The Discovery of Poverty in the United States* (New York: New York University Press, 1956), pp. 201–203.
17. Friedlander and Apte, *Introduction*, pp. 63–71.
18. Ibid., pp. 82–90.
19. "Military Counsels Families," *Des Moines Register*, March 22, 1981, p. 7E.
20. Donald Brieland et al., *Contemporary Social Work: An Introduction to Social Work and Social Welfare*, 3rd ed. (New York: McGraw-Hill, 1985), pp. 8–13.
21. Alvin Toffler, *Powershift* (New York: Bantam Books, 1991).

Additional Suggested Readings

Abbott, Edith. *Public Assistance*. Chicago: University of Chicago Press, 1940.

Abbott, Grace. *From Relief to Social Security*. Chicago: University of Chicago Press, 1941.

Addams, Jane. *Twenty Years at Hull House*. New York: Macmillan, 1922.

Axinn, June, and H. Levine. *Social Welfare: A History of the American Response to Need*. 4th ed. White Plains, NY: Longman, 1997.

Breckinridge, Sophonisba P. *Public Welfare Administration in the United States*. Chicago: University of Chicago Press, 1927.

Chambers, Clarke. *Seedtime of Reform*. Minneapolis: University of Minnesota Press, 1963.

Day, Phyllis J. *A New History of Social Welfare*. 2nd ed. Needham Heights, MA: Allyn and Bacon, 1997.

Devine, Edward T. *When Social Work Was Young*. New York: Macmillan, 1939.

Ehrenreich, John. *The Altruistic Imagination: A History of Social Work and Social Welfare Policy in the U.S.* Ithaca, NY: Cornell University Press, 1985.

Leiby, James. *A History of Social Welfare and Social Work in the United States*. New York: Columbia University Press, 1978.

Lubove, Roy. *The Professional Altruist*. Cambridge, MA: Harvard University Press, 1965.

Trattner, Walter I. *From Poor Law to Welfare State*. 5th ed. New York: Free Press, 1994.

Part 2

Social Problems and Social Services

We come now to the largest part of our endeavor—the study of the major provisions made in response to our principal social problems. What we have covered so far lays a foundation for this next ambitious undertaking.

In the historical overview in the last chapter, we saw that much of the history over the centuries had to do with poverty and attempts to deal with it. This is still a primary concern as will be seen in the next chapter, which addresses public welfare and income maintenance. As will become apparent, considerable unfinished business remains on this matter. Other chapters deal with social work in relation to families and children, schools, physical and mental health, disabilities, substance abuse, and criminal justice. Still others cover the elderly, social services in business and industry, and various emerging and nontraditional settings of social work practice.

As was noted in the Preface, you may wish to read Part 3 on methods of social work practice before Part 2 dealing with programs and services. This will not be necessary if you keep in mind that most social work encountered in the various settings described in Part 2 is with individuals and families, groups, or communities.

4

Public Welfare and Income Maintenance

H. WAYNE JOHNSON

In this chapter we are concerned with the basic social problem of poverty and with public welfare, the constellation of services created in response to poverty. Actually, we will examine some programs that are outside the federal-state-local tax-supported measures usually termed *public welfare*, but all are collectively concerned with poverty and its alleviation or prevention. Not all are income maintenance programs in the usual sense, but all contribute, directly or indirectly, to economic betterment of individuals and families. In some cases this is through a positive impact on purchasing power, in others through increasing employability, and in still others by improvements in health, housing, nutrition, or other major aspects of life.

POVERTY

It may facilitate our understanding to examine poverty in terms of its *nature, causes, extent*, and *solutions*—important considerations in any social problem. On the nature of contemporary American poverty, what Michael Harrington wrote in *The Other America* in 1962 is still essentially accurate today.[1] Poor people in this country tend to fall into certain groups and possess discernible attributes. Among these are migratory agricultural laborers, Appalachian hill people (farmers, miners), racial and ethnic minorities, the elderly, the physically and/or psychologically handicapped, children, alcoholics and addicts, the poor who have migrated to the city from rural areas, and the only group that, according to Harrington, is voluntarily poor—intellectuals, bohemians, beats.[2] Some modifications in Harrington's categories must be made to update the picture (for example, adding other addicts to alcoholics), but the basic scene is essentially unchanged—millions of Americans continue to be poor in a land of affluence. This is not to say that all people occupying any one or several of these groups are poor but that most poverty-stricken Americans possess one or some of these qualities and that a disproportionately large number of people who are elderly, to cite one example, are poor. It is also true that one child in four under age six is poor today.[3]

John K. Galbraith has made an important distinction between what he calls *case poverty* and *insular poverty*. Case poverty refers to those situations in which individuals or families remain poor, unlike most of the people in their surroundings. Certain attributes of the individuals involved relate to their poverty-stricken status. They may be intellectually, physically, or emotionally limited, undereducated, or alcoholic to cite some examples. Insular poverty, on the other hand, Galbraith compares to an island, a situation in which "everyone or nearly everyone is poor." The "colonias," rural slums in Texas and the southwest, are an example. Individual characteristics or inadequacies do not explain such poverty. Both kinds of poverty, or sets of causative factors, are found today. Both present obstacles to alleviation of the condition.[4]

Cause and effect is often a difficult matter and certainly is here. Is a person alcoholic because he or she is poor or is he or she poor as a result of the alcoholism? Often such conditions go hand-in-hand, aggravating and reinforcing each other. It is clear that many people who suffer poverty are born into it and have greatly constricted opportunities and lives from the beginning. For such persons, poverty is the only way of life they have ever known or probably ever will, given our present economic and social welfare systems.

Harrington correctly emphasized that much poverty in this nation is invisible. Modern highways often go through urban slums above or below ground level, and the motorist sees little of the shambles along the way. Rural poverty is frequently tucked away in out-of-sight locations and may even be viewed as quaint and picturesque. The beauty of the landscape may conceal the human suffering. The elderly poor are often restricted to cheap hotel rooms, boardinghouses, and store fronts where they live out their days and years in fear, loneliness, and misery. Skid rows containing some of our alcoholics and inner-city jungles and their junkies are not part of the experience of most Americans. Skin-and-bones starvation is fortunately not characteristic of American poverty, although the poor may frequently be hungry. Rather, our poor are often obese as the result of cheap starchy foods, and the fat may go unrecognized as a sign of poverty. Finally, the fact that many of America's poor are not dressed in rags as is true in some countries, thanks to relatively inexpensive discount stores and second-hand shops, makes our poverty inconspicuous.[5] Out of sight and out of mind is certainly an aspect of modern poverty and a factor contributing to its persistence. If more Americans were aware of its existence and prevalence there would possibly be greater sensitization to poverty and more interest in its reduction. This is not a certainty by any means, however, in view of the general apathy and indifference toward many social problems.

Listing some of these most pronounced features of poverty reveals a good bit not only about its nature but also about its causation. We are talking about people, many of whom are too young, too old, or too disabled to work. This is important to know when we see victim-blaming bumper stickers and placards announcing "I fight poverty—I work." Some could work if employment were available, but given the rates of unemployment we have frequently experienced

W. Hill, Jr./The Image Works

Poverty in America takes a fearful toll in human misery. A jobless man holds up his child and asks desperately for money or other assistance.

in recent decades, it is obvious that there often are not enough jobs to go around or the jobs are unevenly distributed geographically or people are automated out of work. Other chronically poor people work hard, sometimes full-time year after year. But the jobs they are able to obtain pay so poorly they are chronically impoverished. Many poor people have limited education, skills, and sophistication and hence bring little to an industrialized urban labor market. Lack of experience or ability in planning one's life is an element of poverty. The large families sometimes seen in the homes of poor people testify to the absence of a future orientation. Why delay gratification when tomorrow is so uncertain or is almost certain to be as empty and unrewarding as yesterday and today?

Some poor people are single parents struggling to raise a family alone. Most of these are women, and they often have had little or no work experience outside the home. And women are still not as well paid as men, generally, in this sexist society. Hence considerable attention is being given at this time to the *feminization of poverty*. Similarly some people are poor *because* of their racial or ethnic minority status in a racist society. Obviously not all minority persons are in poverty but a disproportionately high number are. African-Americans, Hispanics, Native Americans, and other minorities face multifaceted discrimination—in obtaining jobs, in getting promotions on the job, in procuring training or education required for certain employment, in gaining membership in unions, and so forth. Finally, some people simply do not share work-ethic values. Poverty then has many causes and contributing factors. It is a complex phenomenon. For the people experiencing it, poverty is anguish, pain, and defeat.

Unemployment and underemployment are highly related to poverty and have a profound impact on the well-being of individuals and families. This was made painfully clear in the recession of the early 1990s. The average annual employment rate in 1992 was high, 7.4 percent; it is too easy to ignore the fact that this figure represents over 8 million people. By May 1997, the ever fluctuating rate was down to 4.8 percent, the lowest since 1973. There is also a wide variation in joblessness among states, from a high of over 7 percent in Alaska and West Virginia to a low of 2.5 percent in Nebraska, in January 1997.[6] Furthermore, the official jobless statistics do not reflect the many more who exhaust their unemployment benefits and are no longer counted. At one point it was estimated that there were 1.7 million "discouraged" workers who had given up and stopped looking for jobs.[7] Part-time workers are counted as employed even though many of them want full-time work.

Formerly, economists considered a 4-percent unemployment rate *full employment*, since there are always some people between jobs or in other situations without jobs currently. Now the trend is to think of full employment as approximating 6-percent unemployment. In other words people are being conditioned to expect unemployment and to see it as normal. This is not reassuring to a family facing joblessness. In recent decades there has often been an unemployment rate of 7 percent or higher.

With automation and the various technological changes displacing workers, the question is whether there will ever be enough jobs for everyone. Will work, as it has been known traditionally, become obsolete? Various job-creation programs have been proposed, including the idea of shortening the workweek to 4.5 days in order to increase the number of jobs.[8] But whether any of these schemes can be adequate is an open question. In the meantime, wealthy people in high places continue to say that there is an abundance of jobs; that everyone who wants work can find it; and that newspaper ads list plenty of positions. What goes unrecognized, however, is that the vacancies listed in such areas as computer specialists and technical fields requiring advanced training do little for the average person seeking work.

Accompanying the loss of employment and income for many is the loss of such benefits as insurance programs. It was estimated in 1994 that 60 percent of displaced workers who were employed again had health insurance while only 36 percent of those who were unemployed were covered. In 1986 the Associated Press reported that almost 80,000 retirees of LTV Corporation lost their health and insurance benefits when the company filed for bankruptcy reorganization.[9] In 1997 Apple Computer announced it was laying off 4,100 employees, one-third of its staff, the largest cutback in its history and one of the largest ever in California's Silicon Valley. When a family is without health and/or life insurance, it is terribly vulnerable. Studies indicate a variety of negative personal consequences for the unemployed and their families.

Studies indicate that for each 1 percent increase in unemployment there is a 4.1 percent rise in suicides; 5.7 percent in homicides; and 1.9 percent in stress-related disorders, heart disease, and cirrhosis of the liver. There is also an increase in mental hospital admissions of 2.3 percent for women and 4.3 percent for men. Another study showed that there are 318 additional suicides among American men when unemployment increases 1 percent. Various other studies show increases in alcohol and drug abuse, wife and child abuse, and mental illness accompanying joblessness. Research at Boston College found wives of unemployed men experiencing more anxiety and depression, and a Michigan study found children manifesting retarded physical and mental development, irritability, and digestive problems following parental unemployment.[10] The recession of the early 1980s brought a new class of *affluent poor*, those who cannot pay their house mortgages or car loans because of job losses, but have too many assets to be eligible for welfare.[11]

Poverty is relative, and its occurrence varies with time and place. In the United States we have moved in this century from a nation of general poverty to one in which the poor constitute a minority for the first time. Even as recently as when Harrington wrote, perhaps one-fourth of Americans were poor; in 1995 it was 13.8 percent.[12] To the extent that this is a real change, such progress is encouraging and commendable. However, the number in poverty reached a 20-year high in 1991. The amount of poverty remaining in this country of tremendous wealth is shocking and disgraceful. In addition to the 36.4 million Americans living in poverty, another 12.3 million are *near poor* (between 100 and 125 percent of the poverty threshold) so that about one-fifth of our citizens are deprived.[13]

That we cannot count on the inevitability of decline in poverty is seen in developments of the 1990s. The recession and high unemployment took a heavy toll in the decade, making a bad poverty situation worse. The poverty income guidelines are updated each year by the Department of Health and Human Services. In 1997 the poverty line was set at $16,050 for a family of four, except in Alaska and Hawaii where it is higher.[14] Some years ago the late British historian Arnold Toynbee spent some time in the United States. Upon leaving this country he observed that, of all the places in which to be poor, America was the worst because of its vast wealth. To be poor when everyone around you is similarly afflicted is hard, but to be poor when most are comfortable and many are rich can be unbearable.

America is a land of "private wealth and public poverty." *Business Week* reported that in 1996 the average chief executive officer (CEO) of the largest corporations was paid over $5.7 million in total compensation. This was 209 times more than the average factory worker's wage. The CEO's average raises were 54 percent compared to the worker's 3 percent.[15] *Business Week*, on its cover, termed this situation "out of control." Earlier, Boeing Company gave its chairman a $554,000 bonus, raising his yearly pay to over $2 million at the same time that it planned cutting 28,000 jobs.[16] President Clinton proposes raising the minimum wage and the business lobby argues against this and against discouraging extravagant pay for executives. Finally, a baseball player is paid $11.5 million a year,[17] as in a previous such contract, "enough to pay for 55 bone marrow transplants or hire 265 school teachers...."[18] The Reagan administration deeply cut one social program after another in the name of economy. Yet, as the economist Lester Thurow pointed out, welfare represents less than 1 percent of our gross national product.[19]

As is true of some other social problems, poverty is functional, that is, it serves some social purposes. From certain perspectives it is useful. Herbert Gans delineated 15 functions served by poverty as follows: (1) assuring that society's "dirty work" is done; (2) subsidizing through low wages many activities of the affluent, freeing up money for investments and time/energy for other pursuits; (3) creating jobs for occupations dealing with the poor; (4) prolonging the economic usefulness of goods others do not want but that the poor buy and providing incomes for professionals unappealing to more affluent clients; (5) maintaining the legitimacy of dominant norms by identifying the poor as deviants; (6) providing the affluent with emotional gratification by identifying certain groups of poor as deserving; (7) providing vicarious participation for the affluent in the supposed sexual, alcoholic, and drug behavior of the poor; (8) guaranteeing the status of the nonpoor; (9) furthering the upward mobility of the nonpoor; (10) occupying the time and energies of the affluent, hence giving the latter meaning; (11) making "high" culture possible by providing labor and creating surplus capital; (12) providing "low" culture, which is frequently adopted by the affluent; (13) acting as symbolic constituencies or needed opponents for some political groups; (14) absorbing the political and economic costs of societal growth and change by providing the foot soldiers for wars, land for urban renewal, and other activities; and (15) since the poor participate less in the political process, adding to political stability and a more centrist politics.[20] Gans's article helps one understand that poverty persists partly because it serves the remainder of society. Hence, it will be difficult to remove from the societal scene.

We are sometimes told of the biblical pronouncement "The poor you always have with you," and it is suggested that poverty is inevitable.[21] The question is not whether there will always be a bottom rung on the income ladder; there clearly will be in the American economic system. Rather the issue is what this means. Does it necessarily have to mean lack of human decency and dignity in housing, health, education, nutrition, and other primary life areas, or can relatively low income and human dignity be reconciled? It is the author's position that they can be. There should be no place in a wealthy advanced society for a permanent underclass.

ANTIPOVERTY PROGRAMS

We turn our attention now to those social services that have been devised as antipoverty measures. Prior to the Great Depression of the 1930s, public relief programs in this country were very modest and piecemeal. They were generally local or state in funding and structure, as we saw in Chapter 3. Such arrangements proved to be grossly inadequate for the massive unemployment and misery of the 1930s. At the peak of the Depression as many as 15 million—between one-quarter and one-third of the adult labor force—were out of work.[22] The older notions of poverty as the result of personal immorality or character defect could no longer be sustained. It is not surprising, then, that more and more people came to believe that what were required to keep the nation on an even keel economically were broad-scope income maintenance programs stressing (1) prevention, (2) permanence, and (3) federal leadership. The federal Social Security Act of 1935 was the outcome. It has been amended numerous times since then, generally in the direction of covering (protecting) a greater proportion of Americans and doing so at a more adequate economic level, although there were exceptions to this in recent years. Much unfinished work remains, however, as we will see.

Originally the Social Security Act encompassed three groups of provisions: (1) social insurances, (2) public assistances, and (3) health and welfare services. Only the first two of these groups of programs are directly concerned with maintaining income.

Social Insurances

Social Security.   Under insurances, two programs were originally included: retirement insurance, which the general public has come to equate with "social security," and unemployment compensation. Through the amending process the first of these insurances has been expanded to protect covered people from loss of income due to retirement, disability, and death leaving survivors. The acronym OASDHI is used now in reference to the social insurances with "OA" representing old age (retirement), "S" equaling survivors, "D" disability, and "H" standing for health (Medicare), which we will discuss shortly. These insurances are entirely federal and hence uniform among all states. The contributions to the federal trust funds are money withheld from workers' earnings and matched by the employer or paid by self-employed persons at a rate double the employee rate. Starting in 1997, the first $65,400 earned in a year is taxed at 7.65 percent and is matched by the employer, and self-employed persons pay 15.30 percent.[23] These funds are used to pay benefits to covered persons in the case of any of the three exigencies mentioned, which otherwise generally reduce or eliminate one's income and may create great hardship. The approximate monthly OASDHI benefits are shown in Table 4.1. Retirement can come at a younger age than 65, as early as 62, with reduced monthly benefits.

Numerous technicalities affect the exact benefits received, and these approximations are not actual figures of beneficiaries. The contributions to the trust funds have increased significantly between 1935 and the present, in both the amount of earnings taxed (from $3,000 in 1937 to $65,400 in 1997) and the rate at which they are taxed (1 percent in 1935 to 7.65 in 1997). So, also, have the benefits increased substantially during this time, reflecting the greater cost of living.

OASDHI is administered on the local level through some 1,300 offices staffed by federal employees, who are essentially similar to private insurance

TABLE 4.1   Old Age Survivors and Disability Insurance Benefits

	Maximum Benefits 1997[24] (Maximum Earning Coverage)	Average Benefits December 1996[25]
Retired worker alone*	$1,326	$ 746†
Retired couple*	1,989	1,118†
Spouse and two children (survivors)	2,385	1,478
Disabled worker	1,363‡	705
Disabled worker, spouse, and child	2,044‡	1,169

* Retirement at age 65.
† Composite retirement age.
‡ Age 55.

claims representatives and are not social workers. The offices are often in post offices and other federal facilities and are separate from county welfare departments. The terminology of this program is that of the insurance field, that is, claims, benefits, and so forth. Herein lie some of the controversies surrounding Social Security. Unlike some private insurance, benefits received today by a Social Security beneficiary do not come directly from trust funds accumulated by that specific person who earlier was a contributor to the fund. Rather they come from monies being received in the trust funds currently from other (mainly younger) contributors. The system is one of transfer payments rather than a trust insurance. However, it does use the insurance idea of spreading the risk and does pay beneficiaries regardless of need, another concern of some critics who oppose what they perceive as the high cost of the program.

Clearly its cost, whether termed a "tax" or a "contribution," has increased substantially. In fact, this is now one of the largest taxes paid by the ordinary working individual. As of 1997, a person with an income of $65,400 or more has over $5,000 withheld. As a flat percentage withholding from a designated portion of an employee's earnings, it is not a progressive tax; that is, a person earning $65,400 in 1997 and a person earning $1 million pay exactly the same amount and, if their ages are the same and they retire at the same time, will receive the same benefits. One answer to the increasing costs of such protection is to finance the program, at least partially, through general revenues rather than entirely through wage and salary deductions. The critics of this idea argue that this would convert an "insurance" program into a "welfare" program. But as John Romanyshyn notes, there is considerable mythology in Social Security as social insurance.[26] Other countries use general revenues, and it would be a more equitable program with some reliance on a more progressive tax. Another criticism by some is that participation in the Social Security program is mandatory. This would seem necessary if the program is to accomplish its broad purpose of assuring a minimum level of living for most people. To require that all people obey traffic signs is an infringement on individual freedom, but it does prevent the chaos that could result from a voluntary compliance system.

A concern about Social Security is the low level of the benefits for some people. To expect an elderly individual to live on a few dollars monthly, as some must do, is unrealistic. It is not enough to say that Social Security was not intended to be the sole source of income and that it should supplement other monies. Given the high costs of living in an inflationary era and the modest earnings of millions of Americans, it seems unlikely that many can rely on sources of income other than Social Security in their later years. A serious limitation in the law is the lack of survivors' benefits for widows under age 60 who have no children under 18. A person widowed at, say, 56, who has not worked outside the home for a long time, or perhaps ever, may experience great difficulty in obtaining a job and hence face grave problems financially.

Still another weakness is the penalty imposed on paid employment if the Social Security beneficiary works. Between retirement at age 65 or later and age 70, benefits in 1997 are penalized one dollar for every three dollars earned over $13,500 yearly. People under 65 who earn over $8,640 have their benefits reduced one dollar for every two dollars earned. After age 70 there is no penalty. This penalty reflects the Great Depression era during which Social Security was created. At that time, an overriding concern was unemployment, so that the program was designed to discourage older people from working in order to make more jobs available for younger people needing them. Many observers today believe that it is unwise to maintain this stipulation.

One controversy in the Reagan administration era was focused on Social Security disability beneficiaries. In order to reduce costs, Congress in 1981 instructed Social Security to review the 2.7 million people receiving disability benefits. By March 1984 more than 1 million cases had been investigated and almost half a million people ordered removed from the rolls.[27] Thousands of totally disabled persons lost their sole means of support and Medicare as a result of this action. The repercussions were so severe that, starting in December 1982, beneficiaries were allowed to continue receiving benefits while they appealed cutoff notices. Interestingly almost two-thirds of the persons who appealed were reinstated.[28] Finally a federal judge ruled in July 1984 that disability payments must be reinstated to 15,000 to 20,000 persons whose denial of benefits had been appealed to federal court.[29]

More than nine out of ten workers are earning protection under Social Security. When the program was initiated, only workers in industry and commerce were covered. In the 1950s, coverage was expanded to include most self-employed persons, most state and local employees, household and farm workers, members of the armed forces, and clergy. About one out of every six persons receive monthly benefits. These 44 million people were divided as follows in 1997:

- 26.9 million retirees
- 3.4 million retirees' family members
- 7.3 million survivors
- 4.4 million disabled
- 1.6 million spouses and children of disabled[30]

Social Security is a massive "entitlement" program. Like any large system, it has its deficiencies, but for millions of Americans it provides a much greater degree of security than would otherwise exist.

Changes in the Social Security Act in 1983 resulted in the taxing of benefits for the first time. Retirees have half of their benefits taxed if their income plus half of their benefits exceeds $25,000 for individuals or $32,000 for couples. Another change is gradually raising the retirement age from 65 to 66 in the year 2009 and to 67 in 2027.

Seemingly small changes in Social Security in order to conserve funds can have major repercussions for people. The American Association of Retired Persons reports that a Social Security cost-of-living adjustment (COLA) freeze for one year would move over 300,000 people into poverty. COLA was created to tie Social Security benefits to the cost of living. To deny such raises in an inflationary period is tantamount to cutting benefits.[31]

In recent years there has been growing concern about the federal deficit and debt. There is much controversy surrounding the part Social Security costs play in the deficit and whether this program, too, should be subject to federal cuts or be immune. Over $70 billion was cut from Social Security mainly as a result of the restrictive 1983 amendments. Later $30 billion more was cut from Medicare.[32]

Actually the federal deficit has nothing to do with Social Security, which, until 1969, was not even included in the budget because of the program's independent funding through payroll deductions. It has no connection to the general revenues and expenditures and hence is unrelated to a balanced or unbalanced budget. It may be that the only reason for the 1969 change was to create the appearance of a more balanced budget by including Social Security surpluses. Since Social Security was approaching a $500 billion surplus in 1995, it is unlikely that these funds will be removed from the unified budget as recommended by the National Commission on Social Security. To do so would make the federal deficit even larger.

Medicare.   Medicare (Title XVIII of the Social Security Act) was designed to provide for an unmet need. Becoming effective in 1966, it provided compulsory hospital insurance and supplementary voluntary medical benefits to persons 65 and over and, more recently, to younger people in certain other specified situations, such as those with serious kidney disorder requiring dialysis or a transplant. The latter is an interesting development that points out the piecemeal nature of publicly supported health measures in the United States. Medicare was created for a particular age group, the elderly, and not for all people, although people of all ages have unmet health care needs. A 65-year-old is covered; a 64-year-old with a similar health problem or equally high medical costs has to somehow struggle along without assistance. Of the 7.65 percent Social Security payroll tax on employers and employees each, 1.45 percent on yearly earnings is for Medicare hospital payments. The medical insurance part of Medicare, which pays primarily doctors' fees, was paid for by the insured person at the monthly rate of $43.80 in 1997.

Congress became aware of the immense financial costs for kidney disease patients and amended Medicare to cover this hazard. But what of persons with cancer, heart disease, or many other financially costly conditions? Unless such persons have been entitled to Social Security disability benefits for 24 or more consecutive months or have been disabled since childhood, there is no help for them under this social insurance program. Serious illnesses and injuries have a way of not complying with the legislators' pigeon holes and definitions. If a particular health problem has sufficient visibility to gain political clout, provisions may be made to offset its financial consequences. Otherwise the victim must rely on his or her own resources, inadequate though they may be in relation to the costs of treatment. Even for those included in Medicare there are large costs not covered. For example, in 1997 the patient paid the first $760 of hospital charges. From the 61st through the 90th day in a hospital the patient had to pay $190 per day. After 90 days the patient paid $380 daily. Similarly with the physician's charges there were substantial costs for the Medicare patient. The first $100 in 1997 had to be paid as well as generally 20 percent of everything else covered. Many people purchased "medigap" insurance for some of the costs not covered by Medicare.

The current horror stories about today's out-of-control health care costs seem endless. A surgeon in a small city charges $3,000 for a 15-minute operation. A man takes a second job as a school bus driver to supplement his earnings and discovers that health insurance for his family under the school district's plan takes all of his earnings as a driver, plus more; he continues the job in order to have insurance.[33] A woman suffering from severe emphysema is denied a Medicaid-funded lung transplant that costs an estimated $100,000. For this mother of four, the denial means death.[34] Americans face the highest prescription prices of any industrial nation. While the pharmaceutical industry attributes these high costs to necessary research, only 15 percent goes to research; profits skyrocket.[35] Hospital bills in the hundreds of thousands of dollars are not uncommon. Americans spent a trillion dollars on health care in 1994.[36]

Although over 40 million Americans have no health insurance,[37] some people argue that private hospital and medical insurance such as Blue Cross–Blue Shield is the solution to this problem. This appears to be a naive position in view of the heavy costs of such coverage. Even if one is in a group package plan, the costs are steep. Some people do not have access to such plans and simply cannot afford the premiums independently. For example, costs in one state in 1997 were $246 monthly for an individual (age 60) and $505 for a family for the most complete coverage. Even with these high premiums there were substantial deductibles to be paid by the patient. Furthermore, most private insurance coverage contains limitations. What happens with massive costs of treatment, which are commonplace currently, when the insurance benefits are exhausted? Still another difficulty is that companies will not insure some people with problematic health histories or conditions. Other modern industrial nations have long since provided institutionalized public health care programs, but the United States still debates "socialized medicine" and devises partial Band-Aid responses rather than comprehensive answers.

Unemployment insurance. The other social insurance under the Social Security Act provides protection for the unemployed. Unemployment insurance is a federal-state cooperative program, which varies among the states. Originally in 1935 it covered persons whose employers had eight or more workers for more than twenty weeks a year and paid wages up to $3,000 a year, excluding certain types of employment. Later, firms with four or more workers were included. Now states generally cover employment with only one worker 20 weeks per year. Although more groups have been included over the years, in some states one or more of the following remain excluded: the self-employed, students, employees of small nonprofit organizations, and a few others.

The money in the trust fund comes from a tax on employers' payrolls; in only a few states do employees contribute. A small portion of the payroll tax is used by the federal government for administrative costs, and the balance goes to the states. States must meet the following requirements to receive federal support: (1) public employment services must handle the benefits; (2) the unemployment trust fund must receive the taxes; (3) the funds must be used only for unemployment compensation; (4) beneficiaries cannot be required to join a company union or join or resign from a labor union; and (5) there can be no denial of benefits for refusal to work where there is a strike, lockout, or labor dispute, or where substandard wages are paid.

To be eligible for unemployment compensation a worker must (1) have worked in covered employment a stipulated period of time; (2) be out of work through no fault of his or her own; (3) be registered for work in the public employment service and apply for benefits in the same system; (4) be able to work and available for employment; and (5) serve a "waiting period," usually one week, which is not reimbursed.

In 1994 the average weekly number of beneficiaries of unemployment insurance was approximately 2.6 million. The average weekly benefit of total unemployment was $182. In the same year 2.9 million claimants exhausted their benefits, pointing up unmet needs.[38] Benefits generally can be received for only 26 weeks in one year with 13 weeks in addition when a state's rate of unemployment reaches a specified point.

A major issue in unemployment insurance is whether it encourages people not to work. In addition to the fact that there are various requirements to be met before one is eligible to receive these benefits and therefore the program is not an open cash drawer, it should also be noted that employment pays much better than this insurance. Unemployment compensation was only 37 percent of the usual earnings in 1993.[39] In an inflationary, high cost-of-living era especially, few would voluntarily choose to live on these benefits rather than have their much larger usual incomes. Some such program appears essential in an industrialized society in which unemployment is an impersonal event that strikes capriciously and often harshly and over which people have little control. In any program of this size, there are bound to be certain abuses, but the need to provide some degree of financial protection for individuals and families against losses from involuntary unemployment is urgent and would seem to offset any problems. Unemployment insurance is a smaller program than OASDHI but performs an important function in the United States.

Worker's compensation.   One public insurance program predated Social Security by a quarter of a century, but is still today less well known and understood. Formerly workmen's compensation, this plan first appeared in 1908 as a program for federal employees who were injured on the job to help with some of their medical expenses. States individually followed the federal example and, by 1920, all but six states had such legislation assisting with hospital and physician fees and paying disability and death benefits. A law and an adequate program are not the same, however, and it was 1948 before all states had coverage approaching adequacy. Worker's compensation is not uniform among the states. Funds for this protection are derived from employers.

The workplace is dangerous, more so in some fields of endeavor than others, but in certain occupations extremely hazardous. The government estimates that 17 workers die each day and 9,000 are injured from work-related causes. Other researchers put the injury figures much higher.[40] Prior to worker's compensation, the only recourse an injured employee had was to sue the employer. This often had unsatisfactory results for the plaintiff for several reasons, including the fact that employers frequently argued successfully (1) that the injury was not their fault but due to the carelessness of a coworker, and/or (2) that when the employee took the job, he or she accepted all of the risks inherent in the employment. This kind of situation calls for collective remedy through public (governmental) intervention. An insurance approach spreads the risks, and the costs are shared broadly by employers, consumers, and the general public. Worker's compensation is an important resource and avenue for meeting need.

Public Assistances

The Social Security Act also provided a supplementary system of categorical public assistances (PA). These are not insurances or entitlement programs, and there are no contributions to trust funds as previously described for OASDHI. These cash grants come from general tax revenues through a tripartite system with federal, state, and local levels. Unlike the insurances, there is a means test, that is, to be a recipient one must prove one's eligibility by demonstrating a need. Public assistances vary among the states in specific content. The terms *aid* and *assistance* are synonymous in these programs. Originally there were three categories, with a fourth for disability added in 1950:

- Old Age Assistance (OAA)
- Blind Assistance (BA)
- Aid to Dependent Children (ADC); later Aid to Families with Dependent Children (AFDC)
- Aid to the Permanently and Totally Disabled (APTD)

Beyond that of need, the major eligibility requirement for each type of assistance is implicit in each label, that is, old age (over 65), a visual handicap of a defined degree, one or more children under age 18, or a disability. Additional requirements for eligibility characterize each program.

The purpose of public assistance is to supplement the insurances under the Social Security Act. An example is a person who is in need, is not covered by Social Security, but meets the eligibility requirements for one of the types of public assistance. Another example is a person who receives some OASDHI benefits but in such a limited amount that he or she is eligible in that state for some public assistance to supplement the insurance and bring the total up to what is allowed. Generally a person may receive both an assistance and an insurance but not two types of assistance. As more and more people were covered by OASDHI and at higher levels, fewer were eligible for public assistance, and for those that continued to be eligible, the amounts were often reduced. The best example is the relationship between Social Security retirement benefits and OAA; as the former (OASDHI) increased, the latter declined.

Assistance for the disabled illustrates how a program can be designed and/or administered so restrictively that it is self-defeating. To be eligible, one had to be permanently and totally disabled. One recipient of APTD was so severely handicapped from crippling arthritis that he had to wear a girdle-like appliance on the trunk of his body. It was necessary to have the help of another person to put on and remove this device daily and it was this dependency, in part, that qualified the man for APTD. But the recipient was determined to become free of this reliance on others for physical care and worked day after day for months. Finally he was successful at getting into and out of this device without help. The result of this courageous and excruciating effort was that he

TABLE 4.2   Supplemental Security Income (December 1996)

Type of Payment	Total Recipients[42]	Average Monthly Payment[43]
Total	6,613,718	$363
Aged	1,412,632	261
Blind	82,137	379
Disabled	5,118,949	391

TABLE 4.3   Recipients of Aid to Families with Dependent Children, 1994

Families	4,981,000
Recipients	13,974,000
Children	9,469,000

TABLE 4.4   Average Monthly Cash Payments, AFDC, 1994

Average per family	$378
Average per recipient	135

lost his eligibility for APTD, though nothing had changed in his economic situation.[41]

Supplemental Security Income.   An important change occurred in public assistance when, in 1974, all but AFDC were federalized and consolidated into Supplemental Security Income (SSI). The Social Security Administration, not state and county welfare departments, handles SSI through the same federal offices administering OASDHI. This change raises an interesting question as to whether SSI is actually public assistance or is more of a social insurance. In addition, there is the issue of supplements in SSI available in some states and not in others.

Table 4.2 shows the numbers of SSI recipients and average payment for December 1996.

AFDC.   AFDC was the only remaining major cash-grant public assistance program that was not federalized in SSI but it was replaced in the "welfare reform" of 1996. AFDC was not uniform among the states. It was a large program in both numbers of recipients and expenditures but small compared to the rest of the public welfare system. It was also the most controversial of the programs we have examined so far. The nation's 1994 AFDC statistics are shown in Tables 4.3 and 4.4.[44]

One problem with AFDC, a program serving over 9 million children, was the great diversity of payments among states. In 1994 the range was from a low of a $123 per family monthly payment in Mississippi to a high of $740 in Alaska and $652 in Hawaii.[45] Hence, the national average of $378 does not very well reflect the wide range. While the cost of living does vary considerably around the country, this factor does not justify the extremely low payments in southern states. It is unreasonable to expect a family of approximately three people (usually one adult and two children) to live anywhere in this country, including Mississippi, on $123 a month.

No program for the needy in this country is more myth-filled than AFDC. As a group, AFDC mothers (most adult recipients are women) are stereotyped and scapegoated. A list of some of the myths and the actual related factors follows; they apply just as well to the new program created by welfare reform in 1996.

Myth	*Fact*
AFDC families are large.	The typical family is a mother and two children, and the trend is toward smaller families. Seven out of ten have only one or two children.[46]
"Adult" AFDC recipients are teenage parents.	The median age for adult female recipients is 29.[47]
Women have more children just to get more money.	The typical payment for an additional child is only $40 to $65 a month. Not much incentive to cover the cost of rearing an additional child when it is estimated that $241,440 is required to raise a child from birth to age 18.[48]
Most AFDC families are black.	Blacks constitute a minority of recipients (37 percent).[49]
Why work when you can live it up on welfare?	The average grant in 1994 was about $4,500 a year for a family of three, almost $9,000 below the poverty line. Only 23 percent of cases had non-AFDC income.[50]
More money will be spent on alcohol and large cars; i.e., recipients are poor managers.	Studies show that recipients would spend any extra money received on essentials like food, clothing, better housing. Many AFDC adults are excellent managers—they have to be! They buy used clothing and use donated goods.
AFDC youth should earn income.	Seventy-nine percent are under age 12.[51]

Once on welfare, always on welfare.	Two-thirds of welfare families have been receiving aid less than three years at any given time.[52] It is painful to be on welfare; hence, for many it is a last resort.
Welfare families cheat.	Repeated studies show tiny numbers of recipients in fraud.[53] Honest errors by staff and recipients do occur mainly because of program complexity. Families are monitored.
Welfare rolls are full of able-bodied loafers.	Only 1 percent of welfare recipients are able-bodied males free to work and most of these want to work.[54] Most AFDC adults are mothers; many work part- or full-time or are in training. More would work if adequate affordable child day care were available and if decently paying jobs existed for women, many with limited marketable skills and experience.
Most welfare children are illegitimate.	Almost half were born in wedlock.[55] Out-of-wedlock births are part of a larger national development. Some mothers of out-of-wedlock children are excellent parents.
Many recipients were not born in the United States.	Eighty-nine percent are U.S. citizens.[56]

What all of this means is that to be a public assistance recipient is to subject oneself to a kind of second-class citizenship. There is another kind of ADC in this country that seemingly raises few eyebrows but costs billions—aid to dependent corporations, for example, Lockheed, Pennsylvania Central, Chrysler, Continental Illinois (a 1984 "bailout" of $4.5 billion), the multibillion dollar program to salvage savings and loan companies, and others. Such governmental largess is replete with abuse; some questioned the appropriateness of paying $600,000 yearly salaries each to the two top executive officers of Continental Illinois, for example. But apparently the large scale adds a social acceptability missing in individual victim-blaming situations.

There is an array of services for children, families, and adults in public welfare agencies apart from money grants. Under the 1975 Title XX of the Social Security Act, states determine what services are to be offered with federal funding. Service possibilities include both concrete provisions such as day care, residential care, and meals on wheels, and less tangible activities like counseling and casework. A variety of professions and occupations are represented in these services. In this country such services are still to be systematized and institutionalized. While still restricted to serving a lower-income population, services can be provided to public assistance recipients and to others up to a stipulated percentage of the state's median income.[57] Fees can be charged for others based on a sliding scale related to ability to pay. The potential exists for public welfare agencies to become our first line of defense as good-quality public family and children's agencies. Large caseloads, heavy paperwork responsibilities, ever-changing bureaucratic regulations, and mixed policies regarding qualifications of persons to staff these programs are obstacles to fulfillment of the potential of the services.

The fact that public welfare agencies offer protective services for both children and adults (handicapped and elderly) and deal with problems such as child abuse points out some of the magnitude of the tasks going far beyond the image of the agency as "the welfare," meaning only money grants. Today's social worker in public welfare may be carrying out tasks with individuals and families in the personal services that are very similar to those in private agencies.

Welfare reform of 1996. In 1996, one of the most significant changes in income maintenance to occur in sixty years in this country took place. The federal legislation was entitled the Personal Responsibility and Work Opportunity Act of 1996. It replaced AFDC with Temporary Aid for Needy Families (TANF).

This new system transfers much power from the federal to the state governments to operate their own welfare programs. Each state receives lump sum block grants that are capped (will not increase in a recession). This idea is to replace "welfare" with "workfare" and ends the "federal guarantee of cash assistance to poor children."[58] Some of the features of this measure are:

1. A five-year lifetime limit on cash assistance is imposed and states are allowed to set shorter time limits.
2. Heads of families on welfare are required to work after two years. States can shorten this time limit. After receiving aid for two months, adults without jobs will do community service unless the state does not require it.
3. For hardship reasons, states may exempt 20 percent of these cases from the time limit.
4. Title XX funding for services was cut by 15 percent.
5. Aid may be denied by states to children born into families already receiving aid ("family cap").
6. Unmarried parents under age 18 must live with an adult and stay in school.
7. Welfare mothers who do not cooperate in identifying the child's father have their benefits reduced.
8. Currently eligible AFDC recipients remain eligible for Medicaid.
9. SSI eligibility is tightened.
10. Food stamps are limited to three months every three years for able-bodied single adults aged 18–50. Three additional months are allowed if laid off job.
11. $55 billion is to be cut from spending over six years.[59]

This complex welfare reform package is extremely controversial. President Clinton vetoed two attempts at legislation in late 1995 and early in 1996 before approving the bill that summer. There is little doubt that the public welfare system needed changing. It was cumbersome on paperwork, meager in support for families in need, and served only about half of those eligible. But to replace the known with an unknown is questionable. The myths and facts about AFDC discussed earlier apply equally well to the system replacing this program as a result of the recent "welfare reform."

Poverty is a national problem requiring national solutions. It became a federal matter in the 1930s, partly because states had not fulfilled their responsibilities. Now it is being given back to the states. It appears that the states in the Deep South, for example, have no more ability nor inclination to respond positively to their poverty today than earlier.

Critics of the new welfare reform argue that children, perhaps as many as a million, will suffer drastically as a result. At this writing (mid-1997), it is too early to know the results. It can be said that:

1. Although the number of welfare recipients is down at the moment, this probably has more to do with the presently booming economy, low unemployment, and so forth than any other one factor. Economic recessions are cyclical and will come again. What will happen then when the jobless rate increases?
2. "Workfare," central to this new plan, may sound better than it is. Some people can find jobs, especially in good economic times, but often even those who are better qualified cannot in economic downturns. With work training and help, others may be able to be employed. But what of the hard-core group that brings the least to the labor market and the greatest number of problems and obstacles?
3. For this plan, or any other, to be effective there must be good-quality affordable child care available; accessible, affordable, high-quality health care for families; and adequately paying jobs, including and especially for women.
4. Finally, humans, particularly children, should not suffer from forces over which they have so little control. To make children suffer is societal cruelty and victimization.

Medicaid.   Medicaid, like Medicare, was enacted in 1965 and took effect the following year as Title XIX of the Social Security Act. It is now the largest federal welfare program for the poor. In the main, it provides medical care for persons who receive public assistance. There are state-to-state variations in benefits and, as is true with public assistance, federal and state governments share the cost of the program based on a formula. Expenses covered may include payments to the hospital, physician, or dentist; nursing services at home or elsewhere; and drugs, laboratory fees, and medical supplies.

Originally Medicaid was designed with the intention that states would define *medically indigent* broadly to cover many low-income people in addition to public assistance recipients. But narrower definitions have tended to prevail, thus depriving a large portion of low-income, medically needy people of health care. Medical indigence is an important concept. Great numbers of people in modern America are able to make ends meet financially as long as illness or injury do not strike. But when medical care is required, they reach an impasse economically. In fact, people may be destroyed financially in a short time, given the present inflation in health care costs.

It should not be necessary to argue for a *right* to health care in the United States. Nor should health care costs be allowed to bankrupt families. Medicaid has not fulfilled its promise and potential in these kinds of situations because of its cautious implementation. Medicaid and Medicare are discussed further in Chapter 8, which deals with the subject of health.

General assistance. Closest to and a direct descendant of the historic poor relief is *general assistance* (GA) or *relief*, also known as temporary, emergency, or home relief. It is entirely nonfederal, being either state, local, or a combination, and is not a provision of the Social Security Act. GA often is relief-in-kind such as grocery, clothing, or utility orders. This program aids people who are in need and are not eligible for more institutionalized measures, or acts as a stop-gap while they await receipt of other benefits for which they are eligible. Some persons who receive other aid that is inadequate for their need may receive GA as a supplement.

A problem with GA in some states is lack of uniformity in its administration, even within one state. It is sometimes granted capriciously without written standards, and the personnel administering this program may be political appointees without qualifications for the job. In at least one state (Iowa), the administrator of general assistance still has the title of "overseer of the poor," a term from sixteenth-century England!

Veterans assistance. Another welfare fragment in some states is veterans assistance, a program entirely separate from the various federal veterans benefits in medical care, education, housing, and so forth. As with GA, it is local relief-in-kind and has the same limitations including, commonly, a "tight purse strings" administration. Examples of the demeaning "less eligibility" ways in which this program is conducted may be useful. In one agency it was the practice to keep better quality clothing apart from less desirable goods for, in the words of the staff person, "the better people." What subjective means are used to determine who is more deserving are unknown, but obviously such a system (or nonsystem) is ripe with potential for abuse.[60]

As a veteran approaches the office of veterans assistance in one county court house, the sign on the door says, "The helping hand you are always looking for is at the end of your wrist."[61] So the very program to help veterans demeans and dehumanizes them in one more example of blaming the victim and trampling on the rights and dignity of poor people because they are poor.

Food and Housing Programs

Food is an obvious basic human need; no one can live without it. There is an abundance of evidence indicating that one aspect of poverty is poor nutrition. Food and nutrition are two different matters, of course, in that one may have enough food but poor nutrition, as is seen with some nonpoor people. Studies of individual cases of poverty often reveal that the poor person must set painful priorities. For example, many poor people who live on small monthly incomes such as from Social Security first pay their rent because they must have a place to live. Whatever is left over is budgeted to get through the month as well as possible. In some months food is meager, and generally there is little meat, fresh fruit, dairy products, or other items necessary to a balanced diet. Little wonder that elderly persons are sometimes observed at supermarket checkout counters purchasing canned pet food when they have no pets. Their pride and feelings of shame may even lead them to say something to the clerk about the nonexistent cat to conceal the unpleasant truth of their source of protein. Such conditions in a land of affluence are shocking to say the least. Two major programs of food distribution are food stamps and school breakfasts and lunches.

Food stamps. Between 1939 and 1943 there was a food stamp program, and it was reinstituted in 1964, growing since that time.[62] The distribution of surplus food commodities to institutions, schools, and needy families, which began in the 1930s, has declined in more recent years. Both of these programs are administered by the U.S. Department of Agriculture (USDA) and originally both had as a major purpose providing an outlet for surplus agricultural produce. More recently, growing emphasis has been placed on the food and nutrition needs of people, especially poor people. But the program still suffers from multiple ambiguous goals, and it can be argued that such programs more appropriately belong in the Department of Health and Human Services where they can be integrated with other human welfare measures rather than in the USDA where the poor's need for food may be subordinated to the farmer's need to make larger profits.

Food stamps are purchased by eligible persons for a portion of their face value or are received without payment, depending upon family size and income, and then are used like cash to purchase food in supermarkets and grocery stores. The idea is to increase the food purchasing power of the poor, but a large portion of those eligible do not participate.

Of course, in-kind assistance is given to some individuals and families by churches, service clubs, and other groups in the form of food baskets and comparable items. The problems in this ancient charity approach include the fact that the gifts are given when the giver determines rather than when they are most needed so, for example, there is the December generosity syndrome of such altruism centering around holidays like Thanksgiving and Christmas. Another shortcoming is the hit-and-miss nature of who is targeted to be the receiver and who is overlooked. Still another limitation of this almslike activity is that while it may contribute to feelings of goodness on the part of the distributor of the largesse, an ambivalent mix of happiness and humiliation may result for the recipient. A further concern is that the nature of the goods given may be questionable and inappropriate for the persons receiving them. This kind of fragmentary giving would be unnecessary if there were an adequate, institutionalized, comprehensive income maintenance system. And some of the basket carriers, in contrast to holiday generosity, take political and economic positions in opposition to more fundamental help for the needy.

Other food programs.   Lunches provided at school assure children one good meal a day, five days a week, nine months a year. While this is obviously limited, its impact on nutrition should not be underestimated. These services are uneven and spotty, sometimes being free or charged on a sliding scale. Many states have not implemented free lunches, and many schools do not provide them, so that once again there is unmet need and unfilled potential. Breakfasts are available in only half the schools that have lunch programs. Surplus foods distributed to schools can play an important role in the program in terms of nutrition, but they are unpredictable.

The Women's, Infants', and Children's Supplementary Food Program (WIC) assists persons of certain status with such nutritionally important substances as milk.[63] Sixty percent of those eligible are not reached. Other measures focus on the food needs of the elderly such as congregate meals and meals on wheels. Again, we see fragmentary approaches rather than comprehensive services directed toward adequate nutrition for all.

Housing.   A more extensive discussion of public housing comes later in Chapter 24. What should be pointed out here is that housing is another fundamental requisite for all humans. Poor people have difficulty obtaining and retaining adequate housing just as they do in meeting other primary needs. Therefore subsidization of housing, as with health and nutrition, can be extremely important even in making survival possible. Generally the United States has not gone as far as have some other modern nations in providing public housing. The reasons are complex but do not minimize the human suffering resulting from lack of decent affordable living quarters for individuals and families.

It should be noted that food and housing programs are forms of assistance in kind, that is, nonmonetary aid. Many people, including frequent critics of public welfare and social insurance, look with favor upon in-kind arrangements. But if there were an adequate income maintenance system, people could make their own decisions about food, shelter, and so on, and these residual programs would be either unnecessary or less needed. It may be that for various reasons, some political and economic, a mix of programs is desirable. A more comprehensive income maintenance system is slow in evolving, and even if it comes, in-kind assistance may persist.

The War on Poverty of the 1960s

In the administration of Lyndon Johnson, a new *war on poverty* was declared and, in 1964, the Economic Opportunity Act (EOA) created the Office of Economic Opportunity (OEO) and initiated a new attack on an old problem unlike the direct income maintenance approach of the Social Security Act. The EOA, amended the following year, contained major provisions that can be briefly outlined as follows, using the format and much of the language of the act itself:[64]

1. *Youth Programs*
   a. Job Corps—education, vocational training, and work experience in residential centers for ages 16 to 21.

    b. Work-Training—programs to improve employability of young men and women.

    c. Work-Study—promote part-time employment for college students from low-income families.

2. *Urban and Rural Community Action Programs*

    a. General Community Action Programs (CAP)—mobilizing communities to combat poverty.

    b. Adult Basic Education—for illiterates over age 18.

    c. Voluntary Assistance Program—for needy children.

3. *Special Programs to Combat Poverty in Rural Areas*—for rural families and migrants.

4. *Employment and Investment Incentives*—assist small business concerns.

5. *Work Experience Programs*—experience and training for the poor.

6. *Administration and Coordination*

    a. Creates OEO.

    b. Volunteers in Service to America (VISTA—commonly termed the domestic Peace Corps).

    c. Coordination of all antipoverty programs.

The EOA opened with a statement of findings and declaration of purpose as follows:

> Sec. 2. Although the economic well-being and prosperity of the United States have progressed to a level surpassing any achieved in world history, and although these benefits are widely shared throughout the Nation, poverty continues to be the lot of a substantial number of our people. The United States can achieve its full economic and social potential as a nation only if every individual has the opportunity to contribute to the full extent of his capabilities and to participate in the workings of our society. It is, therefore, the policy of the United States to eliminate the paradox of poverty in the midst of plenty in this Nation by opening to everyone the opportunity for education and training, the opportunity to work, and the opportunity to live in decency and dignity. It is the purpose of this Act to strengthen, supplement, and coordinate efforts in furtherance of that policy.

This statement set the tone for a piece of legislation that did attempt to take a new approach to the problem of poverty. In some ways, it was a more basic and preventive focus than that of the Social Security Act because it attempted to bring an underprivileged portion of the population back into the mainstream of the culture via such fundamentals as employability, rather than simply providing economic maintenance.

In most respects, the war on poverty never materialized. The nation appeared unable to deal seriously with a war on poverty at home when it was enmeshed in the Vietnam conflict. The poverty war was underfunded, never receiving more than $2 billion in a single year, and withered in the Nixon-Ford-Carter era of the late 1960s and the 1970s. In the Reagan years it was dealt with even more harshly. Although the original idea was a federal unit separate from all existing governmental agencies so that it could concentrate on poverty, bit by bit the OEO programs were dismantled, abandoned, or moved. OEO became the Community Services Administration in 1975. Later this organization was eliminated. Some examples of how much difference programs can make locally around the nation in spite of the dwindling federal commitment are such remaining successful antipoverty efforts as Head Start, Legal Services, and community action programs. Head Start serves only about a third of young children from families who meet income guidelines.[65]

Tax Reform of 1986 and 1997

Within the context of income maintenance, the subject of taxes may not be considered as relevant, but a system of taxation can play a large role in income distribution and in human well-being. For years the United States has had a system of progressive income taxation that in theory taxed high-income persons at a higher rate than low-income people who paid not only less taxes but a lower percentage of their incomes in taxes. Over the years various loopholes and devices were built into the tax structure to benefit the wealthier class, hence diluting the "progressive" quality. The same is true for corporate taxes. Various strategies served to protect moneyed special interests.

Since 1975 there has been the Earned Income Tax Credit (EITC) for lower-income families with children and other qualifying adults. It takes the form of a federal income tax refund although it can be paid incrementally through a worker's regular pycheck.

In 1986 federal tax "reform" finally came but in the name of tax "simplification." While the result was a simplified federal income tax in certain respects (such as reducing the number of loopholes and tax brackets), the system continues to be extremely complex. More important for social welfare purposes was increasing corporate taxes (generating more revenues) and removing 6 million low-wage workers from the tax rolls. Still more important was a major setback for the idea of progressive income taxation; the wealthiest taxpayers are now taxed at a greatly reduced rate that is only slightly higher than that paid by the middle class. These changes did little to reduce the massive federal deficit, the existence of which is frequently used as an argument for reducing programs for the poor.

The "Taxpayer Relief Act of 1997," a mixed bag of provisions, increased tax complexity partly by creating different tax rates for capital gains. It provided a $500 per child tax credit. Noteworthy is extension of health coverage to some of the 10 million children lacking it and aid to some of the disabled legal immigrants who would have been harmed by the welfare reform of a year earlier. The federal budget enacted in 1997 was aimed at a balanced budget by the year 2002, although the improved economy has by itself, through increased tax revenues, greatly reduced the deficit. Of course, a recession could change all of this. Generally these tax and budget provisions increase the vast gap between the affluent and the poor.

PROPOSALS FOR INCOME MAINTENANCE REFORM

Criticisms of the programs discussed here abound, but solutions are not easy. Reforms could be either small-scale or large systemic changes. Beginning with the smaller and more local and moving upward, the following can be noted:

1. The residual welfare fragments like general assistance and veterans assistance should be incorporated into broader jurisdictions, at least at state level, for purposes of funding and administration. These programs should be administered by the same county/state offices handling public assistance and by qualified personnel who work from objective written standards. The aid given should be monetary rather than relief-in-kind.

2. Categorical approaches in public assistance should be dropped in favor of comprehensive, universal programs. SSI is a step in this direction but TANF (formerly AFDC) is problematic. The latter should be replaced with some form of guaranteed annual income. Possibilities include:

   a. The Family Assistance Plan (FAP) proposed in the Richard Nixon administration but not enacted. Originally it proposed $1,600 per year for a family of four, an extremely inadequate level. It did have the virtue of helping the working poor, an important feature. Had this plan been adopted, weak as it was, it is possible that it would subsequently have been expanded and improved as has happened with Social Security.

   b. Children's allowances are found in all Western industrialized nations except the United States. Families are paid based on the number of children. Limitations of this scheme are its cost, its possible encouragement of larger families in the face of overpopulation, and its failure to help needy childless couples and single adults, a weakness shared with FAP.

   c. Negative income tax in one proposed form among many possibilities, would have the Internal Revenue Service paying families below a stipulated income considering family size. If the income cut-off figure used were too low in relation to the cost of living, this would greatly hamper the effectiveness of the program. A major advantage of this approach is that it helps everyone who is poor—single or married, with or without children. The cost of such a program is a major concern, as is protection of the incentive to work. Several experiments with negative income taxes have been conducted by the federal government in both rural and urban communities in Iowa; New Jersey; North Carolina; and Pennsylvania; as well as in Denver; Gary, Indiana; and Seattle. But, as Winifred Bell observes, interest in these possibilities has largely disappeared.[66]

   d. The Jimmy Carter proposal would have replaced AFDC, SSI, and food stamps with a single federal cash grant for families, childless couples, and single adults. Public service jobs would have been provided by state and local governments, and tax credits would have encouraged employment of low-income workers in the private sector. It was not enacted.

3. Whatever form an income maintenance program takes, it should provide an adequate level of income in relation to the cost of living then current. *Adequate* must be defined, of course, but some minimum level assuring human dignity is required as a base.

4. It would be useful to move from public assistance toward social insurance as a general approach. This would represent a move from *means-tested programs* to *entitlement programs*, which have the limitation of being more expensive. Means-tested programs serve the poor, whereas entitlement programs especially assist the middle class. If a program in nature and administration can come closer to treating the poor as middle-class people, it is a major gain for the needy. The opposite of this happened in the 1996 welfare reform. Governmental budgets (federal or state) should not be balanced, nor deficits combated, on the backs of the poor.

5. Financing Social Security (OASDHI) at least in part through general revenues[67] rather than entirely by payroll taxes would strengthen the program actuarially and make it less expensive for ordinary workers. Through some means, more progressive taxes should be used for financing Social Security. Income maintenance fragments like Railroad Retirement should be dropped and consolidated into OASDHI.

6. Comprehensive public health insurance is absolutely essential in any system.

Much of the problem of enacting income maintenance reform in this country derives from the immense difficulty in bringing about legislative compromises in this field. Proposals are often overly generous from the viewpoint of conservatives and inadequate for liberals, so that no action is taken.

The Future

What the future holds for income maintenance is uncertain. The need for reform is real, but changes have been slow in coming and as piecemeal as the programs themselves. Present programs are helpful within their limitations. In fact, most of the reduction in poverty between the mid-1960s and 1980 was due to welfare, food stamps, and antipoverty programs, most of them federal. But what is needed is a fundamental national commitment to removing poverty and its attendant problems from this affluent society. What is most lacking is not money or know-how but will.

One hopeful sign is social and economic development using terms such as microenterprise, individual development accounts, asset building, and others. The thrust of much of this activity is facilitating poor people and welfare recipients in becoming self-employed entrepreneurs. It is occurring in both the United States and in developing nations and will be worth watching in the new century.[68]

As this chapter has shown, a large part of the problem is public attitudes. Not only are the poor stereotyped and scapegoated, but so are programs aimed at alleviating poverty. Perhaps it should not be surprising that 40 percent of people with incomes below the poverty line receive no public help, that is, Social Security, SSI, or public assistance. There appears to be little recognition of the fact that, as Mimi Abramovitz notes, we are all on welfare at one point or another. There are really three "welfare" systems—(1) programs of the welfare state, (2) tax code provisions, and (3) fringe benefits—and the welfare-state measures are a small part of the whole.[69] The latter two benefit tremendously the middle class. The other development that went largely unnoticed is how much redistribution of resources there was in the Reagan administration, shifting money from the poor (budget cuts) toward the wealthy (tax relief).[70] The same thing happened again in the late 1990s. For the present we are left with the realization that ours is a meager, reluctant welfare state, as Bruce Jansson terms it, one seemingly aimed more at maintaining a supply of cheap labor than adequately meeting human needs.[71]

SUMMARY AND CONCLUSIONS

In this chapter we have examined the problem of poverty and what has been done and could be done in response to it. Social insurances, public assistances, and other program fragments have been described and evaluated, and a need for a more comprehensive approach has been noted. The chance that these changes will occur soon seems doubtful although reforms in these, along with major changes in the health system and in taxation, are under discussion in the Clinton administration at this writing.

Notes

1. Michael Harrington, *The Other America* (New York: Macmillan, 1962).
2. Ibid., pp. 39–138.
3. Center on Budget and Policy Priorities, "Number in Poverty Hits 20-Year High" (Washington, DC: September 8, 1992), p. 1.
4. John K. Galbraith, *The Affluent Society*, 3rd ed. (Boston: Houghton Mifflin, 1976), pp. 244–254.
5. Harrington, *The Other America*, pp. 1–18.
6. U.S. Department of Labor, Bureau of Labor Statistics, *Monthly Labor Review*, May 1997, p. 10.
7. "Laid-off Workers Return with Changed Attitudes," *Des Moines Register*, August 22, 1983, p. 8S.
8. Barbara Bergmann, "How to Create Jobs by Shortening Work Week," *Des Moines Register*, July 7, 1984, p. 6A. See also Jeremy Rifkin, *The End of Work: The Decline of the Global Labor Force and The Dawn of the Post-Market Era* (New York: G.P. Putnam's Sons, 1995).
9. "Nearly 80,000 LTV Retirees Lose Benefits," *Des Moines Register*, July 19, 1986, p. 5S.
10. Jane E. Brody, "Unemployment: Consequences and Damages," *New York Times*, November 3, 1982, pp. C1, C12.
11. *USA Today*, October 19, 1983, p. 7A.
12. U.S. Bureau of the Census, *Poverty in the United States: 1995* (Washington, DC: Government Printing Office, 1996), p. v.
13. Ibid., p. vi.
14. *Federal Register* 62, no. 46 (March 10, 1997): pp. 10856–10859.

15. *Business Week,* April 21, 1997, pp. 58–102.
16. John Balzar, "Where Is the Public Debate Over Changes in the Workplace?" *Des Moines Register*, April 25, 1993, p. 2C
17. *Des Moines Register*, "Maddux Deal Tops Salary Game," August 11, 1997, p. 1B.
18. Mel Antonen, "Bonilla, Tartabull on Top in Big Apple," *USA Today*, February 28, 1992, p. 62.
19. Lester Thurow, "Whose Income Will Be Cut to Get U.S. Going Again?" *Des Moines Register,* August 17, 1980, p. 1C.
20. Herbert J. Gans, "The Positive Functions of Poverty," *American Journal of Sociology* 78, no. 2 (September 1976): 275–289.
21. Matthew 26:11, Mark 14:7, John 12:8. All of these statements are often taken out of context.
22. Walter I. Trattner, *From Poor Law to Welfare State: A History of Social Welfare in America,* 5th ed. (New York: Free Press, 1994), p. 274.
23. Social Security Administration, "Financing Social Security," SSA Publication no. 05-10094, March 1997.
24. Social Security Administration, "Social Security: Understanding the Benefits," SSA Publication no. 05-10024, January 1997, pp. 35–37.
25. *Social Security Bulletin,* Washington, DC: U.S. Department of Health and Human Services Vol. 60, no. 1, 1997, p. 72.
26. John R. Romanyshyn, *Social Welfare: Charity to Justice* (New York: Random House, 1971), pp. 205–209.
27. "Social Security Halts Cutoffs of Disability Pay," *Des Moines Register,* December 10, 1983, p. 4A.
28. "New Disability Rules Seek to Ease Inequities in Reviews, Termination," *AARP News Bulletin* (July–August 1984): 1.
29. "Judge: Social Security Must Reinstate Benefits," *Des Moines Register,* July 11, 1984, p. 4A.
30. *Social Security Bulletin* Vol. 60, no. 1, 1997, p. 117.
31. Jack Carlson, "Executive Director's Report," *AARP News Bulletin,* January 1988, p. 3.
32. Ibid.
33. Tom Carney, "His Check Is Less Than Insurance Bill," *Des Moines Register,* April 23, 1993, p. 1A.
34. Phoebe Wall Howard, "Transplant Plea Rejected," *Des Moines Register,* June 7, 1993, p. 1A.
35. Senator David Pryor, "High Drug Costs Exact a 'Painful Human Price,'" *USA Today,* March 2, 1993, p. 13A.
36. U.S. Bureau of the Census, *Statistical Abstract of the United States: 1996*, p. 112.
37. U.S. Bureau of the Census, "Health Insurance Coverage: 1995," *Current Population Reports* P60-195, September 1996, p. 1.
38. *Statistical Abstract: 1996*, p. 378.
39. R. Dolgoff, D. Feldstein, and L. Skolnick, *Understanding Social Welfare,* 4th ed. (White Plains, NY: Longman, 1997), p. 199.
40. "Cost of Work Injuries Is Far More Than AIDS," *Des Moines Register*, July 28, 1997, p. 1A.
41. From author's files.
42. *Social Security Bulletin* 60, no. 1, 1997, p. 86.
43. Ibid., p. 88.
44. *Statistical Abstract: 1996*, p. 381.
45. Ibid., p. 382.
46. U.S. Department of Health and Human Services, Administration for Children and Families, "Characteristics and Financial Circumstances of AFDC Recipients FY 1993" (Washington, DC, 1995), p. 1.

47. Ibid., p. 2.

48. Mark Lino, "Expenditures on Children by Families," 1996 annual report, U.S. Department of Agriculture, Center for Nutrition Policy and Promotion, Misc. Pub. No. 15-28-1996 (Washington, DC, 1996); applies to middle-income group.

49. Administration for Children and Families, *Characteristics and Financial Circumstances of AFDC Recipients: FY 1993* (Washington, DC, 1995), p. 1.

50. Ibid., p. 3

51. Ibid., p. 2.

52. Ibid., p. 1.

53. R. Dolgoff et al., op. cit., p. 228. See also "Welfare Fraud-Busters at Work," *Des Moines Register*, November 15, 1996, p. 8A.

54. Charles Zostrow, *Introduction to Social Work and Social Welfare*, 5th ed. (Pacific Grove, CA: Brooks/Cole, 1993), pp. 106–107.

55. *Characteristics and Financial Circumstances of AFDC Recipients*, p. 2.

56. Ibid.

57. Winifred Bell, *Contemporary Social Welfare*, 2nd ed. (New York: Macmillan, 1987), pp. 227–232.

58. *NASW News*, 41, no. 8 (Washington, DC: September 1996), pp. 1, 12.

59. Ibid.

60. From author's files.

61. From author's files.

62. Diana M. DiNitto, "Hunger, Nutrition, and Food Program," in *Encyclopedia of Social Work*, 19th ed., vol. 2 (Washington, DC: NASW, 1995), pp. 1428–1437.

63. Iowa State Department of Health, "Special Supplemental Food Program for Women, Infants, Children" (a pamphlet) (Des Moines, IA, no date).

64. Economic Opportunity Act of 1964.

65. *Des Moines Register*, Editorial, May 30, 1993, p. 1C.

66. Bell, *Contemporary Social Welfare*, p. 166.

67. Martha N. Ozawa, "The 1983 Amendments to the Social Security Act: The Issue of Intergenerational Equity," *Social Work* 29, no. 2 (March-April 1984): 131–137.

68. Deborah Page-Adams and Michael Sherraden, "Asset Building as a Community Revitalization Strategy," *Social Work* 42, no. 5 (September 1997): 423–434. See also Salome Raheim, "Problems and Prospects of Self-Employment as an Economic Independence Option for Welfare Recipients," *Social Work* 42, no. 1 (January 1997): 44–53.

69. Mimi Abramovitz, "Everyone Is on Welfare: The Role of Redistribution in Social Policy Revisited," *Social Work* 28, no. 6 (November–December 1983): 440–445.

70. Bell, *Contemporary Social Welfare*, pp. 235–251.

71. Bruce S. Jansson, *The Reluctant Welfare State*, 3rd ed. (Pacific Grove, CA: Brooks/Cole, 1997).

Additional Suggested Readings

Berrick, Jill Duerr. *Faces of Poverty*. New York: Oxford University Press, 1995.

Block, Fred, F.A. Cloward, B. Ehrenreich, and F.F. Piven. *The Mean Season: The Attack on the Welfare State*. New York: Pantheon Books, 1987.

Chatterjee, Pranab. *Approaches to the Welfare State*. Washington, DC: National Association of Social Workers, 1996.

Citizens for Tax Justice. *The Hidden Entitlements*. Washington, DC: Author. May 1996.

DiNitto, Diana M. *Social Welfare: Politics and Public Policy*. 4th ed. Needham Heights, MA: Allyn & Bacon, 1995.

Dobelstein, Andrew W. *Social Welfare: Policy and Analysis*, 2nd ed. Chicago: Nelson-Hall, 1996.

Ewalt, Patricia L. "Income Security for Children." *Social Work* 42, no. 3 (May 1997): 221–222.

Frank, Mark Robert. *Living on the Edge*. New York: Columbia University Press, 1995.

Kahn, Alfred J., and Sheila B. Kamerman. *Child Care: Facing the Hard Choices*. Dover, MA: Auburn House Publishing Co., 1987.

Karger, Howard Jacob, and Davis Stoesz. *American Social Welfare Policy*. 2nd ed. New York: Longman, 1997.

Rose. *From Client to Individual...Rose's Story*. Milwaukee: Family Service America, 1991.

5

Services to Families and Children in the Home

TERESA K. FULLER KULPER
GILBERT J. GREENE

The concern for the well-being of children and families has been a major part of social work tradition and present-day social work practice. From the early days of the "friendly visitors" of the Charity Organization Societies (COS) and the workers in the settlement houses, both the enhancement of family functioning and childhood development have been major goals of social work.

Social work's primary focus is on the social functioning of clients, and since one's basic level of social functioning is acquired within the family context, or a substitute family situation, it is only fitting that family and child welfare are of major importance to the profession. The dual concerns of strengthening family life and enhancing the welfare of children are inextricably interwoven. This relationship is indicated by Costin and Downing's definition of child welfare, which they state is "concerned with the well-being of individual children, the strengths of family life, and the rights of all children and young persons."[1] Therefore, family and child welfare are inseparable. Though most social programs and policies affect the family in some way (for example, tax laws), only those social services directly oriented to the enhancement of social functioning of families and children will be discussed in this and the next chapter.

THE NEED FOR SOCIAL SERVICES TO FAMILIES AND CHILDREN

In the United States the responsibility for the welfare of children has traditionally been the primary concern of the family. Families tended to rely on friends, the church, the labor union, neighborhood, or relatives when they needed help, rather than seek assistance from the government or formal voluntary agencies. However, in today's complex and mobile society, informal voluntary sources of assistance frequently are not available, and reliance on formal social agencies for assistance is necessary. In addition, laws and policies have been established in more recent times pertaining to child and family welfare.[2] This has led to the creation of more social services for families and may allow for their involuntary involvement in them.

Corresponding to these changes have been changes in the makeup of families and their life circumstances. These changes have resulted in families needing the support provided by social services more than ever. First, in any one year there is one divorce for every two marriages. Only 8 percent of all families with children consist of one parent working outside the home and one parent in the home full-time. In 1991, of all children under the age of 18, 22 percent lived with their mothers only, 3 percent lived with their fathers only, and 3 percent lived with neither parent. The number of one-parent families has been steadily increasing from 12 percent of all families in 1970 to 25 percent in 1991. In 1993, 57.9 percent of mothers with children under six were working. Between 1980 and 1987, the gap between the poor and the wealthy widened considerably, in part due to worldwide changes that impacted American corporations. In 1987, it was estimated that the poorest one-fifth of Americans earned 4.6 percent of the nation's income while the wealthiest one-fifth earned 43.6 percent. Real median income decreased, with 13.5 percent of the population living in poverty. Of the single-parent families described above, approximately half were awarded child support and only half of those actually received the full amount awarded. Those who received child support had significantly lower poverty rates.[3]

It is obvious that families and children in the United States, especially those with low income, are under increasing pressure. This stress has increased with the federal budget cuts of the last several years. Even as the need for services to families has increased, the funding for these services has decreased.

When are families and children seen as needing social services? Kadushin and Martin, referring to a position of the Child Welfare League of America (CWLA), state that child welfare services are provided when parents are unable to fulfill their child-rearing responsibilities to their children or when communities fail to provide the resources and protection required by families and children. Child welfare services are designed to support, supplant, or substitute the functions that parents have difficulty in performing and to improve conditions for children and their families by modifying existing social institutions or organizing new ones.[4]

American society tends to be oriented to change and future growth. If the children in our society are able to maximize the use of their skills and abilities, then so much the better for society. There are, however, many conditions necessary for successful growth and development. Children need to have proper nutrition and clothing, the nurturance and security of caring parents, adequate housing in safe neighborhoods, regular access to quality education, and so forth. Society has a vested interest in attempting to meet these needs.

Social work has been sanctioned by society to help remove many of the barriers children and families encounter in trying to carry out the tasks just mentioned. Throughout the rest of this and the next chapter, we will discuss the major social services that have been created as means of overcoming the barriers to adequate social functioning of families and children, along with social work's role in the provision of such services. These services have been designed to *support* parents in caring for their children at home, to *supplement* the care of children in their homes by their parents, or to provide *substitute* care for children outside the home when parents are deemed unable to do so, temporarily or permanently. Such a classification scheme—supportive, supplemental, substitute—will be used for the discussion of the family and social services, with supportive and supplemental services discussed in this chapter and substitute services in the next chapter.

SUPPORTIVE SOCIAL SERVICES

The assumption that whenever possible it is best to provide services to children in their own homes, where they are cared for by their own parents, is the basis for supportive services. With the prevention of out-of-home placement being the goal, supportive services are provided at three levels of intensity on the basis of risk. Primary prevention services are provided to families without serious signs of distress. These include various types of casework and group work services, both therapeutic and educational, provided by family service agencies and child guidance clinics. Secondary prevention services are child protective services that focus on safeguarding the lives of children from the detrimental effects of abuse and neglect. Tertiary prevention services—the most intense level—are provided to families at serious risk of out-of-home placement or for the reunification of families from which one or all of the children have been temporarily removed because of abuse or neglect.[5] The ultimate goal is to safely allow the child to continue living in his or her own home.

PRIMARY PREVENTION SERVICES

Family Service Agencies and Child Guidance Clinics

Two of the principal kinds of agencies providing supportive services are the family service agency and the child guidance clinic. Such agencies have many similarities and some differences. Both attempt to help families by direct intervention with the child; however, the family service agency is more apt to help the child through helping the parents. Basically, there are no major differences in the cases coming to these agencies; however, the more severely disturbed children tend to be referred more often to the child guidance clinic, primarily because it has psychiatrists on the clinic staff who can prescribe medication. Regardless of any differences, both types of agencies share the same goal of enhancing social functioning of the family and its individual members.

Family service agencies. The origin of the family service agency was in the COS developed in the United States in the late 1880s. Prior to the Great Depression, these agencies provided economic aid and some counseling services to the economically deprived. With the federal government assuming primary responsibility for economic relief during the Depression, family service agencies began to put their energies into providing casework counseling services to help clients deal with noneconomic problems. Consequently, these agencies began helping clients from all socioeconomic groups. The bulk of the noneconomic problems consisted of emotional and interpersonal concerns, parent-child conflict, and marital problems. The workers in the early days were primarily untrained volunteers. Gradually, more workers were added to the payrolls of these agencies and more training for the job was requested and provided. Thus, professional social work began. The bulk of the services provided by these agencies continues to focus on problems in marriages and parent-child interactions.[6]

The major coordinating and standard-setting organization in the family service field is Family Service America (FSA), which was called the Family Service Association of America (FSAA) until the name change in 1983. FSAA was organized in 1946 after going through several previous name changes and reorganizations, beginning in 1911. In 1992, FSA had 230 fully accredited member agencies and an additional 43 provisional and affiliate members.[7]

Child guidance clinics.   The child guidance clinic origins reside in the efforts in 1909 of Dr. William Healy, a psychiatrist, to deal with juvenile delinquency. In his work on this problem, Healy attempted to apply the concepts of Freudian psychology. He took into consideration physical, psychological, and social factors together with parent-child interactions as contributing to the delinquent behavior of children. The basis for this approach was the premise that delinquent behavior arose out of problems in parent-child interactions and that not only did the child's behavior have to be changed, but also the behavior of the parents.[8]

Treatment Services Provided by Family Service Agencies and Child Guidance Clinics

Casework services.   Counseling tends to be the principal service requested by clients of both agencies. Initially, a psychosocial assessment is done by conducting interviews with the child, his or her parents, and significant others. In this assessment phase, child guidance clinics are more likely to use psychological tests and psychiatric consultation. From all the data gathered in the assessment, a treatment plan is formulated.

Because of differential staffing patterns—family services headed by and predominantly staffed with social workers, and the child guidance clinics being staffed by teams of psychiatrists, pediatricians, psychologists, and social workers—treatment may be implemented differently while maintaining similar goals. Family service is more likely to routinely see both parents and children together, at least part of the time, while in the clinic the psychiatrist may interview only the child, and the social workers may interview only the parents.[9]

Traditionally, both family service and child guidance agencies based their treatment approaches on psychoanalytic principles. In recent years, however, there has been an increasing use of behavior modification methods based on learning theory and techniques derived from family systems theory. Another trend is the use of short-term, problem-focused casework services as opposed to long-term psychotherapy, which has personality change of the client(s) as the primary outcome goal. The provision of sex therapy for the treatment of any sexual problems couples may be having is another trend. Sex therapy is most likely to be provided in family service agencies, rather than in child guidance clinics, with children being excluded during the therapy sessions.

Group work services.   The use of a group approach in working with families has been employed by both family service agencies and child guidance clinics. At times a group experience is used in conjunction with casework services and at other times it is the only service provided. Two different types of group services are used, one with an educational focus and the other a treatment focus.

The first type of group is called *family-life education.* This approach uses group discussion and/or lecture to strengthen the functioning of "nonproblematic" families and thus prevent serious family disturbance in the future. The discussions and lectures center around such topics as improving child-rearing practices, parent-child interactions, marital communication, and stress management in order to enhance the participants in their roles of parents and spouses. Some family-life education classes are offered to address situational stress to reduce negative effects. One such class is Children of Divorce, designed to prevent serious problems by normalizing the divorce process for children going through it. Family-life education is based on the belief that problems may frequently arise in family relationships that can be alleviated with increased knowledge or skills. In these groups the leader is more concerned with the participants learning content and skills rather than dealing with the interactional processes among the participants; therefore, the leader serves in the role of educator-expert on family relationships.

Group counseling services in family service agencies often deal more with the needs of parents, usually those with some type of personal disturbance. Growing areas of group counseling are groups for adult women who have experienced sexual abuse as children or groups for adults to develop skills in specific areas such as anger management or interpersonal relationships. Child guidance clinics, on the other hand, frequently provide group counseling services only for children. Unlike family-life educators, the group counselor is not task-oriented but sees the processes of interaction among group members as the primary means of effecting change. The counselor must help create an environment within the group that results in high levels of trust, cohesiveness, and openness about feelings. In contrast to family-life education, group counseling has a rehabilitative rather than a preventive purpose. Group leaders encourage members to set goals or form contracts for change that become a working consensus. Fees are agreed upon and periodic evaluation of progress is possible.[10]

Family therapy.   Family therapy has its origin in the early 1950s in the work of Ackerman, Bateson, Haley, Jackson, Bowen, and Satir, who studied the interactional patterns of families having one member diagnosed as schizophrenic. Therapeutic techniques have been developed by these researchers and other family therapists and have been used with other types of problematic families.[11] In family therapy the family problems and their resolution are viewed from a systems perspective. This perspective is that families share the following attributes of a system: (1) the unified whole consists of interrelated parts; (2) the sum of the parts is different from the interrelated whole; and (3) a change in any one component affects the entire system. Rules affect family functioning, such as how information is shared and processed, adaptation to events, and information and self-maintenance.[12] A family, like any other system, has an innate tendency to seek a balanced state, called *homeostasis*. These characteristics—self-regulation, adaptation, goal-directed behavior, and homeostasis—are respected, and change is introduced in accordance through family therapy. Thus, the problematic behavior of the family or one of its members is viewed within the family context, leading to defining the family rather than just one member as having "the problem." Just as the identified problem did not affect only one part, neither can the solution be focused on that part. Family therapy involves the social worker seeing the family together for interviews rather than the problematic family member alone. The worker is able to observe the interactional patterns of the family that reinforce problematic behavior, which allows the worker to intervene directly in the family system in a way that will facilitate the development of more functional interactional patterns.

Family advocacy.   Traditionally, family service agencies and child guidance clinics provided only clinically oriented treatment services. However, in the late 1960s and early 1970s many of these agencies, especially the family service agencies, broadened their scope of services to consider the impact of community conditions on families and children. *Family advocacy* is a term that describes "the variety of techniques social workers employ to help clients having difficulty obtaining necessary assistance from community resources."[13] Whether the social worker is advocating for an individual family (*case advocacy*) or groups of families (*community advocacy*),[14] the community is included in the problem definition. When community conditions are identified as having a detrimental effect on the social functioning of families and family members, these agencies attempt to create new community resources and to mobilize present ones to correct these situations.

Family advocacy may involve active intervention on behalf of families who do not receive needed social, economic, emotional, or psychological services because of social problems such as racism.[15] Doing family advocacy "requires gathering data to document unjust policies or serious gaps in institutional programs and developing advocacy actions in concert with both the families affected and other available resources."[16]

Community Mental Health

Almost all of the services provided by the family service agencies and child guidance clinics are also provided by Community Mental Health Centers (CMHC). As we will see in Chapter 9, CMHCs were established as a result of federal legislation in 1963. Special provisions for children are made in section 271 of this legislation.[17] Family therapy, family-life education, and group counseling are primary services provided. Prevention is emphasized, with CMHC staff frequently giving presentations and classes to various community groups on topics such as parenting skills and stress management.

SECONDARY SERVICES

Protective Services

The primary purpose of protective services is to deal with situations in which a child has been either neglected, abused, or exploited. Protection of children from such treatment is provided by state statutes; however, this has not always been the case. While the reporting of criminal cases of child abuse is dated as early as 1655, it was not until about 1825 that states began passing legislation addressing the maltreatment of children. There were still no formal services to protect children in 1874, when the extreme abuse and neglect of a child named Mary Ellen was brought to the attention of the director of the Society for the Prevention of Cruelty to Animals—because there was a system in place to protect animals. Public outcry as a result of this discrepancy spurred creation of the New York City Society for the Prevention of Cruelty to Children. This was replicated in several states and started a children's rights movement.[18]

Protective services provided by the states increased, with varied quality, in the 1960s. By 1978 all 50 states provided protective services as a result of Title XX of the Social Security Act, which mandated such services. The provision of protective services is primarily the responsibility of state agencies, variously called, for example, the Department of Social Services, the Department of Human Services, or the Department of Children and Family Services.

Despite the passage of child protection laws, cases of serious abuse went unreported. Frequently neighbors, relatives, schoolteachers, physicians, and others did not want to become involved or risk litigation by the parents or want to believe that abuse of a child was occurring within a certain family. Consequently, various statutes were instituted in some states, *mandating* the reporting of suspected child maltreatment. The passage of the Child Abuse Prevention and Treatment Act by Congress in 1974 was the catalyst for all states to pass such reporting laws. The National Center on Child Abuse and Neglect (NCCAN) was developed to help define the problem and identify who should be mandatory reporters.[19] Because these guidelines offer broad parameters and permit each state to define maltreatment, there is still variation from state to state.[20] These mandatory reporting statutes pertain primarily to professionals such as physicians, nurses, dentists, day-care workers, social workers, and schoolteachers, who are likely to have contact with children and to be the first ones to become aware of suspected maltreatment. When a report of child maltreatment is made, it is usually sent to the state department of social services or the local legal authorities who have the responsibility for investigating the report further. While in most states the reporting of suspected child maltreatment is compulsory, these professionals are also protected from litigation by the parents if the maltreatment is unfounded.[21]

The Child Abuse Prevention and Treatment Act also provides financial assistance to states that comply with guidelines stipulated in the legislation. The purpose of this act is to allow states to develop demonstration programs that will prevent, identify, and treat child abuse and neglect. This availability of federal funds facilitates the necessary development of treatment facilities for children and their parents that are necessary to fulfill the intent and purposes of all child abuse and neglect laws.[22] The Child Abuse Prevention and Treatment Act

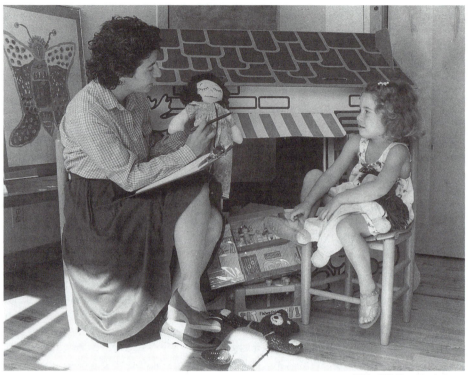

Play therapy is used by social workers to detect and treat child abuse and sexual abuse.

was updated in 1988 by the Child Abuse Prevention, Adoption, and Family Services Act.[23]

Child abuse has been defined as a nonaccidental physical injury that causes substantial risk of death or disfigurement, impairment of health, or loss of function of any bodily organ. More ambiguous is the definition of neglect, which ususally involves the lack of proper care, supervision, or discipline to the detriment of the child's health.[24] A very simple, but helpful, distinction between abuse and neglect to be used here is that abuse is an act of commission and neglect is an act of omission.

Child Abuse

The number of reported cases of child abuse and neglect has been steadily increasing in recent years, 331 percent between 1976 and 1992. The increase in reported cases could be because of an increase in the actual number of abuse and neglect cases, increased public awareness, or expansion of society's definition of maltreatment—or an increase in reporting. Yet many cases of child maltreatment go unreported. Almost 3 million children were reported abused in 1992. About one in three reports are confirmed. Physical abuse and neglect combined are the most frequently reported maltreatment, possibly because they are the most observable. Sexual abuse is next, comprising 14 percent of child abuse reports, with emotional maltreatment and medical neglect following in number of reports.[25]

Maltreating families are disproportionately poor, single-parent, and young (under age 27). Studies have contradicted each other, so it is still unknown if ethnicity is related to abuse. Single fathers are more often abusive than single mothers, particularly when they are also poor.[26]

Complex environmental factors positively correlate with child abuse: poverty, inadequate health care, inadequate housing, and violent communities.[27] The fact that a disproportionate number of perpetrators are low-income, young, and single-parent points to the importance of economic distress as a stressor and contributing factor.

In addition to socioeconomic factors, there are several personal characteristics that child abusers frequently, but not always, are found to have:

1. A history of abuse and/or rejection in childhood
2. Low self-esteem
3. A rigid, domineering, impulsive personality
4. Social isolation
5. A record of inadequate coping behavior
6. Poor interpersonal relationships
7. High, unrealistic expectations of children
8. Lack of ability to empathize with children[28]
9. Lack of parenting and behavior management skills
10. Poor nutrition
11. Educational failures[29]
12. Problems in relationships with extended family
13. Inappropriate developmental expectations for children
14. Ill health[30]

It has been noted that abusers tend to have a limited ability to tolerate frustration and delays in gratification. They become angry very easily, which, together with low self-esteem, contributes to their reacting impulsively and intensely to even minor provocation. Though only approximately 10 percent of all abusers are actually psychotic or sociopathic, research has found that abusive parents suffer from considerably more psychological dysfunction than do control groups.[31] One study found a positive correlation between number of arrests for narcotics and number of child abuse reports, suggesting that communities with major drug problems might be areas in which to allocate services to reduce child abuse.[32]

Children found to be at high risk for child abuse include premature babies, babies with low birth weight, and babies born to vulnerable, unsupported families.[33] A baby with birth problems may remain in the hospital after the mother goes home, which can result in attachment problems.

The event of child abuse, therefore, can be seen to be the result of interaction among four sets of variables:

1. A parent who has the potential for abuse.
2. A child who may be ill, difficult to discipline, and who fails to respond in a manner expected by the parents.

3. An environment of social isolation, cumulative stress, and a community context that tolerates violence.
4. A crisis situation, which triggers the abusive act.

A Case of Child Abuse

Jane, age 21, was the youngest of four children, and her siblings were all boys. Her parents were both well educated and led very active lives. The responsibility for her upbringing was left largely to her older brothers, who alternated between ignoring her and "picking on" her. Jane felt that she was the result of an unwanted pregnancy. Her parents were both emotionally distant, with her father frequently criticizing her and using her as a "scapegoat" for other problems within the family. She has feelings of dislike and hostility toward men in general and her father, brothers, and husband in particular. She admits to feeling inadequate and worthless as a person and especially as a mother.

Jane was married at the age of 20 as the result of an unwanted pregnancy. She had strong ambivalent feelings about having an abortion and put off making a decision until it was unsafe to have one. She admits that she does not even like her son, Bobby, age one-and-one-half, much less love him. She feels that he is the cause of her not having "her own life" and resents that he is helpless and cries so much. She thinks that Bobby often does things to irritate her and refuses to learn how to do things for himself just to make her do them for him. She states that she wishes she never had him. She is left at home all day with Bobby while her husband is at work, and receives no help from her husband when he is at home. Since Bobby's birth, Jane has slapped and shaken him many times, resulting in bruises and cuts. This case of child abuse was reported by a hospital emergency room physician who treated Bobby for a concussion and broken arm. This was Jane's worst attack on Bobby and appears to have been precipitated by the discovery of her husband's involvement in an extramarital affair.

Neglect

Polansky and his associates define child neglect as:

> a condition in which a caretaker responsible for the child either deliberately or by extraordinary inattentiveness permits the child to experience avoidable present suffering and/or fails to provide one or more of the ingredients generally deemed essential for developing a person's physical, intellectual and emotional capacities.[34]

Child neglect tends to be a chronic and long-term problem that can, like child abuse, sometimes be fatal. As mentioned previously, neglect is more frequently a matter of omission in child care. Neglect involves a lack of action by and the indifference of the parents. The failure in parenting may then result in "poor feeding, uncleanliness, extremely bad housing, filthy circumstances which make the children prone to infections, lack of medical care, inadequate supervision and protection from danger, lack of intellectual stimulation, inattentiveness to the children bordering on rejection—one could go on."[35] Educational neglect is the failure to send a child to school as state law mandates.[36]

Families where children are neglected are similar to those described in our maltreatment section in income, parenting status, race, and gender. Other studies have found neglectful parents to have experienced more psychological problems such as depression, poor impulse control, and deficient problem-solving skills. Substance abuse is often a factor. Neglect is more likely to occur in families where the parent or parents lack skills and knowledge of child development and parenting. They are more isolated and may feel negative toward their children when unrealistic expectations are at fault.[37]

Emotional Maltreatment

Though parents may provide adequate physical care for children, they may do serious harm by starving or abusing children emotionally. The Child Abuse Prevention and Treatment Act of 1974 addresses mental as well as physical injury. Emotional and psychological maltreatment is difficult to establish, and definitions vary from state to state.[38] One of the more comprehensive definitions of emotional and psychological maltreatment has been provided by Garbarino and his associates:[39]

> a concerted attack by an adult on a child's development of self and social competence, *pattern* of psychically destructive behavior, and it takes five forms:
> *Rejecting*
> *Isolating* (the adult cuts the child off from normal social experiences)
> *Terrorizing* (the adult verbally assaults the child, creates a climate of fear, bullies and frightens the child)
> *Ignoring*
> *Corrupting* (the adult "mis-socializes" the child, stimulates the child to engage in destructive antisocial behavior)

Occasional punitive parental behavior is not thought to cause emotional and psychological damage if it occurs within an otherwise positive parent-child relationship. For emotional and psychological harm to the child to be likely, a pattern of aberrant parental behavior toward the child needs to be established that is "persistent, continuous, and cumulative."[40] In addition, for intervention in cases of emotional and psychological maltreatment to occur, the child must exhibit some behaviors indicating emotional problems that can clearly be linked to parental behavior toward the child.[41]

Sexual Abuse

Sexual abuse is said to occur when sexually stimulating contact between a child and an adult takes place, the child is someone under the age of 18, and the adult is at least five years older than the victim. Sexual contact may include exhibiting sex organs, genital fondling, mouth-genital contact, intercourse, rape, and the use of children in creating pornography and prostitution.[42] The sexual contact can also be inappropriate verbal interaction that may be sexually stimulating.

The incidence of child sexual abuse is not easy to determine. Reported cases are difficult to substantiate and much abuse goes unreported, for several reasons. While all sexual abuse is traumatizing to the child, it can appear to be loving and caring, which is confusing to the child. In addition, because of the self-referent nature of the development of children, the child usually feels responsible, guilty, and humiliated. Perpetrators of sexual abuse manipulate abused children by telling them it is their fault or that they deserve it. Lack of action by the nonperpetrating parent and/or authority figures can enhance the child's self-blame and decrease his or her ability to seek help. A third factor in the difficulty of detecting and substantiating child sexual abuse is that a common reaction to the abuse is *dissociation*.[43]

Dissociation is the mental blocking of a traumatic event by pretending, forgetting, or shutting off emotionally. Donovan and McIntyre outline a dissociative behavior checklist that can be the effect of severe trauma:[44]

1. Amnesia; events remembered in one context but not in another
2. Dazes and trances
3. Attention deficit disorder or learning disability
4. Shifts in personality
5. Gets lost easily, loses possessions frequently
6. Unexplainable variations in skill or knowledge
7. Rapid regression in behavior
8. Denial of responsibility for own actions

Because the incidence of child sexual abuse is so difficult to determine, most experts believe that it is underreported and that official figures are a gross underestimation. Many experts cite studies of adults who report having been abused as children. One such study found that 27 percent of the adult women and 16 percent of the adult men interviewed reported sexual abuse in childhood.[45] This discrepancy in official reports versus professional estimation is summed up by Donovan and McIntyre, "We live in a society steeped in contradictions: revulsion and moral outrage at child abuse, especially sexual abuse, and yet a monstrous hesitance to recognize its prevalence."[46]

In fact, one study found that 74 percent of the time sexual abuse allegations were not believed in spite of the evidence.[47] Many child sexual abuse allegations occur in the context of child custody disputes during divorce proceedings, and differentiating between true and false allegations can be particularly difficult in this context.[48]

Social Work Intervention in Cases of Child Abuse and Neglect

As mentioned previously, cases of child neglect and abuse may be reported to law enforcement or social agencies. Mulford states, "There is almost unanimous agreement that a treatment-oriented approach is more successful for the child and more beneficial to the family than a punitive approach."[49] However, despite social work's preference for a treatment approach, the legal aspects of dealing with abuse and neglect cannot be ignored. First of all, it is through the establishment of laws concerning this problem that social workers receive their sanction to provide child protection services against the wishes of parents. Child protection laws provide social workers necessary leverage in gaining the cooperation of parents. This authority, given to social workers by the law, must be clearly understood by them in order to be effective. The social worker must understand its nature and source, and convey it clearly and objectively. In turn, the parents must be able to accept to some degree this authority if their functioning as parents is to improve. To provide support to social workers and to treat parents fairly, the protective service agency must establish clear and objective criteria and guidelines as a basis for intervention into the privacy of a family's life. The development of clear standards and rules as a basis for agency intervention and the proper observance of legal provisions will help to ensure that decision making is reasoned and based upon relevant criteria, thus safeguarding the rights of all involved parties.[50]

Since neglecting and abusing parents are usually involuntary clients, they may be very resistant to and rejecting of any attempts by social workers to help them. They may become hostile, guilty, and defensive since their adequacy as parents is being questioned and the autonomy of the family is being threatened. However, regardless of their initial responses, the basic approach should be one that combines empathy and understanding with firm expectations of improvement. It is very important for child protective service workers to be trained and skilled in developing and maintaining effective worker-client relationships.

The protection and safety of the maltreated child is the first priority in working with abusing and neglecting families. Treatment of the parents should also be a priority. In most cases they experienced neglect and/or abuse in their own childhoods, and they are very needful of nurturance and protection as adults. Therefore, social services must be available at all times in response to crisis situations and the social worker must be a stable, consistent, and reliable force for the family. The social worker must be able to respond to and help the family deal with everyday, tangible problems, behaviors, and reality needs.[51]

Families in which child maltreatment occurs often have many problems and needs. Consequently, a multiservice, multidisciplinary team approach is indicated. A number of services and interventions have been developed for meeting the needs of such families. The following is a brief listing and description of some of these services and interventions.[52]

1. *The hotline.* Parents may find it easier to cope with problems when emergency treatment for crises is available by phone 24 hours a day every day. The workers on the hotline are usually lay people who are supervised by a social worker. The hotline worker will have had specific training in crisis intervention.
2. *Crisis nurseries.* These are facilities where children may be taken when parents are unable to cope or while they themselves go for treatment. The maximum stay should be only 72 hours.
3. *Social service homemakers.* These are people who can help in the home with housekeeping and family care. This may be full-time service for a few days or weeks or for a few hours a week for a period of several months.

4. *Parent aides.* These are individuals who act as supportive and concerned friends to the abusive and neglectful parents. If at all possible, these parent aides should be from the same ethnic and socioeconomic background as the parents. They must be recruited and carefully screened by social service agencies and readily accessible to the parents. The parent aide has regular and flexible in-home contact to teach, offer support, and provide a role model for appropriate interaction with children. They can help the parents understand the child's developmental needs and abilities, control their anger, and manage stress.[53]

5. *Psychotherapy.* Despite the extensive deprivation maltreating parents have usually experienced throughout their lives, they usually do not receive traditional intensive individual therapy that has "personality change" as the overall goal. This type of treatment is expensive, long-term, and is usually not within the scope of the agency providing child protection services. Thus, psychotherapy should have limited and specifically defined goals.

6. *Marriage and family therapy.* With two-parent families, it is usually very beneficial to involve the parents in conjoint therapy since both are usually involved in some way in the maltreatment of their children. Involving both parents allows them to learn to express their feelings to each other, to listen and respond openly, and to learn joint problem solving. With a single-parent family, it may be helpful to include noncustodial parents and/or grandparents for some of the same reasons.

7. *Parent-child interaction.* One of the better ways of intervening with parents of young children, usually less than three years old, is to directly observe and change, when needed, the interactions between parent and child. In the process, the social worker can serve as a model for the parents. Successful intervention is usually accomplished through a combination of observation, modeling, discussion, and teaching positive parenting skills.

8. *Treatment in groups.* Groups are available that are educational, therapeutic, or both. Parents Anonymous, a self-help group of abusive parents, was founded along the same lines as Alcoholics Anonymous and has proved to be very effective. Group members are able to confront each other and are more open about their feelings, which they once assumed were unique, since they have experienced the same problems.[54]

9. *Play and art therapy.* Treatment offered to abused children without the parents' direct participation has the purpose of helping the child cope with difficult situations and his or her reactions to the abuse. This type of therapy is formulated with respect to the developmental capacities of the child. As play is the natural medium of communication for children, play therapy allows the child to express himself or herself in ways other than verbal. The symbolic function of art or play is to change the unmanageable into a manageable situation through self-guided nonverbal expression. The child learns new ways to cope, express feelings, relive frustrations, and/or discharge pent-up energy.[55]

TERTIARY SERVICES

Family Preservation Services

One possible response to child maltreatment is the removal of the child from the home and placement in foster care either temporarily or permanently. However, a placement of this sort is costly and disruptive to the family and community and should be the last resort. Following the Adoption Assistance and Child Welfare Act of 1980, many programs have been established that focus on providing intensive social services in the homes of families who have children at risk for neglect, abuse, or acting out and delinquent behavior, and to reunify families if placement occurred due to abuse or neglect.[56] In 1993, Congress passed the Family Preservation and Support Services Program providing $900 million over five years to develop preservation services and refine preventative, community-based approaches for serving families at risk for abusing children.[57] These intensive services have been referred to as home-based family-centered services, family-based services, and family preservation services. For simplicity, the term *family preservation services* will be used, as this seems the most descriptive of the goal of tertiary services.

Family preservation services have been developed with respect to systems theory. *Systems theory*, as described previously, states that the parts of the system are inseparable from the whole, that their actions and interactions are interdependent. Thus, the actions of family members are interrelated, and change in one member's action will reverberate throughout the family system. In addition the family is viewed as one part of a larger system, interdependent with the neighborhood, community, and society.[58] Consequently, rather than blame one family member and individually treat him or her, family preservation services work with the entire family, extended family, and/or neighborhood if possible.

Treating the family in their own environment, their home, is a common practice of family preservation services. This allows the worker to observe the family firsthand, to talk with extended family, neighbors, or other people significant to the family, and to address neighborhood issues such as safety, availability of public transportation, and other children. Skills needed for in-home family therapy include personal and professional flexibility, planning (such as the use of clear contracts and agendas), and diplomatic assertiveness.[59] One commonly used tool for understanding the family within their environment is called an *ecomap*. The worker and family map out the system, with the family at the center surrounded by other components such as the child welfare agency, work, health care, church, extended family, recreation, friends, school, and so forth. Components that have greater influence on the family are placed closer or are larger, with less significant aspects smaller and farther away.[60]

Nelson, Landsman, and Deutelbaum outline three basic models of placement prevention or reunification services: crisis intervention, home-based intervention, and family treatment.[61] Each will be briefly described and compared.

The first model draws on crisis intervention theory as well as systems theory. That is, families are most open to change during a crisis, when typical patterns of behavior are not working. Thus the services are immediate, intensive, and brief in duration. Treatment goals are set, utilizing the family's priorities and addressing expectations, behavior modification, and skill development. Therapeutic services are enhanced with concrete services such as homemakers, transportation, day care, shopping assistance, and financial aid. One such program in Tacoma, Washington, is called Homebuilders. Three main goals of Homebuilders are to ensure the safety of children, to avoid placement, and to improve family functioning. Homebuilders responds to referral within 24 hours, provides availability 24 hours per day seven days per week, provides services between 5 to 20 hours per week to each family with flexible scheduling, is involved as long as it takes to achieve concrete goals, and then terminates services promptly. Four to six weeks' duration is common. The workers serve as role models, service brokers, and advocates. They emphasize the strengths of the family and respect the family's views and priorities whenever possible. The objectives are limited to safety and stabilization, not perfection.[62]

The home-based model also focuses on the family as a system and provides services in the home. The emphasis is on intense family therapy with accurate assessment, concrete goals and expectations, and behaviorally oriented services. Concrete services are also utilized. The response may not be quite as immediate as in the previous model, and the duration of treatment is typically longer but is still moderately brief. Families, Inc., in West Branch, Iowa, is one home-based family preservation model. Workers emphasize family empowerment, attempt to ease accessibility to community resources, and utilize varied family therapy techniques. Appointment times are flexible with respect to the family's schedule, and the family is centrally involved in setting goals and assessing progress.[63]

The third model, family treatment, is exemplified by Intensive Family Services in Oregon. Its services, offered in the office or in the home, emphasize therapy and teaching much more than do the other models. Referrals for concrete services are made to other agencies rather than being provided by the preservation worker. Three distinct stages of treatment are worked through: assessment, intervention, and termination. Duration is typically three to five months, with utilization of a follow-up contact.[64]

Similarities of these models are many. All are committed to maintaining the children in their biological homes when safely possible. The family system within a larger environment is the focus for change. Last, therapeutic, supportive, and concrete services are offered in a comprehensive package.

Family preservation services have been found to be effective with families with severe relationship problems, including parent-child and parent-parent interaction and child acting out behavior.[65] Specifically, improved family functioning has been documented.[66] These services are offered to a broad range of children and families in the mental health and juvenile justice systems as well as the child welfare system.[67]

Family preservation services have also been found to be cost-effective. However, early projections on cost savings have been criticized as too simplistic. Because there are intrinsic complexities and difficulties in measuring outcomes, more research is needed to understand the comparison of family preservation services and other child welfare services. For a thorough review on evaluating cost-effectivness, see Yaun.[68]

The goal of family preservation has been criticized as overemphasized to the detriment of protecting children. Nelson advocates that social work programs strive to find what types of services work with which families and that the broad continuum of services described in these chapters are needed to protect children.[69]

SUPPLEMENTAL SERVICES

Services that compensate for certain inadequacies in parental care or are necessary additions to such care are considered to be *supplemental*. Ideally these types of services help to facilitate the normal growth and development of children in their own homes. The most widely used supplemental programs that will be discussed here are homemaker and day-care services.

Homemaker Services

An important aspect of services to families in which a child has been maltreated is the provision of homemaker services. These services are offered in situations when the parent(s) is unable to meet all the responsibilities of family life. Such services were provided on a small scale as early as 1903 in New York City. In succeeding years, homemaker services were established in many other cities. A national committee, organized in 1939 to promote these services, eventually became the National Homecaring Council.[70]

Homemaker services are provided by a variety of public or voluntary health or welfare agencies. The homemakers themselves are professionally supervised paraprofessionals who are trained to help the sick, aged, developmentally disabled, mentally ill, physically disabled, and those who are feeling too overwhelmed to maintain themselves and their children in their own homes. The homemaker may go beyond just performing housekeeping duties and have some responsibility for meeting the emotional and security needs of the children. Serving as a model to the parent(s) for good parenting and housekeeping skills, the homemaker works with the parents in order to enhance their functioning.[71]

Homemakers must be sensitive to cultural aspects of the family's performance:[72]

> The homemaker's relationship with the family must be predicated on the knowledge and acceptance of their cultural values and lifestyles. So much of what occurs in a household is bound by culture. Whatever new ideas are introduced to the family must be consistent with this realty.... If the homemaker ignores culturally determined patterns of relationship or insists on changes which are incongruent with the family's values, the homemaker's help will surely be rejected either overtly or passively.

A homemaker may be part of a professional team that may include a nurse, a nutritionist, or a physician in addition to a social worker. It is usually the social worker who is responsible for the training and supervision of the homemakers. A crucial aspect of this supervision is to ensure the initial and ongoing acceptance by the family and homemaker of each other so that the homemaker services are maximally effective.

Day-Care Services

Day care is a social welfare service that usually provides child care for some part of the day. Primarily it is a supplemental service that is sought out by families in which the mother and father are both employed. Day-care services for children have been in existence in this country since 1854, when a day nursery was established at the Nursery and Child's Hospital in New York City. Day-care services continued to grow, and in 1898 the National Foundation of Day Nurseries was founded. From 1900 to 1960 federal legislation supporting day care fluctuated with the crises of the times.[73] Federal legislation supporting day care began to expand with the 1962 and 1967 amendments to the Social Security Act; these amendments provided some funding for these services to welfare recipients. Much of the recent focus on day care has had the goal of increasing employment and decreasing dependence on AFDC. Examples of this trend are the Family Support Act of 1988 and the Child Care and Dependent Block Grant of 1990.[74] A 1993 survey indicates that federal money seems to be having a positive effect in improving monitoring activities to safeguard children in day care—by developing referral networks, training day-care workers, and funding prekindergarten programs to help four-year-olds at risk for failure in school.[75] Most day care in the United States, however, is still paid for by the parents of the children receiving such services.

Day care is an important service for families at risk of having a child removed from the home. Day care provided by drop-in centers and crisis nurseries may be helpful for such families under stress. For at-risk families, day care goes beyond the daily care and supervision of children; it is also an important part of an individualized case plan that helps to meet the developmental, educational, and health needs of children as well as to enhance the total functioning of the family. Day-care programs should provide high-quality services that include:

> (1) a strong educational program geared to the age, ability, interest, and temperamental organization of each child, (2) adequate nutrition, (3) a health program and health services when needed, (4) an opportunity for social and emotional growth, including a balance between affectional support, control, and the joy of meeting new challenges and between group experiences and appropriate time for solitude and internalization of ideas and experiences, (5) opportunities for parental education, participation, and involvement, (6) social services as needed by the child and his/her family.[76]

Social work roles in a day-care setting might include helping a mother with any feelings of ambivalence, doubt, fear, or guilt that she may have about going to work and leaving her child. The worker may help the family to become sensitive to the changes the mother's working may have on the family and in exploring ways they can accommodate their daily activities to the employment demands placed on the mother. The need for day care may be embedded in other problems the family is facing such as divorce, low income, illness, inadequate housing, or death, and the worker can help the family in dealing with these problems. The social worker can help the parents prepare for and deal with the child's reactions during the adjustment period in beginning day care. Later behavioral problems may be a response to stressful changes at home, such as a recent job loss by the father. The social worker in a day-care facility may help the family deal with this situation or refer them to other social agencies for needed services. In addition, the worker may act as consultant to the day-care staff on dealing with problematic children and/or parents. Though the need for social work services in day-care facilities is obvious, only a small percentage of day-care centers employ social workers.

SUMMARY AND CONCLUSIONS

The discussion in this chapter has focused on services to families and children with a variety of problems and needs that vary in degrees of severity. The primary goal of such programs is to reduce the various stresses impinging on families and children so that the families may remain intact and their social functioning hopefully be enhanced. If these services are at least minimally successful, all the family members will be able to continue living in the home. Keeping families intact is not, however, always possible because of the nature and severity of their problems and needs. The next chapter will discuss services to families and children in which one or more of the children must live out of the home, either temporarily or permanently.

Notes

1. Lela B. Costin and Rupert Downing, "Child and Family Welfare," in Donald Brieland et al., eds., *Contemporary Social Work: An Introduction to Social Work and Social Welfare* (New York: McGraw-Hill, 1980), p. 197.
2. For example, the Child Abuse Prevention and Treatment Act, 1974; the Community Mental Health Centers Act, 1963; Title XX of the Social Security Act, 1974; and the Adoption Assistance and Child Welfare Act, 1980.
3. Statistics are drawn from Leon Ginsberg, "Selected Statistical Review," in *Encyclopedia of Social Work*, 18th ed. (Silver Spring, MD: NASW, 1990 supplement), pp. 256–288; "Childhood and Early Development," in *Children's Defense Fund: The State of America's Children Yearbook* (Washington, DC: Author, 1994), p. 31; Geneva B. Johnson and Maureen Wahl, "Families: Demographic Shifts," in *Encyclopedia of Social Work*, 19th ed. (Washington, DC: NASW Press, 1995).
4. Alfred Kadushin and Judith Martin, *Child Welfare Services*, 4th ed. (New York: Macmillan, 1988), pp. 9–27.
5. Kristine E. Nelson, Miriam J. Landsman, and Wendy Deutelbaum, "Three Models of Family-Centered Placement Prevention Services," *Child Welfare* 69 (1990) 1: 5–6.
6. Salvatore Ambrosino, "Family Services: Family Service Agencies," in *Encyclopedia of Social Work*, 17th ed. (Silver Spring, MD: NASW, 1977), p. 429.
7. Diane Elias Alperin, "Family Service Agencies: Responding to a Conservative Decade," *Families in Society: The Journal of Contemporary Human Services* 73 (1992) 1: 32–39.
8. Kadushin and Martin, *Child Welfare Services*, p. 88.
9. Alfred Kadushin, *Child Welfare Services*, 3rd ed. (New York: Macmillan, 1980), pp. 78–91.
10. Janice H. Schopler and Maeda J. Galinsky, "Group Practice Overview," *Encyclopedia of Social Work*, 19th ed. (Washington, DC: NASW Press, 1995), pp. 1129–1142.
11. For example, see Nathan W. Ackerman, *The Psychodynamics of Family Life* (New York: Basic Books, 1958); Gregory Bateson, Donald D. Jackson, Jay Haley, and John Weakland, "Toward a Theory of Schizophrenia," *Behavioral Science* 1, no. 4 (1956);

Jay Haley, "Marriage Therapy," *Archives of General Psychiatry* 8 (1963); Don D. Jackson, "Family Therapy in the Family of the Schizophrenic," in Morris I. Stein, ed., *Contemporary Psychotherapies* (New York: Free Press, 1961); Murray Bowen, "Family Relationships in Schizophrenia," in Alfred Auerback, ed., *Schizophrenia—An Integrated Approach* (New York: Ronald Press, 1959); and Virginia Satir, *Conjoint Family Therapy* (Palo Alto, CA: Science and Behavior Books, 1964).

12. Herta A. Guttman, "Systems Theory, Cybernetics, and Epistemology," in Alan Gurman and David P. Knistern, eds., *Handbook of Family Therapy II* (New York: Brunner/Mazel, 1991), p. 41.

13. Salvatore Ambrosino, "Integrating Counseling, Family Life Education and Family Advocacy," *Social Casework* 60 (1979): 581.

14. Jon Conte, "Service Provision to Enhance Family Functioning," in Brenda G. McGowan and William Meezan, eds., *Child Welfare: Current Dilemmas—Future Directions* (Itasca, IL: F.E. Peacock Publishers, 1983).

15. Ambrosino, "Family Services," p. 431.

16. Ambrosino, "Integrating Counseling," p. 581.

17. U.S. Congress, Senate, Committee on Labor and Public Welfare, *Community Mental Health Centers Act: History of the Program and Current Problems and Issues,* 93rd Cong., 1st sess., Comm. Print, 1973.

18. Sallie A. Watkins, "The Mary Ellen Myth: Correcting Child Welfare History," *Social Work* 35 (1990) 6: 500–503.

19. Elizabeth D. Hutchinson, "Mandatory Reporting Laws: Child Protective Case Finding Gone Awry?" *Social Work* 38 (1993) 1: 56–63.

20. Phyllis T. Howing and John S. Woodarski, "Legal Requisites for Social Workers in Child Abuse and Neglect Situations," *Social Work* 37 (1992) 4: 330.

21. Susan W. Downs, Lela B. Costin, and Emily J. McFadden, *Child Welfare and Family Services* (New York: Longman Publishers, 1996) p. 171.

22. McGowan and Meezan, *Child Welfare,* p. 99.

23. Lela B. Costin, Howard J. Karger, and David Stoesz, *The Politics of Child Abuse in America* (New York: Oxford University Press, 1996).

24. Ibid., p. 5.

25. Downs, Costin, and McFadden, *Child Welfare and Family Services,* pp. 162–163.

26. Ibid., p. 195.

27. Vanessa G. Hodges and Betty J. Blythe, "Improving Service Delivery to High Risk Families: Home-Based Practice," *Families in Society: The Journal of Contemporary Human Services* 73 (1992) 5: 259–265.

28. Kadushin, *Child Welfare Services,* p. 178.

29. Hodges and Blythe, "Improving Service Delivery," pp. 259–265.

30. Gary L. Darmstadt, "Community-Based Child Abuse Prevention," *Social Work* 35 (1990) 6: 487–489.

31. Kadushin, *Child Welfare Services,* p. 178.

32. Vicky N. Albert and Richard P. Barth, "Predicting Growth in Child Abuse and Neglect Reports in Urban, Suburban, and Rural Counties," *Social Service Review* 70 (1996), pp. 58–82.

33. Darmstadt, "Community-Based Child Abuse Prevention," pp. 487–489.

34. Norman A. Polansky, Carolyn Hally, and Nancy F. Polansky, *Profile of Neglect* (Washington, DC: Public Services Administration, Department of Health, Education and Welfare, 1975), pp. 3–5.

35. Norman A. Polansky, Mary Ann Chalmers, David P. Williams, and Elizabeth Werthan Buttenwieser, *Damaged Parents: An Anatomy of Child Neglect* (Chicago: University of Chicago Press, 1981), p. 5.

36. Howing and Woodarski, "Legal Requisites for Social Workers," pp. 330–336.

37. Downs et al., *Child Welfare and Family Services*, pp. 182–183.
38. Howing and Woodarski, "Legal Requisites for Social Workers," pp. 330–336.
39. James Garbarino, Edna Guttman, and Janis Wilson Seeley, *The Psychologically Battered Child* (San Francisco: Jossey-Bass, 1986), p. 8.
40. Kadushin and Martin, *Child Welfare Services*, p. 239.
41. Howing and Woodarski, "Legal Requisites for Social Workers," pp. 330–336.
42. Ibid.
43. Denis M. Donovan and Deborah McIntyre, *Healing the Hurt Child: A Developmental Approach* (New York: W.W. Norton, 1990), pp. 166–172.
44. Ibid., p. 178.
45. Howing and Woodarski, "Legal Requisites for Social Workers," p. 330.
46. Donovan and McIntyre, *Healing the Hurt Child*, p. 163.
47. Ibid., p. 164.
48. Richard A. Gardner, "Differentiating Between True and False Sex-Abuse Accusations in Child-Custody Disputes," *Journal of Divorce and Remarriage* 21 (1994), 3–4: 1–20.
49. Robert M. Mulford, "Protective Services for Children," *Encyclopedia of Social Work*, 17th ed. (Silver Spring, MD: NASW, 1977), p. 1117.
50. Downs et al., *Child Welfare and Family Services*, pp. 163–165.
51. Ruth S. Kempe and C. Henry Kempe, *Child Abuse* (Cambridge, MA: Harvard University Press, 1978); Carmine J. Magazino, "Services to Children and Families at Risk of Separation," in McGowan and Meezan, *Child Welfare*, pp. 211–254.
52. McGowan and Meezan, *Child Welfare*, pp. 19–20.
53. Darmstadt, "Community-Based Child Abuse Prevention," pp. 487–489.
54. Kempe and Kempe, *Child Abuse*, pp. 19–20.
55. Garry L. Landreth, *Play Therapy: The Art of the Relationship* (Muncie, IN: Accelerated Development, 1991), pp. 7–23.
56. Nelson et al., "Three Models of Family-Centered Placement Prevention," p. 4.
57. Children's Defense Fund, "Children and Families in Crisis," *The State of America's Children Yearbook* (Washington, DC: Author, 1994), pp. 21–22.
58. Kristine E. Nelson, "Family-Based Services for Juvenile Offenders," *Children and Youth Services Review* 12 (1990) 3: 194.
59. Hodges and Blythe, "Improving Service Delivery," pp. 259–265.
60. *Intensive Family Services: A Family Preservation Service Delivery Model* (Annapolis, MD: Department of Human Resources, 1987), pp. 23–24.
61. Nelson et al., "Three Models of Family-Centered Placement Prevention Services," pp. 3–21.
62. Peter Forsythe, "Homebuilders and Family Preservation," *Children and Youth Services Review* 14 (1992): 37–47.
63. Nelson et al., "Three Models of Family-Centered Placement Prevention Services," pp. 8–9.
64. Ibid., pp. 9–11.
65. Nelson, "Family-Based Services for Juvenile Offenders," pp. 208–209.
66. Maria Scannapieco, "The Importance of Family Functioning to Prevention of Placement: A Study of Family Preservation Services," *Child and Adolescent Scoial Work Journal* 10 (1993) 6: 509–520.
67. Jane Knitzer and Susan Yelton, "Collaborations between Child Welfare and Mental Health," *Public Welfare* 48 (1990) 2: 25–33.
68. Ying-Ying T. Yuan, "Cost Analysis," in Ying-Ying T. Yuan and Michele Rivst, eds., *Preserving Families: Evaluation Resources for Practitioners and Policy Makers* (Newbury Park, CA: Sage Publications, 1990), pp. 102–131.
69. Kristine E. Nelson, "Family Preservation—What Is It?" *Child and Youth Services Review* 19 (1997) 1/2: 101–118.

70. Kadushin and Martin, *Child Welfare Services.*

71. Downs et al., *Child Welfare and Family Services*, pp. 90–92.

72. Marjorie Ziefert, "Homemaker and Day-Care Services," in Joan Laird and Ann Hartment, eds., *A Handbook of Child Welfare: Context, Knowledge, and Practice* (New York: Free Press, 1985).

73. Arthur C. Emlen, "Child Care Services," *Encyclopedia of Social Work*, 18th ed. (Silver Spring, MD: NASW, 1987), p. 232.

74. Gary L. Bowen and Peter A. Neenan, "Child Care as an Economic Incentive for the Working Poor," *Families in Society: The Journal of Contemporary Human Services* 73 (1992) 5: 295–303.

75. Children's Defense Fund, "Childcare and Early Development," *The State of America's Children Yearbook* (Washington, DC: Author, 1994), pp. 30–31.

76. Therese W. Lansburgh, "Child Welfare: Day Care of Children," *Encyclopedia of Social Work*, 17th ed. (Silver Spring, MD: NASW, 1977), p. 134.

Additional Suggested Readings

Boyd, Jennifer, Patrick Curtis, and Michael Petit. *Child Abuse and Neglect: A Look at the States—1997 Stat Book*. Washington, DC: Child Welfare League of America, 1997.

Campbell, Lynda. "Child Neglect and Intensive-Family-Preservation Practice." *Families in Society* 78 (1997) 3: 280–290.

Danzy, Julia, and Sondra M. Jackson. "Family Preservation and Support Services: A Missed Opportunity for Kinship Care." *Child Welfare* LXXVI (1997) 1: 31–44.

Delgado, Melvin, and Sharon Tennstedt. "Puerto Rican Sons as Primary Caregivers of Elderly Parents." *Social Work* 42 (1997) 2: 125–134.

Field, Tracey, "Managed Care and Child Welfare." *Public Welfare* 54 (1996) 3: 4–10.

Gelles, Richard J., and Lucy Berliner. "Family Reunification/Family Preservation. Are Children Really Being Protected?" *Journal of Interpersonal Violence* 8 (1993) 4: 557–562.

Helfer, Mary Edna, Ruth S. Kempe, and Richard D. Krugman, eds. *The Battered Child*. 5th ed. Chicago: University of Chicago Press, 1997.

Helton, Lonnie R., and Maggie Jackson. *Social Work Practice with Families*. Needham Heights, MA: Allyn & Bacon, 1997.

Janzen, Curtis, and Oliver Harris. *Family Treatment in Social Work Practice*. 3rd ed. Itasca, IL: F.E. Peacock Publishers, 1997.

Markward, Martha J. "The Impact of Domestic Violence on Children." *Families in Society* 78 (1997) 1: 66–70.

O'Neill, William J., Jr., ed. *Family: The First Imperative*. Cleveland: The William J. and Dorothy K. O'Neill Foundation, 1995.

6

Services to Families and Children Outside the Home

TERESA K. FULLER KULPER
GILBERT J. GREENE

The thrust of supportive and supplemental services is to help families in their own homes so that they can remain permanently intact. When supportive and supplemental services are not sufficiently effective and/or available, it may be necessary to rely on substitute-care services designed to replace the biological parents, either temporarily or permanently. Though some have contended that the availability of adequate supportive and supplemental services can practically eliminate the need for substitute services, several studies show that a majority of substitute-care placements are necessary, appropriate, and in all probability, unavoidable.[1] The indication, then, is that supportive and supplemental services cannot entirely eliminate or replace substitute services. The services usually referred to as *substitute-care services* are adoption, foster care, and institutional care, which we will discuss in this chapter. Also to be discussed will be *miscellaneous services*, which, though not substitute, are usually provided to families outside their homes. Afterward, we will include a listing of some present and future trends in programs for families and children, and the chapter will conclude with a brief discussion of family policy.

PERMANENCY PLANNING

Substitute care of children has a long history in the United States. The placing of a child in a family as an indentured servant or apprentice was extensively used in the United States from its earliest days. This practice, which was imported from Britain, lasted in this country until the first decade of the twentieth century. The origin of modern foster family care is attributed to Charles Loring Brace, a minister and the first secretary of the New York Children's Aid Society, which was founded in 1853. His approach involved the moving of "needful" children from the cities to rural areas, usually in the Midwest, where the environment was considered to be "more moral." This procedure, never popular with everyone, was abandoned in 1929. Charles Birtwell, the leader of the Boston Children's Aid Society from 1886 to 1911, further refined foster care. He was very systematic and planned carefully, considering the real needs of the child and viewing foster family care as long-term and usually replacing the biological parents in a "pseudo-adoptive" situation.[2]

As substitute care became an ingrained component of our current child welfare system, some problems arose. For many children, the length of time to be spent in substitute care has been unclear. A number of children in foster care never knew when they might be returned to their biological parents or moved to another set of foster parents. It has not been uncommon for such children to spend numerous years in continuous foster care, experiencing placement with several different families without the benefit of a case plan for a permanent living situation.[3] Children in such living situations are said to be experiencing "foster care drift." For other children there have been adoptions that were disrupted as a result of poor planning. One study found that the likelihood of a child returning to his or her home decreased after the first few weeks in substitute care and greatly reduced in the first three transitions from the parental home.[4]

In response to the problem of children drifting in and out of placement, Congress enacted the Adoption Act of 1980 (P.L. 96-272), which specifies the following national priorities for children in need of child welfare services:

1. Preservation of the child's biological family
2. Reunification of the child's biological family if removal has been necessary
3. Permanent adoption
4. Long-term foster care, preferably with the same foster family[5]

Thus the practice of permanency planning became of utmost importance. P.L. 96-272 mandated permanent planning nationwide. Permanency planning in child welfare has been defined as:

> the systematic process of carrying out, within a brief time-limited period, a set of goal-directed activities designed to help children live in families that offer continuity of relationships with nurturing parents or caretakers and the opportunity to establish lifetime relationships.[6]

The current emphasis is on making reasonable efforts to prevent out-of-home placements. Permanency planning means that when such placements are deemed necessary they should be in the "most family-like" setting available and in close proximity to the parents' home. Every effort should be made to rehabilitate the home of the biological parents and return the child as soon as possible. If rehabilitation and reunification are not possible, parental rights should be terminated and subsequent adoption of the child should be pursued. When neither option is possible, then the child should be placed in long-term foster care, preferably with one family.[7]

Continuity and nurturance in relationships are important for the healthy development of a child. She or he needs to know that, regardless of crises and problems the family may encounter, its integrity is assured. Some scholars have advocated that the "best interests of the child" should take precedence. This may then necessitate termination of the rights of the biological parent(s) and the permanent placement of the child with parents who may or may not adopt but will then become the "psychological parents." The intent is that the ultimate plan will be the "least detrimental alternative."[8]

Permanency planning is most effective at the outset of substitute care. The social worker must formulate a written plan outlining clear goals for placement and a time line estimating the progression of services. A treatment contract is developed with the biological parents, detailing specific goals toward resolving the problems resulting in need for placement, expectations of the parents, and actions anticipated from the worker. The permanency plan, then, provides for intensive services for the biological family with an emphasis on frequent parental visits supervised by the worker.[9] If the problems that required placement of the child are not resolved, parental rights may be terminated and the child becomes available for adoption. The intent is that these actions will be taken in a timely manner so as to reduce the time spent in foster care.

The permanency planning process requires input from many people who share in the decision making. The social worker, however, is the key person who performs the following roles, in addition to those described above:

1. *Case planning*—Involves the development and maintenance of fairly long-range plans (e.g., for the next four to six months).
2. *Therapeutic*—The worker provides the necessary clinical services to increase the chances of a successful placement in line with a preferred plan.
3. *Case management*—Involves tasks such as keeping services coordinated among multiple providers and bringing clients into contact with various community and social resources.
4. *Client advocate*—Workers may need to advocate within the legal and service system to be certain that the rights of parents and children are maintained.
5. *Role of court witness*—Workers are called on to provide testimony as a result of their working with cases involving custody issues.

Thus, the 1980s involved an emphasis to preserve families where possible and provide permanence for children. As a result of P.L. 96-272, preservation services increased, court reviews of children were established, and attempts to secure adoptions sooner were made. While the services emphasized during this legislative period were admirable, the funds needed to implement them were not appropriated; in fact, they were often cut.[10] Therefore, implementation of comprehensive services to children and their families has been compromised.

One response to the need to provide more services with less money is outlined by Katz. She describes an agency that developed a two-pronged approach in which the parents understand that permanency is the ultimate goal. The plan for the child's return home and a plan for the child's adoption occur simultaneously rather than sequentially. This involves a holistic agency structure to provide for continuity and expediency; all contracts are written and communicated to the parents and their attorney; the reunification services, foster care services, and adoptive services are provided by the same worker; the foster family may become the adoptive family if reunification fails; and if the child is adopted, the process is very open, with the biological parents often continuing supervised visits. Permance for the child is achieved and contact with the biological family is maintained.[11] Effectiveness of this type of organizational approach needs further research.

The next section will describe traditional and innovative social work services geared toward providing substitute care with permanency as the goal.

SUBSTITUTE SERVICES

Foster Care

Foster care provides noninstitutional, substitute family care to a child for a planned period, either temporary or long-term, when the child's own family cannot care for him or her and when adoption is neither desirable or possible.[12] Children in foster care are placed either in the homes of foster families or in group-home living situations. Research projects indicate that children in foster care are often "rescued from intolerable circumstances and survive relatively well."[13]

Foster family care use has varied in recent years. In the mid-1980s there was a decrease in the use of foster care. There was, however, a tremendous growth of 68 percent in the use of foster care between 1982 and 1992. It was estimated that in June 1992 approximately 442,000 children were in foster care.[14]

The decrease and then sharp increase in the use of foster care was caused by many factors—one related to public perception. Reports of foster care drift, abuse of children in foster care, and awareness of the problems of some adults who are former foster children have led to laws restricting such use. Laws like P.L. 96-272, which were described in the previous section, advocated permanency planning, which resulted in a decline of foster care.[15] The increase of foster care usage can be attributed to the following societal trends: increased reports of severe abuse and even death of children; increased use of extremely addictive drugs such as crack cocaine, with babies being born drug-addicted; the spread of AIDS; extreme poverty; a large increase in the number of adolescent pregnancies; and financial incentives.[16] Financial incentives are the result, in part, of the government actions described previously. The federal government advocated for preserving families and at the same time for cutting child welfare funding. Because of limited funds, the available money is spent serving cases with the most dramatic needs. Thus placement services are often funded and supportive services are cut.

Children are most likely to enter foster care as a result of a family breakdown. General reasons for foster care placement include poverty and lack of resources, inadequate housing, drug abuse, and homelessness. Familial reasons involve parental inability or unwillingness to provide care; the neglect or abuse of children; mental illness, chemical addiction, or incarceration of a parent; family violence; the child's behavioral problems, illness, or handicap; parental refusal of supportive services; drug-affected babies; and AIDS diagnosed in the parent or the child.[17] Typically the reasons for placement differ, depending on the age of the child. The placement of younger children is usually related to family situations and parental problems. Older youth are often placed as a result of their own difficulties, for example, behavioral problems, crime, or violence.[18] The family problems behind foster care are usually multiple, making it difficult to locate one primary reason for each individual placement in foster care. Usually a specific crisis precipitates the need for foster care placement. However, many of these families had frequently been functioning marginally, trying to deal with multiple problems and high levels of stress for sometime prior to the crisis. Other resources for child care, such as friends and relatives, are either unavailable, unwilling, or unable to provide care. Supplemental social services such as homemaker services may be unavailable or inadequate.[19]

According to Steinhauer, all foster care programs must satisfy the following requirements:

- meet the basic physical and emotional needs of all children;
- meet the special emotional needs of children in care such as reaction to separation, abuse, and uncertainty of the future;
- be proactive in the planning process;
- inform children of the planning process when it is developmentally appropriate;
- protect attachment relationships such as parents, siblings, extended family, ethnic community;
- protect continuity as feasible, e.g., utilize the same worker throughout the process;
- coordinate all components of child's life, including biological parents, foster care parents, service agencies, school, etc.[20]

A social worker in foster care needs to be highly competent in the skills of diagnosis and assessment, counseling and psychotherapy, and case management and advocacy.[21] The role of a social worker in foster care is varied and multileveled. Since the removal of a child from his or her own home is such a serious step, it is important for the social worker to develop, as soon as possible, a good working relationship with the biological parent(s), the foster parent(s), and the child. There exists a triangle between the biological parent and the foster parent, with the child in the middle. The worker must foster open communication, flexible and clear boundaries, and specific expectations to ensure that the child is not pulled into potential conflict between the two sets of parents.[22]

Once a decision has been made for foster care placement, the social worker develops with the parents a realistic service plan for improving conditions and making changes necessary for the return of the child(ren). According to Blumenthal, a service plan includes specific changes required; specific actions to be taken by the worker, parent, and child; services offered; visitation arrangements; and a time schedule, including anticipated length of care and dates for periodic assessment of progress.[23] This service plan is similar to the permanency plan discussed previously.

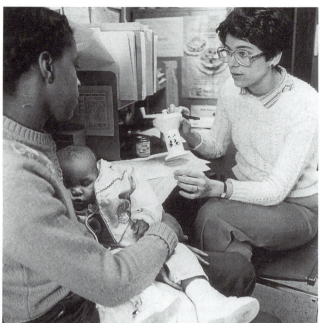

Bryce Flynn/Stock, Boston

Foster care programs seek to meet the needs of children. A mother consults a nutritionist from a federal supplementary food coupon program at a health center in Boston.

Both the selection of foster parents and subsequent agency supervision are important ingredients in successful foster care. A social study of people who apply to be foster parents serves as the primary basis for selection. Preferably, new foster parents receive training from the agency to help them prepare to deal with the problems of foster parenting as well as to learn effective ways of performing this role. Foster parents receive payment for the child's board as well as payments for medical and dental expenses and clothing. Usually, foster parenting is not a financially rewarding occupation, especially considering its high level of demands.[24]

Treatment Foster Care

In the 1950s and 1960s, models for specialized foster care were developed to supplement psychiatric hospital services and as an alternative to residential treatment centers during the deinstitutionalization movement.[25] *Specialized foster care*, also called *therapeutic* or *treatment foster care*, has been described as a preferred service for children with special needs.[26] For the purposes of this chapter the term treatment foster care will be used.

Treatment foster care is similar to the foster care described above in that a foster family is paid to provide substitute services when it is unsafe or impossible for the child to live with his or her biological parents. Problem-focused specific contracts are written in an attempt to modify situations, behaviors, or home conditions.

Treatment foster care is unique in several ways. The foster parents are highly trained; in fact, they are considered a part of the agency's professional team of service providers. The foster family itself is the focus of intensive therapy services, as is the biological family. Many of the services are geared toward the health and behavior management of the special-needs child, rather than focusing solely on the functioning of the biological family.[27]

As mentioned previously, children placed in treatment foster care have special needs—for example, sexually abused children with acting out behaviors,[28] mentally or physically handicapped children or children with Down's syndrome,[29] autistic children,[30] teen moms and their babies,[31] and children with AIDS.[32] In fact, any child who needs out-of-home placement, needs specialized care, or is at risk for more restrictive care might benefit from treatment foster care. Children who may require more restrictive care, such as in an institution, include those with extremely unpredictable behaviors such as irrational violence toward other people, compulsive firesetting,[33] or sexual perpetration.

Treatment foster care social workers perform all of the roles described in permanency planning and foster care. The therapeutic services are more intense and comprehensive; as a result, workers have a decreased caseload and usually no more than one or two children are placed in one home. Crisis intervention services are included.[34]

Group Foster Home Care

Foster home care, regular or treatment-focused, is the preferred type of foster care placement for children who can form family ties and actively participate in family life as well as live in the community without major disruptions. However, this is not the only type of foster care. *Group foster home care* is another type of foster care that may be seen as standing between foster family care and institutional care. It is primarily for children who are not appropriate for foster homes as described above or for institutional care. Group arrangements can also be used for temporary respite from foster family care for children with extreme anger that results in acting out behaviors.[35] It provides some of the closeness experienced in family living while allowing some of the interpersonal distance, especially from adults, that is possible in institutional care. This type of setting is usually better suited to adolescents of all ages, particularly those who have continuing conflicts with parental figures. It is also well suited for adolescents because the primary developmental tasks at this stage involve establishing independence from parents and parent figures.

The group home, which is usually agency-operated, is generally a single dwelling located in a residential area of the community in a house or apartment; it provides care for four to twelve children at a time. The child care staff members may be considered either foster parents or counselors. The staff are salaried employees, and at least one staff member is present in the home at all times. Each home will have certain rules for daily living, but overall the atmosphere should be relaxed and informal. The residents of the group home, if able, will be allowed to participate in the usual larger community social activities and will attend local schools and religious services.[36]

Institutional Care

Another type of substitute care sometimes considered a form of foster care is the *children's institution*. An institution differs from a group foster home in that it is larger, caring for 15 or more residents at a time; it may consist of more than one building; it may provide formal education on its premises; and it may or may not be in a residential part of the community.

Institutions take on various forms serving different kinds of children. Among them are institutions for:

1. Physically handicapped children.
2. Mentally retarded children.
3. The confinement and rehabilitation of juvenile delinquents; these are often called *training schools*.
4. Emotionally disturbed children; these are known as *residential treatment centers*.[37]

The juvenile justice system is responsible for children in correctional institutions; physically and mentally handicapped children are usually the responsibility of the health care system; and dependent children in institutions and emotionally disturbed children in residential treatment centers are the responsibility of the child welfare system. Though social workers deal with all types of problematic children in various institutions, the primary concern here is with dependent and/or emotionally disturbed children since the focus in this chapter is family and child welfare services.

The primary reason for institutional placement tends to be the problematic behavior of the child. Excluding delinquency and physical or medical handicap, the child may be unable to develop a satisfactory emotional relationship with parental figures, or the child may be homeless, severely abused or neglected with resulting violent behavior, and/or drug and alcohol dependent.[38]

The social worker in institutional care services provides the previously mentioned roles such as completing a psychosocial study of the child and family, helping the family and child cope with transitions, and encouraging contact between family members. In addition, she or he will consult closely with the institutional staff on an ongoing basis to ensure that all aspects of the daily activities and institutional environment are therapeutic. This may require regular in-service education with the staff. A further aspect of social work in an institutional setting may involve liaison with other community agencies to ensure that the child and family have the community supports needed to allow the child to return home permanently.

Adoption

Adoption is the legal and social process through which a parent-child relationship between persons unrelated by birth is established. This involves a child born to one set of parents, the biological parents, becoming the child of a different set of parents, the adoptive parents, and thus having the same rights and responsibilities as if they were biologically related. Adoption means a permanent family change, allowing children to have the benefits of long-term, intense family ties that they otherwise would not have. It is an appropriate step when a child's biological parent(s) cannot or will not provide care and other adults are capable and willing to assume, for various personal reasons, the legal responsibility of parenthood. For a child to be eligible for adoption, the parental rights of the natural parents must be legally terminated. Therefore, adoption requires cooperation between social workers and the legal system.

Adoption has a long history dating back to the ancient Egyptians, Greeks, and Romans. It was used to provide family heirs to assure the continuity of a family name and to enhance a family's political power. Therefore, adoption was frequently used for the benefit of the adopter rather than the adoptee. In the early history of the United States, adoption was not a common occurrence. The English common law, which was the basis for the laws in this country, did not provide for adoption. The use of indentured servants and the relation between master and apprentice further hindered the development of legal adoptions. Massachusetts, in 1851, was the first state to pass an adoption law, which became the model for adoption legislation in other states. This legislation made the welfare of the child the primary concern.

Though the welfare of the child was foremost in state laws, there was considerable variability in the legal provisions for investigation and control of adoption by unsuitable parents. In 1891, a Michigan law began requiring that an investigation by a judge be made before finalizing an adoption. Minnesota, in 1917, was the first state to require a detailed investigation and recommendation by a social welfare agency concerning the suitability of adoption.[39] Over the last several decades, social welfare agencies, the Child Welfare League of America, and the social work profession in general have further developed professional guidelines and standards for adoption agencies.

Adoptions can be categorized in different ways. One method of classification is to divide them into adoptions by *relatives* and by *nonrelatives*. Social agencies are seldom involved with the former but are highly involved with the latter. One form of relative adoption is informal adoption, that is, the absorption of a daughter's child into the immediate or extended family as a temporary or permanent solution for unwed teens. Informal adoptions are common in the African-American community. The practice of informal adoption has roots in African culture, in which the boundaries of extended family are flexible, often with three generations living together and sharing parental responsibilities. Shared parenting responsibilities and flexible family boundaries might be seen as a "creative adaptation to poverty," often allowing the teen mother to complete high school. Sandven and Resnick implore social workers to develop innovative and culturally sensitive services, utilizing extended family support for pregnant teens without nuclear family support.[40] Brown and Bailey-Etta note, however, that these arrangements should not be pursued as cost-effective ways to avoid providing supportive services and subsidies to these families. These families are often poor, but receive fewer services than their white counterparts.[41] In addition to adoption by relatives and nonrelatives, there are several other types.

Statistics on adoptions are not consistently kept. In 1986, the last year for which any national statistics are available, there were approximately 51,157 nonrelative adoptions.[42] It appears that the 50,000 per year number has been fairly stable since the 1970s. There have been approximately the same number of formal relative adoptions. Additionally, approximately 10,000 children are adopted from other countries to American families (see section on international adoptions).[43]

    Independent adoption.   This form of adoption is one in which a social agency is not involved. Most independent adoptions are relative adoptions, many of which involve a stepparent adopting a spouse's child(ren). Two other types are *intermediary-not-for-profit* and *intermediary-for-profit*. These are usually arranged by a physician or attorney and involve adoptive parents not known to the biological parent(s). The intermediary-not-for-profit adoption is legal in 46 states, but the intermediary-for-profit form ("black market adoptions") is illegal in every state.[44] These latter types are frequently used by adoptive parents frustrated with the formal adoptive process. Lacking the involvement of a social service agency in independent adoptions can be risky for the child and the success of the adoption. However, it has been found that such arrangements do not necessarily have serious problems.[45]

    Agency adoption.   Many unrelated adoptions are under the auspices of a social service agency. Therefore, the responsibility of the majority of adoptions in this country belongs to the social work profession. The social worker carries out society's responsibility to children in need of an adequate, permanent home. This involves seeing to it that society's responsibilities to the child, the biological parent(s), and the adopting parent(s) are met.

    The selection of adoptive parents is vitally important. The social worker is actively involved in assessing their personal qualities and the kind of home they will provide to the child, as well as in preparing the adoptive parents to meet their new responsibilities. A number of variables are considered: age, physical and emotional health, motivations, marital adjustment, financial stability, and others. Once the agency approves applicants for adoption, the next task is to select a child appropriate for that couple/parent.[46]

    After a child is selected as a possible adoptee for a couple/parent, the social worker is very active in preparing adopters and the child for the initial meeting. The social worker provides information about one to the other and any support and/or counseling needed during this sometimes anxious and exciting period. Older children being adopted may have more conflicts and questions about the process, thus requiring more skills and time from the social worker.

    A "trial" period of approximately six months follows after placement of the child in the home. During this time, the social worker maintains some contact with the adoptive parents and the child by making home visits. This contact serves a protective function for both the child and the parents, for it ensures that the child has been placed in a desirable home and is developing normally. The emphasis during this period should be on helping the parents and the adopted child develop "a sense of kinship" and to help them with the problems that are sure to occur during this period of dramatic change in their lives.[47]

    The type of child most in demand in the United States as an adoptee tends to be a white infant. Though there has been a shortage of this type of child for adoption, other types of children who have traditionally been harder to place are in more than adequate supply. To deal with the situation, agencies and potential adoptive parents have made some changes.

Children with Special Needs

Many children who are free for adoption are not in great demand, for various reasons, by most prospective parents. These children include those who are members of minority groups, are older, are handicapped, or are members of a sibling group.[48] In more recent years, adoption agencies involved in outreach to the community to recruit adoptive parents have been willing to relax standards and procedures to increase the attractiveness of adopting such children with special needs. Of the approximately 50,000 nonrelative adoptions mentioned earlier, 26 percent involved children with special needs.[49]

The nonwhite child.   The demand for minority children for adoption has not been proportionate to the numbers available. For example, African-American children make up 14 percent of the child population but are 25 percent of the foster care population and 33 percent of the children free for adoption.[50] It has been much easier for agencies to find homes for white children than for African-American children. Recent years have shown substantial progress in recruiting minority families and matching them with young, healthy children. Nonwhite couples financially able to adopt do so proportionately more than whites.[51] Successful agency recruitment practices have been identified, including utilizing minority social workers, taking steps to include the minority community, making the agency accessible, and offering services that are individualized and flexible, with the inclusion of the extended family.[52] Adequate funding is necessary for agencies to be able to staff these programs in culturally competent ways.[53]

Older children.   Since most adopting families tend to prefer infants, it is not surprising to find that children over the age of two are hard to place. The placement of older children requires more services, time, and effort, and is therefore more costly. However, in the long run the savings are substantial, considering the costs of foster care and other maintenance costs. Therefore, because of the financial savings and the shortage of infants for adoption, older children are increasingly being placed for adoption.[54]

In placing older children in adoptive homes, the role of the social worker is to reduce potential problems. The older child is likely to have experienced abuse and thus may have emotional problems and acting out behavior. Adoptive parents need to be aware of this and develop realistic expectations. They can be helped to see the child's problems within the overall context rather than as a reflection on their abilities. The child can be more active in the adoption process, with the social worker assisting in transitions and adjustment. Research on success of older youth adoption indicates that, in terms of impact on the youth, adoption is preferable to group homes or institutional care.[55]

Handicapped children.   There have always been children with physical and/or mental problems in need of adoption. However, finding an adoption placement for them is extremely difficult. Such children require considerable time and energy from the parents in addition to extra expenses for medical care and other specialized treatment.

Children with all types of physical handicaps of varying degrees can be placed and reared successfully in adoptive homes. Factors that increase the likelihood of successful adoption of handicapped children include the following: (1) the parents had first been the foster parents; (2) the parents have previous experience with the handicap; (3) close cooperation among the agency, the parents, and medical personnel and facilities; and (4) knowledge of rehabilitative, educational, and counseling services in the community.[56]

Sibling groups.   Another type of special-needs children are groups of siblings who want to be adopted together. While it is preferable for them to remain together, it is difficult to locate adoptive parents willing and able to take on the special demands of more than one adopted child. Parents best suited for adopting a sibling group are those with the following skills: (1) the ability to organize, set priorities, and cope with emergencies; (2) the ability to provide both group activities and meet individual needs; (3) adaptability and flexibility; and (4) families with support from their extended family, friends, and/or community.[57]

An Adoption Case

At the age of two, John Stevens was placed in foster care after his father was killed in a building construction accident and his mother, who has a severe drinking problem, became unable to provide for him adequately. John was placed in foster care after neighbors reported Ms. Stevens to the Department of Social Services for neglect. For a year after placement, Ms. Stevens visited John periodically, but her living conditions did not change, primarily because she refused treatment for her drinking problem. Eventually her visits stopped, and she could not be found by the department's social workers. John was able to live in the foster home for the next four years and the relationship with his foster parents was very close. The agency sought termination of parental rights after the foster parents indicated a desire to adopt John. In the process, Ms. Stevens was found living in a nearby city; she expressed an interest in caring for John again. A social study found that Ms. Stevens no longer was drinking heavily and held a steady job. As a preliminary step, visitation was again arranged for Ms. Stevens to see John on a regular basis. However, Ms. Stevens soon afterward began drinking again, became sporadic in her visits, and lost her job. The Department of Social Services then petitioned the court for termination of parental rights. The agency argued that John had been deserted by his mother, who had become a stranger to him, and therefore should permanently remain with the people he perceived as his "real" parents. The petition was granted and John was adopted by his foster parents.

Outreach Efforts for Adoption of Special-Needs Children

Transracial adoptions.   One way that has developed to help meet the adoptive needs of minority children is the transracial adoption, which is usually the placement of nonwhite children in white adoptive homes. Transracial adoption had its beginning in the 1950s, increased considerably in the late 1960s, and peaked in 1972 when 468 agencies made 2,574 placements.[58]

This trend, however, was not widely supported by everyone and eventually met considerable opposition from minority groups. In 1972, the National Association of Black Social Workers issued a strong protest against transracial adoptions involving African-American children, fearing that this threatened the integrity and the preservation of the African-American family. Questions were also raised regarding how a minority child raised in a white family would form a cultural identity and learn to cope with racism.[59] There was considerable controversy about this issue among social work professionals. Consequently, there was a consistent decline in the number of African-American children adopted by white parents. The positive result of this controversy has been the active recruitment of minority families by adoption agencies mentioned previously. The converse argument is that transracial adoption is preferable to no adoption at all.[60]

Subsidized adoptions.   To help increase the adoptability of children with special needs, most states have passed legislation that provides financial assistance to adoptive parents beyond the traditional legal responsibilities. New York passed the first adoption subsidy legislation in 1968. At present, all states provide some type of adoption subsidy. Funding for adoption subsidies was further aided by passage of the Adoption Assistance and Child Welfare Act (P.L. 96-272) in 1980, which we discussed previously.[61]

Subsidies can be provided for a variety of purposes, such as specialized medical care and/or special education, to offset increased expenses of child care and other costs. It allows for some families to adopt who otherwise would not be financially able to do so. The majority of these adoptions consist of children being adopted by their foster parents. Previously foster parents would lose necessary financial assistance that was available for foster care but ceased after adoption, which discouraged their adoption decisions. Subsidized adoptions have been shown to be more cost-effective than long-term foster care.[62] Because special-needs adoptions have been so successful in lower-income families, subsidies are considered a crucial postadoptive service.[63]

Single-parent adoption.   Since children with special needs are harder to place for adoption, many agencies now consider unmarried applicants as a way of providing permanent homes for these children. Single adults—never married, divorced, or widowed—tend to be accepted as adoptive parents only when two-parent homes are unavailable. In most cases the adoptive parent is a single woman, but occasionally single males also adopt.

The results of such adoptions have tended to be quite positive. Single-parent adopters have been found to be older than other adoptive parents; many of the single-parent adopters have better incomes and more education. In addition, single-parent adopters tend to be self-aware, child-oriented, and to have strong connections with relatives and friends.[64] Consequently, single parents have been able to provide stable, nurturing environments for adoptive children that allow for their positive growth and development.

Some single-parent adoptive families might benefit from social work intervention in dealing with any feelings the child might have about not having a two-parent family. However, sometimes this type of adoption is seen as the placement of choice since the single adopter does not have to give support and attention to a spouse and instead can devote his or her energies to meeting the needs of the adopted child. Groze compared single- and two-parent families that adopted special-needs children. He found that, while both reported satisfaction, the single-parent families showed a slightly more positive outcome.[65]

Adoption outcomes. Adoptions are termed disrupted if the child is removed from the home before the legalization of the adoption. Disruption occurs in 7 to 14 percent of all adoptions and in 24 to 31 percent of special-needs adoptions. There have been only a small number of risk factors substantiated in studies of disrupted adoptions. These include severe acting out behavior, the child's age at the time of removal from parental home (older), and boys who were separated from their siblings.[66]

In summary, the current literature on the adoption of children with special needs reveals similar conclusions:

1. Overall, the majority of special-needs adoptions are successful.
2. Progress is being made to recruit and match minority families with minority children. More effort is needed to find minority families for minority children with other special needs as well. The outreach to minority and low-income families is affirmed.
3. Realistic planning and information sharing are essential.
4. Adoptive families could often benefit from ongoing services, such as financial subsidies, enhancement services, and community support.
5. Creative solutions such as single-parent adoptions, adoption by foster families, and respect for informal systems such as the extended family show promise.

International Adoptions

Since the end of World War II, there has been an interest in the United States in adopting orphan children from other countries. Many prospective parents in this country who are unable to adopt American children turn to this option. Contributing factors involved in the adoption of children from other countries are the mobility of families around the world; the greater ease of communication between countries; the continuing large numbers of American servicemen stationed abroad; and a humanitarian concern for the plight of refugee and other homeless children who may be abused or neglected.[67]

International adoption is not without controversy. Some people view it as "class, race, and national exploitation" of the countries supplying the children.[68]

International adoption can be seen as depriving each such country of its "most valuable resource, its future citizens."[69] After some children, in the 1970s, were removed from their home countries before they were legally available for adoption, most countries have made efforts to ensure that certain guidelines are followed.[70]

Since the movement of a child from one country to begin living in another has potential difficulties, such an adoption should be planned very carefully. An in-depth assessment of the prospective adopters by a recognized child welfare agency in this country must first be completed. The potential problems of adopting a child from another country must be presented to the adopters and explored with them. As with transracial adoption, it is important to assess the parents' commitment to helping the child develop and maintain a racial, ethnic, and cultural identity. In addition, all necessary steps must be taken to ensure that the adoption is legal in both countries. The U.S. Department of Justice and the United Nations have set guidelines to protect the rights of the child and the biological mother, but violations have not consistently been penalized. The child welfare agency should enforce at least the minimum guidelines. A recent extensive review of the literature on the outcomes of both transracial and international adoptions found that these adoptions are quite successful when the guidelines are followed.[71]

The Birth Father

Most social work services in substitute care have focused on unwed mothers, families disrupted as a result of abuse and neglect, and families disrupted as a result of behavioral or medical problems of children. Few services are geared to, or even consider, the unwed birth father. Many stereotypes place blame on him.

Sachdev cites research showing that the majority of adolescent fathers care about their children and remain committed through birth. Most feel guilty and isolated; many birth fathers are conducting searches for their children. In the past ten years the courts have begun acknowledging the rights of birth fathers. Sachdev believes that the negative image of the birth father can hinder the child's identity formation.[72]

Child welfare agencies will need to respond to the increasing court recognition of birth fathers and find ways to involve them in services, when appropriate. Further research is needed, and the best interests of the child should be paramount.

Sealed Records and Open Adoptions

Prior to the 1930s, adoption in the United States was an open process. In the '30s and '40s, there was a very successful movement to increase confidentiality, and to create a more permanent break between the biological parent and the child.[73] Thus, adoption in the United States is highly developed with tightly structured legal safeguards. After the adoption of a child has become a legal fact, the original birth certificate is sealed and replaced by an amended one. Thereafter, papers and records are unavailable for examination except by court order for good cause such as health problems, if then.[74] It has been assumed that confidentiality and anonymity are required in order to encourage both birth and adoptive parents to participate in the adoptive process. There may be potentially embarrassing personal facts that these parents would never want to be available to the public or the adopted child.

This long-established practice is now being challenged in two ways: (1) some adult adoptees are seeking to have their sealed birth records legally opened in order to learn information about their genealogical heritage, with some adoptees wanting to meet their birth parents; and (2) the occurrence of open adoptions, which is defined as follows:

> A process in which the birth parents and the adoptive parents meet and exchange identifying information. The birth parents relinquish legal and basic child rearing rights to the adoptive parents. Both sets of parents retain the right to continuing contact and access to knowledge on behalf of the child.[75]

Unsealing the record.   Adult adoptees seeking to have their birth records opened claim they have a constitutional right to know the identities of their birth parents. Adoptees argue that knowing their heredity background is necessary for further development of their sense of identity.[76] Others, however, believe that the rights of the birth and adoptive parents should also be protected. To open up the record may discourage future unmarried mothers and prospective adoptive parents from pursuing adoption as an option. As of 1985, 35 states had passed laws allowing adult adoptees access to some identifying information about their birth parents. Some states have a reunion registry and a mutual consent procedure that allow adoptive and biological parents to record their openness to meet, if contacted. Other states allow the use of third-party intermediaries, usually social service agencies, to mediate between children and their biological parents.[77]

Open adoptions.   In open adoptions, the birth record is not only open from the beginning, but the birth parent(s) and the adopted child may have periodic contact with each other with the consent of the adoptive parents. Such an arrangement is usually agreed upon from the beginning and often conducted independently of any social service agency.

Open adoption of older children is not very controversial because older children tend to have a past history of contact with their birth parents and extended family. Therefore, it is not realistic and usually not advisable for the adopted child to sever contact unless he or she strongly desires to do so.

Adoption of infants is more controversial. Advocates on both sides agree that the child's best interest should guide the decision. Supporters of closed adoption argue that anonymity and confidentiality are necessary to safeguard the noninterference necessary for permanent attachment and bonding between the adoptive parents and the child. Proponents of open adoption argue that there would be a decrease in the child's tendency to feel rejected by the birth parent. The birth mother benefits in that she is less likely to experience severe feelings of loss and guilt. The adoptive parents' acquaintance with the birth parents can help diminish troubling fears and fantasies they may have and allow for their relationship to the child to be more natural and honest.[78]

In addressing the controversies of the unsealing of adoption records and open adoption, Meezan states that if adoption is "truly a child-centered service, then the rights of the child are paramount."[79] Small proposes that secrecy has led to the denial of differences of adoptive children; they have thus been denied access to information and services. She believes this has served the needs of the adoptive parents to appear the same as the biological parents rather than serving the needs of the child.[80] Curtis believes that before adoption is ever considered, both the adoptive and biological parents should choose whether they wish to participate in an open adoption; this choice could then be used as one of the criteria for matching children and adoptive parents.[81]

MISCELLANEOUS SERVICES

Services to Battered Women and Their Children

At times, children require placement outside of their homes because of domestic violence and wife battering. While women have been physically beaten and psychologically abused throughout history, it has only been since the mid-1970s that domestic violence against women has been recognized as a social problem of major importance.

Davis cites statistics of 1.5 million women abused by their male partners each year. Twenty to twenty-five percent of women in America are physically abused at least once; up to 35 percent of injuries to women treated in emergency rooms are related to ongoing abuse. While 10 to 14 percent of all women experience sexual assault, the figure jumps to 33 to 59 percent of battered women.[82]

The definition of battering has been problematic because it has traditionally been restricted to physical violence resulting in bodily harm. The following definition, however, broadens how this syndrome is to be perceived:

> A battered woman is a woman who is repeatedly subjected to any forceful physical or psychological behavior by a man in order to coerce her to do something he wants her to do without any concern for her rights.... Any woman may find herself in an abusive relationship with a man once. If it occurs a second time, and she remains in the situation, she is defined as a battered woman.[83]

At present, there are no federal or state laws mandating the reporting of spouse abuse. However, in the mid-1980s many states began to legislate protection for women. Most recent progress in protecting women from violence includes laws with some combination of mandatory arrest of domestic violence perpetrators, "no contact" orders, and/or court-ordered counseling. Police have been educated in the dynamics of violence and understand that the perpetrator is likely to abuse children or his next partner. Thus, criminal charges are important.[84] In 1994, the Violence Against Women Act, a subbill of the Omnibus Violent Crime Control and Prevention Act, allocated $8 billion over five years toward curbing domestic violence and mandating arrest of suspected abusers, even when the victim refuses to press charges.[85]

Statewide coalitions have been formed across the nation to increase awareness and to advocate for services to battered women and children. A battered woman seeking help usually requires a variety of services, including law enforcement and legal services, medical services, shelters, social and mental health services, employment services, financial assistance, and/or day-care and housing services. The misconception that the woman is somehow responsible for being battered is an attitude that has long prevailed in society. Blaming the victim is still done subtly and not-so-subtly by traditional service providers. Such an attitude is counterproductive to helping a woman create a new lifestyle in which battering is nonexistent.[86]

To effectively help battered women, it has been necessary to create a service that traditional social agencies have not provided—*safe houses*, which are also called *emergency shelters*. The growth of domestic violence shelters in the United States has been phenomenal. With the Violence Against Women Act, shelters and support services will continue to grow. These programs tend to have three purposes in common:

1. To provide a safe and secure environment for battered women and their children for a limited period of time.
2. To provide emotional support and counseling for battered women.
3. To provide information on women's legal rights, assist with court appearances, discuss housing options, and explore future life goals and directions.[87]

The average length of stay in a shelter may range from a few days to several weeks. During the initial part of her stay, a woman may need crisis counseling and emergency health care. Up to one-third of such women leave the shelters and return to their husbands.[88] The woman's economic dependence on the husband appears to be the primary reason for this decision.[89]

Help from the shelter staff is necessary in obtaining and coordinating needed services. Nonprofessionals and volunteer workers make up the majority of the staff in shelters in this country. However, approximately one-third of the shelters employ full-time social workers; a small percentage of these shelters employ other professionals, full- or part-time, such as attorneys, psychologists, nurses, and vocational counselors.[90] Given the complexity and severity of battering and the wide array of needed services, it is obvious that social work services could be used in each emergency shelter. Saunders also calls for social workers to take the role of expert witness to educate the court about domestic violence and to advocate for gender equality in this country.[91]

Given the seriousness and complexity of the problem of men battering women and the fact that many women who leave shelters return to their husbands, it follows that separate services should be provided for these men; otherwise, the cycle of violence will continue to repeat. It has been suggested that many of these programs are needed but have not been developed because men do not seek help to the extent that women do.[92] As the legal consequences of battering increase, programs for batterers will be needed. Another approach to dealing with this complexity lies in Hamlin's description of the success of combining family preservation services and protective services.[93]

The American Red Cross

The American Red Cross was begun in 1881 by Clara Barton. It is part of an international system that attempts to prevent and ameliorate human suffering. The improvement of the quality of life and the enhancement of individual and family self-reliance are also two of its major concerns. The services provided by this voluntary agency help individuals and families to avoid, prepare for, and cope with crises and emergencies. It is financed primarily by private contributions.[94]

To achieve its goals, the Red Cross provides a variety of services relying heavily on volunteers but also on the full-time employment of social workers. For disaster relief, food and medical care are provided as well as grants of money for rebuilding and restoring homes and businesses. The Red Cross also provides many other community services, such as volunteer blood banks; training volunteers; and transporting medical patients to and from hospitals as well as instructing them in handicrafts and hobbies. In addition, it helps military service personnel, veterans, and their families in emergency situations.

Social workers, working as volunteers or paid staff, provide short-term casework services and crisis intervention for both community service and disaster relief. The Red Cross has been a leader in the development and application of social work methods in such situations. This may involve the provision of information, referral, outreach, and case advocacy, as well as individual, family, and group counseling.

Travelers Aid

This voluntary social service agency was begun in 1851 in St. Louis to help people moving to the West who had problems. Today it continues to focus on assisting people in difficulty away from their homes or who are new to the community. It helps clients by providing casework services, information, and any other needed special services. More specifically, it strives to help individuals and families with problems related to travel or relocation; it also seeks to alleviate social conditions that contribute to such problems. Travelers Aid serves individuals and families who experience economic, social, or personal difficulties in a new environment; who are in flight as a result of behavioral disorders or intolerable physical and/or emotional problems; who are met with unexpected illness, accidents, or incompetence to complete a trip without planned, protective support; who are concerned about the welfare of relatives living elsewhere; who must contact people or resources not directly available to them but important in completing their move; or who are local residents in crisis and have no other available resources.[95]

Present and Future Trends in Services to Families and Children

Because of experience, research, political forces, and other factors, services to families and children do not remain static. There is a variety of trends in this service area, some of which are more developed than others.

1. Public funds for services continue to decrease and costs will be analyzed carefully.
2. Family systems theory and therapy (the ecosystemic perspective) will increasingly be used in assessment and intervention in case management and treatment.
3. The use of home-based, family-centered services by public agencies will increase.
4. Emphasis on providing services that have documented effectiveness will continue. Public and private funding sources will require documentation that the services reached the intended population and that the desired outcomes were reached.
5. For-profit day-care franchises will increase in popularity and numbers.
6. Subsidies for foster care and adoption services will continue.
7. More foster families will adopt, especially children with special needs.
8. Open adoptions will find increased acceptance and use. The debate will also continue, with emphasis on the needs of the children.
9. The need for more outreach and identification of cases involving African-American, Hispanic, and Southeast Asian families and children will grow.
10. The boundaries between currently fragmented services will become more flexible, with coordination of services and continuity of workers for the child and family.
11. Postadoption services with parental support and a family-centered approach are needed. Financial assistance is often needed, especially for children with special medical needs.
12. Agencies and workers entrusted with the safety of children will be held accountable if abuse continues as services are provided.

FAMILY POLICY

Most of the programs and services discussed here are the result of decisions about how to best meet the needs of client groups with specific problems. Policy and program decisions about one problem do not always take into consideration existing or proposed policies and programs designed for other target groups but which may have some bearing on the former. This, therefore, has resulted in a fragmented system of government programs, policies, and services that impacts in a variety of ways on families.

Awareness of such fragmentation and its varied effects on families has contributed to a call for a national comprehensive policy that has a coherent set of principles guiding deliberate and reasoned choices. To have such a policy would require the existence of some consensus about values and goals for strengthening families and protecting children from abuse and neglect, and such a consensus does not exist.

Incorporating a comprehensive national family policy into programs requires dealing with specifics. Given the limited resources now available for social programs and the increasing demands on the social welfare system, operating on a specific level is a lofty goal. This dilemma, however, should not deter social workers from continually striving to better the psychosocial worlds of children and families.

Costin, Karger, and Stoesz suggest that the national policy must go beyond reorganizing all of the services described in the last two chapters into an integrated coordinated system and include the legal system and researchers. They believe that child abuse should have legal consequences congruent with that of domestic violence and that police and attorneys should be included in the coordinated service delivery system. Researchers would be utilized to ensure that data on abuse and neglect are collected, that services are effective, and that policy follows research.[96]

In order to provide for the basic needs of children, parents need supportive communities and neighborhoods. Just as the well-being of children and parents is inseparable, so is the well-being of families and communities.[97] This does not necessarily mean "throwing tax dollars at problems," though there will always be need for public support in this area. As much as anything else, it is a change to a systemic way of thinking about the needs of families and children and thus of society.

SUMMARY AND CONCLUSIONS

In the previous two chapters, we discussed supportive, supplemental, and substitute services to families and children, as well as miscellaneous family and children services. Social work has a long tradition of providing services to families and children, and such programs still are a major focus of the profession today. The need for such services is as great as ever; however, resources are becoming increasingly scarce. It is, therefore, imperative that social work as a profession and individual social workers remain committed to increasing the quantity and quality of such services.

Notes

1. See, for example, Shirley Jenkins and Souber Mignon, *Paths to Child Placement* (New York: Community Council of Greater New York, 1966); Edward Mech, *Public Welfare Service for Children and Youth in Arizona* (Phoenix: State of Arizona, 1970); and B. Bernstein et al., *Foster Care Needs and Alternatives to Placement—A Projection for 1975–1985* (Albany, NY: New York State Board of Social Welfare, 1975).
2. Alfred Kadushin and Judith Martin, *Child Welfare Services*, 4th ed. (New York: Macmillan, 1988), p. 350.
3. Henry Maas and Richard E. Engler, *Children in Need of Parents* (New York: Columbia University Press, 1959); Henry S. Mass, "Children in Long Term Foster Care," *Child Welfare* 48 (1969): 331–334; and Martin E. Bryce and Roger C. Ehlert, "144 Foster Children," *Child Welfare* 50 (1971): 449–503.
4. Roger M. George, "The Reunification Process in Substitute Care," *Social Service Review* 64 (1990) 3: 442–457.
5. William Pierce, "Adoption and Other Permanency Conditions," *Children and Youth Services Review* 14 (1992): 62–66; Robert M. George, "The Reunification Process in Substitute Care," pp. 422–457.

6. Anthony N. Maluccio and Edith Fein, "Permanency Planning: A Redefinition," *Child Welfare* 63 (1983): 197.

7. Richard P. Barth and Marrianne Berry, "Outcomes of Child Welfare Services under Permanency Planning," *Social Services Review* (1987): 72.

8. Joseph Goldstein, Anna Freud, and Albert J. Solnit, *Beyond the Best Interests of the Child* (New York: Free Press, 1973).

9. Linda Katz, "Effective Permanency Planning for Children in Foster Care," *Social Work* 53 (1990) 3: 220–226.

10. Toshio Tatara, "Federal Social Welfare: Recent Trends," *Encyclopedia of Social Work,* 18th ed., 1990 Supplement (Silver Spring, MD: NASW), pp. 102–112.

11. Katz, "Effective Permanency Planning," pp. 220–226.

12. Joyce E. Everett, "Child Foster Care," in *Encyclopedia of Social Work*, 19th ed. (Washington, DC: NASW, 1995), pp. 375–389.

13. Daniel Fanshel, "Foster Care as a Two-Tiered System," *Children and Youth Services Review* 14 (1992): 52.

14. Statistics drawn from Peter Forsythe, "Homebuilders and Family Preservation," *Children and Youth Services Review* 14 (1992): 37–47; Fanshel, "Foster Care as a Two-Tiered System," p. 49; Jane Knitzer and Susan Yelton, "Collaborations between Child Welfare and Mental Health," *Public Welfare* 48 (1990) 2: 26; and Children's Defense Fund, "Children and Families in Crisis," *The State of America's Children Yearbook* (Washington, DC: Author, 1994), p. 20.

15. Fanshel, "Foster Care as a Two-Tiered System," p. 49.

16. Michael Sherraden, "The Business of Social Work," in *Encyclopedia of Social Work,* 18th ed., 1990 Supplement (Silver Spring, MD: NASW); Forsythe, "Homebuilders and Family Preservation," pp. 37–47; and Emily Jean McFadden, "Practice in Foster Care," in Joan Laird and Ann Hartman, eds., *A Handbook of Child Welfare: Context, Knowledge and Practice* (New York: Free Press, 1985), pp. 585–616.

17. Mark F. Testa, "Conditions of Risk for Substitute Care," *Children and Youth Services Review* 14 (1992): 27–36; and Annie W. Brown and Barbara Bailey-Etta, "An Out-of-Home Care System in Crisis: Implications for African American Children in the Child Welfare System," *Child Welfare* 76 (1997): 65–79.

18. Fanshel, "Foster Care as a Two-Tiered System," p. 56.

19. Children's Defense Fund, *Children without Homes* (Washington, DC: Author, 1987), p. 5.

20. Paul D. Steinhauer, "Summary and Review: The Preventative Use of Foster Care," *The Least Detrimental Alternative: A Systemic Guide to Case Planning and Decision Making for Children in Care* (Toronto: University of Toronto Press, 1991), pp. 361–378.

21. Jake Terpstra, "The Rich and Exacting Role of the Social Worker in Family Foster Care," *Child and Adolescent Social Work Journal* 4 (1987): 13.

22. McFadden, "Practice in Foster Care," p. 585.

23. Karen Blumenthal, "Making Foster Family Care Responsive," in Brenda G. McGowan and William Meezan, eds., *Child Welfare: Current Dilemmas—Future Directions* (Itasca, IL: F.E. Peacock Publishers, 1983), pp. 302–303.

24. Lela B. Costin and Charles A. Rapp, *Child Welfare: Policies & Practice* (New York: McGraw-Hill, 1984), pp. 325–384.

25. Joe Hudson and Burt Galloway, "Specialist Fostering: Resources and Activities," in *Specialist Foster Care: A Normalizing Experience,* ed. Joe Hudson and Burt Galloway (Binghamton, NY: Haworth, 1989): 1–16.

26. Hudson and Galloway, "Specialist Fostering," pp. 1–16; and Susan Taylor-Brown, "The Impact of AIDS on Foster Care: A Family Centered Approach to Services in the United States," *Child Welfare* 17 (1991) 2: 193–194.

27. Robert P. Hawkins, Pamela Meadowcroft, Barbara A. Trout, and W. Clark Luster, "Foster-Family Based Treatment," *Journal of Clinical Child Psychology* 14 (1985) 3: 221.

28. Emily Jean McFadden, "The Sexually Abused Child in Specialized Foster Care," in Hudson and Galloway, eds., *Specialist Foster Care*, pp. 91–105.

29. Susan Whitelaw, "Foster Parents of Mentally and Physically Handicapped Children," in Hudson and Galloway, eds., *Specialist Foster Care*, pp. 107–119.

30. Clarice E. Rosen, "Treatment Foster Care for Autistic Children," in Hudson and Galloway, eds., *Specialist Foster Care*, pp. 121–132.

31. Grace W. Sisto, "Therapeutic Foster Homes for Teenage Mothers and Their Babies," in Hudson and Galloway, eds., *Specialist Foster Care*, pp. 195–203.

32. Taylor-Brown, "The Impact of AIDS on Foster Care," p. 193.

33. Reuben Orenstein, "The Therapeutic Home Program," a presentation at the 1st North American Conference on Treatment Foster Care, Minneapolis; Reuben Orenstein, Department of Health and Community Services, New Brunswick, Canada (1987): 4.

34. Pamela Meadowcroft, "Treating Emotionally Disturbed Children and Adolescents in Foster Homes," in Hudson and Galloway, eds., *Specialist Foster Care*, pp. 23–43.

35. Reuben Orenstein, "The Therapeutic Home Program," p. 11.

36. Costin and Rapp, *Child Welfare*, pp. 360–361.

37. Kadushin and Martin, *Child Welfare Services*, pp. 681–685.

38. Children's Defense Fund, *The State of America's Children Yearbook* (Washington, DC: Author, 1996): 91.

39. Kadushin and Martin, *Child Welfare Services*, pp. 535–536.

40. Kari Sandven and Michael Resnick, "Informal Adoption among Black Adolescent Mothers," *American Journal of Orthopsychiatry* 60 (1990) 2: 210–224.

41. Brown and Bailey-Etta, "An Out-of-Home Care System in Crisis," pp. 65–79.

42. William Pierce, "Adoption and Other Permanency Considerations," *Children and Youth Services Review,* 14 (1992): 63.

43. Susan W. Downs, Lela B. Costin, and Emily J. McFadden, *Child Welfare and Family Services* (New York: Longman, 1996): 325–326.

44. Elizabeth S. Cole, "Adoption: History, Policy, and Program," in Joan Laird and Ann Hartman, eds., *A Handbook of Child Welfare: Context, Knowledge, and Practice* (New York: Free Press, 1985).

45. William Meezan et al., *Adoption without Agencies* (New York: Child Welfare League of America, 1987).

46. Costin and Rapp, *Child Welfare,* p. 292.

47. Kadushin, *Child Welfare Services,* p. 484.

48. Vic Groze, "Adoption and Single Parents: A Review," *Child Welfare* 70 (1991) 3: 321.

49. Pierce, "Adoption and Other Permanency Considerations," p. 63.

50. Penelope Maza, *Child Welfare Research Note 2* (Washington, DC: Administration for Children, Youth, and Families), p. 2.

51. Peter Rodriguez and Alan S. Meyer, "Minority Adoptions and Agency Practices," *Social Work* 35 (1990) 3: 528.

52. Sandven and Resnick, "Informal Adoption among Black Adolescent Mothers," p. 223.

53. Brown and Bailey-Etta, "An Out-of-Home Care System in Crisis," pp. 65–79.

54. Costin and Rapp, *Child Welfare,* p. 424.

55. William Reid, Richard Kagan, Alison Kaminsky, and Katherine Helmer, "Adoption of Older Institutionalized Youth," *Social Casework* 68 (1987) 3: 140–149; James Rosenthal, Victor Groze, and Herman Curiel, "Race, Social Class, and Special Needs Adoption," *Social Work* 35 (1990) 6: 532–539.

56. D.S. Franklin and Fred Massarik, "The Adoption of Children with Medical Conditions, Parts I, II, and III," *Child Welfare* (1969): 459–476, 533–539, 595–601; and Laraine M. Glidden, "Adopting Mentally Handicapped Children," *Adoption and Fostering* 9 (1985): 53–56.

57. M. Ward, "Choosing Adoptive Families for Large Sibling Groups," *Child Welfare* 66 (1987) 3: 259–268.

58. Dawn Day, *The Adoption of Black Children* (Lexington, MA: D.C. Heath, 1979).

59. Penny Johnson, Joan Shireman, and Kenneth Watson, "Transracial Adoption and the Development of Black Identity at Age Eight," *Child Welfare* 66 (1987) 1: 45–46.

60. Johnson, Shireman, and Watson, "Transracial Adoption," p. 53.

61. G. Waldinger, "Subsidized Adoption: How Paid Parents View It," *Social Work* 27 (1982): 516–521.

62. P. Hoggan, "Attitudes to Post-Placement Support Services in Permanent Family Placement," *Adoption and Fostering* 15 (1991) 1: 28–30.

63. James A. Rosenthal, "Outcomes of Adoption of Children with Special Needs," *Future of Children* 3 (1993) 1: 77–88.

64. Ethel Brahm, "One Parent Adoptions," *Children* (1970): 17; Joan Shireman and Penny Johnson, "Single Parents as Adoptive Parents," *Social Service Review* (1976): 50.

65. Groze, "Adoption and Single Parents," p. 330.

66. Susan Livingston Smith and Jeanne A. Howard, "A Comparative Study of Successful and Disrupted Adoptions," *Social Service Review* 65 (1991) 2: 249.

67. Downs, Costin, and McFadden, *Child Welfare and Family Services*, p. 362.

68. Cole, "Adoption: History, Policy, and Program," p. 658.

69. Kadushin and Martin, *Child Welfare Services*, p. 602.

70. Ibid., pp. 600–601.

71. Kenneth J. Herrman, Jr., and Barbara Kasper, "International Adoption: The Exploitation of Women and Children," *Affilia* 7 (1992) 1: 45–58; and Kadushin and Martin, *Child Welfare Services*, pp. 626–632.

72. Paul Sachdev, "The Birth Father: A Neglected Element in the Adoption Equation," *Families in Society: The Journal of Contemporary Human Services* 72 (1991) 3: 131–139.

73. Joanne W. Small, "Working with Adoptive Families," *Public Welfare* 45 (1987) 3: 34.

74. Ibid., p. 34.

75. Reuben Pannor and Annette Baran, "Open Adoption as Standard Practice," *Child Welfare* 63 (1984): 437–445.

76. Robert Anderson, "The Nature of Adoptee Search: Adventure, Cure or Growth?" *Child Welfare* 68 (1989) 6: 623.

77. Kadushin and Martin, *Child Welfare Services*, pp. 581–582.

78. Patrick A. Curtis, "The Dialectics of Open Versus Closed Adoption of Infants," *Child Welfare* 65 (1986): 437–445.

79. William Meezan, "Toward an Expanded Role for Adoption Services," in Brenda G. McGowan and William Meezan, eds., *Child Welfare* (Itasca, IL: F.E. Peacock Publishers, 1983) p. 466.

80. Small, "Working with Adoptive Families," pp. 34–41.

81. Curtis, "The Dialectics of Open Versus Closed Adoption of Infants."

82. Liane V. Davis, "Domestic Violence," in *Encyclopedia of Social Work,* 19th ed. (Washington, DC: NASW Press, 1995), pp. 780–789. An example of a critic of the 82 percent figure is Kathleen Parker, who argues that it is exaggerated. "Domestic-Abuse Reports Exaggerated," *Des Moines Register*, September 6, 1997, p. 7A.

83. Lenore E. Walker, *The Battered Woman* (New York: Harper & Row, 1979), p. xv.

84. Daniel G. Saunders, "Domestic Violence: Legal Issues," in *Encyclopedia of Social Work* 19th ed. (Washington, DC: NASW Press, 1995), pp. 789–796.

85. Lela B. Costin, Howard J. Karger, and David Stoesz, *The Politics of Child Abuse in America* (New York: Oxford University Press, 1996), p. 3.
86. Lenora Greenbaum Ucko, "Who's Afraid of the Big Bad Wolf," *Social Work* 36 (1991) 5: 414.
87. Albert R. Roberts and Beverly J. Roberts, *Sheltering Battered Women: A National Study and Service Guide* (New York: Springer Publishing, 1981).
88. Richard J. Gelles and Claire Pedrick Cornell, *Intimate Violence in Families* (Newbury Park, CA: Sage Publications, 1985), p. 142.
89. B.E. Aguirre, "Why Do They Return? Abused Wives in Shelters," *Social Work* 30 (1985): 350–354.
90. Roberts and Roberts, *Sheltering Battered Women*, p. 42.
91. Saunders, "Domestic Violence: Legal Issues," pp. 789–796.
92. Albert R. Roberts, "Intervention with the Abusive Partner," in Albert R. Roberts, ed., *Battered Women and Their Families: Intervention Strategies and Treatment Programs* (New York: Springer Publishing, 1984).
93. Elwood Hamlin II, "Community Based Spouse Abuse Protection and Family Preservation Team," *Social Work* 36 (1991) 5: 402–406.
94. *The Encyclopedia Americana,* International Edition, Vol. 23, s.v. "Red Cross" (Danbury, CT: Grolier, Inc., 1993) pp. 303–304.
95. *The Encyclopedia Americana,* International Edition, Vol. 27, s.v. "Travelers Aid" (Danbury, CT: Grolier, Inc., 1993) pp. 40–41.
96. Costin, Karger, and Stoesz, *The Politics of Child Abuse.*
97. J. Garbarino, "The Issue Is Human Quality: In Praise of Children," *Children and Youth Services Review* 1 (1979): 30.

Additional Suggested Readings

Adoption Quarterly, a new journal started in 1997. Binghamton, NY: Haworth Press.

Bausch, Robert S., and Richard T. Serpe. "Negative Outcomes of Interethnic Adoption of Mexican American Children." *Social Work* 42 (1997) 2: 136–143.

Beggs, Majorie. *In a Day's Work.* San Francisco: Study Center Press, 1996.

Berrick, Jill Duerr, and Ruth Lawrence-Karski. "Emerging Issues in Child Welfare." *Public Welfare* 53 (1995) 4: 4–11.

Bieneke, Richard H., Joseph Leavey, Peggy Mosley, and Marie A. Mataua. "Development and Description of Two New Instruments for Measuring the Impact of Coordinated Social Services for Children." *Child Welfare* LXXVI (1997) 3: 379–391.

Families in Society 78 (1997) 5. Entire issue on foster and kinship care.

Gambrill, Eileen, and Theodore J. Stein. *Controversial Issues in Child Welfare.* Needham Heights, MA: Allyn & Bacon, 1994.

Kamerman, Sheila Boyd, and Alfred J. Kahn. "Child Welfare in the Context of Welfare Reform." New York: Columbia University School of Social Work, 1997.

Kutash, Krista, and Robin Vestena Robins. "Effectiveness of Children's Mental Health Services: A Review of the Literature." *Education and Treatment of Children* 18 (1995) 4: 443–477.

Nelson, Harry. "What is Appropriate Care for the Children of Troubled Families?" New York: Milbank Memorial Fund, 1996.

Roman, Nan P., and Phyllis B. Wolfe. "The Relationship Between Foster Care and Homelessness." *Public Welfare* 55 (1997) 1: 4–9.

7

Social Work in the Schools

MARLYS STAUDT*

Social work and the public schools are closely intertwined, as "public education and social work share a common concern for social problems confronting children and families."[1] While school social work is a specialty area of practice in the profession of social work, all social workers dealing with children find that they must understand and work with the schools. Many children receiving child welfare and child mental health services receive special school services as well, necessitating the need for social workers employed in these arenas also to understand the educational system.

Elementary and secondary schools have evolved into the preponderant socializing institutions in American society. Virtually every citizen has spent significant formative years in these institutions. The fact that you are reading this book indicates that your own schooling experience was successful; you have accommodated to the ways of the school, which are the ways of our society. Many persons, though, have difficulty in this developmental arena, and social work is one of the professions that have proved helpful in a wide range of school-related difficulties.

By 1970 the usefulness of social work within public education was well established. School social work is a field of practice that is analogous to medical social work, in that both medical and school social workers practice in a host or secondary setting. In schools, hospitals, and health clinics, social work is not the primary mission; in these settings, social workers are part of a multidisciplinary team. In schools, other team members include speech and language pathologists, psychologists, guidance counselors, teachers, school nurses, special education consultants, principals, and parents. In education settings the primary profession is education and the central mission is education of youth. Recently,

---

*The author acknowledges Ralph Anderson, the author of this chapter in the first three editions.

there has been increased acknowledgement by the schools that education of youth cannot occur unless the personal and environmental stresses of students are addressed. The primary role of the school social worker is to intervene to ameliorate these social problems so children can fully participate in and benefit from their educational experience.

School social work tends to attract those interested in primary prevention and in assuring developmental opportunities for children. The school provides a unique and comprehensive opportunity for early intervention into the full range of developmental issues. Indeed, in any community the school is the one institution with the potential to come into contact with all its children.[2]

HISTORICAL PERSPECTIVE

The first recorded instances of school social workers appeared in 1906 and 1907 in Boston, Hartford, Conn., and New York City. Interestingly, these first social workers in the schools were financed by community agencies and derived from the burgeoning conviction that the public school was the logical place for early intervention. Not until 1914 did Rochester, New York, become the first city to initiate a program totally funded from public sources. The simple yet elegant justification provided by the Rochester Board of Education continues to be the valid rationale for school social work:

> [This is] the first step in an attempt to meet a need of which the school system has been conscious for some time. It is an undisputed fact that in the environment of the child outside of school are to be found forces which will often times thwart the school in its endeavors.... The appointment of a visiting teacher is an attempt on the part of the school to meet its responsibility for the whole welfare of the child...[and] to secure maximum cooperation between the home and the school.[3]

The title *visiting teacher* continued in vogue for decades and connoted an official school representative who left the school building on behalf of the child, to deal with the child's parents and community agencies. A major function of the early visiting teacher was to attempt to ameliorate situations contributing to school nonattendance. Such activity was consistent with the philosophy of the Progressive Era—that the public school was the key to developing the informed citizenry that is so necessary to a democracy. Education was seen as the agent of social reform; child labor laws (1916) protected children from exploitation and assured their availability for attending school; the elaboration of compulsory school attendance assured that they would attend.

In 1918 the Harkness family established the Commonwealth Fund to "do something for the welfare of mankind." One of the fund's major emphases was delinquency prevention. To further that goal, in 1921 the Commonwealth Fund funded 30 visiting teacher demonstration projects at various sites throughout the United States. These projects provided much input to the development of school social work.

From these early beginnings, school social work slowly developed its acknowledged competence as an integral part of pupil personnel services. The patterns of development varied from state to state, and even from school district to school district. This variation still exists today, despite the goal of all school social work practice to facilitate optimal learning opportunities for children and youth. Student needs vary from district to district and even within districts. Needs also change over time. The current "social era" affects needs. For example, Lela Costin stated that the Great Depression affected the daily activity of school social workers because much emphasis was placed on locating and supplying resources to meet the physical needs of the students.[4] More recently, school social workers have offered group services to students and in-service sessions to teachers on the changing family structure and on coping with loss and change. In the mid-1980s, school social workers in rural areas and small towns needed to be aware of the *farm crisis* and its implications for the students they served. During Desert Storm, school social workers offered group services to help students understand and cope with the war. Today, social issues such as AIDS, homelessness, and violence affect the practice of school social work.

Public policy and the political arena also affect school social work. There have been two occasions of rapid expansion, both resulting from federal initiatives. The first followed from the passage of Title I of the American Education Act in 1965, which recognized the plight of the *educationally disadvantaged*, where the disadvantage is associated with low economic capability and low educational aspirations. The legislation authorized funding to be "targeted" to schools that had a preponderance of such children, mostly inner-city schools, and provided for social services to concentrate especially on home-school relationships.

The second federal initiative having major impact on social work in the schools was Public Law 94-142, the Education for All Handicapped Children Act, which was signed into law by President Ford in 1975. The primary purpose of this law is to ensure that a free appropriate public education (FAPE) be available to all handicapped children aged three through twenty-one. This culminated a series of court decisions, which had established a firm constitutional basis for full educational opportunity, regardless of other considerations. Under the provisions of P.L. 94-142, social work services in the schools include but are not limited to:

1. Preparing a social or developmental history to help determine whether a child qualifies for special education services
2. Group and individual counseling with the child and family
3. Working with those problems in the child's living situation (home, school, and community) that affect the child's adjustment in school
4. Mobilizing school and community resources to enable the child to receive maximum benefit from his or her educational program[5]

Implementation of the provisions of this law has markedly increased the numbers of school social workers in special education units, and in some states and districts social workers work only in the area of special education. In 1990 P.L. 101-476 changed the name of the "Education for All Handicapped Children Act" to the "Individuals with Disabilities Education Act (IDEA)." With this change, autism and traumatic brain injury were added as disability categories that may qualify students for special education services. This law was reauthorized in 1997.

There is some commonality, and so there can be some generalization, in how the role of the school social worker has evolved. In the early decades the primary activities of school social workers were casework with individual children and youth, contact with their families, and contact/liaison with community agencies. During the depression of the 1930s, there was some decrease in the numbers of social workers based in the schools, but the pattern of slow growth was restored following the Second World War. In 1968 Costin found that the primary emphasis of school social work was clinical casework.[6] Paula Allen-Meares replicated Costin's study in the mid-1970s and found a transition in the role from an emphasis on clinical casework to home-school-community liaison and educational counseling with the student and parents.[7] Currently, the role of the school social worker is shaped largely by special education legislation that requires that students receive a comprehensive and multidisciplinary evaluation in order to determine eligibility for special education services.

THE PRACTICE OF SCHOOL SOCIAL WORK

There are different models of school social work. Freeman describes the three major models as the traditional clinical model, the school change model, and the systems model.[8] In the clinical model, the focus is on the problems of the individual student, and the role of the social worker is that of caseworker, counselor, consultant to the teacher, and referral agent. The focus of the school change model is on the dysfunction of the school or district that contributes to student problems. The target of intervention changes from the individual student to school personnel who are in a position to make the needed school changes that will accommodate the learning needs of the student. The school social worker becomes an advocate for institutional change. The third model, the systems or ecological model, is the model to which many of today's school social workers ascribe. This model recognizes that many different social and environmental forces can affect student learning. One well-known school social work text describes the ecological perspective as

> ...the most appropriate perspective for viewing social work practice in schools and for locating the target(s) of intervention. It is appropriate in that it directs attention to the whole and not to any one part, system, or aspect of the client's situation. The focus is on the social process of interaction and the transactions between a child and that child's environment. The environment is defined as the aggregate of external conditions and influences that affect and determine a child's life and development. In addition to the family, some of these determinants are schools, courts, neighborhood, hospitals, clinics, and the mass media.[9]

Social workers today still counsel individual students, but there is recognition and movement toward alternative delivery styles by which more students can be effectively served. These include policy making, teacher consultation, group work, program development, and systems change. Whatever the mode of service delivery, the focus is on the student(s) in the educational setting and eliminating barriers to effective learning.

Even within any one model of school social work practice, there is great variety in the types of problems that school social workers deal with and what they do, since there are vast differences in schools and the communities within which schools exist. As Costin has stated, "School social work is related to a particular school system, the outside community, the characteristics of the pupils, and the social conditions they face."[10] Most of the problems concern students who are not fulfilling expectations of the school, the family, or the community. Such problems may take the form of academic underachievement, difficulties in social interaction with teachers or peers, not attending school, or unacceptable behavior.

The reasons for referral to a school social worker can be organized into three general categories: behavioral/social, academic, and personal. Of course these overlap, and students can and often do experience difficulty in more than one area. Some of the specific problems students experience with which school social workers can help are:

Behavioral/Social	*Academic*	*Personal*
Disruption of class	Lack of organizational skills	Unhappiness or depression
Poor peer relationships	Not completing assignments	Fear of going home
Demands for excessive attention	Off-task behavior	Sexuality problems
Shy and withdrawn behavior	Poor study habits	Eating disorders
Temper outbursts	Short attention span	Chemical dependency
Fear of attempting new tasks	Overdependency on teacher	Experiencing a personal loss
School refusal	Lack of motivation	Psychosomatic complaints
Excessive lying		Suicidal tendencies
Stealing		Hygiene
Impulsive behavior		

School social workers use a variety of interventions, including individual and group counseling, parent and family counseling, parent education and support groups, consultation with teachers, home-school liaison activities, and referral to and coordination with other agencies. In addition, school social workers become involved in program development activities, advocacy, and research.

School social work has long held that its unique contribution is serving as liaison between home, school, and community. Thus, it is necessary to understand the role of each of these institutions in relation to the child. While the

Joel Gordon

School counselors meet with students in an effort to help them fulfill better the expectations of the school, the family, and the community.

school is charged with the responsibility of socializing its youth, the family continues to be held primarily responsible. At the same time, while the family has the primary responsibility to care for and socialize children, the school plays a strong supporting role and provides certain learning that the family cannot; in addition, the school and community monitor and safeguard children's rights if the family is unable to fulfill its function.[11] It is important for the school, home, and community to work in collaboration and for each to support the efforts of the other; the school social worker spans this nexus by working at the interface of all three. This is a unique position. Social workers in other child-serving systems, such as child welfare, juvenile justice, and mental health, also function at these same boundaries. However, these social workers often enter the school as "outsiders" rather than "part of." Similarly, it is not the norm for other professionals in the school to leave the school to interact with the family or other community agencies.

Generally the family, school, or community will tend to blame one of the other two systems if things do not go well. Community members (merchants and citizens) may fault the school if they find groups of youth to be troublesome. They may request stricter monitoring by the school and closer supervision of young people. School personnel often attribute difficulties to the families, especially those who are different from the school or community norm or who do not meet the school's expectations in terms of home-school communication. Families fault the schools for not attending sufficiently to the wants of children and parents. The quality of the relationship between the school, the parents, and other involved agencies is extremely important to children's school success.[12] Social workers are committed to bringing all three systems into better working relations around the developmental needs of the children.

Currently, much school social work activity is devoted to the provisions of P.L. 94-142 to assure that the mandated right to an appropriate education is realized for all those with handicapping conditions. This entails full and close attention to the developmental and educational needs of the individual child and family. This is a multiprofessional effort, with social workers collecting the developmental history and adaptive behavior information and preparing a social history based on the information acquired, interpreting needs and recommendations to the child's parent(s), and assuring parental participation in decision making regarding an individualized educational plan (IEP) for the child.

Role Considerations

As stated earlier, there is a great variation of role definitions, deriving from variations in the educational enterprise. A social worker may be assigned to only one building, a pupil personnel unit serving a number of schools, or an area special education unit. A school social worker may serve only preschool children or only high school students or only students with a certain type of disability. Or he or she may serve students of different ages with various presenting problems. The nature of the assignment is a significant determinant of role expectations.

Often the functions of social work overlap the functions of other professional disciplines found in support services, especially school psychologists and guidance counselors. Much time and effort has been devoted to clearly delineating the functions of these three overlapping disciplines. In fact, most of the research and conceptual development in the field has been on the role of the school social worker. While each profession has particular areas of expertise, there remains a significant common ground based in knowledge and caring about children and their development. The expertise of social workers is acknowledged to be family and community resources, not educational technology. Therefore, one of the main roles of the school social worker continues to be serving as a liaison between school, home, and community.

Because school social workers work in a host setting and work closely with members of other professions, they must possess more than casework skills. They must understand the setting in which they work, be able to function as part of a team, and be able to identify and interpret their role and function to others in the school. School social workers must maintain contact with the teachers of the students they are working with, so teachers are informed of the progress of social work intervention with the student and family and how that may affect the student's school performance. School social workers are part of a team, yet they have access to information from children and families that may or may not need to be shared with other team members. In this regard, school social workers need to be versed in issues of confidentiality that arise in practice in the schools.[13] School social workers must clearly identify and describe their role to educators, yet remain flexible, so that the various and changing needs of the student, school, and community can be met. It is essential that social workers aspiring to practice in the school understand the school as a social institution. As Robert Constable phrased it,

> There is clearly a place and function for school social workers in the education setting but the function is inextricably tied to the education institution. The role cannot be carried out by simply using clinical skills in a school setting. School social workers need to have a thorough theoretical and practical understanding of the American education institution, curriculum and teaching methods at different levels and with different children.[14]

The social work definition contained in P.L. 94-142 establishes a clear set of expectations of social workers, which turns out to be a two-edged sword. It does serve to provide a niche or clear role expectations, but it also puts constraints on role elaboration by limiting the population served to those with suspected handicapping conditions.[15] If school social work is funded by special education monies, then school social work involvement with other students, even though they may be experiencing social or behavioral difficulties, may be limited. District policy often determines which student groups school social workers serve.

The following short case vignettes will give the reader a "taste" of the various ways in which school social workers provide services to students, schools, and communities.

"John"

John is a 17-year-old student who is entering his junior year of high school. This is John's first year at the high school, as he has spent the last three to four years in residential placement in a different community. John now lives with his father. His school file shows that ever since kindergarten John has come to the attention of his teachers because of temper outbursts and aggressive and inappropriate behavior, and was referred numerous times for psychological testing, counseling, and psychiatric evaluations.

John's early family life might be described as chaotic, and his family has experienced a number of personal and environmental problems. For a number of years John has been labeled as a student with behavior disabilities and has received special education services. He reads on a sixth-grade level and has learning problems apart from the behavior disability. In addition, John has complex medical problems, including epilepsy, a drooping eyelid, and a club foot. He is on medication to control seizures. John has few friends, and his appearance is such that others sometimes tease him.

The school social worker attended John's intake staffing and began to see John on a regular basis to help him adjust to his new school and learn how to respond to remarks that might be made by other students. At one point John stopped attending school due to an increase in the number of epileptic seizures, which John's father attributed to stress. The school social worker arranged a meeting with John, his father, the school nurse, counselor, psychologist, and teachers to discuss John's situation. John's schedule was changed and the counselor agreed to mediate with one of John's regular teachers who had unrealistic expectations of John.

As the year ended, John had shown no temper outbursts in school. Soon he will be 18 and a senior.

The school social worker has had regular contact with John and his teachers to monitor his progress. She has referred John to Vocational Rehabilitation, arranged a referral to an epilepsy clinic, and has taken John to see a group home where independent daily living skills are taught. John is on the waiting list to enter this group home. Close contact was maintained with other team members, especially the school counselor and school nurse.

"Amy"

Amy is three years old. Her mother called the Area Education Agency on advice from her family doctor. The mother expressed many behavioral concerns regarding Amy, including not sleeping through the night and eating problems. Amy is "always into things," "very active," and "hard to discipline." There is a history of early medical problems, including surgery involving her stomach. Amy has asthma and has been hospitalized numerous times. Her mother indicates she has been overly protective of Amy. Amy lives with her biological parents, an older sister, and a younger sister.

The social worker and school psychologist worked together in interviewing the mother and family and in observing Amy. Information from Amy's medical doctors was obtained. Parenting information was given during the assessment process.

Amy was temporarily placed in a developmental preschool, so that her behavior could be observed out of the home. Amy's behavior in this structured setting was appropriate. This confirmed the school social worker's and psychologist's initial hypothesis that many of Amy's behaviors were a result of the relationship between Amy and her parents—their overprotectiveness and inappropriate expectations. (For example, Amy's parents had the same expectations of Amy as they had for her older sister in kindergarten.)

The school social worker continued to meet with Amy's mother and provided suggestions and information about child development. Amy's mother wanted services and was eager to make some changes. Amy is now in a regular preschool and her mother reports significant improvement in her behavior at home.

These examples illustrate how school social workers become involved in counseling with students and parents, consulting with teachers, referring to other agencies, and working with teams. Social work services in the two examples occurred in the context of special education. In the first, the student was already enrolled in special education and the social worker provided services to help the student maximize his education; in the second, the school social worker provided assessment to help determine whether the child qualified for special services. The social worker was able to stay involved with the family even when the child did not qualify for special services. Notice that, in both of these examples, the school social worker worked closely with other team members. But, as already noted, school social workers also become involved at the macro level in an effort to meet the needs of groups of students. For example, school social workers may become involved in developing school or community programs. Staudt provides an example of how a school social worker helped develop a big brother/sister program in a rural community.[16] The impetus for such a program came from the recognition by the school social worker that a number of children referred for special school services also had an additional need—for an adult friend and role model with whom to spend time. When school social workers recognize unmet needs, then they become involved in helping to develop and implement new programs.

Issues and Trends

Educational qualifications.   One chronic issue in respect to school social work involves the specification of educational qualifications for such work. Some argue that any professional employed in the school, except physicians and nurses, should have a degree in education and be eligible for certification as a teacher. This argument is firmly grounded in the belief that all school activities are forms of education and should be planned and carried out by educators. Another rationale for such a requirement is that only study in education can provide a thorough understanding of the educational enterprise. Others firmly adhere to a position that professional education as a social worker is sufficient to practice social work in any setting, and that the special characteristics of any particular setting can be learned on the job.

In social work there seems to be a trend toward melding these two polarities. In this view, the professional social work degree continues to be essential but is not necessarily sufficient. Social workers must have an understanding of education as well, and courses in colleges of education are one means toward that end. Work experiences may be another. Some states require school social workers to be "certified." Requirements for certification include that the applicant has taken certain social work and education courses and perhaps completed a practicum in a school setting. There is a related issue in social work education, not unique to school social work. Employing institutions (for example, schools, hospitals, mental health centers) want social work job applicants who have been specially trained for the work of the particular institutions. One of the strengths of the social work profession has been the versatility of its members. How can educational programs be devised that equip graduates to be both highly skilled in one specialty and at the same time competent, or potentially competent, to practice in other settings as well?

Role definition.   Still another recurrent problem is the definition of school social work role vis-à-vis other professions serving the schools. Territorial disputes have occurred and will continue as the various professions sort out their respective areas of competence. Role strain can result if the school social worker's ideas or perceptions in regard to what tasks to perform differ significantly from the ideas or perceptions of others in the school system. There is no overall single description of the specific tasks and functions any individual social worker might provide. School social workers at the building or district level must assess student and community needs and communicate and coordinate with other members of the team and school system. In recent years, working with families has been a subject of contention. However, many have concluded there are more than enough families to go around, and this can also be a multidisciplinary activity.

As in other areas of social work practice, research and evaluation activities are recognized as a necessity in school social work practice. Social workers in all settings have a professional responsibility to be accountable to their clients and other stakeholders. Since social work is not the main function of the school, social workers may be the first to be cut in times of budget cutbacks. Thus, it is wise for school social workers not only to engage in ongoing evaluation but to share the results with principals and other interested parties. Evaluation helps point the way to needed modifications in service delivery; it is difficult for practice to proceed in an effective manner without evaluation findings to inform practice. Three different kinds of evaluation are outcome evaluation of services to individual children, groups, and families; program evaluation; and process evaluation.[17]

It goes without saying (but is too important not to say) that just as in other areas of social work, school social workers must continually develop their skills in working with a diverse client group. School social workers also can provide consultation and workshops to help other school personnel and students understand and accept diversity. Several of the suggested readings at the end of this chapter address diversity in the schools.

Expanding practice.   Services to infants and toddlers with handicaps is an emerging aspect of school social work practice.[18] In 1986, President Reagan signed P.L. 99-457, the Education of the Handicapped Amendments of 1986. P.L. 99-457 amends P.L. 99-142 to include a mandate for the provision of educational and related services for handicapped children aged three to five years. It also provides a discretionary program to establish early intervention services for infants and toddlers (birth through age two) with a developmental disability, and for their families. One of the components of the latter is the development and implementation of an Individualized Family Service Plan (IFSP). In effect, the focus is on the family rather than just the child. The family's strengths and resources in meeting the needs of the handicapped child, as well as the family's needs, must be identified in the IFSP. Other components of the IFSP include statements about the child's developmental level, the intervention services needed, and the plan for evaluation of child and family progress. In addition, a case manager must be named. In short, this legislation recognizes the importance of the family and of coordination and collaboration among agencies in meeting the needs of young children with developmental disabilities. Certainly school social workers will continue to have a role in serving infants and preschool handicapped children and their families. This includes the school social worker assisting in finding, screening, identifying, and serving young children with handicaps and their families.

Systems of care.   Although originating in mental health, the move to develop "systems of care" for children with emotional disturbances affects the educational system. Basically, the systems of care concept exposes that children should have access to a range of coordinated services at the local level and that services should be family focused as well as individualized to meet the needs of each child and family. Traditionally, mental health services to children have consisted of outpatient counseling or residential placement, with few other services available. This is now changing, with family preservation and other family- and community-based services in place in most communities. Any system of care or coordinated service network must include the school; the school social worker will be central in helping to develop each child's plan of care, especially as it relates to the child's schooling.

Inclusion.   Three other recent trends in education must be noted, as school social workers have a role to play in these movements. First, "inclusion" is an effort to educate children with disabilities in the regular classroom rather than in special classes. Rather than "pulling" children with disabilities out of the regular classroom and placing them in special education classes, children with disabilities remain in the regular classroom, and special services that may be needed are provided in the context of the regular classroom. As children with disabilities move into regular classes, school social workers have a role to play in helping them and their families cope with the transition process. Similarly, school social workers can help regular education teachers and other students understand the child with a disability.

Extension of services.   Second, P.L. 100-297, the Augustus F. Hawkins–Robert T. Stafford Elementary and Secondary School Improvement Amendments of 1988, extended the Title I program for disadvantaged children. In addition, it encourages collaboration among families, schools, and communities in meeting the needs of certain students deemed at risk of school failure, and provides monies for these efforts.[19] The amendments explicitly recognize school social work as an appropriate discipline in the planning and delivery of these services.

Service integration.   Third, the school is coming to be viewed as a site to provide social, health, and mental health services to children and families. The availability of social, mental health, and related services in the school is referred to as service integration or one-stop shopping.[20] The role of the school social worker in shaping these services is as yet unkown. While it seems logical that the school social worker would play a key part in the integration of these services in the school setting, Pennekamp notes:

> None of the current restructuring literature known to this writer explores the relationship of the current pupil personnel services staff to services coming onto the campus from the community. The whole potential richness of developing patterns of integrating school-employed student personnel services with outside community human services has not surfaced into a visible agenda.[21]

Institutional change.   Some social workers question whether the public school can be changed significantly from within. Social work values and principles center on the worth and dignity of the individual, and schools sometimes seem to violate those principles as programs are developed for masses of children and youth. School social work is not without critics who suggest that school social workers engage in institutional change efforts all too infrequently. Clancy reminds us that when school social workers focus on clinical intervention with children and families, then they are defining the problem as within the individual and family, and ignoring larger issues such as poverty, racism, and other social problems.[22] Thus, they maintain the status quo. This view is voiced by Leon Williams in a manner that should make every school social worker pause in examination of current social work practice in the school:

> School social work as a professional strategy has not responded to many of the pressing issues that confront schools, and it has failed to act as an effective advocate for children at risk, particularly those who are people of color. The profession needs to give serious attention to its role, domain, function, and purpose in the educational system. Of the potential social work activities within a school or community, the most neglected appear to be client advocacy, political and organizational change, and community development and involvement. In the force of a powerful competing profession, social workers have retreated to the least intrusive levels of practice that place the fewest demands of change or reform on the educational system.[23]

Future

There is no doubt that school social work is here to stay. The importance of the total well-being of both the child and the family to the success of the school enterprise is no longer open to question. The literature of school social work of the past two decades is full of examples of role elaboration, gearing services to the needs of special populations, as well as models for more effective work in school settings. The movement toward inclusion and the development of school-based services are two current reforms that will change the role of the school social worker. The exact direction and loos of that change remains to be seen.

Further into the future it is conceivable that there will be fundamental changes in the school enterprise itself. The push for site-based management has already changed the operation of some schools. Basically, site-based management means more autonomy for the local school, with decision making based at the local level and the involvement of all stakeholders in decision making.[24]

Public education has been under attack on many fronts. The schools have become the battleground for almost all our social controversies. One of the most recent examples is AIDS (acquired immune deficiency syndrome) and the controversy around students with AIDS in school. Some schools refused to enroll children with AIDS; others that did so faced an outcry from parents. Efforts to change institutionalized racism were focused in the schools through busing for integration, rather than through serious attempts to desegregate housing patterns or enrich schools serving predominately minority populations. Controversies about religion (prayer in the schools) and morality (content of textbooks) are centered in the schools. The schools have become the designated agent to eliminate institutionalized sexism and discriminatory practices against the handicapped. Meanwhile the public schools are criticized for not adequately preparing citizens in the "basic" skills (reading, writing, citizenship) that have been the central purpose of the public school since its inception. It is unlikely that the public school (or any single institution) can continue to expand its functions, many of which are contradictory, and maintain a sufficiently steady state to survive. As major institutional changes do occur within the public schools, the place of social work therein will also change.

SUMMARY AND CONCLUSIONS

Social work in the schools is an established field of social work practice. It is one of the very few social work settings where primary prevention is feasible. Trite though it may sound, children are the future, and in our societal structure the school is an institution where the rights of children to develop and thrive can be realized. School social workers have an opportunity to further these purposes.

Notes

1. Cynthia Franklin and Calvin L. Streeter, "School Reform: Linking Public Schools with Human Services," *Social Work* 40, no. 6 (November 1995), 773.
2. Janet Levy, "Schools and Social Services: A Nascent Partnership," *Families in Society* 72, no. 5 (May 1991).
3. *56th Report of the Board of Education*, Rochester, N.Y., 1911, 1912, 1913, as quoted in Lela Costin, "A Historical Review of School Social Work," in *Social Services and the Public Schools* (Bloomington, IN: Midwest Center Consortium for Planned Change in Pupil Personnel Programs for Urban Schools, Indiana University, 1975), n.p.
4. Lela B. Costin, "A Historical Review of School Social Work," *Social Casework* 50, no. 8 (October 1969).
5. See the Education for All Handicapped Children Act of 1975 (P.L. 94-142) and rules and regulations in the *Federal Register*, December 20, 1976, 41:46977, and August 23, 1977, 42:42479–42497.
6. Lela B. Costin, "An Analysis of the Tasks in School Social Work," *Social Service Review* 43 (September 1969).
7. Paula Allen-Meares, "Analysis of Tasks in School Social Work," *Social Work* 22, no. 3 (May 1977).
8. Edith M. Freeman, "School Social Work Overview," in *Encyclopedia of Social Work*, 19th ed. (Washington, DC: NASW Press, 1995).
9. Paula Allen-Meares, Robert O. Washington, and Betty L. Welsh, *Social Work Services in the Schools* (Boston: Allyn & Bacon, 1996), p. 73.
10. Donald Brieland, Lela B. Costin, and Charles Atherton, *Contemporary Social Work* (New York: McGraw-Hill, 1975), p. 152.
11. Robert Constable and Herbert Walberg, "School Social Work: Facilitating Home-School Partnerships," in Robert Constable, John P. Flynn, and Shirley McDonald, eds., *School Social Work: Practice and Research Perspectives* (Chicago: Lyceum Books, 1996).
12. John Victor Compher, *Family-Centered Practice: The Interactional Dance beyond the Family System* (New York: Human Sciences Press, 1989).
13. Toby Berman-Rossi and Peter Rossi, "Confidentiality and Informed Consent in School Social Work," *Social Work in Education* 12 (April 1990).

14. Robert Constable, "Toward the Construction of Role in an Emergent Social Work Specialization," *School Social Work Quarterly* 1, no. 2 (Summer 1979): 147.

15. Lela B. Costin, "Which Children Can We Serve?" *Social Work in Education* 6, no. 2 (Winter 1984): 66–67.

16. Marlys Staudt, "School-Based Program Development in a Rural Community," *Social Work in Education* 9 (Winter 1987).

17. Paula Allen-Meares, Robert O. Washington, and Betty L. Welsh, *Social Work Services in Schools* (Boston: Allyn & Bacon, 1996).

18. Kathleen Kirk Bishop, "Part H of the Individuals with Disabilities Education Act: Analysis and Implications for Social Workers," in Robert Constable, John P. Flynn, and Shirley McDonald, eds., *School Social Work: Practice and Research Perspectives* (Chicago: Lyceum Books, 1996).

19. Paula Allen-Meares, "Elementary and Secondary School Improvement Amendments of 1988 and the Future of Social Services in Schools," *Social Work in Education* 12, no. 4 (July 1990); and National Association of Social Workers, *Expanding School Social Work through Federal Funding* in P.L. 100-297 (Silver Spring, MD: Author, 1989).

20. Paula M. Mintzies, "The Continuing Dilemma: Finding a Place for the Social Work Profession in the Schools," *Social Work in Education* 15, no. 2 (April 1993).

21. Marianne Pennekamp, "Toward School-Linked and School-Based Human Services for Children and Families," *Social Work in Education* 14, no. 2 (April 1992).

22. Jennifer Clancy, "Ecological School Social Work: The Reality and the Vision," *Social Work in Education* 17, no. 1 (January 1995).

23. Leon F. Williams, "The Challenge of Education to Social Work: The Case for Minority Children," *Social Work* 35, no. 3 (May 1990).

24. Calvin L. Streeter and Cynthia Franklin, "Site-Based Management in Public Education: Opportunites and Challenges for School Social Workers," *Social Work in Education* 15, no. 2 (April 1993).

Additional Suggested Readings

Allen-Meares, P. "The New Federal Role in Education and Family Services: Goal Setting without responsibility." *Social Work* 41 (1996): 533–540.

Caple, F.S., R.M. Salcido, and J. diCecco. "Engaging Effectively with Culturally Diverse Families and Children." *Social Work in Education* 17 (1995): 159–170.

Franklin, C., and C.L. Streeter. "School Reform: Linking Public Schools with Human Services." *Social Work* 40 (1995): 773–782.

George R.M., J.V. Voorhis, S. Grant, K. Casey, and M. Robinson. "Special-Education Experiences of Foster Children: An Empirical Study." *Child Welfare* LXXI (1992): 419–437.

Grant, D., and D. Haynes. "A Developmental Framework for Cultural Competence Training with Children." *Social Work in Education* 17 (1995): 171–182

Helper, J.B. "Mainstreaming Children with Disabilities: Have we Improved their Social Environment?" *Social Work in Education* 16 (1994): 143–154.

Knitzer, J. "The Role of Education in Systems of Care." In B.A. Stroul, ed., *Children's Mental Health: Creating Systems of Care in a Changing Society*. Baltimore: Paul Brookes Publishing, 1996, pp. 197–213.

Moody-Maynard, C. "Wraparound Services for At-Risk Youths in Rural Schools." *Social Work in Education* 16 (1994): 187–192.

Pryor, C.B., C. Kent, C. McGunn, and B. LeRoy. "Redesigning Social Work in Inclusive Schools." *Social Work* 41 (1996): 668–676.

Staudt, M., and K.K. Powell. "Serving Children and Adolescents in the School: Can Social Work Meet the Challenge?" *Child and Adolescent Social Work Journal* 13 (1996): 433–446.

Wodarski, J.S., J.S. Kurtz, J.M. Gaudin, Jr., and P.T. Howing. "Maltreatment and the School-Age Child: Major Academic, Socioemotional and Adaptive Outcomes." *Social Work* 35 (1990): 506–513.

8

Social Services in the Health Care Field

GREGORY V. JENSEN,
JAY J. CAYNER,
JAMES A. HALL*

Social workers have been involved in health care systems since 1905, and most of these have worked in hospitals as direct-service providers. As time progressed, social workers have taken on additional roles as policy makers, administrators in health care systems, and program managers. And, at the national level, social workers are serving on review panels for various agencies. Similarly, social workers are obtaining research and service grants as principal investigators or project directors. At the state and local levels, social workers are becoming directors of publicly supported health, mental health, and financial assistance programs. Even as the roles for social workers have broadened significantly, the "core" of social work services has remained remarkably constant.

As this chapter is being written, our health care financing and delivery systems are undergoing massive changes. Health-related costs continue to escalate, while services have been cut, reducing accessibility for many Americans. For example, in 1997 approximately 40 million Americans did not have access to health insurance. Young college graduates, citizens working for employers who do not offer health insurance, and children comprise many of the uninsured. Providing access to health insurance has been particularly problematic due to a lack of public consensus or coherent public health policy. In addition, our country has a combination of public and private health financing that further contributes to a fragmented health care system. The federal government attempted a major reform of the system in 1993; however, not enough public support existed to succeed. Given this lack of public consensus and the failure of the

*The authors wish to thank Julie Spears, Linda Liedke, and Joan Mooney for their assistance with the production of this chapter.

national government to reform health care in the early 1990s, private industry—represented by business and insurance interests—has successfully initiated market-driven reforms designed primarily to reduce the cost of providing health care services.

The purpose of this chapter is to further describe these reforms and identify how social workers have responded to these changes. In the first section, major trends in the American health care system will be identified. The second section will deal more specifically with changes in health care financing. The third section will focus on critical and contemporary social work health care practice issues, including roles that social workers play in health care systems. In the fourth section there is a discussion of future social work opportunities and challenges in health care settings.

TRENDS IN THE AMERICAN HEALTH CARE SYSTEM

The health care system in the United States is not so much a system as it is the outcome of responses to different health needs. The system that has evolved has public and private, charity, not-for-profit, and for-profit traditions. The system of health care has evolved to a large extent as a result of larger social, technological, and environmental trends. These trends directly affect the health care system and social work practice. As this chapter is being written, the following trends at various stages of their respective evolutions are affecting the health care delivery systems and therefore social work practice.

Trend One

People are living longer and facing health problems associated with old age and/or chronic illness. Elderly persons and people with chronic diseases represent an increasing percentage of patients served by the health delivery system.[1] The success of emergency medical services and trauma interventions, medical technology, and public health efforts have all contributed favorably to longer life spans. Individuals with severe trauma and chronic illness require ongoing medical interventions. Chronic conditions such as these account for about three-fourths of the U.S. health care expenditures.[2] Chronic illnesses are extremely complex and have, in addition to the physical issues associated with illness, a variety of psychosocial issues such as dependence or disfigurement. The systems of caring for individuals with chronic conditions are equally complex. For example, payments for health services for individuals with chronic illnesses vary widely in coverage and often place the individual and family at risk. However, patients and families must deal with these systems as well as the day-to-day physical issues associated with their illnesses.

Trend Two

Health care delivery is moving out of its traditional hospital base to community or less restrictive settings. The health care delivery system has evolved over time in response to changes in family composition and size, medical technology, and methods of paying for health services. Hospitals evolved as basic suppliers essentially because they were viewed as the most economical way to provide health care. Secondary to increases in capacity for the health care and medical technology systems, this industry has developed alternatives to acute care settings, such as subacute or home health care, which are now the least expensive options available.[3]

Trend Three

The health care system is being influenced by the marketplace. For years, a debate has occurred in the United States as to whether health care is a right or a privilege. Since the defeat in 1993 of government-sponsored health care reform, the private sector or marketplace economy has driven the changes in health care. Reform efforts in the early 1990s were related to the growing number of persons who had no health insurance and to the rapidly rising cost of providing health care. In response, managed care organizations have proliferated. Because of their control of dollars to pay for or purchase health services, these organizations have affected the place at which care is provided and have made determinations regarding what care is provided. Health promotion and illness prevention have been complementary strategies in the marketplace to controlling costs.

Trend Four

Individuals expect to receive more information and to be more involved in making medical decisions. This trend directly results from an increasing awareness of patients' rights, advances in medical technology, and emphasis on illness prevention and wellness. The complexity of medical decision making includes determinations of best providers—for example, what have historically been considered "alternative treatments" such as acupuncture or chiropractic services for pain. Medical decision making also includes issues such as providing or withholding treatment, organ donations, and the application of innovative medical procedures or invasive/risky surgery. The type of objective information needed by individuals and families to be involved in medical decision making is different from the kind of information that has historically been available to individuals in the traditional physician/hospital–patient relationship.

All of these trends significantly impact social work practice, education, and research. The emergence of longer life spans, chronic illnesses, technology, marketplace reforms, and illness prevention places greater stresses on individuals, families, health care systems, and professionals. As a result of these issues, the demand for psychosocial interventions will increase.[4]

HEALTH CARE FINANCING

The delivery and financing of health care services in the United States have evolved into a complex system, combining public and private enterprises. Fueled by rapid increases in health care spending, both the public and private sectors have sought methods to control these costs. For example, in 1929, the first year such data were available, medical expenditures totaled 3.5 percent of the gross domestic product (GDP). In 1950, health expenditures amounted to 4.5 percent of the GDP, and by the year 2000, medical expenditures are projected to consume 18.1 percent of the GDP.[5] With the advent of rapidly growing health insurance in the 1950s and the establishment of Medicare and Medicaid in the mid-1960s, individuals assumed little responsibility for paying for their health care. This "decoupling" of financing from the delivery system encouraged individuals to seek health care services without being concerned about the costs. Simultaneously, legislation was enacted (for example, the Hill-Burton Act), encouraging hospitals to build expansive facilities. The health care cottage industry grew rapidly and has become one of the largest businesses in the United States. Other factors also contribute to this growth, including population demographics, medical treatment advances, and an increased utilization of services. The rapid expansion of managed care in the 1990s is considered our best opportunity to control and reduce the rapid expansion of health care costs.

Private Health Insurance

The post–World War II development of fringe benefits obtained through collective bargaining and the growth of union/management funds fueled the tremendous growth of voluntary health insurance. This prepayment provision resulted in the lack of cost consciousness by patients who paid little or nothing at the time service was rendered. In 1940, only 9 percent of the population had hospital insurance coverage. By 1992, approximately 212.3 million Americans (84.6 percent of the civilian noninstitutional population) were covered by health insurance.

Private health insurance was initiated and has remained primarily employer based. That is, individuals receive health insurance through their employers as a "fringe benefit." Historically, employers paid 100 percent of the premium for their employees, Increasingly, however, employees are being asked to share the cost of premiums, as well as an increased amount of the actual provision of health care through co-payments and deductibles for health care services used. In addition, employers have tended to eliminate access to benefits, particularly for part-time employees, resulting in an increased number of Americans without access to health insurance, approximately 40 million in 1996.[6]

The private health insurance industry is "for profit" and seeks to provide coverage for healthy working Americans. People with disabling conditions, catastrophic illness, or the elderly are often ineligible for private health insurance. Publicly funded programs were initiated to respond to Americans who could not receive or access private health insurance.

Public Health Insurance

The government has played a significant role in improving access to health care for the most vulnerable U.S. citizens. Following the Great Depression of the 1930s and World War II, Congress enacted several key pieces of legislation that established the government as a major force in the health care industry:

- *The National Institutes of Health* (1887): The federal government established its investment in biomedical research by creating the National

Institutes of Health (NIH). The NIH began as the one-room Laboratory of Hygiene in 1887, with a budget of $300. By the early 1970s, research funding reached the $2 billion level, more than a tenfold increase from the expenditures in the early 1950s, and it continued to rise to over $12.7 billion in 1997.

- *Hill-Burton Act* (1946): The virtual standstill in civilian construction during the war years resulted in an acute deficit in hospital beds—particularly in underpopulated areas. In response, Congress enacted the Hill-Burton legislation, which dedicated substantial sums of federal dollars, matched by state and local funds, into hospital construction. As facilities proliferated, many communities constructed community hospitals, and the accessibility of health services expanded dramatically. For example, in one midwestern state, no one lived more than 25 miles from a community hospital. A tremendous burden was created for the health care system in that we are now supporting substantial excess capacity of hospital beds and related facilities.

- *Health Professions Educational Assistance Act* (1963): As the expansion in the physical capacity of our health system accelerated, it became increasingly apparent that we did not have enough physicians and health professionals to staff the proliferating facilities. Congress quickly responded with an enactment of the Health Profession's Education Assistance Act in 1963. This public subsidy for health science education provided the impetus for a significant expansion in the enrollment of our nation's health colleges.

- *Medicare and Medicaid* (1965): These programs were established with two main goals: (1) to reduce the worry of the elderly as to how they were going to pay for medical expenses, and (2) to provided medical care to the poor. Meeting these goals has proven difficult. Today, Medicaid pays only 40 percent of the medical care expenses for the poor. Coverage has eroded as states—who now share responsibility for the program with the federal government—have restricted eligibility requirements in order to keep Medicaid spending to reasonable amounts. As a result of this federal legislation and private-sector funding, the health care delivery system has evolved into a disjointed patchwork of services and programs. The costs continue to rise, while millions of Americans have no access to health care. Those who do have health care find themselves in an increasingly complicated system of co-payments, second opinions, preauthorization, and a myriad of other laborious and burdensome requirements. All these factors have led to a delivery system that is viewed by many constituents as ineffective in providing comprehensive coordinated care.[7]

Financing Structural Changes

The 1970s and 1980s ushered in an era in which politicians and private industry leaders became very concerned about the rapid increase in the costs of providing health care. Not uncommon were 20- to 30-percent increases in the costs of providing health care per year. Reducing utilization by providing incentives to health care providers and consumers was viewed as the primary means to control costs. In 1983, the Perspective Payment System (PPS) was initiated. Instead of providers being paid the cost they incur for their services, they were paid a fixed rate per procedure.

For example, a patient requiring hip replacement historically may have stayed in the hospital fourteen days, and the hospital would charge Medicare for fourteen days' worth of hospitalization. Under PPS, the hospital might receive $8,000 for the hip replacement. If the hospital could discharge the patient sooner, any of the remaining $8,000 could be retained, even if it did not cost that to provide the service. If the patient remained in the hospital beyond the time at which the hospital extended the $8,000, the hospital could not charge the patient or Medicare for the difference. This change in financing began the era of aggressive discharge planning, as hospitals had tremendous incentives to release patients as soon as possible.

Although the PPS did reduce the rate of increase in health care expenditures, both public and private decision makers were dissatisfied with the reduction in health care costs. In 1993, President Clinton attempted a major health care reform initiative through the public sector. This initiative failed, allowing the private sector to become the dominant force for reforming the financing of the health care system. Private industry endorsed "managed care" as the primary method for health care financing.

Managed care.   The term "managed care" encompasses a range of health care financing and delivery alternatives to traditional fee-for-service medicine. Under managed care, the financing and delivery of health care are integrated through contractual relationships among purchasers, insurers, and providers. Common features of such systems often include circumscribed care to a specific patient population, care delivered by a panel of providers, limitations on benefits to enrollees, and prior authorization requirements. These features are intended to limit and reduce access to health care to ensure that all health care provided is medically necessary.

"Capitated contracts" are also becoming increasingly popular. Under capitation, the health care provider receives a fixed amount of money per member per month, regardless of the extent to which any individual uses services or the costs of providing those services. Providing health care to populations instead of individuals requires providers to become more experienced in actuarial science and more diverse in the types of services they provide. Hospital consolidations and mergers are commonplace. Providers must be able to offer a "continuum of care" because they are at financial risk if too many patients require the most expensive type of health services.[8]

Future financing considerations.   As a society, we have yet to deal with the most vulnerable Americans who do not have access to health insurance. These often include individuals who are temporarily unemployed, people working part-time jobs or who are self-employed, or college graduates just entering the employment market. Access to adequate health insurance for these 40 million Americans must be a priority. With the explosion of managed care, many Americans are beginning to question the underlying philosophy of managing costs by reducing access to health care services. Health care providers and consumers are beginning to advocate for minimum standards to be required of managed care companies. Last, the United States remains the only industrialized country in the world without a comprehensive integrated health care financing and delivery system. This lack of a comprehensive plan fuels individual dissatisfaction with the health care system, which is often viewed as disjointed, fragmented, and difficult to navigate.[9]

SOCIAL WORK PRACTICE IN HEALTH CARE SETTINGS

Over the past 20 years, the field of *medical social work* has grown enormously and developed into a much broader field known as *health and social work* or *social work in health care*. In this section, we review (1) the history of social work in health care settings, (2) social work roles and responsibilities in health care settings, and (3) a case example that portrays the breadth of social work practice in a large hospital.

History of Social Work in Health Care Settings

According to Nacman, the history of social work in health care provides a strong foundation for the current concerns, roles, and issues faced by the profession today.[10] At one point early in the development of the country, the sick were not treated in hospitals but were provided care in their homes—to the best level that could be provided by family and "experts" who were considered the local healers. Before the hospital was the almshouse, in which a variety of persons received care—including those who were physically or mentally ill, criminals, and the poor. This variety of patient types is a far cry from the current system, in which each of these groups is "treated" in different programs. Imagine the challenge for the staffs of those early almshouses as they sorted through the problems of their patients, while they were being exposed to every contagious disease imaginable!

The first almshouse was established in Philadelphia in 1713 by William Penn; the second, Bellevue Hospital, was established in New York in 1736 for the "poor aged, insane, and disreputable." In New Orleans, an almshouse was established in 1737, but it was not until 1815 that a separate unit for children was organized.

Then, also according to Nacman, the physically ill began to be treated in separate facilities from other types of patients around the middle of the eighteenth century. In order to treat these sick patients, between 1751 and 1840, several voluntary hospitals were constructed, which usually started with donations from private benefactors and were a result of middle-class, urban Americans' desire for better health care. Nacman notes that New York Hospital, established as the Revolutionary War Hospital, was the first treatment center to train medical personnel as well as care for wounded. Then, in 1821, Massachusetts General Hospital was instituted, with the majority of funding from state rather than private donations.

In the mid-1800s, some hospitals began to specialize while others remained as almshouses. Although some efforts were made to treat the poor in better conditions during these times, the almshouse approach remained the standard for care. The 1800s ended with efforts aimed at separating the deserving (i.e., those who could pay or whose problems were not considered their fault) from the undeserving (i.e., the poor). The impact of industrialization and urbanization forced the country to look at health care in new and different ways. The medical field became professionalized and more scientifically based.

Social work practice in health care settings developed in the early 1900s, when it became increasingly evident that a relationship existed between a person's health status and environmental conditions (physical and social). In 1907, at Massachusetts General Hospital, Richard Cabot, M.D., hired Ida Cannon, marking the first time a social worker was employed in a health care setting. Cannon observed that a "social worker's function lay in an enlarged understanding of any psychic or social conditions which may be at the root of the patient's distress of mind and body"; this orientation of a hospital social worker remains as valid today as in the early 1900s.

Also at this time, a social work program was established at Johns Hopkins Hospital in Baltimore, with Helen B. Pendleton hired to fill this role. Unfortunately, the role of the social worker had not been very well defined, and she was not allowed on the ward to work with patients. Her replacement also left after a short tenure as a result of the poor working conditions, which were even worse than in the hospital itself. Eventually, the social worker was put in charge of medical records, but she still had her office in a storage area used for various medical supplies.

As the social work profession became better organized, standards for practice in hospitals and for curriculum in schools of social work helped to address many of the problems that had evolved in this transition from almshouses to modern hospitals. In the early 1900s, social workers assisted in efforts to combat tuberculosis, polio, syphilis, hazardous work conditions, and poor treatment of unmarried pregnant women. The Social Security Act of 1935 caused the shift from minimal care of the infirm to public acceptance of responsibility for caring for the ill, disabled, and poor. The reader is referred to Nacman and other readings at the end of the chapter for a more detailed review of the recent history of the social work profession, especially in health care settings. The key point to note from this brief review is that hospitals (the primary mode of health care delivery at this time) were born out of the need to care for the poor and sick—the same need that helped produce the social work profession.

Social Work Roles in Health Care Settings

Several changes, however, have created new and different opportunities and demands for social work services: (1) patient characteristics and needs, (2) technology, (3) lifestyles, (4) popular beliefs, (5) social and health policies, (6) national and local economies, (7) health care costs, and (8) regulation.[11] Today, more than ever, chronic illnesses and their consequences present patients, families, and communities with challenges to which social work practitioners are uniquely qualified to respond. Technological advances continue to extend life and the delivery of health care into home and community settings.

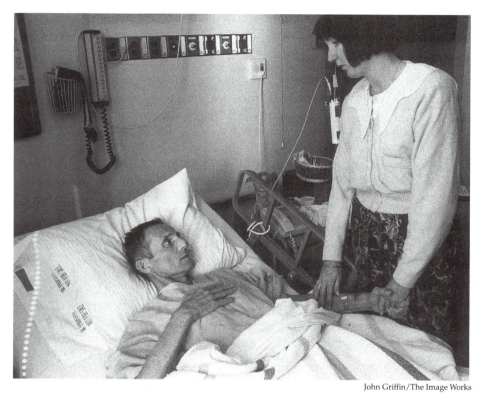

John Griffin/The Image Works

Social workers play an important role in health care systems. A social worker talks with an AIDS victim blinded by the disease at a Veterans Administration hospital in New York City.

Social workers trained in systems theory are able to conceptualize and assist patients and families as they move from one health care resource to another while evaluating the impact the patient's environment has on his or her health care status. Similarly, social workers assist the health care institution by providing internal leadership to meet institutional goals, comply with regulatory agencies, and develop programs and protocols that respond to social and health care legislation. The activities of social workers in health care settings generally include the following three roles: (1) clinical practice activities, (2) interdisciplinary activities, and (3) teaching and research.

Clinical practice activities.   Social workers provide services to patients and their families to enable them to make the best use of medical care within the hospital, home, or community settings. Sometimes referred to as "direct practice," this type of face-to-face work with patients is also referred to as "clinical practice."[12] Specific services often include:

- *Psychosocial Evaluation and Assessment:* Social workers identify demographic, referral, and other information, and a patient's or family's problems and resources that influence the patient's or family's ability to fully utilize medical interventions. All social work interventions are established following a comprehensive assessment.

- *Psychosocial Interventions:* Social workers provide individual, marital, family, and group counseling directed toward enhancing cognitive, emotional, interpersonal, and/or social functioning. This counseling is often aimed at increasing the patient's and family's understanding of the illness and treatment and the impact it has on their lives. Interventions are often aimed at helping them adjust to this illness, disability, or hospitalization so that maximum physical, psychological, and social potential can be reached.
- *Case Management, Discharge Planning, Preadmission Screening, and Outpatient Continuity of Care:* Case management is the clinical coordination of care for high-risk, complex, and/or chronically ill patients. Discharge planning services are provided to patients returning to their homes with in-home services or equipment needed, or to patients requiring placement in a long-term care facility.
- *Facilitating Services, Information and Referral, Financial Counseling:* These types of services are provided to patients and families to assist them with very concrete needs. Assistance with meals, transportation, lodging, referrals for categorical assistance, and emergency financial assistance are services social workers often provide.
- *Protective Services:* Social workers provide services to victims of suspected child abuse, dependent adult abuse, spouse abuse, and domestic violence.
- *Other Specialized Services:* Social workers often provide or coordinate the provision of specialized services, such as interpreter services, teaching and training activities, patient education, coordinating community-based programming, facilitating groups, and social/health policy advocacy.

Obviously, patients/families in health settings will not need interventions in all these areas, so the social worker will use the information gathered during the assessment to develop a plan for service delivery.

Vignette #1

Mrs. Jones, 36-year-old mother of two, was admitted to the hospital following a severe motor vehicle accident. She sustained a spinal cord injury, resulting in paralysis of her legs, and a head injury, resulting in cognitive deficits.

The social worker conducted a thorough psychosocial assessment identifying Mrs. Jones's social resources (i.e., availability of friends, resources through employer, etc.), financial resources (i.e., insurance coverage for inpatient and rehabilitation care, eligibility for Social Security Disability, family income, etc.), and family resources (i.e., husband's/children's understanding of and response to Mrs. Jones's condition, availability of extended family members, etc.). In addition, the social worker further assessed Mrs. Jones's medical status and prognosis according to her physician/nurse/physical therapist/occupational therapist/other team members.

Following this assessment, the social worker decided on the following interventions:

- *Adaptation to Injury Counseling:* Mrs. Jones and her family members need an opportunity to talk about what had happened to her and how these changes will affect her ability to function and changes in the family members' roles.
- *Discharge Planning:* The social worker immediately begins to anticipate Mrs. Jones's health care needs at the time of discharge. The social worker begins contacting prospective rehabilitation centers, attempting to identify a facility of Mrs. Jones's choice that can provide her rehab services.
- *Financial Counseling:* The social worker arranges to have Mrs. Jones's husband apply for Social Security Disability and other possible entitlement programs.
- *Interdisciplinary Team Leadership:* The social worker presents Mrs. Jones's case to the health care team, informing them of her interventions and making recommendations to assist other team members in their treatment of Mrs. Jones's psychosocial condition.

Interdisciplinary leadership.   Providing quality health care requires the skills and talents of many professionals comprising interdisciplinary teams.[13] Interdisciplinary teams usually include primary care physicians, nurses, social workers, nutritionists, psychologists, recreational therapists, occupational therapists, physical therapists, specialty physicians, and others.[14] Social workers, trained in group work practice, often provide organizational and problem-solving leadership to interdisciplinary teams. Specific services include:

- *Patient Care Conferences:* Social workers often plan and lead patient care conferences to assure that the patient and family fully understand the patient's health condition and participate in planning interventions.
- Program Development Teams: Social workers identify gaps in services for specific patient populations and develop programs and services to respond to identified needs (for example, support groups for cancer patients).
- *Institutional Program Development:* As health systems move their services and programs into the communities, social workers lead teams with multiple agency representatives to develop coalitions and partnerships for new programs.
- *Development of Social Health Policy:* Social workers often see the results of failed social health policy in their clinical practice. Using this information to influence the creation and revision of social health policy assures that policy and legislation respond to the psychosocial conditions confronted by patients and families.

Because of their training, social workers are uniquely positioned within the interdisciplinary team to provide leadership, as they routinely interact across boundaries in the hospital and the community.

Vignette #2

Following Mrs. Jones's patient care conference (see Vignette #1), the social worker determines that the Jones family would benefit from educational materials designed for family members, including children. The social worker has determined over the past six months that she has seen several families who would benefit from similar information pertaining to the effect head injury and spinal cord injury have on family members. The social worker presents this issue to the interdisciplinary team and agrees to chair a task force designed to develop these materials. The task force develops these materials and the social worker takes them to the State Head Injury Association and arranges to have them replicated for use throughout the state. The results benefit Mrs. Jones's family, patients seen at the social worker's hospital, and facilities/patients throughout the state. The social worker and the social work profession are seen as providing leadership on this issue, resulting in better understanding of the role social workers can play in health care settings.

Teaching and research.   Social workers practicing in health care settings have a unique opportunity to participate in multiple interdisciplinary training programs designed to equip students with the knowledge specific to their clinical practice. Similarly, social workers routinely act as practicum instructors and provide intensive and relevant training to the next generation of health care social work practitioners. The practicum also increases the capacity for service agencies to provide innovative services that otherwise would not be possible without extra-agency staff.[15]

Social work practitioners and students have exposure to multiple opportunities that combine direct practice and research. Practice-based research not only advances the social work knowledge base but also improves clinical skills. Until recently, social workers in health care had done a limited amount of practice research for reasons ranging from comfort level with research knowledge and skills to lacking the proper time and resources to carry out quality research.[16] Furthermore, dramatic changes in the hospital and health care fields have, in turn, produced growth in the types and scope of services provided by social workers in hospital environments, which now need to be evaluated.[17]

In recent years, many practitioners have conducted research in a health care setting. Several institutions have begun to actively integrate practice-based research into the health care setting through Social Work Service Departments.[18] In one study, the special role of social workers in rural areas impacted by hospital closings was studied through survey means.[19] In several other studies, social work interventions with AIDS patients were discussed and evaluated.[20] Other social workers have studied the psychosocial nature of cancer,[21] homeless women and children,[22] caregivers of the elderly,[23] drug use during pregnancy,[24] and hospice patients.[25]

In addition to research with practice interventions in structured projects, health care social workers also have integrated empirical principles and techniques into their practice settings.[26] Using the research literature as a guide for practice, social workers select assessment and intervention techniques that have been shown to be effective while rejecting other techniques that have not shown positive results. Further, social workers also can use standardized and validated assessment instruments to evaluate the effectiveness of their interventions over time. By implementing empirical practice techniques, social workers are prepared for the conduct of larger research studies in their settings, either as primary investigators or as collaborators with other disciplines.

Vignette #3

Debra, the social worker working with Mrs. Jones in Vignettes #1 and #2, is increasingly pressed for time. Debra is wondering if patients and families could be taught relevant information pertaining to head and spinal cord injuries in groups as effectively as individually. If the group intervention is effective, Debra could save a great deal of time. Debra consults with the faculty at the local school of social work and determines that a student in the advanced research program is interested in assisting in evaluating this intervention. A partnership between the school of social work, the student, and Debra ensues; and they develop a research project to evaluate group interventions for patient education. The outcome yields positive results. Not only is the group intervention just as effective but patients and family members report they like the opportunity to discuss these issues with other families dealing with the same types of challenges.

SOCIAL WORK IN HEALTH CARE: FUTURE OPPORTUNITIES AND CHALLENGES

The emerging health care industry comprises multiple health care providers (hospitals, physicians' practices, nursing homes, etc.) merging their resources into a "health system" capable of providing a full "continuum of care" (home health, hospital, nursing home care, etc.) to patients. Payors (insurance companies, businesses, etc.) are also joining these systems in order to influence their decisions and share financial risk. These "health systems" must effectively provide services and manage resources for entire patient populations. This requires health systems to increase their capacity to provide an array of health services (e.g., prevention, primary care, specialty care, chronic care, etc.) to individuals in multiple settings (home, hospital, or other health settings). Health systems require leaders who can work across boundaries, effectively manage interdisciplinary resources, solve recurring patient care and institutional problems, develop needed services, and provide high-quality patient-focused psychosocial services to patients and families. On can readily see how social workers thrive in this health care environment. Social workers are confronted with many opportunities and challenges in the future environment. These include:

- *Delivery System Development:* Health care systems are increasingly expected to provide "continuum of care" services to patients and families in the home, community, and institutional settings. It is expected that patients will move between and among service components, experiencing "seamless care" and being freed from additional encumbrances of multiple registrations, screenings, assessments, and benefit authorizations. However, most health systems do not currently possess this type of a "continuum of care." Social workers can provide leadership to their organizations in developing these services.

- *Case Management:* Patients who have complex or chronic health conditions benefit from case management designed to more intensely evaluate, plan and monitor, and individualize a treatment plan. A case manager follows the patient throughout the continuum to ensure that necessary services are provided and monitors outcome in terms of health status, utilization of service, and patient/family satisfaction. Social workers have a long professional tradition of providing this type of service.
- *Interdisciplinary Leadership:* Getting people with diverse opinions to work together is a fundamental yet critical function within a health care system. Social workers trained in systems theory and group work practice often assume leadership positions to facilitate interdisciplinary problem solving and program development.
- *Outcomes-Oriented Practice:* All stakeholders in the health care industry are interested in the outcomes of various interventions. The goal is to provide the right service in the right amount at the right time to the right patient. This requires discipline on the part of all practitioners to identify and assess the outcomes of their interventions. Those unable to directly link productive outcomes to interventions will be viewed as a service not adding value, and as a result, will be less likely to remain a viable service provider.
- *Leadership:* The willingness and ability to lead teams and consciously use one's skills to assist an organization to attain its goals may be the most singularly important opportunity for social workers. Institutions continually scan for leaders regardless of their professional affiliations. Social workers need to continually assess their organizations' goals and provide leadership toward the attainment of those goals—which might result in social workers managing functions not traditionally within the scope of social work services. Social workers, however, need to be wiling and able to assume these additional responsibilities. By doing so, they can infuse the social work values into other programs and services.

SUMMARY AND CONCLUSIONS

The health care industry is changing dramatically, both in how it is financed as well as the way health care is delivered. The evolving delivery system will hopefully be more integrated and coordinated, thereby reducing fragmentation of services. Managed care is being viewed as the primary vehicle by which to reduce costs while ensuring adequate care is provided. Ultimately, the success of these initiatives will be evaluated by our children. Nevertheless, social workers remain a valued member of the interdisciplinary team, often presented with new opportunities to provide leadership in areas they had not previously addressed.

The social work role has evolved from that of a direct-patient-care advocate during the tenure of Ida Cannon in the early 1900s to a professional who provides not only direct patient care but develops needed programs and services and provides leadership within the organization. Social workers are trained to work with groups, evaluate systems, and consciously use their own skills to improve the conditions for their clients, their organizations, and their communities. To be effective, social work practitioners must focus on both micro-level issues (i.e., direct-patient-care responsibilities) and macro-level issues (i.e., institutional problem solving and interdisciplinary leadership). By doing so, social workers will be considered critical and necessary providers within their health systems.

Notes

1. U.S. Department of Health & Human Services, *Healthy People 2000,* National Promotion and Disease Prevention Objectives (Washington, DC: Government Printing Office, 1994).
2. Remarks of the AMA Executive Vice President. *Journal of the American Medical Association* 275, no. 10 (1996): 802–803.
3. "Competing in the Maturing Health Care Marketplace: Strategies for Academic Medical Centers." University Hospital Consortium, University of Iowa Hospitals and Clinics, 1993.
4. C.V. Browne, M. Smith, P.L. Ewalt, "Advancing Social Work Practice in Health Care Settings: A Collaborative Partnership for Continuing Education," *Health and Social Work* 21, no. 4 (1996): 267–276.
5. S.T. Burner, D.R. Waldo, and D.R. McKusick, "National Health Expenditures Projections Through 2030," *Health Care Financing Review* 14, no. 1 (1992): 1–29.
6. "Health Care Access and Coverage Initiative," American Hospital Association, 1996. For more information, contact: Liberty Place, Suite 700, 325 7th St. NW, Washington, DC 20004-2802.
7. "Eye on Patients: A Report from the American Hospital Association and The Picker Institute," 1996. For more information, contact: Liberty Place, Suite 700, 325 7th St. NW, Washington, DC 20004-2802.
8. W.J. Simmons and L. Goforth, "The Impact of Managed Care on Cancer Care: Review and Recommendations," *Cancer Practice* 5, no. 2 (1997): 111–117.
9. "Eye on Patients: A Report from the American Hospital Association and The Picker Institute," 1996.
10. M. Nacman, "Social Work in Health Settings: A Historical Review," *Social Work in Health Care* 2, no. 4 (1977): 407–418.
11. See S.S. Bailis, "A Case for Generic Social Work in Health Settings," *Social Work* 30 (1985): 209–212; A.S. Bergman, N. Contro, and N. Zivet, "Clinical Social Work in a Medical Setting," *Social Work in Health Care* 9 (1984): 1–12; A.B. Hatfield, "What Families Want from Family Therapists," in W.R. McFarlane, ed., *Family Therapy in Schizophrenia* (New York: Guilford Press, 1983); H. Rehr, "Health Care and Social Work Services: Present Concerns and Future Directions," *Social Work in Health Care* 10 (1984): 71–83; and K.M. Shevlin, "Why a Social Service Department in a Hospital?" in L. Hubschman, ed., *Hospital Social Work Practice* (New York: Praeger Publishers, 1983).
12. J. Laird, "Revisioning Social Work Education: A Social Constructionist Approach," *Journal of Teaching in Social Work* 8, nos. 1–2 (1993): 1–10.

13. B. Rusnack, "Planned Change: Interdisciplinary Education in Health Care," *Journal of Education for Social Work* 13, no. 10 (1977): 104–111.

14. See R. Fuller and A. Petch, "Does Area Team Organization Make a Difference?" *The British Journal of Social Work* 21, no. 5 (1991): 471–489.

15. C.A. Rapp, R. Chamberlain, and E. Freeman, "Practicum: New Opportunities for Training, Research and Service Delivery," *Journal of Teaching and Social Work* 3, no. 1 (1989): 3–16.

16. N.L. Sidell, P.J. Adams, L.L. Barnhart, N.J. Bowman, V.D. Fitzpatrick, M.L. Fulk, L.M. Hallock, and J.M. Metoff, "The Challenge of Practice Based Research: A Group Approach," *Social Work in Health Care* 23, no. 2 (1996): 99–111.

17. C.S. Berger, J.J. Cayner, G.V. Jensen, T. Mizrahi, A. Scesny, and J. Trachtenbert, "The Changing Scene of Social Work in Hospitals: A Report of a National Study by the Society for Social Work Administrators in Health Care and NASW," *Health and Social Work* 21, no. 3 (1996): 167–177.

18. See the following examples of research in health care settings: A. Gantt, S. Pinsky, B. Rock, and E. Rosenberg, "Practice and Research: An Integrative Approach," *Journal of Teaching in Social Work* 4, no. 1 (1990): 129–143; J.A. Hall, G.V. Jensen, M.A. Fortney, J. Sutter, J. Locher, and J.J. Cayner, "Education of Staff and Students in Health Care Settings: Integrating Practice and Research," *Social Work in Health Care* 24, nos. 1–2 (1996): 93–113; B.D. Rock, M. Goldstein, M. Harris, P. Kaminsky, E. Quitkin, C. Auerback, and N. Beckerman, "Research Changes in a Health Delivery System: A Biopsychosocial Approach to Predicting Resource Utilization of Hospital Care in the Frail Elderly," *Social Work in Health Care* 22, no. 3 (1996): 21–37; and N.L. Sidell, P.J. Adams, L.L. Barnhart, N.J. Bowman, V.D. Fitzpatrick, M.L. Fulk, L.M. Hallock, and J.M. Metoff, "The Challenge of Practice Based Research: A Group Approach," *Social Work in Health Care* 23, no. 2 (1996): 99–111.

19. R.E. Doelker and B.C. Bedics, "Impact of Rural Hospital Closings on the Community," *Social Work* 34 no. 6 (1989): 541–543.

20. See the following for examples of studies with AIDS patients: M. Shernoff, "Why Every Social Worker Should be Challenged by AIDS," *Social Work* 35, no. 1 (1990): 5–8; L.S. Wiener and K. Siegel, "Social Workers' Comfort in Providing Services to AIDS Patients," *Social Work* 35, no. 1 (1990): 18–25; E.J. Ehrlich and P.A. Moore, "Delivery of AIDS Services: The New York State Response," *Social Work* 35, no. 2 (1990): 175–177; D. Stuntzner-Gibson, "Women and HIV Disease: An Emerging Social Crisis," *Social Work* 36, no. 1 (1991): 22–28; K.A. Rounds, M.J. Galinsky, and L.S. Stevens, "Linking People with AIDS in Rural Communities: The Telephone Group," *Social Work* 36, no. 1 (1991): 13–18; F.G. Reamer, "AIDS, Social Work, and the 'Duty to Protect,'" *Social Work* 36, no. 1 (1991): 56–60; K.J. Peterson, "Social Workers' Knowledge about AIDS: A National Survey," *Social Work* 36, no. 1 (1991): 31–37; J.R. McDonell, N. Abell, and J. Miller, "Family Members' Willingness to Care for People with AIDS: A Psychosocial Assessment Model," *Social Work* 36, no. 1 (1991): 43–53; and J. Huggins, N. Elman, C. Baker, R.G. Forrester, and D. Lyter, "Affective and Behavioral Responses of Gay and Bisexual Men to HIV Antibody Testing," *Social Work* 36, no. 1 (1991): 61–66.

21. R.B. Black, "Challenges for Social Work as a Core Profession in Cancer Services," *Social Work in Health Care* 14, no. 1 (1989): 1–13; L. Parsonnet and J. O'Hare, "A Group Orientation Program for Families of Newly Admitted Cancer Patients, "*Social Work* 35, no. 1 (1990): 37–40.

22. A.K. Johnson and L.W. Kreuger, "Toward a Better Understanding of Homeless Women," *Social Work* 34, no. 6 (1989): 537–540.

23. V. Wilson, "The Consequences of Elderly Wives Caring for Disabled Husbands: Implications for Practice," *Social Work* 35, no. 5 (1990): 417–421; and D.J. Monahan,

V.L. Greene, and P.D. Coleman, "Caregiver Support Groups: Factors Affecting Use of Services," *Social Work* 37, no. 3 (1992): 254–260.

24. V.N. Walther, "Emerging Roles of Social Work in Perinatal Services," *Social Work in Health Care* 15, no. 2 (1990): 35–48; and S. Edelstein, V. Kropenske, and J. Howard, "Project T.E.A.M.S.," *Social Work* 35, no. 4 (1990): 313–318.

25. D. Macdonald, "Hospice Social Work: A Search for Identity," *Health and Social Work* 16, no. 4 (1991): 274–280; B. Rusnack, S.M. Schaefer, and D. Moxley, "Hospice: Social Work's Response to a New Form of Social Caring," *Social Work in Health Care* 15, no. 2 (1990): 95–119.

26. Martin Bloom and Joel Fischer, *Evaluating Practice: Guidelines for the Accountable Professional* (Englewood Cliffs, NJ: Prentice-Hall, 1982).

Additional Suggested Readings

Berger, Candyce. *Restructuring and Resizing: Strategies for Social Work and Other Human Services Administrators in Health Care.* Chicago: American Hospital Association, 1992.

Combs-Orme, T. *Social Work Practice in Maternal and Child Health.* New York: Springer Publishing Company, 1990.

Davidson, K.W., and S.S. Clarke. *Social Work in Health Care: A Handbook for Practice.* Binghamton, NY: Haworth Press, Inc., 1990.

Ell, K., and Helen Northern. *Families and Health Care: Psychosocial Practice.* Hawthorne, NY: Aldine de Gruyter, 1990.

Ewalt, Patricia L., E.M. Freeman, Stuart A. Kirk, and Dennis L. Poole, eds. *Social Policy Reform Research and Practice* (especially Part IV–Health and Part V–Mental Health, pp. 345–483). Washington, DC: NASW Press, 1996.

Ginsberg, Leon, and Paul R. Keys, eds. *New Management in Human Services.* 2nd ed. Washington, DC: NASW Press, 1996.

Jackson, V.H., ed. *Managed Care Resource Guide for Social Workers in Agency Settings.* Washington, DC: NASW Press, 1995.

Mailick, Mildred D., and Phyllis Caroff. "Special Issue: Professional Social Work Education and Health Care: Challenges for the Future." *Social Work in Health Care,* 24, nos. 1–2 (1996).

Mullin, Edward J., and Jennifer L. Magnabosco, eds. *Outcomes Measurement in the Human Services.* Washington, DC: NASW Press, 1997.

Poole, Dennis L., ed. *Health and Social Work: A Quarterly Journal.* Washington, DC: NASW Press, 1997.

Schopler, J.H., and Maeda J. Galinsky. *Groups in Health Care Settings.* Binghamton, NY: Haworth Press, Inc., 1990.

Social Work in Health Care: A Quarterly Journal 20, no. 4 (1995). Haworth Press, Inc.

9

Mental Health and Social Work

VERNE R. KELLEY

A view often expressed is that there is a single mental health/mental illness continuum with two opposite poles: mental health at one end and mental illness at the other. In this view there is much that is not revealed: genetic endowment, biological conditions, nutrition, temperament, developmental stages, social support, socially constructed learned behavior, personality traits, cognitive factors, prior experiences, family communication styles, education level, socioeconomic statuses, unemployment, housing, neighborhood, sense of community, race, ethnicity, gender, peer attitudes, family pressures, and other situational stresses that are unique to a particular individual. These influences act simultaneously on a person who may have a greater or lesser array of capabilities, sense of personal competence and empowerment, and other resources to call upon for coping with environmental stresses while attempting to lead an effective life. Actually, almost everyone can become emotionally disturbed at crucial points or crises in life.

EMOTIONAL DISTURBANCE

Because of the numerous influences and patterns involved in emotional disturbances, mental health literature, with good reason, seldom tries to define terms such as "mental disorder." The definitions in the literature typically deal with classifications of types of mental disorders and descriptions of characteristics and traits. As noted in DSM-IV, "no definition adequately specifies precise boundaries for the concept 'mental disorder.'"[1] Concepts of mental illness vary widely, from Szasz, who claims that it is a "myth,"[2] to Torrey, who says it is a "disease of the brain."[3]

Mental Health

Mental health was defined in a 1988 report by National Health and Welfare Canada as "the capacity of the individual, the group, and the environment to interact with one another in ways that promote subjective well-being, the optimal development and use of mental abilities (cognitive, affective, and relational), the achievement of individual goals consistent with justice, and the attainment and preservation of conditions of fundamental equality."[4]

Early attempts to define mental health began with looking at traits exhibited by mental patients and then considering their opposite as being characteristics exemplifying mental health. People with depression felt sad and guilty; therefore, joyous and carefree behavior was a sign of good mental health. Persons with neuroses were anxious and inhibited, so that a "normal" person was gregarious and blithely self-confident. People who were "mentally healthy" seemed incapable of self-sacrifice, which might mean they were having a depression. They did not worry about world problems; to do so could mean that they were being neurotic. Robert White prefers not to use the term "mental health" and instead refers to competence: an "organism's capacity to interact effectively with its environment"[5] and "one's confidence of being able, when necessary, to have desired effects."[6]

In the author's view, White's suggestion leads us to think of competence in certain capabilities, such as:

- coping with problems of your children;
- coping with problems of your parents;
- coping with relationship problems;
- coping with conflicts at work;
- controlling spending;
- controlling use of tobacco, alcohol, and drugs;
- controlling temper;
- managing sexual behavior;
- improving rational thinking;
- improving assertiveness;
- improving racial fairness;
- improving thoughtfulness;
- improving self-understanding;
- expressing feelings constructively.

A person who is feeling confident in his or her competence in such capabilities would probably feel, and be regarded as being, in a good state of "mental health."

Another term, "behavioral health," has entered the lexicon of mental health services. "Behavioral health care" and "mental health care" would appear to have synonymous meanings, yet the behavioral health care term encompasses substance abuse, mental retardation, and developmental disabilities services as well as mental health—reflecting a trend toward integration of health care providers.[7]

Need for Services

Some of the oldest literature cites examples of persons with apparent emotional disturbances. For example, in the Old Testament, Saul, who may have suffered from manic-depressive psychosis, committed suicide.[8] Studies have attempted to estimate the prevalence of present-day emotional disturbance. It is not surprising that findings have varied considerably, because they lack consensus on what is being measured and surveyed. In a 1978 survey, the Mid-town Manhattan Study found that about 75 percent of the people surveyed were considered to have at least some degree of impairment.[9] In a 1979 survey, the Florida Health Study found the prevalence of mental disorder at about 28 percent.[10] A National Institute for Mental Health study released in 1993 by Dr. Darrel Regier and colleagues indicated that about 20 percent of adult Americans had psychiatric disorders, but only about 8 percent were treated.[11] No surveys are yet available concerning the prevalence of mental disorders in children and adolescents. The consistent finding in adults is that the prevalence of emotional disturbance increases with lower socioeconomic status. In another study, more schooling was found to lead to better health in general, controlling for variables of income and intelligence, and a year of schooling contributed about 1 percent to an index of health.[12] This study suggests that the relationship of schooling to mental health is an area deserving research.

MENTAL HEALTH PROGRAMS AND SERVICES

The reaction of Western society to mental health problems is marked by ambivalence: compassion and intolerance. The Old Testament taught social justice in temporal affairs and personal righteousness. Jews and Christians were exhorted to love and care for their families and to have compassion for their neighbors and for strangers.[13] In response to this ideal, mental hospitals were established. The first hospital exclusively for treating people having mental disorders was founded in Jerusalem about A.D. 490.[14] The oldest mental hospital still operating is in Valencia, Spain; it opened in 1409.[15] In the Middle Ages, however, mental illness was linked with witchcraft by two Dominican monks. Many people were tortured and executed as heretics based on the claim that they had freely embraced the devil as their master.[16] This ambivalence has continued to the present day. On the side of compassion, centuries of therapeutic work, research, and advocacy have been devoted to helping people with mental illness and emotional problems. On the negative side, however, neglect, rejection, and skepticism have been simultaneously expressed, a flagrant current example of which is the "dumping" of mental patients out of mental hospitals into cities without adequate preparation or appropriate local services. The streets of most large American cities are now inhabited by numbers of homeless people, many of whom have chronic mental illnesses.

Many ideals have contributed to the development of mental health services. As noted by Rashdall, "Ideals pass into greater historic forces by embodying themselves in institutions."[17] Not only have the ideals of compassion and humane treatment motivated mental health services, the ideals of professionalism (medicine, nursing, psychology, and social work), scientific research, and community care have also become established in mental health facilities. In a later section the roles of social workers in mental health facilities will be discussed.

Mental Hospitals and the First Mental Health Revolution

The first psychiatric hospital in the New World was built in Mexico in 1566. The first general hospital serving people with mental disorders was the Pennsylvania Hospital at Philadelphia, which was founded in 1752.[18] The first mental hospital in America was established at Williamsburg, Virginia, in 1773. The ideals of medical treatment and "moral treatment" were practiced during the colonial period. The Quaker physician, Benjamin Rush, who signed the Declaration of Independence and wrote the first textbook on psychiatry in America, supported the ideal of "moral treatment." The proponents of "moral treatment" held that victims of mental illness were susceptible to morally "right" and humane influences. They taught the use of respect and courtesy with disturbed persons rather than torture and punishment. They established regimens of order and regularity and sought to develop self-respect and responsibility through work and worship. Most of the early mental hospitals did not actually deserve the name of hospital—they were merely places where people with mental illnesses were kept without treatment. Such were the institutions in London: Bethlehem ("Bedlam"), founded in 1247; and in Paris: Bicôtre.[19] The emergence of hospitals with the ideals of treatment and humane care was advanced by Philippe Pinel in 1793 when he released people with mental illnesses from the chains of Bicôtre and Saltpetriére, mental hospitals in Paris, an event often described as the "first mental health revolution." By 1851, "moral treatment" recovery rates were reported as high as 72 percent.[20] Many of the methods of "moral treatment" are still practiced today in concert with other treatments.

Medical treatment of mentally ill persons is an ancient ideal. In the Talmud, insanity was regarded as a disease to be treated by a physician. In the fourth century B.C., Hippocrates described physical causes of "madness" and used diagnostic terms such as "melancholia" and "hysteria."[21] Medical treatment, as we know it now, had not advanced greatly by the mid-nineteenth century; but the ideal of hospital care, rather than jails and almshouses for the mentally ill, was being forcefully advocated by Dorothea Dix of Boston. She pioneered hospital care for the mentally ill in many states. In 1854, she persuaded Congress to enact a bill authorizing grants of public land for use in caring for persons who were mentally ill. President Franklin Pierce vetoed the bill, interpreting the general welfare clause of the U.S. Constitution as reserving such care to the states. This interpretation established a federal policy of nonintervention in social welfare until the various measures of the Great Depression, such as the Social Security Act of 1935.[22] Fighting back from this defeat, Dix took her cause back to the individual states and she won. By the turn of the century, there were 32 state mental hospitals.[23]

The success of state mental hospitals caused them to be overutilized. Early in the twentieth century they started to fill up. Large, overcrowded, and under-

In recent years a great many people have been released from U.S. mental hospitals, with both good and bad results. A retarded adult hugs and clings to his social worker before his release to live in a group residence outside the hospital.

staffed institutions became typical in this "snake pit" era. The average length of stay stretched out to many years, and care was almost entirely custodial. The large facilities had more negative than beneficial effects, and Dorothea Dix's ideal was shattered. While it became clear that new patterns of care were need-ed in local communities, many state mental hospitals were able to improve their methods by using milieu therapy (the ideal that all aspects of the hospital, in-cluding all personnel, should be oriented to the treatment needs of patients), by instituting group methods, and by decentralization of inpatient units according to geographic areas.

Over a period of 28 years, the number of people in residence in mental hospitals in the United States declined nearly 80 percent (from about 558,000 in 1955 to 117,000 in 1983).[24] This is a dramatic decline, but it indicates that there still is a need for state and county mental hospitals. The large decline in hospital-ization is due partially to use of psychotropic drugs and increased community services. Psychiatric medications have played an important role in the commu-nity care of persons having chronic mental illnesses, but medications must be supplemented by community support services—residential and rehabilitation programs.

Hospital-based social work practice has seen dramatic changes caused by the combination of several social policies. Hospital stays based on DRGs (diagnostic related groups) have reduced the length of time a person can remain for inpatient treatment. The number of homeless people is increasing. Mental health services have been cut, the effect of which is that more people with severe and persistent mental illnesses go to emergency rooms. Increasing numbers of working people do not have health and hospital insurance; and the AIDS crisis places additional demands on hospital resources and specialized staff training.

Most mental hospitals also provide outpatient services that can help reduce the number of people who might otherwise need more costly inpatient care. The Veterans Administration, too, operates general hospitals with psychiatric units and also regional hospitals that provide psychiatric services exclusively. In 1985, Veterans Administration psychiatric hospitals provided care in 9.4 percent of all inpatient episodes reported. Public and private general hospitals frequently include psychiatric units and in 1985 provided care in 45 percent of all inpatient episodes.

Dorothea Dix started the voluntary mental health movement and was followed by a recovered patient, Clifford Beers. In 1908, he wrote an influential book, *The Mind That Found Itself,* and a year later he organized the National Committee for Mental Hygiene. He brought in professional and political leaders, and the movement spread. The World Federation for Mental Health (WFMH) was formed in 1948. The WFMH is a mental health coalition of individuals, professionals, and voluntary associations. It is the only nongovernmental organization accredited in consultative status in mental health to all the relevant agencies of the United Nations. Another voluntary advocacy organization is the National Alliance for the Mentally Ill, a national organization with state and local chapters. Its activities include anti-stigma campaigns, support of research on mental illness and advocacy public mental health services.

Sigmund Freud and the Second Mental Health Revolution

The ideal of understanding human motivation and behavior is probably older than the ancient Greek injunction "Know thyself." It was not until the work of Sigmund Freud in the nineteenth and twentieth centuries that systematic knowledge and understanding began to emerge.

Freud studied the connections between the minds of children and the minds of adults, and the associations between images of dreams and perceptions of reality. Freud's work is described as the "second mental health revolution" in attitudes and values regarding mental health. His work has been followed by theorists with different perceptions, such as Carl Rogers and B.F. Skinner, and the quest for understanding and knowledge continues.

Community Mental Health and the Third Mental Health Revolution

Recognizing that the resources of the federal government were needed, the U.S. Congress in 1946 passed the National Mental Health Act. Its purpose was to help states establish community mental health services, and to fund research and the education of mental health professionals. The ideal motivating the community movement was that help could be delivered most effectively in the community or area where troubled people lived, and where relevant concepts could be combined from ecology, epidemiology, anthropology, public health, social systems theory, and community organization.

Mental health authorities were designated in each state to receive and allocate federal funds for the development of community mental health services. In some states the pattern of financing was that federal funds were used as "seed money" to encourage facility development with continuing operational budgets supported by local public funds and patient fees based on a sliding scale of ability to pay. In other states, state appropriations were authorized to match local funds on a continuing basis. Agreements or contracts were signed by local centers with the state for the provision of funds and inpatient and outpatient services. Community mental health centers (CMHCs) operating under these origins are functioning in many states. Social workers make up a substantial portion of the staffs of these centers and they provide services of individual, group, and family psychotherapy; play therapy with children; after-care for former patients of mental hospitals; consultation and education; and administration. The impact of these centers and related services is strong.

In a major new development, Congress in 1955 enacted the Mental Health Study Act, and in 1963 the Mental Retardation Facilities and Community Health Centers Construction Act. These actions set the stage for a "bold new approach" announced by President John F. Kennedy.[25] The Act reconceptualized the federal role in community mental health delivery, providing for the development of comprehensive community mental health centers. The centers were to have a new mission, that is, to reduce dependence on state mental hospitals and to establish facilities in local communities offering a wide range of services, including inpatient, outpatient, partial hospitalization, emergency, consultation, and education services. The ideal that motivated this legislation was that therapeutic care in local communities should replace custodial care in mental hospitals. Key concepts were geographic responsibility, comprehensiveness, continuity, accessibility, responsiveness, community involvement, and prevention. The development of comprehensive CMHCs has been called the third "revolution" in mental health, the creation of integrated facilities where everyone could find skilled help for a wide range of emotional and mental problems regardless of age, gender, race, ethnic disadvantages, color, national origin, diagnosis, or ability to pay. The goal of the program was to establish 1,500 comprehensive CMHCs. By 1981, when the Reagan administration dropped the program, only 754 comprehensive centers had received funding. The roles of social workers in these programs are similar to those noted in CMHCs described above. The community movement was augmented by the enactment of the federal Medicare and Medicaid health care programs for disabled and poor people, which provided funds for the transfer of people from state hospitals to nursing homes and local community facilities.

The community movement was very effective in shifting the proportion of patient-care episodes from inpatient to outpatient services. In 1955, 77.4 percent of all patient services were provided by inpatient facilities, and 22.6 percent were outpatient. In 1979, only 28 percent of patient services occurred in inpatient facilities, while 72 percent were provided on an outpatient basis, almost a complete reversal of the historic reliance on institutional care, and a trend unlikely to be reversed.

The National Institute for Mental Health (NIMH), now called the Substance Abuse and Mental Health Services Administration (SAMHSA), recognized that people having chronic mental illnesses needed much more help in coping with community living. NIMH initiated the Community Support Program, and model programs were established at the Fountain House Psychosocial Rehabilitation Club in New York City and the Program for Assertive Community Treatment (PACT) in Madison, Wisconsin. The services of these programs included case management, social skills training, network building, and resource development. These programs were also highly effective in disseminating information across the United States about their patterns of services. Community support systems were organized to assist people who had major mental illnesses but who could still function in the community if they had the help they needed. Such help is provided by mental health professionals and case managers. A case manager may arrange for unscheduled walk-in appointments with therapists; provide assistance in locating housing, employment, and education; work with families, churches, and volunteer organizations; and engage in advocacy with bureaucracies in helping people qualify for financial assistance and governmental service. These programs were very successful in helping people with chronic mental illnesses to cope with community living and to reduce their utilization of hospital care. Many CMHCs have integrated Community Support Programs into their services and have recognized the value of case management for managed care.

Rural mental health and other human services still lag far behind urban services.[26] The President's Commission on Mental Health, Task Panel on Rural Mental Health, stated that rural areas have unique mental health needs—having higher rates of psychiatric disorders, particularly depression, severe intergenerational conflicts, an acceptance of fatalistic attitudes, and minimal belief that change is possible. Outreach programs to rural elderly are particularly needed.[27]

University Training and Research Facilities

After World War I there began an extensive development of university mental health facilities devoted to research, education, and service. Usually located in major research universities, these programs are typically under the auspices of medical colleges and psychology departments, in conjunction with schools of social work and nursing colleges. Social workers in these facilities are usually employed as university staff, although in some institutions they may have faculty appointments. Roles of social workers usually include research, service, and supervision of graduate practicum students.

Military Social Work

During World War II over 700 social workers participated in the armed services military social work programs. Psychiatric social work was established as a military occupational specialty in 1943, and social workers served with enlisted status in mental hygiene clinics and in psychiatric units of hospitals. Shortly after the end of the war, social workers were commissioned as officers, acquiring the same professional level that had existed for lawyers and physicians. Today, active social work programs are established in the Navy, Air Force, and Army. The programs include drug and alcohol rehabilitation, hospital mental health services, community mental health clinics, and community services for personal and family problems of armed forces personnel.[28]

Private Practice

Private practice of social workers and other mental health professionals has grown in both urban and rural areas. Sometimes social workers are in independent private practice, and sometimes they are employed in a private firm with psychiatrists and psychologists. They may work out of an office or provide services in a psychiatric unit of a community general hospital. The most frequent private practice is part-time, while the social worker is employed full-time in a community facility or agency. The standards of the social work profession are that practitioners in private practice should attain a Master of Social Work (MSW) degree from an educational program certified by the Council on Social Work Education (CSWE) and be certified by the Academy of Certified Social Workers (ACSW). The National Association of Social Workers (NASW) maintains a register of clinical social workers in which many private practitioners are listed. State licensure or registration of social workers is now provided in all states and it is often required for social workers seeking third-party fee payments. Also, the American Board of Examiners (ABE) in Clinical Social Work publishes a directory of Board Certified Diplomates who meet its standards.

Alcoholism and Drug Abuse Services

Alcoholism and drug abuse services are sometimes organized in conjunction with community mental health facilities. Such services often include detoxification, emergency services, individual counseling, group and family therapy, referral to self-help groups, and referral to vocational guidance, occupational rehabilitation, and other needed services. This subject is discussed in greater detail in Chapter 11.

Prevention and the Fourth Mental Health Revolution

Prevention of emotional disorders has been called the fourth and most exciting "revolution" in mental health. It has been a difficult service to establish, and we stand only at the threshold. With regard to the genetic and biological determinants in mental illness, research is sorely needed before prevention can be anticipated. In problems of interpersonal relationships, progress is being made through educational and training approaches. Interpersonal cognitive problem-solving (ICPS) skills, couples' communication, assertiveness, and parent effectiveness training are among the prevention activities in which social workers have made an impact.

Primary prevention is proactive, seeking to build adaptive strengths and coping resources. It is concerned with the total population as well as with specific groups at risk. Its main tools are education and social engineering. It assumes that the best way to ward off maladaptive problems is to equip people with the personal and environmental resources for successful coping. The President's Commission on Mental Health noted that research had supported the efficacy of "[t]hree main areas of primary prevention in mental health: (a) competency training and emphasizing developmental approaches, (b) the impact of social systems on individual development, and (c) the reduction and management of naturally occurring life developmental stresses."[29] While there is considerable support for primary prevention, not enough is being accomplished, partly because there are few linkage institutions that have prevention as their mission and have the collection, integration, evaluation, and dissemination of prevention knowledge in their goals.[30]

Primary prevention of emotional disorders is a time-consuming and complex challenge. It must be approached through a concerted and integrated effort rather than through small research projects and isolated programs. While the costs are substantial, the potential reward is a more effective and healthier next generation.

Helping Disadvantaged Children

Society is discovering that an approach that works is helping poor children in their earliest months and years of life. In the 1960s, the Perry Preschool Project in Ypsilanti, Michigan, began preschool programming to three-year-old children with below-average IQs and from poor homes. Researchers followed 123 of these children until their nineteenth birthdays and found that they did remarkably well. They graduated from high schools, and went on to more education or to jobs at twice the rate of children who did not have preschool education. They also had fewer detentions, teenage pregnancies, and arrests. Early education enhanced the children's sense of control and confidence.[31] "All the more reason," states an editorial in the *New York Times*,[32] "not to wait until a child is 3 or 4 years old. Why not start with prenatal care for frightened mothers, often children themselves? Why not provide classes in basic skills for fathers. An array of such services could save three children at once: The teen-age mother, her baby and the child she is persuaded to defer at least until she has finished school and gained both maturity and job skills." The editorial goes on to state,

> Spend Where It Counts—Americans are generous about social welfare when they know it works, as with Head Start and food stamps.... Why should they react differently to early childhood intervention? Because it is known to work.... Imagine a baby girl born into inner-city poverty today, to a teen-age mother. With an early childhood program, she's more likely to be born healthy; her mother could give her better care; and early schooling would enlarge her self-confidence. In 16 years, she'd probably be starting her last year in high school and have ambitions for the future. Without such a program, she's all too likely to have something else: a baby. And the heavy cycle will start again.

A committee of top corporation executives has recommended:[33]

1. Prenatal and postnatal care for pregnant teenagers and for other high-risk mothers as well as follow-up health care for their infants.
2. Parenthood education programs for both mothers and fathers, including guidance on nutrition.
3. Quality child-care arrangements for poor working parents that stress social development and school readiness.
4. Quality preschool programs for all disadvantaged three- and four-year-olds.

Unless programs such as these are implemented, one wonders how far prevention programs can go, considering the destructive impact that poverty makes on so many children. The poorest segment of the nation's population is children, who are seven times more likely than those over 65 to be poor. Poverty is most likely for those children who live in single-parent families headed by women.[34] While two-thirds of poor children are white, both African-Americans and Hispanics are much more likely to live in poverty: 43 percent of African-American children and 40 percent of Hispanic children are poor.[35] Poor children suffer more frequently from almost every form of childhood deficiency, including infant mortality, malnutrition, recurrent and untreated health problems, psychological and physical stress, child abuse, and learning disabilities. Without early intervention of the kind recommended in the programs mentioned, the volume of these disadvantaged children will continue to grow and create a permanent underclass of people lacking literacy and job skills.

Nontraditional Mental Health Programs

In a variety of nontraditional mental health services, social workers have carried significant responsibilities. Emotional support during disasters is a service that can be provided by CMHCs.[36] Disaster services are organized to help people with the shock of tornados, floods, earthquakes, and other disasters. Psychosocial problems associated with disasters can include (1) initial numbing of the senses, (2) hysteria, (3) intrusive thoughts (nightmares and rumination), and (4) avoidance struggles (grieving, death anxiety, and anger). Mental health professionals can help people work through these feelings and come to "a sense of survivorship and feeling of strength," rather than "psychic numbing."[37]

Telephone and walk-in crisis centers, typically staffed by trained volunteers, offer emergency and short-term assistance for people with a variety of problems: those who are feeling lonely, depressed, or angry, or are seeking referral information. A person who has impulsively swallowed many pills may call a crisis center for help in getting emergency medical care. The staffs of crisis centers often include social workers who may administer the center and organize training for the volunteers.

Women's centers are operated in many parts of the country, providing a variety of services such as support groups, assertiveness training, advocacy, and lobbying. In some areas women's centers have been instrumental in developing programs for rape prevention and support of rape victims. Social workers are often prominent in these programs.

THE ROLE OF SOCIAL WORK IN MENTAL HEALTH

Many schools of social work report that large majorities of their M.S.W. graduates are engaged in the provision of direct services to clients, often in mental health facilities, and in some aspect of family, children, and adolescent services. Most graduates report high satisfaction with their current jobs and their careers.

The usual professions in mental health are social work, psychiatry, psychiatric nursing, and psychology. Members of these professions usually share a commitment: the desire to help people with mental and emotional problems. Social workers, with their commitment to work with and advocate for the poor and vulnerable, often serve as a benevolent and caring arm of a mental health facility. Many engage in social action, working against injustice toward people disadvantaged by poverty, racism, sexism, and membership in sexual minorities. Many social workers also produce new knowledge for the field through scholarship.

Psychiatric social work, which is simply social work practiced in psychiatric and mental health programs or settings, developed from two historical roots: hospitals and child guidance clinics. It began in 1905 at Boston's Massachusetts General Hospital, as well as in Bellevue Hospital and Cornell Clinic in New York City. In 1906, psychiatric social workers were hired by the Manhattan State Hospital in New York City, where they visited patients' families to obtain information on background and life experiences. Later they also performed the function of preparing families and patients for their return home. The principle that treatment of the patient should be performed by a team of peers, including social workers and doctors, was enunciated in 1912 by Dr. Richard L. Cabot, a faculty member of the Harvard Medical School. At the Boston Psychopathic Hospital in 1913, under the leadership of Mary G. Jarrett, psychiatric social work was given its distinctive name.

Another force in the development of psychiatric social work was the child guidance clinic. Based on early work with juvenile delinquents by Dr. William Healy, demonstration child guidance clinics were started in 1922 at Norfolk, Virginia, and St. Louis. In these facilities, the social worker treated the family, and the doctor treated the child who was the patient. Today there is considerable overlapping of these activities. The development of community facilities that are exclusively for child guidance has declined. The current trend is to establish CMHCs that provide a range of services, including those for children.

The term *psychiatric social work* is in decline, and current usage tends to favor *clinical social work.* The NASW publishes a national register of clinical social workers, which has specific professional requirements for listing. Schools of social work now prepare students along generic lines rather than graduating students who are exclusively psychiatric social workers or group workers for example, as was the practice a few decades ago.

Social workers in mental health facilities typically serve on multidisciplinary teams and may provide services of individual, group, and family psychotherapy; consultation; establishing links with community services and groups; advocacy; and administration. In inpatient facilities, social workers are often those in contact with patients and their families to assist them in making plans for patients' return home, and for referral to community services for aftercare. In outpatient facilities, social workers provide a variety of psychotherapeutic services, as well as consultation, education, community organization, and administration. Typically there is much overlapping and diffusion of roles with other members of the professional staff. Social workers serve as case managers and coordinators of community support systems. The role of social workers as administrators of mental health facilities is extensive. Of the 754 comprehensive CMHCs that earlier were federally assisted, more than a third had a social worker as the executive director. This was almost always a person with a master's degree in social work.

Illustration of Clinical Social Work Practice:
*A Hospital-Based Mental Health Group**

A community hospital mental health program developed a specialized group for individuals working to overcome depression. The group leader met each potential group member individually before they joined the group so that the antisickness, antiproblem focus could be explained. The group size of seven to eight members was small enough so that each person had an opportunity to participate in each of the eight weekly sessions. The social worker who served as a facilitator worked in a way that highlighted members' abilities and strengths, and that focused on getting better, overcoming depression, and not talking about problems and illness. This was a new approach for many members, and all of them, including the facilitator, took on the responsibility of talking about solutions, not problems, and how depression tried to rob them of their lives.

In reviewing the group at the last session a member said, "…even though you were all strangers to me and I was afraid at first. As you talked about what it was doing to your lives, I felt right at home." In the third session, the group talked about what had not been stolen from them by depression. Members were able to examine their strengths and skills and were feeling comfortable enough with each other to help each other out on this challenging question for those fighting depression. By the eighth session, as members talked about where they had come over the course of the group, a member commented, "…I thought you were going to teach us to fight depression, but we already know how and we talked about how we are stronger than it is already." Another said, "…this was more like talking than therapy but I sure learned a lot, mostly about myself and how I fight this thing."

Trends and Issues

Changes in society affect the delivery of services. Among such social changes are increased violence in the forms of physical and sexual abuse and other crimes, increased numbers of substance-abusing clients, larger populations of people who are homeless, larger proportions of people who are elderly, and economic trends

*Case illustration by Patrick Clifford, MSW, CSW, Mental Health Program, York County Hospital, Newmarket, Ontario, Canada.

Hazel Hankin

Psychiatric social worker helps retarded men to build shelves in an apartment shared by them. This is an example of psychotherapeutic services in outpatient facilities.

that influence the sources and amounts of agency budgets, leading to cuts in funding and the decimation of public and private services in some jurisdictions. In-depth work and long-term clinical treatment are usually beyond the resources of publicly supported agencies and are increasingly limited to those persons who can pay for service. Some current trends and issues are (1) the self-help movement, (2) a balance between prevention and treatment, (3) centralization of authority, (4) private contracting, (5) accountability, (6) diagnostic labeling, (7) patients' civil rights, (8) deinstitutionalization, and (9) managed care.

Self-help movements have grown in Western Europe and the United States. Conceptually, the self-help movement appears to lie between professional mental health services and natural helper networks. Natural helpers are people who are not mental health professionals but who, by virtue of their occupation or leadership roles, are sought out by those wanting help.[38] Self-help groups allow troubled people to contact others who are like themselves. There are many kinds of self-help groups—for example, survivors of suicide or families who have had a member suicide, bereaved parents who have had children die, and former inpatients of mental hospitals. Mental health professionals can be facilitative to self-help groups by providing them with consultation and referrals.

A balance is needed between prevention efforts and treatment. In most mental health facilities, prevention has received slight attention in program planning and budgeting. There is no doubt that mental health facilities must try to meet current demands, yet they need to look ahead and invest some of their funds for future generations. For example, what can a mental health facility do to aid in the development of curricula for primary grade children to teach them some concepts of family functioning and competent living?

Centralization of authority can be detrimental to the exercise of professional judgment—for example, restrictions on the number of treatment interviews allowed for clients. Yet there are broad substantive issues that are the appropriate concern of a central authority, for example, a state governing body that is responsible for a statewide or federal program. To balance the best of both central and local authority requires good teamwork between a central authority and local facilities.

Some local governments are turning over mental health services to private contractors—for example, social workers and other helping professionals in private practice—and are dissolving offices where large numbers of staff were formerly employed. While this may be bad news for public-sector employment, it is part of a larger trend viewing human relations and educational services as central features of modern life.

Pressure has been building in recent years from funding bodies such as United Way and local government for an additional kind of accountability for private centers, and from state legislatures, federal grants, and others for public hospitals and other facilities. Traditionally, mental health facilities have accounted for the proper spending of funds to substantiate public trust. Recently, mental health facilities have also been pressured to provide evidence that their services are effective, which has raised issues. Reliable measures of organization and treatment effectiveness are still being developed. Sometimes accountability methods jeopardize principles of patient confidentiality and professional autonomy. On the other hand, the expectation of demonstrated treatment effectiveness deserves careful attention and committed effort.

Diagnostic classification of mental disorders is a recurrent issue. Diagnoses reported to insurance companies and computer data systems have possibilities for "labeling" a person for life. Yet, charges to insurance companies need to be substantiated, and computer data systems are needed in accountability. Safeguards need to be observed, and at a minimum the patient's informed consent to the submission of such information should be obtained.[39] Robert Spitzer takes note of the problem of labeling and writes,

> A common misconception is that a classification of mental disorders classifies people, when actually what are being classified are disorders that people have. For this reason, the text of DSM-IV (as did the text of DSM-III-R) avoids the use of such expressions as "a schizophrenic" or "an alcoholic," and instead uses the more accurate, but admittedly more cumbersome, "a person with Schizophrenia" or "a person with Alcohol Dependence."[40]

The civil rights of patients have strengthened during the past decade. Mental disorder is an insufficient basis for involuntary hospitalization unless the person is in need of inpatient treatment and care, and appears to present a danger to her or his own life or safety, or to others. Court rulings have held that the inpatient has a right to treatment in the least restrictive setting available. The trend to strengthen the civil rights of mental patients is a positive contrast with the frightening practice in the former USSR of using mental hospitalization for political detention. Disobedience or resistance to official policies could be regarded as an "abnormal" condition requiring "psychiatric treatment."

The practice of deinstitutionalization, that is, the transfer of mental patients from hospital custodial care to community treatment, is being questioned in many places where there have been excesses and indifference. Patients had been released (dumped) upon communities lacking the facilities to care for them. Neglect, misery, incarceration, and homelessness have resulted for an estimated 150,000 people, conditions reminiscent of those decried by Dorothea Dix in the mid-nineteenth century. Some of the suggestions advanced have been the strengthening of local programs through badly needed financial inducements for local communities, the development of community support systems, and more humanitarian and judicious policies for discharge and release to community living. Much needed, too, are social workers educated to work with people having severe and persistent mental illnesses.

No one universally accepted definition of managed care is in use, but its purposes are clear. Employers and insurers who pay for care are seeking ways to control and manage costs through cost-containment approaches, as well as attempting to balance fiscal viability, control over access to care, and design of benefits. Managed care also aims to increase profits for managed care companies. Clinical social workers often deal with insurance company case managers on issues such as the duration and type of service, frequently resulting in less choice for the subscriber and reduced autonomy for the social worker.

On the face of it, it seems unlikely that quality of services can be improved when financial support is reduced. The impact of managed care on social work practice in mental health may increase the importance of prevention, with a focus on families, as well as strengthening continuity of care and emphases on brief treatment models. Individuals and families requiring long-term care—such as those with chronic mental illnesses—are threatened with insufficient care and neglect. Some improvement, however, may result from the Mental Health Parity Act of 1996, which requires mental health insurance with benefits equal to coverages for physical illnesses. As time goes by, managed care principles are likely to continue, but managed care organizations may decline as direct contracting increases between service providers and payers.

Illustration of Administration Social Work Practice in Mental Health

A CMHC was scheduled for a site visit for its reaccreditation by a state agency. A new aspect of the site visit procedure was a review of a small sample of confidential clinical records to assess compliance with accreditation standards.

There was no question that the state agency had the legal authority to review the records. The professional staff of the center, however, had made commitments of confidentiality to the people they served, which they felt they could not ethically ignore. The administrator of the center was bound by the Code of Ethics of the NASW regarding confidentiality. Also at issue was the possibility of legal suit concerning invasion of privacy or breach of contract.

The administrator of the center sought a problem-solving pattern of collaboration with the state agency. Communication between the two parties led to a solution meeting the requirements of both sides. The

CMHC contacted the persons whose records might be sampled. The issue was described to them, and they were asked to sign statements either of permission or of nonpermission for their records to be in the sample. Eighty percent of the people contacted signed statements of permission. The state agency agreed to pass over those records where individuals had signed a statement of nonpermission. The site visit was smoothly and professionally managed and the center was reaccredited. A further agreement reached was that all new persons served would be advised by the CMHC about the procedure as a preparation step for the next reaccreditation site visit.

Future Prospects

Several policy questions remain:

1. What is the future role of state mental hospitals?
2. Will federal policies further promote community programming?
3. Will state and local governments support programming for the seriously mentally ill?
4. Will preventive programs be provided in local communities?
5. Will the public mental health system increase the involvement of the private sector in publicly funded mental health services?
6. Will the mental health system serve adequately the needs of special populations such as women, children and adolescents, older adults, and members of ethnic minority groups?[41]

The future of mental health programs and services will depend considerably on what role the American federal government assumes, particularly in the arena of overall health policy, on changes in managed care,[42] and upon developments in knowledge and practices of the mental health professions. It is important that the mental health professions continue in their dedication to ethical practice, sense of direction, and discipline to improve mental health professional education programs and services; maintain their determination to service people in the best ways they know; and learn how to work more effectively and efficiently. Some professionals mistakenly believe that they can build bulwarks against the tide of managed care rather than working for improvements. Managed care's for-profit focus could be moderated by a governmental public-service focus. Teamwork through coalitions of selected groups and improved uses of print and broadcast media will be needed for more effective lobbying and political action.

Illustration of Clinical Social Work Practice

The following illustration was derived from clinical practice in the early 1980s. The theoretical model followed was structural family therapy, which was a leading practice theory then, derived from social systems theory as developed by Salvador Minuchin.[43] The period of time in working with the family was about five years, which might not be feasible today under managed care.

A 16-year-old boy was referred to a rural CMHC because of conflicts at home and at school. The precipitating event was that, in the space of one week, he had "totaled" his own car in an accident and had driven his parents' pickup truck into a roadside ditch. For some time he had been associating with friends his parents disapproved of because of their use of alcohol and marijuana. He was failing at school. In contrast, his older brother was doing well in high school and was compliant at home.

The parents and their two adolescent sons lived on a farm owned by the mother's parents. All three generations of the family—the maternal grandparents, the parents, and the adolescent boys—lived together on the farm. The social worker decided to work with the three-generational family, rather than focusing only upon the younger boy. The goal of family therapy was to help the family function better. One of the concepts of structural family therapy is the strengthening of generational boundaries which, in this family, were deteriorating.

The grandmother appeared to be depressed and disengaged from the rest of the family. The grandfather was emotionally invested in the farm, and he also sold seed corn. Both occupations kept him out of the home for long hours, and he did not seem to notice that his wife was depressed. Also, he was ignoring his earlier promise to his son-in-law to turn over the farm to him. The father believed he was being treated like a hired hand and felt denigrated, but when he complained to his wife, she defended the grandfather. The father also seemed to be disengaging from the family and appeared to be developing a drinking problem. The mother and the older son were very close and she saw him as her "good" son. She was very proud of him. She viewed the younger boy as her "bad" son and despaired of his future. Since the parents were not working together well, he was evading their influence and control.

The clinical social worker's goal was to try to strengthen the family along generational boundaries so that it could function better, which was successful. Focusing initially on the grandparents, the social worker was able to help the grandfather recognize his wife's depression and give her some attention and care. While keeping his seed corn business, he gradually turned the farm over to his son-in-law and daughter. The older boy started dating and became less enmeshed with his mother. The 16-year-old dropped out of high school but later enrolled in a course on auto mechanics at the community college. Many of the interviews occurred in the first few months, followed by occasional follow-up contacts as requested.

SUMMARY AND CONCLUSIONS

In this chapter there has been an attempt to indicate the wide variety of services and programs that can be considered under the general rubric of mental health. Because of the many forces involved when people become disturbed, there are a multitude of helping services and patterns of care. The versatility of social workers is particularly valuable in mental health programs, as is their skill and concern. A person entering mental health social work should really care about disturbed people and want to help them.

Notes

1. American Psychiatric Association, *Diagnostic and Statistical Manual of Mental Disorders*, 4th ed. (Washington, DC: American Psychiatric Association, 1994).
2. Thomas Szasz, *The Myth of Mental Illness* (New York: Dell Publishing, 1961), p. 308.
3. E. Fuller Torrey, *Out of the Shadows: Confronting America's Mental Illness Crisis* (New York: Wiley, 1996).
4. National Health and Welfare Canada, *Mental Health for Canadians: Striking a Balance* (Ottawa: Minister of Supply and Services, Canada, 1988), p. 7.
5. Robert W. White, "The Concept of Healthy Personality: What Do We Really Mean?" *The Counseling Psychologist* 4, no. 2 (1974): 5–6.
6. Robert W. White, "Motivation Reconsidered: The Concept of Competence," *Psychological Review* 66, no. 5 (1959): 297–333.
7. Association of Behavioral Healthcare Management, *ABHM Leader* 17, nos. 1 & 2 (March/April 1997): 1.
8. I Samuel 31.
9. Leo Srole, Thomas S. Langner, Stanley T. Michael, Price Kirkpatrick, Marvin K. Opler, and Thomas A.C. Rennie, *Mental Health in the Metropolis* (New York: New York University Press, 1978).
10. John J. Schwab, Roger A. Bell, and George J. Warheit, *Social Order and Mental Health* (New York: Brunner/Mazel, 1979).
11. Darrel Regier et al., "The *de facto* U.S. Mental and Addictive Disorders Service System," *Archives of General Psychiatry* 50, no. 2 (1993).
12. Michael Grossman, "The Correlation between Health and Schooling," in Nestor E. Terleckyj, ed., *Household Production and Consumption* (New York: National Bureau of Economic Research, Columbia University Press, 1975), pp. 147–223.
13. James Leiby, "History of Social Welfare," in *Encyclopedia of Social Work*, 18th ed., vol. 1 (Silver Spring, MD: NASW, 1987), p. 758.
14. N.D.C. Lewis, *A Short History of Psychiatric Achievement* (New York: W.W. Norton, 1941).
15. J. Andriola and G. Cata, "The Oldest Mental Hospital in the World," *Hospital and Community Psychiatry* (1969): p. 20, 42–43.
16. Philip M. Margolis and Armando R. Favazza, "Mental Health and Illness," in *Encyclopedia of Social Work*, 17th ed. (Washington, DC: NASW, 1977), p. 851.
17. Hastings Rashdall, *The Universities of Europe in the Middle Ages* (Oxford: Clarendon Press, 1895).
18. Paul V. Lemkau, "The Historical Background," *Public Mental Health: Perspectives and Prospects* (Newberry Park, CA: Sage Publications, 1982).
19. Gregory Zilboorg, *A History of Medical Psychology* (New York: W.W. Norton, 1941).
20. Bertram J. Black, "Milieu Therapy," in *Encyclopedia of Social Work*, 17th ed. (Washington, DC: NASW, 1977), pp. 921–922.
21. Margolis and Favazza, "Mental Health and Illness," p. 851.
22. Chauncey A. Alexander, "Distinctive Dates in Social Welfare History," in *Encyclopedia of Social Work*, 19th ed. (Washington, DC: NASW Press, 1995).
23. Bernard L. Bloom, *Community Mental Health* (Pacific Grove, CA: Brooks/Cole Publishing, 1977), p. 11.
24. Steven Greene et al., "State and County Mental Hospitals, United States, 1982–83 and 1983–84, with Trend Analyses for 1973–74 to 1983–84," *Mental Health Statistical Note No. 1976* (Washington, DC: U.S. Department of Health and Human Services, National Institute of Mental Health, September 1986), p. 5.

25. John F. Kennedy, "Message from the President of the United States Relative to Mental Illness and Mental Retardation," February 5, 1963 (Washington, DC: Government Printing Office, 0-767-476).

26. President's Commission on Mental Health, *Task Panel on Rural Mental Health*, vol. 3, Appendix (Washington, DC: Government Printing Office, 1978).

27. K.C. Buckwalter, M. Smith, P. Zevenbergen, and D. Russell, "Mental Health Services of the Rural Elderly Outreach Program," *The Gerontologist* 32, no. 3 (1991): 408–412.

28. David L. Garber and Peter J. McNelis, "Military Social Work," *Encyclopedia of Social Work*, 19th ed. (Washington, DC: NASW Press, 1995).

29. *The President's Commission on Mental Health*, vol. 4, Appendix (Washington, DC: Government Printing Office, No. 040-000-00392-2, 1978).

30. Janice Wood Wetzel, "Forging the Missing Link in Social Work." Paper presented at the Council on Social Work Education Annual Program Meeting, Detroit, Michigan, March 4, 1984.

31. Lawrence J. Schweinhart, "Effects of the Perry Preschool Program on Youth through Age 19: A Summary," *Early Childhood Special Education Quarterly* 5, no. 2 (1985): pp. 26–35.

32. *New York Times*, Sunday, September 6, 1987, p. 14E.

33. Committee for Economic Development, Research and Policy Committee, *Children in Need: Investment Strategies for the Educationally Disadvantaged* (New York and Washington, DC, 1987).

34. Daniel Patrick Moynihan, *Family and Nation* (San Diego, CA: Harcourt Brace Jovanovich, 1986).

35. *Children and Their Families: Current Conditions and Recent Trends*, a report of the Select Committee on Children, Youth and Families, U.S. House of Representatives (Washington, DC: Government Printing Office, 1987).

36. Trudy I. Kattner, *The Shock of Disaster* (Des Moines, IA: Iowa State Department of Health, Office for Health Planning and Development, 1980).

37. Ibid., p. 14.

38. Verne R. Kelley, Patricia L. Kelley, Eugene F. Gauron, and Edna I. Rawlings, "Training Helpers in Rural Mental Health Delivery," *Social Work* 22, no. 3 (May 1977): 229–232.

39. Verne R. Kelley and Hanna B. Weston, "Civil Liberties in Mental Health Facilities," *Social Work* 19, no. 1 (January 1974). See also, by the same authors, "Computers, Costs and Civil Liberties," *Social Work* 20, no. 1 (January 1975); and "Release of Confidential Information from Mental Health Records," *Administration in Mental Health* 7, no. 1 (Fall 1979).

40. Robert L. Spitzer, *Diagnostic and Statistical Manual of Mental Disorders*, 4th ed. (Washington, DC: American Psychiatric Association, 1994), p. xxii.

41. Phillip Fellin, *Mental Health and Mental Illness: Policies, Programs, and Services* (Itasca, IL: F.E. Peacock, 1996).

42. King Davis, "Welfare Reform, States' Rights & Managed Care: Impact on Social Work Philosophy, Education & Practice." Paper presented at the National Association of Deans and Directors of Schools of Social Work Annual Meeting, Chicago, Illinois, March 5, 1997.

43. Salvador Minuchin, *Families and Family Therapy* (Cambridge, MA: Harvard University Press, 1974).

Additional Suggested Readings

Andreasen, Nancy C. *The Broken Brain: The Biological Revolution in Psychiatry*. New York: Harper & Row, Publishers, 1984.

Beers, Clifford. *A Mind That Found Itself*. New York: Longman, Green & Co., 1908.

Bentley, Kia J., and Joseph Walsh. *The Social Worker and Psychotropic Medication*. Pacific Grove, CA: Brooks/Cole Publishing Co., 1996.

Chekhov, Anton P. "Heartache." *The Portable Chekhov*. New York: Viking Press, 1969.

Davidson, William B., and Patrick R. Cotter. "The Relationship Between Sense of Community and Subjective Well-Being: A First Look." *Journal of Community Psychology*, 19 no. 3 (1991): 246–253.

Foucault, Michel. *Madness and Civilization: A History of Insanity in the Age of Reason*. Trans. R. Howard. (1961; reissued New York: Pantheon, 1965).

Kirk, Stuart A., and Susan D. Einbinder. *Controversial Issues in Mental Health*. Needham Heights, MA: Allyn & Bacon, 1994.

Mechanic, David. *Mental Health and Social Policy*. 3rd ed. Englewood Cliffs, NJ: Prentice-Hall, 1989.

Rosenhan, D.L. "On Being Sane in Insane Places." *Science* 179 (January 19, 1973).

Webster, Richard. *Why Freud Was Wrong: Sin, Science and Psychoanalysis*. London: Fontana Press, 1996.

White, Michael, and D. Epston. *Narrative Means to Therapeutic Ends*. New York: Norton, 1990.

10

Social Services
and Disabilities

JUDITH I. GRAY
ROBERT VANDER BEEK

INTRODUCTION: A SOCIAL WORK PERSPECTIVE TOWARD DISABILITY

When we picture a person who is disabled, it is usually an image of someone physically or mentally impaired to such a degree that it hinders daily living. That perception is consistent with state and federal guidelines. One estimate is that approximately 3 million people in the United States are living with physical disabilities that they have usually had since birth. Additionally, up to 3 percent of the population, or 2.5 million individuals, are limited by mental retardation.[1] However, almost all of us will eventually become disabled.

Some who are now able-bodied will suffer new limitations due to an accident. Others will confront lost capabilities as a result of aging. For this reason it has been suggested that it would be more realistic for those not currently disabled to think of themselves as "temporarily-abled."[2] While this is a discomforting thought, it is a useful perspective. It helps in realizing that those labeled disabled are not a separate category of humans. Disability in one or more areas of functioning does not summarize the whole person. Disabilities are merely significant long-term obstacles most people will at one time or another face.

Thanks in part to the Americans with Disabilities Act, society has begun a shift toward understanding that barriers are not always entirely due to limitations of individuals. The traditional medical approach has been to conceptualize disabilities solely as biological inferiorities of the person. But frequently obstacles result from the lack of societal accommodation. Think, for example, of an otherwise qualified person not getting a job because the wheelchair does not fit through the office door. The impairment blocking achievement is architectural rather than the individual's ability to do the job.

Appreciating that "the disabled" are more alike than different from the "able-bodied," that a diagnosed impairment does not summarize the person, and that the solution for resulting obstacles is often societally based, is fundamental to a social work perspective toward working with disabilities. It is with these understandings that we can proceed to a discussion of disabilities as defined across a range of professions.

DEFINING DISABILITY

Many circumstances can be disabling. Difficulties with substance abuse and mental health can be as impairing as a stroke. This becomes apparent in the chapters in this book about those problems. As noted above, this chapter will take a narrower focus, defining disabilities as long-term physical or mental limitations due to accident or a characteristic, usually from birth, of the individual. The latter population is referred to as those with developmental disabilities.

It might seem that differentiating between developmental and other disabilities is unnecessary. Whether, for instance, a person's inability to walk is due to a car accident or an accident of birth, severity of need may be much the same. But the faint line between what is and is not considered a developmental disability can have a profound impact upon services to individuals and their families.

DEVELOPMENTAL DISABILITIES

Constructing a separate category called developmental disability resulted in part from a desire to establish a means of identifying people with a wide range of special needs into one diagnostic cateogry, thus establishing eligibility for specialized government assistance. According to the Rehabilitation and Comprehensive Services and Developmental Disabilities Amendment of 1978 (P.L. 95-602):

> The term "developmental disability" means a severe, chronic disability of a person that:
> 1. is attributable to a mental or physical impairment or combination of mental and physical impairments,
> 2. is manifest before the person attains age twenty-two, and
> 3. is likely to continue indefinitely.

As this definition indicates, many persons have coexisting disabilities. About 28 percent of those with one impairment have a second, with disabilities sometimes occurring in both mental and physical areas.[3] But it would be a mistake to assume, for instance, that a physically impaired person also has mental limitations. It is more helpful for social workers to realize that fully 72 percent of those with a disability have no significant coexisting condition. Implications for social work practice are discussed in the following section.

TYPES OF DEVELOPMENTAL DISABILITIES

Due in part to differences between federal and state criteria, as well as criteria between states, conditions considered to be developmental disabilities vary. There are, however, eight broad diagnoses generally agreed upon as constituting developmental disabilities.[4]

Cerebral palsy.   The primary effect of cerebral palsy is to make body movement and posture more difficult, with these symptoms occurring due to an injury to a small part of the brain either prior to or during birth. As a result, the brain is unable to adequately transmit messages to the body to control muscles. Manifestations can be increased muscle tension resulting in difficult or sometimes impossible voluntary movement, involuntary movements of the extremities and rapidly changing muscle tension, or elements of both. Degree of symptoms also vary from mild to severe.

Orthopedic problems.   Difficulties with the functioning of muscles, bones, and joints are orthopedic in origin. One of these is spina bifida, a condition in which the spine has not grown completely, causing inability of nerve impulses to travel to the legs, resulting in an inability to walk. Bone disease, missing limbs, and deformed bones are among other orthopedic afflictions.

Autism.   Although symptoms can easily be confused with those of severe mental retardation, autism is quite different. An autistic child, although often seeming quite normal in the first several years of life, may begin demonstrating repetitive movements, like rocking and hand-flapping, or seem not to be able to hear despite having that capacity. The child may also have language problems and only echo back words that are spoken. As the name implies, autistic children seem to be in a separate world of their own, and seem largely unaware or fearful of their immediate environment.

Epilepsy.   An excessive amount of electrical discharges from the brain causes a person with epilepsy to have seizures. Grand mal seizures result in convulsions, which are episodes of furious and uncontrollable shaking of the entire body for several minutes, usually followed by a period of unconsciousness. Petit mal seizures, on the other hand, may seem to an observer as though the victim is simply daydreaming. The blank stare during a petit mal seizure is really a brief period—perhaps as short as several seconds—of unconsciousness.

Hearing problems.   When an infant or child has a hearing problem it can easily lead to further developmental difficulties. Mastery of speech and language becomes more difficult for a child who is hearing impaired. While hearing loss can range from only very mild to complete deafness, any hearing impairment makes developing verbal communication skills more difficult.

Learning disabilities.   Specific marked problems within areas of calculating, mathematics, listening, reading, speaking, spelling, thinking, or writing are described as learning disabilities. Such difficulties are usually not discovered until a child enters school and sometimes not until adulthood, if at all. Persons with a learning disability usually achieve quite well outside the problem area and, consequently, the developmental problem is sometimes confused with laziness or a gap in educational preparedness. In reality, learning disabilities are symptomatic of physical problems, including visual-motor or visual-perceptual handicaps, minimal brain dysfunction, or dyslexia.

Mental retardation.   A person classified as mentally retarded has tested below average in general intelligence to a degree that it significantly hinders ability to learn in school and, later, to function independently as an adult. The average tested IQ is measured as 100, and the American Psychiatric Association divides those functioning markedly below that level into five categories of mental retardation:[5]

Borderline   (IQ 71 to 84)

Mild   (IQ 50 to 70)

Moderate   (IQ 35 to 49)

Severe   (IQ 20 to 34)

Profound   (IQ below 20)

Many factors, however, can cause standard intelligence tests to be inaccurate. The emotional state, physical health, and educational background of the test taker all might affect the outcome. There is also increased awareness that IQ tests are culturally biased, usually favoring those from a white middle-class background. Because of limitations in accurate testing, there is general agreement that along with a low IQ score, concurrent deficits in adaptive behavior ought to be in evidence prior to a diagnosis of mental retardation.[6] Adaptive behavior refers to the level of social skills and independence that would be expected of other persons the same age and from the same circumstances.

Co-occurring disabilities.   It was previously mentioned that over one-quarter of those with one developmental disability are also impaired by a second. There have been unfortunate cases where individuals with physical impairments have been falsely thought to have mental disabilities. Imagine that you are unable to speak due to motor involvements of your disability and, despite being as aware as others around you, you are treated as though you understand little. People do not talk to you but about you, you are offered no choices about your life, and very little stimulation. Unfortunately, this has been a reality for many, especially before augmentative communication devices of recent times were developed. Although less dramatic, it is not unusual to hear a person with leg braces being talked to in an artificially slow manner, or for a visually impaired person to be addressed in an overly loud voice. One should never assume that a physical disability means that that one is either mentally handicapped or that there are other co-occurring disabilities of any sort.

HISTORICAL DEVELOPMENTS

Historically, treatment of people with disabilities was often harsh in the United States. Although counted among the "deserving poor," the preferred means of support was simply to allow legalized begging. If the severity of an individual's condition did not make begging possible, and if no family members were able to provide, private homes were sometimes given public funds to take the person in. The more severely afflicted, and particularly those with mental retardation, were more likely to be confined by authorities away from public view. Frequently this housing amounted to only a small unheated cell, much resembling a modern dog kennel.[7]

Conditions for those removed from their community marginally improved with the appearance of almshouses. These catchall facilities were unhealthy places for most, and especially threatening to those already suffering physical frailties. Evidence of the degree of risk for inhabitants is found in a description written by inspectors of 55 almshouses in New York in 1856. The almshouses were "badly constructed, ill-arranged, ill-warmed, and ill-ventilated. The rooms are crowded with inmates.... Good health is incompatible with such arrangements."[8]

By the beginning of the nineteenth century, a European trend of creating specialized institutions for the care of people with handicaps influenced social reformers in the United States. Thomas Gallaudet founded the first of these training schools, the American Asylum for the Education of the Deaf and Dumb in Connecticut in 1817.[9] By the middle of the 1800s, a number of residential schools were established, each targeted to needs of children having the same handicaps. Some schools worked with those with mental retardation, others with specific shared physical problems. The goal of training schools was to teach skills that would eventually allow students to return to and function in their home communities.[10] By the late 1800s, social forces leading to increasingly negative perceptions of those with disabilities and pressures to isolate them from the general public impacted training schools. Much like earlier almshouses, the schools became long-term warehouses for those with a variety of disabilities.

Social Darwinism was a corruption of Charles Darwin's theory of natural selection and was used as a mean-spirited rationale for the fortunate not to help the unfortunate. According to natural selection, because weaker members of a herd die and do not reproduce, future herds become genetically superior. Likewise, Social Darwinists held that assisting "inferior" human stock is harmful to the evolution of the human race. While Social Darwinism supported complacency toward the plight of those most in need of assistance, the parallel eugenics movement ignited outright fear of and malevolence toward Americans with disabilities, especially the mentally challenged.

Eugenics asserted that each "feeble-minded" person is a potential criminal, needing only the proper environment of opportunity for development and expression of criminal tendencies.[11] Eugenicists sought a society where those of questionable functional skills would be controlled through methods such as restrictions on marriage, forced sterilization, and confinement in isolated rural institutions.

As with many hate movements, eugenics rapidly expanded the number of citizens thought threatening to the public good. Due to poorly developed intelligence tests, eugenicists found that nearly one-half of the men drafted into World War I, many of whom lacked formal educations, were feeble-minded.[12] Adding to the distrust of the public, research in the 1920s began to show that few people released back into their communities exhibited antisocial behaviors.[13] Regardless of its decline, the legacy of eugenics extended well into the 1950s.

Many Americans who were capable of functioning in the community remained confined in institutions.

NORMALIZATION, DEINSTITUTIONALIZATION, AND THE LEAST RESTRICTIVE ENVIRONMENT

The post–World War II baby boom as well as advances in medicine contributed to a large increase in the number of parents during the 1950s with babies who survived birth, but with physical and/or mental handicaps. The Association for Retarded Children, later to become the Association of Retarded Citizens (now ARC), was established by a network of parents in 1950.[14] The Association became instrumental during that decade in developing community-based (rather than institutional) programming for children with special needs. *Normalization* was the key desired outcome. Originating in Scandinavia, normalization aimed to provide those with disabilities the opportunity to live as normally as possible within the mainstream of society. Development of special education programs within regular public schools, daily living skills training, and community-based vocational and supported living opportunities all resulted in part from lobbying efforts of the Association.

By the late 1960s, a strong trend away from institutionalized care in favor of locally based programming was fully evident. The number of disabled Americans residing in institutions has declined every year since 1967, with the most rapid decreases occurring during the 1980s and 1990s. Several dynamics have influenced this long-term trend.

Deinstitutionalization describes the process of releasing those formerly housed in institutional care settings back into the community. The underlying philosophy is that every individual should be afforded the *least restrictive environment* necessary to support any special needs they have. The term is most often heard in school program planning for students with special needs. For instance, a student having special education needs in some areas is "mainstreamed" into regular classes where those needs are not a barrier to learning. This assists the student in being less segregated from peers.

Similarly, an assumption of deinstitutionalization has been that implementation of community-based supports such as day treatment programs, casework, vocational training, and rehabilitation services would provide necessary supports. Many have been saddened to witness an increase in the numbers of destitute people, particularly with mental health problems, on the streets following deinstitutionalization. It is easy to conlude that deinstitutionalization was not a good idea for many of these people. As was noted in Chapter 3, the failure was not in deinstitutionalizing but in communities not providing sufficient support services.

Successful outcomes through deinstitutionalization have been limited by the lack of accompanying funding that was to have been diverted from the cost of institutional care to development of programs necessary to support transitions to community living. The mood, especially during the Reagan years, was to cut social program spending. Consensus was also lacking between federal, state, and local governments about where funding responsibilities lay. The problem has not been the closing of institutions but an unwillingness to reinvest in the community services needed to replace them.

As we approach the next century, pressures continue to identify ways of cutting expenditures for social programs. However, efforts to cut funding necessary for the basic needs of persons with disabilities will certainly meet with significant opposition, due in part to recent civil rights legislation.

THE AMERICANS WITH DISABILITIES ACT OF 1990

It is frequently said that "you can't legislate morality." Even if this is true, laws can enable more equitable treatment of minority groups. The Civil Rights Act of 1964 placed protections against discrimination on the basis of race, color, national origin, sex, and religion. The Americans with Disabilities Act of 1990 (ADA) extended protection to people with disabilities. At publication of the previous edition of this chapter, the ADA was too new to realize its impact. While it is still early to fully know long-term consequences, there is evidence that the Act has benefited many Americans.

A survey sponsored by the Cerebral Palsy Association in the summer of 1996 found that 96 percent of a sample of people in the United States with disabilities, their families, and their friends believed that the ADA had made a positive difference in their lives.[15] Likewise, according to a Harris survey, the number of disabled Americans who had jobs in 1994 was up 26 percent from 1991, just after the ADA became law. This increase was likely also influenced by economic and other trends. However, the survey also found that approximately 81 percent of employers had modified their workplaces to accommodate special needs in response to the ADA. Clearly, societally imposed obstacles to daily living have lessened due to the ADA, allowing those who are otherwise capable to contribute their skills to society while benefiting from greater self-sufficiency.

Americans' comfort with disabilities also appears to be increasing as more people with such conditions are becoming better integrated into the mainstream. It is widely known that President Franklin Roosevelt felt it necessary to hide his disability from the public. In contrast, during the last presidential campaign, Republican candidate Robert Dole talked openly about being disabled, campaigning that it had made him more sensitive to needs of others. Actor Christopher Reeve, who ironically had played the role of Superman, gave a moving address at the 1996 Democratic National Convention advocating for greater inclusion of handicapped Americans into society. The amount to which increased opportunities for and appreciation of those with disabilities is due to the ADA is immeasurable. Whatever the degree, it is clear that the Act has had a profound positive impact.

Provisions of the Americans with Disabilities Act

Four areas covered within the ADA are employment (Title I), public services and transportation (Title II), public accommodations (Title III), and telecommunications (Title IV). While extending these protections to those with handicaps has been slow in coming, the impact is profound, and will likely be

Despite disabilities, many handicapped individuals have found useful employment. A disabled Hispanic man teaches second-graders in a Texas school.

Bob Daemmrich/The Image Works

especially enabling to the large number of young Americans just entering the world of work.

Legislation in the 1970s opened the nation's school doors to children with handicaps by mainstreaming them into regular school systems. This generation is graduating and is entering the labor market at a rate of 150,000 per year.[16] Like others their age, most would like a chance to apply what they have learned and to earn a living. In fact, why shouldn't the investment in public education for students with handicaps be paid back by allowing each of them assistance in becoming taxpaying citizens? Enabling employment is one aspect of the ADA.

Title I of the ADA protects against discrimination in employment on the basis of disability. A misperception is that employers will be forced to hire people physically unable to do their job. In reality, the ADA only prohibits discrimination against "a qualified individual with a disability." For instance, it would be acceptable not to hire a person who is unable to lift heavy objects for a warehouse job where that is a necessary job requirement. However, it is in violation of the law to refuse employment to an otherwise qualified accountant due to dependency upon a wheelchair. In the first case the disability would significantly affect ability to perform the job, while in the second it would have no effect.

Title II assumes that maintaining a job and success in other areas of community living are dependent upon accessible transportation. This section covers the need for public transportation usable by people with physical handicaps, requiring that all newly purchased buses be accessible, in particular, to wheelchairs. Title II also prohibits discrimination by state or local governments against disabled people within any programs or activities.

Title III attends to consumer needs of the disabled and sets guidelines for eliminating architectural barriers in newly constructed, privately operated public accommodations, as well as modifications to inaccessible commercial facilities such as restaurants and shopping malls. An understanding under the law is that reasonably preventable obstacles to access of the physically disabled to public places ought to be eliminated. This section also prohibits overt denial of services to individuals based upon disability. For example, a restaurant's refusal to serve a person with cerebral palsy because the manager fears a negative reaction by other customers is a violation of the law.

Title IV recognizes the importance of telecommunications to daily living. It requires telephone companies to make available existing devices to the hearing and speech impaired, allowing them to communicate over the phone. A condition of Title IV is also that federally funded public service messages on television be closed-captioned for the hearing impaired.

Clearly the ADA is a meaningful advance for citizens with disabilities. As parents of children with handicaps quickly learn, however, prejudice against their child and the unnecessary barriers faced can affect the entire family. Families of the disabled also experience public stigmatization and physical barriers to family activities. The ADA sends a message to those families as well as the member with the disability that they are accepted and increasingly valued members of society.

PROGRAMS AND SERVICES

Despite deinstitutionalization and judicial mandates for the provision of services in the "least restrictive setting," a small percentage of people with disabilities continue to live in residential state institutions. Efforts continue toward the development of community-based placements for those inappropriately placed, as well as improving the quality of care for those remaining in state facilities. While titles vary among states, each has a branch within state human services charged with overseeing policy implementation and service delivery, regardless of individual placement setting.

It has been learned that early diagnosis and intervention is helpful in reducing the need for out-of-home placements of children with developmental disabilities.[17] Legislation enacted in 1986 has mandated the development of comprehensive early identification, evaluation, and intervention services for children aged birth to three years, through schools or various designated lead agencies. These lead agencies may include local health care providers or social service agencies. Promotion of family empowerment, including collaboration among parents, professionals, and agencies in the development of service plans, is a stated goal of such intervention services. In addition to care coordination, examples of services provided in response to recognized needs include: home-based or developmental day care, physical therapy, parent training, individual and family counseling, and respite care.[18]

For individuals between three and twenty-one years of age, public school programs provide services through an individualized educational plan that also ensures parental involvement in educational decisions related to their children. The overall goal is to assist the person in securing the greatest possible independence in the community. These plans must include education that trains a developmentally disabled person in self-care, social skills, and daily living skills, and enhances vocational potential. Inclusive settings are the current trend in public education, providing supports and adapted curriculum while allowing full access to normal classroom activities and instruction. A noteworthy development also impacting the schools relates to the classification of placements for those with mental retardation. Historically, IQ tests and levels of severity have been used to classify people who are retarded. The American Association of Mental Retardation (AAMR) is now recommending evaluating an individual's needs based upon the level of support systems required (intermittent, limited, extensive, and pervasive) across adaptive skill levels in domains such as communication, self-care, home living, social skills, community use, self-direction, health and safety, functional academics, and work.[19] Schools are also involved in developing transition plans with students and their families to assist with the process of moving the student from school to functional community living and postsecondary education, training, or employment.[20] The adaptive behaviors, mentioned earlier, are also better predictors than IQ scores of successful adjustment in the community.[21] Postsecondary education and training opportunities continue to expand, including many settings with increased flexibility and adaptability.

Beyond the public school experience, developmentally disabled people and their families often have access to a number of other locally based services. Community centers may offer assistance in such areas as independent living skills, vocational training, social and recreational activities, and family support programming. Those needing mental health care may secure services from a local community mental health center. Sheltered workshops and supportive employment provide two methods of offering people work opportunities. Sheltered workshops typically subcontract work, such as sorting or minor assembly, and pay participants based upon their level of productivity, generally at a rate that is a portion of the minimum wage. Supportive employment includes job placement in the community combined with on-site training, assessment, and follow-along services aimed at long-term job retention. Finding a supportive employment setting in which an individual will be successful also requires an evaluation of the work setting, social networks, and workplace cultures.[22]

As defined in the Rehabilitation Act Amendments of 1986, supportive employment clearly provides the more normalized option, and is meant for the most severely disabled. A recent analysis suggests that supported employment has substantially increased the productivity and earnings of people with severe disabilities and has significantly lowered costs for alternative programs. This study also predicted that the economic benefits will eventually be greater than the costs to taxpayers.[23] Even if program costs are more than client earnings, nonmonetary benefits add to the value of the investment. These advantages include the following: (1) gainful employment increases the person's earnings and sense of independence; (2) the person is viewed by family and society as a more productive and integrated member of their community; and (3) integration of those with a variety of disabilities into work settings has the potential to increase social comfort and acceptance of individuals with special needs.[24]

Under the Rehabilitation Act Amendments of 1978, vocational rehabilitation programs are mandated to provide comprehensive services essential to maximizing the independence of disabled people, regardless of their immediate vocational potential. These services included disability assessment and securing of equipment as well as medical and other services essential to enhancing functioning. In addition to the sheltered workshops and supportive employment options mentioned above, vocational rehabilitation provides funding for other types of training, transportation, counseling, and additional assistance helpful in securing employment or meeting appropriate individualized vocational goals.[25]

A range of residential services for disabled persons also exists. Community-based rehabilitation centers or nursing homes offer one alternative to state institutions, often varying greatly in the degree of specialized care available. Small, neighborhood-centered group homes are another alternative. These are often established by private providers or other agencies and usually offer ongoing supervision and programming for residents. Alternative family care for adults can provide a foster care type arrangement with families motivated and capable of meeting an individual's special needs. Semi-independent living programs provide ongoing supports including life skills training and home visits to those individuals living separately in the community. Additionally, people who would otherwise have to live in large-group settings due to the severity of their disability are living in their own apartments or homes with supported living services. These services may include personal assistance or attendant care, residential-based habilitation, and respite care for families.

Medicaid and Supplemental Security Income (SSI), both described in Chapter 4, are also important in meeting basic needs of many people with disabilities. Medicaid assists with reimbursement for medical costs and may provide a daily rate for residential or other community programming. Medicaid waiver monies are also providing funds for the supported living services mentioned above as well as occupational, speech, and physical therapies. However, Medicaid payments have not kept up with the increased costs of medical services. SSI offers further monetary assistance to people found to be totally disabled, but also has not kept pace with the cost of living. Finally, modest yet optimistic improvements have been made in allowing disabled persons to train and begin work without totally losing their benefits. For example, a nine- to twelve-month trial work period is allowed without jeopardizing SSI eligibility. SSI payments are reduced; however, the reduction is slightly less than the amount earned so the worker always comes out ahead financially by working. In some circumstances, Medicaid benefits can continue even when earnings are too high to remain eligible for SSI.[26] Work and supported employment expenses may also be compensated under the SSI program's work incentive provisions.[27]

SOCIAL WORK ROLES AND SETTINGS

Whatever the specific intervention, the primary focus of social work ought to be empowerment. As with any other group, people with developmental disabilities are best served by being allowed the maximum self-determination that individual abilities allow. In fact, empowerment is important for both the individual and his or her family, who are most certainly impacted by prejudicial attitudes and the numerous barriers that restrict the freedom of the disabled member. Considering an empowerment focus, the social worker may serve as an advocate for individuals and families, or model and teach advocacy skills to the person and his or her family.[28] It is imperative that all social workers be involved in continued efforts to secure policies that will enhance the civil rights of people with disabilities. However, all generalist social work roles and skills (direct service, policy, and community practice) are important to effective interventions in a variety of settings. Opportunities are available for the social worker to specialize his or her practice in mental retardation and developmental disabilities.[29]

Social workers will be found on staff at all of the various agencies, programs, schools, and residential facilities that have been mentioned. A social worker may provide indirect services in an administrative capacity or may include direct services to individuals, families, and groups. Administrative functions may include program or policy development, fiscal management, fund-raising, hiring and supervision of staff, as well as board, staff, and community relations. Common direct-service functions are completion of biopsychosocial assessments, doing intake procedures, determining elegibility for services, arranging admissions or planning discharges from facilities, as well as identifying and linking clients to supportive services.

The profession is committed to protective, preventive, and intervention roles in working with children with disabilities who are vulnerable to abuse.[30] In addition, these roles are important in assisting adults with disabilities living in the community who are often victims of domestic violence.[31] Social workers also provide counseling to individuals and families who are in the process of coping and adapting to the multidimensional aspects of their particular situation. Many times, the social worker will be a member of a multidisciplinary team in providing services.

Individual work may focus on issues of low self-esteem, interpersonal problems, or training in vocational or social skills. Families who have given birth to a child with a developmental disability may need help making it through a grieving process. However, the majority of families, while experiencing "chronic sorrow" or a recurring sadness, demonstrate positive coping, adaptation, and growth from the experience of parenting an exceptional child.[32]

For example, a study of mothers of older adult children with mental retardation showed a movement away from disappointment regarding the lack of intellectual achievement of their children to an accommodation to limitations and appreciation of strengths. Additionally, adolescent siblings may experience feelings of neglect or resentment over the time spent by parents on a disabled child's needs or with the expectations and responsibilities of caretaking, or they may express anxiety over the risk of bearing a mentally retarded child. In adulthood, however, siblings emerge as important emotional and instrumental caregivers with positive perceptions of childhood relationships.[33] Family and friends can provide material and physical support, respite care, child care, transportation, and financial resources. Positive adaptation is helped by family, friends, and professionals who become involved, learning about the child's particular disability and establishing a relationship with the child.

Support groups for families offer a safe emotional outlet, current relevant information, an opportunity to learn from other parents, and an arena for social action. Professional social workers are advised to form a collaborative relationship with the family providing informal and formal support. This includes serving as a broker, connecting the family to needed services, or providing education regarding disability information or issue-based forums. It is always advisable to allow the locus of control to remain with the family.[34]

Other issues often mentioned in counseling with such families include being stigmatized, the response of relatives, medical or behavioral problems of the disabled member, as well as difficulties with service delivery and loss of socioeconomic status.[35] As the individual and family move through the life cycle, new issues and needs will arise. Transition points such as moves from the family home or from institutions to other settings are often stressful periods that bring new demands with which families need to cope. For example, elderly parents who have been caregivers for their dependent adult child may need social work assistance in planning for future care needs.[36] Whatever the stage of the life cycle, a variety of social work roles are appropriate to serving needs of the disabled and their families. Overall, the social worker offers a vital understanding of human diversity, an ability to work from a family perspective, and the skills to secure and coordinate services as well as to build interagency collaboration and a supportive community.

SUMMARY AND CONCLUSIONS

Largely as a result of efforts of the disabled and their families, combined with federal legislation resulting in the ADA, a civil rights movement for people with disabilities continues to gain force. Services to this population are becoming more individualized, with continued trends in early intervention, inclusive educational settings, supportive employment vocational services, and providing supports for integrated living in the community. New technologies are expanding educational and work opportunities for people with disabilities. Such advances in augmentative technologies will most certainly continue to increase the ability of people to contribute, regardless of physical or mental challenges.

Without taking into account varying public attitudes or the labels used to define particular characteristics, people with disabilities continue to be a significantly underempowered minority. Therefore, it is increasingly important that social workers become educated to the rights and needs of this population, remaining committed to maximizing the opportunities and enhancing the freedom of each individual.

Notes

---

1. Ruth I. Freedman, "Developmental Disabilities: Direct Practice," *Encyclopedia of Social Work*, 19th ed. (Washington, DC: NASW, 1995), pp. 721–722.
2. Barbara Schram and Betty Reid Mandell, *An Introduction to Human Services Policy and Practice*, 2nd ed. (New York: Macmillan College Publishing Company, 1994).

3. Kevin L. Weaver, "Developmental Disabilities: Definitions and Policies," *Encyclopedia of Social Work*, 19th ed. (Washington, DC: NASW), p. 712.

4. Weaver, "Developmental Disabilities," pp. 712–720.

5. Richard C. Simons, *Understanding Human Behavior and Illness*, 3rd ed. (Baltimore: Williams & Wilkins, 1985), p. 620.

6. Ibid., p. 620.

7. Esco Obermann, *A History of Vocational Rehabilitation in America*, 4th ed. (Minneapolis: T.S. Denison, 1967), p. 77.

8. Martin Judge, "A Brief History of Social Services," Part 1, *Social and Rehabilitation Record* 3, no. 5 (September 1976).

9. James Leiby, *A History of Social Welfare and Social Work in the United States* (New York: Columbia University Press, 1978), p. 57.

10. Phillip Popple and Leslie Leighninger, *Social Work, Social Welfare, and American Society* (Needham Heights, MA: Allyn & Bacon, 1990), p. 390.

11. Walter E. Fernald, "The Burden of Feeblemindedness," *Journal of Psycho-Asthenics* 17 (1913): 90–91.

12. Obermann, *History of Vocational Rehabilitation*, p. 84.

13. For instance, Barry Willer and James Intagliata, *Promises and Realities for Mentally Retarded Citizens* (Baltimore: University Park Press, 1984), pp. 8–9.

14. L. McDonald-Wikler, "Disabilities, Developmental," in *Encyclopedia of Social Work*, 18th ed. (Silver Spring, MD: NASW Press, 1987), pp. 422, 434.

15. Rekha Basu, "After the ADA, A Wider Lens," *The Des Moines Register*, December 8, 1996, p. 36.

16. Richard Thornburgh, "The Americans with Disabilities Act and the Future for Children," *Exceptional Parent* 21, no. 2 (March 1991): W10.

17. Mary A. Alter and Lynn Wikler, "Normalized Family Resources for Families with a Developmentally Disabled Child," *Social Work* 31, no. 5 (September–October 1986): 385–390.

18. Kathleen Rounds, "Early Intervention Services for Very Young Children and Their Families under P.L. 99-457," *Child and Adolescent Social Work Journal* 8, no. 6 (December 1991): 489–499.

19. Mary Beirne-Smith, James R. Patton, Richard Ittenbach, *Mental Retardation*, 4th ed. (Upper Saddle River, NJ: Prentice-Hall, 1994), pp. 57–98.

20. Charles W. Humes, Edna Mom Szymanski, and Thomas H. Hohenshil, "Roles of Counseling in Enabling Persons with Disabilities," *Journal of Counseling and Development* 68 (November/December, 1989): 145–148.

21. Lynn Wikler and Maryanne P. Keenan, eds., "Introduction to Part Two," *Developmental Disabilities No Longer A Private Tragedy* (Silver Spring, MD: National Association of Social Workers, and Washington, DC: American Association on Mental Deficiency, 1983), p. 47.

22. Pat Rogan and David Hagner, "Vocational Evaluation in Supported Employment," *Journal of Rehabilitation* 56, no. 1 (January–March 1990): 45–47.

23. Frank R. Rusch, Ronald W. Conley, and Wendy B. McCaughrin, "Benefit-cost Analysis of Supported Employment in Illinois," *Journal of Rehabilitation* 59, no. 2 (April–June 1993): 31-33.

24. John H. Noble and Ronald W. Conley, "Accumulating Evidence on the Benefits and Costs of Supported and Transitional Employment of Persons with Severe Disabilities," *Journal of the Association for Persons with Severe Handicaps* 12, no. 3 (Fall 1987): 163–174.

25. Dennis L. Poole, "Social Work and the Supported Work Services Model," *Social Work* 32, no. 5 (September–October 1987): 434–439.

26. Mit Amold, *Supported Employment for Persons with Developmental Disabilities* (Springfield, IL: Charles C. Thomas, 1992), pp. 5–17.

27. *Social Security Bulletin* 56, no. 1 (Spring 1993): 44–51.

28. Wolf Wolfensburger, *A Brief Introduction to Social Role Valorization as a High-Order Concept for Structuring Human Services*, 2nd rev. ed. (Syracuse, NY: Training Institute for Human Service Planning, Leadership and Change Agency, Syracuse University, 1992).

29. Rita Beck Black, "Diversity and Populations at Risk: People with Disabilities," in Frederic G. Reamer, ed., *The Foundations of Social Work Knowledge* (New York: Columbia University Press, 1994), pp. 393–416.

30. James Garbarino, Patrick E. Brookhouser, and Karen J. Authier and Associates, *Special Children, Special Risks: The Maltreatment of Children with Disabilities* (New York: Aldine de Gruyter, 1987).

31. Bonnie E. Carlson, "Mental Retardation and Domestic Violence: An Ecological Approach to Intervention," *Social Work* 42, no. 1 (January 1997): 79–89.

32. Lynn Wikler, Mona Wasow, and Elaine Hatfield, "Seeking Strengths in Families of Developmentally Disabled Children," in Lynn Wikler and Maryanne P. Keenan, eds., *Developmental Disabilities No Longer a Private Tragedy* (Silver Spring, MD: National Association of Social Workers, and Washington, DC: American Association on Mental Deficiency, 1983), pp. 111–114.

33. Marsha Mailick Seltzer and Marty Wyngaarden Krauss, "Aging Parents with Coresident Adult Children: The Impact of Lifelong Caregiving," in Marsha Mailick Seltzer, Marty Wyngaarden Krauss, and Matthew P. Janicki, eds., *Life Course Perspectives on Adulthood and Old Age* (Washington, DC: American Association on Mental Retardation), pp. 3–18.

34. Tess Bennett, Deborah A. Deluce, and Robin W. Allen, "Families of Children with Disabilities: Positive Adaptation Across the Life Cycle," *Social Work in Education* 18, no. 1 (January 1996): 31–44.

35. Diane T. Marsh, *Families and Mental Retardation: New Directions in Professional Practice* (New York: Praeger Publishers, 1992).

36. Tamar Heller, "Self-Efficacy Coping, Active Involvement, and Caregiver Well-Being Throughout the Life Course Among Families of Persons with Mental Retardation," in Arm P. Turnbull, Joan M. Patterson, Shirley K. Behr, Douglas L. Murphy, Janet G. Marquis, Martha J. Blue-Banning, eds., *Cognitive Coping, Families, and Disability* (Baltimore: Paul H. Brookes, 1993), pp. 195–206.

Additional Suggested Readings

Ellis, Jon B. "Grieving for the Loss of the Perfect Child: Parents of Children with Handicaps." *Child and Adolescent Social Work Journal* 6, no. 4 (Winter 1989): 259–270.

"The Federal Infant-Toddler Program, New Guide to the Part H Law and Regulation," *Early Intervention Advocacy Network Notebook*. Washington, DC: Mental Health Law Project, July 1992.

Freedman, Ruth I., Leon C. Litchfield, and Marji Erickson Warfield. "Balancing Work and Family: Perspectives of Partents of Children with Developmental Disabilities." *Families in Society. The Journal of Contemporary Human Services* 76, no. 8 (October 1995): 507–514.

Hayden, Mary F., and Jon Goldman. "Families of Adults with Mental Retardation: Stress Levels and Need for Services." *Social Work* 41, no. 6 (November 1996): 657–667.

Jennings, Jeannette. "Elderly Parents as Caregivers for Their Adult Dependent Children." *Social Work* 32, no. 5 (September–October 1987): 430–433.

Kupfer, Fern. *Before and After Zachariah*. Chicago: Academy Chi Publications, 1988.

Lipsky, Dorothy Keruler, and Alan Gartner. "Inclusion, School Restructuring and the Remaking of American Society." *Harvard Educational Review* 66, no. 4 (Winter 1996): 762–796.

McDonald, Thomas P., Graciela Couchonnal, and Theresa Early. "The Impact of Major Events on the Lives of Family Caregivers of Children with Disabilities." *Families in Society: The Journal of Contemporary Human Services* 77, no. 8 (October 1996): pp. 502–514.

Moroney, Robert M. *Shared Responsibility*. New York: Aldine, 1986.

Moxley, David P., Melvyn C. Raider, and Sanford N. Cohen. "Specifying and Facilitating Family Involvement in Services to Persons with Developmental Disabilities." *Child and Adolescent Social Work Journal* 6, no. 4 (Winter 1989): 301–312.

Rimmerman, A. "Provision of Respite Care for Children with Developmental Disabilities: Changes in Maternal Coping and Stress Over Time." *Mental Retardation* 27, no. 2 (April 1989): 99–103.

Wehman, Paul, and M. Sherril Moon. *Vocational Rehabilitation and Supported Employment*. Baltimore: Paul H. Brookes, 1988.

11

Social Services and Substance Abuse

FRANK H. WARE

Substance abuse in the United States has become a chronic problem. Millions of individuals have access, despite a plethora of regulations, to potentially dangerous substances, and a substantial number of these individuals will develop problems as a direct result of the use of these substances.

In 1995, approximately 111 million persons age 12 and over were current alcohol users. About 32 million were engaged in problem drinking, and 11 million were heavy drinkers. Among the heavy drinkers, 25 percent were also illicit drug users. A recent Gallup poll reported 45 percent of Americans say that they or someone in their family or a close friend has used illegal drugs. Families and neighborhoods are being torn apart by the crime and health consequences that often accompany addiction. In 1993, the year from which the most recent data are available, Americans spent an estimated $49 billion on illicit drugs.[1] The social burden in economic costs is quantified by totaling the impact of substance abuse on the health care system, the general welfare and social service systems, the law enforcement and the judicial systems, and the employment market. The economic cost to the nation of alcohol abuse and alcoholism alone is estimated to be $85.8 billion.[2] Billions of dollars in goods change hands for the purchase of substances of all kinds. Substance abuse presents our society with a list of intangibles that cannot be quantified, but the tragedy of human suffering and debilitation, destruction of families, and disruption of communities is immense.

Our perspective of substance abuse is as much shaped by political and moral forces as by scientific evidence. In the United States today, existing side by side (often in conflict), are groups of professionals who view the problem of substance abuse from very different perspectives: (1) as hidden within the individual and his or her attitudes toward self, others, and life in general; (2) as hidden in social conditions that create frustration and deprivations while failing to create opportunities and to control access to dangerous substances; and (3) as hidden in the effects of certain substances and the biology of the user.

We do not really know why individuals abuse substances. What is evident is that such persons present a variety of problems intertwined with substance abuse, and that there are variations in the magnitude of these problems. Substance abuse may appear to be the cause or the result of a problem. Substance abuse touches a variety of human difficulties such as intrapersonal emotional problems, interpersonal conflicts, disruptive family relations, physical disorders, work-related problems, and criminal and civil justice problems.

Many choose to use mood-altering substances for what they feel are positive reasons: curiosity, excitement, aesthetic pleasure, attempts to attain status within society or group acceptance, and attempts to experience personal or spiritual growth. For many, drugs are convenient; they dull the pain and offer elusive pleasure. If escape is the goal, the motivation is usually unhappiness, alienation, depression, or an inability to solve personal or interpersonal conflicts.

It is felt that drug addiction is caused in part by *anomie*, "a state of society in which normative standards of conduct and beliefs are weak or lacking; also, a similar condition in an individual characterized by disorientation, anxiety and isolation."[3] This definition applies to the condition of the ghetto dweller and formless violence of suburban youth. The breakdown of the traditional culture of the Native American may be a factor in the alcohol-related problems of that social group. In general, a marked discrepancy between the goals and ideals of a culture and its ability to achieve those objectives may be seen as a precipitating factor in much substance abuse. Some have promoted the idea that "addicts are the scapegoats of our modern secular, therapeutically imbued societies."[4]

SUBSTANCE CHARACTERISTICS AND TRENDS

The total list of substances abused in the United States is extensive. The following are characteristics of major substances of abuse and observable trends of use and abuse.

Alcohol and Other Depressants

Alcohol is one of a group of highly addictive drugs, the central nervous system depressants. Other depressants similar to alcohol include sedative hypnotics and tranquilizers. Alcohol is the most commonly used psychoactive substance in the United States. More people use alcohol than all other substances combined (excluding nicotine and caffeine).

Alcoholism is also one of the most serious public health problems in the United States today. A slow decline in per capita alcohol consumption began in the early 1980s and continues today. There have been corresponding reductions in liver cirrhosis deaths and alcohol-related traffic fatalities. However, despite these declines, in the early 1990s alcohol was a contributing factor in half of all fatal traffic crashes, and alcohol-related mortality accounted for about 5 percent of all deaths in the United States.[5]

Historically, studies have reported that men drink more and experience more adverse consequences of drinking than do women. Recent analysis has shown that, in younger age groups, rates for alcohol abuse in women more closely approximates those in men.[6] On average, untreated alcoholics incur general health care costs at least 100 percent higher than those of nonalcoholics, and this disparity may exist as long as ten years before entry into treatment.

Alcohol taken with other central nervous system depressants has synergistic effects. One dose of alcohol combined with one dose of other depressants multiplies the effect.

Sedative hypnotics, often prescribed in the treatment of anxiety and insomnia, can cause dependence. Tolerance can develop, requiring more of the drug to produce the desired effect. Minor tranquilizers are the most frequently prescribed substances in the United States, with over 90 million prescriptions filled yearly.[7] Overdose and physical addiction are possible with central nervous system depressants. Depressant addiction is severe, and withdrawal can cause death. No other drug category, including heroin and other opiate addictions, causes death during withdrawal.

Heroin and Other Narcotics

Morphine is the naturally occurring substance found in the opium poppy, producing both sedative and analgesic action. The term *opiate* refers to any natural or synthetic drug that induces morphine-like actions. Opiates include morphine; codeine, another naturally occurring opiate; heroin, a semisynthetic derived from a morphine base; and meperidine, methadone, propoxyphene, pentazocine, and other synthetic narcotics.

Heroin use can induce an intensive state of euphoria. The most common method of administration is injection, which produces the most intense reaction. Heroin and other narcotics are addictive. Heroin withdrawal is similar to a severe case of the flu, usually lasting four to seven days. Though restlessness, craving the drug, chills, cramps, and aches and pains are common symptoms of withdrawal, heroin withdrawal is not life-threatening.

There are many myths regarding heroin use and heroin addicts. Heroin in itself does no physical damage to the body. However, the lifestyle that addicts tend to lead often results in diseases, infections, injuries from unsterile injections, and malnutrition, since the addict spends most of his or her money on procuring the drug.

During the 1990s, heroin purity has tended to increase, and the price of heroin has declined. This trend has developed despite international and domestic control efforts that have sought to reduce the availability of the drug. In 1993, the rate of heroin-related emergency episodes increased sharply. Heroin users are initiating the use of the drug at younger ages, and they are beginning to rely on routes of administration such as smoking and snorting, rather than injecting. This may make heroin use more accessible to a wider range of users.[8]

Methadone began to be widely used for both a detoxification and maintenance treatment of narcotic addiction in the 1970s. Currently, an estimated 111,000 clients are receiving treatment in federally licensed clinics.[9]

Amphetamines and Other Stimulants

Amphetamines have a wide popularity and are used to increase the activity of many body functions. The term "stimulants" may be used to describe Dexedrine

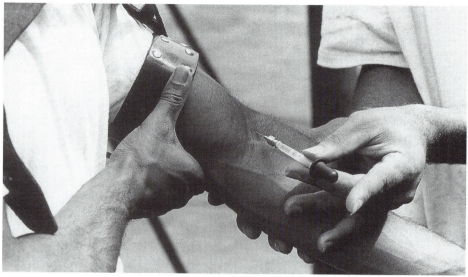

© Joel Gordon

Substance abuse in the United States takes many forms as people in all classes of society "shoot up" with drugs. This problem is particularly severe because of the danger of spreading AIDS through use of contaminated needles.

and other amphetamine drugs, as well as nonamphetamine drugs such as Pre-ludin, Fastin, and Ritalin. Stimulants increase blood pressure, pulse, alertness, and motor and speech activity. Appetite may decrease, and agitation and sleep-lessness are common. Stimulants produce euphoria that may change to anxiety, depression, and fatigue. A speed "run" or "speeding," a continuous pattern of use, can result in sleep deprivation in which hallucinations and/or irritability are common. Withdrawal from amphetamines is only emotionally serious, but the resulting depression is a high-risk time for the individual.

Trends would indicate that, while amphetamines account for a small per-centage of medical emergencies, their nonmedical use has been rising. The drugs are now becoming attractive to young users and are often combined in use with alcohol, heroin, and cocaine. An estimated 4 million persons in the United States have used amphetamines at least once in their life.[10]

Cocaine

Though cocaine is legally classified as a narcotic, it is usually closer to amphet-amines in effect and abuse potential. Cocaine use increased in the United States steadily during the 1980s. Because of the social nature of cocaine, its use was often promoted as harmless, a claim that is not accurate. Steady use slowly in-creases tolerance and can produce strong psychological dependence. Strongly as-sociated with gang-related activities, the widespread use of crack (a cocaine-based drug) increased the popularity and the availability of cocaine. Currently, an estimated 1.5 million Americans use cocaine. Its use has declined from 5.7 million in 1985 (3 percent of the population) to a current .7 percent.[11]

"Mike"

Mike is a 37-year-old professional person who has checked into a psychiatric hospital. His wife is threatening to leave him, and his business partners have informed him that they must terminate their partnership. He experimented with drugs in college without disrupting his life. There is no family history of substance abuse, and he has a strong relationship with his parents. He began using cocaine two years ago and now has a $2,000-a-week habit. Mike reports that "this is the first time in my life things have been out of control."

Hallucinogens

Hallucinogens work by either releasing or inhibiting specific brain chemicals. Though LSD is the best-known hallucinogen, there are other laboratory-produced hallucinogens that include MDA, DOM, and DMT. Some hallucinogens come from the psilocybin mushroom, the peyote cactus button, and morning glory and other seeds. These hallucinogens differ in the intensity of physical effects, though they generally produce an extended vision-induced "trip" lasting anywhere from four to twenty-four hours. Data show that the use of hallucinogens has steadily declined. However, there has been a recent supply and demand for PCP (phencyclidine), which is classified as a "dissociative" anesthetic or as a psychedelic anesthetic, and LSD has regained popularity in some sections of the country.

Marijuana

The use of marijuana had been decreasing steadily in the past decade, though there is evidence that the trend has been reversed. Marijuana remains the most prevalent illicit drug used. Between 1994 and 1995 the rate of marijuana use among youths 12 to 17 increased from 6 percent to 8.2 percent. Since 1992, the rate of use among youth has doubled. Similar trends are evident among both boys and girls and among whites, African-Americans, and Hispanics in metropolitan and nonmetropolitan areas.[12]

Marijuana, once incorrectly legally identified as a narcotic, now shares the "social" status of alcohol, nicotine, and caffeine among many individuals. Marijuana use is no longer seen as an indication for substance abuse treatment.

"Joe"

Joe has disruptive and traumatic circumstances in his life that are created by substance abuse. No members of his family have had substance abuse problems, but his mother has received treatment and medication for nervous tension. As an adolescent, Joe came to experiment with inhalants such as glue; he also "ripped off" his mother's medication and participated in drinking experimentation with his peers. He has recently experienced "blackouts"—periods of time that he is unable to account for once he is no longer under the influence of the substance. He has dropped out of school activities after becoming a frequent absentee from class, and his relationship with members of his family has become strained. Substance abuse has become a problem for Joe and is clearly interfering with his physical health, family life, and social well-being.

———————

The response to the use of drugs and alcohol has not always included the concept of treatment. The following traditional and innovative approaches are found in the fabric of the current substance abuse network.

TRADITIONAL APPROACHES

The Medical Model

I. Alcoholism as a disease.   The disease model, which identifies alcoholism as a progressive illness, has never caught on in regard to other areas of substance abuse. The belief in the disease model has permitted many people to seek help with less fear of being labeled as morally weak. It has permitted society to deal with alcohol-related problems as a treatment issue. The concept has also promoted a fee-for-service system for treatment in recent years, as more physicians become involved in the treatment of alcoholism and as hospitals convert underused bed space to alcoholism treatment units with the support of third-party payments.

The disease model is supported by the contributions of E.M. Jellinek and his description of "gamma alcoholism," although some recent studies question the concept of set stages of alcoholism. At least part of the problem created by trying to develop a single view of alcoholism is the inclusion of women, previously unstudied minority groups, and children and young adults who present few of the symptoms identified by Jellinek. One researcher states:

> Today, after a generation of experience with the clinical intervention approach to alcoholics, and despite the proliferation of expensive alcoholism-treatment centers, alcoholics and alcohol problems persist undiminished. Doubts about the scientific foundation of the disease concept and the efficiency of the clinical intervention model are growing.[13]

II. Detoxification.   One of the first considerations in the treatment of substance abuse is the supervision of the person's withdrawal from the substance. Patients are often brought to detoxification centers by friends, family, or the police. Residence in the detoxification facilities usually lasts from two to five days, during which major withdrawal generally occurs. Detoxification centers provide screening and referral services.

It has often been noted that detoxification facilities are abused by those they are designed to serve—who use the facilities to "clean up" or "dry out" in order to return to abusive patterns of use upon discharge. Physical withdrawal from addictive substances is a necessary approach to rehabilitation but is insufficient by itself. Recently there is a growing interest in the "social detox" model, which is perceived as more cost-effective than hospital treatment. In this model, only patients experiencing severe withdrawal systems are transferred to a hospital setting.

III. Chemotherapy.   Chemotherapy is designed to permit substance abusers to function as socially useful individuals through the use of other chemical substances. Chemotherapy falls into three categories: (1) the use of antagonists that block the effect of the drug or cause adverse reactions when the substance is used; (2) the use of substitutes belonging to the same family as the drug, but having fewer undesired effects; and (3) the use of symptom relievers, such as sedatives, antidepressants, and tranquilizers. Major trends in chemotherapy are as follows:

Antagonists. Antabuse (disulfiram) is often used in alcohol treatment as an adjunct to other therapies. The drug offers a deterrent to resumption of drinking because ingestion of alcohol will, in interaction with antabuse, produce extreme nausea or vomiting. Antabuse is often used for three to twelve months following detoxification.

A major problem with antabuse treatment is that the patient may resume drinking within 24 hours after removing himself or herself from medication. Some research indicates that less than 1 percent of all patients continue to take antabuse after discharge from treatment.[14]

Substitutes. Methadone is itself a highly addictive drug that is used either to stabilize or to wean heroin users from their habits. (Heroin was synthesized in Germany in 1898. It was pronounced as a safe preparation, free from addiction-forming properties, and was widely used in the treatment of morphine addiction.) Methadone in large doses may block the heroin high and does not produce euphoria. Methadone is longer lasting than heroin, and one oral dose will prevent withdrawal symptoms from developing for 24 hours or more.

Addicts report to clinics and receive their medication daily. Because of the lack of euphoria effect, clients maintained on methadone can hold jobs and generally function socially. These clients are, however, strongly addicted to the methadone and would suffer intense withdrawal symptoms if use were discontinued abruptly. Methadone maintenance was pioneered by Dole and Nyswander in 1964.[15] Although administration of methadone is usually accompanied by counseling and support services, it remains a controversial treatment. According to present federal regulations, persons entering methadone programs must be at least 16 years old and must have been addicted to narcotics for at least two years.

While clients are maintained on methadone, they are generally able to get off heroin and lead productive lives. The relapse rate for clients as they begin to undergo detoxification from methadone is substantial.[16] The clients experiencing relapse generally return to heroin or reenter regular methadone maintenance programs.

Nonmedical Approaches

Group and individual therapy.   Unlike the medically oriented technologies, group and individual therapy stresses the client's relating to another person or persons in a therapeutic setting. Many practitioners regard group therapy as an important treatment approach for substance-dependent individuals. Group therapy offers the opportunity for substance abusers to test perceptions, practice new behaviors, receive feedback, and reduce the isolation often associated with substance abuse.[17] The approaches to group or individual therapy are many and varied and are only being suggested here. General readings on major group therapy orientations are explored by Yalom.[18] Group and individual therapy is used nearly universally in substance abuse treatment. Therapy may be provided in outpatient and inpatient settings, both publicly and privately funded. Therapy was found available in 99 percent of the drug-free, methadone maintenance, and multimodality drug treatment programs in the country.[19]

Alcoholics Anonymous and other self-help fellowships.   Alcoholics Anonymous (AA) and other self-help fellowships such as Narcotics Anonymous (NA) are an integral part of many inpatient and outpatient programs. AA was founded in 1935 by two alcoholics for the purpose of providing a fellowship for compulsive drinkers. AA has become a worldwide effort with over 16,000 autonomous groups in North America. Groups hold meetings in which personal narratives concerning the severe problems posed by alcohol consumption are shared. AA is unstructured but is guided by the concept of "Twelve Steps," the first of which is: "We admitted we were powerless over alcohol—that our lives had become unmanageable."[20] Over the years, AA has gained acceptance by many in the professional-treatment community. Some have developed innovative use of the twelve steps as a foundation of counseling the alcoholic.[21]

John Boykin/PhotoEdit

Central to the program of Alcoholics Anonymous are meetings in which personal narratives are offered by individuals in the process of recovery. The "Twelve-Step" philosophy has also been applied in addressing other forms of substance abuse and even to overeating.

Objective outcome data on AA are difficult to obtain, since limited research is conducted. Current data indicate that AA is not as effective as the 60-percent improvement rate reported by AA itself.[22] AA as well as NA demands abstinence as a way of life for the "recovering person." Other offshoots of AA are Al-Anon Family Groups and Alateen for children of alcoholic parents.

Mandatory treatment.   Fostered in part by the belief that the substance-dependent person has diminished capacity to control his or her own behavior, the practice has developed to order persons with "drug problems" into treatment in lieu of incarceration. In many instances, the dramatic change of social attitudes toward recreational drug use has made diversion into "treatment" an absurd parody of its original intent.

A more recent trend in mandatory treatment is emerging out of federal and state welfare reform. Identified substance abusers, including those abusing legal substances such as alcohol, are required to enter and successfully complete treatment in order to retain benefits. Consequences for treatment failure or refusal to enter treatment are severe.

Treatment as an alternative to punishment may be coercion into treatment. From a purely medical or scientific perspective, the decision to use a drug occasionally, even if the drug is not legally available, is not in and of itself a treatable disorder.

"Sue"

Sue is a 35-year-old female. Her family environment was quite dysfunctional, and she was placed in foster care and group facilities from eight years of age until she married for the first time at 17 years. Her first husband physically abused her, and the marriage lasted a matter of months. Her second husband was an alcoholic, and she began to drink heavily with him to "keep the marriage." After the failure of the second marriage, she was treated for depression through a mental health center, but she continues to drink heavily and misuse her medication. Norms, family dysfunction, and social factors are of great importance in Sue's substance abuse problems.

Innovative Approaches

Systems approach.   Systems theory has changed the focus of service to include the network of personal and societal factors that intertwines with the substance abuse problem. As a result of this focus, supportive therapeutic approaches have been added: (1) educational and vocational counseling; (2) job placement; (3) conjoint counseling; (4) recreational counseling; (5) family counseling; (6) income maintenance; (7) public health; (8) clients' rights; (9) legal aid; and (10) prevention services. In addition, those who work from a systems theory perspective advocate social action on a community level to provide the least disruptive services for the client.

Therapeutic communities.   Maxwell Jones began the Social Rehabilitation Unit at Belmont Hospital in England in an attempt to "break away from the doctor dominated world of psychiatry." In this country, the first therapeutic community (TC) was founded by Charles Dederich in 1958. Named Synanon, the community found its base in a self-help model and used recovering persons as staff. TCs receive criticism from professionals for using confrontational techniques and for creating a closed and restrictive treatment environment.

The TC usually calls for a long-term "commitment" from persons who apply for services. Reflecting the elements of a primary social system, the TC stresses group commitment and role modeling as important aspects of treatment. Impressive statistics would point to the TC model's success in rehabilitation for those individuals remaining in the programs for two months or longer.[23] Drug abuse and criminal behavior are viewed as signs of social disenfranchisement, as well as family disturbance and individual maladaptation. Fundamental to the TC concept is the necessity for a total 24-hour community impact to permanently modify lifelong destructive patterns of behavior. The base goals of treatment are somewhat overwhelming: abstinence from drugs, elimination of antisocial behavior, development of employable skills, self-reliance, and personal honesty. Nevertheless, a TC resident wrote:

> This is my view of the TC. I entered after fourteen years of alcohol use and ten years of drug use. These years were filled with misery; five marriages, time spent in prison, time spent in jails, time spent in hospitals, and seven suicide attempts. It is little wonder then that I desired to change my life then.... I am discovering myself and my potential for the first time. I am finding honesty, tears, laughter, joy, peace, love, and most of all hope for the future. I am finding compassion and understanding within a group of people who, like myself, had found themselves lost, but are now finding their way. By helping each other, we help ourselves.[24]

Controlled drinking.   The concept that alcoholics can return to a nonproblem drinking pattern is opposed by groups who see alcoholism as a disease and advocate abstinence as the only feasible choice for recovering alcoholics. Controversy was increased when the Rand Corporation, in June 1976, noted that it was possible for some alcoholics to develop moderate drinking patterns. In a follow-up study published in 1980, Rand said that 61 percent of alcoholics free of drinking problems for four years after admission to treatment had abstained from drinking and that 39 percent were able to drink socially.[25]

Perhaps the strongest precaution comes from the Rand study itself, which concludes that alcoholism is a highly unstable and chronic condition. Although remissions do happen frequently, alcoholics are subject to relapse, and any rate of remission, whether it is aimed at abstinence or nonproblem drinking, is basically unstable over the long term. The subject of nonabstinence goals for individuals is still a matter of controversy, but it is expected that this model will grow in popularity.

Genetic-environmental influences.   The familial pattern in drug abuse is well established. That is, addicts tend to come from families where parents and siblings also have a high incidence of addiction. Approximately 25 percent of the fathers and brothers of alcoholics will likewise be alcoholic, compared to an incidence in the general population of from 3 percent to 5 percent.[26] The relationships are not expressed to the degree that an alcoholic parent will produce an alcoholic biological child, but the statistically significant relationships are indicative of a biological-genetic predisposing condition. Of course, biological factors will interact with environmental conditions. Other biological factors that are subjects of current research include aspects of biochemistry and nutrition.

Industrial substance abuse programs.   Occupational alcoholism programs or employee assistance programs began in the 1940s in a few major companies and have become common in the United States today. AA was a strong influencing factor in the initiation of early programs and still seems to be an integral part of most industrial programs (employed addicts are often referred to NA). Employers and supervisors are being trained to identify substance-related problems and to intervene early.

The most effective approach in the treatment of industrial alcoholism to date has been the "broad brush" approach. Confrontation of employees becomes a legitimate management concern (job performance, absenteeism, lateness, accidents on the job, and so forth). Approximately 50 percent of the cases identified by employee assistance programs are related to substance abuse, with other problem areas—such as marital, financial, psychological, or physiological—making up the remainder of the identified population. In many cases, occupational-based programs have been incorporated into larger health maintenance organizations.

Recovery is more likely with employed persons than with unemployed or disenfranchised persons. The help provided by employee assistance programs is generally short-term, pragmatic, and oriented toward problem solving.[27] Occupational social work is discussed in Chapter 14.

THE ROLE OF THE SOCIAL WORKER

As many of the traditional medically oriented treatment efforts are moving toward a multidisciplinary approach, the scope of addiction studies has moved from a limited view to an interactional perspective. The social worker is uniquely qualified to view the addict or alcoholic as part of a living system that includes the subsystems of family, employer, employing organization, and, in some cases, the court and its legal sanctions. It is obvious that substance abuse is a problem for the individual, family, subgroups of society, and society in general.

Substance abuse as presented today will call for dedicated efforts of (1) the providers of individual, family, and small-group services; (2) program administrators; and (3) planning groups and policy makers. Social workers find themselves encompassed in all of these efforts.

It must be noted that social workers themselves are as likely to develop substance abuse problems as any other segment of society. For social workers who themselves are dealing with their own "recovery," there is often the need to wear "two hats"—to blend their commitment to self-preservation with adherence to their professional code of ethics. Such workers bring to the field invaluable experience and dedication.[28]

Individual, Family, and Small-Group Services

The provider of individual, family, and small-group services is presented with all the problems and conflicts presented to most frontline workers. Some social workers are initially surprised by the reaction of many clients who express the belief that "you can't help me if you are not an alcoholic/addict." Both recovering abusers and nonabusers can be equally effective in assisting clients with substance abuse problems. Despite their effectiveness, professionals have not always been welcomed in a field that had depended on indigenous paraprofessionals as care providers. Special problems sometimes arose when social workers were assigned supervision of paraprofessionals, but it has been demonstrated that with sound supervision techniques these problems can be overcome. Limited resources and decreased social commitment often are frustrating for the worker, who is expected to provide social actualization, family reunification, job and educational capabilities, and abstinence from criminal and/or substance abuse behavior. Over the years, social workers have sought recognition for their professional skills through certification and licensure. Social workers in the substance abuse field today often seek additional certification or licensure as professional substance abuse workers.

The number of substance abusers is far larger than the number of persons who seek treatment. Some of these users may have substance abuse problems but are able through one means or another to bring their lives under control. Many others may be addressed through other social services or the judicial system. Prejudice and skepticism are still present after years of perceiving the substance abuser as depraved and incurable. It becomes the job of the social worker to advocate for the rights of the substance abuser and to demythologize society's view of the individual behind the label.

Administration

Administration of substance abuse programs must face an abundance of critical management issues. These issues may result from problems within the organization, from the local community, and from government funding. Within the program, issues of paraprofessional/professional differences, overworked staff, and facility obsolescence are often cited. Within the community, issues of public opinion, local judicial customs and codes regarding substance abuse and substance users, and the availability of other community services are critical.

The social worker as administrator brings a perspective uniquely different from the management style of the business administrator, a perspective needed to handle three important categories of obligation:

1. He or she must create effective treatment environments.
2. He or she must keep the environment accountable to funders, staff, and clients.

3. He or she must create ways to network with other community services that support the clients' recovery.

Creative and unique administrative designs have developed in substance abuse programming. Some programs have fully integrated the client population into the planning, operation, and funding of the programs, and the blend of professional and "recovering" staff is a model for other human service systems.

There has been a prevalent trend toward efficiency and effectiveness in treatment. Citing many studies that show relatively little difference in the outcome of inpatient versus outpatient care, funders, both public and private, have influenced the utilization of the least costly options. From 1980 to 1994, there was a gradual shift to use of outpatient services. The share of outpatient treatment went up from 84 percent in 1980 to an estimated 87 percent in 1994, while the share receiving 24-hour care declined from 16 to 13 percent. Over the same period of time, privately funded providers shifted more rapidly. In 1980, 20 percent of their daily clients were in 24-hour care; in 1994 it had dropped to an estimated 6 percent.[29]

Another trend is the move toward Behavioral Health Care. Citing high comorbidity of substance abuse and mental health disorders, many have supported the incorporation of the two fields under a behavioral health label. In many states the concept of "one-stop shopping" also includes child protection and health services.

Because of a reduction in social interest, and inflation and funding cutbacks, the challenging question for the future may be: "Can good administrative procedures offset the demoralization of those administrators and their staff when current funding structure puts a premium on client numbers and the cheapest possible way to provide treatment?"

Planning and Policy Making

The nature of substance abuse treatment will change in accordance with changes in knowledge and shifting social priorities. The federal strategy recently has intended to provide balanced and flexible means to reduce the supply of drugs, discourage use, and make treatment available. To keep a balance between treatment and the social-control aspects of substance abuse policy may be the most challenging task for planners.

Currently access to substance abuse care for Americans has lagged behind general medical care. This inequality has had the following consequences:

- Many cannot afford care, especially the underinsured and the working poor.
- The profitable private sector has historically diverted many clients with severe and persistent substance abuse disorders to the overburdened public sector. This same sector in many states now sees public dollars as a likely funding source.
- The failure to access treatment leads to the overuse of general medical resources.[30]

Access to substance abuse services for every American is clearly needed as part of health care reform in the United States. The emerging issues of managed care, welfare reform, privatization, and consolidation of health care services all present planning and policy-making challenges.

SUMMARY AND CONCLUSIONS

Substance abuse was in the past viewed as a moral defect, a weakness of will, a view that created for many the symbol of the abuser as a social deviant in need of either salvation or incarceration. Though self-help efforts and treatment programs have requested dignity for the substance abuser, old views still haunt the memory of many persons who feel, "But really, don't these people bring it upon themselves?"

To discount one's behavior entirely would be in error; to discount society's obligation would be irresponsible. Huge profits are made by those who grow crops for the production of alcoholic beverages; by brewers, distillers, and distributors; by pharmaceutical companies; by the medical and treatment profession; and by federal, state, and local governments receiving tax revenues through their control and distribution of alcohol.

The availability of social service programs for substance abuse is symbolic of society's view of the human condition. Views regarding substance abuse have changed from those held in the past. The question is whether new views will reflect a deeper understanding of the human condition or reestablish a standard hidden somewhere in history.

Notes

1. SAMHSA, Substance Abuse and Mental Health Services Administration Office of Applied Studies, *Preliminary Estimates from the 1995 National Household Survey on Drug Abuse,* Advance Report Number 18, August, 1996 (Rockville, MD: U.S. Department of Health and Human Services Public Health Service, 1996), pp. 20–21.
2. U.S. Department of Health and Human Services, *Eighth Special Report to the U.S. Congress on Alcohol and Health,* September 1993 (Rockville, MD: U.S. Department of Health and Health Services, 1993), p. xxi.
3. White House Strategy Council on Drug Abuse, *Federal Strategy for Drug Abuse and Drug Traffic Prevention, 1979* (Washington, DC, 1979), p. 6.
4. Thomas Szasz, *Ceremonial Chemistry* (Garden City, NY: Doubleday, 1975), p. 2.
5. U.S. Department of Health and Human Services, *Eighth Special Report to the U.S. Congress on Alcohol and Health,* p. xxii.
6. U.S. Department of Health and Human Services, *Eighth Special Report to the U.S. Congress on Alcohol and Health,* p. 259.
7. White House Strategy Council, *Federal Strategy for Drug Abuse,* p. 11.
8. The White House, *The National Drug Control Strategy: 1996* (Washington, DC: 1996), p. 12.
9. SAMHSA, *National Drug and Alcoholism Treatment Unit Survey (NDATUS): Data for 1994 and 1980–1994* (Rockville, MD: U.S. Department of Health and Human Services Public Health Service, 1996), pp. 22–24.

10. SAMHSA, *Preliminary Estimates from the 1995 National Household Survey on Drug Abuse*, p. 17.

11. SAMHSA, *Preliminary Estimates from the 1995 National Household Survey on Drug Abuse*, p. 27.

12. SAMHSA, *Preliminary Estimates from the 1995 National Household Survey on Drug Abuse*, p. 16.

13. Harold Mulford, "'Natural' or 'Scientific' Alcohol Treatment," *Des Moines Register,* March 15, 1988, p. 7A.

14. B.S. Labetkin, P.C. Ribers, and C.M. Rosenberg, "Difficulties of Disulfiram Therapy with Alcoholics," *Quarterly Journal of Studies on Alcohol* 32 (1971): pp. 168–171.

15. Richard C. Schroeder, *The Politics of Drugs: An American Dilemma* (Washington, DC: Congressional Quarterly Press, 1980), pp. 89–92.

16. Peter G. Bourne, *Methadone: Benefits and Shortcomings* (Washington, DC: Drug Abuse Council, 1975), p. 11; Hunter Conway, Jr., testimony before the Senate Labor and Human Resources Subcommittee on Health and Scientific Research, September 10, 1979.

17. Judith A. Lewis, Robert Q. Dana, and Gregory A. Blevins, *Substance Abuse Counseling, An Individualized Approach* (Pacific Grove, CA: Brooks/Cole Publishing Company, 1994), pp. 126–142.

18. Irvin D. Yalom, *Theory & Practice of Group Psychotherapy*, 3rd ed. (New York: Basic Books, 1985).

19. National Institute on Drug Abuse, *Psychotheraphy and Counseling in the Treatment of Drug Abuse* (Rockville, MD: U.S. Department of Health and Human Services, 1990), pp. 1–5.

20. Alcoholics Anonymous, *Twelve Steps and Twelve Traditions* (New York: Alcoholics Anonymous World Services, 1952), pp. 21–24.

21. D.L. Thompson and J.A. Thompson, "Working the 12 Steps of Alcoholics Anonymous with a Client: A Counseling Opportunity," *Alcoholism Treatment Quarterly* 10, nos. 1/2 (1993): 49–61.

22. Alcoholics Anonymous, *Profile of an AA Meeting* (New York: Alcoholics Anonymous World Services, 1972).

23. M.V. O'Brian and D.V. Biase, "Therapeutic Community: A Coming of Age," in J.H. Lowinson, P. Ruiz, R. Millman, J.G. Lamgrod, eds., *Substance Abuse: A Comprehensive Textbook*, 2nd ed. (Baltimore: Williams & Wilkins, 1992), pp. 446–457.

24. Anonymous, "Letter," *Pterodactyl Press III*, April 1980, p. 6.

25. Jon Newton, "Non-problem Drinking Data from Rand Tells Critics," *Toronto Journal,* no. 9, September 1, 1980, pp. 1–4.

26. SAMHSA Substance Abuse and Mental Health Services Administration, *Drug Use Among U.S. Workers: Prevalence and Trends by Occupation and Industry Categories* (Rockville, MD: U.S. Department of Health and Human Services Public Health Services, 1996), pp. 1–7.

27. J.A. Lewis and M.D. Lewis, *Counseling Programs for Employees in the Workplace* (Pacific Grove, CA: Brooks/Cole Publishing Company, 1986), p. 88.

28. "For Members Employed in the Alcoholism Field (Those Who Wear Two Hats)," *AA Guidelines* (New York: G.S.D., no date).

29. SAMHSA, *National Drug and Alcoholism Treatment Survey: 1996* (Washington, DC: 1996), pp. 19–25.

30. Recommendations of the Little Rock Working Group on Mental Health and Substance Abuse Disorders in Health Care Reform (Little Rock, AR, February 3–5, 1993).

Additional Suggested Readings

Bender, L., and B. Leone, eds. *Chemical Dependency, Opposing Viewpoints*. San Diego, CA: Greenhaven Press, 1991.

Collett, L. "Step by Step: A Skeptic's Encounter with the Twelve Step Program." *Mother Jones*, July-August 1988.

Harris, J. *Drugged America*. New York: Maxwell Macmillan International Publishing Group, 1991.

Kinney, Jean. *Loosening the Grip*. 5th ed. St. Louis: Mosby, 1995.

Masing, M. "Desperate over Drugs." *New York Review of Books*, March 30, 1989.

Richmond, C. *Twisted*. Chicago: Nobel Press, 1992.

Schuckit, M. *Drugs and Alcohol Abuse*. New York: Plenum Medical Book Company, 1995.

Stramper, L. *When the Drug War Hits Home*. Minneapolis: Deconess Press, 1991.

Verburg, C. *Substance Abuse in America*. Washington, DC: National Academy Press, 1989.

Wholy, D. *The Courage to Change*. Boston: Houghton Mifflin, 1988.

Wisotsky, S. *Beyond the War on Drugs*. Buffalo, NY: Prometheus Books, 1990.

Yoder, B. *The Recovery Resource Book*. New York: Simon & Schuster, 1990.

12

Criminal and Juvenile Justice

H. WAYNE JOHNSON

Public opinion polls in the last two decades have repeatedly found crime to be among the top concerns of Americans. By almost any standard it is a major social problem. The programs created to deal with offenders constitute a large constellation of social welfare provisions. Their limitations, both in social policy and in programs, are part of the topic of the following discussion. These limitations will be seen to characterize one of the most interesting and important, yet troubled and troubling, social welfare fields.

In this chapter we will consider the social problems of crime and delinquency, the persons accused or convicted of committing these norm violations, and the various social measures, for example, corrections, that society has devised as responses to this deviancy. The "clients" in the justice system supposedly have one thing in common—that they are in difficulty with the law. But they are anything but a homogeneous group. The illegal behaviors leading to the labeling of these persons run a wide range from the "status offenses" of youth (acts legal for adults but illegal for youth) who run away, are truant, and violate curfew or liquor laws or have trouble with their families, to public intoxication and the more serious offenses of theft, burglary, assault, embezzlement, or murder, regardless of age. Such disparate persons may have few similarities apart from their socially defined deviance. There is a world of difference among white-collar criminals, professional check writers, juvenile car thieves, and persons convicted of manslaughter, to cite some examples, and there are probably equally great differences among the individuals constituting just one of these offense categories.

In spite of the image of the offender as a menacing, dangerous creature (requiring bars and cages for containment), the fact is that the vast majority of American crimes consists of property offenses rather than violent crimes against the person. As can be seen in the FBI figures in Table 12.1, the ratio of personal (violent) offenses to property offenses is about 1 to 7.

TABLE 12.1   Index of Crime in the United States, 1991[1]

	Offenses	Rate per 100,000 population
Murder and nonnegligent manslaughter	24,700	9.8
Forcible rape	106,590	42.3
Robbery	687,730	272.7
Assault	1,092,740	433.3
Burglary	3,157,200	1,252.0
Larceny	8,142,200	3,228.8
Motor vehicle theft	1,661,700	659.0
Arson	*	*
Total	14,872,900	5,897.8
Violent crime	1,911,770	758.1
Property crime	12,961,100	5,139.7

*Insufficient data.

Other qualifications of the often assumed homogeneity of this group of persons are that not all offenses are detected or reported; not all reported offenders are apprehended; not all of those apprehended are arrested; not all of those arrested are adjudicated; not all of those adjudicated are convicted; and not all of those convicted are penalized. There is, then, a social selection process all along the route from offense to final disposition with far fewer offenders being handled in institutions and probation offices than being convicted. This process profoundly impacts upon the makeup of the group of persons under consideration in this chapter.

Within those social welfare activities constituting the justice system, some significant distinctions are made that go beyond those in almost any other social welfare field. Two of these classifications are by age and sex. Few other areas in social welfare or social work divide people according to age to the extent that we have labels like *juvenile delinquent*. Urban police departments frequently have special juvenile units. Juvenile courts are set apart from those for adults. Correctional services, too, are delineated by age, whether these are community-based or institutions. Similarly, there is a marked division based on the sex of the offender. In fact, probably no other social welfare field has made as great a sex distinction in its societal responses. While we do not generally have separate welfare departments, hospitals, and family agencies serving males and females, most correctional institutions are still one-sex places although training schools for delinquents are sometimes coeducational. Probation and parole caseloads are often, though not always, largely single-sex, both for children and adults. The sex barrier is changing, but it persists.

Social work as a profession has generally played a larger part with juvenile offenders than with adults, although it is active in both. Historically this activity with youth has often been seen as an aspect of "child welfare" broadly. But juvenile courts, to cite one corrections facet, not only hear delinquency cases but in some states also deal with other family-related matters such as child neglect, paternity, and nonsupport.

Our concern in this chapter is with justice—not social justice in the broader sense addressed by this book generally, that is, in housing, health, education, and other basic areas of human well-being—but justice specifically related to the accused and convicted. We need to examine the elements of the criminal and juvenile justice systems maintained by the society to provide, hopefully, "justice" for all people, including those labeled as deviant.

THE CRIMINAL JUSTICE SYSTEM

Three major subsystems constitute the criminal justice system: *law enforcement,* the *judicial system,* and the *correctional system.* Although social work plays the largest role in corrections, it is also related to the other subsystems, and all three must be considered to understand societal reactions to law violation and offenders. All three are involved in the treatment of these kinds of deviant persons, whether juvenile or adult. The order is significant in that, in general, first contact with suspects and the accused is usually by law-enforcement personnel, whether municipal police, county sheriff's staff, or state or federal agents. In many cases this contact, alone or with others, ends the action without further activity requiring involvement of prosecution and the courts. In other situations police work is only the first step that activates a series of events; the next phase is judicial.

Law Enforcement

One newer development in law enforcement especially pertinent for our purposes is police social work. Early in this century the first police social workers were policewomen. They were to provide certain social services primarily to juveniles and women. The movement then faded.[2] Starting in the 1970s, largely through the efforts of Harvey Treger at the Jane Addams College of Social Work, University of Illinois at Chicago, significant social work roles have appeared in the police departments of several Chicago suburbs and elsewhere, especially in Illinois.[3] The role of the police as commonly portrayed on television is quite distorted. It has been reported that, whereas the typical police officer on TV shoots many people a year, police in the United States actually fire their guns once every 27 years on average.[4] Many police personnel do not spend most of their time pursuing criminals. Rather, a large part of their job is dealing with traffic, or with family and neighborhood squabbles such as disputes between spouses and conflicts between parents and children.[5] It is also true that domestic disputes are among the most dangerous aspects of police work, activities for which police training is generally problematic and for which police may have little enthusiasm.[6] Based on recent FBI statistical reclassification of "disturbance calls," there is some question as to whether police work in domestic disputes is as dangerous as what had been assumed from prior records.[7] However, the new statistical results still show such work to carry a high risk for police.

In some communities, police social workers work in the juvenile unit. In others, their assignments are broader, working generally with family problems. Police social work typically is teamwork, involving the worker, other police personnel, and community agencies and resources. Referrals and follow-up contacts are important in this context.

The acid test of innovative and experimental programs like these is what happens when the federal grants that brought them into being are exhausted. All too often the services die. This has not happened in some of the communities around Chicago and elsewhere, and nonfederal funds have become regular parts of the city and police department budget.[8] These programs can no longer be considered experimental.

Judiciary

The second subsystem in criminal and juvenile justice is the judiciary, the whole area of the courts, prosecution, defense, and disposition of cases by court officials. Here it is necessary to distinguish between adult criminal adjudication procedures and those of the juvenile court.

As noted, social work is more closely identified with work with juvenile offenders than adults. Nowhere is this more clear than in the juvenile court movement itself. Born in Chicago in 1899 in the Progressive Era, the juvenile court personified a principle central to modern social work—individualization. Prior to this development, there was no distinction based on age among persons accused of committing offenses. Youngsters were handled the same as adults when in trouble with the legal authorities. There are records of young children even being put to death not so many decades ago for acts that today would be viewed as relatively minor. This was the way adult law violators were handled, and the same held true for youth. The juvenile court changed all of this through the assumption that each youngster could and should be treated individually toward the goal of rehabilitation. The legal principle involved here was *parens patriae*, the court acting as the ultimate parent.

As a result, the juvenile court, in appearance and procedures, became different than the adult criminal court. Hearings rather than trials were conducted, and they were private and informal, aimed at determining what was best for the youth rather than simply ascertaining guilt or innocence and prescribing sentence. Bail bond was not a part of the juvenile process nor was an arraignment, a grand jury indictment, or proceedings based on the filing of a prosecutor's information, as is done with adults. Until recent years, the presence of defense attorneys in juvenile hearings was the exception rather than the rule. Juries are still not part of the ordinary process for juveniles.

For the first two-thirds of the century, then, the juvenile court was a major social institution operating generally in this way. Beginning in the 1960s, profound changes began to occur with the 1966 *Kent* and 1967 *Gault* U.S. Supreme Court decisions. This grew out of growing concern nationally that the court systems designed to protect children might actually in some ways be detrimental to them. Specifically, there was (and is) reason to be concerned that in the name of helping the child and acting on his or her behalf, the youngster's rights may sometimes be violated. For example, there were occasions when a youth's denial of involvement in illegal acts was ignored or treated lightly because of the obvious presence of problems with the child and/or family, which were seen as requiring intervention. Or, as in the Arizona case of 15-year-old Gerald Gault, a youth was ordered into "treatment" that denied him his freedom until his twenty-first birthday, when an adult convicted of a similar offense could have been fined between five and fifty dollars or incarcerated up to two months.[9] This sense of injustice has transformed the juvenile court into a more legalistic, traditional kind of judicial entity in which more attention is paid to youngsters' constitutional and legal rights. Rules of evidence are now being followed more closely, the atmosphere in the juvenile hearing is more formal, and a defense attorney is present. The only major adult right not so far extended to juveniles in this context is a trial by jury.

Some critics of the juvenile court would take the extreme position of essentially abandoning it and making no distinction between adult offenders and at least many delinquents.[10] To do so would be to go back to the nineteenth-century practices and reject major protections for youth in the modern world. That some adolescents are violent and/or seem not to be amenable to available treatments is little justification for discarding a significant social innovation and "throwing the baby out with the bath water." Hirschi and Gottfredson argue for one justice system rather than two, pointing out that "of the models currently available, the juvenile system seems preferable to the adult."[11]

While the juvenile court is more of a *social work institution* than is the adult criminal court, the latter, too, has been influenced by legislative acts and judicial decisions. The historical direction has been generally toward devoting more attention to the individual offender as a human being and to the rights of the accused, although a more recent countertrend has been toward more severe penalties for offenses. James Q. Wilson and Ernest van den Haag were among the "new conservative" proponents of this latter thrust.[12]

Recently new attention has been devoted to victims and witnesses, often with services for such persons being provided by the prosecutor's office. Traditionally much attention was given to the accused or convicted person, and the victim might be lost in the judicial shuffle. These new programs keep victims and witnesses informed of developments throughout the often long, complex process, provide support in frequently tense situations, and provide other services as needed. Social workers could fill this role, and social work students currently have practicum placements in this setting.

Corrections: Institutions

The third criminal/juvenile justice subsystem is corrections. By the time an individual reaches this point, much has often happened at the hands of law enforcement and/or court personnel. These events have frequently left their mark on the person who has been convicted of committing an offense or, if a youth, found to be delinquent and in need of court intervention. For example, if an offender manifests bitterness, anger, defeat, resignation, or other attitudinal or behavioral attributes, part of the reason may lie within experiences he or she has had with police, judges, or other officials. Such experiences are often less than positive from the offender's view.

Corrections has two major aspects, *community-based* services and correctional *institutions.* Examples of traditional community services for both delinquents and adult offenders are probation and parole. Correctional institutions, on the other hand, run the gamut from short-term jails and juvenile detention centers to reformatories for young adults, and from training schools for youth to prisons mainly for adults. Various political jurisdictions are represented, with jails and detention facilities tending to be city- or county-operated and prisons generally state or federal.

It is important to understand the difference between short-term and long-term institutional care of juvenile delinquents. Detention refers to the former. It is temporary care of a child alleged to be delinquent who requires secure custody in physically restricting facilities pending court disposition or execution of a court order.[13] When properly used, the persons for whom juvenile detention may be appropriate are: (1) some youths from other communities who, it is determined, present too great a risk to hold in less secure arrangements such as foster family care; (2) certain youngsters detained by the police or court pending a hearing are held because their parents could not be reached or because of the seriousness of the offense, the risk to self or others, or likelihood of subsequent illegal conduct; and (3) some youth who have had hearings and have been committed to longer-term institutions and are awaiting transportation and/or admission. Detention is often overused. While by definition it is short-term care, it all too often drags on indefinitely. The physical conditions of detention are another concern. Children should rarely, if ever, be detained in jails with adults, but all too often this is exactly what happens. In mid-1996 an estimated 8,100 juveniles were in jails on one day.[14] The distinction between detention and shelter care is that the former is physically secure and is for delinquents, whereas shelter care is not secure and is for dependent/neglected youngsters. These two groups overlap, and unfortunately some youngsters are in detention who do not require it in spite of delinquency.

While institutions are referred to frequently as *correctional*, they might still today just as well be termed *penal*, the traditional term, because of their typically primitive, punitive nature. All-too-frequent outbreaks of violence such as the infamous Attica (New York) riot of 1971, the New Mexico State Prison riot in 1980, or the one in Ohio in 1993 remind the public of the vastly greater potential dangers on the broader prison scene. In the New Mexico tragedy, at least 33 inmates died and dozens of persons were injured.[15] Among the common problems of correctional institutions contributing to their explosive potential are overcrowding; idleness; indiscriminate grouping; poorly qualified, trained, and paid staff as well as shortage of personnel; poor sanitation, food, and physical conditions; and lack of adequate educational, recreational, and treatment programs, to cite only a few. One of the fundamental attributes of prisons that is so problematic is that they tend to be physically bastille-like containing operations: they are warehouses—a place for holding people involuntarily for long periods of time under conditions marginal at best. Often such facilities are ancient architectural monstrosities unsuited for housing, let alone reforming, persons who have engaged in illegal conduct.

The dangers of incarceration can be summarized as follows: (1) risks of bodily injury or death for inmates and staff in such volatile environments; (2) the phenomenon of "institutionalized personality" through which the inmate becomes so accustomed to and dependent upon the highly structured environment that he or she is rendered unsuitable for living outside this narrow world;

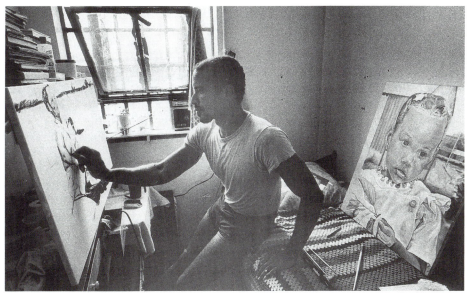

Despite the bad reputation of most maximum security prisons, some institutions allow prisoners to rise above their incarceration and to explore a higher self-expression through art.

(3) the related labeling process in which one is branded by others as a convict, with all that goes with this, and sees oneself accordingly, self-esteem being very much bound up in and affected by labeling; and (4) correctional institutions by their very nature serve as training grounds or "schools" for crime in which techniques are shared among offenders.

It is true that today's American prison is typically not the place of open official brutality of an earlier era. But there are other often more subtle deficiencies. Idleness is its own brutality, so that the disappearance of the leather strap as a punishment instrument (to the extent that it is not as actively used as formerly) does not necessarily signify a renaissance. The problem continues to be serious. Some of the positive changes that have taken place in American prisons have resulted from external pressures as federal courts have found conditions to be intolerable and unconstitutional, constituting cruel and unusual punishment.[16] The prisoners' rights movement has attained some significance in this context.

One response to such prison problems as overcrowding is more brick and mortar—to build new facilities. In recent years, numerous institutions have been erected by the Federal Bureau of Prisons and by state governments. But a parallel social movement in the opposite direction is epitomized by the formation by several groups in the 1970s of the National Moratorium on Prison Construction and some of the activities of organizations such as the National Council on Crime and Delinquency (NCCD). These groups contend that incarceration in American prisons is so dysfunctional (destructive, expensive, and so forth) that the solution is fewer, not more, prisons, and greater emphasis on alternatives to incarceration and on community-based correctional programs.[17] Significantly, at least part of the moratorium movement disappeared in 1987 with the demise of the National Moratorium's newsletter that had, since its start in 1975, opposed new prison construction.

There appears to be consensus that not all people locked in our prisons and penitentiaries require the high walls, guard towers, and other elements of maximum security. One of many examples is the statement of the director of adult corrections in a midwestern state having difficulty with its prison. He indicated that "40 percent of the people we have locked up today don't need to be in prison."[18] Some criminologists have placed the figure much higher. Clearly these architectural artifacts are extremely expensive to build (averaging almost $80,000 per bed) and maintain ($20,000 annually per inmate);[19] they are often counterproductive; they are unnecessary for many of the people on whom they are imposed; and they often serve no useful purpose. Even as we continue to move to greater use of medium- and minimum-security facilities, as has been done to some extent, there still tends to be overuse of incarceration. A major factor in our bulging prison population is the lengthy incarceration of many nonviolent low-level drug offenders.

As critics have often pointed out, the trouble with building more prisons is that they will be used, whether appropriately or not; whether needed or not they will fill up. An Abt Associates 1980 study found a correlation between prison population and prison capacity: "Additions are filled to rated capacity by the second year after opening," and "within five years the occupancy of the new space averages 130% of rated capacity."[20] In addition, once they exist, the state is "stuck" with them for decades to come, no matter how much lay and professional thinking may change in the meantime about the appropriateness of such treatment. Evidence of this is that institutions over a century old are still in use today in spite of the fact they are considered unacceptable by virtually everyone inside and outside the walls. Because they exist and nothing else appears available, they are used and misused. As William Nagel, an ex-warden and prison abolitionist, has said, "So long as we continue to build [prisons], we will have neither the pressures nor the will to develop more productive solutions."[21]

A current controversy has to do with privatization of prisons.[22] Some states are beginning to purchase some or all prison services from private entrepreneurs. The idea is to obtain better or cheaper (or both) prisons. Strong arguments are being made for and against privatization, and it is a significant issue for the entire social welfare field to watch.

Modern social work thinking is somewhat anti-institution and favors community-based programming in general. This is true not only in juvenile and criminal justice but up and down the social welfare line—children, the handicapped, mentally ill, elderly, and others. This is not to say that there is no place for institutions in contemporary thinking. In some fields, perhaps corrections most especially, there continues to be need for a minority of offenders to be institutionalized on a rational, purposeful basis, if for no other reason than the protection of the community and/or the offender from himself or herself at a time when there is still much that is unknown or not fully understood about human behavior. This acknowledges, then, the social control function of corrections, which is perhaps only a more overt demonstration of an aspect of other social welfare programs going far beyond criminal justice. Control is inherent in some programs in mental health, public welfare, and retardation along with other fields.

The question then is not institutions or no institutions but their kind and quality. The dismal truth of correctional institutions generally in this country is that they are deadly, violence-prone places of defeat, apathy, and, all too frequently, suicide and homosexual rape. The latter phenomenon, rape, needs further explanation in order to understand better the "prison problem." There is reason to believe that rape in prison is not as much a sexual matter as one of power in a one-sex, macho environment.[23] Rape is a kind of ultimate degradation, by people desperately attempting to hold or gain self-esteem, of others generally even more vulnerable physically and in terms of self-esteem. To speak of rehabilitation in such an environment seems somewhat unrealistic. What positive changes do occur with inmate attitudes and behaviors would appear to be often in spite of rather than because of incarceration in such settings. There is immense room to humanize such environments, but no matter what positive steps are taken to improve prisons, they always have certain inherent disadvantages, dangers, and limitations. It is important to be realistic and honest when we talk "rehabilitation" under these conditions. There tends to be more rhetoric than reality in such rehabilitation.

Community-Based Corrections

Alternatives to institutions, or "community-based corrections," have been developed. Recently some of these measures have been seen as *intermediate sanctions*, that is, penalties between incarceration and probation. But they are little more than a euphemism in many parts of the country. Words can be very deceiving and may mask business-as-usual practices with the appearance of change, progress, and innovation. Fortunately, our knowledge is greater than our performance, and change is possible, even in this difficult field, if there is the will to bring it about.

Alternatives run all the way through the criminal and juvenile justice systems and processes, from pretrial activities to postincarceration measures. They differ somewhat, just as do traditional services, depending upon whether the target group is juvenile delinquents or adult offenders. Another variable that has some significance in program alternatives and much in traditional programming is sex, as was noted earlier.

Early in the process of apprehending and adjudicating possible offenders there is a set of innovations in some communities aimed at streamlining and modernizing the procedures for handling adult suspects and offenders. Bail bond is an ancient practice of release from jail designed to guarantee the appearance of the accused at a later trial. By its very nature it discriminates blatantly against the poor, people unable to put up money ("make bond") to gain their release. Beginning in the 1960s with efforts of the Vera Foundation and the Vera-Manhattan Bail Project there were a number of experiments around the country in bail bond reform.[24] It has now been conclusively demonstrated in various locations that many persons accused of committing crimes can be released on their own recognizance to await their trials without putting up money and that they will reappear later at the time of the trial. In some studies the rate of appearance for trial is even higher than with bail.[25]

The advantages are obvious: Less incarceration in jail awaiting trials means less expense to the taxpayer and more productivity on the part of the suspect, who can keep or get a job and support his or her family; keeping the accused in the community or returning him or her there more quickly increases the likelihood of some community-based disposition such as probation being ordered for the convicted following the trial rather than more expensive and destructive incarceration. There are other virtues, one of which is the question of justice. In a system that supposedly assumes innocence until proof of guilt and one in which guilt is supposed to be demonstrated in the courtroom, not in the police station, street, media, or elsewhere, it would seem crucial to detain prior to trial only that small portion of suspects who present genuine risks of serious law violation or failure to appear for the trial. In other words, the principle of the least drastic or least restrictive alternative is operative as is individualization, an idea important to social work and one that should be important in criminal justice. These pretrial services facilitate the offender's reintegration into the community without sacrificing public safety.[26]

Safety is always one of the central concerns for the general public—protecting itself from the actions of persons perceived as a threat. People need to learn that they do not achieve security when an offender is incarcerated behind steel and stone. Incarceration is, in most cases, only a temporary measure; the vast majority of those sentenced to prison will be back in the community. Hence, the appropriate question is not whether we will be exposed to him or her because we will be; rather it should be asked under what conditions he or she will return and if he or she will have changed for the better or for the worse as a result of his or her "correctional" experience. The public pays a very high cost for its *in*security, mistakenly believing it to be security.

This matter is even more complex than implied thus far, however, because of other dimensions. For example, it can be argued that a major part of the answer to the previously noted problems in state institutions such as overcrowding and violence is to incarcerate more of these offenders in local (city or county) jails and/or in multicounty regional jails. There could be a number of advantages in this action, including having most offenders closer to home and hence making family contacts easier to develop or maintain and strengthen. Such facilities would be or are smaller, which would generally be an improvement, since a major problem of many American prisons is their large size. More efforts could be made to involve inmates in viable employment programs in the community through work release or partial confinement measures. There are other advantages, too. Regional jails and juvenile detention facilities can be highly appropriate when two or more counties cannot or should not justify their own facilities, as in many rural areas, and can develop centralized, consolidated services cooperatively. In other words, there can be strong, sound arguments for erecting jails, if for no other reason than to reduce the need for large state prison construction. But this approach is appropriate only for the small portion of offenders who truly require incarceration. Other noninstitutional measures are most effective and least expensive for most offenders.

Other Alternatives to Incarceration

In addition to the innovations and alternatives to institutions so far discussed, others include diversion, restitution, community service, work release, partial confinement, house arrest, mediation, two large traditional services—probation and parole, and prerelease centers and halfway houses. Both inside institutions and in communities there also are various counseling, educational, recreational, and employment programs. The social work role in all of these developments varies from almost nil to extensive and extremely significant.

Diversion provides for the routing of the accused or convicted person away from the usual units and steps in the justice system in order to prevent the stigmatizing, labeling, and destructive experiences that tend to accompany the traditional process. In some programs diversion comes early and is a police function; in such cases an offender may be diverted from going to court. In other programs, diversion comes at a later stage involving prosecution and/or the court; then the person charged is diverted from some or all court or subsequent experience. When diverted, the person normally goes into a substitute program such as restitution.

There is a paradox and potential problem that has been pointed out by the critics of diversion. If the accused juvenile or adult is required to admit guilt without benefit of full legal protection in order to gain the opportunity for diversion, there is a real danger that innocent persons may be placed in diversion programs as a result. Another concern is that diversion will simply widen the juvenile/criminal justice net, resulting in more rather than fewer people involved, as is the intention.[27]

As is true of some other social welfare innovations, restitution as a program in the justice system is a fairly simple idea that was not entirely new in the 1970s, the time of its reemergence.[28] Restitution has the advantage of restoring the victims' losses and making amends, both tangibly and psychologically. With the increased interest in victims, victimology, and victim compensation and assistance,[29] it can be seen that to make restitution can be valuable attitudinally and behaviorally for both the abused and the abuser. To be on the receiving end of crime is to feel intimidated and demeaned, whether as a victim of burglary, assault, or purse snatching. To be the perpetrator of such acts may be guilt- or anxiety-producing. The anxiety and anger of both parties can be alleviated at least to some degree through making restitution in some form. In the new programs, restitution is often monitored by a court or administrative agency, and it may be just one aspect of a larger overall treatment plan for the offender.

In some situations, it is not an individual or group of persons who have been harmed by the offender but a collectivity or impersonal entity. An example is vandalism to public property. In such cases, the most appropriate penalty may well be community service such as painting in a courthouse; cleaning a public cemetery or park; helping in a day-care center, nursing home, or neighborhood center; or working with the handicapped in a treatment facility.[30] Although community service offers no panacea for crime and delinquency, it is appealing in several obvious respects, sharing some advantages and attributes of restitution. It is restorative both for the community or persons who suffered loss

Jim West/ Impact Visuals

Volunteers work with juveniles to clean up empty city lots and build playgrounds as part of a Detroit summer project.

at the hands of the offender and for the norm violator. It is relatively easy and inexpensive to administer in contrast to many correctional activities. Further, it avoids the stigma and negative influences of incarceration, and it offers the possibility of facilitating changed attitudes on the part of the general public toward offenders in a more positive, useful direction. Citizens seeing their public buildings and grounds improved by law violators may acquire less harsh and punitive stances toward such persons.

An important issue with community service and some of the other related programs is whether they are actually used as alternative sanctions to institutionalization and hence reduce the number of persons who would otherwise be confined or whether they are used mainly with minor offenders who would not be incarcerated anyway. In the latter case the total number of persons in the overall criminal justice network is increased rather than decreased. In that case the net is widened, and community service would be expansionary rather than diversionary. That this net widening occurs is the conclusion of Irwin and Austin, who advocate shorter prison terms as a more effective way of dealing with prison overcrowding.[31]

Work release is another option that provides some of the same positive features of other alternatives to incarceration. Its roots date back to Wisconsin's Huber law of 1913. Persons on work release experience partial confinement in that they are incarcerated in a jail or some other kind of secure institution but are released during specified time periods to obtain employment, work, or attend school or college. For example, they may work eight hours daily Monday through Friday, spending evenings, nights, and weekends in jail. They may be charged for their meals and jail lodging out of their earnings, thus reducing the taxpayers' burden. Money sent home to families may make public assistance such as AFDC unnecessary or reduce the amount needed. While turning the jail into a "hotel" in this sense may complicate the life of the sheriff and staff, it has very real benefits for persons accused or convicted of offenses and for the community generally.

A variation and reversal of this treatment measure is the partial confinement that takes the form of sentences to incarceration during defined times such as weekends and/or evenings. This can be useful in individual cases by breaking up or diluting such behavior patterns as problematic weekend drinking, while still allowing the person to function in the community on the job, with his or her family, in the usual environment in many contexts. These kinds of innovations also have the effect of avoiding the total institutional experience, the dependency it may create, and the danger of institutionalized personality. Encouraging, if not requiring, people to carry out their responsibilities for themselves in such day-to-day matters as meals, laundry, family, recreation, and education is encouraging people to be responsible. This alternative provides the opportunity.

A limitation on sentencing offenders to spend weekends in jail is that this tends to be a high population period for jails and may cause overcrowding. Some offenders can spend other days of the week locked up and still keep their jobs. For others partial confinement may need to be in less expensive and less restrictive facilities than jails. Many incarcerees do not require the brick and steel security features anyway.

Still another option for a judge can be sentencing a person to remain at home for specified periods. There are various "house arrest" schemes for restricting persons to their homes as they await trial or as part of the punishment following conviction. Through electronic devices now available and in use in some places, it is possible to monitor these people. Even with the cost of the equipment, such programs are much less expensive than jails. They are probably also less damaging to the offender although it is important that the "Big Brother watching" and civil liberty aspects and potentialities of such measures be considered.[32]

Still another set of options is various mediation/conciliation programs aimed at bringing victim and offender together toward working out adjustments and making amends. The goal in such efforts is restoration. Such measures assume that the real victim in crime is the person, not the state or society, and that it is the actual victim who should be satisfied with the results of the punishment process.

All these newer community-based alternatives to institutions have their critics. People often feel that such measures are unrealistic and an easy out for offenders who are perceived as deserving severe punishment. What needs to be recognized is (1) how dysfunctional incarceration is, (2) how expensive it is, and (3) that various community-based measures can be effective and serve the need for punishment. Both the general public and the offender can experience these programs as severe constraints on the guilty parties. Furthermore, the public is not always as concerned with extracting a "pound of flesh" from offenders as is often thought. Wright notes some of the studies suggesting that in both Britain and America victims, offenders, and the public, including criminal justice personnel, favor compensation/restitution and/or community or personal service over prison terms.[33]

In the contemporary interest in more novel alternatives to incarceration, sometimes the two traditional services of *probation* and *parole* are neglected in spite of the fact that they encompass about three-fourths of all offenders under correctional supervision and continue to possess substantial potential to accomplish the multiple purposes of protection of the citizenry, conservation of public funds, and provision of useful services to those in trouble with the law. To understand what is meant by these terms, we will consider their similarities and dissimilarities. Probation and parole have in common that they are conditional releases under supervision and can be revoked. They differ in that probation is a judicial or "judge-made" decision, whereas parole is an administration decision by a parole board, institutional authority, or some governing body. Probation is a release in lieu of incarceration, and parole comes later in the process after a period of incarceration and in lieu of serving the entire sentence to its expiration.[34]

With probation more than parole, there are two aspects to the job: (1) study or investigation bringing together information used in such situations as by a judge in disposing of a case, and (2) supervision of the person who has been ordered placed on probation. In some probation organizations, one probation officer carries both responsibilities, and in others there is a separation of duties with the worker handling only one set of tasks.

Probation and parole operate with handicaps. The public often thinks of them as an easy out for pernicious people who ought to be dealt with severely rather than given a "slap on the wrist." But good-quality probation and parole are not an easy out for the offender. They place demands on him or her while presenting the opportunity and the assistance to change. Unfortunately, probation and parole are often given a bad name when a crime suspect is identified in the media as a probationer or parolee. When a suspect is not on probation or parole, this is not mentioned, of course.

Much of what is criticized is not quality probation and parole but only mediocre practices called by these terms, passing under the label. It could be argued that, in the main, the United States in all of these years has never really instituted probation and parole and given them a fair trial and that what passes for these services is destined to fail because of such factors as (1) excessive caseloads, (2) poorly qualified and inadequately paid staff, (3) insufficient resources and support services, and (4) conflicting purposes and role ambiguity.[35] Caseload figures alone make the point. The President's Crime Commission study in the mid-1960s found over 88 percent of all juvenile cases, over 99 percent of all misdemeanor cases, and almost 97 percent of all felony cases were the responsibility of probation officers having caseloads in excess of 50 persons. The commission recommended an average ratio of 35 offenders per officer.[36]

In recent years some states have moved to what is termed *intensive probation supervision* in an effort to keep more offenders in the community and still protect the public. Caseloads are smaller, supervision of probationers is closer, contact between staff and clients is more frequent. Obviously it is more expensive than regular probation but still costs taxpayers less than institutionalization. Equally important, the evidence is that it can be effective in controlling illegal behavior.[37]

THE SOCIAL WORK ROLE IN CRIMINAL/JUVENILE JUSTICE

Conflicting role expectations are problematic for probation/parole "officers," "agents," "counselors," and so forth. These diverse expectations come from various external quarters and internally. Some probation/parole staff perceive their jobs as similar to law enforcement and act accordingly. Others see the tasks as social work in nature, and this definition determines their conduct. The position of the author is that, properly conceived, probation and parole are social work activities. Like any social work job, they consist of multiple tasks. In role clusters of this sort, some responsibilities are more directly and clearly social work in nature, such as the counseling aspects, and others less so, such as some of the surveillance-type activities and the clerical duties. But the overall thrust of the probation/parole job is social work, that is, it generally includes information gathering (investigation), assessment, developing a plan of action, intervention, and evaluation. This, of course, is the social work helping or problem-solving process, regardless of setting.

But this does not change the fact that "correctionists" and social workers have a hard time coming together. Some corrections professionals look at social workers as impractical and idealistic, insufficiently oriented or committed to certain aspects of some jobs in corrections, like certain perceptions of surveillance activities, and naive about crime and criminals. Some social workers, on the other hand, seem to see no place for social work in corrections, stressing social work's emphasis on client self-determination and noting that corrections clients are involuntary, arguing that you cannot help people who do not want help, or criticizing the confusion of corrections with law enforcement in facets of the tasks performed and punitive stances frequently held by some workers in corrections.

In light of the latter notions, the author would suggest that involuntary clients exist in many social welfare fields, not just corrections. Self-determination is not an absolute, since no one is a totally free agent and we all have constraints. People who do not want help can in fact be aided in the sense that help is relative, and the helper can and does use it selectively. The job of the helper is to enlist the client's involvement and cooperation, working through resistance and dealing with hostility.[38] If social work refuses to have a role in corrections, then it surrenders this important human service field to other, often more repressive groups. In so doing, it plays into a self-fulfilling prophecy: It criticizes punitive orientations toward offenders but relinquishes work with offenders to frequently more punitive people.

In addition to the direct service (casework and group work) activities accompanying such roles as probation, parole, institution social work, and other functions in corrections, social work is important in the other criminal/juvenile justice subsystems, as has been noted. This is particularly true in some of the innovations such as police–social work teaming. Another example is the use of volunteers. Not only may social workers as direct-services workers use volunteers to help with their own caseloads, but social work may also play a significant role in community education about the need for volunteer programs and their value. Establishing such programs can be a social work task as can the recruitment, training, supervision, and evaluation of volunteers.[39] Similar relationships may develop for social work in such innovative programs as Neighborhood Justice Centers, where problems that otherwise may require official court intervention are resolved through conciliation, mediation, and arbitration.[40]

A Case of Juvenile Offenders

Three 16- and 17-year-old boys were referred to the juvenile court by the police after being apprehended together for a series of burglaries, a serious offense. Adults similarly charged often face years of incarceration. The youths might very well have been institutionalized in the state training school or elsewhere. A court intake worker received the cases from the police, interviewed the boys and parents, attended the preliminary hearing, and recommended to the judge that, based on the seriousness of the offense, the youths be held temporarily in the juvenile detention center awaiting further study and information. At that point, the cases were assigned to the probation officer whose job was longer-term than that of the intake worker. It was to gather all pertinent information about the boys, their delinquency, and the total situation.

The school social worker was contacted at the school the boys had attended (all had dropped out) for information from school records. At the detention center the boys were seen individually for in-depth discussions. Detention staff gave the probation officer their observations, including those having to do with the boys' attitudes and adjustment in detention. The probation officer talked separately with each set of parents.

In a few days, the probation officer decided to recommend to the judge that the boys be released from detention to their parents pending their final hearings, yet to be scheduled. Heavy caseloads generally caused more time to elapse before final hearings than was desirable, and if some youths were not released in the meantime, the population of the detention facility would be too high. Furthermore, releasing the youths made it possible to see how they would get along in the community. There was growing reason to believe that they presented few risks of further illegal activity. Throughout the probation officer's work, both before and after detention, it was learned that in spite of the delinquency and a few other weaknesses in the respective individual/family situations, there were significant strengths. All the boys and their families were concerned and cooperative with the police and the court workers. The youths appeared genuinely remorseful. They all held jobs, and one took evening classes in school.

It was the probation officer's responsibility to pull together all the material gathered into a social history or court summary and to make a recommendation to the judge for disposition of these cases. At the final hearing, the judge used the worker's information and accepted the recommendation, placing the youths on probation. In this court, the practice was for the same worker to continue with youngsters placed on probation, and this was done. There was no further delinquency although one boy married his girlfriend when she became pregnant, illustrating that in social work "success" is a relative matter. Some restitution was made. There were significant gains with regard to improved employment situations.

In this example, the taxpayer was saved the expense of unnecessary institutionalization, and three youths and their families were helped. Potentially damaging incarceration was avoided as the youths worked out their problems in the community.

Issues and Trends

The entire field of criminal and juvenile justice teems with issues, some of which have been noted in our discussion to this point. It is clearly a field of great controversy whether one is concerned with the law enforcement, judicial, or correctional realm. We will not repeat here what has already been explored. Rather, we will point out a few additional issues to increase understanding of these important areas and to illustrate further some of the kinds of problems and trends.

Major philosophical concerns in law enforcement center around the role of the police in a free society. How is one to balance individual liberty with collective order? Some famous (or notorious, depending upon one's views) U.S. Supreme Court decisions since the 1960s such as *Gideon*, *Escobedo*, and *Miranda* have, from certain points of view, complicated the job of law-enforcement officers and worked to the advantage of offenders. On the other hand, it is also argued that the effect of such rulings is to require better quality and more professional law enforcement and that these court decisions are consistent with American ideals and principles and the civil liberties of all.

Another area of practical concern is the extent to which suspects/offenders should be pursued when there are great risks to innocent bystanders, law-enforcement staff, and the suspects. For example, a number of persons each year are injured, some even killed, fleeing from the scene of a crime. Some of these injuries and deaths are inflicted by police. In some of these cases, the people injured or killed have had minimal or no involvement in illegal acts.[41] It is not uncommon for police to pursue at high speed persons who have only violated traffic laws.[42] To chase people in cars at 90 miles an hour through city streets and country roads because they have run through stop signs or lights seems unwise. It is not enough to say that police are held responsible for apprehending offenders. They should not do so *at all costs*; there must be reason and balance. Besides, many times such offenders can be safely arrested later in other places, since their identities are often already known or can be determined from auto licenses and other means.

Still another issue that affects the police but is also a larger matter is the easy availability of firearms to almost everyone in the United States. Because this presents such a great danger to peace officers and because every year so many such persons die or are seriously injured as a result of guns in the hands of other people, it is little wonder that police organizations are advocates of gun control.[43] But in spite of all such efforts, we continue to live in a nation with literally millions of guns available.[44] In many states their availability is indiscriminate relative to some or all variables such as age, mental condition, or legal record. But powerful pressure groups and lobbies such as the National Rifle Association reflecting an older, more rural, frontier-type lifestyle continue to convince (or coerce) legislators that the right to possess firearms is somehow essential even to urban America. The fact that public opinion polls have found the vast majority of those surveyed favoring gun control has not so far changed this picture extensively.[45] Social workers need to be aware of such problems and participate in social action and policy development aimed at their resolution. The difficulty in finally enacting even the mild and innocuous Brady bill in 1993 and the 1997 U.S. Supreme Court decision weakening it further illustrate the need for broad citizen involvement in this effort.

In the judicial arena, issues also abound. The two to be discussed here deal with trials and sentencing. A principle of American jurisprudence has long been the idea of a speedy trial following arrest. In view of this, repeated and prolonged delays often in backlogged urban courts are a matter of concern. There are many reasons for the slow pace of rendering justice such as large caseloads and frequent continuances.[46] Some of these have to do largely with prosecution, some with defense, and some with other aspects of the process. But whatever the reasons, the situation is seen by many as undesirable and problematic.

Possible remedies for this problem are on the horizon with new measures being advanced to speed up the adjudication process. But an important question to raise will always be, at what cost will we have swifter trials? Can this be accomplished largely through streamlining and instituting various efficiencies in established practices, or may there be more fundamental threats to due process presented? Such questions are important to many professions, including social work.

Sentencing has always been problematic and in recent years has involved considerable ferment. There is a move in some states away from indeterminate sentencing toward determinate and/or mandatory sentences. A major reason for this development was growing concern over a perception of sentences as being too capricious and unequal. There is the view that similar illegal conduct should bring similar penalties. This movement then reduces the judge's discretion and options and makes sentencing more mechanical. It attacks the indeterminate sentencing idea that penalties should fit the offender rather than the offense and questions whether individualized justice (differential penalties) is not a contradiction in terms. Since individualization is a basic principle of social work, the field should give these debates thoughtful attention.

It would appear that a middle position may be appropriate in this controversy. Some limitations placed on judicial discretion could prevent the most extreme and blatant inequality and abuses in sentencing. But at the same time judges should retain some degree of discretion in order to humanize the law and make it relevant to persons and situations. For these reasons, it would be wise for legal codes to prescribe some range of possible penalties rather than a totally fixed, flat figure (x dollars fine, years incarcerated, and so forth). Convicted persons who are incarcerated could be given a clear picture of how much time they will spend locked up and hence not have to live with painful uncertainty. This can be done without rigid practices in which a prisoner's behavior has nothing at all to do with the date of release.

The whole sentencing controversy illustrates the historical evolution of social movements. Indeterminate sentencing was a reform when it was first introduced, a reaction against rigid, harsh, punitive practices. Some argue now that a new reform is needed to insure justice and equity—hence the determinate sentencing movement. Some also view indeterminate sentencing as too lenient and, as a result, mandatory minimum sentences as a crime control measure have become common. The resulting more certain incarceration and longer imprisonment are factors in the prison population explosion. The pendulum will undoubtedly swing again in the future.

One term of the U.S. Supreme Court was noteworthy partly for the extreme positions taken by the majority on the Court relative to the Bill of Rights.[47] Now the innocent and guilty alike are subject to increased governmental power. Evidence produced by police searches previously held to be unconstitutional under the Fourth Amendment may now be accepted. In its decision on a jail-conditions case the cherished view of innocent until proven guilty has been ignored by the court. And prisoners' personal property may now be arbitrarily seized and destroyed.

Since future developments will be an extension of the present, it is not difficult to predict ongoing tensions and controversies. For example, there may be a decline in adult parole—even conceivably its disappearance—if the movement to determinate sentences accelerates and becomes widespread. Maine abolished parole in 1976, and some other states have ended parole boards' releasing authority.[48] Federal legislation was enacted in 1984 to phase out federal parole beginning in 1987.[49] Totally eliminating parole is unfortunate in this writer's judgment because, even if one agrees with the idea of flat sentences and hence no parole decision to be made, there are important services to be provided to persons leaving correctional institutions. All persons being released, not just those leaving on parole prior to expiration of sentence, should be afforded assistance in reestablishing themselves in the community. They need help with families, housing, employment, education, recreation, counseling, and other matters to smooth the transition and maximize the chances of a positive readjustment.

Interestingly, some states that have in effect abolished parole are reinstituting or retaining postrelease aftercare programs that sound like parole without the name. The realities of prison overcrowding and the need to protect the community via supervising and assisting convicts returned to the community may preserve or resurrect parole. But most states now have laws establishing mandatory minimum incarceration for specific offenses, and many provide sentences of life without possibility of parole. So it seems likely that for some time to come the United States will imprison more persons for longer periods of time than was true in the past.

In the future persons in the criminal and juvenile justice systems, especially corrections, need to learn not to promise more than can reasonably be delivered. This has to do partially with claims relative to recidivism. Since recidivism is in the minds of so many the real test of effectiveness in corrections, it is tempting to make claims beyond our ability to produce. Realities must be faced—crime and delinquency are complex matters that do not easily lend themselves to our treatment activities. Given social forces and values (for example, acquisitiveness and materialism), our limited knowledge of human behavior, our unsophisticated intervention measures, conflicting community attitudes and goals, and other influences, we are not likely to be able to reduce substantially these deviancy rates in the near future.[50]

A factor that needs to be considered relative to the future of these problems and programs is the role of our leaders. Will they help to inform and enlighten the public, a much-needed service, or will they only obfuscate? A case in point is recent presidential election campaigns in which presidential contenders in the two major parties devoted much attention to crime and pandered to the public's emotions. Candidates attempt to outdo each other in their tough-with-crime stances.

Candidates could aid millions of citizens to understand much about crime: that it is largely a youth and young adult phenomenon and the implications of this fact; that labeling itself is problematic; that it is incredibly expensive in terms of not only the losses caused by offenders but also our generally primitive, punitive, hit-and-miss ways of dealing with it that turn out not to be especially productive; that there are options and alternatives to our traditional treatment measures; that crime and criminal justice are extremely complex; that our own social structure, institutions, and values are inextricably intermeshed in our crime; that we may be expecting too much of our justice apparatus given its lack of sophistication and public support; that decriminalization in such areas as status offenders, public drunkenness, and certain drug and other offenses could go a long way toward affording a "solution";[51] and much more. But in the main this does not happen, and hence the future remains uncertain.

Finally, a consideration in future developments is how wide-ranging our mentality (information and attitudes) becomes or whether we "wear blinders." Examining the experience of other nations can be useful in assessing where we are and where we may go. This does not mean that what works well in a smaller more homogeneous country can necessarily be emulated here with equally positive results. But it is important to be informed as to the possibilities and to be imaginative in innovations and implementation. The Netherlands contrasts vividly with the United States in terms of incarceration; the former has one of the lowest rates in the world and the latter has among the highest. When Dodge did his work in the late 1970s, the Netherlands's incarceration rate was 20 per 100,000 compared to 225 for 100,000 in the United States. The average sentence served in prison there was reduced from 3.2 months to 1.1 months at a time when America's sentences are years and are lengthening.[52]

Sweden presents another interesting picture in which incarceration is a last resort and for short duration. In 1983, 66 percent of all incarcerees were sentenced to less than four months, and sentences of a year or more were ordered for only 12 percent. The day fine is used in Sweden. Through this system consideration is given by the court to the seriousness of the offense and the resources of the offender so that the penalty affords more equity than the usual fine in the United States.[53]

Denmark provides for young adult offenders alternative housing in a youth hostel half-occupied by nonoffenders. Another Danish innovation is placing offenders in the homes of volunteer foster families. Germany has come to favor for minor offenders fines over incarceration and has reduced its institutional population rather substantially.[54]

There are also differences internationally relative to the existence and use of capital punishment. In many nations, the United States included, the death penalty declined historically. Now, however, it is being resurrected in this country. While there were no executions in the United States between 1967 and 1976, the 335th since then occurred in July 1996. Over half of these were in Texas, Florida, and Virginia. Included in these executions was the first woman in 22 years and a retarded man.[55] Three persons were executed on one day, the most on one day since executions returned in 1977. State after state has changed statutes in order to meet U.S. Supreme Court objections, and the death penalties of many states are apparently constitutional according to the present Court's interpretation. Since there was a record of over 3,200 persons on death rows in July of 1997 (one-third in California, Texas, and Florida), many more executions may take place in the near future in the absence of major court rulings impeding such action.[56]

SUMMARY AND CONCLUSIONS

This chapter has examined how deviancy is socially defined and how societal reactions are made in response to crime and delinquency. Just as traditional programs (for example, probation, institutions) were social provisions, so modifications in these and the addition of innovative services are social measures and reactions. The criminal and juvenile justice subsystems have been analyzed, shortcomings noted, and reforms such as deinstitutionalization described. Alternatives to incarceration have been stressed. The social work role in the spectrum of services has been explored. In this connection corrections has been seen as a very difficult field generally and a problematic one for social work, but one badly needing social work knowledge, skills, and values. Criminal justice and juvenile justice have been found to be fields ripe with conflict and controversy and with an uncertain future but substantial potential for positive productivity. Which way these fields go depends to a considerable extent on the ability of professionals and the public to be rational in an often irrational climate. And which way they go is important for, in the words of Dostoevski,

> The degree of civilization in a society can be judged by entering its prisons.

Notes

1. *Crime in the United States, 1995: FBI Uniform Crime Reports* (Washington, DC: Government Printing Office, 1996), p. 59.
2. Albert R. Roberts, "The History and Role of Social Work in Law Enforcement," in A.R. Roberts, ed., *Social Work in Juvenile and Criminal Justice Settings*, 2nd ed. (Springfield, IL: Charles C. Thomas Publisher, 1997), p. 105.
3. Harvey Treger, "Police Social Work," in *Encyclopedia of Social Work*, 19th ed. (Washington, DC: NASW, 1995), pp. 1843–1848.

4. Dave Rhein, "Violence on TV Goes Down the Tube," *Des Moines Register*, January 8, 1988, pp. 1T, 5T.

5. Edward M. Colbach and Charles D. Fosterling, *Police Social Work* (Springfield, IL: Charles C. Thomas, 1976).

6. G.A. Goolkasian, R.W. Geddes, and W. DeJong, *Coping with Police Stress*. U.S. Department of Justice (Washington, DC: Government Printing Office, 1986).

7. Joel Garner and Elizabeth Clemmer, "Danger to Police in Domestic Disturbances—A New Look," U.S. Department of Justice (Washington, DC: Government Printing Office, 1986).

8. Albert R. Roberts, "Police Social Work: Bridging the Past to the Present," *Social Work in Juvenile and Criminal Justice Settings*, pp. 126–132.

9. Larry Siegel and Joseph Senna, *Juvenile Delinquency*, 6th ed. (St. Paul, MN: West Publishing Co., 1997), p. 556.

10. D.C. Dwyer and Roger B. McNally, "Juvenile Justice: Reform, Retain, and Reaffirm," *Federal Probation* (September 1987): 47–51.

11. T. Hirschi and M. Gottfredson, "Rethinking the Juvenile Justice System," *Crime and Delinquency* 39, no. 2 (April 1993): 262–271.

12. James Q. Wilson and Richard J. Herrnstein, *Crime and Human Nature* (New York: Simon & Schuster, 1985); Ernest van den Haag, "The Criminal Law as a Threat System," *Journal of Criminal Law and Criminology* 73 (1982): 709–785.

13. Siegel and Senna, *Juvenile Delinquency*, p. G6.

14. D.K. Gillard and A.J. Beck, "Prison and Jail Inmates at Midyear 1996," U.S. Department of Justice (Washington, DC: Government Printing Office, January 1997).

15. "The Killing Ground," *Newsweek*, February 18, 1980, pp. 66–76.

16. Examples are Louisiana, where an entire prison was ordered shut down and someone appointed to plan drastic reforms, and Arkansas, where the state had to increase the prison's budget 600 percent to meet court demands.

17. See, for example, Board of Directors, National Council on Crime and Delinquency, "The Nondangerous Offender Should Not Be Imprisoned: A Policy Statement," *Crime and Delinquency* 21, no. 4 (October 1975): 315–322.

18. Des Moines Register, June 23, 1980, p. 4A. See also H.E. Allen and C.E. Simonsen, *Corrections in America*, 8th ed. (Upper Saddle River, NJ: Prentice-Hall, 1998), p. 231. These authors state that 80 to 85 percent of incarcerated felons do not need maximum security fortress-type prisons.

19. Allen and Simonsen, *Corrections in America*, p. 218.

20. Carol Bergman, "Criminal Justice Reforms: The Struggle Continues," *Jericho*, no. 44 (Fall 1987): 14. This was a former publication of the National Moratorium on Prison Construction, Unitarian Universalist Service Committee, Washington, DC.

21. William G. Nagel, *The New Red Barn: A Critical Look at the Modern American Prison* (New York: Walker, for The American Foundation, Institute of Corrections, 1973), p. 148.

22. Charles H. Logan, "The Propriety of Proprietary Prisons," *Federal Probation* (September 1987): 35–40. See also U.S. Department of Justice, "Private Prisons," by John J. Dilulio, Jr. (Washington, DC: Government Printing Office, 1988).

23. Wilbert Rideau and Billy Linclair, "Sex, Power, Enslavement in Jails and State Prisons," *Des Moines Register*, June 22, 1980, pp. 1C and 3C; and ibid., p. 2C, Ray Cornell, "It *Does* Happen Here; Rape in Iowa Prisons." See also P.L. Nacci and T.R. Kane, "Sex and Sexual Aggression in Federal Prisons," *Federal Probation* (March 1984): 46–53.

24. David Boorkman, Ernest J. Fazio Jr., Noel Day, and David Weinstein, *An Exemplary Project: Community Based Corrections in Des Moines*, U.S. Department of Justice (Washington, DC: Government Printing Office, 1976), p. 8.

25. James G. Carr, "Bail Bondsmen and the Federal Courts," *Federal Probation* (March 1993): 9–14.

26. Boorkman et al., *An Exemplary Project*, pp. 6–14.

27. Siegel and Senna, *Juvenile Delinquency*, pp. 512–515.

28. Richard Lawrence, "Restitution Programs Pay Back the Victim and Society," *Corrections Today* 22 (February 1990): 96–98.

29. Burt Galaway and Joe Hudson, *Perspectives on Crime Victims* (St. Louis: C.V. Mosby, 1981); *Victim Assistance Programs Report Increased Workloads* (Washington, DC: Department of Justice, 1988).

30. Richard Maher and Henry Dufour, "Experimenting with Community Service: A Punitive Alternative to Imprisonment," *Federal Probation* 51 (1987): 22–28.

31. John Irwin and James Austin, *It's About Time: Solving America's Prison Crowding Crisis* (San Francisco: National Council on Crime and Delinquency, 1987), p. 17.

32. Joan Petersilla, *House Arrest*, U.S. Department of Justice (Washington, DC: Government Printing Office, 1988).

33. Martin Wright, "What the Public Really Wants," *Jericho*, no. 44 (Fall 1987): 9 and 15. See also John Doble, *Crime and Punishment: The Public's View* (N.P.: Public Agenda Foundation, 1987); and R.T. Sigler and D. Lamb, "Community-based Alternatives to Prison: How the Public and Court Personnel View Them," *Federal Probation* 51, no. 2 (June 1995): 3–9.

34. H.E. Allen and C.E. Simonsen, *Corrections in America*, 6th ed. (New York: Macmillan, 1992), pp. 668, 670.

35. The President's Commission on Law Enforcement and Administration of Justice, *The Challenge of Crime in a Free Society*, 1967; see especially Chapter 6.

36. Ibid., pp. 167–169.

37. Freda Adler, Gerhard Mueller, and William Laufer, *Criminology*, 2nd ed. (New York: McGraw-Hill, 1995), pp. 503–504.

38. Elizabeth D. Hutchison, "Use of Authority in Direct Social Work Practice with Mandated Clients," *Social Service Review* 61, no. 4 (December 1987): 581–598.

39. William H. Barton, "Juvenile Corrections," *Encyclopedia of Social Work*, 19th ed. (Washington, DC: NASW, 1995), pp. 1563–1577; and ibid, pp. 2483–2490, Patricia C. Dunn, "Volunteer Management."

40. *Justice Assistance News* 1, no. 5 (June/July 1980): 13. See also E.H. Sutherland, D.R. Cressey, and D.F. Luckenbill, *Principles of Criminology*, 11th ed. (Dix Hills, NY: General Hall, 1992), p. 42; "Conflict Resolution," U.S. Department of Justice (Washington, DC: Government Printing Office, March 1997); and R.F. Cook, J.A. Roche, and D.I. Sheppard, *Neighborhood Justice Centers Field Test*, U.S. Department of Justice (Washington, DC: Government Printing Office, 1980).

41. H. Nugent, E.F. Connor III, J.T. McEwen, and L. Neago, "Restrictive Policies for High-Speed Police Pursuits," U.S. Department of Justice (Washington, DC: Government Printing Office, 1990).

42. "Driver Going 160 Falls Prey to 'Silver Bullet,'" *Des Moines Register*, July 9, 1981, p. 1A.

43. *Crime in the United States: Uniform Crime Reports 1995* (Washington, DC: Federal Bureau of Investigation, 1996), pp. 274–276. See also "Youth Violence, Guns and Illicit Drug Markets," U.S. Department of Justice (Washington, DC: Government Printing Office, June 1996).

44. Bill Leonard, "Handgun Laws," *Des Moines Register*, December 20, 1992, p. 1C.

45. David W. Moore, "Public Wants Crime Bill," *The Gallop Poll Monthly*, August 1994, pp. 11–15.

46. Sue Titus Reid, *Criminal Justice*, 4th ed. (Dubuque, IA: Brown & Benchmark, 1996), pp. 169–171.

47. 1983–84.

48. Dean J. Champion, *Corrections in the United States* (Englewood Cliffs, NJ: Prentice-Hall, 1990), pp. 248–249, 531–532.

49. Reid, *Criminal Justice*, pp. 451–452.

50. Jackson Toby, "The Prospects of Reducing Delinquency Rates in Industrial Societies," *Federal Probation* (December 1963): 23–25.

51. Robert F. Meier and Gilbert Geis, *Victimless Crime?* (Los Angeles: Roxbury Publishing Co., 1997).

52. Calvert R. Dodge, *A World without Prisons* (Lexington, MA: Lexington Books, 1979), pp. 133–157. In 1996, there were 1,112,448 prison inmates in the United States, an all-time high.

53. *How to Use Structured Fines (Day Fines) As An Intermediate Sanction*, U.S. Department of Justice (Washington, DC: Government Printing Office, 1996).

54. Dodge, *A World without Prisons*, pp. 101–114; 159–179.

55. "Death Row, U.S.A." (New York: NAACP Legal Defense and Educational Fund, Inc., Summer 1996).

56. "Barfield Now 1st Woman Executed in U.S. in 22 Years," *Iowa City Press Citizen*, November 2, 1984, p. 6A; "Retarded Man Executed for Rape, Slaying of Girl," *Des Moines Register*, July 31, 1987, p. 4A.

Additional Suggested Reading

Braswell, M.C., B.R. McCarthy, and B.J. McCarthy. *Justice, Crime and Ethics*. Cincinnati, OH: Anderson Publishing, 1991.

Currie, Elliott. *What Kind of Future?* San Francisco: National Council on Crime and Delinquency, 1987.

Fulmer, Richard N. "The Prison Ombudsman." *Social Service Review* 55, no. 2 (June 1981): 300–313.

Irwin, John, and James Austin. *It's About Time: America's Imprisonment Binge*. Belmont, CA: Wadsworth Publishing Co., 1994.

Jerin, Robert, and Laura Moriarity. *Victims of Crime*. Chicago: Nelson-Hall Publishers, 1997.

Journal of Contemporary Criminal Justice 13, no. 1 (February 1997). Entire issue on *Conditions of Confinement*.

Morris, Norval, and Gordon Hawkins. *The Honest Politician's Guide to Crime Control*. Chicago: University of Chicago Press, 1970.

Reiman, J.H. *The Rich Get Richer and the Poor Get Prison*. 4th ed. Needham Heights, MA: Allyn & Bacon, 1995.

Rooney, Ronald H. *Strategies for Work with Involuntary Clients*. New York: Columbia University Press, 1992.

Schwartz, Ira M. *(In)justice for Children: Rethinking the Best Interest of the Child*. Lexington, MA: Lexington Books, 1989.

Van Voorhs, Patricia. "Correctional Effectiveness and the High Cost of Ignoring Success." *Federal Probation* (March 1987): 56–62.

Walker, Samuel. *Sense and Nonsense about Crime: A Policy Guide*. 3rd ed. Belmont, CA: Wadsworth Publishing Co., 1994.

13

Aging and Social Work

JEANNE HOWELL MANN

DEMOGRAPHIC CHARACTERISTICS OF OUR AGING POPULATION

Everyone knows that Americans are living longer now. What that means for our future is the subject of much discussion in the media. Knowing it intellectually is one thing; visualizing it is another. Try to imagine what our world will be like when there are three times as many people aged 85 and older, as will be the case in the year 2030, and seven times as many in 2050. If you want to see the future, think about the "gray wave" of senior citizens in the shopping malls, the restaurants, the parks, hotels, and senior centers in Florida, where one out of every five people is over 65. By 2025, the proportion of older Americans throughout the rest of the country will be the same as it is today for Florida, and by 2040, that proportion will be one in four.[1] Eight states will double their elderly population by 2020: Georgia (the only one not in the West), Colorado, Arizona, Utah, Nevada, Washington, California, and Alaska.[2] The slowest-growing elderly population states are expected to be in the Midwest and Northeast.[3]

THE CONSEQUENCES OF DEMOGRAPHIC CHANGE FOR SOCIAL WORK WITH OLDER PEOPLE

Social workers frequently deal with the effects of social change on individuals and families. The profession can expect to see both positive and negative consequences of such a profound demographic change in the structure of our society.

The positive consequences of people living longer may come from:

1. A larger family circle that extends over four or five generations. Families will have the opportunity to know their members over time in a way that heretofore has been rare. More children will know their

grandparents. Grandparents will be able to help their own children with parenting and have the opportunity to influence the lives of their grandchildren. Great-grandparents, undoubtedly frail at some point, may help the growth of compassion and caring in their grandchildren and great-grandchildren as well as contributing to the development of family history. These circumstances have the potential for enriching family life. Social work roles growing from these positive consequences will rely on specialized knowledge about resources that these families may need in terms of care of dependents and community support systems.

2. People who are part of the baby-boom generation will be the best-educated seniors in the nation's history. Education is correlated not only with higher incomes but with better health in later life. Baby boomers have different attitudes toward physical fitness than did their parents and grandparents; their nutrition and health habits are better as well. Common wisdom holds that success in later life depends on good health and sound finances. The "boomers" are learning that it is not age that is the enemy as much as it is our own bad habits.

The negative consequences mean at least two things:

1. At the family level, there will be difficulties for middle-aged children caught in what is called the "sandwich generation." This is a term used to describe people who have parents, children, and grandchildren, or for middle-aged children trying to care for parents with incapacitating disabilities. At the turn of the century, less than 50 percent of the population had a living parent. Today, 80 percent of the people between the ages of 45 and 55 have at least one living parent. Among people in their sixties, 20 percent have a surviving parent. More and more families are facing the challenge of caring for people over 85, where the prevalence of disability is 58 percent.[4] The demographics involved are detailed in Table 13.1.

2. At the societal level, as responsibilities for caregiving grow, so will the cost of providing health and long-term care, now largely provided through government programs such as Medicare and Medicaid. These costs rise along a steep curve for older age groups. The ratio of Medicare and Medicaid spending on people 75 and over to spending on those 65 and over is about 2.5 to 1.[5] The 85+ population may need massive amounts of expensive medical care that will severely strain the nation's health care system. Who will pay for this care? For many people, there is no more important issue in our political and economic life than the resolution of this question. The federal government struggles with health and long-term care budget projections while states implement new ways to deal with the cost of caring for people who are dependent and without the funds to pay for their own care. This is a time of change and innovation in health and long-term care financing. The care that poor dependent elderly receive may depend on in which state they live and whether they have someone acting in their

TABLE 13. The Demographics of Caregiving

Who gives care to aging family members?	Nearly 80% of caregivers are women, who provide the majority of hands-on care
	Among adult children who are primary caregivers, daughters outnumber sons 3 to 1
	80% of family caregivers provide an average of 4 hours of care a day, 7 days a week
	One-third of caregivers are age 65 and older
	Women today can expect to spend 18 years of their lives helping an aging parent and 17 years caring for children
	Less than 10% of caregivers report the use of paid services
	Almost 75% of caregivers live with their disabled elderly relatives
Who resides in nursing homes?	Less than 5% of those 65 and older live in nursing homes, but more than 25% will be in a nursing home at some point during later life
	25% of placements are precipitated by the caregiver's illness or death
	Almost 10% of older people living in private homes would require nursing home placement if family support were withdrawn
	Nearly half of the elders in nursing homes have no close relatives
	Over 70% of nursing home residents are women
Where do older people live?	43% have lived in their present home for over 20 years
	5% live in retirement communities
	Almost 30% live alone (32% of women, 22% of men)
	33% of men and 50% of women over age 65 who are widowed, separated, or divorced live with adult children or other family members

Chart from Wendy Lustbader and Nancy R. Hooyman, *Taking Care of Aging Family Members* (New York: The Free Press, 1994), p. 14. Copyright 1994 by Wendy Lustbader and Nancy Hooyman; copyright 1986 by The Free Press.

best interests who is close at hand. The care for the middle-class and the wealthy will depend on how Congress and the states deal with what Lester C. Thurow calls the "double-40 whammy," by which he means that today the average person over 65 receives 41 percent of his or her income from the government—while another 40 percent have incomes of which 80 percent is from the government. The elderly don't want their benefits cut, but if these entitlements are to continue, taxes will have to be raised, not just a little bit more than the 15 percent paid today, but "…boosted to 40 percent by 2029 to provide the benefits that have been promised."[6] Consider the difficulties involved in resolving these problems at the voting booth when, in 1992, 70 percent of the elderly in this country voted in the presidential election,[7] compared to 43 percent of the people aged 18 to 24.[8]

THE CONCEPT OF AGEISM

Social work is frequently concerned with the effects of negative stereotypes. They get in the way of thinking clearly, whether they are about racial groups (racism), women and men (sexism), or the elderly (ageism).

Ageism is characterized by three distinguishable yet interrelated aspects: "(1) Prejudicial attitudes toward the aged and toward the aging process, including attitudes held by the aging themselves; (2) discriminatory practices against the elderly, particularly in employment, but in other social roles as well; and (3) institutional practices and policies, which, often without malice, perpetuate stereotypic attitudes toward the elderly, reduce their opportunities for a satisfactory life, and undermine their personal dignity."[9] All three contribute to the transformation of the aging process from a stage in the life span into a social problem.

Although people in the helping professions tend to notice "ageist" representations in the media, perhaps they are not as aware that ageism can occur in their own work. In the field of health care, for example, in 1992, the University of Wisconsin Comprehensive Cancer Center published a study concluding that patients over 75 were one-third as likely to be offered radiation and chemotherapy as younger people. And yet, the overall cancer death rate has gone up 13 percent for people 65 and over and declined 5 percent for younger people in the last fifteen years.[10] Another recent study has found that women who are over 65 tend not to be treated as aggressively for ovarian cancer as are younger women. Many older people don't get the screening tests they should. Some doctors overload their patients with pills; others fail to prescribe needed medications. Still others order lab tests when the results of these tests cannot be compared with what is normal for old age because, as yet, these criteria have not been determined, which makes treatment problematic.[11] In the medical world, social workers can play an important role for older people by encouraging them to ask for second opinions, learn more about their own health problems, and become more assertive about the kind of care they need.

Ageism is not confined to young people. Many older people have attitudes about being old that hinder their ability to rehabilitate their bodies after serious illness. They may think that being old means being sick and that rehabilitation is not going to help. They may think that because they have never engaged in daily exercises they cannot do them, or perhaps should not have to learn in old age. They may think that they have earned the right to be dependent, and that their family members have an obligation to take care of them. Sometimes they are afraid that if they are too independent, their families will not care for them and they will be neglected. These attitudes can often sabotage a rehabilitation program after a stroke, a heart attack, or surgery. Doctors describe patients as "poorly motivated" when the patients express the belief that their physical condition is just what should be expected in someone their age and otherwise demonstrate that they lack faith in rehabilitation efforts.[12] In today's world an attitude like this one can have unintended consequences. Insurance companies are quick to act when patients don't demonstrate "timely and progressive improvement" in a rehabilitation program. If reimbursement is terminated, the patient goes home and can be left at a lower level of functioning than is necessary. The ageist attitudes of the elderly patient will then become a self-fulfilling prophecy.

A social worker working with such a case must articulate persuasively the medical/technical regimen of the hospital and work with the belief systems of the patient and the family. The goal in such an intervention would be to help clarify thinking about the mutual expectations among family members, discuss the consequences of not committing oneself to a rehabilitation program, and stimulate thinking about life after rehabilitation. However, once all the options have been set forth, the older person makes the decision and the social worker helps implement it.

Fear of the nursing home haunts many older Americans, even though recent legislation has improved conditions in these institutions. Elderly people are sometimes so afraid of losing their independence that when they have problems they isolate themselves. The suicide rate among elderly Americans climbed nearly 9 percent between 1980 and 1992; one speculation was that the rise might have been due to social isolation.[13]

Many older people do not know that no one can put them in a nursing home without permission from a judge. Social workers often work to protect an elderly person's rights in such a case. One of the most important things to learn about civil rights in our country is how difficult it is to take them away. Our system of laws holds that no one has the right to make any decision for another person unless the courts find that person incompetent to handle his or her own affairs. Eccentric lifestyles do not indicate incompetence, nor do violations of the middle-class dress code. Today, courts move in the direction of what is termed the "least restrictive alternative," which means that if an older person is having trouble balancing a checkbook, or remembering to pay the bills, a representative payee from Social Security or a power of attorney may be set up. Each one has strictly defined tasks limited to one area, compared to an all-inclusive conservatorship, which assumes control of all financial matters. A guardianship, which means surrendering all rights to the oversight of another person, is looked upon with less and less favor unless it can be proven that there is no other viable option.

When an older person needs round-the-clock care, and estimates are that 43 percent will at some point in their lives,[14] a nursing home is the right place to be. Sometimes the need may only be for a short time—to recuperate from an operation, for example, or during rehabilitation after a broken hip. A social worker can make a difference by working to allay the fears of an elderly person, to provide a range of options in nursing homes, and to act as an advocate to ensure that the older person is able to make a desirable choice. Nothing is more important for a person in a nursing home than to have a family member there a good deal of the time, acting as an intermediary and an advocate. When family members and friends are scarce, the role of a social worker can be critical.

IMPORTANT ISSUES AND CONCEPTS

To think about aging without falling into the trap of stereotyping involves learning about the natural consequences of age, as opposed to the consequences of lifelong bad habits, and learning to recognize successful aging patterns.

Biologists use the word "senescence" to refer to the process of aging for all life forms. The process involves deterioration over time, during which viability decreases and vulnerability increases. Increasing chronological age brings an increasing probability of death, although the rate varies at which the changes occur. There are changes in the aging body that are essentially universal, gradual, and irreversible. Senescence is a more useful term for this process than senility because it is free of the prejudices and myths.

Senescence produces obvious changes in how we look and how well we function. But the age at which physical functioning drops below that required for an independent lifestyle varies considerably. Most adults have no serious problems until they are well over 75. And no two individuals are apt to confront exactly the same changes at the same stage in life. We all grow old, but we don't do it in the same way or at the same time. But we can say that there are obvious changes:

1. As the skin ages, it tends to become wrinkled, mottled in color, and dry. It is more subject to bruises, malignancies, and loss of hair than is the skin of a younger person. Sweat glands are reduced in number and diminish the aged body's ability to sweat and cool itself. Hot weather means increased risk for heat exhaustion and stroke.

2. Joints stiffen, particularly in the hips and knees. Degeneration and erosion of the joints are accompanied by a loss of resilience and elasticity of ligaments and cartilage. Muscles lose their strength, although exercise helps slow this process. As people age they become shorter in height because the discs between the vertebrae are flatter. Stooping posture and a slight bending of the knees and hips is common. There is a reduction in the total amount of bone in the skeleton.

3. The nervous system does not process information or send signals for action as quickly as it did. Reflexes are slower than they are in younger people. Changes in cognition occur.

4. People commonly suffer benign senescent forgetfulness (BSF). This form of forgetfulness is different from dementia in the following ways: (1) It involves unimportant data—details such as the name of the person at a party rather than that the party took place; (2) the person knows and apologizes for forgetting; and (3) the person usually remembers later, meaning that the problem is with recall rather than memory.

5. Coronary artery disease increases, but in some instances disease and lifestyle may have greater impact than age.

6. Kidney and bladder capacity drop by 50 percent by the time most people reach age 70.[15]

7. Eyesight may dim. Farsightedness (presbyopia) becomes more pronounced after age 40. The eye can't adapt as quickly to darkness—hence the problem with night vision. Visual acuity may not be as sharp as it is in younger people. Older people may need as much as eight times more light to be able to see as well. Cataracts (clouded vision) are a common and serious problem, and some people develop macular degeneration (the loss of central vision) or glaucoma (optic nerve damage leading to vision loss).

8. Touch isn't as sensitive; taste and smell may decline.

9. Hearing may not be as sharp. There is a tendency to lose the ability to hear high-frequency sounds (the tick of a watch, birds singing). Volume loss may occur because of wax buildup in the ear canal. Earlier hearing loss (due to jackhammers, rock music, etc.) is accentuated with age. Only 22 percent of the people who need them wear hearing aids.[16]
10. Sleep may be disturbed by insomnia, sleep apnea (struggling to breathe, shortness of breath, gasping, snorting, and snoring), and leg movement.

Psychological aging is a developmental process that occurs in tandem with biological aging and an interactive process that occurs between the social environment and the perceptions of self held as a person grows older. Old age was once thought inevitably to bring a decline in self-esteem because of the losses with which it is associated. Some scholars today think that, if such a loss of self-esteem occurs in older people, it may be more a product of ageism than that of changes in personality. The consensus on psychological changes with aging is that: (1) There is a continuity in personality. Individual differences in typical thoughts, motives, and emotions tend to be maintained over time (There is some truth in the saying that as we age we grow "more so"—more opinionated, more exuberant, more the way we have always been.); and (2) the only internal dimension that changes systematically with age is introversion—turning one's interests and attention inward on the self, rather than toward external objects and action.[17]

THE YOUNG OLD, THE AGED, AND THE OLD OLD

Terms like "senior citizens" or "the elderly" cover such a broad span of life (from ages 55–60 to over 100) that they are almost meaningless. Social workers involved with older people routinely deal with the complexity of issues one would expect to find in a period of time that can cover a good part of life. Three stages now used to differentiate among older people are the "young old" (ages 65–74), the "aged" (ages 75–84) and the "old old" (85 and over). The term "frail elderly" refers to the group of people 65 or older who have significant physical and cognitive health problems. It is used to emphasize that not all elderly people have serious health problems.[18]

People at the younger end of the age continuum, the "young old," most often are fully independent. As a consequence of the national obsession with exercise, diet and cholesterol, and giving up smoking, people who have changed their habits have the reward of more energy, fewer heart and blood pressure problems, and a more active lifestyle. Of course some of the natural consequences of aging begin to show themselves (e.g., gray hair, wrinkles, bifocals) but among the "young old" these are more of an inconvenience than a real limitation of abilities.

At the other end of the age continuum are the "old old." Their social, economic, and health characteristics differ greatly from the "young old," and most of the "aged." The "old old" are having a major impact on the nation's health and social service systems because they are the fastest growing part of the population.[19]

As people move through the "aged" toward the "old old" stage, their physical abilities begin to change. As a consequence, many older people experience changes in their abilities to perform ordinary acts of everyday life, like driving or shopping. Night vision becomes problematic for some people. Joints may stiffen to the point at which climbing steep stairs may be difficult or even impossible. Hearing loss can make it hard to follow conversation in a crowd, or to hear the honk of an oncoming auto. However, new and exciting services have developed over the last ten years to serve people who are beginning to suffer limitations in their abilities.

SOCIAL WORK SERVICES TO THE ELDERLY AND THEIR FAMILIES

Case Management

Managed care has had a ripple effect through the long-term care system in the United States. One of the most interesting areas of work for social workers is in *case management*. There are many different ways case management is implemented. Social workers often have the opportunity to work with case management teams of health care professionals to design a plan of care for older people who want to stay in their own homes but are having some difficulty managing it. A recent study commissioned by the State of Hawaii compared case management systems in nine states of the United States. The study found that case man-

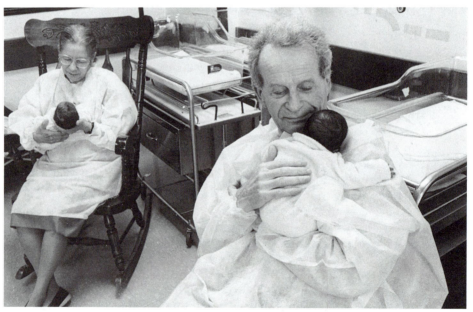

© Joel Gordon

Members of RSVP—Retired and Senior Volunteers Program—in the South Bronx, New York City, are providing love and nurturing for institutionalized crack babies. These caregivers both extend familial affection to the infants and gain the satisfaction of extending their own parenting and grandparenting roles.

agement serves two primary functions in the long-term care system. From the perspective of frail, older adults, it provides access to multiple services. From the perspective of the state, it ensures that public monies are allocated in a fair and appropriate manner to those in need.

The purpose served by a case management system is to coordinate support services so as to provide continuity of care over time and to provide each service as part of a system of help. That system of help is made up of many components, any and all of which can be tapped in the client's best interests. Case management may include, but is not limited to: hospital discharge planning, information and referral, cost control under managed care, social work, public health nursing, and friendly visiting.

The process of case management includes case finding through an entry-level screening tool that often evaluates abilities to perform ordinary activities of everyday life. On the basis of the screening-tool findings, a standardized assessment may be administered if the older person signs a release of information, which is a statement saying that he or she wishes to undergo the assessment and setting out with whom the information found may be shared. A standardized assessment is a document that contains questions on health, physical, cognitive, and affective status as well as social well-being; the current use of services and involvement of the family in care; and a more in-depth look at the person's abilities with activites of daily living.

Standardized assessments act as a safety check to ensure that nothing is overlooked. They also establish a common language providing communication across disciplines and agencies. The purpose of the assessment is to develop meaningful information on the physical, psychological, and social well-being of clients over time and to analyze the outcomes of services set up to help the clients remain independent. This information is used to develop a care plan that is both acceptable to the older person and possible within the framework of available resources.

A care plan starts with a process involving the establishment of the problems to be overcome, what kind of an outcome is to be achieved (what does the client want to happen?), and what kinds of services, both formal and informal, are needed. This process is coordinated by a case manager, who is usually a nurse or a social worker from the agency that provides the most services at the time. The case manager makes referrals approved by the older person to various service providers and assists in setting up whatever might be needed. To be useful both to the client and to the service providers, the care plan must be time-limited, cost-effective, and well documented.

Care plans are monitored in a timely manner and, if changes occur, such as a hospitalization, a reassessment is administered and the care plan redone. If no changes occur, most states require reassessment at least annually.[20]

Direct Services

Social workers are also involved in human service program planning for communities as a whole. Funding for these programs comes from a variety of sources, which can include the federal, state, county, and city governments, in addition to support from United Way and private fund-raising events.

Ulrike Welsch

Senior centers, such as this one in Boston, Massachusetts, provide meal service, preventive health care, adult day care, and counseling.

Examples of these kinds of services include chores, home repair and modification, respite care (which provides relief to family caregivers), congregate meals and meals-on-wheels, assessment and intervention, the Retired Senior Volunteer Program (RSVP), senior centers, and adult day care, among others. Putting together programs to serve the needs of older people can be very creative work. For example, people with cognitive impairments from Alzheimer's disease or strokes, or suffering from mental illnesses like depression, can make use of programs like adult day care, where activities are planned and conducted by a staff, meals are provided, and transportation arranged to and from the program site so that the family can be free of those responsibilities during the day. As part of the system of care involved, often social workers set up caregiver's support groups to help family members, such as the wife who put her dangerous, Alzheimer's-demented husband in a nursing home. Often, having to take a step like this one produces guilt, anxiety, and a loss of self-esteem in the caregiver. Children may not realize how difficult it is to care for a demented person, or they may argue that the behavior is to be expected with age, or they may resent the expenditure of funds for nursing home care. The spouse may feel beleaguered. A support group provides an environment in which people can counsel each other through their common problems as caregivers. It is in such instances that the provision of direct services can become entwined in advocacy.

Senior centers in one form or another exist in most cities and towns across the country today because funding from the Older Americans' Act and state block grants was available in the 1970s and 1980s. Ideally, the services provided include congregate meals, home-delivered meals, transportation, adult day care, preventive health care, and peer counseling in the same facility that offers classes in computers, crafts, and creative writing. Younger seniors traditionally begin their association with senior centers as volunteers, teaching classes, sitting on boards, helping to provide services, and taking part in occasional short-term services. A senior center social worker might be involved in programming, administration, counseling, running an adult day-care program, or training elderly people to act as mental health lay persons among their peers.

A social worker's primary role is to empower people to do what they want to do. As older people age, they become concerned with remaining as independent as possible. In the context of a senior center, they frequently shift from being volunteers who aid in the delivery of help through the center's agencies to recipients of that help. A person who at 60 volunteered to deliver meals to the homebound at 80 might be a recipient of that service. As people reach their mid-70s and 80s, they see many of their friends either move away, become incapacitated, or die. At that point, relationships with other people at the center and with its staff become important in affirming their self-worth. They belong; they are needed; they have a reason to get up in the morning. When a senior center program attracts younger seniors, who bring vitality, power, money, and education, these attributes enrich the lives of those who no longer have as much strength and energy to contribute as much as they once did. This symbiotic relationship occurs when the staff recognizes these diverse needs and responds with programming that is creative and sensitive.

Advocacy

As the "old-old" become more dependent, social workers may find themselves involved in cases of elder abuse (neglect, denial of proper care, extortion, physical and/or emotional abuse, etc.). Drug and alcohol abuse are often part of the problem, and an appropriate referral in such a case would be for treatment of addiction. Sometimes these cases involve an overworked, severely stressed caregiver who feels trapped by a very dependent older person, or perhaps a person who suffered abuse during childhood from the parent she or he is now abusing. One of the most energetic efforts at public education across the country is taking place in several states with task forces developed to combat elder abuse. Laws are being revised to make it easier to prosecute offenders, and multidisciplinary task forces serve to help in abuse situations where the law is not broken but intervention is badly needed. These multidisciplinary teams are made up of representatives from social service agencies, members of the police and sheriff's departments, attorneys, mental health advocates, and hospital staff, among others.

GOVERNMENT FUNDING FOR AGING PROGRAMS

Federal programs for the elderly are very new in our nation's history. Social Security was designed in the 1930s; housing programs, Medicare, and Medicaid in the 1960s; and SSI (Supplemental Security Income) in the 1970s. Despite the fact that they are new, however, their influence on our country is profound. To a large degree they define the range of economic possibilities for older people without substantial resources.

Social Security

Social Security, discussed in detail in Chapter 4, is the most successful and important program in the history of social legislation. Dark clouds are on its horizon, however. Instead of only one in twenty-five Americans being over 65, as was the case in 1900, as stated earlier, by 2040 that ratio will be one in four. What that means is that there are far fewer taxpaying workers to support each Social Security beneficiary. Today there are 3.3. By 2040, there may be as few as 1.6. This is happening at the same time as the extraordinary growth of the "old old" population, with its heavy need for medical care.

> The economist...Herbert Stein once said, "If something is unsustainable, it tends to stop." Or, as the old adage advises, "If your horse dies, we suggest you dismount."
>
> We cannot sustain the unsustainable. Nor can we finance the unfinanceable. By 2013 when Baby Boomers will be retiring en masse, the annual surplus of Social Security tax revenue over outlays will turn negative. By 2030, when all the Boomers will have reached sixty-five, Social Security alone will be running an annual cash deficit of $766 billion. If Medicare Hospital Insurance is included, and if both programs continue according to current law, the combined cash deficit that year will be $1.7 trillion. The horse, in other words, will be quite dead....[21]

Various proposals to resolve these difficulties are being discussed.

The Older Americans Act

In 1965, the Older Americans Act (OAA) brought the Administration on Aging (AOA) into being to serve as the central administrative office for aging programs under the provisions of this legislation. The OAA provided funding for local government and nonprofit agencies for nutrition programs (a national lunch program for seniors), employment and chore services, funding for planning and coordinating functions, and programs like the Retired Senior Volunteers, among others. The list of services expanded during the 1970s to include transportation, home repair, and legal and other counseling services, as well as the setup of "area agencies on aging" (AAAs). All of these services came to be known as "the aging network," and entry into this network provided not only the delivery of services, but activities on behalf of older people, which came to be known as "advocacy."[22] Then the political and economic climate changed. The costs of services became more important and appropriation growth halted. A smaller, subgroup of older people emerged as the focus of attention, and the watchword became "home and community-based care." In the recent past, the aging network has shifted its attention to keeping the frail elderly safely in their homes (and out of institutions). Today, aging network funding is much more reliant on state dollars and Medicare-Medicaid waiver funds than on OAA dollars, which have remained stagnant.[23]

Housing

The Department of Housing and Urban Development (HUD) is charged with meeting the housing needs of people 62 years of age or older who have low incomes and/or disabilities. A thorough discussion of housing issues is to be found in Chapter 24.

Under HUD's Supportive Housing for the Elderly Program,[24] specialized housing for the elderly is available as well. These small cottages (ECHO housing) are free-standing, barrier free, energy efficient, removable, and designed to be installed adjacent to existing one- to four-family dwellings. This Act seeks to enable older people to be independent by expanding the supply of supportive housing designed to meet the special needs of older people and to provide a range of services to meet these needs for the people who live in the subsidized housing.

The White House Council on Aging made recommendations in 1971 that federally subsidized housing projects include long-term care facilities, congregate housing (where assistance with activities of daily living is provided), and personal or homemaker services, as well as recreational and activity programs. We are not there yet. Personal and homemaker services and recreational and activity programs are provided by outside agencies in most subsidized housing today. Assisted living and long-term care facilities are still dreams for the future.

SUMMARY AND CONCLUSIONS

Faculty in social work and in other social sciences in universities across the country are studying the changes that accompany aging. These changes are manifested in social status, roles, living arrangements, and political participation. As people grow older, their religious commitments may change. Their experiences after retirement or on entering the labor force again as a part-time worker are also being studied, as are racial and ethnic experiences and death and dying. All these areas need further research before an accurate picture of the last part of life can be drawn.

What has been presented here is a brief overview of the situation in which most older people find themselves: their current numbers and projections for the future; the kinds of stereotypes and negative attitudes we all carry about aging; the role of federal legislation on what is available to elderly people in the form of services and support; and the role the social worker can play amid the diversity that makes up the world of older people in America.

Notes

1. Peter G. Peterson, "Will America Grow Up Before It Grows Old?" *The Atlantic Monthly* (Boston: The Atlantic Monthly Company, May 1996), p. 55.
2. U.S. Bureau of the Census, Current Population Reports, Special Studies, P23-190, *65+ in the United States* (Washington, DC: U.S. Government Printing Office, 1996), pp. 5–8.

3. Bureau of the Census, *65+ in the United States,* p. v.
4. Wendy Lustbader and Nancy R. Hooyman, *Taking Care of Aging Family Members* (New York: The Free Press, 1994), p. 13.
5. Peterson, "Will America Grow Up," p. 58.
6. Lester C. Thurow, "The Birth of a Revolutionary Class," *New York Times Magazine,* May 19, 1996, p. 46.
7. Bureau of the Census, *65+ in the United States,* p. vi.
8. U.S. Bureau of the Census, Current Population Reports, Special Studies, Series P-23, No. 187, *How We're Changing* (Washington, DC: U.S. Government Printing Office, January 1994), p. 2.
9. Robert N. Butler, "Ageism: A Foreword," *Journal of Social Issues* 36, no. 2 (1980): 8.
10. Doug Poldolsky and Joanne Siberner, "How Medicine Mistreats the Elderly," *U.S. News & World Report,* June 18, 1993, pp. 72–79.
11. Ibid., p. 72.
12. Katherine A. Hesse, Edward W. Campion, and Nassar Karamouz, "Attitudinal Stumbling: Blocks to Geriatric Rehabilitation," *Journal of the American Geriatrics Society* 32, no. 1 (October 1984): 748.
13. *Mobile Press Register,* January 12, 1996, p. 12-A.
14. *The Wall Street Journal,* December 3, 1992, p. 1.
15. Robert J. Rieske and Henry Holstege, *Growing Older in America* (New York: The McGraw Hill Companies, Inc., 1996), p. 75.
16. Ibid., p. 69.
17. Robert C. Atchley, *Social Forces and Aging,* 7th ed. (Belmont, CA: Wadsworth Publishing, 1994), p. 77.
18. Bureau of the Census, *65+ in the United States,* p. 1-1.
19. Ibid., p. 2-8.
20. *Case Management for Hawaii's Older Adults* (Honolulu: State of Hawaii, The Executive Office on Aging, Office of the Governor, January 1991), pp. 7–12.
21. Peterson, "Will America Grow Up," p. 58.
22. Robert H. Binstock and Linda K. George, *Handbook of Aging and the Social Sciences,* 4th ed. (San Diego, CA: Academic Press, Inc., 1996), p. 452.
23. Ibid., p. 453.
24. Cranston-Gonzalez National Affordable Housing Act & Housing and Community Act of 1992, Public Law 102–550, 106 Stat. 3672, October 28, 1992.

Additional Suggested Readings

Allen, Jessie, and Alan Pifer, eds. *Women on the Front Lines: Meeting the Challenge of an Aging America.* Washington, DC: The Urban Institute Press, 1993.
Beaver, Marion L., and Don A. Miller, eds. *Clinical Social Work Practice with the Elderly.* 2nd ed. Belmont, CA: Wadsworth Publishing Company, 1992.
Byers, Bryan, and James E. Hendricks, eds. *Adult Protective Services: Research and Practice.* Springfield, IL: Charles C. Thomas, 1993.
Davis, Nancy D., Ellen Cole, and Esther D. Rothblum, eds. *Faces of Women and Aging.* New York: Harrington Park Press, Inc., 1993.
Hayes, Christopher L., ed. *Women in Mid-Life: Planning for Tomorrow.* New York: Harrington Park Press, Inc., 1993.
Herzog, A. Regula, Karen C. Holden, and Mildred M. Seltzer, eds. *Health and Economic Status of Older Women: Research Issues and Data Sources.* Amityville, NY: Baywood Publishing, 1993.

Jensen, Leif, and Diane K. McLaughlin. "The Escape from Poverty Among Rural and Urban Elders." *The Gerontologist* 37, no. 4 (1997): 462–468.

Lopata, Helena Znaniecka. *Circles and Settings: Role Changes of American Women.* Albany, NY: State University of New York Press, 1994.

Moody, Harry R. *Aging: Concepts and Controversies.* Thousand Oaks, CA: Pine Forge Press, 1994.

Prudino, R.A., C.J. Burant, and N.D. Peters. "Understanding the Well-Being of Care Receivers." *The Gerontologist* 37, no. 1 (1997): 102–109.

Roy, F. Hampton, and Charles Russell. *The Encyclopedia of Aging and the Elderly.* New York: Facts on File, 1992.

14

Occupational Social Work

GLENDA DEWBERRY ROONEY*

Occupational social work is a field of practice in which professional social workers provide social services sponsored by an employer or a union. Social workers in occupational settings provide direct services to individuals and their dependents, and are involved in policy and program development and the administration of policies or programs that ensure a safe, supportive work environment. They also work with medical and personnel departments to improve fringe benefits and working conditions, and provide consultation to management or labor unions concerning the effects of company policies on employees.[1]

The broad practice functions that comprise occupational social work are described as policy; planning and administration; training; direct practice with families, individuals, and special populations; and practice that combines direct service and administration.[2] Program administration includes affirmative action programs and corporate social responsibility initiatives.

WELFARE CAPITALISM AND OCCUPATIONAL SOCIAL WORK

Social work's contribution to the world of work goes back more than a century. Occupational or industrial social work can initially be traced to an era referred to as welfare capitalism. Defined as "any service provided for the comfort or improvement of employees which are neither a necessity or required by law," welfare capitalism began in the late 1890s and lasted through the middle of the 1920s.[3] The system of employer-sponsored welfare services gave rise to the earliest form of occupational or industrial social work practice.

Beginning in the 1890s in England, Germany, and the United States, some industries hired "welfare secretaries," *consuls de famille* or *conseillers du travail* in

---

*The author would like to acknowledge Irl Carter and Nancy J. Johnston, the coauthors of this chapter in earlier editions.

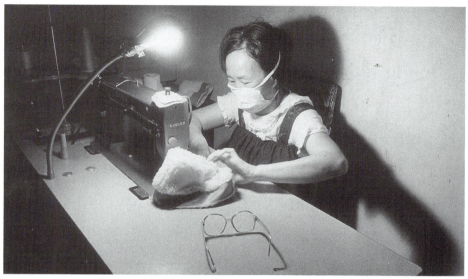

Kathleen Foster/Impact Visuals

New immigrants are often subject to poor working conditions and inadequate wages. Pictured here is a Vietnamese refugee sewing sheepskin slippers in her home in New York, on a contract basis for $1 a pair.

France, and *sozialarbeiten* (from which the term social work is derived) in Germany. In the United States, such individuals were employed by textile mills, as well as International Harvester and National Cash Register, among others.[4] They provided a wide variety of services, including establishing restrooms and washrooms, improving sanitation, introducing safety devices, and supervising visiting nurses. During the height of welfare capitalism in the United States, company programs provided housing, benefit societies, kindergartens, schools for children and adults, sewing and cooking classes, dairy and vegetable farms, visiting nurses, orphanages, and recreational facilities.[5] Support for employees and their families under welfare capitalism, although linked to the production goals of employers, may also be viewed as responses to the social and economic issues of the workforce.

Severe economic conditions during the Great Depression, and the period that followed, significantly influenced the decline of welfare capitalism. Few companies initiated new welfare programs, others dropped those that had been started earlier. Trends toward specialization under "scientific management" gave rise to a group of experts who assumed the role and function of the welfare secretary. In some instances, the welfare secretary was replaced by specialists such as nurses, personnel—or human resources—officers, or administrators. Also, some of the activities performed by the welfare secretary became part of the larger field of social services undertaken by the community, specifically the emergence and growth of community chests between 1920 and 1940.[6]

Following the economic downturn of the Depression, the federal government enacted a series of legislative measures that changed the way in which employers related to employees. The National Labor Relations Act (1935) paved the way for employees to form unions, which would negotiate uniform work-related benefits. Income support programs such as old age pensions and unemployment insurance under the Social Security Act (1935) provided for some rudimentary safeguards in the event of loss of employment. The Fair Labor Standards Act (1935) established a minimum wage. These measures effectively addressed some of the benefit provisions that had been on the agenda of workers and unions since the turn of the century. In effect, they replaced the welfare system, which was viewed as patronizing, feudal, and at the discretion of the employer. Combined, the various measures in essence contributed to a system of employee benefits that met the objectives of earlier welfare capitalism schemes.

The post-Depression era also gave rise to the human relations ideology that is considered to be the second phase of social services in the workplace.[7] The human relations movement emphasized employee well-being and the human dimension as being important to job performance. Many employers, influenced by the human relations movement, accepted occupational social welfare and benefits as good business sense.

SOCIAL WORK PRACTICE AND WORLD WAR II

Attention to employee production, training, and needs resurfaced as the nation prepared to enter and sustain itself through World War II. Manpower shortages and demands of production forced attention to a new group of employees, mainly women and minorities, who had not been previously represented in large numbers in industrial jobs. Large numbers of African-Americans exiting from the violent oppression in the South accelerated their migration to northern and western industrial centers, creating a ready supply of labor.[8] The wartime period is one of the few times in U.S. history that African-Americans enjoyed expanded economic opportunities. Even so, the majority of the new workers were nonminority women and, despite efforts of the War Manpower Commission, there was widespread discrimination in both hiring and working conditions.

During the wartime period, welfare programs similar to those initiated under welfare capitalism once again forged a relationship between social work and business and industry. Unprecedented numbers of social workers were hired in industrial settings, creating shortages in a majority of social service agencies. To meet the demands for social workers, schools of social work offered curricula or training programs in industrial practice, supported by federal funds.[9] The use of social workers during World War II, however, was different from welfare capitalism schemes because the stimulus was the federal government. Except for World War II, during which social services were provided to employees in the defense industries and to merchant marine and military personnel, there were few social workers in occupational settings until the 1970s.

In recognition of occupational social work as a growing field of practice, the Council on Social Work Education and the National Association of Social Workers jointly established a committee in 1975 to study the field and to make recommendations; this led to the first national conference for industrial social workers in 1978. In the decades that followed, the old/new practice of occupational social work emerged as an exciting field of practice. Many social work programs have since offered curricula and field placements in occupational social work.[10]

GROWTH OF OCCUPATIONAL SOCIAL SERVICES

Emphasis on worker well-being and productivity resulted in social workers gaining prominence in occupational settings over the last several decades. The growth of social workers in the workplace may be attributed to the development and expansion of occupational social service programs, an increase in the acceptance of social work practice within business and industry, and progressive changes in organizational cultures. Legislation ensuring equal access to employment—for example, Title VII of the Civil Rights Act, 1964; the Discrimination in Employment Act, 1967; and the Americans With Disabilities Act, 1990—significantly influenced growth in occupational social services. Other factors include the expansion of workers' compensation, increased health care costs and coverage of handicapping to include alcoholism and other chemical dependency, and the broadening of employee benefits to include counseling or therapeutic services. Legislation enacted to ensure a safe working environment, such as the Occupational Safety and Health Act of 1970 (OSHA) and the Drug-Free Workplace Act of 1988, also advanced the development and expansion of employee assistance programs (EAPs) in organizations that received federal funds.

WHAT DOES THE OCCUPATIONAL SOCIAL WORKER DO?

Defining occupational or industrial social work practice is complicated by the diversity of roles and functions as well as by the context in which services occur. Bertha Reynolds, a developer of occupational social welfare, once wrote that the philosophy of social work cannot be separated from the prevailing philosophy of a nation as to how it values people, and what importance is set upon their welfare: "practice is always shaped by the needs of the times, the problems they present, the fears they generate, the solutions that appeal, and the knowledge and skill available."[11] Although Reynolds's reflection dealt with changes in the profession in general, social work practice in occupational settings has similarly shifted with the needs and demands of the times. During the welfare capitalism and wartime periods, social workers assisted with meeting production goals by providing a variety of employee services related to workers' interests, both on and off the job. They helped wartime production through assisting women and minorities in meeting the work and family demands. Concerns related to alcohol use and abuse, the personal problems of employees and their effects upon productivity and job performance, and spiraling health care costs gave rise to occupational alcohol programs (OAPs) and EAPs in which occupational social workers found employment.

Contemporary social workers continue the legacy. Although the services provided are much narrower than those that existed earlier, social workers contribute to humanizing the workplace by providing direct practice for individuals, seminars for employee groups, resource information and referral, and consultation and training to management and labor unions. Social workers in occupational settings are involved in policy development and administration, including the administration of affirmative action programs; the development of fringe benefits in conjunction with personnel or human resource departments; and policies related to occupational health and safety, a drug-free workplace, sexual harassment, and managed care. Occupational social workers have also influenced corporate social responsibility through community relations, corporate philanthropy, and community programs.

Although social workers are engaged in a variety of roles and functions in occupational settings, most are involved in direct-service programs, also commonly called EAPs; other names are OAPs, personnel assistance, or human resources. EAPs and other fringe benefits such as health insurance, vacation, and sick leave are forms of indirect employee compensation.

Employee Assistance Programs

Each decade has witnessed a continual evolution of EAPs. The EAP is conceptualized as a short-term, cost-effective intervention and treatment strategy as well as a human resource tool for dealing with personal problems. OAPs were initially intended as a response to the problem of the alcoholic employee and to concerns about safety and production. Over times, services previously associated with OAPs came under the umbrella of services provided by the EAP.

Although linked, in general, to job performance, EAPs have diminished over time their exclusive focus on impairment. Their scope has expanded to include other problems that employees have, as well as services for family members. Services with a focus on prevention—for example health and wellness and educational seminars—are among the services now provided by EAPs. During the 1980s, EAPs added drug testing, utilization reviews of health services, and managed care—in essence, widening their scope. "Critical incidents stress debriefings" help employees cope with crisis situations such as violence in the workplace and are another service provided by EAPs. Some programs provide resources for care of children and elders.

The development and expansion of EAPs and other occupational social services that assist employees or their dependents with personal and interpersonal problems has coincided with a general trend by work organizations to place more emphasis on human need while maintaining profitability.[12] In addition to their support of the profit motive, EAPs are also viewed as humanitarian in that they are one means to guard against job loss by allowing employees to seek assistance for personal problems.[13]

The following case examples are composites of situations that may be presented to an EAP.

Employee Issues

Situation A.   Margaret is employed as an assembly line worker in a midsize manufacturing company, earning an annual salary of $25,000. She is a single parent, the sole support for her two children, aged eight and fifteen. She is currently eligible for three sick days per quarter and ten vacation days per year.

Margaret has used all of her sick and vacation days. Because she is facing suspension for excessive absenteeism, her supervisor has referred her to the EAP. The supervisor reports that Margaret is having financial problems, and believes that the EAP can help her cope better and manage her finances. According to the supervisor, Margaret earns a good salary, so it is difficult to imagine why she can't manage.

Margaret said that making ends meet on her salary is difficult; she runs low on food before each payday and often chooses between gas, car repairs, clothes for the children, and food. Sometimes she uses a local food shelf. Her car quit running two months ago, and it has been difficult to get to work. Margaret and her older child take turns staying home with the younger child, who has been ill throughout the year. Most often, the older child stays home so that Margaret does not miss work. Margaret can't always afford to take the child to the doctor because she can't afford the dependent health care coverage that is available through her employer.

Situation B.   Geraldo is employed in a poultry processing plant in a rural community. Previous to this job, he and his family were migrants, working on sugar beet farms in an adjacent community. He was born in the United States, but his parents came from Mexico. Geraldo has called the EAP counselor asking for assistance in dealing with what he terms unfriendly coworkers. He is anxious about going to work, and he has difficulty sleeping and concentrating while at work. Several times in the past, he has found graffiti on his locker, and his children are having trouble in school. He has not approached the supervisor for fear of losing his job.

Situation C.   Jane is the eldest daughter of a large family. She is employed as a technician in an electronics company. In the past, the EAP has helped her find affordable day care for her two young children. The issue now concerns her father, who is ill, and her mother, who is unable to meet the constant demands for his care.

Jane has used the majority of her vacation time providing care for her parents. Through an information session conducted and sponsored by the EAP, she learns that the EAP is connected to a network of services that includes elder care home health services. After the session, Jane meets with the EAP counselor who helps her locate a resource for her parents in the community.

Situation D.   John is eligible for EAP services through the benefit program of his wife's employment. He had previously completed treatment for alcohol use and has remained sober for two years. Recently John began using alcohol again. For a time, he did not believe that having a good time with his drinking buddies was a problem. He attributes the problem to being bored. John's supervisor is concerned about the decline in productivity and gave him the option of seeking assistance.

Each of these situations represents a different face of employee assistance services. The range of issues presented by each of the case situations demonstrates the complexity of concerns that employees may have and which may be conceptualized as affecting job performance and well-being. Jane, for example, is in need of a concrete resource. Geraldo's difficulties illustrate the result of discrimination, isolation in the workplace, and an organizational tolerance of harassment. The fact that his children are also experiencing problems in school adds to the stress level of the family. He and his family need support. Perhaps the employer and other workers need sensitivity-to-diversity training as well as an understanding of the effects of harassment.

Margaret may be familiar to a significant number of single-parent families, the majority of whom are women. Both Jane and Margaret represent the growing number of women attempting to balance work and family demands. Linking them to resources are first steps. Within their organizations, consultation with supervisors and managers could include educating them about the multiple roles women manage as well as the financial constraints faced by families in Margaret's circumstances.

In each situation, intervention with the employee is indicated. Each suggests intervention at the macro level as well. A criticism of EAPs and occupational social work is the tendency to focus on the assessment and treatment of the individual to the exclusion of social or economic conditions and environmental or organizational dynamics. These situations are illustrative of issues faced by employees that may affect their performance in the workplace and cause stress in their home and community lives. Social workers and other helping professionals in occupational settings must therefore be knowledgeable about resources, as well as the structure and culture of organizations, and able to assess and intervene in a variety of person-and-environment situations.

AUSPICES AND SERVICE DELIVERY

The auspices of social services in the workplace are trade unions and work organizations, both for-profits and non-profits (such as hospitals, government, and universities). Social services may be among the fringe benefits made available to employees and family members as a result of the employment contract. Delivery of services such as EAPs may be in an office at the work site or at an accessible off-site location. Employers may establish in-house programs and hire professionals to staff them. Many employers purchase off-site employee assistance services from external contract providers such as mental health centers, family service agencies, specialized employee assistance organizations, health maintenance organizations (HMOs), and managed care organizations.

Issues in Occupational Social Work

Occupational social work comprises traditional social work values, knowledge, and skills. However an uneasiness has existed throughout the history of social work's relationship to work organizations; it may seem that the values of the profession are counter to those of work organizations. The profit motive behind the emergence of occupational social work, within the context of welfare capitalism, is also a tension. Welfare secretaries, the early occupational social workers, were not without antagonists. For example, workers pressing for benefits, improved wages, and working conditions sometimes interpreted occupational social services as measures to discredit union organizing, foster dependency, and control the workforce.

Contemporary debates question the compatibility of social work and business partnerships, and point to the motives of organizations and social work as being polar opposites. Three assumptions are evident in this argument. First, there is the assumption that individuals who are employed are not social work's traditional clients—the underclass or vulnerable populations. Second, social work is seen as opposing the profit motive, which is perceived as having a lack of concern for social betterment. Finally, social work has been criticized for what is perceived as an alignment with the agenda of management. These assumptions have some basis, considering the origins and present context of social work in occupational settings. However, social work is also an opportunity to humanize the workplace and support workers' interests. The ongoing discussion of social workers' roles, functions, and responsibilities in occupational settings raises some important issues:

- Possible conflict of the goals of the organization with the welfare of employees; and with equity, social justice, and social work ethics.[14]
- Confidentiality: Who is the client, the organization (or union) or the employee, and what right do various third parties have to information about employees and their situations?
- The social worker's professional responsibility as an advocate versus the obligation to remain neutral.
- In EAPs, who is referred, and why? Why are some employees identified as "being" or "having" a problem? In part, the issue is whether (or how) the social worker should act as an agent of social control.
- The narrowness of the direct-practice focus on the individual in a majority of occupational settings. Social workers are not typically involved in policy or organizational issues, and the range of services or activities in occupational settings is also narrower.
- Despite the profession's "dual focus" on the person and the environment, social workers and other helping professionals providing services in work organizations have tended to emphasize psychological problems as the causes of unsatisfactory job performance.[15]
- The assumption that problems with productivity originate in an employee's life outside of the workplace does not sufficiently recognize stressors that may exist in the work environment.[16]
- The isolation of the social worker in a "host" or secondary setting as the only human service professional, and the importance of social workers understanding their roles and professional obligations as distinct from those of personnel, medical, benefits, or employee relations staffs of the work organization, or from that of a union.

THE FUTURE OF OCCUPATIONAL SOCIAL WORK

The evolution and growth of social services in the workplace have been influenced by increasing health care costs, by the linking of dysfunctional work patterns to personal problems, and by the social and economic forces that affect work organizations and their workers. Since the 1980s, a significant shift in the labor force has occurred. This sift is expected to continue; the workforce of 2000 and beyond will include a larger portion of older workers, women, people of color, and immigrants.[17] Concerns and needs specific to each of these groups will dominate the agenda of occupational social workers. These needs will include child care for single and dual wage-earner parents; elder care for family members of workers; information and referral for immigrants, with efforts to find housing, health services, and schools, and to link them with their communities; and intensive remedial services for workers with deficits in education or training.

Child care needs are likely to increase as a result of welfare reform and welfare-to-work programs. Welfare reform and tax credits for employers will create an expanded labor pool, bringing many nontraditional workers into the workplace. Former welfare recipients may constitute a protected class in categories such as age, sex, and gender. The integration of new employees into the workplace as a result of welfare reform as well as services that are consistent with the needs of minorities, women, and immigrants are issues that will require attention.

Social workers may also play an important role in assisting organizations to develop services consistent with the Family Leave & Medical Act (1993), and other supportive family policies, particularly as women cope with the need to balance work and family, as well as with multiple role demands, stress, role strain, and overload. Gender role demands and outside employment may have particular nuances for immigrant and minority women, for whom family role expectations may be more traditional.[18] In addition, concerns related to cultural awareness and sensitivity to race, culture, and gender may be delegated to occupational social workers as a result of a more diverse workforce.

The general trend to limit governmental involvement and to rely on the private sector to meet human needs will no doubt increase the pressures to provide occupational social services. Specific health conditions may demand the attention of social workers in work organizations; AIDS is the most obvious example, however, diminished physical conditions associated with aging workers are to be considered. Older workers who delay retirement because of changes in Social Security will also have distinctive needs. Diverse family forms—for example, extending benefits to domestic partners and wage disparities for welfare recipients—raise concerns of social justice and equality that will have to be addressed in work settings.

These issues will afford occupational social work opportunities to follow its historical constituency into the workplace. In doing so, it will be important for social workers to use professional knowledge, values, and skills to influence the ideologies and strategies that shape social welfare provisions in occupational settings. It will be important that the occupational social worker is knowledgeable about the work lives of workers and the interpersonal and organizational dynamics in the workplace, including an awareness of the influences that social, economic, environmental, and political factors play in the lives of workers and the dynamics of organizations.

SUMMARY AND CONCLUSIONS

Welfare capitalism was an industrial scheme of social services that began in the 1890s. It is in this context that occupational social work emerged. Some industries in Western Europe and the United States began to hire welfare secretaries or social workers. Their job was to offer a wide variety of services to workers, which may be considered a humanitarian response to human condition and need. These services were also influenced by the organizations' goal to ensure production and profits. By the mid-1920s, economic factors and the emergence of other professionals such as nurses, personnel officers, and administrators, as well as shifts in the focus of the profession, decreased the specialized function of the welfare secretary. Significant legislation also contributed to a system of employee benefits, wages, and working conditions replacing those that had previously been provided at the discretion of employers. The practice of occupational social work reemerged during World War II, however few social workers were employed in occupational settings again until the 1970s. Concerns of employee well-being and productivity contributed to the increased presence of social workers in occupational settings, many of whom are employed in EAPs. The growth of occupational social work in the United States may also be attributed to income supports, occupational safety, ensuring equal access to employment legislation, and concern for employee well-being.

The U.S. workforce has become more diverse. The population of employees includes more older workers, women, minorities, and immigrants. With the exception perhaps of older employees, the workforce may resemble in both composition and human need the individuals who comprised the available labor during the welfare capitalism and World War II eras. In the future, occupational social workers may be called upon to deal with increasingly diverse employee needs and concerns. How can social workers help? First, social workers can use their knowledge and skills to help individuals cope with or resolve their situations. Second, and perhaps more important, social workers can help create an organizational climate that accommodates and supports diversity, and that recognizes that employees' personal and social needs affect their job performance.

The future of occupational social work both resembles past challenges and presents exciting opportunities. Social workers can continue the legacy of humanizing the workplace by exerting their competence in understanding of social conditions, human behavior, the social environment, and diversity. Among the various professional groups involved in occupational social services, it may be social workers who are best able to resolve employee difficulties or concerns that originate from either within or outside of the workplace.

Notes

1. Irl E. Carter, *Industrial Social Work: Historical Parallels in Five Western Countries* (Dissertation, University of Iowa, 1975).
2. See Sheila H. Akabas, "Occupational Social Work," in *Encyclopedia of Social Work* 19:2 (Washington, DC: NASW Press, 1995); and B.K. Googins and J. Godfrey, *Occupational Social Work* (Englewood Cliffs, NJ: Prentice-Hall, 1987), p. 5.

3. Stuart D. Brandes, *American Welfare Capitalism: 1880–1920* (Chicago/London: University of Chicago Press, 1976); David Brody, *The Rise and Decline of Welfare Capitalism, Workers in Industrial America, Essays on the 20th Century Struggle* (New York: Oxford University Press, 1980); and Philip L. Popple, "Social Work Practice in Business and Industry: 1875–1930," *Social Service Review* 55:2 (1981).

4. Carter, *Industrial Social Work.*

5. Brandes, *American Welfare Capitalism.*

6. Louise C. Odencrantz, Employment Manager, Smith Kaufman, Inc., "Social Casework and Industry: Personnel Work in Factories" (*Conference Proceedings,* National Conference of Social Work, Washington, DC, May 1923).

7. Googins and Godfrey, *Occupational Social Work,* pp. 22–23.

8. Nicholas Lemann, *The Promised Land* (New York: Vintage Books, 1992).

9. Family Welfare Association of America (FWAA) War Time Problems Files, Employee Counseling; Impact On Agency Programs (1943); and American Schools of Social Work, War Time Committee on Social Services (1943), *Social Welfare History Archives,* University of Minnesota, Minneapolis.

10. See Michael E. Mor-Barak et al., "A Model Curriculum for Occupational Social Work," *Journal of Social Work Education* 29, 1 (Winter 1993): 63–77, for an example of one school's program; and A. Hoeffer, "Educational Ingredients for Occupational Social Work Practice," *Journal of Social Work Education* 25 (1989): 212–223.

11. Bertha C. Reynolds, "Social Work and the Life of Its Time." Unpublished paper cited in Carel B. Germain, "Social Context of Clinical Social Work," *Social Work* 6 (1980): 483–488.

12. H.M. Trice and J.M. Beyer, *The Culture of Work Organizations* (Englewood Cliffs, NJ: Prentice-Hall, 1993): p. 73.

13. W.J. Sonnesthul and H.M. Trice, *Strategies for Employee Assistance Programs: The Crucial Balance* (Ithaca, NY: ILR Press, 1986); and P.H. Roman and T. Blum, "The Core Technology of Employee Assistance Programs: A Reaffirmation," *The ALMACAN,* 15:3 (1988): 8–19.

14. M. Abramovitz and I. Epstein, "The Politics of Privatization: Industrial Social Work Practice and Private Enterprise," *Urban and Social Change Review* 16:1 (1983): 13–20; R. Balinsky, "People vs. Profits: Social Work Practice in Industry," *Social Work* 25 (1980): 471–475; and M.N. Ozawa, "Development of Social Services in Industry: Why and How?" *Social Work* 25 (1980): 464–470.

15. Bradley Googins and Bruce N. Davidson, "The Organization as Client: Broadening the Concept of Employee Assistance Programs," *Social Work* 38:4 (1993): 477–488; C.S. Ramanathan, "EAP's Response to Personal Stress and Productivity," *Social Work* 37 (1992): 234–239; P.R. Balgopal, "Occupational Social Work: An Expanded Clinical Perspective," *Social Work* 34:5 (1989): 437–442; H. Yamantani, "Client Assessment: A Cross-sectional Method," *Social Work* 33:1 (1988): 34–37; G. Davis, "Retooling Clinical Social Work to Occupational Social Work," *Social Casework* 66, no. 8 (1985): 499–503; and R. Donovan, "Stress in the Workplace: A Framework for Research and Practice," *Social Casework* 68 (1987): 259–266.

16. H.M. Trice and J.M. Beyer, *The Culture of Work Organizations,* pp. 71–72; J.G. Gonyea and B.K. Googins, "Linking the World of Work and Family: Beyond the Productivity Trap." *Human Resource Management* 31:3 (1992): 209–226; K.H. Briar and M. Vine, "Ethical Questions Concerning EAP: Who Is the Client? (Company or Individual?)," in Samuel H. Klarreich, ed., *The Human Resource Management Handbook* (New York: Praeger Publishing, 1984); M.D. Stern, "Economic Changes and Social Welfare: Implications for Employees' Assistance," *Employee Assistance Quarterly* 3:3/4 (1988): 7–19; and B. Googins, *EAP: An Ecological Perspective,* in H. Grimes, ed.,

EAP Research: An Annual of Research and Research Issues (Troy, MI: Performance Research Press, 1984).

17. W.B. Johnston and A.H. Packer, *Workforce 2000: Work and Workers for the 21st Century* (Indianapolis: Hudson Institute, 1987); R. Marshall, *The State of Families,* vol. 3 (Milwaukee, WI: Family Service of America, 1991); and E. Galinsky, J. Bond, and D. Friedman, "The Changing Workforce," Highlights of the National Study (New York: Families and Work Institute, 1993).

18. Glenda Dewberry Rooney, "Concerns of Employed Women: Issues for Employee Assistance Programs," in Alfrieda Daly, ed., *Workplace Diversity: Issues and Perspectives* (Washington, DC: NASW Press, 1997); G. Marlow, "Management of Family and Employment Responsibilities by Mexican American and Anglo Women," *Social Work* (1990): 259–265; E.L. Bell, "The Bicultural Life Experience of Career-Oriented Black Women," *Journal of Organizational Behavior* 1 (1990): 459–477; and K.C. Kim and W.M. Hurh, "The Burden of Double Roles: Korean Wives in the USA," *Ethnic and Racial Studies* 11:2 (1988): 150–167.

Additional Suggested Readings

Balgopal, P. R., and J. E. Pirzynski. "An Analysis of Pre-retirement Planning: Challenges for Occupational Social Work." *Employee Assistance Quarterly* 5, no. 3 (1997): 13–31.

Bargal, D., A. Back, and P. Ariav. "Occupational Social Work and Prolonged Job Insecurity in a Declining Organization." *Administration in Social Work* 16, no. 1 (1992): 55–67.

Bargal, D., and H.J. Karger. "Occupational Social Work and the New Global Economy." *Administration in Social Work* 15, no. 4 (1991): 95–109.

Crawley, B. "The Transformation of the American Labor Force: Elder African Americans and Occupational Social Work." *Social Work* 37, no. 1 (January 1992): 41–59.

Daly, A. *Workplace Diversity: Issues and Perspectives.* Silver Spring, MD: NASW Press, Fall 1997.

Mor-Barak, M.E., and M. Tynan. "Older Workers and the Workplace: A New Challenge for Occupational Social Work." *Social Work* 38, no. 1 (January 1993): 45–55.

Popple, P.R., and L. Leighninger. Chapter 13, "The Workplace." *Social Work, Social Welfare and American Society.* Needham Heights, MA: Allyn and Bacon, 1993.

Ramanathan, C.S. "Occupational Social Work and Multinational Corporations." *Journal of Sociology and Social Welfare* 18, no. 3 (September 1991): 135–147.

Ribner, D.S. "Crisis in the Workplace: The Role of the Occupational Social Worker." *Social Work* 38, no. 3 (May 1993): 333–337.

Rooney, G.D. Chapter 12, "Employee Assistance Programs." In L. Grobman, ed., *Days in the Lives of Social Workers.* Harrisburg, PA: White Hat Communication, 1996.

Root, L.S. "Computer Conferencing in a Decentralized Program: An Occupational Social Work Example." *Administration in Social Work* 20, no. 1 (1996): 31–45.

Social Work 33, no. 1 (January–February 1988), this issue focuses on "Social Work in Industrial Settings"; and *Employee Assistance Quarterly* 5, no. 1 (1989), entire issue on Occupational Social Work; and Families in Society, *Journal of Contemporary Human Services* 6:71 (June 1990).

15

Emerging and Less Traditional Contexts of Social Work Practice

H. WAYNE JOHNSON

So far in this section we have examined what may be regarded as the traditional or usual contexts for social work practice. Now we turn our attention to some innovations, both because they represent further uses of social work currently and also because they may suggest something about the future. We will look at nontraditional services, both actual and potential. Some of these were discussed earlier, but they are sufficiently important to mention again.

First, a word about the use of the term *nontraditional*. Obviously there would not be consensus among social workers as to what constitutes traditional social work practice and its opposite. Each would speak from his or her own context. What is nontraditional is relative. Variables are the part of the country and the community concerned, among many others. What is commonplace in one region may be rare in another part of the country. The preceding chapter dealt with industry, which many would see as an unusual setting for social work. But as was pointed out, it is considered unusual, though now less so, for the United States whereas in some nations such as England, social work has been present in business and industry for a long time. The author has learned of a social work administrator of an urban family service agency who left this position to take a job managing a large law firm. He is not an attorney. So the use of social work is not even and consistent but is a matter of degree. Dichotomous-sounding terms like *traditional* are admittedly problematic, given this unevenness, but they do serve a purpose in differentiating the generally ordinary from uncommon or less common settings.

Still a further aspect of the relativity is seen if we ask just how new a service needs to be in order to be termed nontraditional—one year, ten years, or what? Generally, programs that have originated since the 1960s or at least the 1970s

probably should be considered nontraditional because they are so much more recent than programs like medical, psychiatric, or school social work; foster care or
adoption; and probation or parole, all of which date back most of a century and
in some cases much longer. The newer the program generally, the greater the
likelihood that its presence will not be universal in society. It also should be acknowledged again that in most of the fields of service discussed in previous
chapters, there is a mix of traditional and newer, creative kinds of activities.

DEATH, DYING, AND GRIEF

One area of significant new developments in recent years is in dealing with
death and dying. This subject has become somewhat less taboo, and there is
more openness about it. A literature on the subject has appeared, and services are
being created. In 1996 a "World Gathering on Bereavement" was held in Seattle.[1]
While much of this is focused on the elderly, of course, it cuts across age lines to
include all terminal illness and injury situations and death. This interest includes
the dying patient as well as the family of the dying and significant others. Therefore, a major concern is the grief process. Human service staff members in a variety of agencies encounter persons experiencing grief who need assistance in
coping.

An announcement of a conference on grief suggests how multifaceted this
subject is.[2] The intended conference audience includes social workers, nurses,
clergy and church schoolteachers, school personnel, psychologists, counselors,
other mental health workers, personnel officers, and funeral home staff. Included in the topics of group discussion are 15 different subjects. Clearly death,
dying, and grief are complex phenomena.

A recent appearance on the scene holding promise for social work is the
hospice movement. *Hospice* is a "philosophy of care, value orientation, and service delivery system for people with life threatening illnesses and their families."[3] Services differ from unit to unit, but the trend is toward services that are
both inpatient and home-based, or a combination. These services supplement
and work with those provided by physicians, nurses, ministers, and other professionals. Hospice care begins with patient admission and continues throughout
the mourning period. The purpose is twofold: "(1) to help the terminal patient remain comfortable, alert and able to participate in life as fully as possible for as
long as possible until death occurs naturally and peacefully; and (2) to enable the
family to remain lovingly attentive to the dying person throughout the dying
process."[4]

The social work role relative to hospice is multifaceted. Social workers,
along with others, may help to plan and organize new hospices, work in administration, train volunteers and staff, raise funds, evaluate services, and function in many other capacities. Fitting hospice into the network of services in a
community and working for maximum use of these services can be an important
activity. A primary role for social work is serving on the hospice team along
with other specialists.[5]

The funeral home may represent a new setting for social work practice.
Thus far, such arrangements are not common, but they seem to afford an obvious
means of meeting needs and a way of providing service at a critical point. Help-

ing survivors deal with pain, anxiety, depression, possible guilt, and a mélange of other potential feelings along with assisting in the reorganizing of lives after a loss and all that may entail can be the job of a social worker.

An issue of growing importance is the movement for physician-assisted suicide. In September 1996, in Darwin, Australia, a 66-year-old man suffering from prostate cancer became the first person to legally kill himself under the only voluntary euthanasia law in the world.[6] Dr. Jack Kevorkian, a retired Michigan physician, assisted in 45 suicides from 1990 to early 1997 and is extremely controversial. His lawyer, in August 1997, put the number at "nearly 100."[7] In 1990, the U.S. Supreme Court held that life-sustaining medical treatment may be refused by terminally ill people, but only Oregon permits doctor-assisted suicide. In 1994, Oregon voters approved this by a 50 to 49 percent margin. However, the American Medical Association continues its opposition to medically assisted suicide.[8] On January 31, 1997, a judge in Florida held that a 35-year-old AIDS patient can be helped by his doctor to commit suicide. This ruling is limited to the one case only.[9] A June 1997 U.S. Supreme Court decision found no right to doctor-assisted suicide. This difficult issue is bound to continue and grow, and fields such as social work are and will be deeply affected. With heart disease, cancer, and strokes being the three major killers of Americans, and with these afflictions accompanying aging significantly, it is predictable that life-ending questions will increasingly appear.

CRISIS INTERVENTION CENTERS

Crisis intervention centers and suicide prevention programs were alluded to earlier. These have come into being since the 1960s and early 1970s, and in this sense may be thought of as less traditional services. Some crisis centers operate only telephone services, whereas others also maintain walk-in programs. Services included are counseling, other intervention, and information and referral. Among the calls received are those from distraught or depressed persons who consider or threaten to take their own lives. Hence, suicide prevention becomes one of the problems such centers deal with. In one midwestern center, the most common types of calls by frequency received in 1996–97 were (1) relationships (boy/girlfriend, parent/child, marital), (2) administrative (agency services, donations), (3) venting, (4) financial/employment, (5) transportation, (6) housing/shelter, (7) medical/health, (8) depression, (9) psychiatric, (10) loneliness, (11) sexuality, and (12) suicide.[10]

When crisis centers were started, one of the concerns was drug abuse and help for persons involved with drugs. Hence "hot lines" came into being.[11] Some services have been established as specialized suicide prevention per se, beginning with efforts concentrated in Los Angeles.

One characteristic of crisis intervention is its time-limited nature and short-term duration. Some centers are finding that callers are of two types, the true crisis caller and the regular, repeat, or chronic caller. Different needs may be manifested in these two groups, and they may call for divergent responses. The situation is complicated somewhat with the telephone callers in that, in many centers, neither the volunteer nor the caller reveals his or her identity, but they use first names only to maintain anonymity.

This bridge in Poughkeepsie, New York, the site of numerous suicides, advertises a suicide prevention hotline.

Mark Antman/The Image Works

An interesting feature of crisis centers is their use of small paid administrative staffs and relatively large volunteer staffs. Social work students are often heavily represented among the volunteers in crisis centers located in or near college or university communities. In one university community, for example, the Crisis Intervention Center has a pool of approximately 180 volunteers. Of these, about one-third are undergraduate or graduate social work students or fairly recent graduates of these programs.[12]

Often students, alone or in concert with practitioners and others, have initiated such programs. Social workers frequently are employed as administrators or staff members. In this case, major functions typically are related to obtaining community support and funding, recruiting and training volunteers, and general administrative tasks.

HEALTH AND MENTAL HEALTH

Previous chapters dealt with health and mental health (see Chapters 8 and 9). A good example of the difficulty of differentiating traditional and nontraditional settings is illustrated by nursing homes, a topic previously alluded to. Some American nursing homes have employed social workers for years, but in others this profession is still not represented. Much has depended on federal and state policies and requirements. Practices of nursing homes and extended-care facilities reflect changes in these external regulations. The trend does seem clear toward use of social work in this setting. Interestingly, when social workers are employed in nursing homes, they are used in a variety of ways.

Recently, for example, in one midwestern state, nursing homes in communities in close proximity to each other demonstrated the following patterns: (1) full-time combined social worker/activities director in a single nursing home, (2) full-time social worker serving one facility, (3) part-time worker serving one nursing home, and (4) a social worker whose services are purchased by two or more facilities for a few hours each week. In one convalescent facility, the social worker prepares social histories on all residents, does ongoing work with a few residents individually, and conducts reality orientation groups and remotivation sessions with small groups.

An example of innovations in organizations that were themselves innovations in the early 1970s is seen in *free medical clinics* that are now providing AIDS (acquired immune deficiency syndrome) counseling and HIV (human immunodeficiency virus) antibody testing. This is a critically important service today. The author has worked with social work practicum students who are engaged in HIV counseling in a free clinic. The clinic is determined by the state Department of Public Health to be an alternate site for such testing. Patients remain anonymous by using fictitious names in most cases. A former director of the clinic, a social worker, refers to AIDS-related activity as, sadly, a "growth industry" for social work. Recently, separate organizations have been created especially to focus on problems related to HIV/AIDS and to serving this population.

Physicians in private practice are potentially large employers of social workers. Family doctors typically see many patients a day, spending only a few minutes with each on average. Many patients need to talk with someone more than they need any medical procedure or medication. They need to ventilate pent-up feelings, or have someone objectively discuss options in problematic situations, or any one of many other possibilities. The physician is unlikely to be able to do this for all persons needing it. Therefore, the social worker provides a likely resource. Although this has not yet happened on a large scale, there are precedents.[13]

In one medical clinic composed of 21 physicians, a social worker was added. One hundred cases referred by the physicians to the social worker were classified as follows: in 20 there was a diagnosis of organic disease that was accompanied by emotional stress; with 60 cases there were physical symptoms of psychogenic origin; in the other 20 cases there were no physical complaints but there were individual problems such as anxiety or depression or family problems.[14]

A more common arrangement is for social workers to be employed by psychiatrists or psychologists who are in private practice. These are generally experienced workers with graduate degrees who, along with other professionals, engage in psychotherapy. With considerable variations, they work with individuals, couples, and families.

In these contexts, as well as private practice, a new endeavor is working with compulsive gamblers. There is controversy over the definition and extent of this phenomenon; are these addicts or "undisciplined gamblers"? In 1994 the American Psychiatric Association termed compulsive gambling an addictive disease. Its characteristics have been identified as progression, intolerance for losing, preoccupation, and disregard for consequences. Sensation-seeking may be one of the personality factors involved. Gambling has to be seen within the context of its popularity in the nation and its encouragement by states eager for revenues from lotteries and other schemes. Gamblers Anonymous is a useful treatment approach.[15]

As dental practice changes its emphasis on restorative work to preventive and specialized care, another new role for social work may appear. Fields such as orthodontics sometimes present situations of patient or family expectations for patient transformation that exceed the constraints of reality. This may call for social work intervention. Another aspect has to do with pain and its alleviation in this era of "pain clinics" and related measures. Dentists are increasingly interested in the phenomenon of pain because of the association of dental care and pain in negative ways. Since social work addresses the whole patient, including the psychosocial realm, this may be an area for natural expansion.

Social workers have also been used in university student health services and counseling programs. Because of the struggle that certain students experience in "finding themselves" vocationally and in other ways, and because of the stresses of academic success and other problems of the student role, it is not uncommon for them to seek professional assistance. To request such help is to be considered a strength on the student's part. Another development in some communities is women's clinics. Family planning is another setting for social work, partly traditional and in part newer. An emerging area is genetic services, and social work roles are developing here.[16]

Some practitioners from helping disciplines such as social work and psychology have moved (part-time or full-time) into the field carrying such labels as sports medicine/therapy. The broader idea is to provide various services to athletes to enhance their athletic ability/performance and to facilitate their development and functioning in a holistic way. The author is aware of a master's level social worker employed by a university full-time in sports medicine and of another who works part-time using such approaches as hypnosis with athletes.[17]

Social workers are sometimes employed in university health complexes to teach medical students and/or other personnel such as nurses. The content of such teaching may aim at sensitizing health care professionals to the whole spectrum of needs of patients as biopsychosocial beings and to the importance of humanizing the medical environment. This environment with all its technical paraphernalia, which physicians and others may take for granted, is often extremely threatening to the patient. Part of the job is to demystify such a setting for patients. Helping to make patients and their families informed consumers can pay large dividends in the well-being of the patient. Patient advocacy, not in an adversarial sense but in the sense of family support for patients, can make it much easier for the medical staff to get its job done.[18] In other words, there are good pragmatic reasons for this enabling function.

An example of work with medical students is a midwestern medical school and hospital in which workshops on interpersonal skills were conducted by a social worker. These were funded in part with a mental health grant and partially by a chapter of the American Medical Student Association and other student groups. It is significant that the request came from medical students themselves, probably out of realization of the importance of communication for physicians and the difficulties frequently present in communication.

A development in mental health is the Veterans Administration Readjustment Counseling Service for veterans experiencing posttraumatic stress disorders (PTSD).[19] Veterans, especially of Vietnam, and others sometimes face difficulty in adjustment even years following their military experience. Inpatient and outpatient programs can be useful in helping people cope in these situations.

EDUCATION

The preceding discussion overlaps with education although it has been treated under health. Social workers have been used in other parts of colleges and universities beyond those already noted. One university psychology department, for example, operates a research and training clinic, which employs a social worker to teach graduate students interviewing skills and to supervise some of their work.

Another way social workers are sometimes involved in higher education is to staff student personnel units, counseling/advising services, or in residence halls. Others work with foreign students in international programs or in special support units with minority, handicapped, and otherwise disadvantaged students or those with special needs. Some people with social work training have been employed in college/university admissions, orientation, family housing for married students, placement services, student union administration, affirmative action offices, women's centers, recycling programs, and faculty/staff services. The author has had contact with all these in at least one university.

As far as teaching is concerned, traditionally social work faculty were in graduate schools of social work. More recently, major growth has been in undergraduate programs and even in two-year community and junior colleges. The expansion of social work education on all levels has necessitated drawing more people into teaching and educational administration. Generally, at least the master's degree is required as the base educational requirement for such assignments. More programs offer doctorates, and more MSW programs, especially, require faculty to hold Ph.D.s or DSWs.[20]

School social workers are moving more and more from direct service to such activities as consultation and education. This approach enables them to educate the educators and hence to impact on greater numbers of children and youth. That this trend goes beyond the United States was observed in 1984 by the author in Australia.

The development of alternative schools has expanded considerably in recent years, even in rural communities.[21] These are for youth for whom regular schools are ill-suited. Programs are highly individualized, often with an emphasis on mastering certain competencies outside of the usual school structure. Social workers often assist in identifying needs for such schools, establishing them, and serving on the professional team staffing them.

FAMILIES

As was noted in Chapters 5 and 6, working with families and children constitutes a large part of social work. We want to consider now only those aspects of this field that are recent arrivals in the social services. Among these is divorce counseling and *mediation*. Marriage counseling is a long-established practice, but divorce on a massive scale has come into general societal awareness only more recently. In spite of the growing acceptance of divorce, it is still often traumatic for the persons involved. Hence, help for people in such circumstances may be useful before, during, and following the divorce. Some agencies are providing much more service in relation to marital and family breakdown than formerly. Developments such as the joint custody of children following marriage dissolution is an example of innovations in traditional legal practices holding significance for the human services.

Among the many current changes related to the family, its establishment, maintenance, and dissolution, are those pertaining to sex roles in marriage and divorce. An example is husbands increasingly asking for alimony in divorce cases.[22] As wives earn more than husbands in some cases, more of these kinds of developments can be expected.

Another modern development is cohabiting couples. Interestingly, there is reason to believe that such couples experience some of the same kinds of problems often accompanying marriage. Thus, another service need and opportunity appears.

Starting first with child abuse, there has come to be major attention devoted to various aspects of family violence. Spouse abuse is now in the national spotlight as a social problem. Another concern is physical and emotional abuse of the elderly, often by adult children. None of these problems are new, obviously. What is new is their discovery and such community responses as spouse abuse shelters. It is estimated by a national coalition that there are about 2,000 shelters in the United States for battered women.[23] Social workers play a significant role in establishing and operating these facilities.

New programs for the elderly are sometimes variations of established ones for other age groups, now being adapted to the aged. Examples are day services and foster care. With day care, an elderly person who should not be left alone or who is living with relatives who are occupied goes to a special facility that will meet her or his needs and provide stimulation. This kind of care can be reassuring for everyone concerned—the aged and the family. Other elderly persons are able to live in family homes, but since no family members are available, substitute family care may be arranged. Still another arrangement for some elderly is house sharing, either between two or more elderly[24] or an aged person/couple with a younger person. Social workers may carry a variety of roles in such programs, from direct service to planning, organizing, and administration.

Day care for children can hardly be considered new; what is nontraditional is incorporating social work into this setting. Brennan suggests some possible roles for the social worker by delineating the following children in a normal day-care population: the hyperactive, depressed, angry, fearful, loner; the "child who has a difficult time separating"; and the "child who is highly sensitive to criticism."[25] All of these require individualization and understanding and may call for work with some combination of the child, parents, and day-care staff.

A newly developing field is family caregivers. In 1988, the school of social work at Case Western Reserve University established a project aimed at this problem, defining the term as "families who provide care for a disabled family member." The project is concerned with addressing the needs of such caregivers as these may be served by human service agencies. Various physical and mental disabilities may necessitate extensive family involvement such as providing care

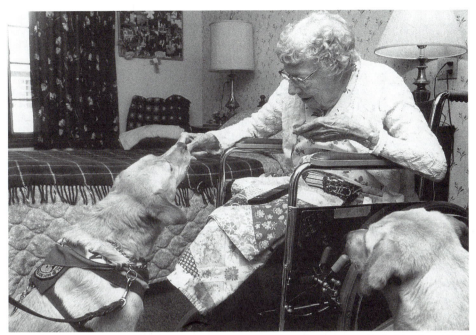

Two registered labrador retriever "pet therapy" dogs visit a nursing home resident at Seminary Manor, Galesburg, Illinois. These visits by dogs are part of a regular program at the home.

for disabled children and youth, people in frail health, stroke patients, and elderly parents with Alzheimer's disease. David Biegel at Case has been extensively involved in research in this field.[26]

THE HUMAN-ANIMAL BOND

Recently an interesting development has occurred relative to the therapeutic use of companion animals and the human-animal bond.[27] There is research evidence that animals fulfill human needs, including those for affiliation and affection. Animals are used for the benefit of people in various settings, including children's treatment centers,[28] nursing homes, rehabilitation programs, schools, and others.

There are now centers for the study of human-animal interaction at various universities: Tufts, Pennsylvania, Purdue, University of California-Davis, and Colorado State (CSU).[29] At CSU is the Argus Center for the Human-Animal Bond and also in Colorado is HABIC (Human-Animal Bond in Colorado). Through the work of Georgia and Ben Granger, HABIC has developed a specific animal-assisted therapy model involving a therapeutic team consisting of a trained volunteer, the companion animal, and a professional staff member (e.g., social worker). The effectiveness of this approach has been documented.[30]

Another aspect of human-animal interaction is the utilization of social workers by veterinarians. A graduate social work student in a practicum placement at the University of Pennsylvania Small Animal Hospital began by donning a white coat and moving about the hospital talking to doctors, students, and pet owners; making herself available to provide support services to Homo sapiens in a hospital designed to treat many other species, but not that one. By the end of her first five months, she had developed a list of twenty-eight different kinds of problems referred to her—problems of communication in which the owner could not seem to understand the physician, or could not follow directions; problems of anger that represented displaced fear or guilt; problems of finances, human health, pet abuse, and/or animal behavior that were affecting family life.[31]

The most difficult problems, or at least the ones with which veterinarians most frequently sought help, were those involving owners who were reacting with strong emotion to the serious illness or death of an animal. The decision concerning euthanasia, for example, is one that is rarely countenanced in relation to humans. Many veterinarians are "uncomfortable in the presence of tears or guilt or anger...and feel they have neither the time nor the skill to deal with clients' emotional outbursts. In these situations, the assistance of a social worker is valued."[32]

JUSTICE

This topic is a mix of various needs and programs in which legal rights and protections are a common core. In modern societies with complex legal and court systems, human well-being is greatly affected by the structure and functioning of these systems. The relationship between law and social work is not entirely new in that some of the early figures in social work were people with legal training. More recently, however, greater attention has been paid to linkages between these two fields. For example, a growing number of universities have developed joint programs between law schools and schools of social work.

Social work students, both graduate and undergraduate, sometimes have field experience or practicum placements in legal settings such as antipoverty legal services. The social worker may assist the legal staff in client advocacy on government benefit matters pending before administrative agencies such as the Social Security Administration, public welfare department, or public employment service. An additional significant role is working with clients and staff in seeking nonlegal solutions to client problems such as locating housing or child care. While these problems are peripheral to the legal ones, they are important. Another social work activity is community outreach. In other words, legal services may be a kind of parallel to the medical field in presenting an array of opportunities for the provision of social services as adjuncts to the central purpose of the organization.

The human rights movement that has taken place in the United States since the civil rights developments of the mid-1950s has had major impact. On the other hand, much unfinished work remains in providing equality of opportunity to racial and ethnic groups and to women. Activities of the Ku Klux Klan, American Nazi party, and other far-right and fanatical groups appear to be increasing and present a serious threat to further assuring the rights of all people. A unanimous U.S. Supreme Court decision in June 1993 held that people who commit "hate crimes" motivated by bigotry may be given longer prison terms.

It is not just in extreme groups such as these that the danger resides, however; it is present to a considerable degree in the apathy of millions of Americans. Social service professionals alone are not enough to alter this situation, but they do have responsibilities in it and opportunities to contribute to its resolution.

The consumer movement is another context of activity for social work and related professions. Some aspects of this movement have roots going back for decades, but there has been a recent impetus with the efforts of Ralph Nader and others. One example is the work in various states of the Public Interest Research Groups (PIRG) engaging in a variety of consumer-oriented efforts, environmental protection, and other activities designed to lend visibility to these needs and to institute and support social action, necessary legislation, and legal action in the public interest.[33] One group of services focus on consumers, credit, debt, finances, and related matters. Social workers sometimes are involved in workshops, counseling, and other activities aimed at helping people in these areas. A related field is work with compulsive shoppers. A study published in 1996 found that compulsive shopping for 5 to 10 percent of Americans results in bankruptcy, divorce, or other serious problems.[34]

It has become increasingly clear that social work must be active politically if the human service system is to be well designed, adequately funded, and effective. This calls for coalitions with a variety of organizations and professions for education of the public and for lobbying, among other endeavors. Some social workers have operated as lobbyists and have provided information to legislators, which can be crucial in the legislative process.

Crime and delinquency were discussed in Chapter 12. Programs for crime victims and witnesses have emerged as have rape victim advocacy programs and centers. Special treatment efforts are being directed to sex offenders, both within institutions and in the community. A new development, albeit controversial, is private corrections in which certain tasks such as the preparation of presentence reports or certain prison functions may be contracted out to profit-making enterprises.[35] Social workers may be employed by such organizations. The appearance of social work in some police departments is encouraging from the point of view of a different kind of intervention and, hence, providing a more preventive service to people. Finally, the addition of various arbitration and mediation programs to resolve intrapersonal, interpersonal, family, and neighborhood issues of both criminal and civil nature is significant.

A few states/communities have youth law centers. These generally are recent innovations employing attorneys and caseworkers aimed at protection, education, and advocacy for children, especially those at risk. These organizations may receive United Way funding.[36]

DISPLACED PERSONS: REFUGEES, IMMIGRANTS, MIGRANTS

In this section, refugees, immigrants, and migrant workers are being grouped together. It is important to note, however, that there are significant differences between these groups and even within one with respect to their characteristics and needs. Migrant farm laborers, for example, often manifest extreme poverty and are vulnerable to factors over which they have little control, for example, weather. The January 1997 freeze in Florida meant no work with vegetable crops

Tuzla, Bosnia-Hercegovina, in 1993. A UNHCR convoy with Muslim refugees from the besieged town of Srebrenica. Civil war in the former Yugoslavia is contributing to hundreds of thousands of refugees.

and hence no income. An estimated 100,000 farmers were affected in 20 counties. Normally these workers move across the country following crops, but with no income they are trapped—unable to stay and unable to move.[37]

While refugee movements have been part of the human scene for centuries, the groups involved have varied. Generally refugees are fleeing repressive totalitarian regimes, persecution, famines, wars, and natural disasters. Forbes indicates that basically there are three solutions for refugees, which, in order of desirability, are (1) repatriation to their own country, (2) settling in a neighboring country in which they find themselves, and (3) resettling in a third country.[38] Since so much of the present world disruption is taking place in poor, developing nations, the first two options are often not feasible.

A major new wave of refugees from Southeast Asia came to this country starting in 1975 as a result of warfare there. This group constituted about three-fourths of the million refugee arrivals in the United States between 1975 and 1985 and was made up mainly of Vietnamese, Laotians, and Cambodians. Other groups are from the former Soviet Union, Eastern Europe, Latin America, and Africa. Refugees tend to differ demographically from Americans in being, on the average, younger, and proportionately more are male.

Refugees from Southeast Asia are hindered in adapting to the United States by major cultural differences, the absence of an established ethnic community that would aid their adjustment, and this country's weak economy when they arrived.[39] It is important to realize that this is not a single homogeneous group of people but a collection of diverse groups in terms of history, language, and culture.

Some of the organizations serving refugees are old established family and/or youth agencies and community centers that expand their programs to serve this population. Others are new and were developed specifically in response to the needs and problems of this group. Some are under the auspices of religious organizations that have become concerned about the well-being of refugees, although some private services are nonsectarian. In addition to all the physical survival needs, people from other countries often experience adjustment problems and emotional difficulties, sometimes requiring mental health services. Enabling clients to see emotional problems as normal reactions to stress that is itself abnormal can be useful.[40]

Southeast Asian refugees often resist using mental health services. Factors contributing to this resistance are (1) language and communication problems, (2) cultural diversity, (3) diversity in migration and resettlement experiences, (4) the stigma attached to mental illness, and (5) a tradition of reliance on kinship and community support networks.[41] Programs to meet the needs of this client population must consider their reluctance to use services and attempt to respond to these factors.

Cultural and value differences and conflict between American mental health professionals and Indochinese Asian patients are presented by Kenzie as follows:[42]

Indochinese Asian Patient Values	*American Psychotherapist Values*
Interdependence and traditional family values.	Autonomy and independence.
"Correct" social relationships.	Relativity in values; situational ethics; rejection of authority.
Holistic culture; i.e., people living in harmony with nature.	People versus nature; the need to master or control nature.
View of mental illness as imbalance of cosmic forces or supernatural events.	View of mental illness as result of psychological and biological factors.
No cultural analogy of extended psychological therapy.	Belief that psychotherapy is valuable and promotes "growth."
Belief that cure should be rapid, healer-active; little history of maintenance therapy.	Awareness that cure will be extended and time-consuming, and therapist will often be passive.
Fear of mental illness.	Comfortable attitude about handling mental illness and symptoms.
"Refugee" status—insecure in language, vocation, and position in society.	Secure status in "society," language, vocation, and position.

Kenzie indicates that the subjects that need to be dealt with in working therapeutically with people who arrive from Southeast Asia are life in the homeland, the escape process, life in the refugee camp, adjustment in this country, and current problems/worries about the future.[43]

People from Central American and Caribbean nations fleeing persecution, totalitarianism, and/or poverty are entering the United States, sometimes illegally. Large numbers of Mexicans enter the country, often illegally ("undocumented aliens"), for employment, and present somewhat different situations from that of actual refugees.

Social workers were involved with immigrants a century ago and are again today active with displaced persons. It is an immense task to help people make the transition and settle into new lives in a strange and foreign land. The adjustment to a new environment with problems of language/communication, education, employment, housing, health, and a hundred other considerations presents a major challenge to displaced persons and to those working with them. Some Americans as individuals or group members were in the 1980s committed publicly to assisting Central Americans (illegally in the United States) who were fleeing oppression. At the risk of arrest and punishment for such acts of civil disobedience, these people acted on the basis of their humanitarian convictions. Complex challenges faced social workers who might be called on to work with such people, and value conflicts abounded for any who might consider participating in illegally assisting others.[44]

More recently (December 1996) the bishop of the methodist denomination in Iowa sent a letter to 900 churches in the state suggesting assistance and sanctuary for Hispanics threatened with deportation by the immigration service. This action followed raids by immigration officials on companies employing undocumented workers. These workers are often exploited by employers who recruit them and frequently pay them poorly for difficult work in undesirable conditions.[45]

A special situation that deserves mention can be discussed within this context. Late in 1987 and 1988 the Orderly Departure Program brought to the United States from Southeast Asia numbers of children and youth who were fathered by American soldiers during the Vietnam War. The program had been suspended two years earlier and was reopened. Relatives of the Amerasians as well as other Vietnamese joining family members in this country were included in this group.[46]

In September 1996, a new federal immigration bill became law. It was a compromise and hence included some repressive measures but dropped others that had been proposed. It denies illegal immigrants benefits such as SSI, Medicaid, food stamps, housing, unemployment benefits, college financial aid, and earned-income tax credit. Interestingly welfare reform, also enacted in 1996, prevents even legal immigrants from receiving many public assistances.[47] The new law also includes extensive security measures, more border patrol agents, increased punishments, and so on. Immigrants, especially those who are in the United States legally, have often been stereotyped and scapegoated. They are here for a variety of reasons such as jobs and uniting families. It is well to remember that children and the elderly who are often parts of these families are humans who need protection, not punishment. Immigration must be regulated and controlled but should be done fairly, humanely, and rationally.

Social workers now play a part in helping displaced people deal with their trauma and loss, their need for support systems, and their coping and adaptation. Some of this occurs through traditional agencies, but some is the work of newer, often more specialized programs and services. The task is made more difficult by a national mentality that is anti-immigration and includes victim blaming with respect to certain ethnic, racial, and nationality groups often characteristic of refugees, migrants, and immigrants.[48]

HOMELESSNESS

Another concern currently is the homeless, a topic to be discussed further in Chapter 24. While homelessness is not a new social problem, it has compounded in recent years and is receiving renewed attention. Estimates of the number of homeless in this country range from 250,000 to 3 million.[49] More exact figures are impossible to obtain, given the nature of the problem. It appears that this highly heterogeneous group tends to be largely young, male, and representative of ethnicity in the local area. On the other hand, the number of women who are homeless is believed to be on the increase. Included in the homeless are individuals and families, adolescents and youth (including runaways), adults, and the elderly. Alcoholism and other substance abuse are common, as is mental illness.

According to Hall, the causative factors contributing to homelessness include periods of recession and high unemployment in the 1980s and early 1990s, a dearth of low-cost housing, deinstitutionalization of the mentally ill, alcohol and drug abuse, and an effort by the federal administration in the early 1980s to reduce the number of Social Security disability insurance recipients.[50] With regard to the recession/unemployment factor, it is important to note that the impact is long-term for some people. Periodic unemployment declines do not benefit all people. Some appear to have become a part of the more or less permanent underclass, and some of these are now without homes.

There is a marked shortage of affordable housing. Such housing is actually declining in numbers, and additional needed units have not been provided. An example of the former is the loss of single-room occupancy (SRO) units on a large scale. Many of the old hotels and other buildings that were being used for this purpose have been razed or converted to other uses. In addition, thousands of people lost Social Security disability benefits as a result of administrative action from 1981 to 1984, and this undoubtedly contributed to loss of housing for some, the effects often becoming permanent.

Deinstitutionalization of the mentally ill is widely thought to be a causative factor in homelessness. The patient population in state and county mental hospitals dropped 77 percent between 1955 and 1981 in the national move to replace long-term custodial care with community-based programs.[51] Unfortunately, no well-organized system for meeting the needs of mental patients on the community level has been funded. The fact that some chronically mentally ill persons are street people without homes is not an argument against deinstitutionalization but the reason for providing comprehensive supportive services in the community to help these people.

A common denominator in much homelessness is poverty (at least temporary) and, in some cases, rootlessness. While Travelers Aid and various temporary lodging provisions of the Salvation Army, missions, and others have been traditional resources, more recently other shelters have appeared. There is now a National Coalition for the Homeless. Shelters are needed in many communities as temporary measures, but they do not provide a permanent solution. What is needed is a range of housing options. As Prock and Taber have noted, the reason for homelessness is irrelevant to the affected person's need for shelter.[52]

HUNGER

Within the larger context of poverty, the problems of hunger and malnutrition persist in a developed nation of surplus agricultural products and general affluence. In the mid-1980s, 20 million Americans were reportedly going hungry, and the problem was worsening. President Reagan in 1986 responded to critics of his administration's inaction on hunger by indicating that people who were hungry lacked knowledge about how to obtain food—the blaming-the-victim implication being that there actually was no problem.

Brown states, "Between 1982 and 1987, a total of 77 studies documented the widespread and serious impact of the increasing hunger in America" and "the evidence shows that there is hunger of dimensions not seen in years."[53] In 1993 it was reported that "12 million American children now experience hunger on a chronic basis."[54] Brown attributes the reasons why one in ten Americans do not have enough to eat to three factors: (1) the national "safety net" was weak to begin with; (2) in the early 1980s the economy soured; and (3) the federal administration made the most severe cutbacks ever in nutrition programs. School meals and food stamps alone were cut over $12 billion. High unemployment, more low-paying jobs, and a tax system that results in more income for the wealthy and less for everyone else add up to poverty and hence to hunger.

Some social workers practice within the context of the newer food and nutrition programs as well as those programs that have been in existence for decades. Both aim at reducing the ravages of hunger, regardless of its causes.

The consequences of the 1996 "welfare reform" for homelessness and hunger remain to be seen. Already there is fear that both may worsen as a result of this change in legislation.

POPULATION AND FAMILY PLANNING

Population is a topic that could be encompassed within health or perhaps with several other subjects but here is being treated separately. Clearly, aspects of the topic relate to education and to such concerns as immigration, considered earlier in this chapter and elsewhere in the book. Obviously population is related to such problems as homelessness and hunger.

Often when maldistribution or population pressures are considered, the assumption is made that it is the international situation being examined and some other country is the focus. But the issues presented are relevant for Americans as well. Certainly the worldwide phenomenon of urbanziation is apparent, and many nations, including the United States, have large cities that appear out of control, environmentally unsafe and unattractive, congested, crime ridden, and so on. That around the globe these urban centers often include shanty towns on their edges or interiors, slums, and pollution is a given.

How many people the Earth can support, with preservation of some semblance of quality of life, is a difficult question. Distribution of population is an important feature. All too often it appears that increasing densities of population around communities (e.g., suburbanization) have had such negative consequences as reduction of available fertile land for crops, which of course are needed to feed the growing number of people. This then leads to pressures for more fertilization and irrigation of agriculturally marginal land and a new set of problems/issues/controversies.

There is a need domestically and internationally for effective, affordable, accessible family planning. Contraceptives have been improved and made more available around the world. But one need go no further than the United States to see some of the conflicts inherent in this value-laden area. In these technologically advanced and sophisticated times, there is still dispute over sex education, family planning methods, and, of course, abortion. On the other hand, there is evidence that the more family planning and contraceptive information and resources available worldwide, the less abortion and AIDS.[55]

This is both an old and a new context for social work. Whether in clinics or in public or private educational or political organizations, there are jobs for social workers to do involving the health and well-being of people in the United States and elsewhere. Spacing of children and size of family is a quality-of-life matter, as are total population dimensions.

INTERNATIONAL SOCIAL WELFARE

Related to several topics discussed in this chapter—but most especially to refugees, homelessness, hunger, and population—is international social welfare. Midgley indicates that research in the social sciences pertaining to the social problems and social welfare institutions of various nations (i.e., comparative social welfare) has recently expanded.[56] What is called "social welfare" in the United States is often termed social development in other nations, especially in Third World countries. Social work and social welfare activity internationally are also likely to increase, according to Healy.[57] Areas that are involved are adoption, family problems encompassing more than one country, refugees, migration, and population. Since the concern is often with living standards and quality-of-life issues, basic human needs are frequently the focus, for example, health, education, housing, and nutrition. This is an exciting, challenging, and important area for the present and future, bearing indirectly and even directly on such issues as world peace.

There is evidence that there is a substantial "mail-order bride" business in the United States. With approximately 200 companies in the United States, an estimated 2,000 to 3,500 American men find wives through mail-order bride catalogs each year. However there are no official statistics available on the number of mail-order brides entering the United States. In 1997, seven different mail-order bride services could be located on the "world wide web" representing in excess of a thousand women from various parts of the globe. There are concerns about spousal abuse with mail-order brides. This problem is apparently so endemic that the legislation proposed in the 1990s called for a waiver of deportation in the event of abuse. Contact with these women is done by purchasing the address from one of these services. In addition to providing the address, several of these companies offer tour packages, so that one can arrange to meet the women with whom one has been corresponding. One web source suggested that an individual should correspond with at least ten different women. After the selection is made, the individual can then marry the woman in her own country or attempt to get her into the United States as her "sponsor." This process is not inexpensive, costing into the tens of thousands of dollars.[58]

SUMMARY AND CONCLUSIONS

In this chapter we have considered some of the less typical social services. A few of these were alluded to in earlier chapters, but it is useful to bring them together in one place and examine them collectively. Here we have attempted also to illustrate and extend what was presented earlier.

Several points must be made in this connection. People employed to work in these nontraditional settings are not always termed *social workers*. Various role titles are found. Some people are employed in these contexts because they are social workers, while others are used with less regard to that fact. Also, not all of what has been described here are actually "settings," as the chapter title suggests. Some are activities or roles of the worker. Furthermore, a distinction should be made between actual and potential social work use, as has been noted. Mention has been made of practicum placements of social work students in a few uncommon contexts. These innovative kinds of arrangements may, on occasion, be indicative of developing fields. Predictions of specific coming professional developments are not being made at this juncture because the future is so uncertain, and what these various human service activities mean for tomorrow is unknown. In some cases, however, the trends appear rather clear.

Notes

1. "Conference Explores Dealing with Grief," *Des Moines Register*, August 18, 1996, p. 2A.
2. Brochure received in March 1988 from Burlington Medical Center, Burlington, Iowa: "Good Grief...A Second Look."
3. Jack M. Richman, "Hospice," in *Encyclopedia of Social Work*, 19th ed. (Washington, DC: NASW), p. 1359.
4. From "Hospice of Central Iowa," a brochure distributed by Hospice of Central Iowa, Des Moines, undated.
5. Richman, "Hospice," p. 1360.
6. "1st Legal Suicide by Australian Reignites Debate," *Des Moines Register,* September 27, 1996, p. 4A.
7. "Kevorkian Aide Admits to 'Nearly 100 Cases,'" *Iowa City Press Citizen*, August 14, 1997, p. 2A

8. "Dying with Dignity," *Corpus Christi Caller-Times*, February 11, 1997, p. B5.

9. "Judge Rules Man with AIDS Has Right to Commit Suicide," *Corpus Christi Caller-Times*, February 1, 1997, p. A6.

10. Iowa City Crisis Center, "Program Statistics: Fiscal Year 1997," Iowa City, IA, July 1997.

11. Leon Brill, "Addiction: Drug," *Encyclopedia of Social Work*, 17th ed. (Silver Spring, MD: NASW, 1977), pp. 39–40.

12. Iowa City Crisis Intervention Center, personal communication with Ellen McCabe, director, June 18, 1997.

13. Theresa W. Barkan, "Private Casework Practice in a Medical Clinic," *Social Work* (July 1973): 5–9. See also Louis H. Forman, "The Physician and the Social Worker," *American Family Physician* 13, no. 1 (January 1976): 90–93; and Ruth L. Goldberg, "The Social Worker and the Family Physician," *Social Casework* (October 1973): 489–495.

14. Barkan, "Private Casework Practice," p. 7.

15. Sayde L. Logan, "Gambling," in *Encyclopedia of Social Work*, 19th ed. (Washington, DC: NASW, 1995), pp. 807, 808–809, 811–812.

16. See, for example, Julia B. Rauch and Rita Beck Black, "Genetics," in *Encyclopedia of Social Work*, 19th ed. (Washington, DC: NASW Press, 1995), pp. 1108–1117.

17. Bryce Miller, "Little Hawk Grapples with Success," *Iowa City Press Citizen*, February 20, 1993, pp. 1D, 4D.

18. Based on discussion with Nina Hamilton, former professor of social work at the University of Iowa.

19. *NASW News*, Classifieds, March 1988, p. 15.

20. According to the Council of Social Work Education, over 50 graduate schools of social work offered doctoral programs in 1996.

21. Mark Sibert, "Troubled Kids Fit Better in New Schools," *Des Moines Register*, December 22, 1996, pp. 1B, 5B.

22. "Worm Turning as More Husbands Seek Alimony During Divorce Cases," *Corpus Christi Caller-Times*, February 16, 1997, p. A25.

23. Personal communication with National Domestic Violence Hotline, June 4, 1997.

24. Carolyn E. Usher and Stephen R. McConnell, "House Sharing: A Way to Intimacy," *Alternative Lifestyles* 3, no. 2 (May 1980): 149–166.

25. Elaine C. Brennan, "Meeting the Affective Needs of Young Children," *Children Today* (July–August 1974): 22–25.

26. See, for example, David E. Biegel and L. Song, "Facilitators and Barriers to Caregiver Support Group Participation," *Journal of Case Management* 4, no. 4 (1995): 165–172.

27. Personal communication with Ben Granger, Dean, Colorado State University, Department of Social Work, June 4, 1997. The Delta Society (a national organization in this field) publishes a multidisciplinary journal, *Anthrozoos*.

28. Gerald P. Mallon, "Dogs in the Dorms: A Study on the Placement of Dogs in the Living Units of a Residential Treatment Center for Children." Paper presented at the Green Chimneys People, Pets and Plants Conference, Brewster, NY, 1991.

29. Ben Granger, personal communication.

30. Kimberly Helmer, Jennifer Fitchett, and Kaili Young, "A New Intervention for Children with Emotional Disorders: The HABIC Human Animal Team Model for Animal-Assisted Therapy," Colorado State University, June 1996, unpublished.

31. Eleanor L. Ryder, "Social Work and Veterinary Medicine," *Sociolog* (Philadelphia: University of Pennsylvania School of Social Work, Spring 1991).

32. Ibid.

33. There were 23 state PIRG offices and 17 field offices listed in 1997 by their national office in Washington, DC.

34. Elizabeth Edwards and Wayne De Sarbo, "Typologies of Compulsive Buying Behavior: A Constrained Clusterwise Regression Approach," *Journal of Consumer Psychology* 5, no. 3 (1996): 231–262.

35. Patrick T. Kinkade and Matthew C. Leone, "The Privatization of Prisons: The Wardens' Views," *Federal Probation* (December 1992): 58–65.

36. Undated brochure, "Youth Law Center," Des Moines, IA. Received January 1997.

37. "Florida Freeze Hits Hardest Among Farm Workers," *Corpus Christi Caller-Times*, February 14, 1997, p. C17.

38. Susan S. Forbes, "Refugees," in *Encyclopedia of Social Work*, 18th ed., vol. 2 (Silver Spring, MD: NASW, 1987), p. 468.

39. Man Keung Ho, "Social Work Practice with Asian Americans," in A.T. Morales and B.W. Sheafor, eds., *Social Work: A Profession of Many Faces*, 8th ed. (Boston: Allyn & Bacon, 1998), pp. 473–491.

40. Hideka A. Ishisaka, Quynh T. Nguyen, and Joseph T. Ikimoto, "The Role of Culture in the Mental Health Treatment of Indochinese Refugees," in Tom Chokin Owan, ed., *Southeast Asian Mental Health* (Washington, DC: U.S. Department of Health and Human Services, 1985), p. 54.

41. Reico Homma True, "An Indochinese Mental Health Service-Model in San Francisco," in Owan, ed., *Southeast Asian Mental Health*, pp. 332–333.

42. J. David Kenzie, "Overview of Clinical Issues in the Treatment of Southeast Asian Refugees," in Owan, ed., *Southeast Asian Mental Health*, p. 119.

43. Ibid., pp. 120–121.

44. Sherry Ricchiardi, "Iowans Help Refugees on Underground Railroad," *Des Moines Register*, July 29, 1984, pp. 1A, 6A. See also "Social Work in the Sanctuary Movement for Central American Refugees," *Social Work* (January–February 1985): 74–76.

45. William Simbro, "Methodist Plea: Give Shelter to Hispanics," *Des Moines Register*, December 13, 1996, p. 1A.

46. "Dozens of Children Fathered by U.S. GIs Head for America," *Iowa City Press Citizen*, January 1, 1988, p. 3D.

47. "Immigration Bill Altered," *NASW News* 41, no. 10 (November 1996): 13.

48. Frederick L. Ahern, Jr., "Displaced People," in *Encyclopedia of Social Work*, 19th ed. (Washington, DC: NASW, 1995), p. 771–780.

49. Judy A. Hall, "Homelessness in the United States," in *Encyclopedia of Social Work*, 18th ed., 1990 Supplement (Silver Spring, MD: NASW, 1990), pp. 159–179.

50. Ibid. See also Jonathan Kozol, *Rachel and Her Children* (New York: Fawcett Columbine, 1988).

51. Steven P. Segal, "Deinstitutionalization," in *Encyclopedia of Social Work*, 18th ed., vol. 1 (Silver Spring, MD: NASW, 1987), p. 377.

52. Kathleen Prock and Merlin A. Taber, "Helping the Homeless," *Public Welfare* 45, no. 2 (Spring 1987): 5–9.

53. J. Larry Brown, "Domestic Hunger Is No Accident," editorial, *Social Work* 32, no. 2 (March–April 1988): 99.

54. Letter from J. Larry Brown, director, Center on Hunger, Poverty and Nutrition Policy, Tufts University, Medford, MA, July 9, 1993.

55. "Panel Urges Sex, Drug Abuse Education to Fight AIDS," *Daily Iowan*, February 2, 1997, p. 6A. See also "Release of Family Planning Funds Urged," *Corpus Christi Caller-Times*, February 8, 1997, p. A7.

56. James Midgley, "International and Comparative Social Welfare," in *Encyclopedia of Social Work*, 19th ed. (Washington, DC: NASW, 1995), p. 1490.

57. Lynn M. Healy, "International Social Welfare: Organizations and Activities," in *Encyclopedia of Social Work*, 19th ed. (Washington, DC: NASW, 1995), pp. 1508–1509.

58. Gary Clark, *Your Bride Is in the Mail* (n.p.: Words That Work Publications, 1997).

Additional Suggested Readings

First, Richard J., Dee Roth, and Bobbie Darden Arewa. "Homelessness: Understanding the Dimensions of the Problem for Minorities." *Social Work* 33, no. 2 (March–April 1988): 120–124.

Harper, Karen, and Jim Lantz. *Cross Cultural Social Work.* Chicago: Nelson-Hall Publishers, 1996.

Kirk, Stuart A., and Susan D. Einbinder. *Controversial Issues in Mental Health.* Needham Heights, MA: Allyn & Bacon, 1994.

Kruk, Edward, ed. *Mediation and Conflict Resolution in Social Work.* Chicago: Nelson-Hall, 1997.

Kübler-Ross, Elizabeth. *Death: The Final Stage of Growth.* New York: Touchstone Books, 1986.

Levinson, Boris M., and Gerald P. Mallone. *Pet-Oriented Child Psychotherapy,* 2nd ed. Springfield, IL: Charles C. Thomas Publisher, 1996.

Mannino, J. Davis. *Grieving Days, Healing Days.* Needham Heights, MA: Allyn & Bacon, 1997.

Midgley, James. *Social Welfare in Global Context.* Thousand Oaks, CA: Sage Publications, 1997.

Rappaport, Bruce M. "Family Planning: Helping Men Ask for Help." *Public Welfare* 39, no. 2 (Spring 1981): 22–27.

Remer, Frederic G. *AIDS and Ethics.* New York: Columbia University Press, 1993.

Shernoff, Michael J. "Family Therapy for Lesbian and Gay Clients." *Social Work* 29, no. 4 (July–August 1984): 393–396.

Whitaker, William H. "A Charity/Justice Partnership for U.S. Food Security." *Social Work* 38, no. 4 (July 1933): 494–497.

Part 3

Methods of Social Work Practice

Now that the various major settings or fields of service—that is, agency and organization contexts—have been covered, we are ready to examine the principal methods of social work practice. We do so not to learn "how-to-do-its" as much as simply to gain an overview of approaches to working with people in helping capacities in a variety of situations.

Therefore, we first consider the idea of the *social work generalist practitioner*. This is the recently emerged way of conceptualizing much of what social workers do, especially in baccalaureate-level practice. Related to this we will examine social systems; the helping process; social work roles, skills, and competencies; case management; prevention; and rural practice.

We will explore working with individuals and families, other groups, and communities. We will also take a look at social work administration and social welfare research.

It should be noted once again that this section may be read prior to Part 2, reversing the order of the two parts. In this case the reader should keep in mind that the practice methods being described are used in a number of diverse agency settings—hospitals, schools, counseling programs, and so forth, and that these organizational contexts influence the professional activity therein, just as the reverse is also true.

16

Newer Approaches in Social Work Practice: The Generalist

H. WAYNE JOHNSON

In the chapters in this section we will consider what traditionally were generally referred to as *social work methods*, the primary ones being casework, group work, and community organization. Whether these are best conceptualized as "methods" is a valid question. They refer to service units or numbers of persons served (case, group, or community) and hence are not really methods in the usual sense of this term as they do not suggest much about a plan of action.

Another limitation of this traditional way of thinking about social work *practice* is that the commonly encountered characterization of casework as working one-to-one does not allow for the vast amount of work done with families. One response is to define casework as activity with individuals *and* families, but the problem here is that the family is a group, a special kind of group, granted, but a group nonetheless. This is one of the reasons for the attention now being given to the notion of the social worker generalist and generic methods.

You may have noticed that the chapters in this section are not entitled "social casework," "social group work," and "community organization." The chapter titles chosen are intended to reflect better the nature of social work practice as it is evolving, particularly the generalist thrust. The latter development was alluded to in Chapter 1, and we return to it here for further examination.

The term *generic* is used here to mean general as opposed to specific. Generic social work has had two connotations over the years. Earlier in the century (1920s and 1930s) most social work education was in casework. Graduate students (social work education then was largely graduate-level) working toward a master's degree in the one-year programs then in existence selected a specialty having to do with a field of service or setting such as psychiatric, medical, or child welfare. One's educational program was tied to this choice of setting specialization. Then because people often moved from one field of practice to another and because of a common knowledge base in all the specialties, social work educational programs were revamped. One change was that the master's degree came to require two years. The other change had to do with the options for students. No longer did one choose a specialty such as psychiatric social work (meaning formerly casework), but now the student selected a "method" (casework, group work, or, in some schools, community organization). If the choice was casework, the idea was (and still is) that the knowledge and skill gained in this area would be transferable across the various settings or fields of service, and that one could engage in the helping process in a variety of agency or problem contexts. This was the first use of the generic social work term, that is, generic relative to setting or field.

More recently, the term *generic social work* has taken on a second meaning, that is, generic relative to method, or what is now often referred to as the social worker generalist. With the recent conception of the generalist, the lines between casework, group work, and community organization are blurred. There is the recognition that many contemporary workers must possess knowledge and skill in all these areas. Assessing individuals, understanding group dynamics, engaging in community planning all may be within one work day of a social worker; hence, the term *generalist* may be particularly appropriate. One may think then of integrated methods or what the worker does as a totality.

Examining some of the common social work skills helps to carry this idea further. Take interviewing, for example. Perhaps no skill is more basic in the social services. It is not just caseworkers in a variety of agency contexts who use the interview. Group workers and community organizers do, too. The common denominator in all these approaches is working with people. How does one work with communities, for example, except through people? It is not possible to deal with the community in the abstract but only by activity with individuals and, most especially, groups. In fact, a community may be thought of as a group of groups. Community organizers spend large amounts of time and energy developing and intervening with committees, task forces, and other kinds of groups toward attaining community objectives and goals.

The increased attention to the generalist practitioner model has been both a cause and result of changes in education and practice. Baccalaureate social work programs arrived on the scene in more recent years and are preparing students for entry-level generalist practice. This is consistent with the Council on Social Work Education (CSWE) accreditation standards, revised in 1994, around the Curriculum Policy Statement approved in 1992. On the graduate level, a variety of educational models exist. One is the master's (MSW) program, which has as its objective the preparation of the advanced generalist. Another is one with two or more tracks, one of which is the generalist. Still another approach in a two-year graduate program is the first year as a generalist base and a second year of specialization. The specialization may center around a particular social problem, field of service, or population.

On the graduate level the term *advanced generalist* is coming to be used by some schools of social work. What this social worker should be and do is not yet entirely clear, nor is there an adequate differentiation between a baccalaureate generalist and the MSW advanced generalist at this time. There are unanswered questions both in education and in practice on these issues, but development is occurring and clarification increasing.[1]

The generalist approach in social work practice is based on the dual nature of the profession, concern with both person and environment. This focus on person-in-environment or person and situation is integral to the generalist way of thinking. Generalists consider the transactions between people and their environments or how people cope with the various life stresses confronting them. In other words the generalist way of thinking is holistic and unitary. As Goldstein points out, the preferred orientation for the generalist is an "adaptational rather than a pathological concept of behavior."[2] From this view a "problems-of-living" perspective is more useful than the medical model of pathology. Among its other advantages, this problems-of-living conception of behavior reflects a systems way of thinking.

In contrast to the traditional orientation regarding methods of social work practice that tended to be seen as separate and distinct, the generalist approach is one of integrated methods. Social work has been termed "inherently generalist" by Sheafor and Landon as a result of the profession's concern with the people-and-their environment interaction. They note that this kind of field focuses on everything from the needs of individuals to social policies broadly.[3]

SYSTEMS

Another development in social work practice is the greater attention being paid to viewing the institution of social welfare, the profession of social work, helping activity, and client situations from a *systems* perspective. The essence of this way of thinking is to view the elements of the social welfare institution and human service professions as interrelated components within a larger network. These interdependent parts are linked to each other and affect one another. They tend toward a state of balance. Impact in one area has influence far beyond the immediate localized point, just as a pebble dropped in water creates ripples moving out in all directions. For social welfare the broader system includes economic and political institutions. Similarly, social work as a profession within the social welfare institution is related to other helping disciplines such as those within education (another social institution) and health, to mention only two. In a systems view social work is seen as boundary work, that is, "at the boundary between the system and its environment."[4]

A much-noted contribution in this systems conceptualization and one that assists in bringing together the helping professions and their social institution context is that of Pincus and Minahan, who delineate four systems present in helping endeavors generally:[5]

1. Change agent system: change agents and the people who are part of their agency or employing organization.
2. Client system: people who sanction or ask for the change agents' services, who are the expected beneficiaries of services, and who have a working agreement or contract with the change agents.

3. Target system: people who need to be changed to accomplish the goals of the change agent.
4. Action system: change agents and the people they work with and through to accomplish their goals and influence the target system.

A particularly utilitarian feature of this conceptual scheme is that it fits and incorporates any and all "methods" in social work. It is as applicable to working with organizations and communities as it is to one-to-one work with individuals. It is then well suited for the generalist.

Related to systems theory is what has come to be termed the *life model* of social work practice, a contribution of Germain and Gitterman.[6] It uses concepts from ecology, which concerns itself with the interactions between living organisms. As with systems theory, this "eco" approach is more a framework for organizing phenomena than an actual theory per se. The key concepts are those having to do with (1) "exchanges" and fit between environments and people, (2) stressors and coping, and (3) relatedness and self-direction.

HELPING PROCESS

It is well to spend at least a little time with the notion of the helping *process*. The idea of process is not new, but new attention has been given to it recently. Traditionally social work education taught a "medical model" of helping. The process consisted of three steps, according to this way of thinking: *study, diagnosis,* and *treatment*. Of course, the study or information gathering was particularly directed to social phenomena, just as the diagnosis and treatment were social.[7] But the terms suggest a medical orientation and a "sickness" model for the consumer of services that some social work scholars and practitioners would prefer now to deemphasize in favor of a broader, more general, and neutral conceptualization with more emphasis on "client" strengths.

One such is the notion of *beginning, middle,* and *ending* stages in helping or problem solving. Whatever labels are used, the helping process inevitably in some way is initiated, continued, and terminated. This is true whether we are speaking of a single interview contact or work with an individual, group, or community over a period of years. *Clients,* to use the word generically, one way or another become involved with workers (usually in agencies) or vice versa, perhaps because the client has sought help or the reverse has happened and the worker has reached out. Once engaged, the two parties work together and, ultimately, separate. Even if the terms are not used, the activities transpire. The more professionals can be consciously thoughtful and purposeful about their part in the process, the more productive and effective the work is likely to be. This is one reason self-awareness is stressed so much for social service workers.

Most scholar/writers who analyze social work practice, including generalist practice, find it necessary to consider what is variously termed the problem-solving, change, or helping process. For Compton and Galaway there are three primary phases in problem solving: contact, contract, and action.[8] The first of these, contact, encompasses problem identification, goal identification, data collection, and initial assessment. Within the contract part of the process is found joint assessment, planning, and prognosis. In the action phase comes implementation of the plan, endings, and evaluation. These authors point out that in implementing a plan, various worker roles are required. Endings entail such possibilities as referral, transfer, and termination.

McMahon, in stressing that the process is a purposeful procedure, sees the components as engagement, data collection, assessment, intervention, evaluation, and termination.[9] Data collection considers all aspects—problems, persons, and environment. Assessment includes problem prioritization and contracting. Intervention often entails teamwork, and evaluation includes reviewing and possibly reformulating the contract.

In writing about the health field, Germain, like Compton and Galaway discussed above, speaks of "phases" in the process. After some preliminary activities, the phases are the initial, the ongoing, and the ending. Encompassed in the initial part are such important activities as engagement, exploration, problem definition and assessment, contracting, goal setting, and planning.[10]

For Johnson the process consists of statement of the problem and of preliminary assumptions, collection and analysis of information, development and implementation of a plan, and evaluation.[11] Siporin's construct is similar to the others: engagement, intake, and contract; assessment; planning; and intervention, evaluation and termination.[12] The change process as formulated by Shaefor and the Horejsis[13] and by Kirst-Ashman and Hull[14] is similar to that of Siporin.

The current way of expressing the process, then, is some variation of this formulation: study, assessment, plan of action, intervention (or action or implementation), and evaluation. As indicated above, this way of thinking is less bound to the medical orientation. It suggests that in attempting to help people, initially there is a need to obtain information, followed by an examination of the information and a tying of pieces together toward an understanding of dynamics, cause/effect, and other relationships. From this assessment evolves a plan. At this point, there may be contracting with a client as to what he, she, or they will do and what the worker's responsibilities will be. The plan is then implemented, action is taken, and there is intervention in whatever directions are indicated. Finally, worker and client analyze in an evaluative way what has transpired and determine what, if anything, to do next. They may decide to repeat the action, to expand or reduce it, or to take some other tack.

We are speaking in the abstract thus far; obviously in the real world of helping, these steps are related to specific problems, people, and activity. Perhaps less obviously it should be noted that any discussion of steps in the helping process has inherent within it the danger of making it appear that the stages are more neat, discrete, and sequential than they are in fact. They are fluid and flow together concurrently as a two-way street. One is often intervening at the beginning contact just as assessment is ongoing and still occurring all the way through the process. One point in all of this is that, regardless of nomenclature, there is a systematic, planful approach in helping and problem solving.

ROLES, SKILLS, AND COMPETENCIES

Recent social work literature has tended to consider the diversity of skills, roles, and activities assumed by the contemporary worker. Federico suggests that six "helping skills" are essential in the social work problem-solving process:[15]

1. Communicating effectively with others
2. Assessing situations
3. Relating effectively to others
4. Planning with others
5. Carrying out plans
6. Evaluating results of the helping effort

Examination of these skills confirms that they are indeed fundamental to all social work functioning regardless of setting or method; in other words, they are generalist in nature. They further refine the process previously discussed.

It is nearly impossible to think of social work activity that does not in some way require relating to people. We relate to others through communication in its several forms. And in relating and communicating we engage in problem solving in an organized way as these skills in totality suggest and as was noted earlier.

Emphasis must be given to the fact that these are generic skills used in working one-to-one, with families and other groups, as well as with organizations and communities. Communication, relating, and systematic helping are vital in all "methods" and approaches in human services.

Although no single list or classification may be entirely satisfactory, some breaking down of helper tasks is useful in understanding the nature of the social work job broadly. Teare and McPheeters identify 12 roles, each of which actually encompasses a constellation of tasks.[16]

1. Outreach worker—identification of need in the community by reaching out and by helping people meet identified needs.
2. Broker—helping people through establishing linkages between people and services within the community.
3. Advocate—advocate entails "going to bat" for clients individually or as a group or class; obtaining needed services from an agency; and acting on behalf of a category of persons in need with a city council, legislature, or other decision makers.
4. Evaluator—evaluation of program effectiveness, assessment of needs and resources, considering alternatives, weighing possible outcomes.
5. Teacher—provision of needed information and skills through instruction.
6. Behavior changer—a whole array of activities aimed at modifying behavior through changing, expanding, or reducing specific behavior clusters.
7. Mobilizer—enlisting existing resources and creating new ones, directed toward problem resolution.
8. Consultant—consultation is working with other agencies, organizations, or persons who possess expertise on a relevant subject.
9. Community planner—planning on the community level toward enhancing human well-being.
10. Care giver—provision of needed supportive services.
11. Data manager—data processing, including collection and analysis to provide a basis for improved decision making.

12. Administrator—the administrative role in program direction and management encompassing planning and other activities essential to operating a program or organization.

This list points up some of the complexity of social work and demonstrates how broad and diverse are the tasks involved in working with people in a helping capacity. Some of these have to do with *counseling* responsibilities that accompany much social work, especially that having to do with what is variously termed direct, personal, or micro services, which are those concerned mainly with individuals, families, and other small groups. In some settings, these are now sometimes labeled clinical. Another set of skills is *educational* in nature. A third set of actions is encompassed under the concept of *community user*. This is intended to cover such varied work as planning, organizing, referral, and linkage activity or what is often now described as *brokerage*. The social worker also has an opportunity and responsibility to serve as an *advocate*, a role borrowed from the legal field. Just as social work identified with the medical model earlier and came to emphasize various psychotherapeutic approaches, so more recently it has rediscovered one of its roots in advocacy. Finally, a group of persons in the social services works partially or largely in *organizational maintenance*, i.e., administration, management, public relations, supervision, fund-raising, and so on.

Within these broad role categories are numerous skills. Examples are interviewing and recording. These basic kinds of skills are essential to virtually all practice. They are necessary in both micro and macro realms and found in both traditional and innovative settings and approaches.

Partly because of fairly recent stress on competency-based education and in approaches emphasizing specific skills for helping professionals, there is now considerable interest in social work *competencies*.[17] This is somewhat related to the *goal-oriented social services* (GOSS) and *management by objective* (MBO) thrust that came into social service administrative staff development and practice largely from business and other fields. A factor contributing to the rise of such activity in the human services is the growing demand for accountability and quality control, both in education and in practice. One of the most influential publications to appear on the competency subject directed specifically toward baccalaureate-level staff is that of Baer and Federico. They propose ten competencies for the baccalaureate social worker.[18]

1. Identify and assess situations where the relationship between people and social institutions needs to be initiated, enhanced, restored, protected, or terminated.
2. Develop and implement a plan for improving the well-being of people based on problem assessment and the exploration of obtainable goals and available options.
3. Enhance the problem-solving, coping, and developmental capacities of people.
4. Link people with systems that provide them with resources, services, and opportunities.
5. Intervene effectively on behalf of populations most vulnerable and discriminated against.

6. Promote the effective and humane operation of the systems that provide people with services, resources, and opportunities.
7. Actively participate with others in creating new, modified, or improved service, resource, and opportunity systems that are more equitable, just, and responsive to consumers of services, and work with others to eliminate those systems that are unjust.
8. Evaluate the extent to which the objectives of the intervention plan were achieved.
9. Continually evaluate one's own professional growth and development through assessment of practice behavior and skill.
10. Contribute to the improvement of service delivery by adding to the knowledge base of the profession as appropriate and by supporting and upholding the standards and ethics of the profession.

The authors of this list have acknowledged that it does not constitute the last word on baccalaureate competencies.[19] But, in spite of the fact that it has been criticized as being so broad that it does not differentiate between levels of practitioners such as BSW and MSW,[20] it is a significant milestone in the ongoing effort to describe and delineate social work practice skills. The next major step may be the twelve goals set forth in the 1992 CSWE Curriculum Policy Statement.[21]

A final thought on the matters we have just been examining—social work process, roles, skills, and competencies. Attention in this text is of necessity focused on the social worker and on the mechanics of the different aspects of the profession. But social work is about helping people and, in the real world, that is where the focus should be. To go back once again to the value base of the profession, the human is at the center of our concern. People are of worth and possess dignity and integrity. And helping must be appropriate to the human needs the people present. The various processes, roles, skills, and competencies are simply devices to be used and applied in helping others.

Case Management

As noted earlier, Goldstein has suggested that one of the several forms generalist social work may take is *case management*. This concept of case manager activity has received considerable attention in recent years and deserves further discussion here. With this managerial role the worker assists the client in determining what services are needed. Then the worker helps locate required resources and facilitates their use. The fragmented social service world is complex and may appear even more so from the client's perspective. Clients are often unaware of what programs are available and/or how to use a service of which they are aware. The worker can provide important assistance in coordinating services on behalf of the client/consumer. In doing so the worker often needs to be involved with the interaction between client and service(s) and between two or more programs providing service to the client. Through this means the client has greater access to service, and the help provided by the service providers is more likely to be appropriate and relevant for the client's needs. Facilitating communication, then, is a central activity, both between client and organization and among the various service providers.

The case management approach is aimed at avoiding service duplication and at filling gaps in service. In some agencies a worker engages in both direct service activities and case management for a client, whereas in other organizations these functions are separated. Either way the case management role is likely at points to entail acting as advocate, mediator, linker, facilitator, and broker.[22] Providing referrals is important in case management, so that knowledge of community resources is essential. The case manager role is one of those expected to grow as the part social work plays in *managed care* expands.[23]

Networking

A currently popular term is *networking*, which refers to communication, informal support, and working together within a group or community or between groups. As often occurs, a new idea (or a new label for old phenomena) may be treated by some as a panacea for many issues, needs, and problems. That networking is not always an answer is confirmed by a recently published study finding that the poor have fewer network resources than have persons from more affluent groups. These researchers caution social workers not to depend only on such networks and to plan with care interventions that use this approach, so that effectiveness is enhanced.[24]

Nonetheless, networking is important and can be extremely useful. This is true both with regard to maximum service for client consumers of social services and for enhancing the strengths and effectiveness of service providers. Potential gains from networking are pointed up in a U.S. Department of Justice research report focusing on activities of police in 12 communities relative to the mentally ill, public inebriates, and homeless. Police must often deal with such persons and can do so more effectively by establishing and maintaining networks with social service agencies, according to this report.[25]

Information and Referral

Related to case management and networking is *information and referral* (I & R). As noted earlier, the social services system is involved, complex, and fragmented. The development of I & R services is a response to the complexity and an effort to make services more understandable and accessible to potential users.

Ours is an information society and, as Haynes notes, "The availability and diversity of human services are meaningful only if there are available avenues to access these services."[26] I & Rs offer advice, make referrals, and provide follow-up. They "steer" clients to appropriate resources and make links. The idea of I & R is organizational; it provides an interagency system or network.

Some I & Rs are independent entities separate from other organizations. Others are part of an existent agency. At this time, many social agencies include I & R in their services. Some communities have centralized I & Rs serving an entire county or state, for example. In others, two or more I & Rs function in one city. Some provide certain kinds of counseling and many afford advocacy. Whatever the arrangement, this "door-opening" activity is important in a complex society.

Empowerment

In recent years new emphasis in social work has been placed on the profession's *empowerment* of people. This is another multimeaning and somewhat ambiguous term having to do with helping people become and feel more effective. Gutierrez suggests that four changes are necessary in enabling people to move from "apathy and despair to action." These are (1) increasing self-efficacy, (2) developing group consciousness, (3) reducing self-blame, and (4) assuming personal responsibility for change. Techniques identified for empowering clients are:[27]

1. Accepting the client's definition of the problem
2. Identifying and building upon existing strengths
3. Engaging in a power analysis of the client's situation
4. Teaching specific skills
5. Mobilizing resources and advocating for clients

These changes and techniques are useful with many populations and situations.

Prevention

A renewed interest in *prevention* has appeared on the social problems/social welfare scene. Professional journals[28] on this subject have emerged, and a significant text[29] became available in 1981. Numerous books and articles on prevention appeared in the 1980s. Every year since 1981 there have been major presentations on prevention at the Annual Program Meeting of the CSWE. Finally, the last three editions of the *Encyclopedia of Social Work* and the 1983–84 *Supplement* carried separate topics on prevention. All indicate the increased attention being devoted to prevention.

Bloom uses the Public Health Service definition of prevention: "Primary prevention refers to those scientific practices aimed at simultaneously *preventing* predictable problems in individuals or populations at risk; *protecting* or maintaining current strengths, competencies, or levels of health and healthy functioning; and *promoting* desired goals and enhancing human potential."[30]

Social work has long been concerned with prevention, though not always by this name. The present thrust is interdisciplinary in nature, involving professionals from a variety of helping fields. For these disciplines, including social work, there are prevention connotations both in reforming social conditions broadly and in direct services.

Prevention holds different meanings for different people. For some it is an absolute activity aimed at totally averting the appearance or emergence of a problem condition from the outset. For others it means intervention directed toward discouraging repetition or continuation of a condition or problem that has already been present. The focus also varies; for some the health field is the context for prevention, whereas for others it is crime and delinquency, and still others are more drawn to families and children when thinking of prevention. Certainly social work, with its family orientation, would argue that whatever supports and strengthens families tends to be generally preventive of social pathology, at least in a broad sense.

The prevention model provided by the public health field includes activities of *primary,* *secondary,* and *tertiary* treatment/prevention. These refer to levels of care in the health field. Suffice it to say that in translating from public health to the social services, there are actual and potential activities in which social work engages or could engage that can be useful and productive on all three levels.

In his discussion, Wittman identifies four prevalent themes that are useful in understanding prevention and what is happening currently on this matter:[31]

1. The recognition of the importance of strengthening the natural interacting systems in which people live.
2. The reaffirmation of the importance of infancy and childhood as a focus.
3. Crisis intervention (useful in early detection and treatment of problems) is closely related to prevention.
4. Many approaches are necessary if services are to be truly preventive.

There are tremendous opportunities for wiser use of funds and greater economy as well as the furtherance of human well-being if priorities emphasize prevention of social problems.

Prevention is an extremely important goal in the human services, but we must be realistic about what is possible, given our present state of knowledge, and must avoid simplistic notions. For example, it is easy to assert that certain youth programs "prevent delinquency." But can this be demonstrated and documented? Often it may be easier, more accurate, and more honest to claim, sticking with the illustration, that a particular provision is useful for youth in general. It is important not to claim more than can be delivered. Social problems such as delinquency are typically too complex to lend themselves to simple solutions. There are no panaceas and therefore prevention, too—appealing and attractive as it is—must be put into perspective and dealt with realistically.

Social Work and the Arts

In recent years interest has developed in using the arts in social work and other helping disciplines. This may be done as part of a therapeutic approach with individuals or in the context of recreation/leisure activities, usually of a group nature. A particular theoretical/treatment orientation (e.g., Gestalt) is sometimes inherent in the use of the arts. This approach is used to facilitate diagnosis and assessment on one hand as well as to provide an aspect of treatment intervention on the other. Just as play therapy is often effective with children diagnostically, it is also useful for ventilation and emotional release. The same may be true of music, dance, painting, sculpting, and dramatics. They provide means of expression for persons who may have greater need for such outlets than most people, as well as presenting an option for working with social work clientele generally.

Spirituality and Social Work

In recent years there has been a reemergence in the helping professions, including social work, of attention to spirituality and religion. One example of this trend is the appearance of a new journal, *Spirituality and Social Work*. Spirituality has reference to "the views and behaviors that express a sense of relatedness to something greater than the self; spirituality connotes transcendence or a level of awareness that exceeds ordinary physical or spatial boundaries."[32] If a holistic approach to and view of people is to be taken, inclusion of the spiritual can be important.

Some medical schools are now offering courses or content on "alternative" or "integrative" medicine focusing on nontraditional practices and treatments, for example, meditation and acupuncture. A survey of the American Academy of Family Physicians found that most doctors surveyed believe that there is an important relationship between mind and body, between faith and healing. The traditional gulf between science and religion may be in the process of being bridged to a degree.[33] Not all alternatives are equally valid, and they should not all be lumped together. Skepticism of some is more warranted than of others that may be more widely studied and practiced.

RURAL SOCIAL WORK

An area for which the generalist model of social work practice is particularly appropriate is the rural community. In the 1970s new interest emerged in non-metropolitan human services.[34] A national rural social work caucus came into being, and national institutes on social work and human services in rural areas are now held annually.

So often both social problems and services are equated with the urban way of life. In a similar vein, the rural environment is frequently thought of as relatively problem-free, static, and quiescent. This is hardly a correct image of what is transpiring currently in nonmetropolitan America. Change is pervasive, and the rural community is often in dynamic flux. Two examples of this are "impact" communities or boomtowns a few years ago in western states mushrooming with coal mining or extraction of petroleum, gas, or minerals in an energy crisis era, and some towns in all regions of the country experiencing rural industrialization.[35] Such developments often transform the affected communities, and immense problems may result, such as shortages of housing, schools, and recreation facilities as well as increases in child abuse, alcoholism, and family dysfunction. This is not to deny that many rural communities are withering and declining, which presents still further problems. The farm crisis of the mid-1980s impacted negatively on towns and cities that are economically tied to agriculture, as well as on farms.

Rural dwellers experience many of the same needs and problems as those of their city cousins: poverty, physical and mental health, education, crime, family relations, and others. Resources for dealing with these problems in small communities may be scarce, although the author has noted elsewhere that it is often not as much a dearth of resources as a different kind and arrangement.[36] For example, rural law enforcement persons, clergy, school staff, and service clubs often perform functions informally that in a metropolitan environment may be handled in a more elaborate, formal network of social welfare agencies and organizations. There is a public welfare agency in virtually every county in the nation, although it is probably small in size and staff in a rural area. This agency is the hub of social work activity. Small-town libraries and librarians are other organizations/persons that may be at the center of human services provision in a rural area.

There are problems that are specific to rural communities. Examples are needs in sparsely populated areas for specialized programs such as services for the chemically dependent or developmentally disabled, or for child day care. People with these needs do exist in rural sections, but their limited numbers deny them visibility and power and make the provision of service difficult. Transportation is a particular concern in nonmetropolitan regions, especially when we consider groups such as the elderly. One problem for aged people is isolation, and lack of transportation may make this even worse. Not only does this mean absence of human interaction and contacts for stimulation and enjoyment, but it may also mean difficulty in meeting basic human needs such as obtaining medical care and groceries.

A disproportionately large part of the rural population is elderly. Four of the eight states possessing the highest percentage of the elderly in 1995 were in the Midwest, a principal rural part of the United States. In all of these, the percentage of the population of persons 65 and over exceeded by far the national figure of approximately 12.8 percent.[37]

In view of the importance of transportation for rural dwellers, the elderly, and others, planners in recent years have devoted attention to either or both of two aspects: how to transport people to services and how to bring services to people. Both are being done successfully in increasing numbers of communities. Examples of taking services to people are mobile libraries, meals, and certain health programs. Transporting people to resources, even in rural communities, is occurring now through scheduling of regular routes using a variety of vans, buses, and other vehicles. Social workers are often among the first persons to become aware of the need for such programs and frequently play important roles in planning, establishing, and administering them.

The energy crisis of the 1970s, with high costs and shortages, raised questions about the future of transportation programs like these. But an energy crisis may provide reason for increasing rather than decreasing such approaches because they may be more energy-efficient than the alternatives, assuming there is to be at least a modicum of service provided.

When a social worker is one of only a few persons in an agency or perhaps the only one, as may be the case in a rural environment, he or she must be versatile and able to function independently and autonomously.[38] Ability to provide direct service, such as counseling, is important, as is skill in serving as an advocate. But at the same time, the worker may need to sensitize the community to its needs and help to establish a needed resource such as a day-care center or program for the elderly. Organizing a self-help group and publicizing its availability could be another concurrent activity of this generalist. In other words, helping approaches in rural communities include both direct services and program/community development and organizing.

Another aspect of rural practice should be commented upon. In a community where it may be quite literally true that "everybody knows everybody," a new professional such as a social worker is highly visible. To gain and maintain acceptance in such places, which are often rather conservative, the worker needs to be conventional and make an effort to fit into the community. An interesting feature of working in nonmetropolitan areas is that the worker is likely to encounter his or her "clients" most anywhere outside the agency, for example, in a supermarket, shop, restaurant, or church, or to find one's children in the same school class as the client or the client's child.[39] These kinds of relationships and contacts along with the usual rural informality may present both obstacles and opportunities in the helping process.

SUMMARY AND CONCLUSIONS

In this chapter we have considered some of the newer approaches to and developments within social work practice. Included have been the generalist model, a systems perspective, increased interest in the helping process, concern with roles/skills/competencies, and a new thrust around prevention and social work and the arts. Finally, rural social work has been examined as an important kind of generalist practice. Not everything discussed represents what the chapter title may suggest to some readers—distinct approaches. Instead, collectively we have examined varying degrees of new directions in professional social work activities.

Notes

1. See, for example, Robert J. Teare and Bradford W. Sheafor, *Practice-Sensitive Social Work Education* (Alexandria, VA: Council on Social Work Education, 1995), pp. 97–117.
2. Howard Goldstein, in Neil Gilbert and Harry Specht, eds., *Handbook of the Social Services* (Englewood Cliffs, NJ: Prentice-Hall, 1981), p. 414.
3. Pamela S. Landon, "Generalist and Advanced Generalist Practice," in *Encyclopedia of Social Work*, 19th ed., vol. 2 (Washington, DC: NASW, 1995), p. 1101.
4. Gordon Hearn, "General Systems Theory and Social Work," in Francis J. Turner, ed., *Social Work Treatment*, 2nd ed. (New York: Free Press, 1979), pp. 333–359.
5. Allen Pincus and Anne Minahan, *Social Work Practice: Model and Method* (Itasca, IL: F.E. Peacock Publishers, 1973), p. 63.
6. Carel Germain and Alex Gitterman, *The Life Model of Social Work Practice,* 2nd ed. (New York: Columbia University Press, 1996), p. 5.
7. This point is reflected in the titles of two significant books, one a pioneer and the other modern: *Social Diagnosis* by Mary Richmond (New York: Russell Sage Foundation, 1917) and *Social Treatment*, 2nd ed., by James K. Whittaker and Elizabeth Tracy (New York: Aldine de Gruyter, 1989).
8. Beulah Compton and Burt Galaway, *Social Work Processes*, 5th ed. (Pacific Grove, CA: Brooks/Cole Publishing Co., 1994), pp. 56–57.
9. Maria O'Neil McMahon, *The General Method of Social Work Practice*, 3rd ed. (Boston: Allyn and Bacon, 1996), pp. 82–336.
10. Carel B. Germain, *Social Work Practice in Health Care* (New York: Free Press, 1984), pp. 70–72.
11. Louise C. Johnson, *Social Work Practice: A Generalist Approach*, 5th ed. (Boston: Allyn and Bacon, 1995), pp. 68–72.
12. Max Siporin, *Introduction to Social Work Practice* (New York: Macmillan, 1975).

13. Bradford W. Sheafor, Charles R. Horejsi, and Gloria A. Horejsi, *Techniques and Guidelines for Social Work Practice*, 4th ed. (Boston: Allyn and Bacon, 1997), p. 131.

14. Karen K. Kirst-Ashman and Grafton H. Hull, Jr., *Understanding Generalist Practice* (Chicago: Nelson-Hall, 1993), p. 36.

15. Ronald C. Federico, *The Social Welfare Institution*, 4th ed. (Lexington, MA: D.C. Heath, 1984), p. 163.

16. Robert J. Teare and Harold L. McPheeters, *Manpower Utilization in Social Welfare* (Atlanta: Southern Regional Education Board, 1970), pp. 34–35.

17. For example, see Morton L. Arkava and E. Clifford Brennen, eds., *Competency-Based Education for Social Work* (New York: Council on Social Work Education, 1976).

18. Betty L. Baer and Ronald Federico, *Educating the Baccalaureate Social Worker* (Cambridge, MA: Ballinger Publishing, 1978), pp. 86–89. Copyright© 1978, reprinted by permission of the author, Betty L. Baer.

19. Ronald C. Federico, *The Social Welfare Institution*, 3rd ed. (Lexington, MA: D.C. Heath, 1980), p. 233.

20. Shirley M. Ehrenkranz, "Report of the Committee on Articulation of Graduate and Undergraduate Social Work Education," March 7, 1981 (to Deans and Directors of Graduate Schools of Social Work), p. 2.

21. Washington, DC: Council on Social Work Education, 1992.

22. Dean H. Hepworth and Jo Ann Larsen, *Direct Social Work Practice*, 3rd ed. (Belmont, CA: Wadsworth, 1990), pp. 449–451. See also Jack Rothman, "A Model of Case Management: Toward Empirically Based Practice," *Social Work* (November 1991): 520–528.

23. Golda M. Edinburg and Joan M. Cottler, "Managed Care," in *Encyclopedia of Social Work*, 19th ed., vol. 2 (Washington, DC: NASW, 1995), p. 1641.

24. Gail K. Auslander and Howard Litwin, "Social Networks and the Poor: Toward Effective Policy and Practice," *Social Work* 33, no. 6 (May-June 1988): 234–238.

25. Peter E. Finn and Monique Sullivan, "Police Responses to Special Populations," U.S. Department of Justice, January 1988.

26. Karen S. Haynes, "Information and Referral Services," in *Encyclopedia of Social Work*, 19th ed., vol. 2 (Washington, DC: NASW, 1995), p. 1464.

27. Lorraine M. Gutierrez, "Working with Women of Color: An Empowerment Perspective," *Social Work* 35, no. 2 (March 1990): 149–153. See also Ruth J. Parsons, "Empowerment: Purpose and Practice Principle in Social Work," *Social Work with Groups* 14, no. 2 (1991): 7–9.

28. Martin Bloom lists 13 diverse journals on prevention in "Primary Prevention Overview," in *Encyclopedia of Social Work,* 19th ed., vol. 3 (Washington, DC: NASW, 1995), p. 1899.

29. Martin Bloom, *Primary Prevention: The Possible Science* (Englewood Cliffs, NJ: Prentice-Hall, 1981).

30. Martin Bloom, "Primary Prevention Overview," p. 1895.

31. Milton Wittman, "Preventive Social Work," in *Encyclopedia of Social Work*, 17th ed. (Silver Spring, MD: NASW, 1977), pp. 1051–1152.

32. Joyce O. Beckett and Harriette C. Johnson, "Human Development," in *Encyclopedia of Social Work*, 19th ed. (Washington, DC: NASW, 1995), p. 1393.

33. "Survey: More Doctors Say Faith Aids Healing," *Iowa City Press Citizen*, December 16, 1996, p. 1A.

34. See, for example, Leon H. Ginsberg, ed., *Social Work in Rural Communities*, 2nd ed. (Washington, DC: Council on Social Work Education, 1993); and H. Wayne Johnson, ed., *Rural Human Services* (Itasca, IL: F.E. Peacock Publishers, 1980).

35. Judith A. Davenport and Joseph Davenport III, eds., *Boom Towns and Human Services* (Laramie, WY: University of Wyoming, 1979).
36. Johnson, *Rural Human Services*, p. 49.
37. "A Profile of Older Americans 1995" (Washington, DC: American Association of Retired Persons, 1996).
38. Johnson, *Rural Human Services*, pp. 147–148.
39. Barbara Lou Fenby, "Social Work in a Rural Setting," in H. Wayne Johnson, ed., *Rural Human Services* (Itasca, IL: F.E. Peacock Publishers, 1980), pp. 149–152.

Additional Suggested Readings

All the practice texts listed here use a more generalist, integrated-methods approach than is true of the traditional- or single-method texts. Traditional-method texts are listed separately after each appropriate chapter.

Brill, Naomi J. *Working with People*. 5th ed. New York: Longman, 1997.

Canda, Edward R. "Spirituality, Religious Diversity, and Social Work Practice." *Social Casework* 69, no. 4 (1988): 238–247.

Epstein, Laura. *Helping People: The Task-Centered Approach*. 3rd ed. New York: Macmillan, 1992.

Gambrill, Eileen. *Social Work Practice*. New York: Oxford University Press, 1997.

Hoffman, Kay S., and Alvin Sallee. *Social Work Practice: Bridges to Change*. Needham Heights, MA: Allyn and Bacon, 1993.

Maguire, Lambert. *Social Support Systems in Practice*. Silver Spring, MD: NASW, 1991.

Martinez-Brawley, Emilia E. *Perspectives on the Small Community*. Silver Spring, MD: NASW, 1990.

Rothman, Jack. *Guidelines for Case Management*. Itasca, IL: F.E. Peacock Publishers, 1992.

Shulman, Lawrence. *The Skills of Helping Individuals, Families, and Groups*. 3rd ed. Itasca, IL: F.E. Peacock Publishers, 1992.

Simon, Barbara Levy. *The Empowerment Tradition in American Social Work: A History*. New York: Columbia University Press, 1997.

Sundet, Paul, and Joanne Mermelstein. "Helping the New Rural Poor," *Public Welfare* 45, no. 3 (Summer 1987): 14–19.

Thyer, Bruce A., ed. *Controversial Issues in Social Work Practice*. Boston: Allyn and Bacon, 1997.

Zastrow, Charles. *The Practice of Social Work*. 5th ed. Florence, KY: Brooks-Cole, 1995.

17

Working with Individuals and Families

JANET JOHNSON LAUBE

Social work with individuals and families was the earliest form of social work practice, and its traditional classification was *casework*. Practitioners of this approach have historically held the professional title of *social caseworker*, and more recently some have used the title of *clinical social worker*. These labels indicate that their specialty is problem solving with persons experiencing personal, interpersonal, or situational stresses. While the goal of balanced social functioning is shared with other methods, caseworkers are primarily engaged with individual or family units and systems that impinge on or interact with these units. The focus is on the "person-in-the-situation," which means that both internal, psychological forces and external, social forces receive consideration in the helping process. Of course, social workers whose practice is with larger client systems often interact and intervene with individuals and families, too, so they must be familiar with the knowledge and skill base for this kind of practice. Probably the largest number of generalist social workers with bachelor's degrees work with individuals and families. The same is true of MSW workers, whether they are thought of as advanced generalists or specialists.

The information that the practitioner working with individuals and families must use concerns a fundamental struggle that all human beings experience, that is, the struggle between the inclination toward independence (autonomy, differentiation, mastery) and the tendency toward dependence (symbiosis, relationship, belonging). Beginning at the point of earliest development, individuals experience the vulnerability of relying on other persons for their sustenance and protection. Survival is at stake. Individuals learn to feel trust or mistrust of their environments as embodied in other persons. Even this early, individuals learn that, however responsive the family and environment may be, there is always a separateness or aloneness inherent in life. The memory of physical connectedness or symbiosis before birth contributes to the desire for reunion, touch, belonging, and/or for eliminating the aloneness. This longing for closeness is met with affection, rejection, or indifference, and individuals early develop an expectation of how well their needs will be met. Competing with the longing for closeness is the biological and psychological push toward differentiation and identity. The individual strives for mastery of physical skills and a sense of self that is distinct from other persons.

As individuals develop through the life cycle, they perform an ongoing dance of steps toward and away from independence and dependence. Their physical development and their culture's imperatives present demands for particular expressions of one drive or the other at specific periods.[1] For example, the physical stage of adolescence is characterized by an intense psychological desire for belonging and acceptance and physical touching with peers; but it also is a time when there is a need for differentiation from family and development of an adult identity that is exacerbated by cultural demands for decisions about careers and values.

Problem solving, which is the aim of any social worker, becomes centered on achieving balance for individuals and families in their relationships—with themselves and with others—between aloneness and connectedness as well as between demands for personal expression and social survival. In order to realize this balance successfully, individuals and families must accomplish four tasks defined by Talcott Parsons: adaptation, or changing and growing to meet internal and external demands; integration, or organizing an identity and relating to other systems; pattern maintenance, or maintaining stability, autonomy, and boundaries; and goal attainment, or self-realization and productivity.[2] Each of the tasks contains an individual and a social mandate for successful accomplishment. Social workers assist in the achievement of these tasks by encouraging individuals and families in their independent functioning and also in their transactions with their environments. For example, they may be educators when helping people to adapt, or liaisons to services when aiding integration, or therapists when facilitating identity development, or advocates when promoting goal attainment. This flexibility on the part of the professionals requires knowledge of life cycle development and cultural contexts.

Social workers who assist individuals and families with personal, relationship, or environment problems make use of the independence/dependence paradox within the professional relationship. They recognize that the authority of the helper offers clients protection and guidance but also challenges their inclination for self-direction. The skill with which the professionals can use that authority to direct the course of intervention, while at the same time mobilizing the clients' initiative, determines the effectiveness of the problem-solving alliance.[3]

HISTORICAL EVOLUTION

Social work with individuals and families has a long history. It first emerged as a method of preventing or reducing pauperism in the 1880s, when "cases" were investigated to identify the "worthy" poor. The Charity Organization Society's *friendly visitors* (discussed in Chapter 3) who conducted these investigations soon recognized that forces other than "morality" contributed to individual and family dysfunction. They could see that strong social forces, as well as individual abilities and characteristics, shaped people's living conditions. Mary Richmond was a pioneer in investigating the causes for and effective ways of resolving people's problems in living.[4]

Social workers began to seek professional knowledge and skill training for improving their ways of dealing with people. While this professionalization resulted in some moving away from the morality model, it tended to keep the focus primarily on problems inside persons and used a study, diagnosis, and treatment paradigm adopted from the field of medicine. This paradigm served to organize the activities of the workers and to unite practitioners in the many fields of social casework practice (medicine, mental health, corrections, child welfare, schools, and so forth). It was limited by its focus on "symptoms," on defects rather than strengths, on labeling, and on the authority role of professionals. Freudian psychology served to enhance the knowledge base but reinforced this individualist perspective. The depression in the 1930s and World War II in the 1940s offered some contrasting evidence of the significance of social forces, so that there was always a counterpoint to the individualist theme.

Not until the 1960s did the developing profession adopt a theoretical perspective that permitted integration of practice wisdom about individual capacities and environmental demands. The social systems model enabled social workers to articulate what they knew about the interactional influences of individuals and their environments. Social workers now know that systems not only have to organize the energy within them but also exchange energy with the net-

Brown Brothers

A visiting nurse social worker visits a poor family in New York in the late 1800s/early 1900s.

work of systems to which they are related. This enables an approach to people that takes into account their individual intelligence, values, coping skills, and communication expertise, as well as their social models, comforts, opportunities, and stressors.

In social work with individuals and families, the *relationship* between client and professional has always been considered a significant aspect of the intervention process.[5] Social systems theory is an umbrella theory that accounts for the significance of the interaction of the helper with the organisms to be helped.

WHAT THIS APPROACH IS AND DOES

Social work with individuals and families consists of helping people confront the day-to-day realities of living alone and together. This means, first, *physical coping*—the quantity, quality, and accessibility of food, clothing, sleep, and medical care; the availability of physical supports, rehabilitation, and institutional care; the safety, spaciousness, and financial assurance of housing; the regularity and motivation for recreation, relaxation, and exercise; and the use or abuse of stimulants, tranquilizers, and inhibitors. Thus, the social worker may be actively engaged with a client in trying to obtain basic food and shelter, as is the worker for the public department of social services. On the other hand, the worker may verbally investigate the influences of physical conditions on psychosocial functioning, as does the individual or family therapist at a mental health center. Example:

"Marie"

In obtaining data about Marie that might reveal why she is feeling depressed, the social worker asks her about her physical self-care: What are the possibilities for her to engage in physical exercise? What are her usual eating patterns? What is her customary use of psychoactive substances and of medications? What are the economic limitations on her access to food, exercise, and medication? Are there any sources of physical, sexual, or emotional abuse in her environment? Have there been any experiences of abuse or violation in her past?

Along with physical well-being, and certainly related to it, is people's *economic coping*. Social workers working primarily with individuals and families may simply assess the influence of or act to alter their clients' economic standard. The drive toward independence may be frustrated by economic hardship, or congenial interdependence may be jeopardized by economic uncertainties. Example:

"Sam"

Sam had had appointments that morning with two clients whose financial situations inhibited them in far different ways. The first, Jim, was frightened by the deepening recession that meant he was not likely to be called back to work by his company for many months. His eligibility for unemployment benefits might not last through his period of lay-off, and his wife's job alone was not enough for them to support their family. Jerry, the second, had a well-paying job in a company where his future was secure, but he had long wanted to start his own art gallery. He was afraid to risk loss of financial assurance by starting his own creative and personally expressive business.

Part of economic coping is educational well-being. Social workers assess and intervene in relation to schooling. Example:

"Kevin"

This school social worker was contacted by the third-grade teacher who was worried about Kevin's self-image as failure-prone. The teacher wanted consultation about behavioral incentives for the classroom, as well as a referral for Kevin to the peer group therapy program run by the social worker. They jointly decided that Kevin's parent needed to be invited to the school for a discussion of the boy's progress and the resources available to him. One of the outcomes of that meeting was a referral for Kevin's mother to the department of social services. She wanted to enroll in college classes, so that she could improve her job-finding possibilities and improve her own self-image. She was eligible for public assistance in this educational effort.

Social work with individuals and families includes attention to social coping. *Social coping* consists of relating the individual self to other persons and organizations, or relating the family to other social systems. It includes the satisfactory negotiation of role relationships, as of student to teacher, employer to employee, parent to child, family to church or synagogue, and/or parents to schools. Social workers help individuals to develop their own interpretations of role requirements, but they often also translate social standards for individuals. Thus, they teach communication skills, parenting skills, organizational skills, assertiveness skills, and budgeting skills. Social workers serve as negotiators between individuals and other groups or between families and organizations to facilitate understanding and exchange. Example:

"John"

John is employed by the department of social services as an outreach worker to abusing parents. He helps Darla and Dave Jensen change their expectations of their young child and also improve their own self-images as individuals and parents. He shows them how to communicate their feelings and desires to each other and how to show affection and tolerance to their child. He is helping them to modify the patterns of discipline that they learned from their own parents so that they can better meet the society's standards for acceptable parenting. As he does so, he helps them distinguish those aspects of their parenting and marital styles that are unique because of their ethnic and cultural backgrounds. John also helps a group of abusing parents start a support system, a Parents Anonymous group, to give them encouragement and understanding in their growth toward better parenting.

———————

Social work with individuals and families also is concerned with psychological coping. *Psychological coping* is developing and maintaining a sense of *self*. This evolves through viewing oneself as reflected by others and then organizing an internally defined and directed self-image. Psychological coping requires that this sense of self grow and adapt to changing physical development and the resultant changing demands of the environment upon the ego. In order to cope emotionally, individuals must be able to (1) distinguish the boundary between their perceptions and the impinging environment; (2) differentiate sensory data from internal symbols; (3) separate thoughts and feelings; and (4) develop a sense of self as having influence on the environment. Social workers aid individuals in clarifying a sense of identity and modifying maladaptive defensive stratagems. Perceptions, interpretations, feelings, and wants are identified. Then individuals are taught effective skills for communicating this self-awareness. Example:

"Anna"

———————

In her work with adolescents, Anna was quite confrontational relative to inconsistencies. She knew these inconsistencies were typical of this development stage, but she also knew that her comments challenged the teenagers to distinguish what was important to them, what their beliefs and feelings were, and what they wanted. They used this increased awareness in their efforts to define themselves as individuals.

———————

In summary, social work with individuals and families requires attention to their physical, economic, social, and psychological coping. For optimum coping on each of these levels, there needs to be a balance between the drive toward independent expression of the self and the drive toward dependence or union. The social worker aids in the supply of energy or supports to effect such a balance. These provisions may be tangible or intangible. Tangible supports for independent functioning may include money, prosthetic devices, education, and physical rehabilitation. Intangible supports for independent functioning may include hope, faith, assertiveness skills, rational thinking skills, psychotherapy for ego development, and growth of self-esteem. Tangible supports for interdependent functioning may include adoption services, child-care arrangements, Parents without Partners meetings, or residential treatment for adolescents. Intangible supports for interdependent functioning may include trust, communication skills, family therapy, and marital counseling.

How It's Done

Social work with individuals and families proceeds through an orderly process despite the varying theoretical orientations about change that are held by practitioners. The process begins with establishment of a *relationship*. This relationship should be a collaborative one, where the client and social worker are partners working for understanding. Such a partnerhsip requires the social worker's acknowledgement of the context of the client's problems. Where there are racial, religious, gender, or ethnic differences between social worker and client, the development of a positive working relationship necessitates cultural competence and respect for diversity on the part of the professional.[6] Services to individuals and families rely on both verbal and nonverbal interaction; therefore, communication of positive regard through language use and nonverbal signals requires a high level of knowledge and skill.

The next step in the helping process is the establishment of the *contract*, that is, the agreement about roles, timing, objectives, confidentiality, grievances, and fees. This may be a formal agreement that is signed by both social worker and client, or it may be an evolving verbal discussion between them that addresses each of these items. Background information about the problem, the desired outcome, and previous problem-solving attempts are all discussed so that an *assessment* may be made jointly between client and social worker. It is important that previous problem-solving efforts be understood as indiciators of possible directions for intervention. Potential problem-solving approaches are reviewed and a *plan* for intervention into the situation is negotiated. This plan and a means for *evaluating* the results are developed through a discussion of "where are we going and how will we know when we get there?" The *intervention* process then proceeds toward a jointly planned *termination* of services. As described earlier, the particular intervention devised for an individual client or client family may be tangible, intangible, or a combination. The intervention services selected will be a function of the particular agency (psychotherapy at a mental health center, parenting services from a family services agency, and so on) and the theoretical predilection of the individual social worker. Careful attention to termination of the helping process enables people to anticipate resolving other difficulties in the future. Example:

"Marilyn and Ben"

Marilyn and Ben came for help with their family's adjustment to Ben's diagnosis of early Alzheimer's disease. Because he was only 48 years old, his disease was expected to progress much faster than in an elderly person. The couple wanted help with their acceptance of the prognosis, with Marilyn's deteriorating ability to sleep and associated symptoms of depression, and with their children's adjustment to Ben's imminent incapacity and death. The social worker's capability for expressing her understanding of the powerlessness ond grief they were experiencing, as well as for exhibiting skills for helping, enabled the development of a trusting and collaborative relationship. The couple decided to come to eight sessions, they made arrangements for payment of fees, and they decided on a combination of individual, couple, and family sessions. They spent time telling the social worker about their reactions to the diagnosis, their attempts to deal with the reactions of other members of their family, and their past problem-solving patterns and successes. They decided on a focus for their work together, which was to *strengthen connections*—within their family as well as with Marilyn's associates outside the family. They decided they would have achieved their goals if Marilyn's depression were reduced and her sleep improved, if Marilyn felt more able to talk with friends and colleagues at work about her grief and needs for support, if their children were able to talk openly with them about their father's illness and impending death, and if Ben were able to develop some resources for estate planning and grief support. At the end of the eight sessions, the family evaluated their progress as adequate on the goals they had set. They had developed a variety of supports in their community for the stages they had learned they would go through, and they had each acquired greater understanding of their particular patterns and capabilities for handling grief. They were ready to terminate with the social work services, but planned to return for additional sessions when Ben's illness brought different challenges to them.

The primary theoretical orientations of individual and family social workers may be classified as psychodynamic, cognitive-behavioral, interactional, ecological systems, costructivist, and/or feminist. When using a psychodynamic approach, social workers as therapists help individuals modify their personality structures with the aim of strengthening ego functioning. This takes place within an open-ended relationship in which the professional offers interpretations of the client's conscious and unconscious needs and motives.[7] When using a cognitive-behavioral approach, social workers and clients identify irrational thinking patterns and maladaptive behaviors. They are taught to alter their catastrophic expectations and to organize new systems of reinforcement for deisrable behaviors.[8] Within an interactional framework, social workers help clients develop authentic relationships in which their self-concepts are strengthened by clear communication.[9] An ecological systems approach focuses on the relationships among biological, social, psychological, and cultural factors affecting and affected by human behavior. Using this model, social workers focus on processes surrounding the emergence and maintenance of problems and pursue an interruption of the problem-maintaining interactions. The focus for intervention is strengthening the relationship between people and resource systems.[10] From a constructivist point of view, problems and their solutions are embedded in interactive processes; thus, social workers collaborate with their clients in ascribing meaning to experience, to problems, and to possibilities for solutions.[11] A feminist approach to individuals and families requires the social worker to recognize and respond to the effects of nonequal power distributions that support oppression and dysfunction.[12]

Who Uses This Method?

Services to individuals and families are offered by social workers in a number of settings. The most prevalent is the family service agency, which may belong to Family Service America; it may be a voluntary, sectarian agency like Lutheran Social Services, Catholic Charities, or Jewish Family Services; it may be a private, nonsectarian agency like a child guidance or a child placement agency; or it may be a department of a government-funded social service center. Social workers at agencies of this sort usually provide family therapy, individual therapy, pregnancy and child-placement counseling of unwed parents, adolescent therapy, play therapy for children, group therapy, and even financial planning and debt adjustment services. Social workers at community mental health centers provide many of the same services to individuals and families, usually in a psychotherapeutic mode, although they also offer educational programs for such skills as assertiveness, parenting, and communication. Within mental health settings, social workers often serve individuals suffering from long-term psychological disability through day treatment or community support programs.

Services to individuals and families are offered by social workers located in several other settings. These professionals may facilitate hospital adjustment, posthospital placement, and rehabilitation when working in medical centers. They help bridge the relationship of families with schools. They conduct orientation and therapy sessions for families of residents in institutions and group homes. They also are increasingly setting up their own practices in private offices and are offering a whole gamut of psychotherapeutic, educational, and advocacy services.

The special knowledge that practitioners offer individuals and families includes personality development through the life cycle, personality dynamics, family structure, family communication process, and resources for problem solving. The special skills that practitioners offer individuals and families includes case-finding, relationship building, communication assessment and change, personality assessment, problem assessment, problem solving, and environmental manipulation.

The Position of the Approach in Social Work

Services to individuals and families have always been a cornerstone in the social work edifice, and they will continue to be demanded by our society in its "pursuit of happiness." The social work profession itself gave short shrift to the fundamental necessity for these services during the 1960s and 1970s when it experienced a much-needed surge of interest in social policy. Direct services to persons were devalued when it seemed that they were only piecemeal attacks against a vast network of destructive social forces. The profession seemed to support the redirection of social workers' energies into social activism and social policy reform. However, individual and family problems persisted, and they often were controlled only partly by external forces. There continued to be a need for direct services, both tangible and intangible. Most recently, the social work profession has returned to the position that social workers must be knowledgeable about effecting change with both individuals and their social environments, although they may choose to specialize in one or the other sphere.

Issues and Trends

The major issue in provision of services to individuals and families is the same as that underlying all social work practice: Is the change effort directed to altering people's behavior and expectations so that they can function in a more adaptive way, or is it directed toward altering the demands and supports in the environment? As with all social work practice, the answer is "both." The effort is directed toward achieving balance, an integration of individual and social functioning. However, in each individual case there will be a choice of emphasis and there must be a selection of where to begin. Working with individuals and families requires the social worker to be adept at locating persons in their unique developmental and relationship contexts. This has traditionally been described as "beginning where the client is." The success of the intervention rests on how well the professional can mobilize reciprocal, interacting powers of individuals *and* environment.

Identifying supports for individuals and families has become an increasingly important social work activity during the end of 1990s, when conservative trends and strained budgets are altering the human service delivery system. Not only is there public questioning of the *means* of delivering services to people in need, there is questioning of the *aim* of ensuring protections for people's health and well-being.[13] A "social deficit" occurs when government economic supports for social programs are drastically reduced.[14] Recent "social disinvestment" has taken place during the period in which the huge baby boom cohort reached adulthood. Traditional family structures reached an apex of transformation through divorce, blending, and unmarried parenthood. Recession dislocated vast numbers of workers. In addition, there was increased incidence of and increased recognition of family violence, child physical and sexual abuse, and AIDS. Social workers have had to rediscover traditional roles of locating and developing social networks, volunteers, and self-help groups to aid the victims of this social disinvestment. In many cases they have become case managers, helping to organize nonprofessional supports for farm families, homeless persons, victims of violence, persons with addictions, single mothers, the chronically physically and mentally ill, and so forth.

An outcome of reduced public funding and limitations in service provision has been the downgrading and declassifying of professional social work positions. The caseworker in the public agency increasingly has had an indirect role in assisting client functioning, as purchase-of-service arrangements have restricted service activity to problem identification, resource location, and monitoring services. Very often, case managers have been stripped of direct helping roles.[15] In contrast, clinical social workers working in private agencies, mental health centers, and private practice have organized effective drives in many states for professional licensure to clarify their practice qualifications.

Another strong influence on the provision of services to individuals and families has been the emergence of the managed care system. Efforts to limit unnecessary health and mental health costs have resulted in restrictions on provider choice, eligibility, frequency, and length of service provision. These restrictions alter many facets of the traditional working relationship, because decisions about length of care or frequency of intervention are made by a case manager, and the agency or practice must be selected as a preferred provider before it can serve people who subscribe to managed care systems.[16]

There is a continuing need within the profession for a unified theory of practice, supported by evidence of effectiveness.[17] Social workers practice in a broad spectrum of settings, and individual professionals function across various practice strata. General systems theory has provided a language to describe the interrelation of individual, family, community, and societal processes, but it is insufficient in articulating direct practice applications. Thus, social work practitioners too often fashion numerous techniques of practice into an "eclectic" point of view, techniques frequently derived from the work of professionals in other disciplines. As social workers become better trained in the scientific method, practitioner-guided research will contribute to development of a testable theoretical approach.[18] The trend in the profession is toward much more rigorous evaluation of service provision, which will enable more specific education for practice and more confident practice.[19]

THE FUTURE

Social work with individuals and families in the next decade will continue to be preoccupied with the outcomes of social structure change and social disinvestment. Outcomes of transformation of the public welfare system will gradually progress in opposing directions: strengthened patterns of self-support with attendant improved personal and family functioning on one hand, and exacerbated patterns of vulnerability and risk on the other. Problems that clients present will continue their recent trend toward the serious challenges of relationship abuse, substance abuse, inadequate and unsupported parenting, chronic and complex health problems due to AIDS, mental breakdown, aging, employment difficulties, and poverty. Social workers will have to arm themselves with information about intricate connections between economics and psychosocial functioning, so that they can more effectively advocate for public policy changes. Social workers who deal with individuals and families are particularly suited to addressing the social costs of inadequate investment in human development. In addition, social work's attention to diversity in ethnicity, gender, sexuality, and ability provides special expertise for addressing societal complaints and costs.

Increased reliance by individuals and their employers (as third-party payers) for social work services is resulting in widespread pressure for short-term services that limit costs; however, these limits in many cases inhibit the provision and receipt of the long-term and in-depth services that are needed to treat the very complex problems that a society in transition has been creating, e.g., sexual abuse, physical violence, substance abuse, and alienation.

Trends toward privatization of many public services will maintain their momentum into the next decade. The social work profession itself has paralleled this trend in the growing numbers of practitioners who are developing their own private practices. Cost-effectiveness is the byword for the decade. Private organizations will propose that they can run public institutions in a more cost-effective, but not necessarily socially just, manner. Third-party payers will determine whether it is more cost-effective to reimburse private social workers for services usually provided by more costly professionals, or less so because social work services are more widely available.

SUMMARY AND CONCLUSIONS

Social work with individuals and families has a prominent history within the profession, having long been known as *social casework*. The professional helper aids individuals and families to balance their inclinations toward both dependence on and independence from their environments. The areas of physical, economic, social, and psychological coping are attended to in assessing and intervening with these clients. The process of helping is a collaborative one between client and social worker and proceeds through the phases of relationship establishment, contract clarification, assessment, planning, intervention, evaluation, and termination. A variety of theoretical approaches are used by social workers found in a variety of settings, including public and private family service agencies, mental health centers, hospitals, schools, institutions, and in private practice.

Social workers have long recognized the significance of the family for human functioning, and they are being joined by other professions in developing practice theory that takes family interaction into account. The social work profession and other professions, as well as lay persons, are currently calling for a greater national recognition of the importance of the family to societal integration. National social policies for family protection and nurturance have been recommended by many groups as vital for our society's continuing health and growth.

Notes

1. Erik Erikson, *Identity: Youth and Crisis* (New York: W.W. Norton, 1968). See also Carol Gilligan, *In a Different Voice: Psychological Theory and Women's Development* (Cambridge, MA: Harvard University Press, 1982).
2. Talcott Parsons and E.A. Shills, *Toward a General Theory of Action* (Cambridge, MA: Harvard University Press, 1967).
3. Allison D. Murdach, "Beneficence Re-examined: Protective Intervention in Mental Health," *Social Work* 41, no. 1 (January 1996): 26–32. See also Ronald Simons, "Stratagies for Exercising Influence," *Social Work* 27, no. 3 (May 1982): 268–274.
4. Mary Richmond, *Social Diagnosis* (New York: Russell Sage Foundation, 1917).
5. Helen Harris Perlman, *Relationship: The Heart of Helping People* (Chicago: University of Chicago Press, 1979). See also Enola K. Proctor, "Defining the Worker-Client Relationship," *Social Work* 27, no. 5 (September 1982): 430–435.
6. D. Harrison, B. Thyer, and J. Wodarski, eds., *Cultural Diversity and Social Work Practice* (Springfield, IL: Charles C. Thomas, 1996).
7. Michael J. Mahoney, *Human Change Processes: The Scientific Foundations of Psychotherapy* (New York: Basic Books, 1991), pp. 235–238. See also Sheldon Cashdan, *Object Relations Therapy: Using the Relationship* (New York: W.W. Norton, 1988).
8. E. Mash and J. Hunsley, "Behavior Therapy and Managed Mental Health Care: Integrating Effectiveness and Economics in Mental Health Practice," *Behavior Therapy* 24, (1993): 67–90. See also Mahoney, *Human Change Processes,* 234–245.
9. Lawrence Shulman, "Developing and Testing a Practice Theory: An Interactional Perspective," *Social Work* 38, no. 1 (January 1993): 91–97.
10. Lisbeth Schorr with Daniel Schorr, *Within Our Reach: Breaking the Cycle of Disadvantage* (Garden City, NY: Doubleday, 1989). See also S.W. Renggeler and C.M. Borduin, *Family Therapy and Beyond: A Multisystemic Approach to Treating the Behavioral Problems of Children and Adolescents* (Pacific Grove, CA: Brooks/Cole Publishing, 1990); K.G. Lewis, *Family Systems Application to Social Work: Training and Clinical Practice* (Binghamton, NY: Haworth Press, 1991); and Greg Yamashiro and Jon K. Matsuoka, "Help-Seeking among Asian and Pacific Americans: A Multiperspective Analysis," *Social Work* 43, no. 2 (March 1997): 176–186.

11. J.L. Zimmerman and V.C. Dickerson, "Using a Narrative Metaphor: Implications for Theory and Clinical Practice," *Family Process* 33 (1994): 233–246. See also R. Neimeyer, "An Appraisal of Constructivist Psychotherapies," *Journal of Consulting and Clinical Psychology* 61, no. 2 (1993): 221–234; B. Rudolph, *A Brief Collaborative Therapy: A Practical Guide for Practitioners* (Westport, CT: Greenwood Press 1996); and Adrienne S. Chambon and Allen Irving, *Essays on Postmodernism and Social Work* (Toronto: Canadian Scholars' Press, 1994).

12. Vincent Fish, "Introducing Causality and Power into Family Therapy Theory: A Correction to the Systemic Paradigm," *Journal of Marital and Family Therapy* 16, no. 1 (January 1990): 21–37. See also Mary Bricker-Jenkins, Nancy R. Hooyman, and Naomi Gottlieb, *Feminist Social Work Practice in Clinical Settings* (Newbury Park, CA: Sage Publications, 1991).

13. Patricia L. Ewalt, "Social Work in an Era of Diminishing Federal Responsibility: Setting the Practice, Policy, and Research Agenda," *Social Work* 41, no. 5 (September 1996): 439.

14. Edith M. Freeman, "Welfare Reforms and Services for Children and Families: Setting a New Practice, Research, and Policy Agenda, *Social Work* 41, no. 5 (September 1996): 521–532.

15. Federico Souflee, "A Metatheoretical Framework for Social Work Practice," *Social Work* 38, no. 3 (May 1993): 317–331.

16. Barbara Berkman, "The Emerging Health Care World: Implications for Social Work Practice and Education," *Social Work* 41, no. 5 (September 1996): 541–551.

17. E.G. Goldstein, "Issues in Developing Systematic Research and Theory," in A. Rosenblatt and D. Waldfogel, eds., *Handbook of Clinical Social Work* (San Francisco: Jossey-Bass, 1983).

18. R. Fuller and A. Petch, *Practitioner Research: The Reflexive Social Worker* (Bristol, PA: Open University Press, 1995). See also Jane F. Gilgun, "A Case for Case Studies in Social Work Research," *Social Work* 39, no. 4 (July 1994): 371–380; and Srinika Jayarnate, Tom Croxton, and Debra Mattison, "Social Work Professional Standards: An Exploratory Study," *Social Work* 42, no. 2 (March 1997): 187–199.

19. Jack Rothman and Edwin J. Thomas, *Intervention Research: Design and Development for Human Science* (Binghamton, NY: Haworth Press, 1994). See also Marlys Staudt, "Pseudoissues in Practice Evaluation: Impediments to Responsible Practice," *Social Work* 42, no. 1 (January 1997): 99–106.

Additional Suggested Readings

Combrinck-Graham, Lee. *Children in Families at Risk: Maintaining the Connections.* New York: Guilford Press, 1995.

Congor, Rand D., and Glen H. Elder. *Families in Troubled Times: Adapting to Change in Rural America.* Hawthorne, NY: Aldine de Gruyter, 1994.

Corcoran, Kevin, and Vikki Vandiver. *Maneuvering the Maze of Managed Care: A Survival Guide for Clinicians in Public and Private Settings.* New York: Free Press, 1996.

Dunst, Carl J., Carol M. Trivette, and Angela G. Deal. *Supporting and Strengthening Families, (Vol. 1): Methods, Strategies, and Practices.* Cambridge, MA: Brookline Books, 1994.

Feldman, L.B. *Integrating Individual and Family Therapy.* New York: Brunner/Mazel, 1992.

Kilpatrick, Allie C., and Thomas P. Holland. *Working with Families: An Integrative Model by Level of Functioning.* Boston: Allyn and Bacon, 1995.

McManus, R., and G. Jennings. *Structured Exercises for Promoting Family and Group Strengths; A Handbook for Group Leaders, Trainers, Educators, Counselors, and Therapists*. Binghamton, NY: Haworth Press, 1995.

Pozatek, Ellie. "The Problem of Certainty: Clinical Social Work in the Postmodern Era," *Social Work* 39 no. 4 (July 1994): 396–403.

Schneider, D. *American Childhood: Risks and Realities*. New Brunswick, NJ: Rutgers University Press, 1995.

Schwartz, Ira M., and Philip AuClaire. *Home-Based Services for Troubled Children*. Lincoln: Univeristy of Nebraska Press, 1995.

Shulman, Lawrence. *The Skills of Helping Individuals, Families, and Groups*. Itasca, IL: F.E. Peacock Publishers, 1992.

18

Social Work with Groups

PATRICIA KELLEY

Social group work was traditionally seen as a method of social work, and it is now considered to be part of generalist practice. Today, for example, social workers lead support groups for victims of assault, education groups for families coping with a chronically ill member, therapy groups for persons experiencing emotional or relationship difficulties, and advocacy groups for disadvantaged persons. Social group work is a method practiced in many fields of social work and in many kinds of agency settings. While group work is a method of practice, the skills and knowledge are basic to all social work practice. No matter what field of practice a social worker may be in and no matter what method is used, knowledge of group dynamics is important. Social workers attend meetings of formal organizations, they work in teams or units in agencies, they serve on committees, and they work with communities, families, or individuals. In all of these situations, it is important to understand people in interaction with others.

DEFINITIONS AND CRITERIA OF GROUPS

First of all, one asks, what is a group? More than a collection of individuals, the group is a social system itself. There are many definitions of the term *group*, with a fair degree of consensus. There are some elements common to most definitions of group. First, there is the idea of plurality: That is, a group must be two or more people. A second element is that there needs to be contact or interaction among these persons. A collection of individuals walking down a busy street in a city, then, would not be a group. If an accident occurs, and those people stop to observe the accident, then those individuals might be considered a group. If they worked together to aid the accident victims and began to talk together about it, then they more clearly becomes a group. A third facet in defining group is the presence of some significant commonality. People join a group for a purpose, and those purposes are sometimes called *goals* or *rewards*. People have always bonded together for a common good. In early times, persons joined together to protect themselves or to find food. In today's more complex society, where an individual may feel isolated, the group can serve as a mediator between the individual and the larger society. Persons still join together to work for a common good; examples of this might be a trade union, a professional organization, or a political group. Through these groups, people believe that they can have more impact on their lives and control over their destinies.

With respect to joining groups for a reward, those rewards may be tangible or intangible. For example, people may join together in a neighborhood group for something very tangible—such as sidewalks, so their children can walk to school more safely. On the other hand, people in that same neighborhood may join together for conversation and coffee, and the reward might be social interaction and finding friends. People may join a group to have a particular problem solved, such as a task force in an organization. Generally, persons can be considered part of a group if any of these criteria are met: They engage in frequent interaction with the others; they define themselves as members of the group; they share norms or values concerning certain matters; they find some group rewards; and they pursue an interdependent goal.

Types of Groups

Having discussed definitions and criteria for groups we now address types of groups and ways in which groups may be classified. First of all, groups are often classified as either primary or secondary. A primary group is a group to which there are primary and lasting ties. The family is considered a primary group, and social workers working with families need to understand group dynamics. A secondary group is one in which the ties are not primary or permanent. An elected city council would be an example of a secondary group.

Groups may be classified as formal or informal. A formal group usually has rules, official members, and stated goals, whereas informal groups are more loosely organized. Let us look at formal and informal groups in the context of social group work. A parent education group led by a social worker in a family service agency would be an example of a formal group in that it would be announced in advance, the social worker would be seen as the professional group leader, specific rules would be made explicit, and there might be an intake procedure for membership in that group. The number of sessions would be spelled out in advance, as would the goals. On the other hand, a youth worker in an inner-city neighborhood house might be available during after-school hours for adolescents to "drop in and chat." There would be no membership lists or rules of order, but simply a notice that popcorn is there and that the worker is available. Different people might attend on different days, there is no official agenda, and the worker here assumes the role of facilitator more than leader.

In social work settings, groups can be classified by objective or goal, by the setting, by the people in it, and by the methods involved. Examples of groups classified by objective or goal are recreational groups, educational groups, therapy groups, support groups, and political action groups. Examples of groups classified by setting would be the "inpatient group" in a hospital, or the "Smith Street Tenants' Rights Group" in a neighborhood. A social worker talking about the youth group or the golden-age group is classifying the group on the basis of the persons in it. When social workers talk about a "stress management" group or a "positive peer culture group,"[1] they are classifying the groups by the methods used.

Historical Antecedents of Group Work

Historically, there have been several ways in which social workers have become interested in working with groups. Traditional social group work in our country can be traced back to the settlement house movement in the late nineteenth century. Grace Coyle, a pioneer in social group work, wrote, "social group work as a defined method developed first in settlements and community centers in low income areas and in the youth serving agencies."[2] Settlement houses served new immigrants to this country, mainly in the large cities. An early and famous example is Hull House in Chicago, which was founded by Jane Addams. It was hoped that new immigrants could better assimilate if they were educated to the norms and ways of our country. Settlement house workers aimed to educate and encourage these new immigrants in their own neighborhoods, and it was thought that this could help to ameliorate the disadvantages that they faced. At the same time, these social workers aimed to change the social conditions and the inequality that oppressed the immigrants who were caught in the sweatshops and squalid poverty that characterized the Industrial Revolution. Main thrusts of the settlement house movement, then, were citizen education and social reform. Neighbors joined together to work on projects for the betterment of all, such as improved conditions in the neighborhood. These settlement houses did provide a haven for the immigrants; they provided an opportunity for people to learn about their new country with their friends and neighbors from their old country, and to work together for social change. The themes in early social group work of social participation, social action, and democratic process remain today as important values in the social work profession.

A second historical antecedent of today's group work theory and practice is the group dynamics movement. Social psychologist Kurt Lewin coined the term *group dynamics.* After escaping to this country from Nazi Germany in the 1930s, he became interested in the effects of social climate on individual attitudes. His students, Ronald Lippit and R.K. White, became interested in studying leadership style. Other social psychologists, adult educators, sociologists, and organizational theorists became attracted to this movement.[3] These researchers studied the behavior of the group as a developmental system itself. They viewed the group behavior as more than, and different from, the summation of individual behaviors of the people in the group, believing that the group develops its own values, goals, set of behaviors, and developmental cycle. They became interested in looking at the application of these groups dynamics to specific settings, especially organizations. These adherents of applied group dynamics set up the National Training Laboratory in Bethel, Maine, in the 1940s to study the practical applications of group dynamics theory further. This laboratory was established to train persons for leadership in business, labor, government, and education. An additional goal was to study group dynamics. The focus of this training and research was to teach people to become more

Jane Addams Hull House Association

Jane Addams, pictured here in 1930 or 1931, reads stories at Mary Crane Nursery, part of the 13-building complex that made up Hull House. The nursery, which opened in 1907, provided one of the best programs in Chicago for preschool children.

aware of their own roles, functions, and patterns of behavior in groups, and to recognize these patterns in others, too. Awareness of self and the development of new behaviors and skills were emphasized, and styles of leadership and decision making were examined.

The third historical antecedent to present-day group work was the group psychotherapy movement that began early in this century, but which became "vastly accelerated" by World War II.[4] The term "group therapy" was coined in 1925 by J.L. Moreno, who also developed psychodrama, but it was not until World War II that the movement received much attention. During the war, there were not enough trained therapists to help all the individuals needing psychotherapy, so persons were treated in groups. While the initial use of group therapy was for efficiency, other benefits quickly became apparent. Therapists discovered that the patients in group therapy were often learning and changing faster than those in individual therapy. These patients learned not only from the therapist but from the others in the group as well. They began to see themselves in relation to significant others, and their social and interpersonal behavior could be examined more easily in groups. The cohesiveness of the group and the support of others with similar problems were also helpful, and it was discovered that people could learn new and more appropriate social behaviors in a group setting.

The group psychotherapists, mainly clinical practitioners, and the group dynamics people, mainly researchers, did not have much interaction or cross-fertilization of ideas until the 1960s, when the *sensitivity movement* became popular. The sensitivity training movement was an outgrowth of the National Training Laboratory and its branches and focused on self-awareness through interpersonal feedback. These growth and human potential groups grew out of the group dynamics movement, but developed in a different direction. The focus of these groups was more on human potential and growth than on leadership training, and they developed out of social forces of the day.[5] Personal responsibility and focus on the here and now were key elements in the human potential groups, and group psychotherapists, moving away from the traditional psychodynamic view, began to incorporate these concepts into their work. The lines between these movements have become less clear, and today group work theory is pulled together from all three historical sources. While many disciplines study group phenomena and many professionals work with groups, this integration of group theory is especially important for social workers because of their wide sphere of practice—from group counseling to community change.[6]

Models of Social Group Work

In the 1960s, Catherine Papell and Beulah Rothman conceptualized three *models* of social group work practice,[7] and their models roughly corresponded to the historical antecedents. They defined *model* as a conceptual design to solve a problem that exists in reality, and they cautioned that the models are theoretical formulations, not discrete categories, and that others might classify them differently.

What Papell and Rothman called the *social goals model* is a direct descendant from the settlement house movement. The purpose of these groups is to teach social responsibility and to raise social consciousness; the role of the worker is that

Hall of History Collection/Boys Town

Boys Town is another example of Papell and Rothman's "social goals model." Here the second executive director of Boys Town, Msgr. Nicholas Wegner, umpires an intramural baseball game. If you really try at Boys Town, you always get another chance: Although Wegner is signalling three strikes to the batter, the boy at bat awaits another pitch.

of an enabler. This kind of group work is carried out in such organizations as Girl Scouts, Boy Scouts, Boys' Clubs of America, YWCA, the settlement houses, and community centers. The second model of social group work practice Papell and Rothman referred to as the *remedial model,* and this is a direct descendant from the psychotherapy movement. Many social workers are involved in group psychotherapy, where the purpose is treatment of individuals involved for personal or social adjustment. The worker here assumes the role of therapist, healer, or change agent. Such work is carried out in psychiatric hospitals, mental health centers, and youth group homes. The third model of social group work practice Papell and Rothman called the *reciprocal model.* Here the individuals work together to help each other. Examples might be support groups, task force groups, and peer supervision groups. The worker here is less of a leader and more of a facilitator, mediator, or resource person, and sometimes the groups are leaderless. The purpose of these groups might be mutual help and support or personal growth rather than treatment of problems. These groups may not have specific goals other than mutual aid and support. The reciprocal model of group work practice is a direct outgrowth of the group dynamics laboratory work, and theory is heavily drawn from Lewin's field theory, which views an individual's behavior as a function of his or her "life space" or "field," and sociological systems theory.[8]

Today, less distinction is drawn between the models, and current social work practice draws from all three of the historical models. As early as 1980, Papell and Rothman distilled common elements from all three models into a more generic *mainstream model.*[9] At about that time, also, Emanuel Tropp's *developmental approach* to group work[10] encompassed both the social goals and the reciprocal models, but he distinguished the developmental approach from group therapy, while admitting some overlap. Gisela Konopka, a major theoretician in the field of social group work, has been identified with both the social goals model and the remedial model,[11] and has worked and written in both areas. More recently, Lawrence Shulman has articulated an *interactional paradigm,*[12] which incorporates many elements of group work practice. Charles Garvin, a contemporary social work educator in group work, has noted the importance of adapting to the needs of a particular group or situation in selecting an approach.[13]

Assertiveness training can be viewed as an example of how these theoretical models mix in practice. Assertiveness training, developed in the 1970s,[14] was a precursor to the *empowerment* movement of today, in which group members develop their own resources and strengths.[15] Assertiveness training is usually conducted in groups, its members are not usually considered patients or clients, and the goal is growth rather than treatment. Differentiating assertive communication and behavior from aggressiveness is taught and practiced. The outcome of substituting assertive behavior (stating your own wants and needs so negotiating can occur) from aggressive behavior (trying to push your demands on to others) is the aim of such training. While its growth goals would place it in the reciprocal category, its emphasis on personal change would place it in the remedial category. Such training is carried out in industries, agencies, and schools as communication and conflict management tools (reciprocal), and in mental health centers and other treatment agencies (remedial). Its leaders may be teachers (reciprocal) or clinicians (remedial).

Group Work Practice Today

Social group work keeps changing in response to societal changes and needs. For example, in the affluent '60s and '70s, group work focused more on maximizing human potential, while group workers today address serious problems as they respond to the challenges of the 1990s. Thus, we see social workers leading groups for AIDS patients, for victims and perpetrators of sexual abuse and other forms of violence, for abandoned and neglected children, for homeless persons, for displaced persons and refugees, and for families of seriously disabled persons no longer cared for by the community.

As social workers meet these new challenges, they continue to work with many kinds of groups, in many fields, and in many ways. There are many self-help groups (for example Alcoholics Anonymous or Parents Anonymous—a group of persons who have abused their children) that do not require or want professional leadership, but often look to the professional social work community for consultation or help in getting started. Other self-help groups, such as groups for survivors of sexual assault, more commonly have professional leaders, who are often social workers. Social workers frequently become involved in problem-solving and advocacy groups, such as helping parents of developmentally disabled children organize for better services for their children, or helping them lobby for better legislation for their cause. In these situations, the social worker might serve as consultant or group leader. Medical social workers often organize or facilitate support for educational groups, such as in hospitals with patients or relatives of patients with life-threatening illnesses. These groups offer mutual emotional support and education on disease management. The literature on the use of groups in medical social work has increased greatly in recent years.[16] Social workers often lead educational groups in social agencies, too—groups such as parent education, foster parent training, or couple communication training.

Social workers also become involved in developmental groups, such as in-service training in stress management, team building, or wellness programs at work sites. Clinical social workers often conduct therapy or treatment groups in mental health or family service agencies. In group therapy, the individual benefits from having more points of view, and the other group members benefit by identification with and observation of the helping process. The group interaction itself is also a medium of change.

Social workers also work with recreational groups, such as in nursing homes, in neighborhood houses, and in youth organization clubs such as those historically classified under the "social goals" model. In such situations, their recreational activities are usually the means to achieve ends, not the ends themselves. The ends might be educational (such as learning new skills), therapeutic (such as increasing self-esteem), or social improvement (such as decreasing delinquency). Social workers are also involved in community groups, neighborhood groups, social action, and political groups. Often "task groups" in which specific tasks are undertaken are used in community work.[17] As social workers strive toward changing the social environment as well as helping the individuals within it, they utilize groups at both levels. Working in the political sphere involves sensitivity to and awareness of group process, as does work within agencies and in communities.

ASPECTS OF GROUP DYNAMICS

Since social workers are so frequently involved with groups at many levels and in many fields, it is imperative that they have some understanding of, and some skills in the management of, group process. Furthermore, one criterion for social group work is attention to group dynamics.[18] Some of the elements that social workers need to be aware of in group dynamics will now be discussed.

First, there are natural *stages* or *sequences* of group development, just as there are stages of individual growth and development that the worker needs to understand. Theorists vary in the number and names of stages of group development, but there is agreement as to the general progression.[19] As the group advances developmentally, different interventions and skills are required at different stages.[20] These stages are clearer in time-limited groups than in open-ended groups, where people join and leave while the group continues, but attention to group development is important in both situations. Today, there are even single-session groups,[21] where the stages are more compressed and less important, as the sense of group is less strong.

Other aspects of group dynamics that the leader needs to be aware of are *participation* and *influence* of various members. It is important to be aware of the level of participation, verbal and nonverbal, of all the members. It is important, also, to note which members have influence, how they use that influence, and what style of influence is predominant. It is useful for the leaders and members of groups to be aware of their struggles for leadership and rivalry for power, and to be aware of participation in subgroupings.

How *decisions are made, conflicts resolved*, and *problems solved* are also important group dynamics issues. Sometimes decisions are made by one or more people in the group with others agreeing, sometimes decisions are made democratically with input from all, and sometimes the group takes the path of least resistance by going along with whatever suggestion comes up. Groups may make decisions through a formal vote, through informal consensus, or through a process of evaluating and prioritizing the courses of action.

It is also important to be aware of *roles* that various members play and functions that they serve in the group. Just as we all need to assume various roles in our everyday life, roles have very important functions in group development. Thus, it is important to assess both the task roles (seeing that things get done) and the affective roles (taking care of the emotional needs of the group members) that are taken by various group members.

Membership and *subgroupings* are aspects of group dynamics, also. Who seems in, partially in, or out of this group? Are these patterns consistent or do they vary from time to time? Do the people who are out of the interaction seem to have chosen that position, or does it appear that they have been shut out? Are there subgroups and do they contribute to somebody being left out? Do these smaller units support or subvert the goals of the larger group? Membership may depend on regularity of attendance, also. With the severity of problems being addressed today, such as AIDS, chronic mental illness, and homelessness, groups may not fall into the open-ended or closed-ended classification. Members may come or go as needed or they are able. This situation changes the definition of group membership, and criteria for membership are less clear.

It is also important to be aware of the *atmosphere* and *feelings* in the group. Is the atmosphere friendly and congenial, is there hidden conflict and disagreement, or is there open conflict and disagreement? Do the people seem interested and involved in the tasks at hand or bored by them? Are there signs of anger, warmth, excitement, and/or competitiveness? It is important to be aware of the affective nature of the group.

Another element that is important to look for is the development of *group norms* or *standards*. Corey and Corey have stated that norms are "the shared beliefs about expected behaviors that are aimed at making groups function effectively."[22] Norms express beliefs or desires of the majority of the group members as to what behaviors should or should not take place in a group. Sometimes these rules are very clear, such as when guidelines are voted upon, or when group standards or rules are discussed. However, sometimes these group norms are not so clear and are not made explicit. An example of this might be when certain areas or topics are avoided, or if there is an implicit norm to avoid conflict.

The social worker needs to be aware of individual as well as group needs, and of the *communication patterns* among individuals in the group. The worker also must be aware of development of the group and of the norms and the rules that evolve regarding communication.

The *leader's role* in a group will vary according to the purpose and kind of group. For example, in a community group, it is the goal of the leader to develop leadership from within the people in that community so the group can function after the leader leaves. In a therapy group, on the other hand, the leader will continue the leadership function until the group is terminated.

Leadership styles and *size of group* also affect the group. Both of these variables are heavily reviewed in the literature.[23] There is no "right" style for the leader to have; the choice would depend on the leader, the members, and the purpose of the group. Likewise, the "correct" size varies. As Reid says, "There is no optimal size for a group. The size a practitioner establishes for a group will be based on the group's purpose, as well as the practitioner's own level of comfort."[24] In general, it can be said that smaller groups (under ten for example) tend to have more participation of members, more consensus, and a greater degree of cohesiveness. Larger groups can be broken into smaller subgroups when necessary. For some situations, a larger group—with its increased anonymity and reduced intensity—is preferable. In some educational or community settings, this is often the case. Last, it is important to consider the organizational context in which the group work is conducted.[25]

*A Community Support Program Group**

The community support program (CSP) group meets for one and one-half hours weekly at a community mental health center. It is designed to offer support for persons who have returned to the community after hospitalization in a mental institution. It was begun several years ago and is open-ended in that the membership changes. A few members

---

*Case provided by Veronica Wieland, RN, MA, Department of Family Practice, University of Iowa, Iowa City, IA.

have been with it since its beginning, while others are new members. The group size is usually about eight people.

At the beginning of this particular session, the focus of the conversation was on those the members knew who were patients or employees of the Mental Health Institute. The group leader inquired why the members were focusing on past hospitalizations. The newer members then talked about their fears of living away from the hospital, their difficulties with managing money, and their problems in their jobs. When they felt afraid, the hospital seemed secure and consistent. There they knew the rules.

The group leader encouraged them to share their feelings and then directed the focus of the group on specific, individual goals. Since finances were a major concern for most of the members, the leader, using a chalkboard, had a group member, Joe, plan a monthly budget. Group members were active in helping him budget for food, rent, transportation, and the like. The budget was then broken down to a weekly plan, and Joe was to report back to the group on how this plan worked.

The meeting ended with the leader asking each member to share thoughts and feelings about the meeting and to choose a goal to be worked on during the following week. The members left, several of them getting together for coffee at a nearby restaurant.

A Chronic Pain Group*

A community hospital developed a group program for individuals dealing with a chronic pain condition that is one of the types of arthritis. After attending an education group where participants learned about their illness and about what techniques to use to manage the symptoms even if the pain wouldn't go away completely, they were invited to join a group to talk about how they could dig themselves out from under a blanket of pain. There were about eight members in this eight-week group, along with a social worker who acted as the facilitator.

Even though the members knew in advance that this group was not about the illness, but about what they had been doing and were going to do about having it, many still naturally slipped into talking about being sick. The group was about talking about shaking off the dominating effect of pain and illness, talking about being better, not about what was still wrong. In the first session, members were able to talk not about what hurt, but about how the illness impacted their lives. This was a chance for people who did not know each other to connect by talking of what they had in common—an illness and how the illness affected them—but it didn't allow them to talk about who hurt more or who hurt where. This mapping out of common ground was found by the social worker to be an excellent way to unite the group early on, and with some persistence, members were able to help each other to not talk about what hurt.

As the sessions went on, the group, through a vareity of questions the facilitator would ask, looked at their own strengths and skills and at

---

*Case provided by: Patrick Clifford, MSW, CSW, Arthritis Program, York County Hospital, Newmarket, Ontario, Canada.

what choices they were making that helped them get better, or what tricks of the illness they were falling for that kept them from doing as well as they wanted. A member of the group who was doing well, in separating who she was from who the illness was trying to make her be, used her abilities (that she had talked about earlier as her strengths) to challenge another group member who kept talking about what was wrong. In doing this she took responsibilitiy for the welfare of the group, not leaving it up to the social worker alone. Another group member helped her understand as well that, while this was helpful, she needed to be careful of the role that existed in the rest of her life, as well, of looking after other people before herself. Members were able to understand through these conversations how their own personalities and the impacts of illness worked for or against their getting better and sharpened their skills in detecting those things that were not working in their favor.

Members commented at the last session that this had been an unusual group experience because it encouraged them to look at the glass as half full, not half empty. This was new and hard for many. The experience encouraged personal growth and understanding and at times challenged things people assumed about themselves, and it did this all with a style that made the group members, not the social worker, the experts on getting better. Not only did this group experience not focus on illness but it encouraged the members to see themselves as the experts on their own lives and on getting better, using the health team and the social worker as consultants in their work, not as the people on whom getting better depended.

SUMMARY AND CONCLUSIONS

People learn, unlearn, and relearn behavior patterns from interaction with others. Self-concept is developed in large part from interactions with other people. Since social work deals with persons in interaction, knowledge of group dynamics and group development is important at all levels of intervention. In addition to providing a base for social work generally, group work is also an important method of social work practice used in many fields of practice.

Notes

1. Harry Vorath and Larry Brendtro, *Positive Peer Culture,* 2nd ed. (Hawthorne, NY: Aldine Publishing, 1985).
2. Grace Coyle, "Some Basic Assumptions about Social Group Work," in Marjorie Murphy, ed., *The Social Group Work Method in Social Work Education XI,* Curriculum Study (New York: Council on Social Work Education, 1959), p. 88.
3. For further discussion of this subject, refer to Irvin Yalom, *The Theory and Practice of Group Psychotherapy,* 3rd ed. (New York: Basic Books, 1985), pp. 489–495.
4. Ibid., p. 504.
5. John Shaffer and M. David Galinsky, *Models of Group Therapy,* 2nd ed. (Englewood Cliffs, NJ: Prentice-Hall, 1989), pp. 14–15.
6. Anne Gero and Patricia Kelley, "The Group as a 'Wild Card' in Social Work Education," *Journal of Education for Social Work* 19, no. 1 (Winter 1983): 47–54.

7. Catherine Papell and Beulah Rothman, "Social Group Work Models: Possession and Heritage," *Education for Social Work* (Fall 1966): 66–77.

8. Ibid., p. 66.

9. Papell and Rothman, "Relating the Mainstream Model of Social Work with Groups to Group Psychotherapy and the Structured Group Approach," *Social Work with Groups* 3, no. 2 (1980): 5–23.

10. Emanuel Tropp, "Social Group Work: The Developmental Approach," in *Encyclopedia of Social Work*, 17th ed. (Silver Spring, MD: NASW, 1977), pp. 1321–1327.

11. Catherine Papell and Beulah Rothman, "Social Group Work Models: Possession and Heritage," *Education for Social Work* (Fall 1966): 66–77.

12. Lawrence Shulman, "Social Work with Groups: Paradigm Shifts for the 1990s," in B.L. Stempler, M. Glass, and C.M. Savinelli, eds., *Social Group Work Today and Tomorrow* (New York: Haworth Press, 1996) pp. 1–18.

13. Charles Garvin, *Contemporary Group Work* (Englewood Cliffs, NJ: Prentice-Hall, 1987), p. 20.

14. For further discussion of assertiveness training, see Robert Alberti and Michael Emmons, *Your Perfect Right*, 7th ed. (San Luis Obispo, CA: Impact Publishers, 1995).

15. Janice H. Schopler and Maeda J. Galinsky, "Group Practice Overview," in *Encyclopedia of Social Work*, 19th ed., vol. 2 (Washington, DC: NASW, 1995), p. 1132.

16. Thomas Carlton, "Group Process and Group Work in Health Social Work Practice," *Social Work with Groups* 9, no. 2 (Summer 1986): 6. Also see Patricia Kelley and Patrick Clifford, "Coping with Chronic Pain: Assessing Narrative Approaches," *Social Work* 42, no. 3 (May 1997): 266–277.

17. For fuller discussion, see Garvin, *Contemporary Group Work*, pp. 291–301.

18. Gale Goldberg and Ruth Middleman, "Social Work Practice With Groups," in *Encyclopedia of Social Work*, 18th ed., vol. 2 (Silver Spring, MD: NASW, 1987), p. 721.

19. For a discussion and comparison of several theories of developmental stages, see Paul H. Ephross and Thomas V. Vassil, *Groups That Work* (New York: Columbia University Press, 1988), p. 57.

20. Janet Laube and Veronica Wieland, "Developing Prescriptions to Accelerate Group Process in Incest and Bulimia Treatment," in P. Kelley, ed., *Uses of Writing in Psychotherapy* (New York: Haworth Press, 1990), pp. 5–11.

21. Janice H. Schopler and Maeda J. Galinsky, "Group Practice Overview," in *Encyclopedia of Social Work*, 19th ed., vol. 2 (Washington, DC: NASW, 1995), p. 1133.

22. G. Corey and M. Corey, *Groups: Process and Practice*, 3rd ed. (Pacific Grove, CA: Brooks/Cole Publishing, 1987), p. 119.

23. For example, the Yalom and the Corey and Corey texts previously cited deal with both issues very thoroughly.

24. Kenneth E. Reid, *Social Work Practice With Groups*, 2nd ed. (Pacific Grove, CA: Brooks/Cole Publishing, 1997), p. 180.

25. Edcil Wickham, *Group Treatment in Social Work: An Integration of Theory and Practice* (Toronto: Thompson Educational Publishing, 1993), pp. 3–17.

Additional Suggested Readings

Anderson, Joseph. *Social Work with Groups*. New York: Longman, 1997.

Cartwright, Dorwin, and Alvin Zander, eds. *Group Dynamics: Research and Theory*. 3rd ed. New York: Harper & Row, 1968.

Glassman, Urania, and Len Kates. *Group Work: A Humanistic Approach*. Newbury Park, CA: Sage Publications, 1990.

Konopka, Gisela. *Social Group Work: A Helping Process*. 3rd ed. Englewood Cliffs, NJ: Prentice-Hall, 1983.

Lee, Judith B., ed. *Group Work with the Poor and Oppressed*. New York: Haworth Press, 1988.

Northen, Helen. *Social Work with Groups*. 2nd ed. New York: Columbia University Press, 1988.

Shaw, Marvin E. *Group Dynamics: The Psychology of Small Group Behavior*. 3rd ed. New York: McGraw-Hill, 1981.

Shulman, Lawrence. *The Skills of Helping Individuals, Families, and Groups*. 3rd ed. Itasca, IL: F.E. Peacock Publishers, 1992.

Social Work with Groups, a quarterly journal published by Haworth Press.

Stempler, Benjamin L., Marilyn Glass, and Christine M. Savinelli, eds. *Social Group Work Today and Tomorrow*. New York: Haworth Press, 1996.

Worchel, Stephen, Wendy Wood, and Jeffry A. Simpson. *Group Process and Productivity*. Newbury Park, CA: Sage Publications, 1992.

19

Working with Communities

THOMASINE HEITKAMP
STEVEN KRAFT
MICHAEL JACOBSEN

The profession of social work is unique in its emphasis on generic, not specialized, practice. Social workers require knowledge and skills in a variety of areas to effectively address concerns of individuals, families, groups, organizations, and communities. The emphasis in social work education is to train students to handle a wide variety of social and personal problems in our society.[1] Social workers must be prepared to help people with individual problems as well as to work to solve broad problems in the community.[2] Community work is that portion of generalist social work practice in which the worker focuses on the community as a dimension of the significant environment of the worker's clientele and in which a dimension of the community or the community itself is the client. The Council of Social Work Education (the national accrediting body for baccalaureate and master's programs in social work) standards require integration of content on community systems as a component of generalist practice in both graduate and undergraduate classes. Community practice is central to social work history and development.[3]

William E. Gordon suggests that social work practice is concerned with the interaction between client systems and their significant environments.[4] Not only does the significant environment vary with the identified client, but as the helping process proceeds with the initial client group, the worker is often called upon to shift attention from one portion of the environment to another. For example, as the worker assists an individual who has been hospitalized for psychiatric care with adjustment to an altered family situation, the worker may become aware of community stereotypes and prejudices concerning mental illness that are preventing that client from becoming employed or integrating back into the community. If the worker has several clients experiencing similar difficulties, he or she might consider a community-level intervention focused on altering the attitudes of employers regarding mental illness and conducting a community education forum. In this situation, the social worker responsible for aftercare services with the emotionally disabled will become an educator and community advocate for the mentally ill.

In many respects, community change activities are also organizational change or developmental activities. Most social work practitioners operate within the context of being employed by organizations that provide sanction for their activities, establish the possibilities and limitations of their practice, direct their efforts, and expect accountability. People in communities commonly meet their needs through involvement with organizations such as schools, medical care facilities, retail businesses, churches, economic development commissions, and so forth. Human services as need-meeting mechanisms are typically delivered through organizations. Community-based institutions and organizations such as police departments, city councils, planning and zoning commissions, and probation and parole departments all share responsibilities for providing social order and control within the community. As these organizations were created and are maintained by humans, are dynamic, and may make errors or fail to serve their functional responsibilities, they are often the focus of change activities. Many community change efforts, then, require the development of new organizational forms in communities or the revision of existing organizations, and these efforts require leadership skills.[5] Organizations that serve individuals with disabilities have demonstrated the ability to focus on commuity-based services in response to client need. In those situations, workers are often asked to serve as case managers or as resource individuals in linking needed human services to clients; as consultants toward effective training and engagement of local natural-helper systems; as facilitators of training, self-help, and support groups; as activists to fight stigma that exists among community members; or as advocates engaging in legal action on behalf of clients.

Some social workers are concerned about a decline in community-directed activities in the profession coupled with a decline in community-practice emphasis in social work education. Constricted funding and funding based on specific units of service monitored by budget-driven managed care agencies make it difficult for agencies to develop services directed to the community as client system. A conceptual outgrowth of these changes has been the development of the terms *micro, mezzo,* and *macro* to refer to social work practice with different-size populations. The term *macro practice* combines community work with administration. Since social work is institutionally based, administrative issues are a part of every practitioner's concern. Unfortunately, the administrative part of macro practice may be getting a disproportionate share of attention in the macro practice concept.

Since, however, community practice is viewed as a dimension of generalist practice, it follows that the abilities necessary for successful community intervention develop from the basic values, skills, and knowledge required for good generalist practice. Value considerations often include a belief in the right of access to services, in people's right to choose and participate in helping processes, in citizen rights to participate in decision making, and in a commitment to making social institutions more humane and responsive to people. Good generalist community practice requires application of the problem-solving process to community-based concerns.[6] This requires skills in interviewing as well as involving the community in the change effort. For effective community-level interventions, however, it is also necessary to go beyond basic skills into more advanced activities such as budget preparation, program evaluation, issue analyses, negotiation, community studies, training, needs assessments, network development, organizing social movements, and practice with leadership groups including boards of directors.[7] The knowledge necessary for effective community practice includes basic understanding of human behavior and development, as well as ethnic and cultural diversity,[8] and an understanding of the relationship of social programs to social policies.[9] It also includes knowledge of community and organizational behavior, the legislative process, administrative law, federal and state regulations, and human services, among others.[10]

Social workers may also practice with a range of different types of communities.[11] A common understanding of community is defined by geographic boundaries—the neighborhood, city, small rural town and outlying agricultural area, the county, region, and so forth.[12] However, social workers also practice with "nonplace" communities where geographical identification or location is not of major concern. Examples of this conceptualization include professional communities such as social workers, lawyers, and health or mental health service providers. Other examples would include *client communities* such as Native Americans, the elderly, the disabled, or children and youth.

Community work as the authors understand it also appears under a variety of other names. Included would be community organization (the most commonly used), social planning, community development, social action, and community intervention. Community organization, however, is the most recently formally recognized practice specialty within the field of social work.[13]

Social work is not the only group or profession concerned with the community as the client or in creating community change. The professions of social planning and public administration have been concerned with purposive change at the community level. A number of universities offer advanced degrees in urban and regional planning or public administration. While these fields have historically been concerned with the design and use of public facilities—the physical environment, transportation systems, and urban growth—these professional fields have also begun to address human and social problems such as inadequate housing and ineffective delivery of medical and mental health services. Agricultural extension workers have a long history of community involvement in rural America. The legal profession has also been intimately involved in community change.

Despite its rather recent official recognition, community social work dates back to the beginnings of social work practice in this country.[14] Early social workers in both public welfare and charity organization society settings were involved in social planning efforts. Settlement house social workers were quite involved in urban neighborhoods with both community development and social action processes. Examples of these planning, development, and action processes include the conceptualization and implementation of neighborhood health services, the creation of programs to teach English to immigrants, the formation of local chapters of labor unions, and the organization of self-help neighborhood safety patrols. It is clear that theorists have often differed on the appropriate approach and place of community work within the profession, but nearly all have supported community-level efforts of some form. A historical review of community-based social action can be found in the 1987 edition of the *Encyclopedia of Social Work.*[15]

THREE APPROACHES TO COMMUNITY PRACTICE

While community practice can certainly be viewed as an integral portion of generalist practice, it is also important to recognize it as a legitimate form of specialized social work practice. Jack Rothman has developed a particularly useful conception of three types of community practice: (1) locality or community development, (2) social planning, and (3) social action.[16] This paradigm was developed for the purpose of bringing together three major themes of traditional social work involvement with communities, so that practitioners might have a mechanism for comparison and contrast of those approaches. Rothman has used an "ideal type" format in their development so that the three approaches are intended simply for conceptual and analytic purposes. They are not intended as descriptions of ways that community work *should* be practiced nor as three separate "pure form" approaches to practice.

More commonly, community workers blend various components of all three approaches into an appropriate response to particular practice situations. The three types of community practice represent personal orientations to community work. Some community workers simply are more skilled or comfortable with certain approaches, while others might use a variety of approaches that may be more appropriate to their particular context or organizational setting.[17] The three models are presented in Table 19.1.

TABLE 19.1   Three Community Intervention Approaches According to Selected Practice Variables

	Mode A (Locality Development)	Mode B (Social Planning/Policy)	Mode C (Social Action)
1. Goal categories of community action	Community capacity and integration; self-help (process goals)	Problem solving with regard to substantive community problems (task goals)	Shifting of power relationships and resources; basic institutional change (task or process goals)
2. Assumptions concerning community structure and problem conditions	Community eclipsed, anomie; lack of relationships and democratic problem-solving capacities; static traditional community	Substantive social problems, mental and physical health, housing, recreation, etc.	Aggrieved populations, social injustice, deprivation, inequality
3. Basic change strategy	Involving a broad cross section of people in determining and solving their own problems	Gathering data about problems and making decisions on the most logical course of action	Crystallizing issues and mobilizing people to take action against enemy targets

4. Characteristic change tactics and techniques	Consensus: communication among community groups and interests; group discussion	Consensus or conflict	Conflict confrontation, direct action, negotiation
5. Salient practitioner roles	Enabler-catalyst, coordinator; teacher of problem-solving skills and ethical values	Fact gatherer and analyst, program implementer, expediter	Activist advocate: agitator, broker, negotiator, partisan
6. Medium of change	Guiding small, task-oriented groups	Guiding formal organizations and treating data	Guiding mass organizations and political processes
7. Orientation toward power structure(s)	Members of power structure as collaborators in a common venture	Power structure as employers and sponsors	Power structure as external target of action: oppressors to be coerced or overturned
8. Boundary definition of the beneficiary system	Total geographic community	Total community or community segment	Community segment
9. Assumptions regarding interests of community subparts	Common interests or reconcilable differences	Interests reconcilable or in conflict	Conflicting interests which are not easily reconcilable, scarce resources
10. Conception of beneficiaries	Citizens	Consumers	Victims
11. Conception of beneficiary role	Participants in an interactional problem-solving process	Consumers or recipients	Employers, constituents, members
12. Use of empowerment	Building the capacity of a community to make collaborative and informed decisions; promoting feeling of personal mastery by residents	Finding out from consumers about their needs for service; informing consumers of their service choices	Achieving objective power for beneficiary system—the right and means to impact community decisions; promoting a feeling of mastery by participants

Source: Jack Rothman, "Approaches to Community Practice," in *Strategies of Community Intervention*, 5th ed., Jack Rotham, John L. Erlich, and John E. Tropman, eds. (Itasca, IL: F. E. Peacock Publishers, 1995), pp. 44–45.

Locality or Community Development

In community or locality development, the entire community—typically a geographic entity such as a city, neighborhood, county, or village—is seen as the client system. Community residents tend to be viewed as citizens who have considerable potential as community members and who can assist in solving community problems but whose potential has not been fully developed or used. They may need the services of a practitioner to help them fully realize, develop, and focus on those abilities. The community developer sees each community member as unique, capable of growth, and potentially a valuable contributor to the community.

Community development has been defined as "a process designed to create conditions of economic and social progress for the whole community with it's active participation and the fullest possible reliance on the community's initiative."[18] Community development practitioners tend to assume that social change can best be pursued through broad participation of a wide range of people at the local community level. Community members are seen as acting in their own interest as well as being representative of the entire community's interests. The community members are responsible for both determination of goals and selection of strategies to achieve these goals. The overall purpose is to empower community members. Process goals—those concerned with the community's ability to function over time—tend to take precedence over task goals, those related to specific problem-solving accomplishments. Of particular concern to the community developer is the community's ability to function in cooperative forms, its ability to help itself, and the degree to which it uses democratic procedures in problem solving. Other goals of community development work include the development of indigenous leadership, the use of self-help strategies, the development of an informed and involved citizenry, and enhancing communication between various subparts of the community.

The community developer sees the interests of community subparts as reconcilable. The practitioner tends to place emphasis on the unity and commonalities of community life. It is believed that rational persuasion, democratic processes, mutual understanding and communication, and a focused concern for the welfare of the entire community will bring divergent community groups together. Cooperative strategies and techniques are generally preferred over those encouraging community conflict. Some community developers see community conflict as a natural but temporary process that is to be experienced so that a later consensus can be achieved. Community power actors are viewed as collaborators in the process of community problem solving.

This model requires that the local community identify the problem that the community developer addresses. Therefore, the community concerns tend to vary considerably with the local situation. For example, the community might be seen as tradition-bound and ruled by a small power elite who are very interested in controlling change. Accompanying this situation may be a large group of residents who have been inactive in community decision making because of their own limitations in education, resources, or leadership skills. In this situation, the practitioner might be interested in developing leadership skills as well as in the opportunity to use them in the larger populace.

The community may also be seen as dominated or isolated by the larger society. The community may be perceived as being unable to control its own destiny and make its own decisions. In this situation, the practitioner may attempt to help groups develop and retain local decision-making capacities.

A third area of concern to community developers focuses on the loss of a sense of "community" in contemporary life.[19] This loss is attributed to the effects of industrialization, technological change, urbanization, and an ultimate loss of a sense of culture. The effects of these changes are experienced at the community level as loss of pride and sense of belonging, alienation of residents from one another, isolation, and general loss in community decision-making capabilities. It is further believed that such a situation erodes democracy in America, makes for unresponsive institutions and local organizations, and impedes personal and family development.

In community development the social work practitioner functions in the following roles: enabler, encourager, teacher, and facilitator of the process of problem solving. Throughout the process the practitioner helps people express felt needs and dissatisfactions, encourages and sustains communication and interpersonal relationships among community members, helps to organize community individuals to act upon needs, and serves to identify and emphasize commonalities in the community. The practitioner may be seen as the catalyst for change, but the responsibility for change rests with the community.

Small task-oriented groups often emerge from within local organizations that are sanctioned by those organizations. These organizations may be the basis of a new community-based organization that is one outcome of the community development process. Biddle and Biddle, for example, suggest the development of a *steering group* that becomes responsible for the initiation and development of all change efforts.[20] As that steering group matures, achieves some success, and begins to broaden its scope or discover new opportunities, it may decide to formalize as an independent organization or as a dimension of an existing organization such as a board of directors or an advisory group.

Social work processes have their detractors and critics. Each of these community models can be criticized by proponents of the other models. Social planners often see portions of community development as basically an "uninformed" approach to community change, an approach that may ignore or refuse more efficient solutions to problems simply because they are developed by "experts" or "outsiders." Social action practitioners have suggested that an emphasis upon cooperation and consensus is, at the best, naive, and at the worst, amenable to cooptation by power actors in communities and society. Development efforts may be easily directed to noncontroversial problems with little real substance. Followers of both approaches may criticize community development for spending countless hours in discussions that yield few true solutions to the problem and do not speak directly to the need for fundamental change in the community. Finally, they might suggest that much of the initiative for community development actually originates from outside the community, which is a clear violation of the principles of community development.

Social Planning

As many of the employers of social planners are public organizations mandated to address specific social problems such as mental illness, unemployment, delinquency, or dependency, the field of social planning tends to be oriented to the prevention, control, or resolution of those social problems. Often social workers serving as administrators or managers—frequently as program or direct-service supervisors—are involved in social planning processes within such organizations. Within social planning, task goals seem to take general precedence over the process goals emphasized in the locality development model. For example, some task goals may include the tangible improvement of the outcomes of a state mental health delivery system, the controlling of costs associated with administering regional public assistance programs, the development of a more efficient child protective system in a county, or tangible improvement of community coordination and referral among health agencies in an urban area.

The client system for the social planner may be seen as the residents of a geographic area. The client system may also be seen as some portion of that geographic region such as the elderly, mentally ill, disabled individuals, or other specific at-risk groups. When the clients are seen as a particular population, the social planner may generally view them as consumers or recipients of services. Consumers or recipients are not necessarily active determinants of social policy, procedures, or goals when using the social planning model. Ultimate control of the activities of planners is often located in city or state government entities, legislatures, the courts, officials within public welfare organizations, or community leaders active in welfare planning at the local level. While representatives of client groups may be involved in an advisory capacity, much of the decision making is left to formal "representatives" of the citizenry who are selected through the political process.

In the social planning approach, social problems are seen as amenable to control and resolution through the process of rational analysis, which leads to deliberately planned and controlled change. Technical or expert roles are emphasized in social planning. The planner is often seen as a technical fact finder, program planner, implementor, and evaluator. As a technical analyst, the social planner is expected to have expertise in empirical research methods, community analysis techniques such as needs assessments, and program evaluation methods, as well as familiarity with fiscal decision making and control. The planner is expected to have knowledge of organizational and community behavior as well as of the range of human service programs available in the community. Since much of the work of the planner is done in a formal organizational context within legal parameters and in conjunction with other professions, the planner is expected to be able to perform effectively within formal organizations and with a variety of professionals from other disciplines.

Advocates for social action or community development might suggest that social planning is by definition a "top-down" approach to community problem solving. The entire problem-solving approach is seen as being dominated by politicians, technicians, bureaucrats, or elites who have little understanding of the situation as experienced by those immediately living with the problem. Social action practitioners might also suggest that planners have a long history of failure in their efforts to resolve or control social problems effectively since most social problems remain. Some suggest that social planning efforts have only increased costs associated with the bureaucracy of human services delivery, expanded red tape, and necessitated more government intrusion into the private lives of citizens. Community development practitioners may reject the formal attempt to solve community problems through technical processes removed from immediate community life when the solution lies with the citizenry. They suggest instead that local individuals acting through community groups must determine and develop their own solutions.

Social Action

The overriding goal of organizers' involvement in social action has been basic fundamental change in organizations, communities, and society. This process generally attempts to redistribute power, resources, and decision making. Most social change efforts include the goal of bringing about social changes in values, beliefs, and attitudes regarding social problems. In order to effect such change, social action practitioners often attempt to secure change in large formal organizations such as the local chambers of commerce, the state and county departments of social service, city councils, educational institutions, professional associations, or state and national legislatures.

The social action practitioner may stress either task or process goals. Common task goals include changes in the law such as enactment of the Americans with Disabilities Act, the modification of hiring practices so that more people of color and women are hired by a particular industry, changes in bureaucratic procedures so that more low-income people may obtain their entitlements, or the political empowerment of unrepresented people by securing their election and appointment to positions in city administration. Common process goals may include a series of "open forum" discussions about the need for change in city government, identification and organization of people of color or women in a professional organization to identify and articulate their needs within that organization, or the development of a representative and articulate group of consumers of services in a rural county. A common technique of the social action practitioner is to relate the attainment of a specific goal (either task or process) to the real possibility of making fundamental change in a community, organization, or society generally. Smaller-scale goals or activities may be pursued because they are achievable, do make a difference (task), and help to build the organization (process).

The social action practitioner tends to see society as being structured through conflict, power, and privilege. Decision making and control of resources are viewed as being dominated by a group of power actors who are often seen as the political and economic elite. The clients or constituents of the social action practitioner are often seen as "victims" of a system of oppression; they are the "underdogs" or the "have-nots" of the community. The practitioner tends to assume that the interests of the two groups are at fundamental variance and are not reconcilable. Those in positions of power and privilege do not easily give up their influence and will attempt to regain their advantage if it is removed.

The power structure is seen as the target for action—an external force opposed to the client. That power structure is often viewed as having considerable influence over community institutions and organizations that directly affect the lives of the clientele. The power structure is to be coerced or overturned, so that the interests of the client population may be furthered. In accord with their understandings of social justice and democracy, social action practitioners tend to see large numbers of disadvantaged or disenfranchised people in society who need opportunities for organization so that they may place demands on the community for just treatment, for more input into decision making, or for an increased share of social resources. Social action practitioners attempt to assist the powerless in that organization so that they can independently pursue and defend their own interests.[21]

The basic strategy of social action practitioners is to bring together their clientele and organize them to take direct action against the power elite. It is then often necessary to facilitate discussion and education within the client group regarding the issues at hand and the possibility of change. The practitioner must have an understanding of the local issues, be adept at group or organizational building activities, and be able to lead discussions focused on the concerns of the clientele. The social action practitioner often employs both the advocate and activist roles and attempts to organize client groups, so that they may better pursue their own interests independent of the practitioner. The practitioner also may become involved as a member of the client group in a partisan social conflict intended to serve only client interests. Social action activities tend to be characterized by confrontation and conflict between the client group and the power structure. Where the activist is interested in attitude change regarding

© Joel Gordon

In response to the promotion of a variety of issues, including education reform, support for health care programs, and control of property taxes, citizens organize and mount effective campaigns to advance their points of view and focus the attention of the electorate.

the identified client group in the general community, the practitioner may use electronic and print media for those purposes. Consensus tactics are commonly stressed within the client group. Other social action tactics include direct action such as boycotts, pickets, sit-ins, or civil disobedience.

As with the other two processes, social action has its critics. The community development practitioner believes that the social action orientation to conflict and confrontation is too disruptive to the community, that rapid changes that are forced on a community are invariably resented and susceptible to retaliatory measures. They might also suggest that many of the issue formulations "imported" by the social action practitioner are developed "outside" the community and are "forced" on residents. As such, they are not accurate representations of either citizen needs or their interests. The social planner might express displeasure with the frequent hostility of the social action practitioner toward formal human service organizations and the "expert" role in decision making. The planner may express impatience with a view that suggests that the planner is not equally as concerned and knowledgeable regarding the conditions of people in communities. Both might combine to attack a view of community that they see as focusing on the "negatives" and ignoring many of the positive changes and features in society. Finally, both are made uncomfortable by a position that "the wars must continue," that client and other community group interests are not basically reconcilable, and that communities will continue to be ordered through oppressive use of power and privilege.

In a subsequent article in 1995, Rothman develops the "Three Models" construct further. He discusses the "Interweaving of Interventions Approaches."[22] In this theoretical refinement we begin to see how aspects of each of the three models can be combined so that strategies and tactics appropriate to the target community, the need being addressed, and the resources available can be formulated. Instead of a strategy determined by value orientation, practitioners are able to use Rothman's refined model to base their strategy development on functional realities. We are further encouraged to move from one model or set of combined models within the same intervention to other models or combinations as needs require. Rothman refers to this change of intervention approach as "phasing."

The challenge to social work is to find concrete ways to include community practice in the mission and programs of social agencies.

Fundraising in Hard Times: Lessons Learned

Srudents enrolled in an undergraduate Macro Practice class at the University of North Dakota are required, as partial fulfillment of the course requirements, to initiate and implement an organizational effort in the community of Grand Forks, North Dakota. The purpose of this assignment is to introduce students to the complexities of organizing, and to give them an opportunity to address community concerns. The community concern that several students chose to address during the winter of 1997 was the needs of families relocating from Bosnia to Grand Forks.

During a previous semester, undergraduate students enrolled in this class prepared a directory of social and human services for refugee families. This project was completed under the supervision of a graduate social work student. As a result, students enrolled in our program were generally aware of the complexities of concerns for families relocating to this area, as well as the need for a knowledgeable resource broker to effectively utilize the formal human services available. It was apparent to the students that an effort to establish continued and enhanced community support would involve coordination with the local Refugee Resettlement Coalition, which was basically a group of individuals representing various church groups in the area concerned about refugee resettlement. The need for community support for the Resettlement Coalition was also obvious because two more families would be arriving in Grand Forks during the month of March and there was a need for basic housing and furnishings for these families. The relocation was also occurring in the midst of some of the worst winter weather recorded in the history of North Dakota, which included eight blizzards. Students were also aware that assisting with immediate needs would help these families to become more economically self-sufficient.

To partially address the need for food and shelter, these students chose to become involved in a creative fundraising effort to raise money for the Resettlement Coalition. The goals of the fundraiser were straightforward: The event would be fun; funds would be secured for a worthy cause; Bosnian families, which are established in the community, would be involved in raising funds; there would be no economic risk; community education would occur; and, the students would secure needed organizational skills as well as learn how to work cooperatively in a task group and educate themselves about the needs of Bosnian families in the area.

The first phase of this organizational effort involved brainstorming about fundraising techniques that would be beneficial to refugee families and about methods to educate the community. A plan was developed to secure up to $2,000 in funds by working with local ceramic artists and other concerned individuals in the community. The plan called for the creation of ceramic bowls that would be made at no cost, filled with chili, and sold at a chili feed sponsored by a local church. Another component of this plan was to have Bosnian families make homemade bread, which they had been marketing in the community. As part of the community education effort, a local author, who had written a book with information about her interviews with Bosnian children, agreed to be present at the fundraiser and to autograph her book. The children featured in the book also agreed to be present at the fundraiser. This effort would involve layers of coordination. Students were aware that this project needed to be completed before the end of the semester.

Students were expected to work coopertively with the local churches, the Department of Art at the University of North Dakota, a human needs committee at a large Catholic church, Bosnian families, and local corporations that would donate products, as well as the local author. Students quickly understood the importance of securing a good location for a fundraiser as well as the importance of planning an event that would not lose money. In that spirit, students met with the human needs committee at the local Catholic church to secure its support. Sample ceramic bowls were dislayed at that meeting by local artists who agreed to donate their time. The church agreed to allow the students to use a large social hall, and to assist in advertising this event in the weekly church bulletin.

Chili, and flour to make the bread, were donated, and a local fast-food restaurant donated drinks. Students were also given permission to sell the chili bowls prior to the event at the church. Two local ceramic artists agreed to donate their time, their resources of clay, and use of a kiln to fire the stoneware pottery. Students agreed to help the artists create the chili bowls, finishing the bowls by stamping "Refugee Resettlement, Grand Forks N.D." on the bottom of the bowls, waxing the bottom of the clay pots, and loading the kiln with pottery. Within one month, 120 ceramic bowls were fully ready to box up for the event.

Unfortunately, the students' fundraising plan could not be implemented because of a historic flood that occurred in Grand Forks. All of the students enrolled in this class and the course instructor were mandatorily evacuated from their homes and themselves became refugees. Six weeks later, the instructor arrived at the church to learn that the ceramic bowls were flooded but could be cleaned. The chili had spoiled, but the books were dry on a shelf.

While this project was never completed, several lessons were learned about community organization. The most important lesson is that you can never anticipate all the barriers a community organizer may encounter. However, there is clearly a need for organizers to plan appropriately. Use of good social work problem-solving skills and having a shared purpose will assist in managing and organizing your efforts. Students quickly discovered that they could become homeless refugees, which increased their empathy for the organizational effort with which they were involved. Another lesson was that there are very limited formal agency-based resources available for these families and that their most immediate needs were being provided for by the local churches.

SUMMARY AND CONCLUSIONS

We have outlined the historical and contemporary involvements of a range of social work practitioners with communities. The relation of community interventions to generalist practice were discussed. Three model "specialist" approaches to community practice were described along with a brief critique of each approach. We mentioned the move toward combining approaches to make community practice more effective. Social work practice with communities is seen as an integral process within the profession that will continue. The case study above showed one example of how skills and techniques learned by students are implemented but also how barriers are encountered.

Notes

1. Charles Zastrow, *The Practice of Social Work*, 4th ed. (Belmont, CA: Wadsworth Publishers, 1992).
2. Karen K. Kirst-Ashman and Grafton H. Hull, Jr., *Generalist Practice with Organizations and Communities* (Chicago: Nelson-Hall, Inc., 1997).
3. David A. Hardcastle, Stanley Wenocur, and Patricia R. Powers, *Community Practice and Skills for Social Workers* (New York: Oxford Univeristy Press, 1997).
4. William E. Gordon, "Basic Constructs for an Integrative and Generative Conception of Social Work," *The General Systems Approach: Contributions toward a Holistic Conception of Social Work* (New York: Council on Social Work Education, 1969), p. 7.

5. Si Kahn, *Organizing: A Guide for Grassroots Leaders* (Silver Spring, MD: National Association of Social Workers, 1991), pp. 21–49.

6. Beulah R. Compton and Burt Galaway, *Social Work Processes*, 4th ed. (Belmont, CA: Wadsworth, 1989).

7. John E. Tropman, John L. Erlich, and Jack Rothman, *Tactics and Techniques of Community Intervention*, 3rd ed. (Itasca, IL: F.E. Peacock Publishers, 1995).

8. Felix G. Rivera and John L. Erlich, *Community Organizing in a Diverse Society*, 2nd ed. (Needham Heights, MA: Allyn and Bacon, 1995).

9. Kathleen McInnis-Dittrich, *Integrating Social Welfare Policy & Social Work Practice* (Pacific Grove, CA: Brooks/Cole Publishing Company, 1994).

10. Karen S. Haynes and James S. Mickelson, *Affecting Change: Social Workers in the Political Arena*, 3rd ed. (White Plains, NY: Longman, 1997).

11. Herbert J. Rubin and Irene S. Rubin, *Community Organizing and Development*, 2nd ed. (New York: Macmillan, 1992), pp. 83–94.

12. Emilia E. Martinez-Brawley, *Perspectives on the Small Community* (Silver Spring, MD: National Association of Social Workers, 1990).

13. Recognized as a practice subspecialty by the National Association of Social Workers in 1957.

14. Frank Bruno, *Trends in Social Work* (New York: Columbia University Press, 1948), p. 194.

15. Board of Editors, "Community-based Social Action," in *Encyclopedia of Social Work*, 18th ed., vol. 1 (Silver Spring, MD: National Association of Social Workers, 1987), pp. 293–298.

16. Jack Rothman and John E. Tropman, "Models of Community Organization and Macro Practice Perspectives: Their Mixing and Phasing," in F.M. Cox, J.L. Erlich, Jack Rothman, and John E. Tropman, eds., *Strategies of Community Organization*, 4th ed. (Itasca, IL: F.E. Peacock Publishers, 1987), pp. 3–26.

17. See, for example, Jacobsen's argument for community development in rural areas in H. Wayne Johnson, ed., *Rural Human Services* (Itasca, IL: F.E. Peacock Publishers, 1980), p. 196.

18. United Nations, *Social Progress through Community Development* (New York: United Nations, 1955), p. 6.

19. Paul Leinberger and Bruce Tucker, "Individuals Are the Conscience of the Crowd," *Utne Reader* 52 (July–August 1992): 86–88.

20. W.W. Biddle and L.J. Biddle, *The Community Development Process* (New York: Holt, Rinehart & Winston, 1965).

21. Saul D. Alinsky, *Rules for Radicals* (New York: Random House, 1971).

22. Jack Rothman, John L. Erlich, and John E. Tropman, eds., *Strategies of Community Intervention*, 5th ed. (Itasca, IL: F.E. Peacock Publishers, Inc., 1995).

Additional Suggested Readings

Biklen, Douglas P. *Community Organizing: Theory and Practice*. Englewood Cliffs, NJ: Prentice-Hall, 1983.

Brody, Ralph, and Murali D. Nair. *Macro Practice: A Generalist Approach*. 3rd ed. With websites. Wheaton, IL: Gregory Publishing Company, 1997.

Brueggemann, William G. *The Practice of Macro Social Work*. Chicago: Nelson-Hall, 1996.

Burghardt, Steve. *Organizing for Community Action*. Newbury Park, CA: Sage Publications, 1982.

Fellin, Phillip. *The Community and the Social Worker*. 2nd ed. Itasca, IL: F.E. Peacock Publishers, 1995.

Flora, Cornelia Butler, Jan F. Flora, Jacqueline D. Spears, and Louis E. Swanson, with Mark B. Lapping and Mark L. Weinberg. *Rural Communities: Legacy & Change.* Boulder, CO: Westview Press, 1992.

Flynn, John P. *Social Agency Policy: Analysis and Presentation for Community Practice.* 2nd ed. Chicago: Nelson-Hall, 1992.

Ginsberg, Leon H. *Social Work in Rural Communities.* 2nd ed. Alexandria, VA: Council on Social Work Education, 1993.

Lee, Judith A.B. *The Empowerment Approach to Social Work Practice.* New York: Columbia University Press, 1994.

Levine, Murray, and David V. Perkins. *Principles of Community Psychology: Perspectives and Applications.* 2nd ed. New York: Oxford University Press, 1997.

Richan, Willard C. *Lobbying for Social Change.* New York: The Haworth Press, 1991.

Specht, Harry, and Mark Courtney. *Unfaithful Angels: How Social Work Has Abandoned Its Mission.* New York: The Free Press, 1994.

20

Social Service Organizations: Administration and Management

WILLIAM P. McCARTY

All organizations are made up of people who come together to work toward a common purpose. As a result, each person within the organization has some measure of responsibility for helping the organization achieve its goals. Depending upon the type of organizational structure and the style of management employed, any particular individual's role and responsibilities within the organization may be very narrowly and specifically defined, or more broadly and generally defined.

Social service organizations are established specifically for the purpose of delivering social services to people who need them. As in any organization, each member of a social service organization (employee, volunteer, manager, board member, or client) has a role to play, and shares responsibility for the achievement of the agency's goals.

Social services management, at the close of the twentieth century, is about management of change. Economic, political, and social pressures; technological developments; and evolving management theory all combine to redefine the social service organization, how it is managed, and the services it provides. Indeed, management guru Peter F. Drucker, among others, argues that the nature of society itself is changing, and thus, the nature of all organizations.[1]

In this chapter, we will not attempt to analyze and compare differing organizational structures and management theories in depth. Rather, we will attempt to give an overview of current theory and practice in social services management, identifying common issues and problems, and placing them in the context of the larger body of knowledge about organizations and management in general.

TYPES OF SOCIAL SERVICE ORGANIZATIONS

Social service organizations can be divided into three general categories: public, private nonprofit, and private for-profit. *Public* social service organizations are those operated by a unit of government—federal, state, or local. Public agencies often have citizen advisory boards or commissions, but the ultimate policy-making authority usually rests with one or more elected officials.

Private nonprofit organizations are operated by a self-perpetuating board of directors. By self-perpetuating, we mean that the board has a system for recruitment, selection, and election of its own members. They are not appointed or selected by some outside authority, such as is often the case with an advisory commission to a public agency.

"Nonprofit" is a tax status conferred by the Internal Revenue Service of the United States government that signifies that the organization performs some charitable purpose; that any "profits" are **not** distributed to "shareholders" or owners; and that individuals and corporations may receive a tax deduction for gifts of value (goods, services, property, or money) made to the nonprofit organization. Nonprofits also do not have to pay income and certain other taxes that for-profit corporations and individuals must pay.

It is important to understand that "nonprofit" status does *not* mean that the organization cannot or should not make a profit. It merely means that the organziation is not required to pay taxes on whatever profit it makes. In fact, it is essential that nonprofit human service organizations take in more money than they spend, so that excess dollars can be redirected where needed to provide more and better services. This concept is widely misunderstood by the public, funders, and even by human services boards, staff, and managers, who believe that "nonprofit" literally means that social service agencies should not make, retain, or accumulate capital. Peter Brinkerhoff refers to this belief as "poverty chic" and calls it "probably the most shortsighted social policy of our generation."[2]

Private for-profit organizations are established for the purpose of making money for the owners or shareholders. For-profit organizations take many forms. They may, for example, be wholly owned by one individual, a partnership of two or more individuals, or a corporation, with an elected board of directors, representing the shareholders who own stock in the company.

In the United States, most social services are delivered by public or private nonprofit organizations. However, participation by for-profit corporations is becoming much more common.

There has been an increased recognition in recent years that good management and administrative practices apply to all types of organizations. It is our contention that a businesslike approach to human services management and sensitivity to social work values are *not* mutually exclusive. In fact, they are quite compatible. This is equally true whether the agency is public, private nonprofit, or private for-profit. A social services agency is a *business*, and it needs to be run in a businesslike manner.

The delivery of social services is essentially a labor-intensive activity. In other words, the amount of the organization's *output* (the volume of services provided to clients) is directly related to the number of employees, because employee/client interaction is necessary to deliver the services. This is in contrast to some industrial organizations in which output is a product or products, and production can be highly automated. If output of a product needs to be increased, it may be possible to speed up the production line, or to add a second production line, with little or no increase in employees. In social services, however, significant increases (or decreases) in output of services usually necessitate increases (or decreases) in the number of employees.

The labor-intensive nature of social services delivery, coupled with the need and desire to treat all clients fairly and equally, leads to the development of large social service bureaucracies. Bureaucracies are characterized by hierarchical organizational structure (i.e., employees are ordered vertically, with each level reporting to the level above them), specialization of functions, and elaborate sets of rules and procedures governing how employees may deliver services.[3] Such bureaucracies are most evident in public social services organizations, but they also occur in private nonprofits and private for-profits.

Over the past 50 years, substantial research has been devoted to how bureaucratic organizations function. During the '50s and '60s, bureaucracies were widely seen as highly dysfunctional and antithetical to social services values reflected in the dignity and worth of each individual human being (both clients and employees). During the '70s and '80s, a more balanced viewpoint developed.[4] The value of rigidly regulated processes and procedures was emphasized.

Certainly, there are inherent drawbacks to this organizational structure. However, if these limitations are known and understood, there are techniques that can be employed to minimize the problems. The systematic, consistent, and fair application of good management techniques, coupled with a basic understanding of how people function in groups and organizations, enables the social services manager, or any manager, to be effective. Today, the emphasis is on empowering workers and quality improvement, techniques that can make all organizations more effective.

MANAGEMENT DEFINED

Management can be defined as the process by which an individual or group of individuals directs the work of others toward certain shared organizational goals.[5] Management can also be defined as those individuals whose role and responsibility it is to direct the work of others toward common organizational goals. So, management is both the people and the process. Both these definitions imply authority over, and responsibility for the work of, others, as opposed to responsibility solely for one's own work.

The terms *administration* and *management* are often used interchangeably, although some scholars have tried to distinguish between the two.[6] Many definitions identify them as synonyms. However, Webster's definitions of "administration" often refer to a public or governmental organization while "management" is distinguished as a business activity.[7] The term *management* is preferred because it implies a more proactive and team-oriented process. Also, sound principles of management cut across the public, private nonprofit, and private for-profit sectors, despite some organizational differences.[8]

Although different names are sometimes used, there is general agreement as to the four broad functions, or duties, of management. They are (1) planning, (2) organizing, (3) evaluating, and (4) leading.

Planning is the process by which organizational goals are identified and the means for achieving those goals are determined.

Organizing is the process by which the necessary resources are gathered and coordinated in order to achieve the identified organizational goals.

Evaluating is the process by which progress toward achieving identified goals is measured.

Leading is the process by which the manager motivates, directs, and supervises the activities of the organization members in order to achieve organizational goals.

THE MANAGER'S ROLE

In small social services organizations, the manager may take on many roles—providing direct services to clients, supervising staff, and performing administrative functions such as budgeting, planning, and public relations. In larger social service organizations, managers are more specialized, each performing a narrow, specific function. For example, there may be "first-level" supervisors who oversee the work of direct-service staff. These first-level supervisors may report to "middle managers" who oversee the activities of an entire program or unit.

At the highest level of the agency's management structure is the chief executive officer (CEO). The CEO goes by various titles. In public agencies she or he may hold the title director, administrator, or commissioner. In private non-profits, executive director is commonly used to distinguish the position from that of the board of directors. CEO or president are common titles in for-profit organizations, including profit-making social service agencies.

Regardless of the title or type of organization, the CEO is the individual who has overall responsibility for all aspects of the organization's activities. She or he reports to the board of directors (or elected official[s] if the agency is a public one), and manages and directs (either directly or through middle managers) the work of all employees. In larger agencies, the CEO may have a number of specialists who assist in the managing of the organization. Positions such as human resources director, business manager, public relations director, director of professional services, and office manager are common in such organizations. It is possible, even likely, that, within the management team, only the director of professional services will have education and experience in social work or a related field. This individual typically oversees the delivery of the agency's social services, usually by supervising middle managers who in turn supervise other middle managers, first level supervisors, or direct service staff.

In smaller agencies, the CEO herself or himself must perform many of the tasks associated with the specialists listed above. In any case, either directly or through others, it is the CEO's responsibility to synthesize these diverse specialties into an effective management team.

Many, if not most, social service managers began their careers providing social services directly to clients. Over time, opportunities for advancement arise, and providers of services to clients move into supervisory or middle-management roles. Eventually, some become specialists in top management positions or CEOs. Yet, a relatively small portion of professionally prepared social workers obtain a concentration in management or administration.[9] While there is a great deal of carryover of social work skills and values to good professional management, there are additional skills, practices, and values to be learned. The professional social worker who wants to become a good manager will pursue additional training when accepting a management position. Likewise, social service agencies that make a practice of promoting direct-service staff to management positions need to have a thorough and comprehensive training program for new supervisors and middle managers.

Earlier, four primary functions, or duties of management, were identified: planning, organizing, evaluating, and leading. All of these activities are closely interrelated. However, it is helpful to consider them separately and in more detail, in order to understand the responsibilities of a manager and the process of management.

Planning

A common planning mechanism used in all types of organizations is strategic planning. Strategic planning is a process by which the organization's mission and goals are established. When fully implemented, a strategic plan can be a blueprint for the future and a tool for evaluating individual and organizational performance. It can focus the entire organization (staff, volunteers, managers, board members) on the organization's goals and what must be done to achieve them.

There are five steps to strategic planning:

- Establishing a mission and goals
- Situational analysis
- Strategy development
- Implementation
- Evaluation

The key to establishing organizational direction is the development of a clear, purposeful statement of the organization's *mission*. This statement answers the question, "Why does this organization exist?" From this statement, organizational goals can be developed. Organizational goals are the targets set up by the organization to help it accomplish its purpose or mission.[10] Thus, goals should flow clearly and logically from the mission statement.

Situational analysis involves studying the organizational environment to identify factors that significantly influence the organization's operations.[11] These include both external and internal factors, developments, and trends. For a social service agency, external indicators to consider might include client needs, economic conditions, available funding, and other social service agencies. Internal factors might include staff, financial resources, agency culture and values, and existing programs and facilities. There are several methods for assessing all this information, but the one that is applicable to most social service agencies is SWOT analysis. SWOT is an acronym for strengths, weaknesses, opportunities, and threats.

Strategy development answers the question "How can we achieve our goals?" By carefully considering the identified factors in terms of the organization's internal strengths, weaknesses, and external opportunities and threats, a strategy (or strategies) for implementing the goals can be developed. The strategy can be a written statement or a set of objectives that more specifically defines the goals.

Implementation involves operationalizing and carrying out the strategy. It must be determined who is going to do what, and by when, in order to accomplish the goals and objectives. This can be expressed as a series of tasks to be accomplished, with due dates and person(s) responsible for carrying them out. When this has been completed, the plan can be put into effect.

Evaluation is the process of monitoring performance and determining whether goals are being met. Each objective or task should have measurable criteria in order to determine progress toward accomplishing agency goals. Evaluation is discussed in more detail later.

Because today's environment is characterized by rapid and sometimes unanticipated change, traditional strategic planning is becoming obsolete. As frequently practiced in the past, strategic planning could be a lengthy and laborious process through which management would try to predict what was most likely to happen over a three- to five-year time span. In today's world, a carefully crafted strategic plan can be rendered obsolete overnight by an unanticipated event. Planning now tends to be more tactical (short-term) in nature. The same five steps are applied, but the time frame for implementation may be little more than a year. Drucker says that organizations must now "plan for uncertainty" by asking the question, "What has already happened that will create the future?" Analyzing an organization's strengths and matching them with changes that have already taken place creates the plan of action.[12]

Management by objectives (MBO) is a tool popularized by expert Peter Drucker. It is a method for implementing the organization's strategic plan that involves every individual in the organization. MBO embodies five steps:[13]

- Review organizational goals
- Set worker objectives
- Monitor progress
- Evaluate performance
- Give rewards

Notice the similarities to the steps in the strategic planning process. Drucker's model moves from very broad, general organizational goals to specific objectives for each individual worker. The worker is involved in setting her or his own objectives, and is evaluated and rewarded based upon whether or not they are achieved. Though now considered somewhat obsolete, the MBO model has been successfully implemented in thousands of for-profit and nonprofit organizations.

Organizing

Classical organizing theory deals primarily with how human resources are coordinated to meet organizational goals. In its broadest sense, organizing also refers to coordination of financial, material, equipment, and other resources. However, human resources is the most important and most difficult aspect of organizing.

One of the most important organizing skills a manager must learn is that of delegation. Delegation is the process of assigning tasks to members of the organization. To do so successfully, the manager must understand the difference between responsibility and authority.

Responsibility is the obligation to perform assigned or delegated tasks. Authority is the right to make necessary decisions in order to accomplish assigned tasks. The most common delegation mistakes are:

- Delegating a task without committing the necessary decision-making authority to accomplish the task
- Delegating (or trying to delegate) responsibility

Managers can, and must, delegate authority to subordinates in order to get the work done, but they can never delegate responsibility for accomplishment of the tasks. It is the manager's responsibility to accomplish assigned tasks through the work of others.

Current management theory often uses the term *empowerment,* rather than delegation. Empowering employees means giving them the training, information, resources, and authority to make important decisions that affect them and their work. The effective social services manager will learn to support her or his employees and allow them to make their own decisions, within appropriate organizational parameters.

Evaluating

Evaluating is often referred to in the business management literature as *controlling.* We prefer the term *evaluating* because we think it accurately describes the process and it lacks the negative connotations sometimes associated with "control" or "controlling." Evaluating answers the question "How are we doing?"

Until recently, evaluating organizational performance (as opposed to individual employee performance) was not very important in social service agencies. Today, there is enormous pressure on social service agencies to justify their existence and their need for funding. This pressure has prompted social service managers to place new emphasis on organizational evaluation.

There are many acceptable techniques, standards, and methods for evaluating organizational performance. However, not all of them are applicable to, or appropriate for, social service agencies. Rino Patti contends that there are five types of performance indicators for social service agencies:[14]

1. Service effectiveness (quality of service)
2. Output (quantity of service)
3. Productivity (efficient use of resources)
4. Resource acquisition
5. Minimizing budget cuts

Patti argues convincingly that service effectiveness, or quality of service, should be the measure of highest priority in any social service agency.[15] Such a view is entirely consistent with much of the currently popular thinking regarding management in the for-profit business sector. We will discuss quality in more detail later.

How does the social services manager know how her or his agency is doing? How does one measure any of the above performance indicators? In order to evaluate the agency on these, or any, objective criteria, the manager needs a good management information system (MIS). Management information systems are data collection systems that monitor and analyze numerous aspects of the organization's operations—such as finance, production, sales, quality, and so forth—and produce periodic reports that managers use to help make business decisions. In a small social service organization, the MIS may be charts and records, tabulated by hand, or a personal computer on the CEO's desk that is used to compile monthly agency financial and statistical data.

In today's competitive, rapidly changing, cost-conscious environment, social service managers can't assume that what was working well yesterday still works today. They can no longer afford to make "seat of the pants" decisions—guesses about what to do, based upon past experience or unproven assumptions. Managers need to use structured decision-making techniques. Structured decision making involves the use of factual information and systematic processes. In order to use structured decision making, managers need accurate, current data, which requires an up-to-date MIS.

Large or small, for-profit or not, social service organizations must constantly seek to enhance their structured decision-making capacity. Social service agencies have been slow to adopt computer technology, primarily because of its cost. However, steadily increasing pressures to cut costs and demostrate effectiveness necessitate ever greater use of the computer as a management tool. New software is being developed contiunuously that not only enables social service managers to perform accounting, billing, word processing, and data collection and analysis more efficiently, but also simplifies case management, quality assurance, and client assessment functions.

Managed care is a collection of management policies, procedures, and technologies that are intended to limit the costs and improve the quality of services. Introduced to control health care costs, managed care techniques are now applied to a wide range of health, mental health, and social services. Managed care uses computerized databases to analyze costs and outcomes and assess the effectiveness of specific treatment modalities and programs. The development of managed care systems requires sophisticated, networked computer databases to track clients, service providers, outcomes, and costs. Smaller social service agencies without sophisticated MIS may find themselves in the awkward position of dealing with managed care companies who know more about the agency's clients, services, and outcomes than the agency does.

Leading

There are at least three important types of leadership behavior performance by managers: *motivating* (or *influencing*), *managing groups*, and *communicating*. Until recently, leadership was considered to be the result of certain personality and behavioral characteristics; thus the cliché, "Leaders are born, not made." However, more careful study of leadership behavior has indicated that leaders can, indeed, be "made."

Most modern leadership theory asserts that leaders develop from some combination of leader behaviors, follower expectations, and situational circumstances. There are several contemporary models, but the important point to remember is that the effective leader adjusts her or his leadership style to fit the circumstances and the needs of the followers.

How to motivate employees is a perpetual mystery and a constant challenge to managers. Motivation is the incentive(s) that causes an individual to behave in certain ways. The manager is trying to motivate employees to perform assigned tasks in a way that will help the agency achieve its goals. There are many theories of motivation, but suffice it to say here that the better the social services manager understands human behavior, the more likely she or he will be successful in motivating employees. The social services manager must use all of her or his creativity and skills to identify employee needs, and ways to meet those needs, within the financial, ethical, and political constraints of the agency.

Directing groups is an important management function because so much of an organization's work is done in groups. There are board committees, task forces, staff team meetings, departmental committees, focus groups, and community meetings, to name just a few common groups that social services managers may be asked to attend or lead. Managing organizational work groups may be a new experience for the inexperienced manager. Those who are familiar with group dynamics and group process will find themselves able to apply these principles in many group management situations. Good group facilitation skills are essential management skills.

Communicating is such an important management skill that it is often listed as a fifth basic management function, along with planning, organizing, evaluating, and leading. It is discussed here under leading, but obviously virtually all management activities are accomplished, at least partially, through communication. Good communication skills are just as important for the effective manager as they are for the good social worker. One important difference is that when a manager communicates, it may be received differently by others within the organization, because of his or her *role* as a manager (as opposed to employee, peer, friend, etc.). Anything a manager can do to improve her or his communication skills (written and oral) will be a great asset to the manager and to the organization.

Transformational leadership is a theory that, as the name implies, advocates fundamentally changing the way work organizations function. Transformational leadership can be defined as, "…a process of inspiring change and empowering followers to achieve greater heights, to improve themselves, and to improve organization processes."[16] Koehler and Pankowski identify eight principles of transformational leadership:[17]

- View organizations as systems.
- Establish and communicate organization strategy.
- Institutionalize a management system.
- Develop and train all associates (employees) in process managment.
- Empower individuals and teams.
- Measure and control processes.
- Recognize and reward continual improvement.
- Inspire continual change.

QUALITY

Earlier, we noted the increasing emphasis placed on evaluation in social services agencies. There is a related trend in the for-profit business sector today: the emphasis on quality. It is incumbent upon the contemporary social services manager to examine the quality management movement in American business and industry, to determine the lessons it holds for social services.

In the for-profit business world, the ultimate goal is clear and measurable—to make a profit for the company, the owners, the shareholders. This is the proverbial "bottom line,"[18] the principal criterion by which all for-profit businesses are measured. When the "product" or output of a for-profit business is social services, an additional dimension is added. Some practitioners and scholars argue that the provision of social services by for-profit organizations is compromised by the inherent focus on the goal of turning a profit. This line of thinking also argues that the "bottom line" for any social service organization should be the quality and effectiveness of the services provided.[19]

Indeed, a primary performance criterion for any organization must be the quality of its output. In fact, contemporary adherents to the principles of total quality management (TQM) go so far as to maintain that *quality of output* must be the all-consuming focus of any business, and that profits will accrue to the for-profit businesses that do so. This perspective suggests that a well-managed social service organization can deliver high-quality services, be it a public, a private nonprofit, or a private for-profit agency.

Joseph M. Juran and W. Edwards Deming were two of the founders of the quality movement in the manufacturing field. Their theories gained wide acceptance in Japan following World War II and became popular in the United States during the 1980s, when Japanese manufacturers were consistently beating American companies in quality, growth, and profitability. TQM principles have now been adopted by all kinds of businesses and many governmental organizations, including public and private nonprofit social service agencies.

Juran and Deming taught that the mission of any business organization should be quality, not profit, because quality assures long-term survival (and long-term profitability), while pursuit of profit at the expense of quality is shortsighted and can ultimately lead to a decline in sales and profitability. The key point here, for the social service manager, is that *quality must be the central mission of the organization.* For Juran and Deming, the manager's role, from the CEO to the first-level supervisor, is to focus everyone in the organization on that central mission; to plan it, to teach it, to measure it, to support it in word and deed, and to lead everyone to believe in it.

Certainly, measuring quality in a social service agency is not as simple as counting defects on an assembly line. Patti suggests several courses to pursue,[20] including success in generating client change, timeliness, consistency, human- ness, proficiency, and client satisfaction. Some of these factors are easier to count and measure than others. Nevertheless, the pursuit of quality, and the measure- ment of it, is just as essential for social services agencies as it is for manufactur- ers and for-profit businesses. It is no longer good enough to demonstrate need. Funders demand *results.* Outcome measurement in social services has become a major issue in the 1990s. It will be a fundamental expectation of all human ser- vice agencies by the beginning of the new century.

How does one achieve an organizational commitment to quality? Deming outlined "Fourteen Points" or principles of his philosophy of total quality man- agement:[21]

1. Create constancy of purpose for improvement of product and service.
2. Adopt the new philosophy. We are in a new economic age.
3. Cease dependence on inspection to achieve quality.
4. End the practice of awarding business on the basis of price tag alone.
5. Improve constantly and forever the system of production and service.
6. Institute training on the job.
7. Institute leadership.
8. Drive out fear, so that everyone can work effectively for the company.
9. Break down barriers between departments.
10. Eliminate slogans, exhortations, and targets for the workforce.
11. Eliminate work standards (quotas); eliminate management by objective. Substitute leadership.
12. Remove barriers that rob the hourly worker of his [or her] right to pride of workmanship.
13. Institute a vigorous program of education and self-improvement... for everyone.
14. Put everybody in the company to work to accomplish the transformation.

Not all of Deming's principles and barriers are applicable to social service agencies, nor are they all universally accepted by management experts. But they have undeniably worked in a variety of companies, and many of them are con- sistent with the philosophies of other recognized thinkers in the field. In simplest terms, TQM, as postulated by Deming, is a marriage of statistical control meth- ods (developed to monitor war production during World War II), fundamental principles of organizational behavior, and basic management and supervision techniques.

Social service managers and educators are adopting TQM principles and adapting them to social service agencies. Application of quality management to social services is not without problems, however. Service production systems are fundamentally different from the production of tangible goods.[22] Furthermore, social service agencies typically have multiple customers. Often the consumer of the service (the client) is not the payer. The payer may be a governmental unit, an insurance company, a private contributor, or a combination of these. Each payer has its own set of expectations, which may be very different from the client's. The social service agency must be sensitive and responsive to all the relevant, and potentially conflicting, customer expectations. Another common dilemma for social service agencies is the fact that, for some clients, the potential for positive, or at least desirable, outcomes is limited. This does not mean, however, that quality cannot be improved.[23] There is a growing body of work focusing on the use of TQM in social services and related organizations. The reader is referred to the readings at the conclusion of this chapter for other resources.

What constitutes a well-run social service agency? There is no simple answer to that question. However, Peters and Waterman conducted a study of for-profit businesses to determine the common characteristics of well-run companies.[24] They identified eight characteristics:

1. A bias for action (do it, fix it, try it)
2. Closeness to the customer (learn from the people you serve)
3. Autonomy and entrepreneurship (foster creativity and innovativeness)
4. Productivity through people (treat your employees as a resource, with respect)
5. Hands-on, value-driven (clear mission, top management close to the work)
6. "Stick to the knitting" (do what you know how to do best)
7. Simple form, lean staff (simple organizational structure, not top-heavy with management)
8. Simultaneous loose-tight properties (decentralized decision making, but very strong allegiance to the company's central values/mission)

Notice how Peters and Waterman's characteristics contrast with those of bureacracies, described earlier (hierarchical structure, specialized functions, elaborate rules and procedures). Nonprofit management specialist Peter Brinkerhoff identifies nine characteristics of successful nonprofit organizations.[25] They are:

1. A viable mission
2. A businesslike board of directors
3. A strong, well-educated staff
4. A tight set of controls
5. A bias for marketing (*everything* is marketing)
6. A vision for where they are going

7. Financially empowered (diversified, nontraditional income sources)
8. Social entrepreneurs (willing to take risks to perform mission)
9. Rapid response to changing circumstances

Notice the similarities between Brinkerhoff's list and Peters and Waterman's. Clearly, well-managed, successful social service agencies have much in common with well-managed, successful for-profit businesses.

SUMMARY AND CONCLUSIONS

By now it should be evident that contemporary managment theory is not only compatible with social work values, it mirrors many of them. The dignity and value of each individual (worker or customer), the emphasis on customer (client) needs, systems theory, the value of teamwork, and the assumption that people can and will change if properly motivated are all essential components of both bodies of knowledge.

Social service agencies are similar to other types of organizations in general and to business organizations in particular. Although there may be differences in organizational mission and goals, much current business management theory and technology has some application to social service agencies. Social service managers perform the same basic functions as managers in any business—planning, organizing, evaluating, and leading.

Social service managers who have social work education and experience will find that their backgrounds are helpful in the human relations aspects of management, but they may need additional training in some of the other skills required. Depending upon the size of the agency, the social services manager may be a specialist, or may perform many different kinds of tasks.

The current emphasis on outcomes in social services is compatible with the total quality movement to the extent that social service managers can identify appropriate measurements of service quality. The effective social services manager today is skillful in adapting the tools and methods of modern business management to the social services setting, without compromising social work values or agency mission.

Notes

1. Peter F. Drucker, *Managing in a Time of Great Change* (New York: Truman Talley Books/Dutton, 1995), pp. 75–76.
2. Peter C. Brinkerhoff, *Mission-Based Management* (Dillon, CO: Alpine-Guild Inc., 1994), pp. 12–13.
3. Richard M. Wiess, "Organizational Structure in Human Service Agencies," from *Managing Human Services Organizations*, Lynn E. Miller, ed. (Westport, CT: Greenwood Press, 1989), pp. 21–22.
4. Ibid., pp. 36–38.
5. Joseph L. Massie, *Essentials of Management* (Englewood Cliffs, NJ: Prentice-Hall, 1979), p. 4.
6. Stephen P. Robbins, *The Administrative Process* (Englewood Cliffs, NJ: Prentice-Hall, 1976), p. 14.

7. Frederick C. Mish, ed., *Webster's Ninth New Collegiate Dictionary* (Springfield, MA: Merriam-Webster, Inc., 1983), p. 57 and p. 722.

8. Samuel C. Corto, *Modern Management* (Needham Heights, MA: Allyn and Bacon, 1992), p. 15.

9. *Statistics on Social Work Education in the United States: 1996* (Alexandria, VA: Council on Social Work Education, 1997), p. 34.

10. Samuel C. Corto, *Modern Management*, p. 110.

11. Ibid., p. 191.

12. Peter F. Drucker, *Managing in a Time of Great Change*, p. 43.

13. Samuel C. Corto, *Modern Management*, p. 120.

14. Rino J. Patti, "Managing for Service Effectiveness in Social Welfare Organizations," *Social Work* (September–October 1987): 377.

15. Ibid., p. 377–380.

16. Jerry W. Koehler and Joseph M. Pankowski, *Transformational Leadership in Government* (Delray Beach, FL: St. Lucie Press, 1997), p. 16.

17. Ibid., pp. 17–21.

18. Rino J. Patti, "In Search of Purpose for Social Welfare Administration," *The Child and Youth Care Administrator* 5 (1): 17.

19. Ibid., p. 17.

20. Rino J. Patti, "Managing for Service Effectiveness," p. 377.

21. Mary Walton, *The Deming Management Method* (New York: Perigee Books, 1986), pp. 34–36.

22. Stephen T. Moore and Michael J. Kelly, "Quality Now: Moving Human Services Organizations Toward a Consumer Orientation to Service Quality," *Social Work* (January 1996): 34.

23. Ibid.

24. Samuel C. Corto, *Modern Management*, pp. 10–11.

25. Peter C. Brinkerhoff, *Mission-Based Management*, pp. 26–27.

Additional Suggested Readings

Au, Chor-fai. "Rethinking Organizational Effectiveness: Theoretical and Methodological Issues in the Study of Organizational Effectiveness for Social Work Organizations." *Administration in Social Work* 20, no. 4 (1996).

Brashears, Freda. "Supervision as Social Work Practice." *Social Work*, September 1995.

Drucker, Peter F. *Managing the Nonprofit Organization*. New York: Harper Business, 1992.

Edwards, Richard L., Philip W. Cooke, and P. Nelson Reid. "Social Work Management in an Era of Diminishing Responsibility." *Social Work*, September 1996.

Emenhiser, David, Robert Barker, and Madelyn DeWoody. *Managed Care: An Agency Guide to Surviving and Thriving*. Washington, DC: Child Welfare League of America, 1995.

Kluger, Miriam P., and William A. Baker. *Innovative Leadership in the Nonprofit Organization: Strategies for Change*. Washington, DC: Child Welfare League of America, 1994.

Martin, Lawrence L. *Total Quality Management in Human Service Organizations*. Newbury Park, CA: Sage Publications, 1993.

Martin, Lawrence L., and Peter M. Kettner. "Performance Management: The New Accountability." *Administration in Social Work* 21, no. 1 (1997).

McCready, Douglas J., Stephen Price, Sheldon L. Rahn, and Kirk Were. "Third Generation Information Systems: Integrating Costs and Outcomes." *Administration in Social Work* 20, no. 1 (1996).

Menefee, David. "Strategic Administration of Nonprofit Human Service Organizations: A Model for Executive Success in Turbulent Times." *Administration in Social Work* 21, no. 2 (1997).

Moore, Stephen T. "Efficiency in Social Work Practice and Administration." *Social Work*, September 1995.

Pecora, Peter J., William R. Seelig, Fotena A. Zirps, and Sally M. Davis. *Quality Improvement and Evaluation in Child and Family Service*. Washington, DC: Child Welfare League of America Press, 1996.

21

Social Work Research

JAMES A. HALL*

Social work research is usually conducted by social work researchers who are very similar in overall orientation to social work practitioners. Rubin and Babbie argue, however, that social work researchers are a "breed apart" from other academic researchers in that they conduct research that improves knowledge about social work practice.[1] That is, the purpose of most social work research is to help improve practice whether that practice be direct (e.g., counseling individuals, families, or groups) or indirect (e.g., community organization and policy development). In the social work research literature, we can find many studies that are agency-based and in which the practitioners assist the researcher with the project. Although some master's-level social workers conduct their own research, more often social work faculty work with practitioners to develop, implement, and evaluate projects of various kinds.[2]

The empirical literature has been the place in which social workers have published their results about social work–related populations and problems, and about the effectiveness of practice techniques. Later in this chapter we will review some of the populations and problems of interest to social work. Unfortunately, the practice effectiveness results have not always been clear nor have they always been positive. Fischer has reviewed the empirical literature related to casework effectiveness.[3] Based on a review of eleven studies, he concluded that the data did not support the effectiveness of social casework but that the research methods used seriously undermined the significance of the research. Later reviews of the casework effectiveness literature ranged from mixed to optimistic.[4] Other authors criticized the reviewers because of other methodological issues[5] and one researcher even expanded the scope of social work research

---

* The author wishes to dedicate this chapter to the late Professor John L. Craft, author of this chapter in the first editions. Dr. Craft's concise style of writing and sense of humor served as guidelines and inspiration as this was first written and then later revised for this edition. Thanks to Julie Spears for her assistance with the research.

to include research conducted with problems of concern for social work (rather than requiring that a social worker conduct the research).[6]

What can be concluded from these and other studies is that practice effectiveness is very difficult to "prove." Rather than give up on conducting research, however, social work researchers have intensified their efforts to assess populations, study practice, and evaluate social policy. Over the past few years, the quantity and quality of social work research have improved greatly, although even this conclusion would be debated if presented to a group of social work researchers and practitioners.

Thus, the purpose of this chapter is to introduce readers to social work research and hopefully provide inspiration to review or even conduct research sometime during their careers. To facilitate understanding, we shall describe the process of developing social work research in a step-by-step format. Examples of social work research from the literature will be included along the way, as will four specific examples from this author's experience.

THE PROCESS OF SOCIAL WORK RESEARCH

In this section, the process of social work research will be described in a step-by-step format so that each component can be identified and explained. We shall give examples from the empirical literature to help explain each step; we shall also describe a framework for categorizing social work research.

In the previous edition of this book, Craft reviewed the history of social work research, using the text by Zimbalist as a key source.[7] Craft noted that social work research was not distinctly separated from other research areas until the 1930s and 1940s. Other distinguishing landmarks were noted for social work research, which was defined by Zimbalist as: *"the production of knowledge that can be utilized in planning and carrying out of social work programs."*[8] Thus, in order to understand social work research, one must understand social work programs and practice. Patterson observed that while the practice and research communities share some common goals and processes, these branches of social work have often been deeply divided and have described the causes of problems and possible solutions in dramatically different ways.[9] For example, the purpose of social work practice is to improve conditions for individuals, families, groups, or communities of peoples. The purpose of social work research is to improve knowledge about practice, even if individual clients or communities might not be helped (i.e., some experimental or untested interventions might not be effective). In practice, we can change procedures if we find that a client was not being helped. In research, unless we have some very compelling reason, we cannot change the rules of helping if one or more persons are not making improvements. Other similarities and differences will be discussed as we review this area.

So what do social workers study? One way to think about the topics of social work is to consider what makes this profession unique. Frankel contended that social work research should utilize three characteristics that distinguish the profession from others.[10] First, social work practice and therefore social work research are based on the social welfare institution. Second, social work uses a practice paradigm that emphasizes the *person-in-environment* principle—that is, we not only work with an individual, but we also recognize the enormous impact of family, groups, communities, and other forces in that individual's environment. Finally, social work is unique in that *practitioners and those engaged in policy analysis* are in the *same* profession—that is, social work includes both direct and indirect practitioners.

Step #1—Determining the Purpose and Goals of Research

The first step in any research project—social work included—is to determine the purpose of the study. In social work, studies have been conducted to (1) describe, (2) explain, and (3) predict.[11] This process is basically one of building theory or knowledge so that we can help our clients and communities achieve better lives. Social workers engage in various types of studies depending on the quality and quantity of knowledge in that particular area. For example, when social workers first began working with HIV-positive clients, not much research or practice wisdom existed to help guide their activities.[12] By using social work practice principles and by adapting procedures used with other client groups, *exploratory studies* were conducted to gather basic information about the needs of these clients and about interventions that would help those needs.[13] As more social work practitioners and researchers become involved with this population, more sophisticated studies will be conducted.

Some researchers conduct *surveys* of specific groups (called *samples*) of HIV-positive clients, using self-administered questionnaires or by interviewing these clients individually (using an *interview schedule*). Typically, surveys are conducted either to (1) describe the needs and characteristics of a sample at a given time (called a *cross-sectional* survey) or (2) describe the needs and characteristics of a sample over time (called a *longitudinal* survey).[14] A survey might seem like a fairly simple type of research project, but the identification of a sample and the construction of reliable and valid measurement instruments (e.g., questionnaires) make this a very complex process. Depending on the type of data collected and the size of the sample, the social work researcher might also analyze the data to *explain why* something happens within a sample or population.

Besides these exploratory and descriptive studies, social workers also conduct evaluative studies that focus on interventions and programs. To evaluate an intervention, the researcher usually studies two or more groups of study participants (who are also called *subjects*). If two groups are included, one group sometimes receives a special intervention (called the *experimental group*) and the other then receives standard treatment or a placebo (called the *control* or *comparison* group). The second group is called a control group if the researcher randomly assigns participants to a group. If the researcher uses an existing group, this second group is called a comparison group. Many difficulties exist when evaluating an intervention, and these will be reviewed later.

Current topics for social work research. In preparation for this chapter, we conducted a computer-assisted review of the empirical literature related to social work research using the data base *Social Work Abstracts*, which is published by the NASW. This data base was selected because the research cited would most likely be conducted or written by social workers, or of interest to social workers in general.

A few years ago, the editors of *Social Work Abstracts* divided the literature into four main categories: (1) the social work profession, (2) theory and practice, (3) areas of service, and (4) social issues and social problems. Although these categories might not be used as much in today's computerized data base searching, these four major categories and subcategories help organize the social work literature conceptually—as in Table 21.1. As you can see, these categories represent a wide range of interests for social workers; both practitioners and researchers work in and study these areas.

TABLE 21.1 Four Major Categories of Social Work

1.	*The Social Work Profession*	
	a.	General
	b.	Education and training
	c.	History
	d.	Interprofessional relationships
	e.	Organizations and associations
	f.	Personnel issues
	g.	Quality assurance and standards
2.	*Theory and Practice*	
	a.	Administration and management
	b.	Case management
	c.	Casework and psychotherapy
	d.	Community organization and community development
	e.	Family and couples therapy
	f.	Consultation and supervision
	g.	Group work and group therapy
	h.	Research methodology
	i.	Theory and conceptual frameworks
3.	*Areas of Service*	
	a.	General
	b.	Aging and the aged
	c.	Children and families; child and family welfare
	d.	Crime and delinquency; justice
	e.	Developmental disabilities and mental retardation
	f.	Education and schools
	g.	Health and health care
	h.	Mental health and mental illness
	i.	Substance use and abuse; alcoholism
4.	*Social Issues and Social Problems*	
	a.	Civil and legal rights
	b.	Economics and poverty
	c.	Employment and affirmative action
	d.	Legislation and lobbying
	e.	Rural and urban issues
	f.	Social policy and social action
	g.	Special populations

1. The social work profession.   For research about the social work profession since 1990, we present the following recent examples. Hall and colleagues developed a cooperative program between a hospital department of social services and a school of social work to integrate the faculty and students with clinicians for both practice and/or research internships.[15] This project helped clinicians conduct research, provided students with practical research experience within a clinical setting, and increased the likelihood that both staff and students would participate in research. All of these aspects enhance the various areas within the social work profession.

In another profession-related study, Gasker focused on the development of a professional identity for the field of social work education.[16] For many faculty, the desire to be an effective teacher is sometimes limited greatly by the pressure to publish and to engage in other scholarly activities. This study provides insights regarding educational and clinical practice, as well as general professional development. Thus, this research addressed an important issue relevant to the academic wing of the profession including what we have to learn and to teach in the practice of social work.

2. Theory and practice.   Research on theory and practice focuses more on the methods of practice and the methods of research. Within social work research, some debate exists between the qualitative and quantitative researchers. Allen-Meares and Lane studied this issue by comparing both approaches with social work practice.[17] On the basis of a review of the literature, they concluded that both quantitative and qualitative methods were necessary in social work research—mainly because social work practice focuses on events (such as human interactions) that cannot be measured adequately by one method alone. Qualitative methods typically work with the actual words people use in their interactions and draw conclusions from the themes that are noted across time or people. Rosenthal argued that since qualitative description allows sensitivity to context, it facilitates data interpretation and communication particularly for nonstatistical audiences (e.g., beginning social work students, administrators, and practitioners).[18] Quantitative researchers, on the other hand, might count the number of positive statements made by each person who is talking about personal issues and draw their conclusions from these data.[19]

Also within the theory and practice area, researchers have studied why practitioners have tended to underutilize research results to improve social services. Bonuck concluded that the social work profession, while proficient at the assessment process, has paid insufficient attention to the research concerning unmet client needs.[20] This study illustrated the value of using research methods for administrative programming and policy development in the human services.

3. Areas of service.   In social work, areas of service have been defined as special groups or settings that have been historically associated with our profession. Within the "child and family welfare" subcategory, Arditti and Madden-Derdich studied types of child custody among divorced mothers.[21] Based on family organization variables, results indicated that parenting stress, coparental relationship quality, custody satisfaction, and age of children in the household were predictive of custody type. With this information, we can recommend that social workers should carefully examine these issues when working with children and families so that they can provide better social work services.

In the service area of "aging and the aged," Choi studied the social support systems and characteristics of never-married and divorced elderly men and women.[22] This researcher collected data using the Longitudinal Survey of Aging and found that those with higher education were less likely to lack social support than those with lower education. In addition, results indicated that women were more likely to experience economic hardship than men. Thus, by conducting a descriptive but explanatory study over time (i.e., a longitudinal survey), this researcher concluded that individual attributes and family environment (i.e., number of children and siblings) were better predictors of the economic and health status of an elderly person than marital status. In addition, practitioners can use this information as they assess client needs and eventually provide services.

4. Social issues and social problems.   Within this area, we can find many of the policy studies and more "macropractice" or "indirect" practice studies. Social workers have not only concerned themselves with the needs of individuals, families, and groups but they have also worked with the larger picture—thus, the category, social issues, and social problems.

Focusing on a macropractice topic, Mulroy and Ewalt studied the impact of Federal cutbacks on housing programs.[23] This study predicted that pending cuts in the U.S. Department of Housing and Urban Development (HUD), combined with deep funding cuts in public assistance, would have a profound effect on low-income households. Conclusions from this study included the interrelation of employment and housing from which social policy, social work methods, and research will all be affected. Mulroy's previous research on this issue supported the training of social workers in community organization, administration, and planning to assume leadership in developing better policies and programs to help this population's (single-parent mothers) access to affordable housing.[24] Although the researcher would probably support micropractice efforts, such as counseling these mothers using empowerment strategies, the main focus was on social policy that would improve programs to help a disadvantaged population.

Finally, Crawley studied changes in the American labor force by focusing on elder African-Americans.[25] Due to the projected changes in the labor force (i.e., fewer workers in the age group of 18- to 34-year-olds), other labor sources may be needed. This researcher surveyed the needs of 165 African-Americans aged 60 years and older about their work interests and needs. Besides concluding that this segment of the labor force is a national resource, the author also believed that one type of social work practice (called occupational social work) is the most appropriate to conduct research and to work with this population.

So how does a social worker select a topic for study? Usually, the worker has some connection to that topic through practice or through an opportunity related to the practice of others. Many direct-practice researchers collaborate closely with practitioners to describe practice problems and to evaluate interventions to alleviate negative situations. Indirect-practice researchers might also select a topic based on collaboration with direct practitioners, but they also might decide on topics based on their knowledge of the literature.

Step #2—Reviewing the Empirical Literature

After selecting a topic, no matter how general or specific that topic might be, social work researchers must also become familiar with the research conducted by others in that area. Thus, practitioners and researchers should read the literature to find what others have studied and what they have concluded. Their knowledge base is then changed by the interaction of personal experience and the experience of others as described in the literature.

"The literature" is made up of various sources of printed materials and electronic data bases. With the advent of the computer and accessibility of massive data bases (e.g., *Social Work Abstracts*), our conception of the literature is apt to change over the next five years. In fact, a great deal of attention and research have emerged on the use of computerized searches of the empirical literature. For example, the World Wide Web offers resources related to research on social work practice and which can be focused from general to the social work specific.[26] Further, Patterson proposed and described an international information resource linkage for the advancement of social work education and practice.[27] This kind of Internet-accessible repository would allow for the creation of peer-reviewed electronic journals, immediate retrieval of recent papers, and perhaps a forum for addressing emerging social problems. Social work researchers can use these recent and pending technological innovations to advance the field of social work into the twenty-first century.

Currently, however, social workers can review textbooks and monographs related to their study topics, as well as review "empirical literature" that is published mainly in periodicals or journals (found through the "reference desks" in most libraries at colleges and universities). In the computer-assisted review of the literature for this chapter, the data base, *Social Work Abstracts*, was searched using the key word phrase *research and social work* and focused on the publication years of 1993 through 1997. Through this process, a substantial number of articles was identified—all containing the words *research* and *social work* somewhere in their bibliographic listing.

After reviewing these listings that included an abstract, about 25 were selected for inclusion in this chapter. All articles were related to social work research, but some were "more related" than others, based on the goals for this chapter. Social workers who review the literature usually follow a similar process of searching a data base using a computer, printing out the bibliographic listings, and then reviewing those listings for relevancy.

Then, the researcher must locate the literature sources—periodical or textbook—and review the actual article. Essentially, the researcher must treat each literature source as a "subject" in the study of the literature related to the overall topic. As themes become clear from the review of the literature, the researcher can then develop a theoretical argument for looking at the study topic or for studying more specific aspects. Thus, theory can be developed from conclusions drawn from a review of the literature or from data collected by the researcher.

The main type of study found was the *literature review*, which usually examined a particular issue or problem and then proposed practice principles or research for the future. For example, Lyons and colleagues reviewed literature on ten different risk assessment models for child-protective services.[28] Copeland

and Wexler reviewed the literature on implementing federal-state partnership programs and addressed the importance of research on policy implementation on social welfare while presenting a framework for analysis.[29] And finally, Mason reviewed the literature on the consensus of a "best" method for upholding feminist principles in research by looking at the application of those principles.[30] These three studies and several others not only looked for themes in the literature but also proposed responses to acknowledged problems exposed from these reviews.

Asking good questions. As the researcher both thinks about the proposed study purpose and reviews the empirical literature, he or she usually develops a set of research questions. The cornerstone of good research includes asking questions and then refining those questions over time. Once the questions are asked, however, the research design and data analysis procedures are usually determined to a great extent. If the researcher asks, "What are the needs of those who attend a legal clinic?" then a cross-sectional survey is most likely implied. If, on the other hand, the researcher asks, "Is this housing program effective for meeting the needs of the targeted population?" then a program evaluation study is most likely selected as the general design.

Step #3—Deciding on a Design for the Research

So, what is a "research design"? Simply put, a research design is the *basic plan for the collection of data*. This plan includes *general descriptions* of the study population and sample (including recruitment procedures), assessment procedures, intervention procedures (if the study includes an intervention component), and data analysis procedures. Researchers typically develop the design to control for possible sources of bias that could affect the possible conclusions of the study.

Types of research designs. Rubin and Babbie describe three purposes of research that, in turn, determine the most appropriate types of research design.[31] The first type, *exploratory*, is typically used to study a new topic of interest; therefore, the research serves to explore that subject. While exploratory research can be extremely useful in becoming familiar with a new topic, it rarely gives more than insights for further research possibilities. The second type of research, *descriptive*, is used in both quantitative and qualitative research. Quantitative research uses description to describe the characteristics of the study population, which should, in turn, be a representative sample of that population. Descriptive attributes that can be quantified include age, race, gender, income, education, and so on. In qualitative research, investigators may describe the environment in narrative fashion (rather than in numbers), or the interactions of a group of people by recording exactly what is said. The third purpose of research, *explanatory*, intends to determine why a phenomenon happens, as opposed to simply describing the rates or the population surrounding that issue, or to predict the occurrence of an event or characteristic in a sample.

In reality, most studies will have elements of all three research purposes, therefore making it difficult to characterize the exact purpose of a particular study. The time frame of a study helps to determine its purpose. A *cross-sectional* study is based on observations made at one point in time and may be exploratory, descriptive, or explanatory. On the other hand, *longitudinal* studies may conduct their observations over an extended period to describe changes within a sample or population over time. The overall goal of each design, however, is to understand phenomena so that our quality of life can be improved.

Participants or data source.   The researcher must choose the source of the study data, which will obviously be dependent on the study purpose. Typically, if human subjects are involved, a *sample* representing the study *population* is recruited from a *sampling frame*. If case records or some other existing data bases are the source of data, then the researcher must decide how to sample from these data bases. Specific plans are developed so that the researcher can describe who are included and who are not included as potential participants or data elements (e.g., case records). Not all potential human subjects are usually recruited into a research project. Although this factor might create some bias in the research (by not having a representative sample), the rights of human subjects are predominant—as will be seen later.

Data collection.   The next issue for the researcher is how to collect the data. Data are usually thought of as *variables*—or, in other words, key characteristics or topics related to the study purpose. Usually, the key variables of the study must be operationalized or put into words that allow them to be measured. In most studies, the researcher first describes the variables that are related directly to the study topic. For example, one study focused on the psychosocial needs of those who attend a legal clinic. The researcher operationalized "psychosocial" to mainly include "distress," which was measured with a specific research instrument.

In some research, "cause and effect" variables are included. Within descriptive studies, some variables might be causative factors—such as family conflict, which might be theorized as leading to physical abuse of family members. Within evaluative studies, these variables would be the actual *intervention* that is being evaluated.

Further, we will include *other variables* in studies if those variables are seen as important. For example, a researcher might include demographic variables (such as age, ethnicity, and gender), psychological variables (such as self-esteem and depression), and social variables (such as social support and household characteristics). The guiding principle is to collect enough data to answer the key study questions but not so much data that the researcher becomes lost in the collection or analysis procedures.

Another question in the data collection step is the source of the data. If human subjects are involved, the researcher can collect data from the targeted study participant, or from a significant other of this targeted participant, or from existing records in the community (such as school achievement). The choice of one or more data sources is again related to the study purpose and goals.

As part of this focus on data collection, the researcher must also select the instruments to measure the study variables. Basically, two types of measurement instruments can be used: direct and indirect. Direct measures record the targeted variable at the time the variable is occurring. For example, the researcher could observe a parent talking with a teen and count the number of times the parent said something positive to the teen. The other type of instrument is classified as indirect: Data are collected retrospectively or are collected on variables that are not directly observable (such as depression or self-esteem). In addition, existing sources of data (e.g., a data base) are usually considered indirect sources of data, and the researcher might develop a data collection form that would be used to collect data on certain variables from this existing source (e.g., counting arrests for drug possession from juvenile court records).

Finally, the researcher must decide *who* will collect the data. Sometimes, the researcher or trained assistants will collect the data. In other situations, the targeted participants or their "significant others" will record information about the participant—using either questionnaires or observation systems.

Controlling bias.   The social work researcher, as mentioned above, must try to control sources of bias using the plan for the collection of data (i.e., the research design). In *descriptive research*, possible bias is counteracted by the use of standardized instruments and prescribed recruitment procedures (hopefully randomly selected participants from the targeted population). In *evaluative research*, bias is counteracted through (1) random assignment to groups, (2) using an adequate sample size, (3) sample selection procedures, and (4) the use of standardized instruments.

Step #4—Describing the Procedures

As indicated above, three or four types of procedures are usually included in the research design: (1) recruitment, (2) assessment, (3) intervention (optional), and (4) data analysis. Recruitment and sampling procedures have already been discussed above.

Assessment procedures.   Assessment procedures include descriptions of the instruments used to collect data and the steps used to implement them. Researchers usually select one or more of the following types of instruments: (1) questionnaires or inventories (completed by the participant), (2) observation systems (structured observations of participant activities), (3) interview schedules (plans for interviewing participants), and/or (4) secondary data forms (templates used to collect data from existing data bases). Although these instruments usually have standard implementation procedures, some researchers ask participants to complete questionnaires by entering their answers directly into a computer—thus eliminating a separate data entry step and possible errors.

In addition, some researchers collect behavioral or physical samples from the participants using prescribed procedures. For example, studies focusing on drug use typically employ a combination of means to assess drug use—including self-report by clients, analysis of urine samples, or analysis of hair samples. Or, in studies of interaction skills, participant behavior might be recorded with audiotape or videotape and then rated at a later time for positive and negative behaviors. The reader is referred to Rubin and Babbie for a more extensive discussion of assessment procedures.[32]

Intervention procedures.   If an intervention is being evaluated, then the researcher must describe the principles and procedures of the intervention. For example, in the skills-training study described below, a session-by-session treatment manual was developed to describe the program being tested. In the study of case management described below, a session-by-session manual is inappropriate—thus, our manual describes case management activities and case manager functions. As inferred from above, the intervention must be described in detail so that the researcher and audience know what is being evaluated, and the implementation of this intervention must be recorded (this is called *process recording*).

Data analysis.   Finally, we need to describe data analysis procedures. The basic question here is, how will data will be presented to determine their significance? Many social workers rely on visual analysis, which is the basis for all data analysis.[33] The researcher must be able to describe the tables and figures used to present the data at the end of the project, and be able to describe what is held to be clinically significant. In most descriptive research, a large sample is desirable in order to support generalization to other groups of targeted participants.

Finally, although visual procedures are the "backbone" of data analysis in general, researchers must also pay attention to statistical testing. Most doctoral-level social work researchers study statistical procedures and are familiar with several of them. The appropriate statistical test is chosen based on the research question being asked, the size of the sample, the levels of measurement of the variables involved, and the characteristics of the theoretical variable distributions. Beginning researchers typically consult extensively with a statistician in the planning phases of the research as well as in the analysis phase. And, some studies do not rely on statistical analysis, but rely almost entirely on observation (visual analysis)—for example, qualitative reviews of case records for common themes and discontinuities, and single-subject research evaluating intervention effectiveness.

Step #5—Determining the Significance of the Research

The final step in the research development process is the determination of significance. Obviously, this activity should have been occurring during all the previous steps, but the researcher usually focuses on the potential study significance by comparing potential risks and benefits.

Potential risks.   Initially, the researcher must assess the potential risks for the human participants. For the targeted sample or population, six potential risk topics are usually considered: (1) psychological (e.g., distress or anxiety), (2) social (e.g., embarrassment or breech of confidentiality), (3) economic (e.g., loss of income from being part of the study), (4) legal (e.g., reporting of parents to Child Protective Services for suspicion of child neglect or abuse), (5) physical (e.g., injury from attending a group treatment session with an abusive person), and (6) violations of normal expectations (e.g., telling the participant that the study is about student achievement when the study is actually about heterosexual interactions in the waiting room of the research office). In most public institutions (such as a university), researchers are required to apply for human subjects' approval from an institutional review board (IRB), which is charged by the university with the protection of human subject rights. Theoretically, the researcher works cooperatively with the IRB to make sure all study procedures respect the rights of all potential subjects and that risks are minimized and acceptable.

Potential benefits.   Besides potential risk, the study must also have some potential benefit—otherwise, why conduct the research? Potential benefits can be discussed in three ways. First, for the actual participants, the potential benefits that directly emanate from the study might be minimal. Especially if a participant is interviewed, the chances of benefiting are quite low unless the person arrives at an insight that improves his or her life. Second, potential benefits can also be projected for the researcher. These benefits can be a potential source of bias (e.g., by publishing results, the researcher will obtain a raise in salary) and need to be controlled through the research design. Finally, potential benefits should exist for the scientific community. If the researcher actually obtains positive results in the study, what will we now know that we didn't know before? By predicting these potential benefits, we can acknowledge both the possible sources of bias and the potential significance of the study.

Comparing potential risks and benefits.   At some point, the researcher must compare the potential risks and benefits to see if the study is truly worthwhile. Some studies have been conducted without much consideration to potential risk. For example, Rubin and Babbie described the infamous Tuskegee syphilis study begun in 1932.[34] Researchers told a sample of poor African-American men who had syphilis that they would receive free treatment for their disease, but then only assessed these men over time to see how the disease affected their physical and mental health. Other inappropriate studies have been described elsewhere, and the reader is referred to those sources for other examples.

Protections for risk.   The researcher does have some basic procedures available for protection of participants from risk. First of all, potential participants must be informed about the study purpose and procedures *before* they actually consent to participate. As indicated, most institutions now have review boards in place to approve the consent procedures before they are implemented. Thus, participation must be voluntary and based on informed consent.

As part of the study procedures, the researcher also must address the protection of the participant's identity in the study records. If the study participants complete and return a questionnaire without any identifying information, then this procedure usually guarantees the strongest form of protection, called *anonymity.* Just because a participant's name is not on the questionnaire, however, does not mean that the study is anonymous. If a social work instructor were to survey a classroom of social work students that included only one male, then presentation of the results using gender as a category would absolutely identify this male.

The next level of protection is called *confidentiality* and involves coding data using a number and restricting access to the data to only the research team. In addition, in all study reports, the identities of participants should be protected through presentation of only grouped data and by changing names and key information when case reports are used.

> **Backup counselors.** Besides these procedures, many studies also include *backup counselors* prepared to help participants who react negatively to study procedures. For example, a participant could be interviewed about a previous episode of family violence that occurred in the home. By thinking about this episode, the participant could become significantly depressed or anxious—a direct result of participating in the study. In these situations, the researcher is obligated to respond to this problem by supplying a counselor who will assist the participant in coping with this negative emotional reaction. Obviously, since other negative consequences might occur, the researchers also need the backing of malpractice insurance.

The Final "Step"

When the metaphor of "steps" is used with research, the reader is cautioned not to believe that research is a totally linear process; that is, research does not occur in a lockstep fashion from beginning to end. Good research follows the scientific process but might involve several processes at the same time. The researcher might be working on the possible research designs while the literature is being reviewed. Or the research questions might be revised at several points during the study development. Once the data collection process has started, however, the development phase is over and revisions to the research *proposal* would be inappropriate.

FOUNDATIONS OF RESEARCH: EMPIRICAL PRACTICE

Much of the difficulty faced by social workers wanting to conduct research stems from how they conduct their practices. Rather than gather clinical data, a social worker might assess a client's problem by "beginning where the client is at." The main attention is given to the principle of practice rather than the procedure. In order to conduct research, the social worker must pay attention to both principles and procedures—even by "collecting data" rather than only "listening to my client."

One label given to this type of practice in which principle and procedure are both emphasized is "empirical social work practice." This approach uses the empirical literature (i.e., published articles about problems and clinical effectiveness) and stresses the evaluation of clinical procedures with standardized measures. When empirical procedures are not available, the practitioner relies on clinical wisdom—or the principles of experienced clinicians in this problem area. Empirical practice, then, can be thought of as a key part of the foundation of social work research. If data are being collected with standardized instruments and in a systematic way, then the social worker has a much easier time conducting the research due to the history of quality measurement and the overall acceptance of structure in practice.

Case Study

Over the years, I have counseled teens and their families usually through the adolescent medicine divisions of teaching hospitals. Adolescent medicine is a subspecialty of pediatrics and focuses on the special needs of teens. Many of the teens referred have been supported through public funds for health care. One such teen was referred due to concerns about depression and family conflict.

Susie (not her real name) was a 14-year-old at the time of referral and was living with her maternal grandparents. She had dropped out of school and never seemed to have the energy to get up in the morning or to keep to a weekly schedule. Her mother, Nancy, suffered from bipolar depression and led an "up and down" life, according to Susie. After two failed marriages and several failed jobs, Nancy became pregnant with Susie but did not tell Susie's father. Since Nancy could not keep a job for very long, she asked her parents to help with raising Susie for a while. Although they expected to help for only a short time, the grandparents have had custody of Susie on and off for the past twelve years.

As part of my empirical practice, our clinic intake worker had mailed a "Parent Questionnaire" to the grandparents. This screening instrument was completed by the grandmother and covered several areas: (1) vital statistics about the teen, (2) referral information, (3) family and household, (4) description of parenting persons, (5) school, (6) developmental history, (7) areas of concern (e.g., hearing, vision, behavior, sexual activity, etc.), (8) survival skills (e.g., earns allowance, cooks own meals, makes friends, visits relatives, etc.), and (9) previous counseling history. I used this completed questionnaire at the first interview with Susie and her grandparents to help orient me to their family and to their concerns.

At the end of their first assessment interview, I asked them to complete a questionnaire packet and to be videotaped while discussing conflict-arousing, problem situations. After this first session, I reviewed these instruments and videotapes with a social work intern and tried to describe their problems based upon the data. As a result of their scores, we concluded that (1) most likely Susie was mildly depressed but had good self-esteem; (2) they all had mainly negative attitudes about each other; (3) marital conflict was low; (4) the grandparents were probably not depressed; and (5) the three differed about communication problems at home. After viewing the videotaped conversations, we found that Susie was a good listener (e.g., good eye contact, did not talk while others were speaking, good body orientation, etc.). Her grandfather dominated the conversations (based on how many times each person talked and for how long), and her grandmother did not state her opinions very often. The grandfather tended to lecture for two to three minutes at a time on various topics, using an ineffective communication approach: "You should do better in school, Susie. You should listen to your grandparents more." When asked at a following session, all three stated that they didn't feel listened to and that the others only wanted to talk.

Then, based on these assessment data, we used specific intervention procedures (e.g., providing information, modeling, role-playing, supportive feedback, and homework assignments) to help them improve their attitudes about each other, convince the others that they were actually listening, increase the number of positive statements given to the others, and balance the conversations so that the grandfather spoke less and the other two spoke more. After eight sessions, the three displayed much better communication skills, had much more positive things to say about each other, and reported that the tension at home had decreased significantly. Susie even claimed that she didn't feel like running away from home now. Although many of the other problems presented by these three were still present, they did have a positive start in working on their own problems and felt somewhat confident that they could continue to improve.

In addition to these noted interventions, there were others that will not be reviewed here. Although this family improved in various ways, not all teens and families respond in this way to this counseling approach. Based on my practice experience, about 30 percent of adolescent clients and their parents came in for one interview and felt helped enough not to come back. Another 30 percent did not come back because one or more members of the family did not want to participate. And the final 40 percent continued counseling from two to sixteen sessions—with the mean number of sessions about four.

Practice procedures were based on social work principles and a specific practice orientation or paradigm called cognitive-behavioral. By reading the literature related to adolescents and parent-teen communication, we identified both standardized instruments and effective interventions. By collecting data at each session, estimates of intervention effectiveness were obtained.

Beginning Research: Social Skills Training

Based on these clinical experiences with communication-skills training with parents and teens, I began reading about social skills that could help teens. As a result of a request for help from a community practitioner, a new project was developed to help improve the social skills of developmentally disabled adults in an employment training setting. The training staff identified several problem areas: (1) inappropriate reactions to negative feedback from a supervisor, (2) inappropriate sharing of personal information with strangers in public settings (e.g., at the bus stop), and (3) poor cooperation at home. To further operationalize the problem, the employment training center staff was asked to rate the importance of several training-related problems and then to assess the problems and strengths of the specific trainees in the program.

Next, the empirical literature was reviewed. We found a study by Bates that paralleled our concerns and that described a specific treatment program.[35] By contacting Dr. Bates, we were able to use his assessment and treatment procedures and apply them to our setting. Because our main concerns were with the improvement of each individual trainee, we evaluated the effectiveness of the intervention by using special evaluation designs for individual clients or client systems. By sequentially focusing on each of the four targeted social skills, we were able to demonstrate that the intervention was effective: Skills for each of the trainees improved following the implementation of treatment.[36] We even tested the generalization of these skills using a "real-life" test in a local snack shop.

Clinical Trial: Iowa Case Management Project

Given funding from the National Institute on Drug Abuse (DA08733), we began an evaluation of an enhancement for rural clients in substance abuse treatment—the Iowa Case Management Project for Rural Drug Abuse. Clients who volunteered for this study are being randomly assigned to one of four groups: (1) case managers working at the drug agency, (2) case managers who work for an outside agency, (3) case managers who work with clients using a computerized telecommunication system (i.e., voice mail, phone reminders, etc.), and (4) a standard drug treatment or "control group." By randomly assigning participants to groups in this clinical trial, we will be able to make stronger conclusions about the effectiveness of case management by the end of this study. Our preliminary results show that the drug treatment program (with or without our case managers) is associated with a significant drop in drug use at two follow-up assessment points—three and six months after intake into drug treatment. By the end of this study, we will have screened more than 1,000 drug clients and recruited more than 600 into the research study.[37]

Program Evaluation: CADS Adolescent Drug Treatment

Sometimes, researchers are asked to evaluate existing programs rather than develop most of the research project—such as in the Iowa Case Management study. When we work with existing programs, we use a program evaluation research design to collect our data. By focusing on the program's stated (and often unstated) goals, we suggest measurement instruments to an agency so that goal achievement can be evaluated. The best program evaluation designs happen when the evaluator is involved from the very beginning of the planning stages and provides information for ongoing program improvement (i.e., how can we improve the program over time?) as well as outcome evaluation (i.e., does it really help the clients?). In many instances, however, the evaluator is called in after the fact and must rely mainly on existing data. As part of the Center for Alcohol and Drug Service (CADS), the Adolescent Drug Treatment program was funded by the federal Center for Substance Abuse Treatment (CSAT) through the state of Iowa. The project was initially designed as a comprehensive and collaborative effort targeting substance-abusing youth (and their families) who had engaged in or were at risk of engaging in drug use and criminal acticity.[38] Our evaluation team asked the treatment staff to administer several standardized assessment instruments as one source of data and, in addition, we collected data from existing agency records. Based on our analysis, we found that teens in day treatment reported significant decreases in substance use (teen self-report) and deliquent and criminal behaviors (juvenile court records), and that family and individual functioning improved (teen and parent reports).

These three studies represent some, but not all, of the research designs that are used by social work researchers. Most social work research is based on social work practice, although many researchers study social welfare policies using existing data sets. Readers are encouraged to pursue topics of interest to them through social work research textbooks or through a computerized search of the social work literature.

SUMMARY AND CONCLUSIONS

As was indicated earlier, the basis of most social work research has been empirically oriented practice. The examples cited in this chapter show the range of activities possible including direct practice with clients, cross-sectional and longitudinal surveys, clinical trials involving various numbers of participants, and program evaluations. Thus the principles of social work practice also hold for social work research: Social workers study "people in environments," conduct research in applied settings (usually community-based agencies), and strive to empower clients to solve their own problems.

Notes

1. Allen Rubin and Earl Babbie, *Research Methods for Social Work*, 3rd ed. (Pacific Grove, CA: Brooks/Cole Publishing Co., 1997).
2. Gerard Hogarty, "Aftercare Treatment of Schizophrenia: Current Status and Future Direction," in H.M. Pragg, ed., *Management of Schizophrenia* (Assen, The Netherlands: Van Gorcum, 1979), pp. 19–36.
3. Joel Fischer, "Is Social Work Effective: A Review," *Social Work* 18, no. 1, (1973): 5–20.
4. For a "mixed" review, see Katherine M. Wood, "Casework Effectiveness: A New Look at the Research Evidence," *Social Work* 23, no. 6 (1978): 437–458. For an optimistic review, see William J. Reid and Patricia Hanrahan, "Recent Evaluations of Social Work: Grounds for Optimism," *Social Work* 27 no. 4 (1982): 328–340.
5. Betty J. Blythe and Scott Briar, "Direct Practice Effectiveness," in *Encyclopedia of Social Work*, 18th ed. (Silver Spring, MD: National Association of Social Workers, 1987), pp. 399–408.
6. Allen Rubin, "Practice Effectiveness: More Grounds for Optimism," *Social Work* 30 no. 6 (1985): 469–476.
7. John L. Craft, "Social Work Research," chapter in H. Wayne Johnson, ed., *The Social Services: An Introduction*, 3rd ed. (Itasca, IL: F.E. Peacock Publishing, 1990); Sidney E. Zimbalist, *Historic Themes and Landmarks in Social Welfare Research* (New York: Harper & Row, 1977).
8. Zimbalist, *Historic Themes and Landmarks*, p. 24.
9. D. A. Patterson, "Research and Practice: The Great Divide in Substance Abuse Treatment," *Reflections* 2, no. 2 (1996): 4–10.
10. S. Frankel, "What Is Unique about Social Work: A Brief Think Piece," *The Social Worker–Le Travailleur-social* 58, no. 2 (1990): 61–68.
11. Craft, "Social Work Reseach," p. 420.
12. D. Scott, "Practice Wisdom: The Neglected Source of Practice Research," *Social Work* 35, no. 6 (1990): 564–568.
13. Elaine J. Ehrlich and Paul A. Moore, "Delivery of AIDS Services: The New York State Response," *Social Work* 35, no. 2 (1990): 175–177.
14. Rubin and Babbie, *Research Methods*, Chapter 11.
15. James A. Hall, Greg Jensen, Mark A. Fortney, Joy Sutter, Jan Locher, and Jay J. Cayner, "Education of Staff and Students in Health Care Settings: Integrating Practice and Research," *Social Work in Health Care* 24, nos. 1–2 (1996): 93–113.

16. J.A. Gasker, "The Making of a Social Work Instructor: a Qualitative Research Study," *Journal of Teaching in Social Work* 13, nos. 1–2 (1996): 93–109.

17. P. Allen-Meares and B.A. Lane, "Social Work Practice: Integrating Qualitative and Quantitative Data Collection Techniques, *Social Work* 35, no. 5 (1990): 452–458.

18. J.A. Rosenthal, "Qualitative Descriptors of Strength of Association and Effect Size," *Journal of Social Service Research* 21, no. 4 (1996): 37–59.

19. Rubin and Babbie, *Research Methods,* Chapter 1.

20. K.A. Bonuck, "Theory and Method: A Social Work Approach to Unmet Needs," *Administration in Social Work* 20, no. 2 (1996): 29–40.

21. J.A. Arditti and D. Madden-Derdich, "Joint and Sole Custody Mothers: Implications for Research and Practice," *Families in Society* 78, no. 1 (1997): 36–45.

22. N.G. Choi, "The Never-Married and Divorced Elderly: Comparison of Economic and Health Status, Social Support, and Living Arrangement," *Journal of Gerontological Social Work*, 26, nos. 1–2 (1996): 3–25.

23. E.A. Mulroy and P.L. Ewalt, "Affordable Housing: A Basic Need and a Social Issue," *Social Work* 41, no. 3 (1996): 245–249.

24. E.A. Mulroy, "Single-Parent Families and the Housing Crisis: Implications for Macro-Practice," *Journal of Independent Social Work* 35, no. 6 (1990): 542–548.

25. B. Crawley, The Transformation of the American Labor Force: Elder African Americans and Occupational Social Work," *Social Work* 37, no. 1 (1992): 41–46.

26. G. Holden, G. Rosenberg, and A. Weissman, "World Wide Web Accessible Resources Related to Research on Social Work Practice," *Research on Social Work Practice* 13, nos. 1–2 (1996): 93–109.

27. D.A. Patterson, "An Electronic Social Work Knowledge Base: A Strategy for Global Information Sharing," *International Social Work* 39, no. 2 (1996): 149–161.

28. P. Lyons, H.J. Doueck, and J.S. Wodarski, "Risk Assessment for Child Protective Services: A Review of the Empirical Literature on Instrument Performance," *Social Work Research* 20, no. 3 (1996): 143–152.

29. V.C. Copeland and S. Wexler, "Policy Implementation in Social Welfare: A Framework for Analysis," *Journal of Sociology and Social Welfare* 22, no. 3 (1995): 51–68.

30. S. Mason, "Social Work Research: Is There a Feminist Method?" *Journal of Women and Social Work* 12, no. 1, (1997): 10–32.

31. Rubin and Babbie, *Research Methods,* Chapter 4.

32. Ibid., Chapter 7.

33. Martin Bloom, Joel Fischer, and John G. Orme, *Evaluating Practice: Guidelines for the Accountable Professional,* 2nd ed. (Boston: Allyn and Bacon, 1995).

34. Rubin and Babbie, *Research Methods,* p. 59.

35. Paul Bates, "The Effectiveness of Interpersonal Skills Training on the Social Skill Acquisition of Moderately and Mildly Retarded Adults," *Journal of Applied Behavior Analysis* 13 (1978): 237–248.

36. James A. Hall, David Schlesinger, and John Dineen, "Social Skills Training in a Group with Developmentally Disabled Adults," *Research on Social Work Practice* 7, no. 2 (1997): 187–201.

37. James A. Hall, Christopher Carswell, Mary S. Vaughan, James E. Rohrer, Robert I. Block, and Thomas Vaughn, Iowa Case Management Project for Rural Drug Abuse—Preliminary Results. Paper presented at Social Work's Contribution to NIH Research, conference sponsored by NIH and the Institute for the Advancement of Social Work Research (IASWR), Bethesda, MD; September 5, 1996.

38. James A. Hall, Miriam Landsman, and Brad Richardson, *Day Treatment for Drug Abuse with Juvenile Offenders.* Unpublished manuscript, University of Iowa, 1996.

Additional Suggested Readings

Blythe, Betty, Tony Tripodi, and Scott Briar. *Direct Practice Research in Human Service Agencies*. New York: Columbia University Press, 1995.

Brower, Aaron M., and Sheldon D. Rose. *Advances in Group Work Research*. Binghamton, NY: Haworth Press, Inc., 1990.

Craft, John L. *Statistics and Data Analysis for Social Workers*. 2nd ed. Itasca, IL: F.E. Peacock Publishers, 1989.

Ginsberg, Leon. *Social Work Almanac*. 2nd ed. Silver Spring, MD: National Association of Social Workers, 1995.

Grinnell, Richard M. *Social Work Research and Evaluation: Quantitative and Qualitative Approaches*. 5th ed. Itasca, IL: F.E. Peacock Publishers, 1997.

Mark, Raymond. *Research Made Simple: A Handbook for Social Workers*. Thousand Oaks, CA: Sage Publications, Inc., 1996.

Pecora, Peter J., Mark W. Fraser, Kristine E. Nelson, Jacquelyn McCroskey, and William Meezan. *Evaluating Family-Based Services*. New York: Aldine de Gruyter, 1995.

Rothman, Jack. *Guidelines for Case Management: Putting Research to Professional Use*. Itasca, IL: F.E. Peacock Publishers, Inc., 1992.

Royse, David, and Bruce Thyer. *Program Evaluation: An Introduction*. 2nd ed. Chicago: Nelson-Hall Publishers, 1997.

Sherman, Edmund, and William J. Reid. *Qualitative Research in Social Work*. New York: Columbia University Press, 1994.

Tripodi, Tony. *A Primer on Single-Subject Design for Clinical Social Workers*. Silver Spring, MD: National Association of Social Workers, 1994.

Part 4

Special Groups, Issues, and Trends

We approach the final section of this book having come a considerable distance. We have covered background information, the major social service settings and the social problems to which they relate as well as some nontraditional settings, and the principal social work practice methods, including some innovative approaches.

In the remaining section, we will take up a few special considerations and trends such as human diversity; oppression and empowerment; women's, men's, and gender issues; and housing, a basic human need but not a large area of employment for social workers until now.

We will examine a special newer focus in the human services termed *social development* that has particular significance internationally. We will also discuss the educational preparation of social service personnel and their organization and professionalization in the field. Finally, we will conclude with a chapter on the future that projects beyond the reach of most such commentary and leads us to look ahead, just as early in the text we looked back historically.

22

Human Diversity and Empowerment

N. YOLANDA BURWELL

I have a deep seated bias against hate and intolerance. I have a bias against racial and religious bigotry. I have a bias against war, a bias for peace. I have a bias which leads me to believe no problem of human relations is ever insoluble.

—Ralph Bunch[1]

Achieving social justice, equity, and dignity for people who are systematically denied these attributes by systems of service and helping agents is an important social work objective. Social justice refers to an assurance of equal access and equal quality of services to consumers.[2] Discriminatory practices and attitudes must not be tolerated. Equity means fairness: Provision of balanced access to and distribution of resources and services is equity. When groups receive their proportional share of goods and benefits, equity is realized. Everyone has the right to be treated with respect. Recognizing the intrinsic worth and viability that people and communities bring to any helping situation imparts dignity. The absence of these qualities breeds racism, sexism, homophobia, ageism, and discrimination against the disabled, poor, and uninformed—bad lessons taught in society.[3] The positive combination of these qualities heightens opportunities for diversity. Human potential thrives in tolerant environments. Social workers must play a critical role in ensuring the presence of these attributes in all types of social settings.

Too often social justice, equity, and dignity are withheld because of a trait of birth or circumstances. A person's race or gender or sexual orientation can disqualify him or her for full benefits, resources, goods, or services. Individuals are stigmatized because they have acquired immune deficiency syndrome (AIDS), or because they are homeless or uneducated. A person's religion or way of managing life can target him or her for overt acts of prejudice or exclusion from participation. Over time, people become increasingly disempowered because of the constancy of these acts where they work, live, play, or buy/use services. These cumulative acts of disempowerment are costly. They lead to poverty, homelessness, civil disobedience, unemployment and inadequate education, crime, disenchantment, and senseless deaths. Acts of intolerance put everyone at risk.

Social workers are primary empowering agents in ameliorating many of these problems. They are well positioned to promote diversity and tolerance in all types of human interactions. Through empowerment, social workers can maximize opportunities for justice, equity, and dignity for individuals, families, agencies, and communities. Empowerment enhances diversity and culturally sensitive social work practice.

DEFINING EMPOWERMENT

Helping stigmatized/victimized groups or individuals to increase and exercise interpersonal skills or community influence is empowerment.[4] Opening up resources and minimizing service barriers are also empowerment activities.[5] Social work practice, policy, and research must facilitate the removal of personal and institutional blocks to power. Social work policy statements,[6] curriculum standards,[7] and codes of ethics[8] support diversity and dignity. Therefore, advocacy and social action *for* human diversity are expected of social workers today.

Social work interventions for diversity and tolerance are greatly needed. Deep cultural divisions and etiquette systems, double standards, and policies mark groups for discrimination here and abroad. Hate violence acts were on the rise in America just as UN investigation teams found graves where mass killings occurred in Croatia.[9] As apartheid was slowly dismantled in South Africa, there was an awareness of a rise of militia and separatists' groups in the United States. Nationally, we were stunned on a psychological and social level by the World Trade Center and Oklahoma City bombings. As the first females successfully completed their first year at the Citadel in South Carolina, military officers were convicted of rape and sexual harassment charges at various military bases. Persons with AIDS face housing, employment, insurance, and educational discrimination.[10] Impoverished families are subjected to increased scrutiny under the new federal and state welfare reform initiatives.[11]

Businesses and schools grapple with issues of human interaction and diversity daily. Future trends point to more diversity in these settings. Employment projections forecast that more people of color and women will comprise the American workforce than any other groups by the year 2000.

> The demographics of the American workforce are changing rapidly. Of the 25 million people expected to join the workforce in the next dozen years, 85 percent will be minorities, immigrants, and women. Will today's youngsters be able to function effectively in a rich mixture of races, religions, languages, ethnicities and lifestyles? Sadly, the answer all too often is a resounding "No!"[12]

Empowerment and diversity are worthy goals for social work practitioners. Achieving social justice, equity, and dignity in all helping processes and delivery systems is an important agenda in modern society.

UNDERSTANDING DIVERSITY IN AMERICA

Diversity is a natural, inescapable characteristic of America's social and physical landscape. Culturally, each state and territory sees itself as unique. America boasts a variety of languages, dialects, and communication styles. Localities are proud of their distinctive art, foods, music, recreation, festivals, celebrations, and historic attractions—in a nation of numerous religions.

Regional and geographic distinctions emerge within states and across the country. Rural America is just as diverse in social and ethnic composition as metropolitan America. Migrations between rural and urban and suburban areas continually occur. Social work in rural areas offers unique perspectives on practice and service delivery.[13]

Demographically, America is populated by people with a variety of experiences.

> About 43 million people in the U.S. are disabled or 1/16 of the population, constituting the nation's largest minority. Eighty percent of Americans at some time will be personally involved with someone who has a disability or long term illness. One in three Americans can expect to experience a temporary or permanent disability sometime in her or his life.[14]

AIDS and HIV infection are additional phenomena Americans will encounter directly or indirectly. AIDS poses new challenges about intolerance. It does not discriminate. Individuals and families across all ages, socioeconomic, geographic, and racial lines are affected. "An estimated 650,000 to 900,000 persons in the United States are HIV-positive—approximately 1 in every 325 Americans."[15]

American is enriched by its ethnically and racially diverse native-born and immigrant population:

> Census Bureau preliminary reports show an increase in all populations of color. Out of a total of over 248 million people in the United States, almost 30 million are African American, representing 23 percent of the total population and an increase of 64.6 percent over the 1980 census. Native American, Eskimos and Aleuts share .08 percent of the population, almost two million people, representing an increase of 33.7 percent from the last census; Asians and Pacific Islanders, about 2.9 percent of the total at over seven million strong, show an increase of 144.9 percent over the 1980 count; Latinos represent 8.9 percent of the population with over 22 million people, an increase of 87.3 percent over the 1980 census.[16]

Immigrants arrive daily in the United States. Their sheer numbers are changing educational, political, cultural, and social welfare arenas. In the 1980s, the United States admitted about 8.5 million people; predictions are higher for the 1990s. In 1989, the top ten source countries for legal and amnestied admissions were Mexico, El Salvador, Philippines, Vietnam, Korea, China, India, the Dominican Republic, Jamaica, and Iran.[17] Immigrants from Asia, Latin America, and the Caribbean accounted for about 40 percent of new entrants during the past decade.[18]

Immigration has also had a significant geographical impact. About three-fourths of all legal immigrants in 1991 ended up in six states—California, Texas, Florida, New York, Illinois and New Jersey. These states have been leaders in receiving immigrants since 1971, with California leading the pack every year since 1976.[19]

Sexual orientation is another variation. Conservative figures vary from 4 million to 20 million gays and lesbians in the United States. This impreciseness points to the abivalence, silence, and fear many have about openly ackowledging their sexual orientations. Many gays and lesbians experience harsh reprisals from jobs, relatives, religious groups, military establishments, and educational systems when they come out.

Some gains have been realized for this population group.

By 1993, 24 states had decriminalized homosexual acts between consenting adults, several municipalities had passed some type of nondiscrimination law tht included homosexuals, and some major companies and universities had provided benefits to the partners of lesbian and gay employees. On April 23, 1993, supporters of lesbian and gay rights—estimated at more than 1 million—marched on Washington, D.C.[20]

Unfortunately, the irrational fear of same-sex relationships continues to produce atmospheres of humiliation, retaliation, and intolerance. Gays and lesbians are denied the same rights as heterosexuals in mariage, child custody and adoption matters, insurance and inheritance benefits, and employment and educational opportunities. Media portrayals are stereotypical or sensationalized. Gays and lesbians are the frequent targets of hate crimes and harassment.

Modern technology offers increased opportunities for diversity. America is a young and growing nation of diverse regions, cultures, and traditions as it actively competes in a rapidly changing global economy. The "world" is shrinking in this technological and information age. Telecommunications systems and satellite capabilities allow us to view world events as they occur. Our understanding and awareness of other lands, cultures, and problems are transformed. International travel exposes us directly to cultures that were once distant and remote. The opportunities to learn and reach out to other people are greater than ever before.[21]

Diversity is an American quality. Differences in heritage, socialization, cultures, viewpoints, and preferences are inevitable. Yet, America has had an ambivalent and contradictory history in handling its diversity.

CHALLENGES TO DIVERSITY: DISEMPOWERMENT AGENDAS

America's ambivalence to human diversity has been greater than its acceptance. America welcomed immigrants from other lands while divesting descendants of her original inhabitants. Early "newcomers" came to the colonies escaping poverty, persecution, and oppressive conditions—only to enslave African and Caribbean people and their descendants. Equality and opportunity have not been afforded to all equally, despite the Constitution. In fact, individual rights have been awarded in a piecemeal fashion. Women gained the right to vote in

1920. Native Americans gained citizenship rights in 1924, and the Voting Rights Act of 1964 guaranteed voting privileges to African-Americans.

Modern discriminatory patterns and actions against various groups are residuals of history; today's treatments echo past responses to other unfavored groups. Blocks to power became institutionalized against populations deemed "unfit," dangerous, or inferior. Historically, four official agendas and treatments have been used against unwanted or "different" groups. These agendas were extermination, expulsion, exclusion, and assimilation.[22] Systematically, legal, scientific, and religious bodies justified these agendas as "helping" or as the best solution to a thorny problem. However, these four agendas block empowerment.

Extermination

The destruction of undesirable populations has been a pattern in America and around the world. Whether called mass murder, genocide, or the final solution, methods and implementation of extermination have occurred through disease, slavery, and warfare. The infamous Salem, Massachusetts, witch trials and murders were used against odd or defiant people; Native American tribes experienced a decimation of their cultures and populations; and the slaughter of over 6 million Jews during the Holocaust is an example from this century.[23]

Expulsion

Removing populations is another approach. The Removal Act of 1830 called for the relocation of all Eastern Native American tribes to the west of the Mississippi River. Of the 16,000 Cherokee who moved west in 1838, 4,000 died. Half of the Creek nation died during the migration and their first years in the West. Over 70,000 Native Americans were relocated by 1840. Known as the Trail of Tears, this forced migration cost untold lives and created a disintegration of cultural heritage.[24]

Over 110,000 Japanese-Americans were involuntarily interned to relocation centers by Presidential Executive Order in the early 1940s, after the Pearl Harbor attack. No trials were held, no charges were made.[25]

At one time, women educators were dismissed from teaching positions once they married. Only single women were permitted to teach school. Today, gay and lesbian military personnel are honorably discharged if their sexual orientations are known.

Exclusion and Segregation

This government policy takes many forms, but the results are the same. Separation is the goal, not equality. Native Americans were assigned to reservations, and other groups were affected by this policy. "Conquest, segregation, a distinct language and culture, and to some extent, skin color, kept Mexican-Americans from full participation in the American experience."[26]

Jim Crow laws, disenfranchisement, and unchecked activities of the Ku Klux Klan quickly nullified any positive effects people of color might have envisioned after the Civil War and during Reconstruction. These state laws and court decisions restricted movement and participation in public affairs. Racial segregation was enforced in social service systems, cemeteries, public accommodations, schools, and the courts.[27]

Historically, women were assigned their "place" socially, economically, and politically. Gaining the right to vote in 1920 did not improve their life chances. Until recently, women were excluded from employment opportunities, sports, politics, and military advancements because of their gender.

The disabled were institutionalized or placed in special schools under exclusionary policy. A residual of this philosophy was a belief that little could be done for this population.[28] Disability carried such a societal stigma that President Roosevelt took great pains to present himself as able-bodied to the American people.[29]

This policy continues today. Residuals are seen in recruitment and employment patterns, housing, and educational systems. The omission of women, homosexuals, persons with disabilities, and people of color in history books, science, and intellectual life articulates blatant practices of exclusionary intent. A subtle form of this policy is found repeatedly in public waiting rooms, where magazines and printed materials seldom mirror the wide diversity of consumers using these facilities.

Assimilation

The "melting pot" metaphor comes to mind with this policy agenda. One's cultural integrity and distinctiveness are suppressed or relinquished in favor of the dominant culture. Consensus and conformity to the dominant culture is the goal. It was thought that the dominant culture was better in every respect than one's culture of origin. Americanization involved becoming like "them" and being less like "us," and assimilation involved more than learning English. Removing accents or other traces of differences to "make it" in America has embodied assimilation.[30]

Civilizing the less fortunate was sanctioned. Large boarding schools for Native American children who lived on reservations were established after the Civil War. Children between the ages of three and thirteen were separated from their families and tribes. It was illegal for Native American children to use their native language in federal boarding schools. Modern educational practices continue to be at cross-purposes with the goals of Native Americans for their children.[31]

Social work has an ambivalent history about diversity as well. Racial segregation was as much a part of social work's history as its activism for civil rights and suffrage. Early settlement house workers like Jane Addams used assimilation processes with newly arrived immigrants to urban centers. Similarly, early African-American settlement house workers and labor agents engaged in "uplift work" by teaching proper behaviors and good work habits to young men and women of color coming to the cities from the rural south.[32]

Until very recently, the American educational system and media have espoused this policy through myopic presentations of "American culture and history and people." Generations of school children learned "See Spot run" and a

Caucasian "Dick and Jane." The SAT exams are standardized from one experience, not various cultures. Policies of "We are all the same" contradict the wide diversity in this country.

SELF-DETERMINATION: CHALLENGES TO INTOLERANCE

Parallel developments in American social history deserve illumination because they provide instruction about empowerment and give a more balanced view. People did and do not simply submit to degradation. People stood up for themselves in the face of oppressive conditions. Protest and defiance are just as much a part of our country's social fabric as discrimination. Group self-determination was present during slavery, on and off reservations, and in city halls and county seats. Slave insurrections, sabotage, and escapes were prominent dimensions of the institution of slavery.[33] The 1973 Wounded Knee conflict was an extension of the protest Native American tribes consistently mounted against removal from their lands even before the 1890 tragedy.[34] The gains made by the disabled and the recent enactment of the Americans with Disability Act came about because of concerted social action activities by Americans with disabilities and allies of disability rights.[35]

Social workers have played pivotal roles in many of these protest movements. Historically, social workers were strong catalysts for environmental change in local, state, and national arenas. They organized, lobbied, marched and petitioned against poor workplace conditions, child labor and welfare, sexual and reproductive abuses to women, and lynching. Like other reformers, Jane Addams was a prolific woman, active on many fronts besides settlement house work. Her protests for peace as the country went to war deserve equal illumination.

The work of Lawrence Oxley, while Director of the Division of Work Among Negroes with the North Carolina State Board of Charities and Public Welfare in the 1920s, gives testimony to self-help and activism among African-Americans. An African-American trained in community organization, Oxley was instrumental in successfully organizing citizens on a local level to raise monies for the salaries of some of the first African-American social workers in county after county in the state.[36] This is not an isolated example of self-help, philanthropy, or community development; these activities were duplicated in numerous ways across the country by people fighting intolerance and discouragement.

The modern Civil Rights movement has stimulated sweeping social changes for the disabled, women, elderly, and gays and lesbians, as well as people of color. Activism by grassroots and advocacy groups, like Mothers Against Drunk Driving, have transformed policies and practices nationwide regarding alcoholism, driving, and crime. The environmental movement and peace movement are viable in America.

There is worry within the profession that social work is losing sight of its history and need for community organization and environmental change because this focus gets less notice in social work curricula, professional meetings, and employment opportunities.[37] Yet the need for talent, skills, and courage in these arenas has never been greater.

EMPOWERMENT AND SOCIAL WORK PRACTICE

> "Give a person a fish, they eat for a day. Teach a person to fish, they eat for a lifetime."

Since Barbara Solomon's groundbreaking work on the topic in the early 1980s, empowerment has become a social work objective in helping all persons or communities in need. Empowermats is not given or enforced. It is allowed to happen. Empowerment occurs when people feel a mastery and competency in managing their many social environments. Removing subtle and blatant blockages to power is a critical step.

Blocks to empowerment are numerous. Blocks can occur in the form of policies, attitudes, perceptions, and incompetence. The following discussion identifies five common environmental blocks to empowerment in social work practice and four enhancers to empowerment. Blocks to empowerment impede social justice, equity, and dignity for clients and communities alike. This is not an exhaustive discussion, but it is intended to stimulate new thinking about barriers to social work practice and service delivery with diverse populations.

The enhancers to empowerment borrow from new and emerging perspectives as well as from standards in practice that are often overlooked or taken for granted. The enhancers support social justice, equity, and dignity in helping relationships.

Blocks to Empowerment

1. Missing the consumer's view of service.   All the procedures, structures, and service continuums are in place. The doors of the agency are ready to open. Providers of service know what they have to do. Interventions have been designed with a full understanding of "the problem." Everything is set, except that the consumer's view is missing. Priorities on getting the job done ignore "service" to consumers.

> When non–English speaking people attempt to locate services, they often end their search in anger and frustration. From the client's point of view, concrete difficulties interfere with their gaining access to service from agencies: arbitrary denial of services; institutional inflexibility; red tape with long delays and silences; undignified or callous treatment; complex forms and procedures of eligibility; long waiting lists; inaccessibility by telephone or in person; runaround from agency to agency; lack of simple clear directions and explanations…. This list of problems is multiplied many times when the person who needs help cannot speak English.[38]

For the disabled or illiterate or a first-time consumer, these problems multiply. Agencies are work habitats for providers of service. They can be intimidating, complex, and depersonalizing experiences for consumers.

2. Dominance thinking.   Dominance thinking cuts off other views, cultural ideas, and experiences, as explained in the works of Anne Wilson Schaef and Robert Terry.[39] Dominance thinking and operation are pervasive in social re-

© Joel Gordon

Elderly and disabled demonstrators attempt to influence Medicare and Medicaid policy.

lationships and service delivery systems. Someone has power and control over another. It explains and justifies all forms of discrimination and drives assimilation. Tenets of this approach include superiority and singleness of ideas. There is only one way of doing things or understanding experiences, and that way is superior to all others. Holders of "the way" know everything there is to know about everything, and they are rational, logical, and objective to others. Beliefs or groups that exist outside of the "norm" are defined as inferior, deficient, and/or dangerous. Obedience and submission are expected outcomes of dominance.

Preoccupation with the idealistic nuclear family is a good example of this thinking. The perception is that nuclear families can do no harm or wrong. Everyone should aspire to the traditional family values embodied in this family type. Other family forms, which are increasingly numerous in America, are considered inappropriate or problematic.

3. *Marginalizing or homogenizing groups.* An artifact of dominance thinking and operation is marginalizing groups. The token "representative" is invited to speak to issues only around his or her trait. The total person or the full range of a group's experiences are ignored. Marginalizing occurs when the presence of difference is restricted to one at a time—one person of color, or one female, or one course on diversity, or one event during Disability Awareness Week. Full diversity is kept to a minimum. When the largest of goods and resources is systematically denied to a neighborhood or school, a marginal identity results.

Homogenizing refers to lumping all people together as one. Terms like *homeless* or *Asian-American* fail to describe these groups accurately.[40] The rich heterogeneity within these populations is lost. Providing accurate and balanced descriptions of people and their communities counters this trend.

4. Privilege.   Peggy McIntosh's writings expose privilege as a block to empowerment.[41] Privilege is described as unearned advantages that various groups enjoy over another because of the color of their skin or gender. Automatic benefits accrue to preferred groups. Others cannot advance because benefits are automatically withheld from them.

Modern physical environments are designed for literate people and, increasingly, for computer-literate people. Many buildings and public accommodations were originally designed for only able-bodied people. Driving an automobile gives individuals many privileges over those who do not or cannot drive. The privileged are sheltered from seeing and experiencing numerous barriers in society that less-fortunate people experience constantly.

Staying alert to blocks of power becomes an important social work activity. Increasing the opportunities for equity, social justice, and dignity requires a constant focus on environmental influences. If these qualities are achieved, then helping relationships are enhanced as well.

Enhancers to Cross-Cultural Practice

> "A prized aspect of human growth is becoming an open, authentic person. Open, authentic behavior by social workers fosters like behavior in clients."[42]

Social work literature is replete with content on working with other cultures. Diversity is an important topic within the profession. Effective cross-cultural practice requires an awareness of openness and authenticity on the part of consumers and workers. Support of dignity and worth entails attention to the "lived experience," priority to consumer rights, a respect for multiculturalism, and tapping into energies for change. Cultural sensitivity is an ongoing professional work.

1. Lived experiences.   McBride and McBride write about the paradigm of the lived experience.[43] Borrowed from feminist writings and theory, the lived experience acknowledges that "the personal *is* political." The personal story is more meaningful than the sociology of the problem. Listening and validating how a person describes his or her experience empowers. Individuals—not providers—are the experts on their own experiences. For many, patriarchy, racism, homophobia, sexism, and other types of discrimination are integral conditions in their lives. The ways and means by which individuals manage or resist constant acts of disempowerment and the consequences deserve visibility and attentive ears.

2. Consumer and personal rights

> *You have the right to be treated with respect.*
>
> *You have the right to set your own priorities.*
>
> *You have the right to ask for what you want.*

You have the right to get what you pay for.

You have the right to say "no" without feeling guilty.

Encouraging ownership and the assertion of personal rights helps the empowerment process. When personal rights are exercised, self-determination and personal worth rise. People are then able to act in their own self-interest and self-protection. Helping people regain personal rights is empowerment.

We live in a rights-conscious society. The past decade has seen a rewriting of this entire area of service delivery: Knowledge and information are power. Consumers have numerous rights and should be informed of them.[44] Providers must be vigilant that agencies and other systems do not usurp these rights. Providers of service also have rights and protections. Personnel manuals and agency policies need constant review to ensure those rights.

3. Multiculturalism.   For purposes of this discussion, multiculturalism refers to possessing an openness to diversity and translating that to practice behaviors with consumers seeking services. Openness to diversity involves seeking answers through new avenues of learning. For example, shifting stigmatized groups to the "center" of political, economic, and educational agendas is one aspect of multiculturalism. Multiculturalism amplifies diversity rather than suppresses it. This defies dominance systems thinking and operation.

Multiculturalism recognizes that stigmatized or disempowered groups come with their own definitive and authentic cultural resources to manage their daily lives. Indigenous helping networks are potent resources in times of need for many populations.

Multiculturalism requires learning what you don't know and unlearning what you thought you knew. It means being open to others' ways of being, thinking, and reacting to circumstances. Become an avid consumer of literature and information on various groups. All groups speak "for themselves" through their *own* newspapers, journal articles, and other publications. Effective social work practice with culturally diverse persons means having a familiarity and knowledge of mainstream *and* indigenous resources. The inclusion of bilingual services and options must became a natural component of service delivery.

4. Tap into energies for change.   Social workers are fate-makers and catalysts in all types of human dramas as they unfold. They quicken processes of change that were waiting to happen. Therefore, their task becomes one of stirring up a sense of discovery, creativity, and wonderment in others and self. It helps to stay fascinated by the human spirit; dreams and hopes are natural to human experiences. Social workers begin where the person is and believe that people desire better for themselves. Empowerment is supported by a belief in human potential for change.

SUMMARY AND CONCLUSIONS

Rather than focusing exclusively on the oppression and victimization of people, this chapter directed attention to the need to achieve equity, social justice, and dignity in helping systems and helping processes. A tolerance for diversity and well-being is urgently needed in society. Social workers are engaged in the work of empowerment and social change in all sectors of society. They are well positioned to advocate for the presence of social justice in agency practices, policies, and operations. They can give voice to fair and balanced distribution of goods and services in community affairs. They can ensure that people recieve respect and decency—regardless of race, ethnicity, religion, gender, sexual orientation, or class.

This chapter outlined America's rich human diversity as well as "bad lessons taught in society," whereby social justice, equity, and decency are withheld because someone is different. Advocacy and social action for human diversity remain critically germane to social workers.

Social workers are well positioned to advance empowerment and social justice as agendas in agency practices, policies, and operations, and the heritage of social work supports these objectives. Social workers must become visible advocates for dignity, social justice, and equity to ensure a decent quality of life and well-being for all. To do less puts all of us in jeopardy.

Notes

1. Taken from *I Have a Dream: A Collection of Black Americans on Postage Stamps* (Washington, DC: U.S. Postage Service, 1991), p. 58.
2. Dean H. Hepworth and Jo Ann Larsen, *Direct Social Work Practice: Theory and Skills* (Pacific Grove, CA: Brooks/Cole Publishing Company, 1993), p. 6.
3. "Hatred, intolerance, bigotry, chauvinism are never innate—they are bad lessons taught in society," from speech given by Ralph Bunch. See Ben Rivlin, *Ralph Bunch* (New York: Holmes and Meier, 1990), p. 236.
4. Barbara Solomon, *Black Empowerment* (New York: Columbia University Press, 1976), p. 6; Elaine B. Pinderhughes, "Empowerment for Our Clients and for Ourselves," *Social Casework* 64, no. 6 (June 1983): 331–338.
5. Hepworth and Larsen, *Direct Social Work Practice*, pp. 495–500.
6. National Association of Social Workers. *NASW Speaks* (Washington, DC: National Association of Social Workers, 1991).
7. Council on Social Work Education, Commission on Accreditation. *Handbook for Accreditation Standards and Procedures* (New York: Council on Social Work Education, 1984).
8. Since the late 1960s many professional social work organizations have evolved with their own codes of ethics. Besides the National Association of Social Workers, these include the National Association of Black Social Workers and the Association of American Indian and Alaskan Native Social Workers.
9. "Klan Watch Reports Hate Violence at Record Levels Last Year," *Southern Poverty Law Center Report Newsletter* 23 (April 1993), p. 1.
10. New York City Commission on Human Rights' Law Enforcement Bureau, *Report on Discrimination Against People with AIDS and People Perceived to Have AIDS January 1986–June 1987* (New York: Commission on Human Rights, 1987).
11. Mimi Abramovitz, *Regulating the Lives of Women* (Boston: South End Press, 1988).
12. "The New Ethnoviolence Haunts New Generation," *Forum* 6, no. 1 (March 1992) p. 1; See John Naisbitt and Patricia Aburdene, *Megatrends 2000—Ten New Directions for the 1990s* (New York: William Morrow and Company, Inc., 1990), pp. 118–153; 216–240.

13. National Association of Social Workers, "Social Work in Rural Areas," in *NASW Speaks* (1994) pp. 160–171; see Creigs Beverly, Carole Hartman, and Carole Wheeler, "Social Work Practice in Urban Communities: An Independent Study," *Black Caucus* (Spring 1993), pp. 30–39.

14. John Molnar, "Disabled Travelers Break Emotional, Physical Barriers," *The Daily Reflector*, Greenville, North Carolina, 10 January 1993, p. G7.

15. The North Carolina AIDS Advisory Council, *The NC AIDS Index*, 1997, p. 3.

16. Felix G. Rivera and John Erlich, "A Time for Fear, A Time for Hope," in Felix G. Rivera and John Erlich, eds., *Community Organizing in a Diverse Society* (Boston: Allyn and Bacon, 1995), p. 2; Rafael Valdivieso and Cary Davis, *U.S. Hispanics: Challenging Issues for 1990s* (Washington, DC: Population Reference Bureau, 1988).

17. Peter Schuck, "Welcoming Immigrants Will Enhance Our Future," *The Daily Reflector*, 5 May 1991, p. E5.

18. Kyung-Hee Nah, "Perceived Problems and Service Delivery for Korean Immigrants," *Social Work* 38, no. 3 (May 1993), p. 289.

19. Pete Carey and Steve Johnson, "Immigration System Patchwork of Pork-Barrel Deals and Abuse," *The Daily Reflector*, June 27, 1993, p. E1.

20. Carol Thorpe Tully, "Lesbians Overview," in *Encyclopedia of Social Work*, 19th ed. (Washington, DC: NASW Press, 1990), pp. 1591–1596; Victoria Brownworth, "Not Invisible to Attack," in *Experiencing Race, Class and Gender in the United States*, Virginia Cyrus, ed. (Mountain View, CA: Mayfield Publishing Co., 1993), pp. 323–326.

21. Naisbitt and Aburdene, *Megatrends 2000*, pp. 118–153.

22. Brewton Berry, *Race and Ethnic Relations* (Boston: Houghton Mifflin, 1958), pp. 181–299.

23. Gerhard Weinberg, "The 'Final Solution' and the War in 1943," in *Fifty Years Ago: Revolt Amid the Darkness* (Washington, DC: U.S. Holocaust Memorial Museum, 1993), pp. 1–15.

24. Phyllis Day, *A New History of Social Welfare* (Englewood Cliffs, N.J.: Prentice-Hall, 1989), p. 181; Theda Perdue, *Native Carolinians: The Indians of North Carolina* (Raleigh, NC: North Carolina Department of Cultural Resources, 1985), p. 40.

25. Ibid., pp. 291–292; Diana DiNitto, *Social Welfare Politics and Public Policy* (Englewood Cliffs, NJ: Prentice Hall, 1995), p. 259; Harry Kitano and Roger Daniels, *Asian Americans: Emerging Minorities* (Englewood Cliffs, NJ: Prentice-Hall, 1988), pp. 61–62.

26. Miguel Montiel and Felipe Ortego Y Gasca, "Chicanos, Community, and Change," in *Community Organizing in a Diverse Society*, Rivera and Erlich, eds.

27. Kitano and Daniels, *Asian Americans: Emerging Minorities*, pp. 59–60; Paul Finkleman, "Exploring Southern Legal History," *North Carolina Law Review* 65 (November 1985), pp. 77–116.

28. Evelyn P. Tomaszewski, *Disabilities Awareness Curriculum for Graduate Schools of Social Work* (Washington, DC: National Association of Social Workers, 1992), pp. 6–11.

29. Hugh Gregory Gallagher, "FDR: Handicapped American," *Public Welfare* (Summer 1984), pp. 19–25.

30. Michael Novak, "Neither WASP nor Jew nor Black," in Cyrus, ed., *Experiencing Race, Class and Gender in the United States*.

31. See Shirley Hill Witt, "Pressure Points in Growing Up Indian," *Perspective* (Spring 1980), pp. 24–31.

32. See Susan Chandler, "Industrial Social Work: African American Origins," paper presented at APM Council on Social Work Education, February 1993 in New York; Beverly Jones, "Mary Church Terrell and the National Association of Colored Women, 1896 to 1901," *Journal of Negro History* (Spring 1982), pp. 20–33.

33. See Adele Logan Alexander, *Ambiguous Lives: Free Women of Color in Rural Georgia, 1789–1879* (Fayetteville, AR: The University of Arkansas Press, 1991).

34. Day, p. 358; Perdue, p. 40; Scott Derks, "We Can't Turn Back," *Southern Exposure* 13, no. 6 (November/December 1985), pp. 67–71.

35. See DiNitto, *Social Welfare Politics*, pp. 149–152.

36. N. Yolanda Burwell, "Shifting the Historical Lens: African American Philanthropy," *Journal of Baccalaureate Social Work* (October 1995), pp. 25–37.

37. Rivera and Erlich, "A Time for Fear," pp. 3–4.

38. J. Donald Cameron and Esther Talavera, "An Advocacy Program for Hispanic Speaking People," *Social Casework* 57, no. 7 (July 1976), p. 427.

39. Ann Wilson Schaef, *Women's Reality: An Emerging Female System in a White Male Society* (San Francisco: Harper and Row, 1985), pp. 1–20; Robert Terry, "The White Male Club," *Civil Rights Digest* (Spring 1974), pp. 66–77.

40. Carel Germaine, *Human Behavior in the Social Environment: An Ecological View* (New York: Columbia University Press, 1991), pp. 83–91.

41. Peggy McIntosh, *White Privilege and Male Privilege: A Personal Account of Coming to See Correspondences through Work on Women's Studies*, Working Paper no. 189 (Wellesley, MA: Wellesley College, 1988).

42. Hepworth and Larsen, *Direct Social Work Practice*, p. 24.

43. Angela Barron McBride and William C. McBride, "Theoretical Underpinnings for Women's Health," *Women and Health* 6, nos. 1–2 (Spring/Summer 1981), pp. 37–55; Patrick Haney, "Providing Empowerment to the Person with AIDS," *Social Work* 33, no. 3 (May/June 1988), pp. 251–253.

44. Alexis A. Halley, Judy Kopp, and Michael Austin, *Delivering Human Services—A Learning Approach to Practice* (White Plains, NY: Longman, 1992), pp. 228–241.

Additional Suggested Readings

Carlton LaNey, Iris, and N. Yolanda Burwell. *African American Community Practice Models*. New York: Haworth Press, 1996).

Cowger, Charles D. "Assessing Client Strengths: Clinical Assessment for Client Empowerment," *Social Work* (May 1994): 262–68.

Dalton, Harlon, Scott Burris, and the Yale AIDS Law Project. *AIDS and the Law—A Guide for the Public*. New Haven: Yale University Press, 1987.

Devore, Wynetta, and Elfriede Schlesinger. *Ethnic-Sensitive Social Work Practice*. Boston: Allyn and Bacon, 1996.

Drachman, Diane. "Immigration Statuses and Their Influence on Service Provision." *Social Work* (March 1995), pp. 188–197.

Iglehart, Alfreda, and Rosina Becerra. *Social Services and the Ethnic Community*. Boston: Allyn and Bacon, 1995.

Ryan, Angela Shen. "Cultural Factors in Casework with Chinese-Americans." *Social Casework* (June 1985), pp. 333–340.

Shilts, Randy. *And the Band Played On*. New York: Penguin Books, 1987.

Song, Young I., and Eugene C. Kim. *American Mosaic*. Englewood Cliffs, NJ: Prentice-Hall, 1993.

Three Rivers, Amoja. *Cultural Etiquette: A Guide for the Well-Intended*. Distributed by Market Wimmin, Box 28, Indian Valley, Virginia 24105.

Weatherford, Jack. *Native Roots: How the Indians Enriched America*. New York: Crown Publishers, 1991.

Zinn, Howard. *A People's History of the United States*. New York: Harper and Row, 1980.

23

Tides and Tensions of the Women's and Men's Movements: Entering a New Millennium

B. ELEANOR ANSTEY

Swelling tides of concerns about women's and men's issues have rolled across the land since the nineteenth century. Each movement had its own characteristics and its own tensions. The tides were followed by low ebbs, but female and male issues were never washed out to sea, nor were they beached on land. A curious phenomenon is currently developing in women's and men's movements as this century draws to a close. What once were seen as gender issues in these movements have now become gender tensions.

Before describing the origins of the separate movements, a distinction must be made between gender and sex. *Gender* refers to the social definitions of female nd male.[1] Sociologists see gender as a product of culture, not biology. Social scientists use the word *sex* to refer to the biological status of being female or male. Gender ranks with race, religion, class, and ethnic background as one of the great divisions in a fractured society. The values, behavior, and life opportunities of people on one side of the division line are distinctly different from those people on the other side. To understand the significance of gender, the research of anthropologist Margaret Mead is enlightening. In her study of three primitive societies in New Guinea she noticed that, even though in every culture certain tasks, responsibilities, and privileges were assigned by gender, those assignments were not identical. In one, the military task of protecting the village was assigned to males, but in another both sexes had to go to war if the village was threatened. In still another tribe, food production by agriculture was assigned to women and the men who had to do hunting and gathering had much more free time. When the males were not away, they were home unemployed and were able, and indeed expected, to sit around conversing with each other.[2] An understanding of this research enables one to see that every culture does not have the same rigid expectations of definitions of women's and men's roles and work as in the United States. Many of the tensions in the United States between men and women have arisen over this assignment by society of tasks and responsibilities.

The women's and men's movements have changed the way we think about gender in this country. A survey of recent social work textbooks, journals, and even bookstores reveals a change in the treatment of both movements. For the most part, paragraphs instead of chapters are allotted to the topics. In bookstores previously having an entire section devoted to male studies, the books are diminished or absent, although there are still sections for female studies. Web sites on the Internet have increased information on culture and gender, and current literature is available about both male and female interest groups, as will be indicated later. However, both of these movements are radically changing, if indeed they are still alive. A splintering into interest groups has occurred, thus giving rise to gender tensions. This splintering is centered around perceived needs of women and men today in the United States. This chapter will address how this phenomenon has happened by looking at the historical origins and issues of both movements, and the current tensions for both females and males.

Sheila Tobias describes three waves or generations of the women's movement in the United States: (1) the postcolonial movement, culminating with women attaining the right to vote; (2) the rise of feminism in roughly 1960–1975; and (3) 1975–to the present.[3]

WOMEN'S STATUS IN THE POSTCOLONIAL ERA

In the 1830s and 1840s, before the first tidal wave of the organized women's rights movement, middle-class, educated, moral, Protestant women were aware of their own status in society. Each was aware in her personal life that a married woman did not have property rights, which meant:

- She could not own her own farm.
- She could not have her own bank account.
- She could not do business as an independent contractor.
- Even if she inherited property from her father or earned income if she worked outside the home, the income belonged to her husband.
- She and the children were the property of the man she married.
- The father had custody of the children.

A wife's marital status made her wholly dependent on her spouse.[4] This unequal status and power of women was simply the result of gender-assigned roles of the society which, until now, were not questioned.

Despite these handicaps, the nineteenth-century women's rights activists began their reform activities as participants in campaigns to enhance the rights of others. Alice Rossi details three social roots of the women's movement: temperance, antislavery, and social reform.[5] Temperance entailed a drive to criminalize the sale of alcohol. Antislavery attracted moralists from North and South who knew slavery first hand and could expose it in print and in meetings. Social reform found response among privileged women for the downtrodden, the mentally ill, and the immigrant.

Without power and influence, in seeking money and support for their causes due to lack of civil rights, these women's efforts were ineffective. Elizabeth Cady Stanton and Lucretia Mott, women activists struggling to be useful on behalf of other people's movements, traveled as United States delegates to the World Antislavery Conference held in 1840 in London, and were not allowed to sit with their delegation, speak to the assembly, or to vote on resolutions. In fact, they were asked to sit out of sight in the balcony. Lack of status, respect, and power drove women toward the position that abolitionist Angelina Grimké expressed in 1838, when she said that she could not make the contributions she was capable of making toward the emancipation of the Negro slave until and unless she achieved her own emancipation.[6] Grimké's statement was interpreted as selfish and abandoning abolition; however, until she had civil rights she was powerless to help others.

When Stanton and Mott organized the first women's rights meeting in a Methodist church at Seneca Falls, New York, on July 19 and 20, 1848, the highlight of the convention was Stanton's proclamation of a "Declaration of Sentiments." Using the Declaration of Independence as a model, she addressed the grievances of women and proclaimed 18 rights, including:

> in the universities, in the trades and professions; the right to vote, to share in all political offices, honors…equality in marriage, to personal freedom, property, wages, children; to make contracts; to sue, and be sued; and to testify in the courts of justice.[7]

One consequence of the women's rights meeting was the movement of women from the singular role of homemaker to participant in cultural, educational, and political activities. Despite conflicts and divisions regarding the way to achieve the rights of women, thousands made contributions toward the achievement of their rights. Sojourner Truth, a freed slave and one of the most prominent African-Americans in this period, gave her famous "Ain't I a Woman" speech at the Akron Convention in 1853. Women thought that if they could get the right to vote they would be able to bring about the reforms for which they were fighting.

For 20 years there had been close political and personal relationships between the abolitionist and the suffrage movement. After the Civil War, pressure was strong within Republican ranks to ensure national strength for the party by granting the vote to the Southern Negro. Republican men feared that support for the vote for women would jeopardize the chances of securing the vote for the Negro, whose votes were needed to strengthen Republican representation in the Congress.[8] This defeat for women not only took its toll on morale but caused a splintering among the women themselves in how to reach their goals. The result was that they dropped their efforts for any rights except suffrage. The single most impressive fact about the attempt by American women to obtain the right to vote is how long it took. From its earliest beginnings in the public speaking of Fanny Wright in the 1820s and the Grimké sisters in the 1830s through the complex history of equal rights and suffrage associations, it was indeed a "century of struggle"[9] before women could first participate in a national election. Of the first-generation pioneers, only Antoinette Brown Blackwell lived to cast her ballot in that first election in 1920.[10] Seventy-two years after the Seneca Falls meeting, men had finally given women the right to vote. And who had given this right to men? Clearly it is a case of societal gender assignment of roles, but a privilege begrudgingly relinquished to women.

After suffragist feminism came to an end, enthusiasm ebbed, and there is no question that a younger generation chose not to join the 2 million older women who had struggled valiantly and successfully to win the vote. However, feminist scholars have unearthed new findings to contradict the perception that nothing happened for the next 40 years of women's history.

MEN'S STATUS IN THE POSTCOLONIAL ERA

To describe the status of men in the colonial and postcolonial period is to describe not a tide, but the whole ocean. Rotundo, in his history of American manhood in the colonial period until present day, describes how men dominated every aspect of life such as:

- Men were employed to support the family.
- Men served in the military.
- Men were the employers.
- Men had the right to vote and to enact the laws for the country.
- Men were the religious leaders.
- Men owned the property and the businesses.
- Men were the physicians and attorneys.

Rotundo sees this dominance arising from three different phases of manhood, each of which included its own languages and expectations of men: communal manhood, self-made manhood, and passionate manhood.[11]

Communal Manhood

Communal manhood developed in the social world of colonial New England. A man's identity was not separated from the duties he owed to his community. Rotundo tells us that men fulfilled themselves through public usefulness more than by economic success. The social status of the family to which a man was born gave him his place in the community more than those things he personally achieved. This social role as head of the family expressed his value to the community and gave his wife and children their social identity. Manhood was closely entwined with the needs and expectations of his neighbors. His creditors were neighbors, and his relatives were clients, so his failure in work would never be a private concern. Likewise a man's failures in his family were of concern to the community. Any deviant actions of his children were charged directly to the father who had brought them into the community.

People understood manhood not only in terms of the social setting but also in contrast with womanhood. The fundamental belief about men and women before 1800 was that men were superior. In particular, men were seen as the more virtuous sex. They were credited with greater reason, which enabled them to moderate passions like ambition, defiance, and envy more effectively than could women. This belief in male superiority provided a foundation for other forms of inequality before the law and in the household.[12]

Self-Made Man

Many social factors accounted for the new manhood at the end of the eighteenth century: the birth of republican government, the spread of a market economy, and the concomitant growth of the middle class itself. Free play of individual interests was at the root of the changes in economic and political life. In this era, a man took his identity and his social status from his own achievements, not from the circumstances of his birth. A man's work role, not his place at the head of the household, formed the essence of his identity.[13] Men's passions were now given freer rein. Ambition, rivalry, and aggression drove the new system of individual interests, and a man defined his manhood not by his ability to channel his passions, but rather by his ability to moderate them. Reason was still seen as a male trait, but in addition he was expected to be jealous of his autonomy and free from reliance on external authority. "In this world where a man was supposed to prove his superiority, the urge for dominance was seen as a virtue. These male passions provided the driving force in the lives of nineteenth century men."[14]

Passionate Manhood

The most dramatic change for men in the late nineteenth century was the positive value put on male passions. Ambition and combativeness became virtues for men. Toughness was admired and tenderness was scorned. The male body became a vital part of manhood: strength, appearance, sexual desire, and athletic skill were legitimate concerns for men. "Where 19th century had regarded the self and its passions suspiciously…20th century opinion exalted them.… A man defined his identity not just in the workplace but through modes of enjoyment and self-fulfillment outside of it."[15]

Nineteenth-century men and their concepts of manhood shaped many of our current institutions. Modern legal education is based on the nineteenth-century case method; many customs of the United States Congress, particularly male domination, only elaborated masculine culture of the 1800s; the medical profession swept women to the margins of health care. With this new set of institutions and ideals came the growing emphasis on "male" reason and authority in the practice of medicine and a diminishing focus on "female" nurture. Since men have held predominance of power over the last two centuries, a study of recent gender tensions must be placed in this historical context.

Men have often acted thoughtlessly, sometimes viciously, and nearly always for their own advantage, in dealing with women *as a sex*, but this simple picture does not do justice to the varieties of male behavior or the complexities of inner motive. Consequently few men recognize themselves in such a generic portrait. Because of this pervasive male dominance in social institutions and personal lives, there did not seem to be the same reflectiveness on gender issues as there was for women in the next period under study.

THE SECOND WAVE OF THE WOMEN'S MOVEMENT, 1960–1975

The resurgence of activity in the 1960s ushered in the second tidal wave of the women's movement, from the 1960s to about 1975.

To understand why women united in sisterhood for a second time, the following were conditions for women before 1965—not even 40 years ago.

- Married women could not establish credit in their own names, which meant no credit cards or mortgages or other financial transactions were possible without a husband's agreement.
- Rape charges required a corroborating witness to be convincing in court—a woman's word alone was not good enough. A woman's past sexual history was allowed as testimony, usually to prove that she was "promiscuous" and had been "asking for it." A husband who raped his wife was not a rapist.
- Newspapers carried sex-segregated help-wanted ads. Employers routinely assigned certain jobs to women, others to men, with the women's jobs paying far less.
- There were few women in law or medical school, a fact visibly prominent in those professions.
- Women were addressed as "Miss" or "Mrs." even in irrelevant situations like booking airline seats, where there were obviously not special sections for married or unmarried women.
- Abortion was illegal. Sterilization without a woman's consent was common. Birth control was not much discussed in public discourse, and dispensing contraceptive information, even to married couples, was against the law in some states.
- "He" and "man" were considered universal words, applying to all humankind.
- Under most state laws, women were routinely not allowed to be administrators of estates.
- Most schools and colleges had few, if any, organized competitive sports for women. Male teams always had priority in terms of athletic scholarships, budgets, equipment, and playing time. Marathon running was considered too strenuous for women, who were barred from such competitions even in the Olympics.
- Working women who became pregnant could be fired.
- The marriage contract was understood to be that men supported women financially and women provided domestic and sexual service to their husbands.
- An employer who insisted that in order to keep her job, a female employee have sex with him or submit to fondling was not breaking the law.
- No woman anchored the news on television. Most women reporters wrote for the women's pages of newspapers. All women in media were paid less than men, except for those who owned the company.
- There was a 2-percent cap on enlisted women in the military, and no women at the rank of general or admiral.[16]

The second generation of the women's movement was characterized by legislative, economic, military, and social action. As Tobias notes, "In the heady first dozen years of the revival of feminism in America, differences between women—by class, by race, by position in or out of the labor force, by age, by marital status, even by political affiliation—seemed less significant than a shared sense of previous isolation and a powerful agenda for change."[17]

As in the postcolonial period, women worked on behalf of others, not simply for themselves. In sisterhood, women participated in all phases of public outcries to end oppression—marches for civil rights, rallies, protest sit-ins, and other public demonstrations to point to injustices. They worked on a wide range of issues that seemed to be of common interest and importance. Issues such as sex discrimination in employment, housing, and credit resulted in enforced legislation at the federal and state levels. In 1961, President John F. Kennedy established the first President's Commission on the Status of Women, and eventually 50 parallel state commissions were also established. In 1964, Congress passed the Civil Rights Act, including Title VII, which prohibits discrimination in employment on the basis of race, color, religion, national origin, or sex. The Equal Employment Opportunity Commission was created to enforce the Title VII provisions. In 1965, President Lyndon B. Johnson signed Executive Order 11246, which required companies doing business with the federal government to undertake affirmative action in hiring minorities. In 1972, Congress passed Title IX of the Educational Amendments to the Civil Rights Act to enforce sex equity in education. Title IX generated enormous resistance, not because it provided equality of access, scholarships, and hiring in public schools and universities, but because it challenged the privileges of men-only athletics on college campuses. When women were fully integrated into the United States military after the draft was abandoned, similar resistance occurred. And when feminists insisted on redefining rape as a crime of assault, rather than one of unbridled passion, this challenged age-old prejudices. Date rape, sexual harassment, and a new definition of pregnancy for the sake of workplace benefit payment plans, as another illness or disability, were added to the feminist agenda.

Title VII of the 1964 Civil Rights Act, through the 1978 Pregnancy Discrimination Act, requires employers to apply the same standards to pregnancy as to any other temporary "disability"; the worker is not fired and is reinstated with continuing seniority and benefits. The 1974 Federal Equal Credit Opportunity Act, as amended, prohibits discrimination in access to credit on the basis of sex or marital status.

Women were further unified as they began a process of sharing stories that later became known as "consciousness-raising." This process gave rise to the popular slogan, "The personal is political," which meant that women were incorporating the power of their personal stories and experiences as vehicles for bringing about social change. Shirley Chisholm was elected the first African-American woman to the House of Representatives in 1968. The National Organization for Women (NOW) was formed; feminist publications began to appear in the United States (500 between 1968 and 1973).[18] A rebellion by homosexual patrons of Stonewall Inn in New York City against treatment by police launched the gay and lesbian rights movement. The first large-scale women's studies course was offered; the North American Indian Women's Association was founded; Chicana feminists founded Comisión Feminil Mexicaná and held their first national conference; the first conference of Puerto Rican women was convened.

In 1923, Alice Paul, suffragist and founder of the National Woman's Party, had introduced a constitutional Equal Rights Amendment "that no rights would be abridged on account of sex." Not until 1972 did Congress pass the Amendment, which was sent to the states for ratification. Conservative opposition began raising money and organizing, bringing the process to defeat on June 30, 1982, only three votes short of passage.

THE THIRD WAVE OF THE WOMEN'S MOVEMENT, CIRCA 1980 TO THE EARLY 1990s

The euphoria of the 1960s and 1970s was beginning to atrophy. So much had been accomplished to redress women's grievances, but, despite the formation of the first of four International Women's Congresses uniting women globally, the momentum was beginning to wane. A second ebb followed the huge 1960s tidal wave. No amount of gender solidarity could erase real social-class differences among women in the degree and kind of oppression they experienced. First-generation issues, which involved role change, took on greater urgency as the movement matured, but these changes also brought controversy. Tobias states, "…it was probably inevitable that once equal access to jobs, pay, credit, and education was legislated, once abortion was at least protected by law…it would be harder to get activists to follow a single 'feminist' path." Tobias continues to describe on which issues feminists would divide: "Working with those issues myself in the 1970s and 1980s, I came to believe that issues such as women in the military, pornography, comparable worth, the 'Mommy Track,' and unwed motherhood challenged feminists to come to grips with differences in outlook and priorities that had not surfaced before."[19]

How were women who had worked so zealously in the peace movement to come to grips with and support women who now wanted to be active in the military? How were women who had invested so much of themselves in the fight against pornography to unite with the women who saw the right to pornography as a "free-speech" issue? During the 1980s, many women redefined pay equity to mean not just equal pay for equal work as used in the 1963 Equal Pay Act, but also equal compensation for jobs of "equal value" to the employer. Women who disagreed with this position, even though they were only receiving about $0.64 to $0.72 for every $1 men earned, saw the comparable worth argument a threat to the positions they held. In addition, proponents for comparable worth pointed out that job categories in which women predominate would be revalued, presumably upward to allow for better pay.[20]

The "Mommy Track" issue also divided feminists. Women today are compelled to work outside the home to support their families as single parents or to make ends meet in two-paycheck families. Many poor or unmarried mothers would be eager to have the job security, health and retirement benefits, and upward mobility that come with full-time jobs, but they cannot compete with other job applicants because of time constraints. They have accepted a disproportionate share of part-time, underpaid employment in the service sector because they saw their first obligation to their children. Professional workers can afford to purchase child care, which is a luxury service workers cannot. In 1989, Felice Schwartz, a long-time advocate of women and business, made a proposal intended to assist women on the professional fast track who were trying to accommodate work and child rearing.[21] Immediately denounced as the "Mommy Track," women opponents saw this suggestion to give women greater flexibility with "family" time to mean that child care was a "woman's issue" rather than a parental issue.[22]

Some wives and husbands, concerned about family atmosphere for their children as well as themselves, were working to refine their relationships so that women did not shoulder household responsibilities alone while employed outside the home. These couples could see the emasculation of men who, trying to share household tasks, were in effect becoming as one more of the children because their "sharing tasks" ended up doing what the mother knew needed to be done, rather than the males' making the doctors appointments, buying the school clothes, and taking children to their activities. Both females and males thought they were sharing household tasks, but as shown in the following figure, increasing effort toward equalization still needed to be made.[23]

Women in sisterhood would agree that their roles were confining, unrealistic, and sexually charged. The nature of women's inequality would not be a subject of dispute among feminists. "But the origins of women's differences,

FIGURE 23.1

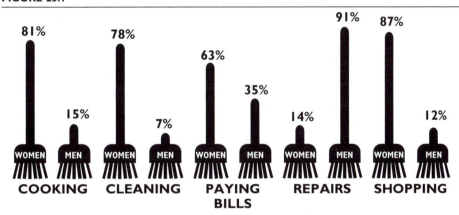

81%   78%   63%   91% 87%

15%   35%   14%   12%
7%

WOMEN MEN WOMEN MEN WOMEN MEN WOMEN MEN WOMEN MEN

COOKING   CLEANING   PAYING   REPAIRS   SHOPPING
                        BILLS

Who's Pushing the Broom?

The Families and Work Institute has conducted a five-year national study that confirms even though women have joined the work force outside the home, they are still shouldering most of the housework. The study reports who women and men think takes the greater responsibility for household tasks in two-income families.

The first column shows the percentage of women who reported doing more around the house; the second column shows the percentage of men who reported doing more around the house.

Source: *Self* magazine and Families and Work Institute.
(Because the men and women were polled separately, the numbers don't add up to 100 percent.)

from one another as well as from men, would lead to competing explanations, different perspectives, different political priorities, and different scenarios for change."[24]

MEN'S MOVEMENT IN THE LATE 1970s TO PRESENT

Earlier studies of gender relations, in which a unitary notion of masculinity was often employed, largely concentrated on women and girls. Masculinity was assumed to be a monolithic unproblematic entity, with patriarchy encompassing a universal status as the single cause of the oppression of women.[25] This attitude, often rancorous, left little space for men who were rethinking their relationship with women. Walter Farrell's *The Liberated Man: Beyond Masculinity, Freeing Men and Their Relationships with Women* was a popular and early source of many ideas helping men to reflect upon their own situations rather than attacking the women's movement.[26] Many of the writings of this period were written in the light of feminism.

Joseph Pleck, analyzing the men's movement in North America, discovered an antisexist bias in the late 1970s. While the men's movement was not as widely known as the women's movement, it generated a variety of books, publications, and organizations.[27]

Two of the more popular books on masculinity, John Stoltenberg's *Refusing to Be a Man*[28] and Robert Bly's *Iron John*,[29] represent two extreme poles of the current reaction to changes in gender roles inspired by feminism. Unlike some authors who reject or attack feminism, both claimed to take feminism seriously and to respond to it supportively. Stoltenberg states that men should give up completely on the traditional model of masculinity, and Bly proposes a return to an even more traditional model. Stoltenberg believes that manhood has been so connected with patriarchy and injustice toward women that he claims "The male sex is socially constructed. It is a political entity that flourishes only through acts of force and sexual terrorism."[30]

Robert Bly is primarily concerned with overcoming the historical changes in men's relationships brought about by industrialization. While Bly claims that he is not opposed to feminism, he states that the women's movement must bear some of the blame for the current state of emasculated manhood. Most of the myths Bly retells place a woman, normally the mother, at the center of the men's difficulties.[31] Bly thinks that there are essential differences between women and men, and the model of masculinity that he sketches has gone too far in the opposite direction. Instead of envisioning new ways for men and women to interact, ways that resolve the problems he discussed with insight, he turned uncritically to the past. Stoltenberg does not see great differences between women and men, and consequently he believes that men can choose something different from the traditional roles that have been assigned to them.[32]

While women were united in their movement by what they saw as oppressions, men began searching for their identity. Clatterbaugh, in *Contemporary Perspectives on Masculinity: Men, Women and Politics in Modern Society*, coins the term *masculinist* to apply to any point of view that offers an analysis of the social reality of American men and an agenda for them.[33] The following offer a sampling of topics about which men have written in this period:

- Real men
- What's manly
- Masculinity and race: the dual dilemma of black men
- Age and change in the adult male sex role
- Sports and war: rites of passage in male institutions
- Men and work
- Man as victim
- The rise and demise of the sensitive man
- Masculinities and families
- Men, masculinity, and the challenge of long-term unemployment
- Masculinity, power, and identity
- The rise of homophobia
- Aggression and violence
- Pornography and sexuality
- Fatherhood and manhood
- Paternity and responsibility
- The oppression of men
- Chicano men and masculinity
- Judaism and masculinity

Many books written about men end with a chapter variously titled "What Happened to the Men's Movement?" or "Is the Men's Movement Dead?" The titles themselves point to a diminution of print materials in books and magazines. Many books were written about men's lives, manhood, and masculinities in the late 1980s and early 1990s. A search for authors' works on the topic in the late 1990s shows a break in the volume of literature now being produced. This does not mean there is no interest in issues affecting males. Searching the Internet, one finds a plethora of writings, which might mean that for those more in tune with the Information Age, speed, availability, and rapid communication are more important than waiting for more traditional forms of publication. Material for 1997, updated by the month in some cases, is maintained by a designated person.

The Society for the Psychological Study of Men and Masculinity (SPSMM), a division of The American Psychological Association, promotes the critical study of how gender shapes and constricts men's lives and is committed to an enhancement of men's capacity to experience their full human potential. SPSMM acknowledges its historical debt to feminist-inspired scholarship on gender, and commits itself to the support of groups such as women, gays, lesbians, and peoples of color who have been uniquely oppressed by the gender/class/race system. A research Project Page on the Internet is designed to facilitate the process of planning research, linking colleagues, and organizing presentations.[34]

Men Against Racism and Sexism (MARS) is another group seeking concrete ways to end sexism among men. It presents specific suggestions such as the recognition that men's and women's views of each other and of themselves have been shaped by sexist conditioning in our society; provides education on the ways that women have been oppressed; and encourages men to feel and express natural feelings or to model nonsexist behavior everywhere.[35] Individuals who are involved in scientific and scholarly work in the area of men and masculinity are presented. This current use of the Internet might explain why book-

Hazel Hankin

A female police officer and male day-care center worker challenge traditional roles for men and women.

Elizabeth Crews/The Image Works

stores are not investing in books about the men's movement. The concern about men's issues is not dead; many writers have moved to another arena.

THE EBBING INFLUENCE OF THE WOMEN'S MOVEMENT

During the Reagan and Bush administrations in the 1980s, feminism moved quickly from the offense to the defense. The defeat of the Equal Rights Amendment in 1982 was a symptom of the nation's moving to the political right. "The silent majority," "the born-again Christian Right," and the conservative "middle" invested themselves in politics to the detriment of the feminist movement. Affirmative action—the requirement that employers make extra efforts to hire in accordance with the numbers of minorities and women in specific labor pools—continued to be challenged individually by white males and collectively by their unions. But the 1980s were full of ironies: Legislative setbacks and judicial reversals were accompanied by the appointment of Sandra Day O'Connor as the first woman to the Supreme Court, and women continued to be elected to more and higher local, state, and federal offices. Poverty was now being analyzed in terms of gender, described as the Feminization of Poverty. The data showed gender discrimination as well as women of color, females heading households, and older women abandoned by their husbands or left without adequate support when they were widowed being those at highest deprivation.

In the United States, African-American and Hispanic single mothers suffer poverty rates 50 percent greater than those of their white counterparts, and African-American women are three times as likely as white women to be in the economically vulnerable position of single motherhood.[36] Right-to-life women split with pro-choice women over abortion. The public debate about the availability of the "abortion pill," RU 486, touched personal values and religious beliefs of women who disagreed about its use.

Women were busy defending feminist issues during the 1980s and were distracted from the central policies of the current administrations. Feminists were absent from the political scene, and three military involvements within 12 years—in Grenada, in Somalia, and in the Persian Gulf—did not evoke the response and protest from feminists it once would have. Feminists, busy defending their own issues, ignored the increased military spending, tripling the national debt, and other political realities. Feminists began asking themselves if their only issues were related to gender and sex—to the exclusion of the rights of women that affected their economic, domestic, and political lives. This splintering into interest groups for women is evident by such committed groups as: National Women's Law Center; 9 to 5 National Association of Working Women; Older Women's League; Women's Economic Agenda Project; Women Employed; Women's Legal Defense Fund; and Institute for Women in Trades, Technology and Science, to name a few.[37]

THE EBBING INFLUENCE OF THE MEN'S MOVEMENT

The late 1990s appear to be a time of dissipated energy for a single movement but not a lack of interest in men's issues. David R. Throop reports that there is not a single men's movement today in the United States, but there are at least seven:

(1) Mythopoetic Men's Movement, which is interested in men's inner work. It is somewhat critical of "traditional" male roles, but generally open to the idea of different roles for men and women. (2) Feminist Men's Movement, which is much more political and identifies with the more militant end of feminism. (3) Fathers' Rights Groups, which organized primarily around issues of single and divorced fathers. (4) Men's Rights has a broader spectrum of interests (including the draft, men's treatment in prisons, choice for men) and an opposition to gender roles. It is generally sympathetic to egalitarian feminists but extremely critical of most of current feminism. These men are opposed to affirmative action and all-male draft. (5) Christian Men's Movement is antifeminist as it favors traditional gender roles. (6) Men's Recovery focuses on the problems of men who have grown isolated from their fellows and are trapped by their sex roles. (7) The Fatherhood Movement, which focuses particularly on the problem of the absent father.[38]

The first ten years, at least, of what is called the men's movement was about repairing the wounds to the soul created by dysfunctional relationships between fathers and sons, according to Stephen Johnson, director of the Men's Center of Los Angeles. Now he thinks men have done enough of their personal work and need to be of service to their communities. He thinks men need to create mentor relationships for fatherless boys that are at high risk, that are about to drop out of school, and/or that are about to become involved with a gang or with drugs. Men need to be working with men who are caught up in the prison system or helping those coming out of prison in terms of rehabilitation and reentry into society. They also need to be working with men who are sexual violators, and who have questions and issues having to do with sexual addiction or inappropriate sexual behavior. Johnson believes men should be creating a social justice network of men working together in a hands-on way to stabilize their communities.[39]

Men's groups have splintered, much as have women's groups. The Internet reveals these titles of men's organizations: American Men's Studies Association; Coalition for the Preservation of Fatherhood; Men Against Domestic Violence; Men's Health and Well-being Association, Inc.; Pot-Bellied Men of America; and the Society for the Psychological Study of Men and Masculinity.[40]

THE PRESENT LOW EBB OF THE WOMEN'S AND MEN'S MOVEMENTS

From the 1820s to the 1990s there have been high tides and low tides for women as they have sought to obtain their equal rights. Men are progressing from "movements" and personal need to specialized groups and community awareness of the need for men to work with other men. Susan Hartmann suggested that if feminism was to proceed "from margin to mainstream," then mainstream issues, and not just gender inequity, deserved more of the feminists' attention.[41] Much of male talk is taking place quietly, in men's groups and other forums somewhat out of the media's distorting glare. Men did not like the media flash, and once the flash became intense, they began to back away. Men are not ready to go public because they are having to change something that has been fundamental to the meaning of masculinity for centuries. Men are not instigating anything remotely comparable to the political and social uproar that defined the women's movement.

AREAS OF GENDER TENSIONS IN THE LATE 1990s

Women and Men and Violence

Violence against women, both nationally and globally, is the greatest violation of human rights issues. On January 21, 1993, Senator Joseph R. Biden, Jr., introduced "The Violence Against Women Act," quoting these statistics:

> Every week, 21,000 women report to police they have been beaten in their homes.

> Every day, over 2,500 women visit an emergency room because of violence.

> Every hour, as many as 70 women across the country are attacked by rapists.[42]

In August 1997, according to a new Justice Department report, almost half of the 1.4 million victims of violence or suspected violence treated in hospital emergency rooms in 1994 were hurt by someone they knew. The report found that 17 percent of the victims, about 243,000 people, suffered injuries inflicted by someone with whom they had an intimate relationship—a spouse, a former spouse, or a current or former boyfriend or girlfriend. "Among the victims of abuse by spouses or ex-spouses, 7 percent of the total, women victims outnumbered men 9-to-1 according to the report. Nearly 10 percent of the 1.4 million victims of violence were hurt by a boyfriend or girlfriend, and women were almost eight times more likely than men to fall into this category."[43] In the United States, 54,000 women are killed every five years, the same number of men and women killed in the Vietnam war.[44]

Women and Men in the Military

Two Army investigations into the service's handling of sexual misconduct have found widespread discrimination by male commanders against female troops, staffing that left too few drill sergeants to supervise troops, and a selection system that allowed wife-beaters to fill the prestigious job of drill sergeant, Army officials and lawmakers reported.[45] In November 1996, the Army created a sexual-harassment hotline and logged 3,102 calls in less than a week. Callers can talk to a woman if they prefer, and they can be passed through directly to investigators if they desire. Military leaders and civilian authorities say that the hotline is critical in the effort to get to the bottom of all allegations.[46] After much opposition, in 1996, one female student entered the previously all-male Naval ROTC program at the Citadel, in South Carolina. In 1997, 30 women enrolled at the Virginia Military Institute, and much stricter supervision is promised to prevent any sexual harassment or infractions of regulations.

Women and Men in Congress

Although women make up over 50 percent of the United States population, there are only 51 women of 440 members of the House of Representatives[47] and 9 women of 100 members in the Senate.[48] Men still hold the prestigious committee positions and are featured far more often than women in the media reporting congressional business.

Women and Men in Religion

In 1993, feminist issues in religion had somewhat arrived in mainstream American churches and theological seminaries. Most Christian seminaries included at least one woman professor teaching women's issues in theological studies. Faculty women in these seminaries were equipped to do specialized courses on women in the Bible, theology, church history, ethics, pastoral psychology, and worship. At the same time there continued to be backlash movements in both Catholicism and Protestantism seeking to discredit feminist theology and liturgy as heretical. Feminist theology in a Christian context is well established, and now coming of age is a second generation of feminist theologians who have already read the works of earlier feminist writers. New groups of feminist writers are developing in the African-American, Hispanic, and Asian-American communities, as well as among lesbians, challenging the lack of attention to racism, ethnic diversity, and homophobia in established Christian feminism.[49]

Although Jewish women have long been leaders in American secular feminism, feminist critique and reconstruction of religious Judaism has gained momentum in the last third of the twentieth century. Women students in rabbinical colleges and increasing numbers of women rabbis can draw upon Jewish feminist biblical exegesis and reconstruction of women's history in Judaism. With the rise of Jewish women biblical scholars, they have begun to take their places as teachers in the theological schools of the Reformed and Reconstructionist traditions. Jewish women recognize that ceremonies such as circumcision and the bar mitzvah privilege the Jewish male as the normative Jew, and rabbinical laws exclude women from the time-bound commandments of prayer. Jewish feminists work to create inclusive language, ceremonies, and religious observance.[50]

In the early 1990s, Bill McCartney founded a group called Promise Keepers for men of all denominations. At the heart of Promise Keepers' mission is racial and denominational reconciliation. In four short years, 70 men became 230,000 attending meetings throughout the United States. Of this number, 40,000 are committed Promise Keepers who promise to honor Jesus Christ through worship, prayer, and obedience to His Word. Among other promises these men make are: A Promise Keeper is committed to pursue vital relationships with a few other men, understanding that he needs his brothers to help keep his promises. A Promise Keeper is committed to practice spiritual, moral, ethical, and sexual purity. He is committed to build strong marriages and families through love, protection, and biblical values. A Promise Keeper is committed to reach beyond any racial and denominational barriers to demonstrate the power of biblical unity.[51] St. Joseph's Convenant Keepers, a Catholic men's organization similar to Promise Keepers but along denominational lines, meet nationally. Steve Wood, founder and president of the Family Life Center International, explains, "Catholic men want to be better husbands and fathers...to help turn our culture away from death and back to God our Father."[52]

Media and Advertising

The information that people receive through newspapers, radio, and television shapes their opinions about the world. The more decision-making positions women hold in the media, the more they can influence output, breaking stereotypes that hurt women, attracting greater attention to issues of equality in the home and in public life, and providing young women with new images, ideas, and ideals. Women remain poorly represented in the more influential media occupations such as program managers and senior editors. When major networks employ males as anchors for the national evening news and a one woman/three men ratio to present local news, this omission of women is significant. We may ask ourselves these questions: Which serious women's accomplishments are being covered? Are they the peace negotiators in areas of world tension? Which politician's work is being covered? How often do we hear from or about the women who are in Congress? Or is the major news about women relative only to their health? Women continue to be portrayed more anatomically than men in most clothing advertisements. Women are still being viewed as objects in advertisements for perfumes, cosmetics, and personal hygiene products. On the other hand, in recent years, advertisements show more men as care givers for children and helping with the laundry, housework, and in nurturing roles.

Women and Men at Work, in Economics and in Education

Women throughout the world continue to be paid less for comparable work than men, and the wage gap has narrowed only slightly over the past decade. "Women's progress in the work force over the past 10 years has not meant greater access to quality jobs nor has it brought an end to discrimination," according to Mary Chinery-Hesse, International Labor Organization (ILO) deputy director-general. She continues, "Despite gains in some areas, women earn an average of just two-thirds of men's wages and they are often denied access to opportunities leading to the best jobs."[53] By 2000, women will comprise at least half of the labor force in most countries, compared to a third in 1990. Men dominate the highest corporate and institutional positions worldwide. The ILO estimates that, at the present rate of progress, it will take 475 years for parity to be achieved between women and men in top managerial and administration positions. A greater percentage of women than ever are the sole breadwinners for their families, contributing to the feminization of poverty. Women's employment is primarily concentrated in a narrow range of sectors, especially services, where job access is easier but wages are lower and the job security is minimal. Women also make up a greater percentage of workers in the "informal" sector and other precarious forms of employment that often are outside the scope of labor regulations, making them more open for exploitation. Between 65 and 90 percent of all part-time workers are women in industrial countries (65 percent in the United States). Women make up two out of every five workers in industrialized countries.[54]

Education is considered one of the most important means to empower women with the knowledge, skills, and self-confidence necessary to participate fully in society. In higher-education enrollments, women equal or exceed men in many regions. Despite progress in women's higher education, major obstacles still arise when women strive to translate their high-level education into social and economic advancement.[55]

SIGNIFICANCE OF GENDER TENSIONS FOR SOCIAL WORK

The Social Work Code of Ethics challenges social workers to recognize the value and worth of each human being and to seek to empower clients with basic rights. These admonitions take on special significance when one looks at the tension arenas of gender. How can female therapists assist male clients if they make no effort to understand masculine perspectives? How can male therapists understand women's issues if they carry societally ingrained prejudices toward women? Women and men who practice social work will need to continually educate themselves to gender issues pertinent to their clients through professional meetings, the Internet, the printed word, and media.

Social workers might profit from the insights of Joe Schriver[56] as he discusses the traditional/dominant paradigm or worldview long accepted by social work educators. This paradigm embodies scientific, objective, and quantitative knowledge expressed through white, patriarchal, competitive, privileged lenses. Rather, social workers might consider adopting the alternative paradigm, which stresses information gained through an interpretive, intuitive, qualitative approach. This view includes feminism, diversity, interrelatedness, and integration of new information. When social workers no longer only receive information in the curriculum according to the traditional paradigm, it will be easier for them to view gender tensions from new perspectives. Students need to search elsewhere for the information—professional meetings, the Internet, and magazines containing articles about gender.

The 1995 *Encyclopedia for Social Work* lists a number of areas of practice in which gender is an issue. Some of the areas are job stressors;[57] men, women, and alcohol;[58] and men, women, and divorce.[59]

Social work as a profession has its roots in the early movements of social reform in this country. Challenging the existing social order has been the role of social workers throughout history. The changing attitudes about roles of women and men in this country can be augmented by social workers who are willing once again to expand existing societal boundaries. The task of both women and men in the field of social work is to live actively as individuals unwilling to accept the powerless roles assigned to those who suffer discrimination because of their gender. Informed social workers are central to assisting both female and male clients as they continue to attempt resolution of contemporary tensions, for only then will they constantly be in touch with the pulse of their client's gender needs.

SUMMARY AND CONCLUSIONS

Although neither the women's nor men's movements have the kind of momentum exhibited 25 years ago, the issues affecting both groups are still vital as society prepares for the next millennium. The daughters of the 1960s–1970s feminists have not experienced the same deprivation of rights as their mothers and therefore do not feel the urgency of political and social involvement. The low ebb of enthusiasm is similar to that shown by women in 1920 after women had achieved the right to vote, and that fire about women's causes will not be rekindled until young women experience their own personal loss of rights. This does not mean that younger women do not care about rape, sexual harassment, violence, and unfair treatment in the military or religion. However, there is no longer a unified movement to confront these issues.

Leadership for women's issues today seems to be much stronger in developing countries. Latin American, Asian, African, and Pacific Rim women at grassroots levels have been working to create new awareness of women's rights, including their rights within the family. Rapid population changes, combined with many other social and economic changes, are being accompanied by considerable changes in women's household and family status. As a result of these changes, many more women than men spend a significant part of their life without a partner, with important consequences for their economic welfare and their children's. Since men have higher rates of remarriage, marry at an older age, and have a shorter life expectancy, most older men are married, while many older women are widows and suffer from a low standard of living.

Both females and males have profited from participation of diversity groups. The African-American Million Man March on Washington could not have taken place in an earlier era; Native Americans and Latinos would not have been strong enough to reclaim their heritage when legal and societal prejudices deter them. The generation of women and minorities who resurrected our darkest memories challenged us to seek a brighter future.

The uniqueness of America has come from its founding in optimism, its assumption that human beings can transform their lives and alter the past. The past demands our attention, but not our energy, because it cannot be undone. The future is another matter, and Americans usually are at their best when they turn their faces toward tomorrow. The new millennium gives us an opportunity. That future will not be perfect, but if we live in it with renewed hope and unity, we will be closer to realizing the American dream than at any moment in history.

Notes

1. José B. Ashford, Craig W. Lecroy, and Kathy L. Lortie, *Human Behavior in the Social Environment* (New York: Brooks/Cole Publishing Company, 1997), p. 126.
2. Margaret Mead, *Sex and Temperament in Three Primitive Societies* (New York: William Morrow, 1935).
3. Sheila Tobias, *Faces of Feminism: An Activist's Reflections on the Women's Movement* (Boulder, CO: Westview Press, 1997).
4. Ibid., p. 12.
5. Alice Rossi, ed., *The Feminist Papers* (New York: Bantam Books, 1973).
6. Gerda Lerner, *The Grimké Sisters from South Carolina: Rebels Against Slavery* (Boston: Houghton Mifflin, 1967). See also the description of Angelina Grimké's conversion in Catharine Stimpson, *Where the Meanings Are: Feminism and Cultural Spaces* (New York: Methuen, 1988), pp. 16–19.

7. Elizabeth C. Stanton, Susan B. Anthony, and Matilda J. Gage, eds., *History of Women's Suffrage*, vol. 1 (Rochester, NY: Charles Mann Publishers, 1981), pp. 67–74, 88–94.

8. Rossi, ed., *The Feminist Papers*, pp. 411–412.

9. Eleanor Flexner, *The Century of Struggle: The Woman's Rights Movement in the United States* (Cambridge, MA: Harvard University Press, 1959).

10. Rossi, ed., *The Feminist Papers*, p. 407.

11. Anthony Rotundo, *American Manhood: Transformations in Masculinity from the Revolution to the Modern Era* (New York: Basic Books) 1993, pp. 2–9.

12. Ibid., p. 3.

13. Ibid., p. 3.

14. Ibid., p. 4.

15. Ibid., p. 6.

16. Louise Bernikow, *The American Women's Almanac* (New York: Berkley Books, 1997), pp. 43–44.

17. Tobias, *Faces of Feminism*, p. 170.

18. Ann Mather, "A History of Feminist Periodicals," *Journalism History* 1 (Autumn 1974): 82.

19. Tobias, *Faces of Feminism*, p. 171.

20. Tobias, *Faces of Feminism*, p. 176.

21. Felice N. Schwartz, Margaret H. Schifter, and Susan S. Gillotti, *How to Go to Work When Your Husband Is Against It, Your Children Aren't Old Enough, and There's Nothing You Can Do Anyhow* (New York: Simon and Schuster, 1972).

22. Sylvia Ann Hewlett expressed these views about motherhood in *A Lesser Life: The Myth of Women's Liberation in America* (New York: Warner, 1986).

23. *Who's Pushing the Broom? (September 1994). The KWWL 7 Newspaper* 2, 17, Waterloo, IA.

24. Tobias, *Faces of Feminism*, p. 194.

25. Martin Mac an Ghaill, ed., *Understanding Masculinities* (Philadelphia: Open University Press, 1996), p. 1.

26. Walter Farrell, *The Liberated Man: Beyond Masculinity, Freeing Men and Their Relationships with Women* (New York: Random House, 1974).

27. Joseph H. Pleck and Jack Sawyer, eds., *Men and Masculinity* (Englewood Cliffs, NJ: Prentice-Hall, 1974).

28. John Stoltenberg, *Refusing to Be a Man* (Portland, OR: Breitenbush Books, 1989).

29. Robert Bly, *Iron John* (Reading, MA: Addison-Wesley, 1990).

30. Stoltenberg, *Refusing to Be a Man*, p. 30.

31. Larry May, Robert Strikwerda, and Patrick D. Hopkins, eds., *Rethinking Masculinity, Philosophical Explorations in Light of Feminism*, 2nd ed. (Boulder, CO: Rowman & Littlefield Publishers, Inc., 1996), p. xii.

32. Stoltenberg, *Refusing to Be a Man*, p. 32.

33. Kenneth Clatterbaugh, *Contemporary Perspectives on Masculinity: Men, Women and Politics in Modern Society* (Boulder, CO: Westview Press, 1990), p. 2.

34. Internet/Yahoo/http://www.Society and Culture:Gender:Men:Organizations only. SPSMM. Page maintained by James L. Campbell, last updated October 26, 1997.

35. Internet/Yahoo/http://www.Society and Culture:Gender:Men:Organizations only. Men Against Racism and Sexism.

36. Quoted in Gertrude S. Goldberg and Eleanor Kremen, eds., *The Feminization of Poverty: Discovered in America* (New York: Greenwood Press, 1990), p. 5.

37. Carol Kleiman, "List Names Groups Committed to Women," *The Cedar Rapids Gazette*, March 18, 1996, p. B3.

38. Internet http://www.Society and Culture:Gender:Men:Organizations:Alta Vista Pages: Men's Movement History: What are Men's Issues? A survey by David R. Troop. Updated May 19, 1997.

39. Ellis Cose, *A Man's World* (New York: HarperCollins, 1995), p. 79.
40. Internet http://www.Society and Culture:Gender:Men:Organizations Search all of Yahoo. 1997.
41. Susan M. Hartmann, *From Margin to Mainstream: American Women and Politics Since 1960* (New York: Knopf, 1968).
42. Biden-statement@www.inform.UMD.edu.Microsoft Internet. p. 1.
43. "Violence Is No Stranger," *The Cedar Rapids Gazette*, August 27, 1997, pp. 1A, 5A.
44. Christie Fortmann Doser, "Domestic Violence and the Workplace," *The DVIP Advocate*, Iowa City, IA, Summer 1997, p. 1.
45. Eric Schmitt, "Army Inquiries Find a Wide Bias Against Women," *New York Times*, July 31, 1997, pp. A1, A19.
46. Charles Pope, "Praise for Army's New Sexual-Harassment Hot Line," *The Cedar Rapids Gazette*, November 15, 1996, p. 9A.
47. Internet http://clerkweb.house.gov/members/OALMbr.html. Official Alphabetical List of the House of Representatives of the United States 105th Congress compiled by Robin H. Carle, Clerk of House of Representatives. Last modified May 30, 1997.
48. Internet. http://www.senate.gov/senator/members.html. Senators of the 105th Congress, Directory of Senators by Name. Last modified on May 30, 1997.
49. Rosemary Ruether and Rosemary Skinner Keller, eds., *In Our Own Voices* (San Francisco: Harper, 1995), pp. 428–429.
50. Susannah Heschel, ed., *On Being a Jewish Feminist: A Reader* (New York: Schocken, 1993).
51. Promise Keepers, *Men of Action* (Fall 1994), pp. 2, 8–9.
52. "Covenant Keepers Set Date," *The Catholic Messenger*, Davenport, IA, August 21, 1997, p. 1.
53. Microsoft Internet Explorer. 6.html@www.essential.org Women Earn Less than Men in Comparable Jobs. ILO Washington Focus, Fall 1995 Issue. p. 1.
54. Ibid., pp. 2, 3.
55. "The World's Women 1995: Trends and Statistics" (New York: United Nations Publication no.95.xvii.2).
56. Joe M. Schriver, *Human Behavior and the Social Environment* (Boston: Allyn and Bacon, 1995), Chapter 2.
57. W.C. Lesch and J.E. Hazeltine, "Pathways to Labor Force Exit: Work Transitions and Work Instability," *Journal of Health and Social Polity* 7, no. 2 (1995), pp. 47–60.
58. J.L. Kunz and K. Graham, "Life Course Changes in Alcohol Consumption in Leisure Activities of Men and Women," *Journal of Drug Issues* 26, no. 4 (Fall 1996), pp. 805–809.
59. A.V. Horwitz, H.R. White, and S. Howell-White, "The Use of Multiple Outcomes in Stress Research: A Case Study of Gender Differences in Responses to Marital Dissolution," *Journal of Health and Social Behavior* 37, no. 3 (September 1996), pp. 278–291.

Additional Suggested Readings

Baines, Donna. "Feminist Social Work in the Inner City: The Challenges of Race, Class, and Gender." *Affilia* 12, no. 3 (1997): 297–317

Basu, Amrita, ed. *The Challenge of Local Feminisms: Women's Movements in Global Perspective.* San Francisco: Westview Press, 1955.

Boyd, S.B., W.M. Longwood, and M.W. Muesse, eds. *Redeeming Men: Religion and Masculinities.* Louisville, KY: Westminster John Knox Press, 1996.

England, Paula, ed. *Theory on Gender: Feminism on Theory.* New York: Aldine de Gruyter, 1993.

Goldberg, Joan E. "Mutuality in the Relationship of Homeless Women and Their Mothers." *Affilia* 12, no. 1 (1997): 96–105.

Internet. Yahoo http://www.Society and Culture:Gender:men:Issues/history.

Internet. Yahoo http://www.Society and Culture: Gender:Women:Issues/organizations.

Jesser, Clinton J. *Fierce and Tender Me: Sociological Aspects of the Men's Movement*. Westport, CT: Praeger Publishers, 1996.

Martin, Susan E., and Nancy C. Jurik. *Doing Justice, Doing Gender: Women in Law and Criminal Justice Occupations*. Thousand Oaks, CA: Sage Publications, 1996.

Messner, Michael A. *The Politics of Masculinities: Men in Movements*. Thousand Oaks, CA: Sage Publications, 1997.

Rapping, Elayne. *The Culture of Recovery: Making Sense of the Self-Help Movement in Women's Lives*. Kansas City, MO: Beacon Press, 1996.

24

Housing, Homelessness, and Social Welfare

GARY ASKEROOTH

Housing, like food, is so important in the everyday life of people all over the globe. Housing is of concern to the social welfare profession because the location, condition, and cost of shelter is a major determinant of our mental and physical health. The fight for better, more affordable housing has been important in the history of social reform in the United States, as entire generations of citizens and immigrants have endured degradation and disease partly caused by deplorable housing conditions.

Housing is the primary environment for most of the world's inhabitants for much of their lives. This is especially true for people who live in temperate climates that cause them to spend substantial periods in the shelter of their homes. Through personal experience and social research we know that housing has significant influences on human development and the quality of life. Populations at risk—such as young children, the frail elderly, and the disabled—are especially influenced by the circumstances of their housing. Adequate space, temperature, facilities for food preparation, sleeping, and toilet and bathing facilities are crucial to human beings' welfare.[1]

In the United States, fully one-third of all fixed capital is invested in housing. For the typical middle-class family, housing is the single largest asset they will own throughout their lives.[2] For most of renters as well as homeowners, housing is by far the largest monthly expense. Where and how we house ourselves is as important as any decision we make, because our homes are fixed to pieces of ground that are parts of neighborhoods—small geographic places that express great variation in key aspects of social welfare, including access to education, recreation, transportation, jobs, and public safety.

SOCIAL SYSTEMS AND HOUSING

In societies such as the United States that are dominated by capital markets, a family's housing is determined by their economic status. Owning an ever-larger, more modern home is the means by which people stake out their place in the territory of the American Dream. People who cannot achieve the wealth and income needed to reach this territory are often consigned to live in low-quality housing in undesirable areas, or are driven to homelessness as the result of losing the competition.

In centrally planned societies, housing is often drab and crowded, but is provided to everyone as a right, often at minimal cost to the family. Countries such as Cuba, for example, provide an apartment for almost every family for rent of a few dollars a month, but this right can be removed for offenses against the state, such as speaking out against political leaders or government policies.

In societies such as Sweden or Japan, which have blended market and central planning systems, housing is a social welfare benefit that is provided through a variety of direct population and large-scale subsidies based on need. In these countries, the tax system is used aggressively to limit the extremes of luxury housing in order to prevent the scourge of homelessness and the deprivation that comes with living in dilapidated housing.

American social reformers and advocates for the poor have promoted housing policies similar to European countries for nearly all of the twentieth century. Reformers have consistently argued for a number of mechanisms that would modify the forces of the capital and real estate markets that have led to widespread homelessness and burdens for millions of poor renters and homeowners. This admiration for foreign models is not surprising. Homelessness in Britain, for example, is miniscule (2,852 people in 1991)[3]—fewer for the whole nation than for a single large American city.

With the coming of the twenty-first century it is clear that these reforms have had a very small impact on our housing problems. The exception to this bleak assessment is in the aspect of housing adequacy, especially in the electrical, heating, cooling, and plumbing systems, which have been vastly improved through the development of new technology and the enforcement of housing and building codes. In other aspects our housing policies and housing welfare programs have been weakened considerably in the last two decades of the twentieth century. The needs of investors and taxpayers have become the dominant forces in American housing, as in the social welfare system in general, raising the possibility that increasing numbers of people will have even their most basic housing needs unmet.

THE BASIC HOUSING NEEDS

Territorial Security or Shelter

As with any area of social welfare there is a kind of hierarchy of housing needs. The most basic need is for territorial security. Unless one is a member of a nomadic tribe, to be homeless is terrifying and is to be avoided at nearly all costs. On the other hand, if people feel so threatened even in their own home, they will be-

Burns Archive

THE PRESS CONTINUES TO COVER THE HOMELESS

Kirk Andrews

Homelessness is not unique to the '80s and '90s as this December 1935 photo of the New York City subway illustrates.

come refugees or escapees, but they quickly seek a new home to reestablish their security. For refugees from war or disaster, the most simple shelter is satisfying, but only for a short time. As soon as possible they will explore the environment outside their home, seeking to expand their access to the other human needs that can be met once they have a secure place from which to work and socialize.

People who do not have their basic territorial security needs met often have increased illnesses and problems with social functioning.[4] The importance of this basic need can be seen most graphically in the lives of those who are homeless. Elliot Liebow describes how not having a territory of one's own can cause a person to become disturbed. He found that many homeless women would rather live in a car than a shelter, if they could not safely store their belongings there. Others would spend their last few dollars to store things that other people would think worthless:

> Past and future, then, and even one's self, were embedded in one's belongings. When Louise could no longer pay for storage and lost her belongings to auction, she was surprised at her own reaction to the loss. Her belongings had been so much a part of her, she said, that now she's lost them, she's not sure who she is.[5]

So many things that we who have homes take for granted are big problems for the homeless. Even if a person can sleep in a shelter at night, he or she usually cannot stay during the day, so that receiving telephone calls, following medical advice when ill, or simply retreating to one's home to clean up, relax, or meet with someone important are impossible. The streets and other dangerous public places become the site for routine as well as critical activities in place of one's home.

The causes of homelessness.   Homelessness has grown into a very visible, distressing problem throughout the United States. The homeless seemed to emerge rather suddenly in the early 1980s as a wave of destitute, discouraged, often disturbed people, mostly single men, who were discovered sleeping in parks, huddling over warm exhaust grates, or hiding in trash bins. Local governments and the U.S. Department of Housing and Urban Development (HUD) were at first concerned with minimizing the problem. Their general view was that this was a temporary situation that would be reduced as soon as interest rates fell. HUD estimated that there were only 300,000 homeless in 1984.

Local shelter providers, who were inundated with demand for shelter, believed that there were probably three million homeless.[6] Although an increasing number of the homeless are women and children, the majority are still single men.

The principal causes of homelessness are:[7]

1. Loss of affordable housing units (detailed below)
2. Cutbacks in government income supplements and services
3. Deinstitutionalization of services for the mentally ill
4. Evictions due to loss of job or illness, combined with lack of family support
5. Substance abuse

Large numbers of the homeless are veterans who often have experienced several of the causal factors listed above.

Adequacy

A second housing need is adequacy. Standards of adequacy of housing vary among cultures and over time within a society. Since 1949, the United States government has been committed to "the goal of a decent home for and a suitable living environment for every American family."[8] President Lincoln campaigned proudly on the symbol of the log cabin with an outhouse. One hundred and forty years later, only hermits or seekers of simplicity are proud of such accommodations. In the United States each person should have at least 80 square feet in his or her sleeping area alone, or their housing is considered inadequate. In the tropical country of Belize, houses without sufficient space underneath to escape from the sun and mitigate against flooding are considered inadequate.[9]

Adequate housing in the subsidized or the government-assisted market segment in the United States is measured by two official standards, the first of which is the main focus here: (1) *housing quality standards* (HQS) or *housing codes* imposed by units of government, and (2) building codes applied to new construction and rehabilitation.

Adequate housing is near the top of the list of concerns for both the rich and the poor, but the U.S. Bureau of the Census collects only rudimentary data on the lack of plumbing, inadequate heating, and major structural defects, leaving the more detailed collection of data on housing conditions to local governments.[10]

By the basic Bureau of the Census definition, over 6 million housing units are substandard, with the worst conditions generally in those areas where people are both low-income and isolated due to race, geography, lack of information, or all of these factors. Native American reservations, rural southern and southwestern areas, and central areas of certain older northeastern cities have the highest rates of inadequate housing.[11]

Consumer choice is an additional, unofficial standard.   Lower-income people are consumers, even if they are receiving public or private funds to help meet their housing needs. Most Americans no longer accept housing that lacks toilet facilities, hot and cold running water, heating adequate to keep the living space at 65° during winter, as well as cooking facilities, trash removal, and so on. On the other hand, the recent rise in immigration, both legal and illegal, has led to millions of people living in conditions that native-born Americans consider inadequate. Of course, people can demand more if they have more money, but there is evidence that many new residents are not familiar with either their housing rights or their power as consumers to demand better housing.

Immigrants' housing conditions have often been poor. In 1901 a typical housing inspection found: "Babies, almost like blind fish inhabiting sunless caves, suffer ophthalmia"; and "Tenements in Jewish, Italian, Polish and Bohemian areas were 'a destruction to morals and health.'"[12] Social workers played prominent roles in exposing poor housing conditions. Through community organizing and advocacy and collaboration with housing professionals, these early reformers were able to make slumlords a symbol of disgrace.

By the late '90s many of the same American cities exhibited the same conditions for a whole new wave of immigrants, who in this decade alone added 27 million to the U.S. population, with over 70 percent of them settling in 11 cities, including New York, Los Angeles, Miami, Chicago, Houston, and Washington.[13] Social workers and legal advocates are once again working to expose the evils of slumlords and to educate these new groups about their rights and opportunities to improve their lives.

One measure of how low-income customers view the housing available in their neighborhoods is the rate of abandonment. Certain cities have extremely high numbers of vacant buildings, many structurally sound single-family houses. Houston has over 100,000 vacant housing units, despite a rapid decrease in housing costs, from $90,000 for a single-family home in 1980 to $59,700 in 1994.[14,15] Clearly these houses are considered inadequate by the potential consumers because of a group of factors, including fear of crime, lack of access to jobs, and other negatives that attach to houses in these areas.

HQS is the name for a requirement that HUD imposes as a minimum for all housing that is supported by Department funds. Local governments most often use these standards in conjunction with issuing "Section 8" certificates or vouchers. Low-income renters who receive these certificates select their own rental unit, after which the landlord is required to pass HQS inspection. The tenants pay 30 percent of their adjusted gross income for monthly rent, and the local government pays an additional amount to the landlord to ensure that he or she receives a "fair market rent" set by HUD for the metro area.

Some cities adopt HQS as their housing standard, while others adopt more stringent housing codes. Older cities and rural areas with much poor housing stock and many poor people tend to be flexible in the enforcement of these codes, preferring to use them as a tool to encourage improvement, not as a basis for blanket application of rules.

Excerpts from a recent housing inspection include the following:[16]

- Leaking main water shutoff, evidence of leaking in basement
- Missing flame shield and relief valve pipe on water heater
- Over-fused breaker and subpanel (electrical main service)
- Extension cords used in place of proper wiring
- Rotted window sills, inoperable windows
- Several broken windows, missing storm windows and screens
- No insulation, nor ventilation in attic or walls
- Loose, damaged, missing siding, and lack of paint

Overcrowding.   Overcrowded housing, defined as a ratio of more than one person to a room, is also considered inadequate by the U.S. government. Overcrowding is associated with a variety of negative effects, such as frustration, irritability, violence, decreased individuality, loss of sleep, and sexual dysfunction.[17] The severity of this problem is hard to measure accurately because many overcrowded households are thought to avoid responding to the census.[18] It is believed that in the city of Dallas there are three to four times as many people living in overcrowded housing as are homeless.[19]

Experts also believe that overcrowding has a significant cultural component. In the United States, the standard is closer to four times as much square footage as is considered adequate in Hong Kong.[20] An amazing 19 percent of Native American rental housing is overcrowded (about ten times the national rate), yet the average middle-income American household consumes over 600 square feet of housing per person, about three times the consumption of families in the late 1940s.[21]

Affordability

Affordability is the third housing need. Henry Cisneros, in 1996 prior to resigning as HUD secretary, reported to the Congress of the United States a number of disturbing housing facts:[22]

- The number of very-low-income renter households with the most serious housing needs, 5.3 million, is at an all-time high and continues to grow through both economic recession and recovery.
- Worst-case housing needs are concentrated at the lowest income levels. Over three-fourths of the households with worst-case needs have incomes below 30 percent of the area median income.
- The number of units affordable to those households without rental assistance continues to shrink. Despite large and growing demand, private housing markets are not responding to the acute needs of the lowest-income renters by producing units affordable to them.

Standards of affordability vary through time and across cultures and communities, just as do standards of adequacy. The accepted standard in the United States is an expenditure of no more than 30 percent of monthly gross income for housing. The large numbers of families who pay over this amount are considerably "cost burdened," while those who pay more than 50 percent of their income are considered "severely cost burdened" (or rent burdened).

Due to moderate costs of borrowing money in the 1990s, most areas of the country do not have a shortage of affordable housing for moderate- and middle-income families. The exceptions are in high-cost areas such as parts of the West Coast, Hawaii, New York City, and Boston. Housing markets are sensitive to a variety of business and demographic factors, so markets that are high-cost now could be much cheaper a few years in the future. But there seems to be no improvement for those at the bottom of the ladder, where those whose income is less than 30 percent of the median for their areas are in a continual crisis.

More than 5.3 million households, with over 12 million people, paid more than half their income for rent in a recent year. The primary causes are two: a stagnation of wages and other income within this group, combined with the disappearance of affordable housing units. The growing gap can be seen in Figure 24.1.

So affordability for the poorest families is primarily due to the obvious—not enough money. This is called a "demand-side" problem, which housing vouchers and other income supplements were supposed to rectify. But there are many other forces at work in a capitalist housing market, forces that have unreasonable upward pressure on the cost of lower-income housing, and diminish the actual number of units rather severely.

Additional Forces That Limit Affordable Housing

- **Political and business leaders hostile to "cheap" types of housing in downtown areas.** Ever since the days of urban renewal of the 1950s

FIGURE 24.1 **Affordable Rental Housing Shortages**

Source: Rental Housing Assistance at the Crossroads, HUD report to Congress, 3/96, p. 36.

and '60s, low-cost housing has been unpopular among political and business leaders. Between 1960 and 1990, at least 75 percent of cheap hotel rooms for single poor people were demolished or converted to more expensive uses.[23] Large numbers of cheap apartments were also demolished in many cities to make way for sports stadiums, freeways, parking ramps, hotels, and other commercial and entertainment centers. According to the Joint Center for Housing Studies, "the number of subsidized low-cost units has fallen by more than half" in the northeastern United States between 1974 and 1995,[24] while the number of subsidized low-cost housing units has dropped at an even faster rate. The federal government provided subsidies for 300,000 to 400,000 units during the 1970s, but has recently provided subsidies for fewer than 100,000 per year during the 1990s.

- **Middle-income homeowner's hostility to affordable housing in their neighborhoods.** It is difficult to overestimate the suspicion and resentment that emerge in middle- or upper-class neighborhoods when a developer proposes to build new affordable housing nearby. This general hostility is one reason that the housing industry began calling low-income housing "affordable housing" in the 1980s. The opposition is usually more intense if the housing will be occupied by homeless people, or others who have the greatest need. Property values are thought to be threatened and one's children or spouse are thought to be at great risk. Indeed, it is rare to hear of any community where established citizens, especially homeowners, have encouraged the building of affordable housing. The universal opposition has a well-known name: Not in My Back Yard (NIMBY). The cost of fighting this opposition has made housing the poor and disabled more expensive. Architect Sam Davis believes that NIMBYism is the underlying cause for most of the regulations and delays that add $20,000 to the building of a house in California.[25]

- **Building codes and zoning.** There is general agreement among experts that building codes and zoning ordinances increase the cost of housing as well as limit its availability. HUD and the National Association of Home Builders tested a variety of methods and building materials in the 1980s to reduce the cost of codes and zoning on affordable housing—savings of $6,000 per unit were common.[26] The results were encouraging, but most of the changes have not been widely adopted, primarily because of fears that property values and quality of life will decline along with housing prices. Examples include "zero lot lines" on one side of every house and smaller garages. Greater savings could perhaps be achieved by allowing manufactured housing to be placed on vacant lots in inner-city areas; however, very few cities are willing to try this alternative. Nearly all manufactured housing is placed in rural areas, often on lots that have poor or no water and sewer systems, causing health and environmental problems.[27]

CURRENT HOUSING POLICIES AND PROGRAMS

Most housing problems and opportunities are heavily influenced by housing policies, primarily at the federal level. The U.S. Congress can radically alter the quality and affordability of housing. They do this through a variety of direct nd indirect means. The basic mechanisms are changed every few years, as the government and the housing industry alternate between emphasis on "supply-side" or "demand-side" strategies. Supply-side strategies aim at stimulating developers and builders to produce new housing or rehabilitate existing units, while demand-side strategies aim at giving renters and home buyers more money to shop for housing. Housing policies operate through several interconnected systems, the basics of which are outlined below.

Finance and Tax Systems

The American systems of housing finance and taxation strongly favor the construction of and investment in housing that is much larger and of higher quality than necessary to meet the national goal of a decent affordable home of all Americans. The most significant elements of this systems are:

Mortgage interest deduction.   Approximately $50 billion per year in tax expenditures goes to taxpayers who deduct the full cost of the interest they pay on mortgage loans on their homes. This amount is *more than twice the annual HUD budget!* Much of this goes to people who consume large amounts of housing, well beyond their basic needs. Seventy-five percent of this benefit goes to people in the top 20 percent income group.[28] This subsidy for the wealthy increases each year, as the size and quality of new homes increases steadily. The low-income housing budget could be substantially increased if the deduction were limited (eliminating the subsidy could have a negative impact on home ownership).

Targeted tax credits.   In addition to tax deductions for certain types of housing investment, the U.S. government often prefers to use the indirect method of tax credits instead of directly building or subsidizing the building of affordable housing. The majority of low-income rental housing built in the 1990s has been subsidized by the Low Income Housing Tax Credit, which gives the wealthy ten years of tax credits for investing in qualified projects. Investors' hefty profits on these credits, along with legal and consultant costs, result in less than 60 percent of the money going into the housing itself.[29]

Investor inducements.   Federal and state governments, and some cities, try to stimulate the supply of certain types of housing by attracting investors through guaranteed earnings and reduced taxes on bonds, insurance for lenders, and similar tools. In a typical project, a developer will obtain a variety of loans and grants from five to ten different sources. The loans to the project will cover about 70 percent to 80 percent of the cost, with the balance made up of grants. Recent research shows that investors make a return of 17 percent to 19 percent, with very little risk since the loans are insured by the government.[30]

Promoting home ownership.   Most of our housing policies and programs are designed to promote home ownership, through both supply- and demand-side incentives. Ever since the Federal Housing Administration was established in 1934, our society has consistently viewed home ownership as both a source of stability for communities and families and as the preferred investment among varieties of living arrangements. Veterans of wars, for example, are encouraged to buy homes with zero down payment through VA loan guarantees. No similar assistance is available for renters.

Habitat for Humanity, which organizes groups of volunteers to build low-cost housing for the poor, is the largest nongovernment builder of housing in the United States as well as one of the most popular charities in the country. President Clinton recently declared that increasing home ownership by the year 2000 would be the goal of a national strategy. HUD and Fannie Mae, the nation's largest secondary market organization, are leading a collaboration of 56 groups in this effort. The range of innovative programs involved in this strategy is remarkable, especially when compared to the low-income rental housing problem. Here are a few of the programs:

- Homeownership Zones, in which cities will build entire new neighborhoods of homes supported by $30 million HUD grants
- Youthbuild, in which groups of lower-income youth learn a trade while building affordable housing; also supported with large HUD grants
- Self-Help Housing Opportunities Program, which, along with HUD support for expanding Habitat for Humanity, aims at unleashing volunteer energy and private money for low-income housing.
- Full Cycle Lending programs of Neighborworks© Organizations, in which nonprofits across the United States provide low-interest loans, housing counseling, and neighborhood improvement strategies in low-income areas.

Grants to state and local governments. Much of the production of affordable and special-needs housing in the United States has been financed through categorical grants and block grants from the federal government. *Categorical grants* were made to local and state governments that would agree to produce housing for specific groups of people in need, following detailed guidelines for the funding, building, occupants, and maintenance.

Categorical grants work well for certain groups that have well-known special needs. An example is housing for the mentally ill, which can be provided through grants and loans to specialized nonprofit developers. Community Access in New York City used such a program to build a new 50-unit apartment building for a combination of 22 single, mentally ill people with 28 low-income families. The city provides funding for the on-site provision of many services, including psychiatric care, employment, education, and job training.[31]

Block grants are rapidly replacing categorical grants as the primary source of federal funding for housing as well as for community development in general. Block grants were originally intended as a form of revenue sharing. They are "entitlements" to cities and states for a certain amount of money based on population and severity of poverty and the relative cost of housing in each jurisdiction. The largest of these is the Community Development Block Grant, which has recently totaled about $4.6 billion per year. In a recent year, cities with populations of more than 50,000 used an average of 36 percent of their grants for housing. The balance went to a wide variety of services for lower-income people, including senior and youth centers, child care, rebuilding streets, and other public facilities in distressed neighborhoods.[32]

HUD proposes to consolidate many of the special-needs grants into one large block grant. Housing for Persons with AIDS, Emergency Shelter Grants, Supportive Housing, and other targeted programs would be eliminated, giving cities and states their choice of where to invest scarce housing and related social service funds.

Empowerment zones and enterprise communities. HUD has gone through a major reorganization and downsizing in the 1990s. One of the keys to the new HUD is the emphasis on job creation and other aspects of economic development. One reason is the obvious relationship between income, wealth, and the quality of family and neighborhood life, including housing. Another is that as welfare reform and reduction in housing programs remove billions of dollars from poor communities, community development experts are desperately seeking new solutions to long-standing problems.

Empowerment zones are being created in cities and rural areas to stimulate job creation—investment in local people's skills—based on locally designed comprehensive plans. The tools used in these zones are familiar, mostly tax credits, bond programs, and other incentives to lure businesses back into depressed areas. HUD is also sponsoring a smaller version of this program called enterprise communities. These programs are all supposed to be coordinated through an antipoverty strategy that is outlined in a community's consolidated plan. Look at any of these plans and you will see a great disparity between the needs of the homeless and very-low-income people and the proposed programs.

Regulatory Pressure

One way for governments to improve housing without investing large sums of money is to pressure private developers and public housing providers through regulation and court actions. Some of these regulations are initiated by private citizens, some by public interest groups, and others are enacted after court challenges or at the request of industry groups. In addition to housing codes, pressure for equal access to housing is most common.

Equal access (equal opportunity).   Equal access to housing continues to be a problem for certain groups of people in many communities. The legal view of this problem is that enforcing laws requiring equal opportunity in housing is the means by which equal access can be achieved. There are, however, factors other than simple discrimination that keep people from equal access to decent, affordable housing. Business and governments sometimes limit people's access to affordable housing by locating jobs and transportation systems in remote suburban or exurban areas, forcing lower-income people to choose between paying for excess commuting or excess housing costs.[33]

Even public housing was completely segregated until the 1950s. The city of Buffalo at one time had a waiting list of over 1,000 blacks, at the same time they had over 4,000 empty public housing units waiting for white tenants.[34] In 1948, the NAACP won a Supreme Court case that rules restrictive covenants unconstitutional.[35] A typical covenant read "No lot shall ever be sold, conveyed, leased or rented to any person other than of the white or Caucasian race."[36]

HUD has aggressively pursued equal opportunity in both public and privately owned housing. One such case occurred in Yonkers, N.Y., where a federal court found that the city had deliberately segregated both its schools and housing by locating 96 percent of its public housing in one area.[37] The city was ordered to create a *Scattered Site Public Housing* program, which has been copied in a number of cities in the 1990s.

The Fair Housing Act of 1968 requires that virtually all landlords take action to achieve equal access to decent housing for nearly all Americans. In 1974, HUD began to require that all communities begin removing *architectural barriers* to handicapped access, beginning with public buildings and federally assisted housing. Accessibility for the handicapped was extended in the 1992 Americans with Disabilities Act to all except the smallest multifamily housing developments in the country.

Equal opportunity in housing is currently enforced by HUD, primarily through the activities of *fair housing councils*, voluntary organizations that receive some HUD funding. They employ staff and volunteers to do research and investigate complaints. They often send testers of different races to compare their treatment by landlords and real estate agents. These testers continue to report widespread discrimination, especially in rental housing. Some cities also operate *housing courts* where tenants and landlords argue their competing claims. Usually low-income tenants are assisted in these courts by organizers or advocates.

Inclusionary zoning.   Court action has made exclusionary zoning illegal.[38] Advocates for social justice and housing professionals have used this and other court decisions to build programs for *inclusionary zoning*, which requires developers of new housing to include a certain number of affordable housing units in each development. Montgomery County, Maryland, has used this method to produce over 10,000 affordable units in the last 25 years.[39] In other communities the developer is allowed to propose alternative social investments instead of building all the required affordable units. This method, called "linkage," includes such innovations, as in San Francisco, where the city collects a fee for all new, large developments that is dedicated to child care centers and vouchers.[40]

Lead paint. Another focus of significant regulatory intervention is lead paint. Young children, especially those in older inner-city housing, are often harmed by lead paint poisoning. All government-assisted housing must be inspected for lead, which must be removed or encapsulated according to strict specifications. This, of course, raises housing costs.

Community Reinvestment Act. The Community Reinvestment Act (CRA) is another tool that government and advocates are using to improve housing opportunities for disadvantaged groups. This law requires federally regulated banks to assess community credit and development needs in the bank's market area, and design programs to meet those needs. The CRA was passed in 1975, after community organizers exposed the practice of *redlining*, in which financial institutions were accused of drawing a red line around neighborhoods that were mostly poor and minority.

Many banks have now set up departments to deal with the demands of community groups for reinvestment, and have produced collaborative programs with governments and community-based organizations that make creative loans to low-income home buyers, develop housing for the homeless, and even support social services and local cultural programs. The CRA is enforced by the Federal Reserve and the Comptroller of the Currency.[41]

SOCIAL SERVICES IN HOUSING

Social workers have been involved in the housing sector primarily as social reformers and community organizers. Social services have been provided to people with special needs, such as persons with AIDS or those with disabilities. Service roles have usually been those of service coordinator, such as in the case of tenants who are displaced through government actions. Relocation staff work with families to help them find new homes and solve other needs caused by involuntary displacement.

Several programs in public housing developments use social staff to help tenants improve their life skills and economic circumstances. Tenant leaders are organized into *resident management councils*, where they learn how to manage maintenance of some parts of their housing, and may even be trained to develop small businesses such as day care and laundry services.

Some of the most successful social services in public housing have been pioneered by private groups, such as the LeClaire Courts redevelopment in Chicago, where tenants develop and manage businesses that increase their income and control over their lives.[42] HUD has promoted this type of program in several ways. Local housing authorities are encouraged by rules and with small grants to employ low-income tenants, especially females, in nontraditional jobs such as construction. Housing authorities also are required to provide social and employment services under the *Family Self-Sufficiency* program.

Property owners and managers seem to agree with HUD that supportive services help maintain property values, reduce crime (especially drug dealing), empower residents, improve the surrounding neighborhoods, and save money on security and repairs.[43] HUD requires service coordinators to have a background in social work or psychology. They use a combination of self-help group work, case management, and individuals counseling.

The quality and types of social services offered through assisted housing providers vary greatly from one city to another. In New York City, nonprofit housing managers are required to deliver a wide range of services to low-income tenants, which they pay for out of the rent they receive from government vouchers. In Oakland, California, "few, if any, dollars automatically flow into social services," causing nonprofit housing managers to find private sources of funding to pay their own social service staffs for services.[44]

Continuum of Care

HUD is promoting an approach called continuum of care, in which all providers of housing and social services for the homeless would be designed and managed as a comprehensive system with four components:

- Prevention, outreach, and assessment of needs and linking the homeless to service
- Emergency shelter for people on the streets
- Transitional housing with supportive services to develop homeless people's capacities
- Permanent housing, with or without supportive services

NEW DIRECTIONS

Continued Reduction of HUD

HUD continues to reduce its role and its staff. By the year 2000 the department expects to have reduced its workforce by 50 percent since the early 1980s. HUD plans to consolidate all its programs to perhaps three, through a combination of strategies, among which are:

- **Devolution of authority to state and local governments and private companies.** This will be accomplished by asking states to share risks of insurance programs; match HUD funds with local money; and invest in alternative networks of nonprofits, such as Habitat, Youthbuild, Neighborhood Reinvestment Corporation, and the National Community Development Initiative.
- **Conversion of subsidized housing to market rates.** HUD is lowering the guaranteed rents of nearly one million housing units, while nego-

tiating financing deals with the owners, with the goal of removing the government from any support for these projects. HUD expects that low-income tenants will have to pay more for rent, and some owners will walk away from their buildings as these conversions occur.

Deregulation of Public Housing

The Congress and HUD are both pursuing deregulation as this is written. It is aimed at allowing local housing authorities to compete with private landlords for more desirable tenants, while reducing the level of federal funding. Some of the changes that are already affecting the lives of lower-income renters include:

- **Increased tenant opportunity to live where they choose.** Housing authorities will be required to compete for housing vouchers that are given to tenants, which could result in large numbers of tenants moving out, leaving units vacant and resulting in bankruptcy of some housing authorities. HUD is experimenting with one version of this, which is called *Moving to Opportunity*, based on the assumption that low-income families will move to suburban areas where they will find jobs and will be positively influenced by the new social environment.
- **Eliminating one-for-one replacement.** Congress recently removed the requirement that any low-income government-assisted housing that is demolished must be replaced by another unit somewhere in that community. Public and private owners of such housing immediately began to destroy their least profitable housing units, adding to the shortage. The law requiring that low-income people pay no more than 30 percent of their income for housing is also under attack, and is likely to be eliminated soon.

The Impact of Welfare Reform

The relationship between this housing crisis and the social welfare system is clear and direct. Large numbers of welfare recipients are also rent-burdened. The system operates sort of like a lottery. Those who qualify for one of the mainstream programs such as public assistance may also be lucky enough to get a Section 8 certificate, as well as food stamps and possibly reduced-cost day care if they work or go to school. Such families might have an officially recognized income of only a few hundred dollars a month, while effectively receiving more than double that amount in cash equivalents.

Those who are less fortunate, for example a Supplemental Security Income (SSI) recipient who is on the waiting list for assisted housing, are very likely to pay a majority of their meager income for rent. The HUD Crossroads report estimates that "the SSI results imply that the worst case needs among adults with disabilities are more than five times as great" as in the general population.[45]

Much of this will change with welfare reform. Those who are dropped from public assistance will have a number of poor choices, including doubling up with other households, paying a much larger portion of their income for rent, or relocating to rural areas or other communities where housing is cheaper.

SUMMARY AND CONCLUSIONS

Providing decent, affordable housing for all Americans will probably continue to be an important social policy goal that is not fully met. Indeed, the future of housing and related social services in the United States seems likely to be tied more than ever to the ability of the private market systems to provide housing for lower-income people and those with special needs. States and cities will face pressures to replace some of the federal programs that will disappear as HUD continues to be downsized. Nonprofits will probably produce a larger portion of affordable housing, especially for the homeless. The cost of providing enough new and rehabilitated housing for groups in need is likely to far outstrip the willingness of taxpayers and politicians to respond.

To improve this picture dramatically, and eliminate homelessness, as has been done in many other countries, would require either a moral revolution or a radical change in our system of distributing income and wealth. There are some signs that in certain communities local civic and religious leaders are attempting to inspire such changes. It is, however, more realistic to hope that the recent gradual improvements in jobs and income of the working poor will eventually lead to increased family purchasing power, and a long-term trend toward greater social justice in housing.

Notes

1. From the lowest-income peoples to the highest, having a secure shelter of some sort seems to be universal, as seen in the range of housing types and residents' other possessions. See Peter Menzel, *Material World: A Global Family Portrait* (San Francisco: Sierra Club Books, 1994.)
2. Stuart A. Gabriel, "Urban Housing Policy in the 1990s," *Housing Policy Debate*, vol. 7, issue 3 (1996): 675.
3. Duncan MacLennan, "Housing to 2001: Can Britain Do Better?" *Housing Policy Debate*, vol. 6, issue 3 (1995): 675.
4. Kai T. Erickson, in *Everything in Its Path,* describes the results of a huge flood that left 4,000 homeless: "Nearly everyone left in the community has recurring fears of future invasions of their homes by unexpected forces. Psychosomatic illnesses have dramatically increased, families, friendships and neighborhoods are no longer close-knit, as if the loss of their homes required new personalities" (Englewood Cliffs, NJ: Simon & Schuster, 1976).
5. Elliot Liebow, *Tell Them Who I Am: The Lives of Homeless Women* (New York: Penguin Books, 1995), p. 35.
6. Personal communication with several emergency shelter directors during the late 1980s, including Andy Raubeson, executive director, SRO Housing, Los Angeles, and Ruth Schwartz, executive director of Shelter Partnerhsip, Los Angeles.
7. Thomas I. Kenyon and Justine Blau, *What You Can Do to Help the Homeless* (New York: Simon and Schuster, 1991), p. 12.
8. National Housing Act of 1949, which established many goals that have never been achieved.
9. Personal observation and discussions with personnel in the Department of Social Development, Belmopan, Belize.
10. I have discussed this issue with numerous local government officials for many years. Most local governments rely on "windshield surveys" to estimate housing

conditions for specific project areas. They also analyze housing inspection reports to derive averages. This does not reveal what the residents think of their housing, which can more easily be estimated by observing their behavior when they have choices.

11. National Commission on American Indian, Alaska Native and Native Hawaiian Housing, *Building the Future: A Blueprint for Change* (Washington, DC, 1993), p. 11.

12. Robert Hunter, *Tenement Condition in Chicago: A Report by the Investigating Committee of the City Homes Association,* 1901, pp. 18, 52.

13. Joint Center for Housing Studies, Harvard University, *The State of the Nation's Housing* 1995, p. 4.

14. U.S. Census of Housing, 1990. Available @ www.census.gov.

15. Houston Consolidated Plan Executive Summary, 1996. Available @ www.hud.gov/cpes.

16. A 1994 housing inspection provided to the author prior to purchase of a substandard house in Alexandria, VA. Correcting all the cited deficiencies required an investment of over $20,000.

17. Walter A. Friedlander and Robert Z. Apte, *Introduction to Social Welfare* (Englewood Cliffs, NJ: Prentice-Hall, 1980), pp. 339–340.

18. Average household size among Hispanics is now 40 percent higher than among white, non-Hispanic households, and these households are known to be underreported in the census. See Amy Bogdon, Joshua Silver, and Margery Austin Turner, *National Analysis of Housing Affordability, Adequacy, and Availability: A Framework for Local Housing Strategies,* report by the Urban Institute for U.S. Dept. Of HUD, November 1993, p. 18.

19. Consolidated Plan, Dallas, TX, FY 1995–96 through FY 1997–98 @ www.hud.gov/cpes, page 3.

20. Jonathan Freedman, *Crowding and Behavior* (New York: Viking Press, 1975), p. 104.

21. The average new single-family home is now 1800 to 2000 square feet, with an average of just under three persons. In the '40s and early '50s, when war veterans were buying millions of homes in new subdivisions, the averge home was about 600 to 800 square feet. What was four rooms and a bath has grown to be four bedrooms and three baths.

22. HUD, office of Policy Development and Research, *Rental Housing at A Crossroads: A Report to Congress on Worst Case Housing Needs,* March 14, 1996. Introductory letter. I rely on this report, along with data from the U.S. Census Bureau @ www.census.gov, and the Annual Housing Survey, for much of the analysis of affordability.

23. Peter Dreier, "Philanthropy and the Housing Crisis: The Dilemmas of Private Charity and Public Policy," *Housing Policy Debate,* Vol. 8, Issue 1 (1997), p. 248.

24. Joint Center for Housing Studies, *State of the Nation's Housing 1995* (Cambridge: Harvard University), p. 20.

25. Sam Davis, *The Architecture of Affordable Housing* (Berkeley, CA: The University of California Press 1995), pp. 40–41.

26. Barbara Bryan, "The For Profit Homebuilder's Perspective on Affordable Housing," in Jess Lederman, ed., *Housing America* (Chicago: Probus Publishing Co., 1993), p. 122.

27. A three-bedroom manufactured house costs an average of $39,000. Certain western and southern cities do permit new manufactured housing. In Las Cruces, New Mexico, 25 percent of the housing is of this type, and the majority of new units in that city have been of the manufactured type every year since the 1990s. See HUD, U.S. Housing Market Conditions, 4th quarter, 1996, p. 28. Published February 1997 @ http://huduser.org.

28. National Coalition for the Homeless, *Why Are People Homeless?* Fact Sheet #1, January 1997, p. 5 @ http://nch.ari.net/causes.

29. *Tax Credit Returns Questioned.* Housing Affairs Letter, May 2, 1997, page 4 (Silver Spring, MD: CD Publications). For an overview see Jennifer Blake, Low Income Housing Tax Credits, Neighborhood Reinvestment Training Institute, 1997, @ www.nwo.org.

30. James E. Wallace, "Financing Affordable Housing in the United States," *Housing Policy Debate,* vol. 6, issue 4 (1995), p. 800.

31. Community Information Exchange, *Case Studies on Special Needs Housing* (Washington, DC: Community Information Exchange, 1995): 43.

32. HUD, Office of Community Planning and Development, Renewing Government, *1996 Consolidated Annual Report,* p. 114.

33. This often becomes a public policy issue because the government subsidizes the business investment and the transportation system that result in a lack of equal access to decent affordable housing.

34. William L. Evans, *Race Fear and Housing in a Typical American Community* (New York: National Urban League, 1946), p. 40.

35. *Shelly* v. *Kramer,* 334 U.S. 1 (1948).

36. Minnesota Governor's Interracial Commission, *The Negro and His Home in Minnesota: A Report to Governor Luther W. Youngdahl* (1947): 66.

37. *U.S.* v. *City of Yonkers* et al. (1985).

38. The major decision was *Southern Burlington NAACP et al.* v. *Mt. Laurel,* 67 NJ 151 (1975).

39. Nico Calavita et al., "Inclusionary Housing in California and New Jersey: A Comparative Analysis," *Housing Policy Debate,* vol. 8, issue 1 (1997), p. 111.

40. *Linking Development Benefits to Neighborhoods: A Manual of Community-Based Strategies* (Washington, DC: Community Information Exchange, 1989), p. 51.

41. For an account of the evolution of the CRA, see *From Redlining to Reinvestment,* Gregory D. Squires, ed. (Philadelphia: Temple University Press, 1992).

42. Thomas Rodenbaugh, *Human Services: An Economic Development Opportunity* (Washington, DC: National Congress for Community Economic Development, 1992).

43. Glenn L. French, *Government Assisted Housing* (Chicago: Institute of Real Estate Management, 1997), p. 101.

44. Rachel Bratt et al., *Confronting the Management Challenge: Affordable Housing in the Nonprofit Sector* (New York: New School for Social Research, 1994), p. 99.

45. *Rental Housing Assistance at the Crossroads,* p. 29.

Additional Suggested Readings

Atlas, John, and Ellen Shoshkes. *Saving Affordable Housing.* Orange, NJ: National Housing Institute, 1997.

Downs, Anthony. *New Visions for Metropolitan America.* Washington, DC: The Brookings Institution, 1994.

Fannie Mae Foundation. *Using Housing Policy to Build Healthy Communities: A Response to Devolution and Welfare Reform,* Proceedings of the Fannie Mae Foundation 1997 Annual Housing Conference. Washington, DC, April 30, 1997.

Gilderbloom, John I., and Richard P. Appelbaum. *Rethinking Rental Housing.* Philadelphia: Temple University Press, 1988.

Hecht, Bennett I. *Developing Affordable Housing.* New York: John Wiley and Sons, 1994.

Kotlowitz, Alex. *There Are No Children Here.* New York: Doubleday, 1991.

Kozol, Jonathan. *Rachel and Her Children: Homeless Families in America.* New York: Random House, 1988.

Kozol, Jonathan. *Amazing Grace.* New York: HarperCollins, 1995.

Medoff, Peter, and Holly Sklar. *Streets of Hope: The Fall and Rise of an Urban Neighborhood.* Boston: South End Press, 1994.

Vissing, Yvonne. *Out of Sight, Out of Mind: Homeless Children and Families in Small Town America.* Lexington, KY: University of Kentucky Press, 1996.

25

Social Development: An International Perspective

JUDITH LEE BURKE

Societies differ in how they view development, and controversy exists about the nature and definition of social development.[1] Social development workers note that "the individual is affected by...social circumstances and that political and economic factors have a great impact in shaping the social circumstances of individuals and groups."[2] The goal of social development workers is to change such circumstances by reforming institutions, policies, and programs; they advocate for units of people such as communities, unions, or networks of common interest. These workers take a broad systems view of the structural inequities underlying socioeconomic problems. Social development is based on such core values as global awareness, popular participation and collective action, and economic redistribution.[3] The highest priority is to fulfill basic human needs through equalizing access to opportunities.

The United Nations has described social development as a process involving "the structural transformation of societies, rather than measures that merely stimulate economic growth."[4] In order to appreciate this perspective, other concepts need elaboration. Development in this chapter refers to planned growth in a previously underdeveloped sector of society. Development can be domestic—that is, limited to changes within one country—however, the examples described here will apply to international development, in which one or more countries or nongovernmental agencies assist people who live abroad. Targeting areas of the world for social development requires knowledge about the great inequities that exist.[5] Regions differ vastly as measured by economic indices, such as per capita income or the gross national product (GNP); by social indices, such as health indicators and educational levels attained; or by material standards, such as how many people own cars, bikes, or indoor plumbing. The base upon which development builds is often referred to as infrastructure. This can mean "the specific ecological and geographical conditions within which a society exists and from which it extracts its material means of existence."[6] Infrastructure also commonly includes human additions to natural resources, like roads or communications systems in place. A goal of development is for residents to become less dependent upon outside help; for this, infrastructure must increase.

PLANNED INSTITUTIONAL CHANGE

One model of social development has been proposed by a social worker to exemplify development through existing institutions (see Figure 25.1). Hollister described social development as "planned institutional change to bring about a better fit between human needs and social policies and programs."[7] Hollister depicted social development as a process in which the institutional mechanisms for service delivery are improved. At the base of the treelike model are human needs. Virtually all who have worked for social development and recounted their experiences or research warn against assuming what people need. Needs should be self-defined, although professionals can aid the process of need definition through community discussion and self-surveys. Methods exist to help community groups define their needs. Local traditions of social order may demand flexibility on the developer's part: Go-betweens may express local people's needs, for instance, rather than their speaking directly in public meetings.

Cultural limits (the "trunk" of the model) determine which needs are recognized and put forth as legitimate concerns for social action. Social and organizational constraints further affect the next stage of the model, in which recognized needs may become organized as community demands. Political forces enter into each part of the social development process. Hollister urged social workers to recognize political influences upon policy formulation, planning, and program implementation. Politics characteristic of the region in which social development is attempted greatly affect the strategies employed and the outcomes. Groups targeted for social development projects display self-interest and conflicting values, like all groups. A community problem may reflect general concern, but factions typically arise among people of unequal power and visibility. If no factions appear among prospective participants, the social development worker may learn afterwards that the representation was biased, with only an elite group attending. The field has recognized risks associated with elitism and struggled with ways to reach the poorest and least-represented people, as case illustrations will show. Participants' value conflicts require open analysis to bring about change. Lackey has described a process of development that involves the optimization of conflicting values.[8]

SOCIAL DEVELOPMENT LINKS SYSTEMS

Organized community demands formed the center of Hollister's model, suggesting that a distinctive feature of social development is its creation of linkages among multiple systems. For this to succeed, workers must establish collaboration between traditional agencies and institutions and often must work beyond their boundaries. This is a challenge when human service agencies divide into separate empires, with few incentives to work jointly. One of the tasks of social development workers is to help create systems that are broad enough in scope to

FIGURE 25.1 A General Model of the Social Development Process

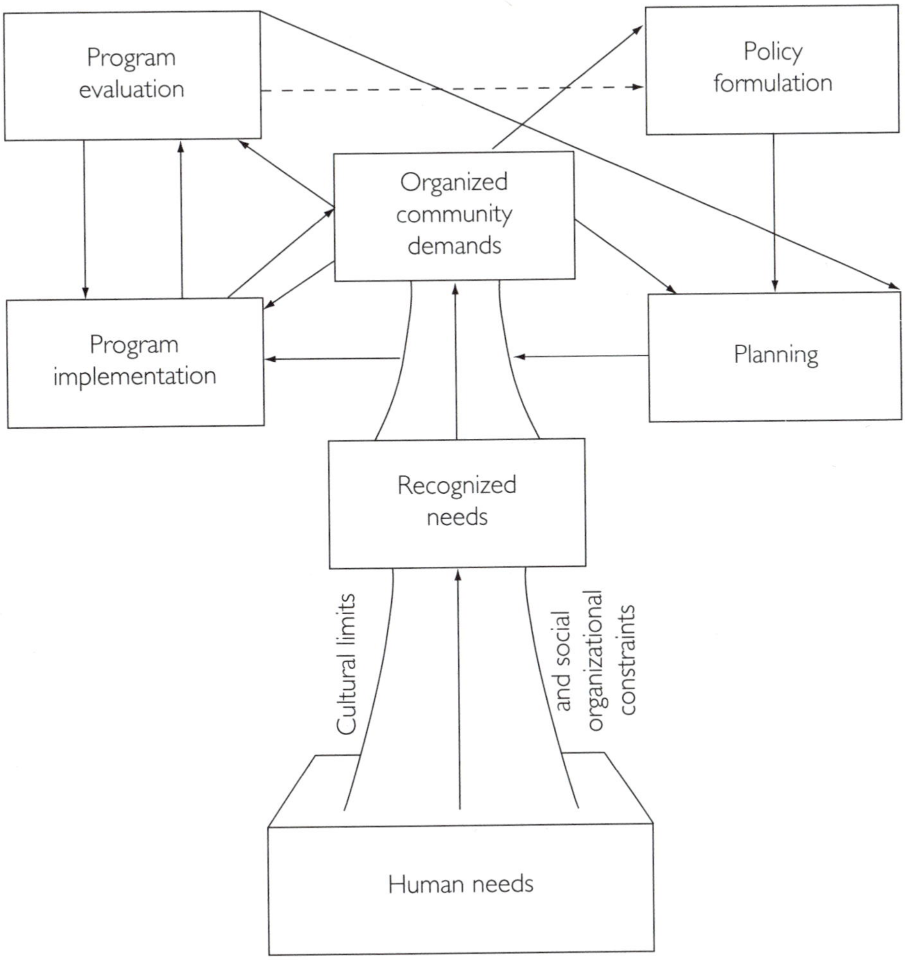

Source: Hollister model reproduced by permission of *Social Development Issues*, The University of Iowa, School of Social Work.

provide needed links. Communication and transportation systems must be in place for localities to receive materials and maintain contact with central offi-cials. To attain these links, the relations between dominant decision makers and the people must permit feedback among citizen participants and multi-agency staff with support and resources. Intermediate institutions at the community or regional level provide a measure of popular control when the stimulus may be a national or international plan. Working in an industrialized country with reliable travel, phone, fax, or Web connections contrasts sharply with the scant resources of a poor region.

TECHNOLOGY

Technology, put simply, is how things are done. Privileged owners and users of technology may consider modern machinery and computer applications as the equivalent of technology; however, processes of doing work are also part of technology. The role of technology in social development is complex. New and sophisticated tools that Western consumers welcome may fail to apply elsewhere. Finding what technological changes are preferred and are feasible and affordable, both immediately and in the long run, is a key effort in the process of implementing development. Just as in social work generally, cultural values and customs must be considered when trying to fit a technology to its potential users. Failures, or partial failures, have included the export of machinery to countries without the means to maintain it, or the export of infant formula to areas where the water mixed with it was impure.[9]

In contrast, the term *appropriate technology* describes apt technological solutions—culturally acceptable and useful—to human problems. Examples of successful introduction of technology are many and varied. They have included tailoring of resettlement dwellings to residents' customs,[10] as well as devising, in Africa, a mill to process a grain that is easily grown but difficult to convert to food. Technology rarely *automatically* transfers from one setting to another. Potential adopters of the new methods and tools must have input. Moreover, concerns about technological impact upon the environment of a locale are being expressed. Sustainable development entails the issue of whether the pace and the by-products of growth can be sustained given the ecology of the systems that it affects.[11] A world summit sponsored by the United Nations Conference on Environment and Development met in 1992 in Brazil to help address this critical issue.[12]

ACTORS IN DEVELOPMENT PROGRAMS

Who are the people targeted for social development? A full answer would require familiarity with United States foreign policy and history.[13] In 1944, the Bretton Woods conference etablished a financial system known as the International Monetary Fund (IMF) to regulate world currencies; it created the World Bank. The direct aid relief or loans that followed were tied to the U.S. dollar. The United Nations Relief and Rehabilitation Administration (UNRRA) provided aid for those impoverished by war, but Europe's economy grew worse. The Marshall Plan was introduced to Congress in 1947, as a means to help Western Europe rebuild its industries and recover economically through the United States' investment. The Marshall Plan set precedent for peacetime foreign aid; it initiated long-term planning for development, as well as offering temporary relief for dire needs. The aid was often unilateral, from the United States as donor country to the governments of the recipients.

Drafters and supporters of the Marshall Plan had humanitarian values, yet they also believed that the welfare of the United States depended upon having economically viable world neighbors. Both motives have persisted in the field of international development. Social workers can usually identify enthusiastically with the humanitarian values. Yet sometimes the argument in support of helping people in other countries must be made in economic terms. One response to critics of international development is that citizens who live in areas where the chances for their livelihood have improved are potentially consumers. Another is that the monies designated for foreign aid by Congress help purchase and export U.S. agricultural products and equipment for development; now it is estimated that close to 80 percent of the United States Agency for International Development's contracts and grants go directly to this country's firms, organizations, and institutions for work overseas.[14] The foreign policy of the United States has determined and will continue to dictate which countries benefit from funding for social development. The Cold War dominated such policy for decades. Now in the era after the Cold War other national security and economic interests prevail.

The United States has not been the sole donor of aid for development. In fact, when measured by GNP per capita, it is one of the smallest donors. With post–World War II economic recovery, other wealthy donor nations emerged. Collectively, these came to be known as "the North," while many recipient countries traditionally known as "the South" were viewed as "developing," as the "Third World," or, for the poorest countries, as the "Fourth World."[15] Low per capita incomes and low GNPs were conditions targeted for development in the host countries where programs and projects took place.[16] Between approximately 1950 and 1975, international agencies like the Agency for International Development and the World Bank promoted economic approaches to raise the GNP of poor countries.[17] Many social workers and others working for social development did not embrace this model for Third World nations because they disagreed with growth economists' assumptions.[18] One assumption being tested was that overall economic gains for developing countries would trickle down to their poorest citizens. The problem with trickle-down theory has been that poor people have rarely received the products of growth. Large-scale capital-intensive programs did not target the poorest people in plans except to provide labor. Corruption has also contributed to the failure of development programs that were meant to build infrastructure and to reach intended beneficiaries.[19]

In addition to dissatisfaction with the trickle-down approach, an important critique exists of the controlling economic forces that may underlie inequalities. World system theorists argue that exploitation by colonial and postcolonial rich countries has kept poor regions poor.[20] They have cited excessive mining of natural resources, labor exploitation, loan policies that create staggering debts, and other practices by outsiders as evidence. The globalization of world economies in which multinational corporations conduct business has created new systems of control over the world's poor.[21]

An alternative to the administration of development policies and programs through central governments of countries has been growing in numbers and influence. Nongovernmental organizations, known as NGOs, may meet the needs of host country citizens in ways that governmental bureaucracies cannot. Both secular and religious-affiliated nongovernmental agencies exist. Many fund small-scale projects and may be freer to pursue social development than those agencies that are saddled with political agendas.

Village Networks

Korten analyzed development programs that had specifically dealt with the engagement of local participants.[22] These included models of villager or union input and contact with influential leadership in settings as diverse as an Indian dairy cooperative, the Bangladesh multipurpose Rural Advancement Committee, and a Sri Lankan village network. Korten illustrated the strengths and weaknesses of programs that had shown objective signs of success, such as spontaneous replications. Critical of programs built from the top down and administered from afar, he selected case examples that derived from local people's expression of their needs. The Dairy Council built upon a bureaucrat's skills in collaborating with small farmers (e.g., those owning one cow) to improve union practices in marketing their products. Korten noted that a strength in this organization was the close monitoring of growth, experimenting as it proceeded. Equal access through setting up a system to wait in line to sell milk, for example, altered some of the social interaction among caste members. Later the World Bank funded the Dairy Council to expand its products and membership. Its originator became its national administrator. Development programs in Sri Lanka and Bangladesh were studied by reviewing participants' evaluations and other data. Typical problems included biased appointments of participants rather than elections; failure to share funding with the intended recipients; failure to identify the poorest vilages; and corruption. Responses to the evaluation led to better screening of trainees and to inclusion of villagers in data collection. Other solutions involved the support of collective, self-help activities, rather than giving direct benefits or handouts. Where cliques interfered, regional groups were reconstituted to invite broader participation. Korten stressed that using participants' input and modifying the program over time was an improvement over projects dominated by centralized government requirements.[23]

Women of Self-Employed Women's Association (SEWA)

Microenterprise makes credit or loans available to people who ordinarily would have been turned away because they were too poor to have collateral or to appear worth the risk to lending institutions.[24] Another case example involved organizing the means to give small loans or microcredit to very marginally self-employed Indian women.[25] Many belonged to unions that had done little for their membership. The leaders felt that autonomy and self-help were necessary but could be boosted with formal union status in the Self-Employed Women's Association or SEWA. Individuals' dues were combined to hire social workers who served the women and their families. They assisted women in meeting loan repayments and did crisis intervention. These women, Jain noted, got "closer to members and assured them of SEWA's financial and moral support in all cases of genuine distress."[26]

Credit was established at local banks for small loans. SEWA generated many empowering activities such as teaching about banking; changing bank procedures for illiterate customers; and controlling its own vendor carts, which the women had formerly been forced to rent at high rates. SEWA also offered maternity, widowhood, and death benefits for families; day care to supplement poor government facilities; and occupational training and health education for workers. Leadership training was available to women who displayed interest in extending SEWA's work and their skills. This helped ensure participation and continuity when professionals turned activities fully over to members.

The case of SEWA shows how the processes of social development intertwine. The women's basic needs were evoked in a series of organizational meetings. Cultural and social institutions, including existing but weak trade unions, informal networks, and banks were used to guide expression of these needs in a form that society could accept. Microcredit was extended with ready loans for poor woman who lacked credit histories. SEWA maintained an ongoing evaluation of workers' experiences with its programs. The group orginally formed to meet one set of needs tried to remain responsive to new needs. Although SEWA provided a comprehensive structure beyond small loans, microcredit itself is a viable way to empower poor people to help themselves. In fact, microenterprises, funded by small loans, have been so encouraging overseas that domestic projects within the United States based on the same principle are now receiving attention. Technology can transfer to the United States.

SKILLS FOR SOCIAL DEVELOPMENT

Most social workers learn to do community organization and planning. These skills are basic for workers in social development. Further, the field demands knowledge of economic and political processes. The history of a region is vital to know. Practitioners should prepare to honor differences in customs—a process helped not only by reading and prior exposure to audiovisual material, but also by contact with residents of the area who can brief social workers. Information from the State Department about the "post" or region in which the development project is to take place may also assist with this educational process. Other social work skills useful for practice include the analysis and reform of social policy, research, and evaluation. With the addition of group work skills, workers can facilitate social development and assess its effectiveness. Facility in the language of the region may permit more open access to key personnel and to participants.

Social development demands change. Vested interests resist change. Powerful people fear ownership reforms, credit reallocations, and expansion of opportunities that may have been monopolized. Familiarity with mediation and with conflict resolution methods and roles will be essential.

PREPARATION FOR AN INTERNATIONAL PERSPECTIVE

To practice social development requires knowledge of different social welfare systems and alternative ways to meet human needs. Anders depicted international study as a weak component of U.S. social work education,[27] and some international social work students have also questioned its applicability.[28] A test is whether a social work curriculum restricts itself to one nation's—or region's— practices. However, study abroad and overseas seminars and field experiences have begun to help address comparative social development and social welfare issues. Students interested in comparing national programs may do so with resources like Estes's *Trends in World Social Development*,[29] *Journal of International and*

Comparative Social Welfare,[30] and *Community Development Journal: An International Forum.*[31] Associations of social workers practicing social development form a worldwide network. The International Association of Social Welfare meets yearly and publishes *International Social Work.*[32]

SUMMARY AND CONCLUSIONS

Social development is an order of social work that spans policy analysis and change, social service systems modification, and the empowerment of people to help themselves by establishing alternative institutions. Its goals are to provide conditions in which people can meet basic needs and, beyond that, to improve the quality of their lives in ways that they select. Workers in social development place great value on collective action and economic redistribution to make opportunities more accessible to poor people. Another value held by social workers in this field is that of global awareness. Practitioners of social development are able to see connections between problems of people in developing countries who are vulnerable in the existing economies and welfare systems and similar problems faced by people in the United States. Indeed, since this book was first published, the movement toward a gobal economy and trade agreements that cross national boundaries, as well as the impact upon workers in the United States, help to bring these connections home. Social development programs are staffed by social workers, along with professionals from other disciplines who may have gained experience in the Peace Corps, in Vista, or with NGOs and found that they were committed to helping solve worldwide human problems.

Notes

1. R. Harris, "Beyond Rhetoric: A Challenge for International Social Work," *International Social Work,* International Council on Social Welfare (1990): 213–223.
2. Salima Omer, "Social Development," *International Social Work* (Bombay: International Council on Social Welfare, 1979).
3. Dennis R. Falk, "Social Development Values," *Social Development Issues* 5 (1981): 67–83.
4. Hazel Henderson, *"International Social Development Review"* (New York: United Nations Publications, Department of Economic and Social Affairs, No. 3., 1971, p. iii).
5. York Bradshaw and Michael Wallace, *Global Inequalities* (Thousand Oaks, CA: Pine Forge Press, 1996).
6. Maurice Godelier, "Infrastructures, Societies, and Histories," *Current Anthropology* 19 (1978): 763.
7. David C. Hollister, "Social Work Skills for Social Development," *Social Development Issues* 1 (1977): 9–20.
8. Alvin S. Lackey, "Defining Development," *Journal of Rural Development and Administration* 22, no. 4 (1990): 63–75.
9. Sandra L. Huffman, "Determination of Breastfeeding in Developing Countries: Overview and Policy Implications," *Studies in Family Planning* (New York: Population Council, 1984), pp. 170–183; see also "Nestle Gives In—Again," *Interdependent* 10, no. 1 (January–February 1984).

10. Pamela R. Johnson et al., *Egypt: the Egyptian American Rural Improvement Service, A Point Four Project, 1952–63.* A.I.D. Project Impact Evaluation No. 43 (Washington, DC: U.S. Agency for International Development, April 1983).

11. Richard J. Estes, "Toward Sustainable Development: From Theory to Praxis," *Social Development Issues* 15 (1993): 1–29.

12. Drafts Agenda 21; Rio Declaration; Forest Principles. United Nations Conference on Environment and Development (New York: United Nations, June 1992).

13. Diane Kunz, *Butter and Guns: America's Cold War Economic Diplomacy* (New York: Free Press, 1997).

14. *SAID Development* (Washington, DC: U.S. Agency for International Development 3, No. 2, 1997), p. 4.

15. The South Commission, *The Challenge to the South: The Report of the South Commission* (Oxford: Oxford University Press, 1990).

16. Satish Sharma and Thomas Walz, "Social Development in Third World Nations: A Reflective Assessment in the Shadow of the 21st Century," *Social Development Issues* 14 Nos. 2/3 (1992): 13–27.

17. Lane E. Holdcroft, *The Rise and Fall of Community Development in Developing Countries, 1950–65,* MSU Rural Development Paper No. 2 (East Lansing: Michigan State University, 1978).

18. Sharma and Walz, "Social Development."

19. Alvin S. Lackey, "Why Development Projects Don't Work as Planned: Pitfalls and 'Solutions,'" Special Studies Series on Global Development, no. 5 (College Park, MD: World Academy of Development and Cooperation, 1987); see also Nicholas D. Kristof, "Why Africa Can Thrive Like Asia," *New York Times,* Sunday, May 25, 1997, Week in Review, Section 4, pp. 1 and 6.

20. Bradshaw and Wallace, *Global Inequalities.*

21. Mitchell A. Seligson and John T. Passe-Smith, eds., *Development and Underedevelopment: The Political Economy of Inequality* (Boulder, CO: Lynne Rienner Publishers, 1993); and Peter F. Drucker, *Managing for the Future: The 1990s and Beyond* (New York: Truman Tally, 1993).

22. David C. Korten, "Community Organization and Rural Development: A Learning Process Approach," *Public Administration,* September/October 1980, pp. 480–511.

23. Ibid.

24. Lisa D. Steven, "Credit as a Women's Issue in Social Development: The Janashakthi Banking Society in Sri Lanka," *Social Development Issues* 16, no. 1 (1994): 107–118; and "Microcredit—An Emerging Tool for Fighting Poverty," *USAID Developments* (Washington, DC: U.S. Agency for International Development 3, No. 2, 1997): 2.

25. Devaki Jain, *Women's Quest for Power* (New Delhi: Vikas House, 1980).

26. Ibid., p. 39.

27. J.R. Anders, "Internationalism in Social Work Education," *Journal of Education for Social Work* 11, no. 2 (1975): 16–21.

28. M. Cetingok and H. Hirayama, "Foreign Students in Social Work Schools: Their Characteristics and Assessment of Programmes in the U.S.," *International Social Work* 33, no. 3 (1990): 243–253.

29. Richard J. Estes, *Trends in World Social Development: The Social Progress of Nations, 1970–87* (New York: Praeger, 1988).

30. *Journal of International and Comparative Social Welfare* (Baton Rouge: Louisiana State University School of Social Work).

31. *Community Development Journal* (Manchester, England: Oxford Univeristy Press).

32. *International Social Work,* International Council on Social Welfare (London: Sage Publication).

Additional Suggested Readings

Black, Jan Knippers. *Development in Theory and Practice: Bridging the Gap*. Boulder, CO: Westview, 1991.

Development Dialogue. A journal of international development cooperation published by the Dag Hammarskjöld Foundation, Uppsala, Sweden.

Human Development Report. New York: United Nations Development Program, annual publication.

Lowe, Gary R. "Social Development," in *Encyclopedia of Social Work*, 19th ed. (Washington, DC: NASW, 1995), pp. 2168–2173.

Midgley, James. *Social Development: The Developmental Perspectives in Social Welfare*. Thousand Oaks, CA: Sage, 1995.

Nagel, Stuart S., ed. *African Development and Public Policy*. New York: St. Martin's Press, 1994.

Nayak, Radhakant, ed. *The Fourth World: Appraisal and Aspirations*. New Delhi: Manohar Publishers, 1997.

Schneider, Bertrand. *The Barefoot Revolution: A Report to the Club of Rome*. London: Intermediate Technology Publications, 1988.

Tinker, Irene. *Persistent Inequalities: Women and World Development*. New York: Oxford University Press, 1990.

Weaver, James H. *Achieving Broad-Based Sustainable Development: Governance, Environment, and Growth with Equity*. West Hartford, CT: Kumarian Press, 1997.

White, Louise G. *Implementing Policy Reforms in the LDCs: A Strategy for Designing and Effecting Change*. Boulder, CO: Lynne Rienner Publishers, 1990.

26

Professionalization, Education, and Personnel in the Social Services

H. WAYNE JOHNSON

Not surprisingly, at a time of pervasive ferment in American society and the world, social work, like many other professions, is undergoing major changes. It is experiencing change in educational preparation, in personnel standards, and in a number of aspects of professionalization.

Whether or not social work is actually a profession—or the extent to which it is—constitutes a long-standing question. Abraham Flexner, an educator, speaking to the 1915 National Conference of Charities and Corrections, advanced criteria for a profession and contended that on some of these measures social work did not qualify.[1] Greenwood, in 1957, noted that professions possess five attributes: a knowledge base, authority, sanction of the community, regulative codes of ethics, and a professional culture.[2] Based on these, Greenwood found social work to be a profession.

The issue was also dealt with by Etzioni, in 1969, in his work on what he called *semi-professions*, which dealt with teachers, nurses, and social workers.[3] All three are fields in which women outnumber men in contrast to most of the older, more established and recognized professions in which males predominate, although less so recently.

In the Etzioni book, Goode predicted, "These semi-professions will achieve professionalism over the next generation: social work, marital counseling, and perhaps city planning."[4] Interestingly, in a reference to this statement he writes:

> Perhaps it should be emphasized that we are referring to the social worker, who has undergone professional training which culminates in the M.S.W. or the doctorate in social work. By contrast, the welfare or case worker in urban

departments of welfare is much less likely to have been trained in a formal curriculum and, of course, does not fall into this category.[5]

It should be stressed that while in some respects Goode's comment is still applicable today, recent undergraduate social work education developments and expansion have, to some degree, transformed the picture. This does not change the fact, however, that considerable numbers of persons without social work education are employed to staff the human services.

One essay in Etzioni is based entirely on a sample of social workers from one county welfare department.[6] In view of this, it should be pointed out that public welfare agencies nationally do not constitute a uniform homogeneous entity and that they are probably more bureaucratic than at least some other fields of service in the extremely broad, diverse, and complex field of social work totally. The author of the essay acknowledged that the group was not presented as representative or typical of social work generally.[7]

THE PROFESSION OF SOCIAL WORK

Understandably, the reader may have difficulty appreciating the significance of this whole professionalization subject. The point is that questions, debates, and struggles over whether or not a particular field, in this case social work, is or is not a profession are indicative of the professionalization process itself. Some occupations obviously developed much earlier as professions whereas others, such as social work, did so later or are still emerging.

Regardless of how social work is perceived relative to its position as a profession, clearly it is in the process of professionalization. Just as clearly it has come a long way in the twentieth century, the time of most of its maturing, but it still has a distance to go. One step along the road of professionalization came in 1996 when the U.S. Supreme Court ruled 7 to 2 that "confidences shared in therapy between licensed social workers and their clients are protected under the federal Rules of Evidence." This was an important development for social work and the people it serves.[8]

Characteristics of the Profession

The Bureau of Labor Statistics counts 557,000 social workers in the United States.[9] Of these 155,000 are members of the National Association of Social Workers (NASW). NASW estimates that, in addition, an equal number of nonmembers are employed in the field who have social work degrees, a requirement of membership. Hence, totally about two-thirds of those in the Labor Department's figures are "trained" social workers.

A 1995 survey of NASW membership produced some interesting findings. In terms of setting, 22 percent of the respondents worked in social service agencies, 17 percent in inpatient health, 16 percent in outpatient health, 14 percent in private solo practice, and the remainder in other settings.[10] About 39 percent worked in private not-for-profit service, 27 percent private for-profit, 17 percent public local, 13 percent public state, 3 percent public federal, and 1 percent public military.[11] With regard to function, 69 percent of the respondents were in direct service, 15 percent in administration, and 6 percent in supervision. The balance was scattered over several other functions.[12]

These social workers' primary practice areas were also tabulated as follows (in round numbers):[13]

NASW Members by Practice Area, Shown in Percentage

Mental health	38	Services to elderly	5
Family services	26	Occupational social work	1
Medical clinics	13	Other	12
School social work	5		

Organizations for the Profession and for Education

NASW is the principal professional organization in this field today. It emerged in 1955 as a consolidation of seven previously separate organizations: the American Association of Group Workers, American Association of Medical Social Workers, American Association of Psychiatric Social Workers, American Association of Social Workers, Association for the Study of Community Organization, National Association of School Social Workers, and Social Work Research Group. In 1997, the NASW membership was 155,000 compared to 22,500 in 1955. There are 55 state chapters in the United States, Virgin Islands, Puerto Rico, and Europe. Another example of marked growth during the twentieth-century push toward professionalization was in the old American Association of Psychiatric Social Workers, which started out with 99 charter members in 1926 and had grown to 2,200 in 1955 when it combined into NASW.[14]

Like many organizations of professionals, NASW engages in activities having to do with (1) standards, (2) professional development, and (3) social action as well as (4) providing services to individual members. Standards include such endeavors as personnel classification and protection. Development includes continuing education, conferences, publications, and other related pursuits. Action encompasses lobbying and political activities. Member services range from insurance programs to travel plans.

Originally NASW membership was restricted to persons holding the graduate Master of Social Work (MSW) or equivalent degree. As a result of the recognition of the facts that (1) large numbers of people occupying social work positions did not hold graduate degrees in this or any other field, and (2) undergraduate social work educational programs were growing rapidly in number and enrollment, membership in NASW was opened in 1970 to people with social work baccalaureate degrees from programs approved by the Council on Social Work Education (CSWE). In 1974, this program approval evolved into accreditation paralleling the existent CSWE accreditation of graduate programs.

As of 1997 there were 406 accredited undergraduate programs in American colleges and universities. At the same time there were 125 master's level programs. A number of new programs are in candidacy at both levels.[15] More than 50 schools offer post-master's and doctoral programs. For many of the latter, offerings beyond the master's are relatively new. These figures are interesting in realtion to our neighboring countries. In Mexico there are social work programs in 30 universities, but only one offers a graduate master's program. In 125 schools there are technical social work programs.[16] In Canada the basic degree for practice is the bachelor of social work. Some universities offer graduate degrees ranging from one to two years.[17]

There are still social workers who believe that either or both the inclusion of Bachelor of Social Work (BSW) workers in the national organization and/or the accreditation of undergraduate programs were mistaken actions. Some contend that this reduces the viability of the profession. The opposite view argues that such actions merely recognize the realities of the social services workforce and attempt to build in some basic guarantees of quality social work practice and protection for the service consumer. The recency of many of the issues under discussion should be kept in mind. If we remember that neither admission of baccalaureate level workers to the national professional organization nor accreditation of undergraduate programs appeared until as recently as the 1970s, it is not surprising that some issues and controversies are still present.

For an undergraduate program to be accredited, it must have as its objective preparing students for entry-level practice. An exposure to social work/social welfare is not sufficient, but there must be at least 400 hours of field experience as well as classroom instruction aimed at preparing people to enter the profession. The curriculum must include content on social work practice, social welfare policy and services, human behavior and social environment, social research, social work values and ethics, diversity, social and economic justice, and populations at risk.[18] In other words such a program may be very different in content today than just a few years earlier or than another nonaccredited social work program today with differing objectives.

Social work education is changing as is the world around it. Distance learning models are expanding in many locations,[19] and part-time programs have become common. In education generally there is a move to more experiential activity, which has always been significant in social work training, and there is a National Society for Experiential Education.

Differentiating Levels of Personnel

It is noteworthy that the traditional NASW definition of the professional social worker identified the master's degree as the base educational level. Now that this has been expanded to include the baccalaureate practitioner, the idea is that undergraduate education prepares one for the entry level, for beginning professional practice, seen as a generalist. This development, along with others, presents questions as to the proper role for the MSW worker. So far, this matter is unresolved, but it appears that in general it is thought that the graduate degree worker moves ahead in one or both of two directions: specialization and advanced practice. Examples are supervision, administration, psychotherapy, or teaching/research. Another way of organizing specialization/advanced practice is around fields of service such as certain roles in the health field, for example, alcoholism.

Two attempts to come to grips with the problem of differential use of personnel in the social services will be examined briefly. In the early 1960s, before some of the major changes we have just described occurred, Richan proposed that the roles of *professional* and *nonprofessional* workers be delineated based on two factors: (1) client vulnerability and (2) worker autonomy.[20] From this base he classified four levels of workers: (1) the professional, (2) the specialist, (3) the subprofessional, and (4) the aide. When Richan equated high client vulnerability and high worker autonomy with his professional, he seemed to be calling for the MSW. The specialist, according to Richan, may serve very vulnerable clients but does so in narrower, more technical ways. Hence, the specialist's training could come from "agency-operated schools or community college settings."[21] Richan's subprofessional worker appears to be one with a baccalaureate degree who handles the same kinds of responsibilities as the professional but with clients who are less vulnerable. Finally, the aide deals with the least vulnerable clientele and has only limited responsibilities. Training would be "brief in-service orientation courses."[22] It is important to recognize that this proposal is dated partly because of the NASW and CSWE developments related to undergraduates. But the idea of client vulnerability and worker autonomy as determinants of worker roles and qualifications still seems significant today.

NASW offered a classification plan consisting of two preprofessional and four professional levels as follows:

Preprofessional

Social service aide. Entry is based on an assessment of the individual's maturity, appropriate life experiences, motivation, and skills required by the specific task or function.

Social service technician. Entry is based on completion of (1) a two-year education program in one of the social services, usually granting an associate of arts degree, or (2) a baccalaureate degree in another field.[23]

Professional

Basic professional level. Requires a baccalaureate degree from a CSWE accredited social work program.

Specialized (expert) professional level. Requires a master's degree from a CSWE accredited social work program.

Independent professional level. Requires two years of appropriately supervised post-master's experience following receipt of an accredited MSW degree.

Advanced professional level. Requires proficiency in special areas or ability to conduct advanced social welfare research; usually requires possession of a doctoral degree in social work or a related field.[24]

No matter what the proposal is regarding levels of personnel, the inescapable conclusion must be that the situation is still open and unfinished. A great range and variety of persons are employed in the social services, and a refined, consistent system for using people with certain qualifications exclusively or even primarily for particular responsibilities does not, in fact, exist at this time. There is research suggesting differential functioning and competencies, but further work in this area is needed.[25]

Since the designation ACSW has been used, further explanation is warranted. These letters stand for Academy of Certified Social Workers. Practitioners holding MSW degrees may qualify for ACSW by passing a written examination after completing 3,000 hours of experience under the supervision of a worker who is a member of ACSW. This is another example of the credentialing that tends to accompany professionalization in a field. In 1991 NASW initiated a credentialing system for baccalaureate-level workers with social work degrees (ACBSW). This was not widely subscribed and was terminated in 1995.

Licensing, Certification, and Declassification

Another development is the nationwide appearance on a state-by-state basis of some form of licensing or certification for social workers. NASW and other groups are promoting this development for a number of reasons having to do with protection of the service consumer from quacks and unscrupulous persons, assuring base levels of qualifications/competence, and enabling practitioners to receive "third-party payments" (for example, an insurance company or program paying a professional on behalf of an insured client) for services provided. While only 12 states regulated social work practice in 1972, in 1992 the last state in the nation (Wisconsin) enacted legislation legally regulating social work. In some states, workers are licensed, and in others there is provision for registration or title protection. Some state laws cover both registration and licensing.

While the trend would appear to be toward more licensing in social work, the future on the matter is difficult to predict in view of the Carter, Reagan, and Bush administrations' push for governmental deregulation generally. Another potentially complicating factor is the presence in some states of so-called "sunset" laws that require legislatures periodically to reconfirm the existence of state governmental regulations, provisions, or programs or, if legislatures fail to do so, their automatic termination at specified times. This system has not been significant for social work licensing so far, but the potential to impact negatively upon it would seem to be real. In 1980 Kansas became the first state to conduct a "sunset" review of an existing social work licensing law; another licensing law was enacted.[26]

A related issue is the advent in some states of "declassification," that is, state merit or civil service systems modifying the requirements for employment of staff in the public social services. This modification may take the form of reducing, diluting, or dropping the requirements that must be met to obtain positions in the system; hence, the term *declassification* is used. The concern of some professionals is that this will mean poorer-quality services for the consumer. A Kentucky study found that staff with BSW or MSW degrees were better prepared than workers lacking degrees in social work.[27] This is another area in which more hard data and solid documentation would be most useful.

THE SOCIAL SERVICE WORKFORCE AND SPECIAL PERSONNEL

A group of developments having to do with the helping disciplines revolves around the diversity of people who staff the social services. This personnel matter has been alluded to earlier but warrants special attention here. There is a tendency when discussing social welfare to consider only the profession of social work and within that to focus narrowly on "mainstream" professionals, ignoring many closely related occupations and different levels within broad employment groupings. The lines between some of these occupational categories are often unclear, and there are gray areas as to who does what. For purposes of

Habitat for Humanity International

Community volunteers contribute to a housing project for Habitat for Humanity.

discussion, we will divide this topic into four interrelated and overlapping parts: self-help, indigenous workers, paraprofessionals, and volunteers. They represent four special groups in the workforce. They are in addition to those staff that carry the title of social worker. The latter are largely baccalaureate- and master's-level workers whose titles, too, are multiple and hence part of the ambiguity in this field as to who does what.

Self-Help

The modern self-help movement is a striking development of recent decades although its roots date back through centuries of mutual-aid endeavors. Gitterman and Shulman not that "self-help groups explicitly use such concepts as mutual aid and helper therapy in an ideology which emphasizes peoples' need for each other."[28]

In earlier years, there were few such groups formalized, and Alcoholics Anonymous, which was founded in the 1930s, is generally viewed as one of the first. More recently, the number and kind of self-help groups have grown rapidly. The central ideas of these are reciprocal relationships and interaction toward the benefit of all involved in the group. It has been estimated that there may be 500,000 to 750,000 of these mutual support groups in the nation involving 10 to 15 million people.[29]

Currently, there are self-help groups of the "anonymous" nature such as alcoholics, gamblers, overeaters, and others; groups with various physical or mental health problems or histories; dieters; addicts; ex-prisoners; homosexuals; persons with certain family characteristics such as parents of handicapped children; single parents; and many others.

Among the values noted in this kind of helping approach is the phenomenon of everyone "being in the same boat" and being able to identify with and support each other because of shared experiences and feelings, past, present, or both. This can be a powerfully supportive force and can help to alleviate anger, anxiety, guilt, and other dysfunctional feelings. Another advantage points up the overlap between self-help and indigenous workers, a category to be discussed next. When a poor person who is a welfare recipient helps another poor person with meal planning, budgeting, child care, or whatever, there can be a tremendous psychological boost for that person in being a "giver" instead of a receiver. The same is true of an ex-offender working with offenders.

In the past, social workers have not generally played a large direct role in self-help groups. They may help to organize them, refer others to them, and provide consultation. An article based on the experience of a large family service agency makes a strong case for the consultation role. Defining self-help as "the process whereby people with similar problems come together to alleviate their distress, independent of professional intervention," this agency employed a self-help coordinator whose job was to provide consultation service to self-help units in the agency's catchment area. This service was both for people wishing to start a group and for existing groups. Important among the worker's activities were assessment and linking the groups with the agency and community.[30]

Indigenous Workers

A distinction is being made here that is not always made in the literature. Paraprofessionals and indigenous workers are being differentiated because of the formalized (for example, community college) training programs that often exist for the former and may not for the latter. The two groups may be combined, however. During the 1960s, particularly within the context of the antipoverty movement, considerable attention came to be given to involving people in the human services who knew from experience the hardships of being "clients" or potential clients. An example is employing welfare recipients or former recipients to work with the poor. Hiring unemployed or underemployed persons to work in income maintenance programs or in any one of a variety of social welfare areas has two major potential benefits: it is helpful to those persons requiring service, and it is also useful to the person wanting to move into or up within the labor force. Many of these so-called "indigenous" workers (that is, people from client groups served by social work) were at points employed in fields other than social welfare either as an employment end in itself or as a means toward stable work. But often various roles within the helping service systems themselves were occupied by such people.

With the passage of time in the 1970s and 1980s, there appears to have been diminishing enthusiasm in certain quarters for such approaches, and some critics have asked whether social work has lost its commitment to this effort.[31] To the extent that this activity has declined, a number of factors are undoubtedly present. One of these is the current concern within the social work profession over "declassification" of professional social work positions in state merit and civil service systems. There is now the desire to protect the earlier gains made by the professionals and to argue that quality service to the consumer requires fully qualified professional staff. There is a dilemma in this.

In one state, the merit system developed a plan in which a person with an undifferentiated baccalaureate degree qualified for employment at the Social Worker I level, whereas persons with bachelor's degrees from accredited social work programs were hired at the Social Worker II level. This arrangement later was changed, in the name of affirmative action, so that Social Worker II was opened to others. Experience and education are often equated so that a job applicant may count specified amounts of experience toward educational requirements. But this raises a question as to the qualifications of the persons employed at this level and whether, for example, minority clientele are well served by movements in this direction. Whatever the outcome of such issues and controversies, it is likely that there will continue to be a diversity of persons working in the human services.

Somewhat related to these personnel issues is the use of so-called natural helpers, particularly in rural areas.[32] Bartenders, beauticians, barbers, ministers, school personnel, law enforcement persons, and others are often cast into helping roles in communities. Social workers in some communities have established programs to enhance the knowledge and skills of such persons to make them more effective helpers.

Paraprofessionals

Although it is difficult to generalize on social work credentials, it can be said that, from the point of view of the NASW and the CSWE, the four-year college degree in social work is now viewed as the base educational requirement for beginning professional practice. The content of that undergraduate education presents another set of issues dealt with earlier in this chapter. In spite of this consensus, there are many people in social work–type positions with less formal education, often persons who meet a state's merit system or civil service experience alternative requirements or persons with a college education but not in social work.

Beneath the baccalaureate degree there are various levels of workers employed in the social services, often under the collective rubric *human services*. One group includes persons with two-year degrees from junior or community colleges. In general, these are relatively new arrivals on the social welfare scene. In the main, such persons fall into one of two situations. They either have rather undifferentiated degrees such as Associate of Arts (AA) or something similar, which tend to be made up of basic arts and sciences or liberal arts content, or they are somewhat specialized along a certain vocational line. Often the two-year degree based on vocational areas leads to some sort of certificate in human services or a related area. One such program illustrates the latter phenomenon. The community college offering this "Human Service" program describes it in its bulletin:[33]

> The Human Services program prepares students for entry level jobs or for transfer to a four-year degree program. By the end of the program students will be able to interact effectively with clients in a human services agency.
> The program emphasizes skills needed in working with clients such as interviewing, determining eligibility for services, making appropriate referrals, and assisting with counseling. A supervised field experience allows students to apply their skills in a work setting.
> Specializations are offered in chemical dependency counseling, mental health, social services, and psychosocial rehabilitation.
> When the program is completed, students may find employment in a wide variety of settings including public and private social service agencies, treat-

ment centers, group homes, institutions, hospitals, community centers and state or county departments of social services.

Some agencies and organizations require personnel with the specific educational backgrounds just described. Others with, say, one, two, or three years of college but less than a baccalaureate degree, end up in human service positions in either a planned or unplanned way. It is common practice for certain kinds of social welfare organizations to employ college students on either a part-time or full-time basis in specified roles, depending upon the personnel needs of the agency. Here, again, the result is sometimes a mix with the same job title in an agency being held by college students, persons with some college training, and people with undergraduate degrees who may qualify for higher-level positions but, for varying reasons, hold the lower-level jobs.

Use of so-called paraprofessionals results from many factors, chief of which is the fact that not all social welfare jobs working directly with people require a high level of formal education. Even if this were not the case, there are not enough professionals to fill all of these job slots nor are there sufficient funds to employ the higher-paid persons.

A concern with this paraprofessional category of workers has to do with their somewhat marginal status. Few people want to be thought of or think of themselves as subprofessional, and to be in a nonprofessional category may be equated with being a less significant worker. Yet the responsibilities of such persons are often immense and of critical importance to the well-being of the people with whom they work. Child-care workers or youth workers in group homes or children's residential centers may be, in important respects, the most significant persons in the lives of the youngsters. They work closely with them many hours a day, every day, in contrast to the professional therapists (social workers, psychologists, psychiatrists) who may see the child once a week or less often for an hour or so. The same is true of a worker in a mental hospital whose job is on the ward with the patients on an ongoing basis. In the latter situation, we are referring to essentially nursing-type personnel rather than social work, but the point about time and responsibility is as valid as it is in another context, nursing homes.

The role of the social worker in relation to these paraprofessionals is noteworthy. Often social workers have partial or total responsibility for the orientation and supervision of paraprofessionals. In-service training and staff development may be significant social work roles with a variety of personnel.

Volunteers

Volunteers have been defined as individuals who "choose to act with an attitude of social responsibility when a need is recognized, without concern for tangible gain. To volunteer means to go beyond one's basic obligations."[34] Typically, in the complex and challenging social services there is more work to do than there are people to do it. Added to this is the fact that some of the tasks to be done do not require special educational backgrounds. Since most social services are governmental or nonprofit, funds are not sufficient to employ personnel to cover all tasks. Volunteers are a partial response to this situation. Among other contributions, they can free the time of professionals and other staff from assignments not requiring professional skills. Other volunteers shoulder such significant responsibilities as serving on agency boards and making policy. President Clinton has been an enthusiastic advocate of the use of volunteers, including at the April 1997 national summit in Philadelphia on volunteerism.[35] Compared to other countries, volunteering is a striking characteristic of the U.S.[36] There is now even an emphasis on making community service a part of learning for students at all levels.[37]

Sieder and Kirshbaum have suggested the following possible roles for volunteers: (1) identifying problematic conditions requiring services; (2) policy making; (3) providing direct services; (4) fundraising; (5) acting as spokespersons for an organization, interpreting its programs and the problems with which they are concerned; (6) reporting and evaluating community reactions to programs; (7) community planning activities; (8) developing new service-delivery systems; (9) advocacy for the poor and disenfranchised; and (10) protest and public action.[38]

One of the largest users of volunteers is hospitals. In a hospital, volunteers often perform a range of more or less routine activities that may greatly improve the quality of the hospitalization experience for the patient and his or her family. Volunteers also have a large role in nursing homes and often in programs for the elderly. They are also used as "friendly visitors" in some public welfare departments, where they may help to humanize the large bureaucracy and provide some personal individual attention in an otherwise mass system. Other contexts in which volunteers are even more essential to the total operation are crisis intervention centers and big brother/big sister organizations that provide adult companions for children and youth. In these, the volunteer is the person who delivers the service. Similarly, volunteer leadership is conspicuous in scouting, YMCA/YWCA, church groups and similar activities, and in United Way fundraising and community organization.

Social workers often constitute the paid professional staff in some of these programs that depend on volunteers for staffing. In such cases, the worker's job may include recruitment of volunteers, orientation and training, program planning, and evaluation of volunteers and the program. Training of volunteers takes on added importance where the volunteer becomes the service deliverer, because the quality of the program hinges directly on his or her knowledge, skill, and ability.

While volunteers make major but undetermined contributions to social welfare, social work as a profession has a somewhat ambivalent position relative to them. NASW did, in 1977, approve a policy statement on "Volunteers and the Social Service System." This organization, along with CSWE, the Association of Junior Leagues,[39] and other groups are working together in a project "to enhance the effectiveness of volunteers and to improve the means of preparing social work students to work with volunteers."[40] Because of the cuts in human service budgets, there is some fear that volunteers might replace professionals. On the other hand, there is an important place for volunteers in social welfare, and they should be made an integral part of the whole.

Volunteerism has an uncertain future, partially because a major source of volunteers in the past has been women. As more and more women take paid employment, there may be fewer available as volunteers. On the other hand, the growing number of elderly and retired persons may provide a major new source of volunteers, at least in some social welfare areas.[41]

From this discussion of special social welfare personnel, which has been somewhat arbitrarily divided into self-help, indigenous workers, paraprofessionals, and volunteers, it is apparent that there is considerable confusion in the field. It is useful, therefore, to keep in mind that social work is a relative newcomer to the professions, and that some students of the subject see it as a semi-profession.[42] However it is viewed, clearly it is still evolving and is in transition.

Burnout

In recent years there has been growing attention to and concern about what has come to be called *burnout*. The term is used in reference to a condition, actual or potential, of workers in the social services. One definition of burnout is that by Maslach: "a syndrome of emotional exhaustion, depersonalization, and reduced personal accomplishment that [occurs] in response to…the chronic emotional strain of dealing extensively with other human beings, particularly when they are troubled or having problems."[43] Social work is a challenging and often stressful occupation. Dealing with human and social problems in heavy doses over prolonged periods of time can, and sometimes does, take a toll on employees in helping professions. Among the numerous specific situations that may contribute to burnout are working in relative isolation in private practice[44] and in HIV/AIDS settings.[45]

A study of counselor burnout in 17 family agencies found a relatively small incidence. What there was appeared to be associated with such factors as work pressures, job dissatisfaction, lack of support, authoritarian administration, and personal vulnerabilities.[46] There may be more burnout than that characterized in these private agency findings in public agencies that so often have heavier workloads.

Burnout can be prevented, reduced, or treated through various measures that tend to enhance the workers' coping abilities. Included are assuring adequate rest, nutrition, diversion, and exercise for individuals. Reorganizing the workday to include such things as mini-breaks can be useful. *Time management* is a significant aspect in minimizing burnout, among other benefits, and is receiving growing attention in many fields. A positive self-image for professionals is important, so that support groups of peers in and out of the agency and supervisory support are helpful. Improved communication within organizations is important as is identifying sources of stress and taking appropriate action. An example of the latter might be for a worker to take assertiveness training. Also it is often essential to help workers maintain detached concern for clients with reduced personal involvement in clients' problems and more emphasis on client self-responsibility.[47]

Related to burnout is the phenomenon of *impaired workers* that has received increasing attention in recent years. Social workers, like others in all professions, sometimes fall victim to addictions, emotional and mental health problems, or other difficulties. The focus then is to protect the public and consumer of services and to restore the professional so that he or she may return to effectiveness if possible. One state licensing board has instituted "Impaired Practitioner Rules" providing that all action remains confidential if the worker self-reports and cooperates with the board's findings. Otherwise, any action becomes public information.[48]

SUMMARY AND CONCLUSIONS

In this chapter we have examined the phenomenon of professionalization. As with any field, this has included such considerations as professional organizations and education. In this particular field it has also been important to examine the various levels of existing personnel and issues around regulations. Special workforce developments included the use of volunteers, paraprofessionals, indigenous workers, and the self-help movement. It should also be noted that most of the chapters in this book deal with professionalization in the social services without necessarily addressing the matter specifically.

Notes

1. Abraham Flexner, "Is Social Work a Profession?" *Proceedings of the National Conference of Charities and Corrections* (Chicago, 1915), pp. 576–590.
2. Ernest Greenwood, "Attributes of a Profession," *Social Work* 2, no. 3 (July 1957): 45–55.
3. Amitai Etzioni, ed., *The Semi-Professions and Their Organization* (New York: Free Press, 1969).
4. William J. Goode, "The Theoretical Units of Professionalization," in *Semi-Professions*, Etzioni, ed., p. 280.
5. Ibid., p. 310
6. W. Richard Scott, "Professional Employees in a Bureaucratic Structure: Social Work," in Etzioni, ed., *Semi-Professions*, pp. 82–140.
7. Ibid., pp. 83–84.
8. *NASW News* 41, no. 8, "Supreme Court Upholds Social Work Privilege (Washington, DC: National Association of Social Workers, September 1996), p. 1.
9. *Occupational Outlook Handbook*, 1996–97 ed. (Washington, DC: U.S. Department of Labor, 1996), pp. 132–134.
10. Margaret Gibelman and Philip H. Schervish, *Who We Are: A Second Look* (Washington, DC: National Association of Social Workers, 1977), from Table 2.5, p. 32.
11. Ibid., from Table 2.6, p. 34.
12. Ibid., from Table 2.7, p. 36.
13. Ibid., from Table 2.4, p. 30.
14. Chauncy, A. Alexander, and David N. Weber, "Social Welfare: Historical Dates," in *Encyclopedia of Social Work*, 17th ed. (Washington, DC: NASW, 1977), pp. 1501–1502.
15. *Social Work Education Reporter* 45, no. 2 (Alexandria, VA: Council on Social Work Education, Spring/Summer 1997), p. 8.
16. *Newsletter*, Issue 4 (West Hartford, CT: North American and Caribbean Regional Association, International Association of Schools of Social Work, Summer 1996), p. 3.
17. Merl C. Hokenstad and Katherine A. Kendall, "International Social Work Education," in *Encyclopedia of Social Work*, 19th ed. (Washington, DC: NASW, 1995), p. 1518.

18. *Handbook of Accreditation Standards and Procedures,* 4th ed. (Alexandria, VA: Council on Social Work Education, 1994).

19. Bruce A. Thyer, Gerald Polk, and James G. Gaudin, "Distance Learning in Social Work Education," *Journal of Social Work Education* 33, no. 2 (Spring/Summer 1997): 363–367.

20. Willard C. Richan, "Determining Roles of Professional and Nonprofessional Workers," *Social Work* (October 1961): 27.

21. Ibid.

22. Ibid., pp. 27–28.

23. NASW Policy Statement 4, "Standards for Social Service Manpower" (Washington, DC: NASW, undated), pp. 6–11.

24. "NASW Standards for the Classification of Social Work Practice" (Silver Spring, MD: NASW, 1981), p. 9.

25. Patricia L. Kelley, "The Relationship between Education and Socialization into the Profession of Social Work" (Ph.D. diss., The University of Iowa, 1981), pp. 39–49. An exception to the inconclusiveness and mixture of findings in studies is the doctoral dissertation of Walter H. Baily, "A Comparison of Performance Levels between BSW and BA Social Workers," Catholic University of America, 1978. He found a higher performance on the part of BSW graduates than of undifferentiated BA persons.

26. *NASW News* 25, no. 6 (June 1980): 19.

27. S.S. Dhooper, D.D. Royse, and L.C. Wolfe, "Does Social Work Education Make a Difference?" *Social Work* 35, no. 1 (January 1990): 57–61.

28. Alex Gitterman and Lawrence Shulman, eds., *Mutual Aid Groups, Vulnerable Populations and the Life Cycle,* 2nd ed. (New York: Columbia University Press, 1994).

29. Alfred J. Katz, *Self-Help in America* (New York: Twayne Publishers, 1993).

30. Brian A. Auslander and Gail K. Auslander, "Self-Help Groups and the Family Service Agency," *Social Casework* 69, no. 2 (February 1988): 74–80.

31. Edward A. Brawley, "Social Work's Diminished Commitment to the Paraprofessional," *Journal of Sociology and Social Welfare* 7, no. 5 (September 1980): 773–788.

32. Patricia Kelley and Verne Kelley, "Training Natural Helpers in Rural Communities," in H. Wayne Johnson, ed., *Rural Human Services* (Itasca, IL: F.E. Peacock Publishers, 1980), pp. 130–139.

33. Des Moines Area Community College Catalog (Ankeny, IA: 1996), p. 64.

34. Patricia Dunn, "Volunteer Management," in *Encyclopedia of Social Work,* 19th ed. (Washington, DC: NASW, 1995), p. 2483.

35. "Volunteers Strain to Reach Fragile Lives," *New York Times,* April 27, 1997, pp. 2, 13.

36. Patricia Dunn, "Volunteer Management."

37. "Educators: Teach Kids Volunteerism," *Chicago Tribune,* April 15, 1997, Section 1, p. 4.

38. Violet Sieder and Doris C. Kirshbaum, "Volunteers," in *Encyclopedia of Social Work,* 17th ed. (Washington, DC: NASW, 1977), p. 1582–1583.

39. "Volunteerism and Social Work Practice," an announcement from the Association of Junior Leagues, New York, February 1981.

40. Gordon Manser, "Volunteers," in 1983–84 *Supplement to the Encyclopedia of Social Work* (Silver Spring, MD: NASW, 1983), p. 172.

41. Ibid., pp. 169–170.

42. Etzioni, *Semi-Professions.*

43. As quoted by Dorothy Fahs Beck, "Counselor Burnout in Family Service Agencies," *Social Casework* 68, no. 1 (January 1987): 3.

44. Robert L. Barker, "Private Practice," in *Encyclopedia of Social Work,* 19th ed. (Washington, DC: NASW, 1995), p. 1908.

45. Gary A. Lloyd, "HIV/AIDS Overview," in *Encyclopedia of Social Work*, 19th ed. (Washington, DC: NASW, 1995), p. 1277.

46. Beck, "Counselor Burnout," pp. 5–15.

47. Ibid.

48. *NASW Iowa Update* 22, no. 4 (December 1996): 6.

Additional Suggested Readings

The Community Services Technician: Guide for Associate Degree Programs in the Community and Social Services. New York: Council on Social Work Education, 1970.

Gartner, Alan, and Frank Riessman. *The Self-Help Revolution*. New York: Human Science Press, 1984.

Jones, Martha L. "Role Conflict: Cause of Burnout or Energizer." *Social Work* 38, no. 2 (March 1993): 136–141.

Katz, Alfred H. *Self-Help: Concepts and Applications*. Philadelphia: Charles, 1992.

Kurtz, Linda Farris. "Recovery, the 12-Step Movement, and Politics." *Social Work* 42, no. 4 (July 1997): 403–405.

"Network Helps AIDS Caregivers to Cope." *NASW News 33*, no. 5 (May 1988): 3.

Ratliff, Nancy. "Stress and Burnout in the Helping Professions." *Social Casework 69*, no. 3 (March 1988): 147–154.

Richan, Willard C. *Beyond Altruism*. Binghamton, NY: Haworth Press, 1988.

Richan, Willard C., and Allan R. Mendelsohn. *Social Work: The Unloved Profession*. New York: New Viewpoints, 1973.

Sherman, Susan R., Russell A. Ward, and Mark LaGory. "Women as Caregivers of the Elderly: Instrumental and Expressive Support." *Social Work* 33, no. 2 (March-April 1988): 164–167.

Teare, Robert S., and Bradford W. Sheafor. *Practice-Sensitive Social Work Education*. Alexandria, VA: Council on Social Work Education, 1995.

Thomlison, Barbara, Gayla Rogers, Donald Collins, and Richard M. Grinnell, Jr. *The Social Work Practicum: An Access Guide*. 2nd ed. Itasca, IL: F.E. Peacock Publishers, 1996.

27

Social Work:
A Futures Perspective

CRAIG ABRAHAMSON
THOMAS WALZ

OVERVIEW

Both a century and a millennium are drawing to a close. The profession of social work belongs to the century, but its roots are traceable through the millennium. Yet, if it is the future we are to discuss in this chapter, why begin by looking backward? It is our perspective that the future is shaped by both the present and the past. The future comes with a history. A futurist must do more than look forward.

Two era shifts have taken place within the present millennium. The first occurred roughly in midmillennium and was the outcome of three revolutionary developments—the Protestant Reformation, the Industrial Revolution, and the Scientific Revolution. The combined forces of the Industrial and Scientific Revolutions then set the stage for a second "high-tech" driven industrial revolution. The benchmark for the arrival of this next era shift was shortly after World War II. Its metaphor is the mushroom cloud produced by the dropping of the atomic bomb.

The principal social changes forthcoming from the first industrial era shift included: the rise of the nation states; the rapid material development of society; the increase in the scale of organizational life; the subsequent division of labor and specialization in society; and the shift in power relationships among the growing number of social institutions that characterize modern society.

Social changes associated with the current "post industrial" era shift include: the rise of consumerism, the globalization of the economy, the aging of the world's population, and the destabilization of the family as a social institution. Social work as a profession bridges both the industrial and postindustrial periods.

The profession of social work makes its formal appearance in the first decades of the twentieth century. Its early influences were both religious and secular. Ties with the churches were reflected in its Judeo-Christian heritage, while its secular ties were through its philanthropic sponsors. Both connections contributed to the moralistic intonations present in the early days of social work practice. The arrival of the Depression brought the federal government into social welfare delivery. Government's role in welfare became so pronounced that the term *social worker* became synonymous with public welfare worker. By mid-century, social work was practiced under a mix of public, private nonprofit, and private for-profit auspices.

The point of this historical reflection is that these institutional connections inevitably influenced the location and practice of social work. Social work practice remains in a constant dynamic relationship with sociopolitical-economic environment.[1] Even more than other professions, social work is an expression of culture. It reflects the social attitudes and values of society.

A current sociocultural trend in society, for example, is the privatization of social and health services. Privatization reflects the power of the market economy to turn services into "commodities"—products that can be bought and sold. Not surprisingly, this has been followed by the advent of managed care, in which insurance companies control the distribution of health and social services to maintain their profitability.

Social work has tended to adapt and adjust to the market economy's role in the delivery of services, even to the point of taking on its entrepreneurial behaviors. It is the dominant power of the market economy over health and social services that could influence the direction of social work in the years to come.

POSTINDUSTRIAL CATALYSTS

The increase in material goods for consumption and the availability of social services outside the family are central features of postindustrialism. According to Washington, the postindustrial society is a service society, with the central values of social work influenced by this ideology.[2] It is the increased role of the market economy in the delivery of health and social services that is new and different.

Unfortunately, the influences of the market economy come with attendant defects. Public policy is largely shaped to serve bottom-line interests, private profit, and growth, and often disserves the needs of many citizens, especially the less powerful persons and groups in society.

Part of the growth of the market economy's influence on society has come at the expense of government. The lessening of government's role in welfare and civil protections has produced some serious distributive injustices.[3] The observation that the rich get richer and the poor poorer in a postmodern economy has been frequently documented.

Postindustrial developments share some correspondence to the rise of selected social problems, for example, poverty, destabilization of family, increased domestic and societal violence, employment problems, stress-related mental health problems, problems associated with nonfamily child care, and problems associated with longevity. The challenge presented by these social problems will inform social work's future.

With this as an overview, we shall present a framework for analyzing probable future developments in social work. The analysis will be restricted to probable futures rather than a preferred futures perspective.

The framework chosen is a reconfiguration of similar frameworks used by Daniel Bell[4] and Torres-Gil[5] in their efforts to forecast social change. In our framework, three catalysts of social change are selected for analysis: technological changes/global economic developments; demographic shifts in population size and makeup; and observable modifications in the cultural paradigm (shifts in societal attitudes and value orientations). Each will be explored with reference to its impact on the future of social work as a profession and as a practice.

ADVANCED TECHNOLOGY AND THE GLOBAL ECONOMY

Advanced technology is distinguished from industrial technology by its enhanced power and scale. The tools of advanced technology (computer, video, laser, nuclear energy, etc.) simply can do more things, faster. While there are many new high-tech tools, few are as significant in defining the culture as the computer.[6]

The impact of the computer on society is evident. Its impact on social work practice is equally dramatic.[7] Intake interviews are often directly entered into computers for storage, case planning, and record keeping. Reports and analyses of agency data are prepared using a variety of new software. With the advent of the Internet, E-mail, bulletin boards, and websites, a whole new information exchange is taking place within professional practice.

There is a common misconception that computer technology, like the telephone, has arrived at a stage of development at which the only advances yet to be made are cosmetic. Clearly this is not the case. The interface of computers with video laser technologies will produce further developments in the way in which we communicate electronically. More and more client-worker communication in the future will be mediated electronically.[8]

The culture of practice is obviously affected by such changes. Picture, for example, a depressed client whose husband has left her with three small children. Out of money, in desperation, she goes to the local welfare department for assistance. The intake worker hears her story with her eyes affixed to a computer into which the tragedy is being recorded. The client may feel as if she is speaking to a machine. Her story becomes only so many words to be recorded. Here a tool of efficiency is used in a way that questionably enhances practice.[9]

Another example of puzzling use of the computer is the disturbed client who puts drawings of his terrifying nightmares on his website each morning for the world to see. What therapeutic impact may this have? What consequence may it have for his own privacy? In fact, the whole privacy and confidentiality issue is raised to new levels with computer-based record keeping, storage, and information transfers.[10]

The computer also has had an impact on the way social work faculty are prepared and selected. Traditionally, faculty brought a strong practice background to teaching. More recently, the graduates of social work doctoral programs bring a strong background in empirical research, but with much less practice experience. Along with other changes in academia, this has impacted preparation for practice. The future generations of practitioners can be expected to be more entrepreneurial and research-focused.

There are many other impacts of the computer in social work practice. The computer has enabled disabled clients to communicate in new ways, allowing more possibilities for rehabilitation work with disabled clients. It has helped workers record efficiently, hopefully freeing up time for more direct contact with clients. Agency administrators have found the computer a useful tool in budget management and general accounting.[11] Agencies have been able to do some remarkable desktop printing. Faculty have been able to analyze data quickly and explore new databases. The contributions of computer technology to social work are limitless.

The computer, along with a host of other new technologies, also had considerable impact on today's mode of production. The exchange of capital-intensive technologies for human labor has become a distinguishing feature of the new economy. This has resulted in greater productivity and availability of low-cost goods, but at a cost to worker job security.[12] The instability of labor and the restructuring of labor has been deeply felt by society. Social workers daily cope with workers and families experiencing unemployment, underemployment, and induced early retirement.

A key feature of the current postindustrial economy has been the commodification of social and health services. As noted, this has allowed the market economy to become a major player in the delivery of social and health services. Profits can now be made from human misfortune.

The new service economy has opened up new employment opportunities for women.[13] The mass employment of women has come at a time when birthrates in industrial nations were dropping and when a second income in the family was deemed necessary to sustain an accustomed standard of living. Women are now an integral part of the American workforce.

With the rise of dual occupationalism, structural and functional changes in the family followed.[14] Families had to buy child care, dependent adult care, precooked foods, recreation, and a variety of other social commodities. A host of new providers responded to replace what families could no longer do for themselves. Prominent among these providers were social workers. Moreover, the buying and selling of services to families has hardly reached its maximum. Serving families will be a large part of social work's future. Social workers will continue to be involved in the provision of child care, out-of-home placements, in-home family services, family counseling, and the long-term care of dependent adults.

Like other commodities, social services are now part of the international marketplace. Already there has been an increase in the international market for adoptions and mail-order brides. Worldwide refugees are knocking on the doors of safe houses. Others are paying heavily to be smuggled into industrial societies as illegals. Despite overtones of creating an iron door to entry, immigration into the United States is brisk. Social work has never been more international and cross-culturally demanding.

There are many other high-tech developments that directly or indirectly impact on social work. Some of these will be covered in the sections that follow.

DEMOGRAPHIC CHANGES

The small planet on which we live is shared by more than five billion people. Until recently, most nations were experiencing high birthrates. Fortunately this trend has shifted, and for the first time in history, the world may experience a birth dearth. The birth of fewer children relieves population pressures and reduces the need to absorb large numbers of new persons into the economy. On the other hand, fewer children also means fewer mouths to feed, bodies to clothe, and minds to educate—an unwelcome development as far as a growth economy is concerned.

Not all families opt for low birthrates. Many low-income and minority families have large families. Overall, however, the drop in birthrates often translates into a drop in child welfare supports. Typically these cutbacks have greatest impact on low-income families who have the most children.[15] Welfare reform has reduced both transfer payments and in-kind programs in the safety net for poor children.

Ironically, the drop in birthrate has been somewhat offset by an increase in longevity. In the century about to close, we have witnessed nearly a 40-percent increase in life expectancy. The population bubble has shifted from young to old. The fastest-growing part of the population in the United States is the very old, those over 85. Thus in the face of an ever-growing, reluctant welfare state, the growing elderly population places a demand on society for support. This results in a growing competition for social welfare resources between young and old and among the care providers who specialize in one or the other population.[16]

The drop in birthrate is also offset somewhat by dramatic improvements in infant mortality. Death at birth or in the neonatal period is rare. While this is a welcomed development, it also explains a substantial increase in the survival rate of developmentally disabled persons. Not only do more children disabled at birth survive, but they live considerably longer than they did in the past.[17] In the future, social workers can expect an increasing number of persons with disabilities who will require long-term health and social services.

Lifestyle changes have an impact on the status of the population. Substance abuse directly or indirectly affects the birth status of many children. The number of fetal alcohol syndrome children has been growing, as has the number of children born HIV-positive.[18] These changes add to the growing numbers of persons with developmental disabilities in the society.

Returning to the increase in life expectancy, high-tech health has played a part. Old people rarely die suddenly. Dying and death are protracted affairs. The new medical science can keep people alive without necessarily being able to assure them quality of life; technology in this case addresses bodily needs better than the needs of the spirit. In doing so, in many ways it increases the need for social services. Social work with the very old and the dying will continue to expand. The hospital, hospice, nursing home, and home health agency will be common settings for social work practice. The expected doubling of the aging population by mid–twenty-first century assures this.

A potent new technological development that comes out of biomedical science is DNA technology. While much public attention has been directed toward the issue of cloning, DNA technology has many other applications. Some observers are convinced that DNA procedures will replace chemical and surgical medical interventions, especially in the treatment of cancers. DNA has also been conceived of as a tool in the prevention and repair of selected recessive genes. Regardless of application, many ethical considerations associated with the new genetic science have been raised. At a minimum, any assessment or treatment interventions in medical genetics will require much interpretation to consumers and their families. Genetic counseling is likely to be a major growth area for social workers in the coming century.

Apart from population trends in the United States, trends in world population growth and recomposition have significance for the future of social work. The world population is clearly aging. The greatest relative growth ironically is in the Third World, where birthrates also remain high. The high dependency ratios in these countries suggest that Third World poverty is likely to get worse before it gets better. In addition, these same countries contribute heavily to refugee movements. The destabilization of families due to civil and regional conflict is ubiquitous in the Third World. The resettlement of these families has opened up new service arenas for social workers. Again, there is nothing on the world vista to suggest that refugee movements will subside or even decline in the coming decades.

In a global world, diversity is the rule, not exception. The ease and speed of communications truly creates a global family, which can at times be a mixed blessing. Whatever the case, knowledge and skill in working with multiple cultures become requisites for social workers. The ability to deal with cross-cultural tensions also demands special skills of mediation and an ability to work with groups.

CULTURAL PARADIGM SHIFT

In a society experiencing rapid social change, continuous shifts in cultural trends can be expected. The new cultural trends we are undergoing have been accompanied by the emergence of "managed cost organizations" and the transfer in part of social work from the public to the private sector. To cope with this transition, clinical social work will need to integrate financial and clinical decision making.[19] Moreover, these trends will increase a sense of powerlessness in that the clinician's choices will be limited by corporate decisions.

The major catalysts of the current cultural paradigm seem to be consumerism and the economic values that gave it birth. This can be seen in the profession's current infatuation with fee-for-service practice.[20] The broader repercussions are seen in the privatization of the nonprofit sector, in cost-containment efforts, in emerging practice domains, and in vendorships in social service delivery.

The new consumer economy brings with it its own set of social problems. Not surprisingly, one of these problems is overconsumption, particularly the abuse of food and substances. Some believe overconsumption to be symptomatic of the deeper problem of meaninglessness and emptiness associated with patterns of daily living. People experience a disappointment that comes from the failure of material things to satisfy the spirit. Frankl suggested such in his book *Man's Search for Meaning*.[21] The search for meaning is often behind the pursuit of counsel and therapy by many clients.

Social work has responded to these existential dilemmas through clinical interventions. Helping persons cope with a troubled culture, however, is only one aspect of social work. Therapy is not a fundamental solution to culturally induced problems. It remains to be seen to what extent social work will respond to the deeper-rooted structural problems of a materialist culture. At the moment, there is little evidence of any shift away from dealing with social problems at other than a symptom level.[22] Community work, policy development, and political action are not major centers of social work activity. They may be in the future, but there is currently no basis for making such a forecast.

A question of some importance is the durability of the current consumer lifestyle. Some commentators argue there is evident movement toward gentler living, lighter consumption, and greater harmony with the environment. Should this occur, the impact on social work would be considerable. Any cultural paradigm shift, however subtle, has momentous effects on professions.

As noted earlier, the economic/consumer orientation culture has had a profound impact on family life and function. The restructuring of households and dual occupationalism have made the family increasingly dependent on services outside itself. If some redirection in culture were to occur in which families chose to do more for themselves and reduce their income needs in the process, it could have a huge impact on social work as well as the economy. Social work, like many other professions, has grown at the expense of the lack of family self-sufficiency.

Despite the advances in the availability of material goods, postindustrial society still struggles with how to equitably distribute its goods and services. A growing GNP has not reduced the volume of individuals and families dependent on government transfer payments. The belief that welfare and poverty are bad habits that can be cured with learnfare or workfare approaches is yet to be substantiated. In the meantime, we find more poor families, more homeless, a fourth of the nation's children growing up in poverty, and many disenfranchised individuals showing up among the criminal population. The nation turns its back on entitlements for poor people while doubling its prison cells. The voice of social work is strangely silent in the face of these developments, a silence that would persist in the coming years. The exception has been NASW's Violence and Sustainable Development project.[23]

As the culture goes, so goes the profession. The market-oriented culture spills over into the values and aspirations of those entering the professions. Privatization and commodification of social services and the growth of social work private practice initiatives come from the same source. The motivations of practitioners are increasingly informed by economic values. A market-oriented social work tends toward gentrification (since only better-off people can afford to buy services), except where services to poor people are subsidized in some way. The question has been raised whether social work will again reemphasize its early mission of serving as the voice of poor and disenfranchised people.[24]

This social class bias visible in social work today has mixed effects. On the one hand, social workers are no longer viewed as people who take someone's child away or hand out welfare checks. A host of new clients are finding social workers working as genetic counselors, AIDS counselors, hospice directors, employee-assistance workers in industry, management advisors, and policy analysts, to mention but a few. The profession may be becoming more gentrified, but it is also becoming more diversified and publicly accepted.

Those entering the social work profession in the coming years will discover both opportunity and challenge. Social workers are invited to do many things in society. The weightiest human and family problems are often placed in their lap. There has been no dearth of demand for social workers, nor does this appear to be the case in the immediate future. The pursuit of economies has caused some redistribution of who does what within the different levels of professional education. The BA practitioner may have greater difficulty in finding employment than will the MSW practitioner. Meanwhile, the doctoral programs in social work have never been more attractive. Meritocracy as a part of culture is as much a fixture in social work as it is in other professions.

It is axiomatic that tomorrow's social work is cast into today's social problems and the culture in which these problems are framed. There will always be a few surprises, but the student alert to the moment and its dynamics should have a good feel for what is around the corner. The future, like any other subject, can be studied. There are many good futurists writing in (and outside) social work journals. The key is working on getting the big picture and grasping the social, economic, and political forces driving social change.

SUMMARY AND CONCLUSIONS

Social work and the future, we have argued, are shaped by three catalysts: technological and global economic developments, demographic changes, and the dominant—but subtly shifting—cultural paradigm.

In our framework, social problems are a function of a particular culture, and that culture is heavily influenced by the most powerful social institutions in society. Specifically we suggested that the market economy is the most dominant institution in society and that market values are responsible for the materially oriented and consumer culture in which we find ourselves. We have further argued that social work, as an expression of the culture, is infused with these values and plays a supporting role in helping members of a society adapt to the culture and accept its dominant themes.

The social problems that come with the territory of advanced capitalism include all forms of labor displacement—unemployment, underemployment, forced retirement, and welfare-state transfer payments. The economic changes have altered family structure and function and in some ways set up conditions for a variety of family-based troubles—poverty, violence, and instability. Those marginalized by today's economy or addicted to aspects of consumption often find themselves caught up in criminal alternatives. Half the prison cells are filled with people whose substance addictions or involvements got them there. The existential emptiness and excesses of lifestyle are evident in visits to both doctor and social worker.

The commodification of social and health services has a major influence on social work's future. Where social workers work, with whom they work, and what services they offer, and even the way they offer them are being directed by market decistions. Managed care, third-party payees, government accountability, and the like all impact on both the provision offered and providers' behaviors.

Public funding of social work activities is in flux and uncertain. Nonetheless, there is much to indicate that health, aging, and long-term care will continue to be growth areas for social work, as will employee-assistance programs and private practice. School social work, child welfare, and family services of all kinds should remain steady, despite the drop in birthrate.

Demographic changes are evident in determining social work's future. More elderly than children, greater numbers of disabled persons living and living longer, large numbers of immigrants, and relative increases in minority populations all speak to those with whom social workers will be working in the future.

The cultural values and orientation of society are clearly fixated on material development and economizing behaviors, yet there are hints of the eventual coming of a postcapitalistic society. New age alternatives could eventuate in something of a social movement. The global economy could collapse and, with it, the power and force of the institution of the market economy. Should this happen, much rethinking about such devlopments as postindustrialization, commodification, and the privatization of social services could take place. Whatever happens, social change is more rapid and cultural paradigm shifts more likely than at any other time in human history. Whether we like it or not, as a profession, social workers in the future are in for a roller-coaster ride.

Notes

1. R. Middleman and G. Goldberg, eds., *Social Service Delivery: A Structural Approach to Social Work Practice* (New York: Columbia University Press, 1972).
2. R. Washington, "Social Work in the Future and Implications for Social Work Education," *California Sociologist* 1, no. 2 (1978): 193–204.
3. H. Karger and D. Stoez, eds., *Reconstructing the American Welfare State* (Lanham, MD: Rowman and Littlefield, 1992).
4. Daniel Bell, ed., *Coming of Post-Industrial Society* (New York: Basic Books, Inc., 1973).
5. F. Torres-Gil, ed., *The New Aging* (New York: Auburn House, 1992).
6. D. Dillman, "The Social Impacts of Information Technologies in Rural North America," *Rural Sociology* 50, no. 1 (1985): 1–26.
7. D. Phillips, "The Underdevelopment of Computing in Social Work Practice," in D. Macarow, ed., "Computers in the Social Services: Papers from a Consultation," *International Journal of Sociology and Social Policy* 10, nos. 4, 5, 6 (1990): 9–19.
8. P. Roosenboom, "The Dutch 'National' Curriculum Computer Applications for Schools of Social Work," in M. Liederman, C. Guzetta, L. Struminger, and M. Monnickerendam, eds., *Technology in People's Services, Research, Theory and Applications* (New York: 1993), p. 291.
9. C. Richarson, "Computers Don't Kill Jobs, People Do: Technology and Power in the Workplace," *The Annals of the American Academy of Political and Social Science* 544, (March 1996): 167–179.

10. J. McNutt, "National Information Infrastructure Policy and the Future of the American Welfare State: Implications for the Social Welfare Policy Curriculum," *Journal of Social Work Education* 32, no. 3 (1996): 375–388.

11. D. Phillips, "The Underdevelopment of Computing in Social Work Practice," pp. 9–19.

12. W. Bridges, "The End of the Job," *Fortune* 129 (1994): 673–674.

13. Children's Defense Fund, *The State of America's Children: Yearbook 1997* (Washington, DC: Children's Defense Fund, 1997): 113.

14. Thomas Walz and William Theisen, "The Political Economy of the Family," unpublished paper, The University of Iowa, School of Social Work (1996).

15. Children's Defense Fund, *The State of America's Children: Yearbook 1997*, pp. 16–18.

16. R.C. Sarri and F. Maple, eds., *The School in the Community* (Washington, DC: National Association of Social Workers, 1972).

17. Thomas Walz et al., "The Aging Developmentally Disabled Person: A Review," *Gerontologist* 26, no. 6 (1986): 622–630.

18. Children's Defense Fund, *The State of America's Children: Yearbook 1997*, p. 56.

19. C. Munson, "Social Work Update: The Future of Clinical Social Work and Managed Cost Organizations," *Psychiatric Services: A Journal of the American Psychiatric Association* 48, no. 4 (1997): 479–482.

20. K. Storm and W. Gingerich, "Educating Students for the New Market Realities," *Journal of Social Work Education* 29, no. 1 (1993): 78–87.

21. V. Frankl, *Man's Search for Meaning* (Boston: Beacon Press, 1962).

22. R. Morris, "Persistent Issues and Elusive Answers in Social Welfare Policy, Planning and Administration," *Administration in Social Work* 6, nos. 2–3 (1982): 28–43.

23. National Association of Social Workers, *Violence and Sustainable Development* (1996).

24. Thomas Walz and Victor Groze, "Mission of Social Work Revisited: An Agenda for the 1990's," *Social Work* 36, no. 6 (1991): 500–504.

Additional Suggested Readings

Allen-Meares, P. "Analysis of Tasks in School Social Work." *Social Work* 22 (1977): 135–139.

Allen-Meares, P. "A National Study of Education Reform: Implications for Social Work Services in Schools." *Children and Youth Services Review* 9 (1987): 207–219.

Allen-Meares, P. "Anchoring School-linked Services in Sobering Realities: A Glance at the Past and a Searching Stare at the Present." In E. Wattenberg and Y. Reason, eds., *A Summary of the Proceedings of the Conference Defining Excellence for School-linked Services.* Minneapolis: University of Minnesota, 1995.

Beniger, J. "Information Society and Global Science." *Annuals* 495 (1988): 14–29.

Civille, R., M. Fidelman, and J. Altobello. *A National Strategy for Civic Networking: A Vision of Change.* Charlestown, MA: The Center for Civic Networking, 1993.

Cnaan, R. "Social Work Practice and Information Technology: An Unestablished Link." In R. Cnaan and P. Parsloe, eds., *The Impact of Information Technology on Social Work Practice.* Binghamton, NY: Haworth, Press, 1989.

Murdock, G., and P. Golding. "Information Poverty and Political Inequality: Citizenship in the Age of Privatized Communications." *Journal of Communications* 39, no. 3 (1989): 180–195.

Murnane, R. "Education and the Well-being of the Next Generation." In S. Danziger, D. Sandefur, and D. Weinberg, eds., *Confronting Poverty: Prescription for Change.* New York: Russell Sage Foundation, 1994.

Radin, N. "School Social Work Practice: Past, Present, and Future Trends." *Social Work in Education* 11, no. 4 (1989): 209–272.

Rapoport, L. "In Defense of Social Work: An Examination of Stress in the Profession." In Paul Weinberger, ed., *Perspectives on Social Welfare.* New York: Macmillan, 1969.

Reinhardt, A. "Building the Data Highway." *Byte* 19, no. 3 (1994): 46–74.

Schoech, R. "Human Services: Stages and Issues in Teaching Computing." *Social Sciences Computer Review* 9, no. 4 (1991): 612–623.

Epilogue

H. WAYNE JOHNSON

We have come to the end of a journey that I hope has been instructive and enjoyable. The contents of this book have been arbitrarily organized—as is true to some degree of an introductory text in almost any field. There is some overlap among topics, but when the same subject has been dealt with in two or more places, we have attempted to emphasize aspects appropriately in relation to their context. In other words, a topic has not been given equal and similar attention in two places but an emphasis in one.

Starting with basic principles, concepts, and a historical résumé, we spent considerable time on social services as community and societal responses to an array of social problems. Both traditional and nontraditional programs were studied as we saw that a multiplicity of responses occur to conditions perceived as problematic, themselves numerous. We saw the "3 Ps" construct at work, of problem-policy-program, intermeshed and reciprocally influential. Many measures for assisting people to cope with change and stress were examined as these exist on all levels from micro through macro.

Social work as practice was also considered through our discussion of generalist social work practice and newer helping approaches. Attention was given to working with individuals and families, groups, and communities. Research and administration in a social work/welfare context were also examined. Finally, in the last section we introduced content on racism, sexism, diversity and discrimination, and the social services. Housing as a unique field and social development (particularly on the international level) as special practice areas were explored. Matters related to professionalization in social work constituted one chapter, as did likely future developments in this field. What the future holds for the social services is uncertain, yet is partially predictable. Clearly change will continue to be pervasive and ever-present. Change has been a continuous theme throughout this entire text as it has been historically and inevitably will be in the future.

Although our voyage is over, we have really just begun. The need is for an enlightened, informed, rational citizenry as voters, taxpayers, committee and task force members, and decision makers. This is actually a greater need than for more and better social workers, although the latter is not insignificant. This is especially true at this time, when there are people in high office around the country providing stimulus and leadership to a national mentality that is not conducive to general widespread human well-being.

You can make a difference; we all can. So, in the words of Horace Mann,

"Be ashamed to die until you have won some victory for mankind."

Index

---

*Page numbers with *n* indicate authors referenced in notes found on those pages.

THE SOCIAL SERVICES: AN INTRODUCTION
Fifth Edition
Edited by John Beasley
Picture research by Joanne de Simone and Cheryl Kucharzak
Production supervision by Kim Vander Steen
Designed by Lesiak/Crampton Design, Inc., Park Ridge, Illinois
Composition by Point West, Inc., Carol Stream, Illinois
Paper, Finch Opaque
Printed and bound by Book-mart Press, Inc., North Bergen, New Jersey